BECKETT

STAR WARS

COLLECTIBLES PRICE GUIDE

THE HOBBY'S MOST RELIABLE AND RELIED UPON SOURCE™

FOUNDER & ADVISOR: DR. JAMES BECKETT III

EDITED BY MATT BIBLE WITH THE BECKETT PRICE GUIDE STAFF

BECKETT is a registered trademark of BECKETT MEDIA LLC, DALLAS, TEXAS

Manufactured in the United States of America | Published by Beckett Media LLC

Beckett Media LLC

4635 McEwen Dr., Dallas, TX 75244

(972) 991-6657 • beckett.com

First Printing

ISBN: 978-1-930692-22-0

INSIDE

OUR STAFF

EDITORIAL
EDITORIAL DIRECTOR: Mike Payne

DESIGN
ART DIRECTOR: Lindsey Jones

ADVERTISING
Priscilla Torres
PTORRES@BECKETT.COM
972-448-9131

COLLECTIBLES DATA PUBLISHING
MANAGER, SR. MARKET ANALYST:
Brian Fleischer
PRICE GUIDE STAFF
Lloyd Almonguera, Ryan Altubar, Matt Bible, Jeff Camay, Steve Dalton, Justin Grunert, Junel Magale, Ian McDaries, Eric Norton, Kristian Redulla, Arsenio Tan, Paul Wirth, Sam Zimmer.
SPECIAL CONTRIBUTOR: Kyle Dobbins

BECKETT GRADING SERVICES
DIRECTOR OF BECKETT GRADING SERVICES : Jeromy Murray
JMURRAY@BECKETT.COM

DALLAS OFFICE
4635 McEwen, Dallas, TX 75244
Derek Ficken
DFICKEN@BECKETT.COM
972.448.9144

NEW YORK OFFICE
NORTHEAST REGIONAL SALES MANAGER: Charles Stabile
484 White Plains Rd, 2nd Floor, Eastchester, N.Y. 10709
914.268.0533
CSTABILE@BECKETT.COM

CALIFORNIA OFFICE
WESTERN REGIONAL SALES MANAGER:
Michael Gardner

17890 Sky Park Circle, Suite 250, Irvine, CA 92614
MGARDNER@BECKETT.COM
714.200.1934

ASIA OFFICE
ASIA/PACIFIC SALES MANAGER:
Dongwoon Lee - Seoul, Korea
DONGWOONL@BECKETT.COM
CELL: +82.10.6826.6868

BECKETT AUCTION SERVICES
AUCTIONS MANAGER: Traci Kaplan
TKAPLAN@BECKETT.COM
972.448.9040
DIGITAL STUDIO: Daniel Moscoso

OPERATIONS
MANAGER-BUSINESS ANALYTICS:
Amit Sharma
SR. LOGISTICS & FACILITIES MANAGER:
Alberto Chavez

EDITORIAL, PRODUCTION & SALES OFFICE
4635 McEwen Road, Dallas TX 75244
972.991.6657
beckett.com

CUSTOMER SERVICE
BECKETT MEDIA, LLC
4635 Mc Ewen Road.
Dallas, TX 75244
SUBSCRIPTIONS, ADDRESS CHANGES, RENEWALS, MISSING OR DAMAGED COPIES: 866.287.9383 or 239.653.0225

FOREIGN INQUIRES
SUBSCRIPTIONS@BECKETT.COM
BACK ISSUES: BECKETTMEDIA.COM

BOOKS, MERCHANDISE, REPRINTS
239.280.2380
DEALER SALES & PRODUCTION
dealers@beckett.com

BECKETT MEDIA, LLC
PRESIDENT: Sandeep Dua
PUBLISHER: Jon finkel
VP, BBS & AUCTIONS: Kevin Isaacson

COVER PHOTO COURTESY OF
THE TOPPS COMPANY, INC.

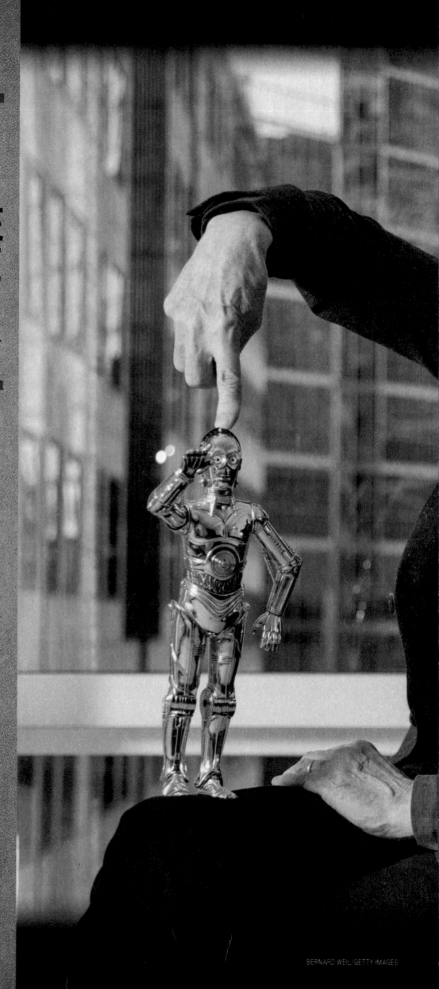

HE LIKES TOYS ... JUST LIKE YOU & ME

Anthony Daniels, the only C3PO the Star Wars franchise has ever known, holds a toy of the character he has brought to life.

TOP 10

VINTAGE STAR WARS ACTION FIGURES

BY KYLE DOBBINS

1

1977-78 STAR WARS BOBA FETT
(ROCKET FIRING PROTOTYPE)

2

1977-78 12-BACKS A JAWA
(VINYL CAPE)

3

1980-82 STAR WARS EMPIRE STRIKES
BACK FX-7 (MEDICAL DROID) PALITOY

4

1983 STAR WARS RETURN OF THE JEDI LUKE
SKYWALKER (JEDI KNIGHT OUTFIT) LILY LEDY

5

1985 STAR WARS POWER OF THE
FORCE YAK FACE

6

1977-78 STAR WARS 12-BACKS A DARTH
VADER (DOUBLE TELESCOPING LIGHTSABER)

7

1977-78 STAR WARS 12-BACKS A BEN (OBI-WAN)
KENOBI (DOUBLE TELESCOPING LIGHTSABER)

8

1985 STAR WARS DROIDS
VLIX GLASSLITE

9

1977-78 STAR WARS
21-BACKS B BOBA FETT

10

1977-78 STAR WARS 12-BACKS A LUKE
SKYWALKER (DOUBLE TELESCOPING LIGHTSABER)

TOP 10

VINTAGE STAR WARS VEHICLES & PLAYSETS

BY KYLE DOBBINS

1

1977-78 STAR WARS VEHICLES MILLENNIUM FALCON

2

1978 STAR WARS PLAYSETS CANTINA ADVENTURE SET (SEARS)

3

1978 STAR WARS PLAYSETS DEATH STAR SPACE STATION (KENNER)

4

1978 STAR WARS VEHICLES X-WING FIGHTER

5

1980-82 STAR WARS EMPIRE STRIKES BACK SNOWSPEEDER

6

1983 STAR WARS RETURN OF THE JEDI VEHICLES TIE INTERCEPTOR

7

1983 STAR WARS RETURN OF THE JEDI VEHICLES IMPERIAL SHUTTLE

8

1980-82 STAR WARS EMPIRE STRIKES BACK AT-AT

9
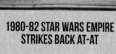
1978 STAR WARS VEHICLES LAND SPEEDER

10

1983 STAR WARS RETURN OF THE JEDI VEHICLES Y-WING FIGHTER

YOUNG STARS

In a photo snapped in May 1980, the stars of Star Wars V: The Empire Strikes Back share a moment together outside of the Savoy Hotel in London. The cast included Harrison Ford (far left), David Prowse (Darth Vader), Carrie Fisher, Kenny Baker (R2D2), Peter Mayhew (Chewbacca) and Mark Hamill.

TOP 20

TRADING CARD SETS

BY MATT BIBLE

1 2007 SW 30TH ANNIVERSARY

WHY THE FORCE IS STRONG:
• Comprehensive in all regards (it even includes cards of the infamous Holiday Special)
• Huge auto checklist, first from Harrison Ford.
• Signers also include behind the camera heroes, legendary composer John Williams.
• Stamped buyback box toppers still very popular, particularly the latter series.
• Lots of high quality sketch cards.

2 1977 STAR WARS

Han Solo and Chewbacca

WHY THE FORCE IS STRONG:
• The set that started it all
• Most recognizable Star Wars set of all-time.
• Still popular with a lot of fans who might not otherwise collect trading cards.
• Later series have some interesting behind-the-scenes shots.

3 2015 SW MASTERWORK

QUI-GON JINN

WHY THE FORCE IS STRONG:
• First high-end Star Wars set.
• Large on-card autograph checklist.

4 1993-95 SW GALAXY

WHY THE FORCE IS STRONG:
• Brought SW cards back after ten-year hiatus.
• Art-based approach laid groundwork for new styles of sets.

5 2001 SW EVOLUTION

WHY THE FORCE IS STRONG:
• First Star Wars trading card set to include actor autos
• Thematically spawned 2006 sequel & another in 2016.

6 1995 SW WIDEVISION

INT. DAGOBAH – TREE CAVE

WHY THE FORCE IS STRONG:
• Introduced oversized Widevision line.
• Backs contain plenty of info and production artwork.

7 2004 SW HERITAGE

FIGHTING AN OLD FRIEND

WHY THE FORCE IS STRONG:
• First set to have sketch cards from Original Trilogy.
• First autographs of Mark Hamill & James Earl Jones.
• Retail-only Letter Stickers still popular with set builders.

8 1980 SW EMPIRE STRIKES BACK

"EMBRACE THE DARK SIDE!"

WHY THE FORCE IS STRONG:
• Original Trilogy set.
• Three series are not as many as first film but still comprehensive as a whole with larger checklists.
• Ralph McQuarrie artwork included on some cards.

9 2016 SW MASTERWORK

DARTH VADER

WHY THE FORCE IS STRONG:
• Features 80 total autograph signers!
• Contains autos of new stars Daisy Ridley and Adam Driver (his first in any product).
• Eclectic relic cards featuring stamps, medallions.

10 1996 SW 3-DI WIDEVISION

WHY THE FORCE IS STRONG:
• One of the smallest print runs of any 1990's SW set.
• First Star Wars cards to use 3-D technology.

11 2015 SW HIGH TEK

WHY THE FORCE IS STRONG:
- Acetate designs and pattern variations make it easy to collect the set several ways.
- First set with a John Boyega autograph.

12 2013 SW JEDI LEGACY

WHY THE FORCE IS STRONG:
- First pack-inserted Star Wars memorabilia cards.
- Different spin on Luke Skywalker, Darth Vader stories.

13 2017 SW 40TH ANNIVERSARY

WHY THE FORCE IS STRONG:
- 62 different autographs including the elusive Six-Person booklet
- Contains medallion relics.

14 2002 SW ATTACK OF THE CLONES WIDEVISION

WHY THE FORCE IS STRONG:
- Large auto checklist which includes the only autos of Frank Oz (Yoda) and Ahmed Best (Jar Jar Binks).

15 1996 SW FINEST

WHY THE FORCE IS STRONG:
- First full chromium Star Wars set outside of inserts.
- Refractors make their franchise debut.
- Takes an all-art approach but each artist did a nine-card group based on a similar theme.

16 2014 SW RETURN OF THE JEDI 3-D WIDEVISION

WHY THE FORCE IS STRONG:
- Limited print run sold out quickly as an online exclusive.
- Autos randomly inserted as bonus hit.
- Technology makes for a stunning base set.
- Some of the greatest packaging ever for a trading card product, Star Wars or not.

17 2004 SW CLONE WARS

WHY THE FORCE IS STRONG:
- First Star Wars sketch cards, period.
- Cool artwork from overlooked Genndy Tartakovsky short cartoon anthology.

18 1977 SW WONDER BREAD

Millenium Falcon

WHY THE FORCE IS STRONG:
- Fresh, memorable design.
- Nice alternative and complement to the original 1977 Topps set.

19 1996 SW SHADOWS OF THE EMPIRE

WHY THE FORCE IS STRONG:
- Based on spinoff novel bridging events between Empire Strikes Back and Return of the Jedi.
- Every card features original artwork from Greg and Tim Hildebrandt.

20 1996 SW BEND-EMS PROMOS

WHY THE FORCE IS STRONG:
- Challenging set available only with toys.
- Most use character images from original 1993 Star Wars Galaxy.
- Popular with set builders.

TOP 20

STAR WARS FUNKO POP VINYL

BY MATT BIBLE

1

#23 DARTH MAUL (HOLOGRAPHIC)/480*
(2012 SDCC EXCLUSIVE)

2

#14 SHADOW TROOPER/480*
(2011 SDCC EXCLUSIVE)

3

#24 BIGGS DARKLIGHTER/480*
(2012 SDCC EXCLUSIVE)

4

#6B CHEWBACCA (FLOCKED)/480*
(2011 SDCC EXCLUSIVE)

5

#32 BOBA FETT DROIDS/480*
(2013 SDCC EXCLUSIVE)

6

#25 501ST CLONE TROOPER/480*
(2012 SDCC EXCLUSIVE)

7

#15 HAN SOLO STORMTROOPER/1000*
(2011 ECCC EXCLUSIVE)

8

#33 DARTH VADER (HOLOGRAPHIC GLOW-
IN-THE-DARK) (2014 DALLAS COMIC
CON/PARIS EXPO EXCLUSIVE)

CONTINUED ON PAGE 16

9

#16 LUKE SKYWALKER
STORMTROOPER/1000*
(2011 ECCC EXCLUSIVE)

10

#54 PRINCESS LEIA (BOUSSH
UNMASKED)/1008* (2015 SDCC
EXCLUSIVE)

11

#128A QUI GON JINN/2000*
(2016 NYCC EXCLUSIVE)

12

7A GREEDO

13

#3A HAN SOLO

14

#26B WICKET THE EWOK (FLOCKED)
(2013 FUGITIVE TOYS EXCLUSIVE)

15

#10A OBI-WAN KENOBI

16

#29 QUEEN AMIDALA

17

#12A GAMORREAN GUARD

18

#43B UNMASKED VADER (2015 STAR
WARS CELEBRATION EXCLUSIVE)

19

#21A CLONE TROOPER

20

#198D PORG (OPEN MOUTH FLOCKED)
(2017 HOT TOPIC EXCLUSIVE)

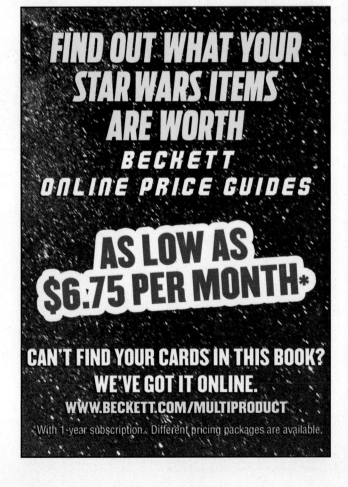

TOP 40

STAR WARS AUTOGRAPHS

BY MATT BIBLE

1

2016 STAR WARS MASTERWORK
AUTOGRAPHS DAISY RIDLEY

2

2007 STAR WARS 30TH ANNIVERSARY
AUTOGRAPHS HARRISON FORD

3

2004 STAR WARS HERITAGE
AUTOGRAPHS MARK HAMILL

8

2016 STAR WARS ROGUE ONE SERIES ONE
AUTOGRAPHS FELICITY JONES

9

2001 STAR WARS EVOLUTION
AUTOGRAPHS BILLY DEE WILLIAMS

10

2016 STAR WARS MASTERWORK
AUTOGRAPHS ADAM DRIVER

15

2007 STAR WARS 30TH ANNIVERSARY
AUTOGRAPHS JOHN WILLIAMS

16
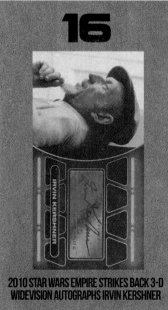
2010 STAR WARS EMPIRE STRIKES BACK 3-D
WIDEVISION AUTOGRAPHS IRVIN KERSHNER

17
2001 STAR WARS EVOLUTION
AUTOGRAPHS PETER MAYHEW

4

2001 STAR WARS EVOLUTION
AUTOGRAPHS CARRIE FISHER

5

2004 STAR WARS HERITAGE
AUTOGRAPHS JAMES EARL JONES

6

2002 STAR WARS ATTACK OF THE CLONES
WIDEVISION AUTOGRAPHS FRANK OZ

7

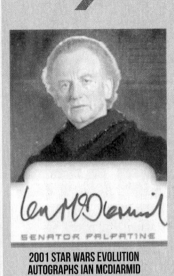

2001 STAR WARS EVOLUTION
AUTOGRAPHS IAN MCDIARMID

11

2006 STAR WARS EVOLUTION UPDATE
AUTOGRAPHS HAYDEN CHRISTENSEN

12

2005 STAR WARS REVENGE OF THE SITH
WIDEVISION AUTOGRAPHS SAMUEL L. JACKSON

13

2001 STAR WARS EVOLUTION
AUTOGRAPHS ANTHONY DANIELS

14

2001 STAR WARS EVOLUTION
AUTOGRAPHS KENNY BAKER

18

2010 STAR WARS EMPIRE STRIKES BACK 3-D
WIDEVISION AUTOGRAPHS RALPH MCQUARRIE

19

2015 STAR WARS HIGH TEK
AUTOGRAPHS JOHN BOYEGA

20

2001 STAR WARS EVOLUTION
AUTOGRAPHS JEREMY BULLOCH

21

2007 STAR WARS 30TH ANNIVERSARY
AUTOGRAPHS DAVID PROWSE

22

2016 STAR WARS MASTERWORK
AUTOGRAPHS ANDY SERKIS

23

DONNIE YEN AS
CHIRRUT ÎMWE

2016 STAR WARS ROGUE ONE SERIES ONE
DONNIE YEN

24

RAY PARK
AS DARTH MAUL

2012 STAR WARS GALACTIC FILES
AUTOGRAPHS RAY PARK

25

FOREST WHITAKER AS
SAW GERRERA

2016 STAR WARS ROGUE ONE SERIES
ONE FOREST WHITAKER

26

K-2SO

AUTHENTIC AUTOGRAPH
STAR WARS: ROGUE ONE

2017 STAR WARS GALACTIC FILES
REBORN AUTOGRAPHS ALAN TUDYK

27

KAYDEL KO CONNIX

2017 STAR WARS THE FORCE AWAKENS 3-D
WIDEVISION AUTOGRAPHS BILLIE LOURD

28

WICKET W. WARRICK

2001 STAR WARS EVOLUTION
AUTOGRAPHS WARWICK DAVIS

29

JAR JAR

2002 STAR WARS ATTACK OF THE CLONES
WIDEVISION AUTOGRAPHS AHMED BEST

30

JAKE LLOYD
AS ANAKIN SKYWALKER

2012 STAR WARS GALACTIC FILES
AUTOGRAPHS JAKE LLOYD

DUAL AUTOGRAPHS

2013 STAR WARS GALACTIC FILES 2 DUAL AUTOGRAPHS FISHER/HAMILL

2013 STAR WARS GALACTIC FILES 2 DUAL AUTOGRAPHS FORD/MAYHEW

2013 STAR WARS GALACTIC FILES 2 DUAL AUTOGRAPHS JONES/MCDIARMID

2016 STAR WARS MASTERWORK DUAL AUTOGRAPHS FISHER/BAKER

2016 STAR WARS MASTERWORK DUAL AUTOGRAPHS HAMILL/RIDLEY

TRIPLE AUTOGRAPHS

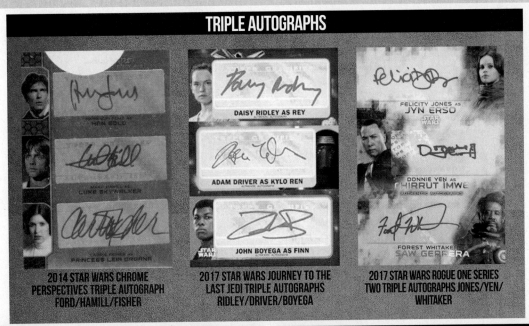

2014 STAR WARS CHROME PERSPECTIVES TRIPLE AUTOGRAPH FORD/HAMILL/FISHER

2017 STAR WARS JOURNEY TO THE LAST JEDI TRIPLE AUTOGRAPHS RIDLEY/DRIVER/BOYEGA

2017 STAR WARS ROGUE ONE SERIES TWO TRIPLE AUTOGRAPHS JONES/YEN/WHITAKER

QUAD AUTOGRAPH

2017 STAR WARS 40TH ANNIVERSARY QUAD AUTOGRAPHED BOOKLET HAMILL/FISHER/DANIELS/BAKER

SIX-PERSON AUTOGRAPH

2017 STAR WARS 40TH ANNIVERSARY SIX-PERSON AUTOGRAPHED BOOKLET FORD/ HAMILL/ FISHER/ DANIELS/ BAKER/ MAYHEW

GREATEST
STAR WARS CHARACTERS OF ALL-TIME

BY RYAN CRACKNELL

After a bunch of films, a couple of television series, dozens of books and lots of other stories in other mediums, *Star Wars* has introduced an entire universe of characters. Many are icons to multiple generations.

And then there's Jar Jar Binks.

Several factors go into great *Star Wars* characters. Story and personality are the big ones. These bring the emotional core that make us relate and feel a connection.

But let's be honest. Some *Star Wars* characters achieve greatness not because they make us feel but because they look cool. In a visual medium like film, an inspired design can make an impact just like a scene that brings a smile or causes our eyes to water.

With those things in mind, here are 40 of the most unforgettable *Star Wars* characters from the saga's first 40 years.

40 GREATEST CHARACTERS

[40] MALAKILI

Malakili has the look of someone who's tough. He's a big guy without much use for shirts. His job is to look after the monstrous Rancor that resides under Jabba the Hutt's throne, gobbling up anyone who wrongs the slimy gangster. It turns out that Malakili's tough exterior is all a facade. When it comes to him and his Rancor, Malakili is all teddy bear.

[39] WICKET

Wicket is the young hero of the Ewoks. The teddy bears with spears may get a bad rap by some who don't want their Star Wars cute and cuddly, but Wicket is different. Between all the yup-nubbing is a tough adventurer who shows little fear and lots of heart. And if your Saturday mornings in the '80s involved the Ewoks cartoon, your respect for Wicket and his adventures is probably even higher.

[38] GREEDO

Greedo's time on the screen may be limited but his legacy is undeniable. He's part of the scum that makes the Star Wars universe so appealing. The Rodian bounty hunter looks as though he's related to the Sleestak's from *Land of the Lost*. It's in his death that Greedo's memorable status is cemented. Originally, Han shot first in their fateful meeting at the Mos Eisley Cantina. But through George Lucas' changing mind, that changed because the creator felt good guys should only protect themselves. With that, the Han Shot First movement was born, rebelling against tinkering with a classic series. And now Greedo is part of an even bigger history.

[37] ADMIRAL ACKBAR

"It's a trap!" It's funny how one line of dialogue can make a character unforgettable. Admiral Ackbar has a lot more going for him, though. He's essentially a humanoid squid

with a uniform that would fit in at a disco. That's hard to pull off. At the center of several key battles, Admiral Ackbar has to be respected for his tactical knowledge and expertise, as well.

[36] PADMÉ AMIDALA

Given her importance in the Star Wars saga, Padmé should rank much higher. However, the way she's introduced in the prequels, it's hard to truly get behind her. Many of her costumes are amazing. But this is Star Wars, a place with strong female leads thrive and inspire. Padmé has a few moments here and there, but many are crippled by the awkward courtship between her and her "Annie."

[35] ASAJJ VENTRESS

Asajj Ventress is not only one of the toughest characters in the Star Wars universe, but she's also one of the scariest. Rising from a slave to apprentice of Count Dooku and bounty hunter, the dark side runs deep in the Dathomirian. Wielding a pair of lightsabers, she participated in several big battles in both the *Clone Wars* micro-series and was a central villain in the later *Clone Wars* series.

[34] CHOPPER

Droids have provided plenty of laughs over the course of all the films and various television shows. For machines, they sometimes offer some heart that makes them endearing. A member of the crew on *Rebels,* the C1-10P droid can be a little bit cranky at times and even do things the way he wants. But Chopper sometimes shows a more playful side. In interviews, Dave Filoni, the executive producer of *Rebels,* has compared Chopper to being like a family cat much like R2-D2 is likened to a dog.

[33] CAPTAIN REX

The story of Captain Rex is an expansive one. It's also fairly complex. He's a central figure in *The Clone Wars*. A clone himself, he's the model trooper. By the time Rebels rolled around, Rex is much older thanks to his accelerated aging. But this simply adds more depth to his personality now that he's grizzled and gone through so much.

It can also be said now that Rex's appearances didn't stop there. Dave Filoni recently acknowledged that Rex may have been fighting for the Rebels once again on Endor during *Return of the Jedi*. Filoni has supported the idea that a noticeably older fighter among the group could indeed be Captain Rex.

[32] SAW GERRERA

Somewhat of a militant extremist, Saw Gerrera's story is filled with personal tragedy. Although best known for his central role in *Rogue One*, he was first introduced on *The Clone Wars*. That's where his tragic origins are laid out. With several years and many battles happening between then and *Rogue One*, Gerrera continued to transform — mentally and physically. In the film, his appearance is somewhat monstrous, adding a bit of a frightening edge to his character.

[31] JABBA THE HUTT

Unless you're one of his prisoners or part of his endless diet, being in the company of Jabba the Hutt means a never-ending party. Pre-Special Edition, Jabba was introduced by name early on as someone Han Solo was running away from. And for good reason as said slug-like creature would later go on to use him as a wall hanging. Jabba, or at least a computer-generated imposter, was later edited back into *A New Hope* but the good one is the original from *Return of the Jedi*. The slime, the laugh, the eyes — he's grotesque and disgusting. But he commands your attention, even if you're not one of his captives.

[30] GRAND ADMIRAL THRAWN

Timothy Zahn's Star Wars novels from the early 1990s helped bring the franchise back into the mainstream. Grand Admiral Thrawn was a big reason why. Heading up the post-Vader Empire, Thrawn led by being a ruthless tactician. He's more of a thinking-person's villain than one who controlled by brute force. As part of the Expanded Universe, Thrawn was no longer part of canon for a period of time. However, he was made official again after being brought back for *Rebels*.

[29] POE DAMERON

Introduced in *The Force Awakens*, there's still a bit to be revealed about Poe. One thing that is obvious about the Resistance X-Wing pilot is his charm. As a character, he's something of an original trilogy hybrid of Luke and Han. It's obvious that Poe has a central role in the new films, but how it plays out is still a bit of a mystery. He has some great moments, particularly alongside Finn. But, there's not quite the same dynamic depth showcased by the former Stormtrooper and Rey.

[28] EZRA BRIDGER

Jedi apprentice with humble beginnings — where have you heard that before? While the parallel to the Skywalker lineage is obvious, Ezra Bridger's journey is a different one. The character that the animated *Rebels* revolves around, Ezra isn't your typical hero. As the show gets ready for its final run, there's a definite darkness about his destiny. That not only makes Rebels more interesting, but Ezra as well.

[27] K-2SO

Droids aren't generally known for their emotion. They know right from wrong, black from white. K-2SO brings a level of sarcasm and feeling not normally

reserved for robots. The result is several laughs and a surprising amount of tender moments with Jynn Erso, Cassian Andor and the Rebel spies. K-2SO's imposing size and spindly arms make for a memorable look that further adds to the characterization. It's almost like the reprogrammed Imperial droid is a confused teenager or young adult coming to grips with what the future holds.

[26] QUI-GON JINN

Make no mistake about it, Qui-Gon Jinn takes up the wise Obi Wan Kenobi role of *The Phantom Menace*. His apprentice? A young, less gray-haired version of Obi Wan. A bit of an outsider among the Jedi, he's still extremely powerful with the Force and swings a strong lightsaber. Without a lot of backstory enjoyed by so many other characters, Qui-Gon can be seen as a little too similar to the older version of Kenobi introduced in *Star Wars*.

[25] BAZE MALBUS

Baze Malbus has a cool factor about him just for the massive gun that he carries. His appeal goes deeper, though. A member of the Guardians of the Whills, it's Baze's friendship with Chirrut Îmwe that makes him memorable. Despite not being seen on screen for long, the two have a deep connection that is both authentic and unique to the saga. Star Wars has its share of pairs, but few feel as genuine as Baze and Chirrut.

[24] SABINE WREN

When we think of Mandalorians in Star Wars, usually the attention shifts to Boba Fett's armor. Over the course of Rebels, Sabine has made a case. She's edgy, she's tough and her role with the Man-

dalorian people is one of destiny. Sabine isn't the lead in *Rebels* but she's the type of character that a lot people have gravitated towards because of her strength. But as the show has progressed, her importance has grown in key storylines. Her strength as a leader brings a sense of destiny and promise, which only makes her more interesting to watch and follow.

[23] LANDO CALRISSIAN

Lando's a suave, cape wearer who seems like the coolest guy ever — until he sells out his friend and becomes the Judas of the original trilogy. But Star Wars has plenty of redemption points with Lando being one of the swiftest. Bits and pieces of Lando's backstory have been worked into the films, books and comics, but perhaps his biggest claim to fame is losing the Millennium Falcon to Han Solo in a game of Sabaac.

[22] MARA JADE

Perhaps the most prominent member of the Expanded Universe, Mara Jade was first introduced in Timothy Zahn's "Heir to the Empire." Trained by Emperor Palpatine, she shared a connection that went beyond his death. Over the course of Zahn's novels, she undergoes a major transformation in attitude. Mara Jade became a focal point of several more Star Wars books in the years that followed. Whether villain or hero, she's one of the strongest females in all of Star Wars. At least she was. With the elimination of the Expanded Universe, Mara Jade is currently not part of canon. However, like Thrawn, that could change as the revised canon grows.

[21] KANAN JARRUS

The rugged leader of the Ghost on *Rebels*, Kanan is a Jedi who never finished his training. It could be argued that he never reached his full potential. As *Rebels* has progressed, Kanan continues to

change and evolve, both physically and with his powers. Watching over and guiding Ezra, the relationship has some similarities to Obi-Wan with Anakin and later Luke. At the same time, it's different. Kanan is on his own journey of self-discovery.

[20] JYN ERSO

Jyn Erso isn't the typical Star Wars hero. She's strong, but she's part of a team. Jyn is the central figure in *Rogue One*, but she's one in a group. She's one of many. And that's what makes her role in the franchise interesting. We learn about her backstory quickly and in a straightforward manner. Jyn is a reluctant soldier, but one nonetheless. Ultimately selfless and dedicated to the important job she has no choice but completing, she gets her big moment and a somewhat surprising sendoff.

[19] FINN

Despite all the Stormtroopers shown on screen over the decades, few glimpses have been offered under the helmet. Because they act as a collective force, it makes it all the more impactful when FN-2187 removes his blood-marked mask to reveal the person we now know as Finn. Brave, funny, dedicated and a risk-taker, Finn is the consummate hero. And yet, there's still plenty we don't know about him — what he doesn't know about himself. A journey awaits, which should make him even more interesting by the time it's done.

[18] DARTH MAUL

When *The Phantom Menace* arrived, Darth Maul was everywhere. And for good reason. His stare was piercing and nightmare-inducing. His skin and horns were devilish. Let's not discount the fact that he swung a double-sided lightsaber. Unfortunately, his appearance in the film was limited. The scenes were memorable, but more from Maul was needed. He was brought back for both the animated *Clone*

Wars and *Rebels*, which helped flesh out his character more and create a character that was interesting for more than just his look.

[17] CHIRRUT ÎMWE

Sometimes you just have to believe. Chirrut Îmwe believed in the Force but he was no Jedi. That didn't stop him from trying to tap into its mystical powers. It'd be easy to overlook the heavily spiritual Chirrut Îmwe. He's an old, blind man who mutters to himself. What could he accomplish? Plenty. Even without Force powers, Chirrut knows how to take care of himself, even when surrounded by a mob of aggressive troopers. On top of all that, there's a quick wit, lots of humor, loyalty and caring demeanor. It's hard not to feel anything but warmth towards him.

[16] R2-D2

Sometimes "beeps" and "boops" can go a long way in establishing a character. R2-D2 may not be a droid of many words, but he has a way of being heard. Whether he's hacking into the Death Star computers, fixing spaceships in mid-flight, carrying messages to or cutting open an Ewok net, Artoo is a resourceful little robot who brings companionship, humor and plenty of heart — even if he doesn't have one.

[15] AHSOKA TANO

Introduced in *The Clone Wars,* Ahsoka was a Jedi Padawan working alongside Anakin. Her training paralleled her personal growth as a teenager. It was a little scary, sometimes frustrating adventure with several turning points along the way. Because we watch knowing Anakin's fate, it's also heartbreaking to see their bond form and know at some point there's going to be a breaking point.

[14] BB-8

When the first clips of BB-8 surfaced, there was a sense

that the robot could be the next Jar-Jar Binks — a character that panders to the youngest of viewers and is nothing but obnoxious. It turns out BB-8 was all right. In fact, he was more than all right. The parallels to Artoo are obvious but they're far from identical. The spherical build of BB-8 adds a sense of innovation. His part in adventures is exciting. And his "flaming thumb" provides one of the biggest laughs of all the films.

[13] EMPEROR PALPATINE

Many layers exist to this evil puppet master. Like any good villain, he plays the long game. Palpatine hides in plain sight as a Senator of the Galactic Republic. In the shadows, he's something much darker. It's Palpatine who is responsible for luring Anakin to the Dark Side and creating the monster known as Darth Vader. But much of this depth comes to light in the prequels.

Even in the original trilogy, when he's simply the Emperor, there's plenty that's frightening about him. He's old and shrivelled. He hides behind a cloak and remains largely mysterious. He shoots lightning bolts from his fingertips. And that voice, a croak that induced many a nightmare to a generation of young viewers.

[12] KYLO REN

Looking to emulate the dark path of his grandfather, Darth Vader, Kylo Ren has the dark outfit and mask that makes him memorable simply by sight. For reasons not fully revealed as of yet, there is a deep-seated rage within him. Even if there is some sort of eventual redemption, it may be hard to forgive him for putting the Dark Side before family.

[11] GRAND MOFF TARKIN

No matter how you look at it, you can't not have strong feelings towards someone who blows up an entire planet and everyone on it. When that planet happens to belong to a beloved character like Princess Leia, clench fists are bound to happen. When it comes to film, that's a good thing. Someone's doing something right if you feel emotion, no matter if it's positive or negative.

Grand Moff Tarkin is the essence of cold and calculating. He always seems to be in deep thought, treating every breath as though it were part of a massive game of chess. He's an intelligent villain who operates on logic over emotion, bring balance to Darth Vader and terror to the Rebel Alliance.

40 GREATEST CHARACTERS

[10] BOBA FETT

Boba Fett was at his coolest when the least was known about him. When he was introduced, he was something of a mystery man who had a cool outfit, awesome blaster and killer spaceship. He had a rocket pack to boot. And the job of bounty hunter? Boba Fett has that aura of cool surrounding him like an intergalactic James Dean. For the first couple of decades of Star Wars, Boba Fett was probably the coolest character in the saga. But through the Special Editions and prequels, we learned a little more about him and his origins. He can't be seen with the same mystery anymore. A less is more approach would have worked just fine for Boba Fett.

[9] C-3PO

C-3PO isn't the most likeable character. Sometimes, the droid can be a little irritating. If he were a kid in class, he'd be the one at the front of the room with his hand up. He's the one who always tells you when you're wrong. But that's by design. Although things may revolve around the Skywalker family, C-3PO is our guide. Precision is in his programming. And sometimes, the golden robot's takes offer up some refreshing honesty the heroes might not want to hear. But it's a reflection of the danger at hand and the excitement of the stories. As far as design goes, C-3PO is impeccable. The classic golden version harkens back to Fritz Lang's black-and-white classic *Metropolis*. It adds a level of iconography for a franchise that is filled with instantly recognizable costumes and designs.

[8] CHEWBACCA

Chewbacca is more a Wookiee of action rather than words — or growls. Primarily working as Han Solo's partner, Chewbacca is a symbol of bravery, companionship and loyalty. He may look imposing and tough (because he is), but there's a warm, cuddly side to Chewie as well that goes beyond his fur. He's a family man, one of the lone takeaways from the infamous Holiday Special.

[7] YODA

For a small, green creature, Yoda carries quite the lightsaber. Throughout the Star Wars saga, whether it's on the big screen, TV or on the page, he's a gatekeeper of sorts for the Force. And while his power and position make him notable, it's his characterization that makes him so memorable. Most of his lines have a Yogi Berra-type of nonsense to them that actually bring forth a sense of wisdom. Yoda is funny, he's cute and, perhaps most of all, he believes in the good of life even when things are at their darkest.

[6] REY

Who is Rey? We still don't fully know. But the glimpse that we've been given is that she's something special. Sometimes mystery works against you. In this online age, the mystery surrounding Rey, which will be fleshed out in *The Last Jedi* and Episode IX, makes for endless discussion and theories. It works to add to the mystique surrounding her. What we do know is that she's strong and resourceful. She's both serious and lends an element of humor. Even she doesn't fully grasp the power that she holds. That's a big part of her intrigue. *The Force Awakens* gave us a taste to show that she fits in with the Star Wars greats and it's exciting to root along with her.

[5] OBI-WAN KENOBI

Introduced as the wise wizard, Ben Kenobi turned out to be so much more. His place in the saga shows the biggest change. When things start out, he's a young jedi. He's learning and still prone to mistakes. Battle after battle, big and small, there's no character that grows more over the course of the saga than Ben Kenobi, except for maybe Anakin. The dynamic with Obi-Wan is different, though. Anakin may share a similar level of loss, but Ben deals with it differently. His place on the Light Side of the Force is never in doubt. He may not be perfect, but he's a hero at every stage.

[4] PRINCESS LEIA ORGANA

Sometimes the term "princess" brings a negative connotation in movies. Princesses have a long history of being portrayed as needing to be saved by a knight in shining armor and a perfect smile. Leia Organa is not your typical princess. Yes, Star Wars sees her getting saved by not one but two handsome gents, but over the course of the rest of the original trilogy and *The Force Awakens*, she's the one giving the orders. Leia is strong. She's comfortable giving orders, making tough decisions and getting into the thick of things. Whether that's as a diplomat, a battlefield warrior, a friend, lover or family member, it doesn't matter.

[3] HAN SOLO

Han Solo is the kind of person many people imagine being in some sort of alternate reality. Free-spirited scoundrel, he does what he wants, when he wants. Han is handsome, funny, speaks his mind and usually gets his way. He's funny, he goes on adventures and he knows how to talk his way out of almost any tough situation. And those that he can't — he has a blaster in his holster and a Wookiee at his side. Even with the tough exterior, Han Solo has heart. He's loyal to his friends, even when it's inconvenient. Of the major Star Wars characters, Han is the closest thing we have to an everyman. He has no special powers, just skills. Flaws and all, it makes him rounded and relatable.

Expand Your Adventure!

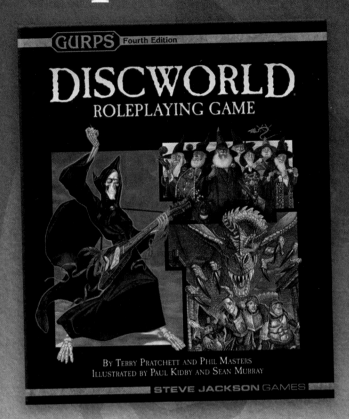

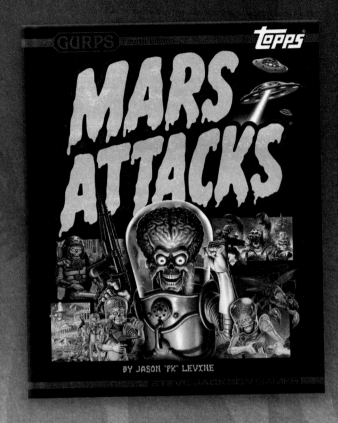

Where the world is round, but also flat!

Journey through the mind of Terry Pratchett . . .

Will you save the Earth? Or – will you conquer it?

Play as either Martians or humans! Wield futuristic weapons and tech! Fly spaceships!

Find these at your friendly local game store today! Or order at warehouse23.com.

STEVE JACKSON GAMES

| sjgames.com
#PlaySJGames

[2] LUKE SKYWALKER

From a whiny desert farm boy to wise, old wizard-type, Luke Skywalker's gone through a lot of changes. A prototypical hero, he answers the call of adventure, making many important stops and discoveries along the way — including discovering that princess he kissed was actually his sister. Luke is our guidepost through the original trilogy. Early on, it looked like he was going to be one of those unbearable leads and kill everything before the Empire got the chance. In particular, it's hard not to cringe (or laugh) when we first meet him. Just listen to him sound like a three-year-old complaining to his Uncle Owen. But then things change. Destiny takes over and a champion emerges. It goes far beyond the first Death Star. In the films and adventures that follow, Luke continues to discover more about himself, his powers and responsibility — not to mention the potential dangers those bring as Light and Dark battle on inside him.

[1] DARTH VADER/ ANAKIN SKYWALKER

Star Wars is formed around Anakin Skywalker and his descent into Darth Vader. It's a story of tragedy, rage,

sadness and hope. It's the eternal struggle of good and evil played out in epic battles, iconic costumes and big moments. Because we met Anakin after we knew what he became, there's always a certain edge about his younger self. But all that lays the groundwork for the infamous villain that he would become. Even in death, he continues to influences the Dark Side through Kylo Ren. Darth Vader's menacing look matches his actions. He's a figure of strength, danger and evil — a recipe for nightmares. The movies give him several big moments, particularly when it comes to turning point battles. But Darth Vader isn't just about lightsabers and heavy breathing. He's a fleshed out and fully realized character. Between the films, TV shows, spinoff books, comics and other stories, we know who he is and how he got there. Despite all the horrible things he does, there's a certain part of us that cheers for him. So even in a universe filled with memorable characters, Vader reigns supreme.

WICKED GOOD

His taste in color runs black and he's a bit of a heavy breather. It's all part of the Darth Vader aura, the most intimidating – and fascinating - presence in the Star Wars galaxy ... *and Hollywood's greatest villain.*

BY ROGER FERNANDEZ

" I had to make Darth Vader scary without the audience ever seeing his face. His character's got to go beyond that. He's done a lot of horrible things in his life that he isn't particularly proud of. Ultimately, he's just a pathetic guy who's had a very sad life."

- GEORGE LUCAS IN AN
INTERVIEW WITH ROLLING
STONE MAGAZINE

DARTH VADER: WICKED GOOD

ACTORS PETER CUSHING, CARRIE FISHER AND DAVID PROWSE ON THE SET OF THE ORIGINAL STAR WARS FILM.

To loosely borrow a famous line the one-and-only Obi-Wan Kenobi used in the original *Star Wars* movie, this is the villain you're looking for.

Darth Vader, it turns out, is in fact the chosen one, the one you hate, you love, you hate to love and love to hate. No, we're not trying to work an old Jedi mind trick on you.

It's the truth. Hollywood and pop culture have never had it so good and so bad when it comes to villains, and the *Star Wars* franchise can take credit for coming up with a dream of a nightmare bad guy.

When you really think about it, the dark-mask-wearing, heavy-breathing, light-saber-wielding, wanna-conquer-the-galaxy-and-fulfill-his-destiny tough guy may be as popular and beloved as any of the heroes in the enduring saga.

Move over, Luke Skywalker, step aside Princess Leia, out of the way Han Solo, and that goes for you too, Chewbacca and Yoda — Lord Vader may have the inside track on all of them in a *Star Wars* adoration contest.

It takes a special kind of evil to get that much love.

DARTH VADER: WICKED GOOD

THERE IS A VADER SIGHTING ...

The world first laid eyes on this fearsome figure in the opening moments of Episode IV – the original *Star Wars* - when Vader stormed through the hallways of a starship, barking out orders, interrogating a rebel and finishing him off with one of his patented choke holds. Viewers didn't exactly know what to make of Vader, who appeared to be some type of man/robot hybrid with a booming voice and top-dog status.

And that's exactly the way Stars Wars creator George Lucas wanted it. The aim was to make the antihero an incomparable unnerving enigma. Vader proved to be a shock to the senses from the very start. The more we saw him, the more we wanted to know about him — from a safe distance, of course.

"I had to make Darth Vader scary without the audience ever seeing his face," Lucas told Rolling Stone magazine. "Basically, it's just a black mask. I said, 'How do I make that evil and scary?' I mean, he's big and black and he's got a cape and a samurai helmet, but that doesn't necessarily make people afraid of him. His character's got to go beyond that — that's how we get his impersonal way of dealing with things. He's done a lot of horrible things in his life that he isn't particularly proud of. Ultimately, he's just a pathetic guy who's had a very sad life."

THIERRY ZOCCOLAN/GETTY IMAGES

ACTOR DAVID PROWSE (SHOWN ABOVE IN AN IMAGE FROM 2013) WAS THE MAN IN THE SUIT FOR DARTH VADER WHILE JAMES EARL JONES (SHOWN BELOW) PROVIDED THE CHARACTER'S IMPOSING VOICE.

JIM SPELLMAN/GETTY IMAGES

Let's start with the character's name, which provided a hidden clue. "Darth" is a variation of dark, and "Vader" is Dutch for father. "So it's basically Dark Father," Lucas added in Rolling Stone. Little could audiences have known that Lucas had provided a sneaky hint to a planet-shaking plot twist that would rattle viewers down the line.

Now let's turn to the obvious: the look. It is the foundation for the character's popularity. The film industry had never seen anything like Vader. In Hollywood, villains were simply troublemakers who more or less looked like someone you might bump into at the grocery store, only they went about their daily life concocting sinister plans.

Perhaps, at the worst, they wore black and maybe an eyepatch, spoke with a British or Eastern European accent or sported a perpetual scowl or unsightly scar. With Vader, we didn't know whether he was chewing bubble gum or even awake, for that matter. The expression-less mask, not to mention his height and dark, flowing cape, made him that much more psychologically terrifying.

Can't forget to mention he's an expert with a lightsaber and has mastered the Force, thus he's able to wring the life out of anyone who crosses him without so much

laying a finger on them. That nifty weaponry and "Force choke" gives him an aura of invincibility.

HE'S A HEAVY BREATHER

Toss in the breathing. How many movie characters would you recognize on their breathing pattern alone? It's unmistakable, one of the most distinct and menacing sounds the film industry has ever produced. If it takes you more than a split second to identify it, perhaps you've stopped breathing. Admit it — as a *Star Wars* fan, you've tried to copy that sound, just as you've tried to emulate Vader's voice.

That voice. That sweet, full-toned, authoritative and ominous sound provided by James Earl Jones. He's the man who told us "This is CNN" and later gave sports fans goosebumps talking about baseball in a middle-of-nowhere Iowa cornfield in *Field of Dreams*. Never mind those other roles. His voice is the one that will speak for the Dark Side for eternity.

Jones admitted to The New York Times Magazine to having a little fun putting Darth Vader's voice to use off the set. Who wouldn't?

"I did that once when I was traveling cross-country," he said. "I used Darth as my handle on the CB radio.

DARTH VADER: WICKED GOOD

The truck drivers would really freak out — for them, it was Darth Vader. I had to stop doing that."

We've got the visuals. We've got the sounds. And just to add to the sensory overload, the powers that be asked composer John Williams, the man who created the eerie *Jaws* theme, to whip up a little tune for Vader. "The Imperial March" nailed it. It's intimidating, apocalyptic and perfectly captures the unpleasant tone in all things Vader and the Empire. The song has become the unofficial anthem for anything or anyone with a despicable side.

Episode IV made it clear that Vader was a bad dude, assuming he was human, and downright cold. The more the films peeled his layers, the more we realized there was a glimmer of humanity behind the darkness. Heck, he was even a cute kid at one time and had what it took to be — spoiler alert — a dedicated Skywalker family man.

In later films, created to unveil Vader's backstory, we meet him as a young Anakin Skywalker, a slave boy thought to be the "Chosen One." The young Jedi in training was supposed to bring balance to the Force. Oops. Not quite. He's the classic case of a good kid gone bad, caught up trying to rule an entire galaxy, far, far, away. It could happen to the best of us.

In The *Empire Strikes Back*, Vader reveals himself as Luke Skywalker's father and asks the youngster to join him as the nastiest pop/son duo in the galaxy. While that reunion didn't pan out, Vader, in *Return of the Jedi*, showed compassion and proved that family always comes first when he saved Luke from the Emperor. See, he wasn't such an evildoer after all, and it's not so tough to sympathize with him.

It's impossible not to jump on the Team Vader bandwagon when he tosses the Emperor into oblivion. For all that venom and rancor early on, Vader rebounds and totally redeems himself. That's part of the attraction to the character, his transformation from a monster into a human. It's like *Beauty and the Beast* in space, only with less fur (outside of Chewie and the Ewoks), less ballroom dancing and a lot more lightsaber battles.

Few are the movie villains who can stand up to that kind of range, which is why Vader is one of best you'll ever see. An impeccable mix of visual awe and character development thrust him into the pop culture pantheon.

Vader pulled off the improbable as the poster boy for both right and wrong. No one wants to be him, yet, at the same time, everyone wants to be him. Look around the neighborhood come Halloween. His is a costume that's been in style since 1977, and it's still as hip as ever.

You'll catch him at sporting events. At Oakland Raiders home games, take a glance at the team's famed "Black Hole" section and you're sure to spot a Darth-Vader-clad fan cheering on the Silver and Black. Vader's theme song is always a go-to tune at stadiums and arenas whenever the home squad wants to take a jab at "vile" visiting teams.

Even Disneyland, "The Happiest Place on Earth," featured Vader in promotional ads. You've come a long way in popularity, and most certainly anger management, when you can make a seamless transition from aspiring to snatch power at all costs to taking a spin on the Dumbo ride. That, folks, is what you call doing a complete 180.

HOLLYWOOD GOLD

He's such a power player that he's the equivalent of a March Madness No. 1 seed. Since 2013, StarWars.com has run an official NCAA-style bracket tournament, called "This is Madness," to determine the franchise's top character. Vader is practically a dynasty. He has dominated the Dark Side's half of the bracket, reached the final in the first four editions and won it in 2015.

Hollywood obviously has an affinity for him. Run an on-line search for the greatest movie villains of all time. Vader frequently comes up the best of the worst. *The Wizard of Oz's* wicked witch can't hang with him, and neither can *Halloween's* Michael Myers.

When was the last time you saw Hannibal Lecter (*The Silence of the Lambs*) on a lunchbox, Norman Bates (*Psycho*) on kids' light-up shoes or Hans Gruber (*Diehard*) featured on a waffle maker? Vader is a merchandiser's dream, and everyone from toddlers to grandparents can't get enough of him. He made it chic to go against the grain in the ceaseless conflict that is good vs. evil.

The thing that makes Vader stand out in a bad bunch on earth, as out of this world as he has always been, is that deep down we can all relate to him on a certain level. That can't be said for most movie meanies.

"The first film, people didn't even know whether there was a person there," Lucas said in Rolling Stone. "They thought he was a person. They thought he was a monster or some kind of a robot. In the second film, it's revealed that he's a human being, and in the third film you find out that, yes, he's a father and a regular person like the rest of us."

Dare tell Vader he's not the most iconic ruffian the world has ever known, and you're likely to get an icy-cold stare and a calculated response that should sound familiar: "I find your lack of faith disturbing." He allowed all of us to believe that sometimes it's good to be a little bad.

1977
STAR WARS

THE SET THAT STARTED IT ALL

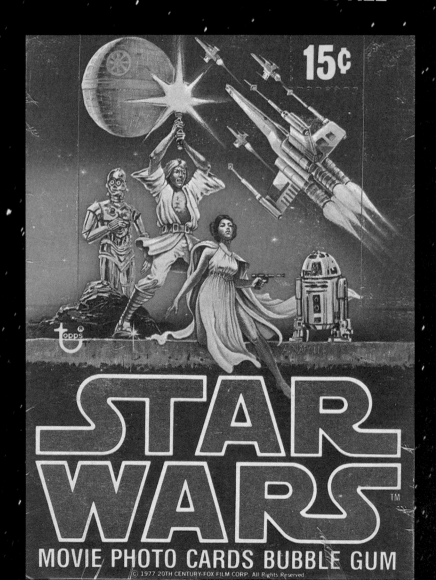

15¢

STAR WARS

MOVIE PHOTO CARDS BUBBLE GUM

1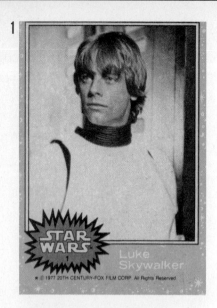

Luke Skywalker

2

See-Threepio and Artoo-Detoo

3

The little droid, Artoo-Detoo

4

Space pirate Han Solo

5

Princess Leia Organa

6

Ben (Obi-Wan) Kenobi

7

The villainous Darth Vader

8

Grand Moff Tarkin

9

Rebels defend their starship!

Princess Leia captured!

★ © 1977 20TH CENTURY-FOX FILM CORP. All Rights Reserved.

Artoo is imprisoned by the Jawas

★ © 1977 20TH CENTURY-FOX FILM CORP. All Rights Reserved.

The droids are reunited!

★ © 1977 20TH CENTURY-FOX FILM CORP. All Rights Reserved.

A sale on droids!

★ © 1977 20TH CENTURY-FOX FILM CORP. All Rights Reserved.

Luke checks out his new droid

★ © 1977 20TH CENTURY-FOX FILM CORP. All Rights Reserved.

Artoo-Detoo is left behind!

★ © 1977 20TH CENTURY-FOX FILM CORP. All Rights Reserved.

Jawas of Tatooine

★ © 1977 20TH CENTURY-FOX FILM CORP. All Rights Reserved.

Lord Vader threatens Princess Leia!

★ © 1977 20TH CENTURY-FOX FILM CORP. All Rights Reserved.

Artoo-Detoo is missing!

★ © 1977 20TH CENTURY-FOX FILM CORP. All Rights Reserved.

19

Searching for the little droid

★ © 1977 20TH CENTURY-FOX FILM CORP. All Rights Reserved.

20

Hunted by the Sandpeople!

★ © 1977 20TH CENTURY-FOX FILM CORP. All Rights Reserved.

21

The Tusken Raiders

★ © 1977 20TH CENTURY-FOX FILM CORP. All Rights Reserved.

22

Rescued by Ben Kenobi

★ © 1977 20TH CENTURY-FOX FILM CORP. All Rights Reserved.

23

See-Threepio is injured!

★ © 1977 20TH CENTURY-FOX FILM CORP. All Rights Reserved.

24

Stormtroopers seek the droids!

★ © 1977 20TH CENTURY-FOX FILM CORP. All Rights Reserved.

25

Luke rushes to save his loved ones

★ © 1977 20TH CENTURY-FOX FILM CORP. All Rights Reserved.

26

A horrified Luke sees his family killed

★ © 1977 20TH CENTURY-FOX FILM CORP. All Rights Reserved.

27

Some repairs for See-Threepio

★ © 1977 20TH CENTURY-FOX FILM CORP. All Rights Reserved.

28

Luke agrees to join Ben Kenobi
★ © 1977 20TH CENTURY-FOX FILM CORP. All Rights Reserved

29

Stopped by stormtroopers
★ © 1977 20TH CENTURY-FOX FILM CORP. All Rights Reserved

30

Han in the Millennium Falcon
★ © 1977 20TH CENTURY-FOX FILM CORP. All Rights Reserved

31

Sighting the Death Star
★ © 1977 20TH CENTURY-FOX FILM CORP. All Rights Reserved

32

Lord Vader's Guards
★ © 1977 20TH CENTURY-FOX FILM CORP. All Rights Reserved

33

The droids in the Control Room
★ © 1977 20TH CENTURY-FOX FILM CORP. All Rights Reserved

34

See-Threepio diverts the guards
★ © 1977 20TH CENTURY-FOX FILM CORP. All Rights Reserved

35

Luke and Han as stormtroopers
★ © 1977 20TH CENTURY-FOX FILM CORP. All Rights Reserved

36

Blast of the laser rifle !
★ © 1977 20TH CENTURY-FOX FILM CORP. All Rights Reserved

37

Cornered in the labyrinth
★ © 1977 20TH CENTURY-FOX FILM CORP. All Rights Reserved.

38

Luke and Han in the refuse room
★ © 1977 20TH CENTURY-FOX FILM CORP. All Rights Reserved.

39

Steel walls close in on our heroes!
★ © 1977 20TH CENTURY-FOX FILM CORP. All Rights Reserved.

40

Droids rescue their masters!
★ © 1977 20TH CENTURY-FOX FILM CORP. All Rights Reserved.

41

Facing the deadly chasm
★ © 1977 20TH CENTURY-FOX FILM CORP. All Rights Reserved.

42

Stormtroopers attack!
★ © 1977 20TH CENTURY-FOX FILM CORP. All Rights Reserved.

43

Luke prepares to swing across the chasm
★ © 1977 20TH CENTURY-FOX FILM CORP. All Rights Reserved.

44

Han and Chewie shoot it out!
★ © 1977 20TH CENTURY-FOX FILM CORP. All Rights Reserved.

45

The light sabre
★ © 1977 20TH CENTURY-FOX FILM CORP. All Rights Reserved.

46

A desperate moment for Ben
★ © 1977 20TH CENTURY-FOX FILM CORP All Rights Reserved.

47

Luke prepares for the battle
★ © 1977 20TH CENTURY-FOX FILM CORP All Rights Reserved.

48

Artoo-Detoo is loaded aboard
★ © 1977 20TH CENTURY-FOX FILM CORP All Rights Reserved.

49

The rebels monitor the raid
★ © 1977 20TH CENTURY-FOX FILM CORP All Rights Reserved.

50

Rebel leaders wonder about their fate!
★ © 1977 20TH CENTURY-FOX FILM CORP All Rights Reserved.

51

See-Threepio and Princess Leia
★ © 1977 20TH CENTURY-FOX FILM CORP All Rights Reserved.

52

Who will win the final Star War?
★ © 1977 20TH CENTURY-FOX FILM CORP All Rights Reserved.

53

Battle in outer space!
★ © 1977 20TH CENTURY-FOX FILM CORP All Rights Reserved.

54

The victors receive their reward
★ © 1977 20TH CENTURY-FOX FILM CORP All Rights Reserved.

55

56

57

58

59

60

61

62

63

64

Governor of Imperial Outlands

65

Carrie Fisher and Mark Hamill

66

Amazing robot See-Threepio!

67

See-Threepio and Luke

68

The Millennium Falcon

69

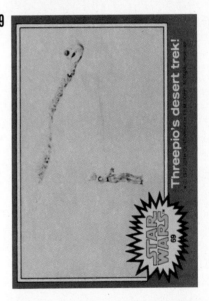

Threepio's desert trek!

70

Special mission for Artoo-Detoo!

71

The incredible See-Threepio!

72

Ben Kenobi rescues Luke!

73 — The droids wait for Luke

74 — Luke Skywalker on Tatooine

75 — Darth Vader strangles a rebel!

76 — Artoo-Detoo on the rebel starship!

77 — Waiting in the control room

78 — Droids to the rescue!

79 — Preparing to board Solo's spaceship!

80 — "Where has R2-D2 gone?"

81 — Weapons of the Death Star!

82

A daring rescue!

83

Aboard the Millennium Falcon

84

Rebel pilot prepares for the raid!

85

Luke on the sand planet

86

A mighty explosion!

87

The droids try to rescue Luke!

88

Stormtroopers guard Solo's ship

89

The imprisoned Princess Leia

90

Honoring the victors!

91

Solo and Chewie prepare to leave Luke

92

Advance of the
Tusken Raider

93

Stormtroopers blast the rebels!

94

Interrogated by stormtroopers!

95

Sighting Artoo-Detoo!

96

The droids on Tatooine

97

Meeting at the cantina

98

See-Threepio

99

Ben with the
light sabre!

100

Our heroes at the spaceport

100

101

The Wookiee
Chewbacca

101

102

Rebels prepare for the big fight!

102

103

Stormtroopers attack our heroes!

103

104

Luke's uncle and aunt

104

105

Imperial soldiers burn through the starship!

105

106

A message from Princess Leia!

106

107

The Tusken
Raider

107

108

Princess Leia observes the battle!

108

109

Ben turns off the Tractor beam

110

Threepio fools the guards!

111

Chewie and
Han Solo!

112

Threatened by Sandpeople!

113

Ben hides from Imperial stormtroopers!

114

Planning to escape!

115

Hiding in the Millennium Falcon

116

Honored for
their heroism!

117

Chewbacca poses
as a prisoner!

118

R2-D2 and C-3PO

119

Threepio, Ben and Luke!

120

Luke destroys an Imperial ship!

121

Han Solo and Chewbacca

122

The Millennium Falcon speeds through space!

123

Solo blasts a stormtrooper!

124
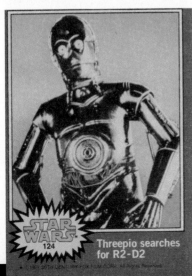
Threepio searches for R2-D2

125

Luke in disguise!

126

A quizzical Threepio!

127

The Rebel Fleet

128

Roar of the Wookiee!

129

"May The Force be with you!"™

130

Pursued by the Jawas!

131

Spectacular battle!

132

Lord Vader and a soldier

133

Ben and Luke help C-3PO to his feet

134

Luke dreams of being a star pilot

135

Cantina troubles!

136

Danger from all sides!
★ © 1977 20TH CENTURY-FOX FILM CORP. All Rights Reserved

137

Luke attacked by
a strange creature!
★ © 1977 20TH CENTURY-FOX FILM CORP. All Rights Reserved.

138

On the track of the droids
★ © 1977 20TH CENTURY-FOX FILM CORP. All Rights Reserved

139

Han Solo™...
hero or mercenary?
★ © 1977 20TH CENTURY-FOX FILM CORP. All Rights Reserved.

140

"R2-D2,"
where are you?"
★ © 1977 20TH CENTURY-FOX FILM CORP. All Rights Reserved.

141

Some quick-thinking by Luke!
★ © 1977 20TH CENTURY-FOX FILM CORP. All Rights Reserved.

142

Darth Vader™ inspects the throttled ship
★ © 1977 20TH CENTURY-FOX FILM CORP. All Rights Reserved.

143

Droids on the sand planet
★ © 1977 20TH CENTURY-FOX FILM CORP. All Rights Reserved.

144

Harrison Ford
as Han Solo™
★ © 1977 20TH CENTURY-FOX FILM CORP. All Rights Reserved.

145

Escape from the Death Star!™
★ © 1977 20TH CENTURY-FOX FILM CORP. All Rights Reserved.

146

Luke Skywalker's™ aunt preparing dinner
★ © 1977 20TH CENTURY-FOX FILM CORP. All Rights Reserved.

147

Bargaining with the Jawas!™
★ © 1977 20TH CENTURY-FOX FILM CORP. All Rights Reserved.

148

The fearsome stormtroopers!
★ © 1977 20TH CENTURY-FOX FILM CORP. All Rights Reserved.

149

The evil
Grand Moff Tarkin™
★ © 1977 20TH CENTURY-FOX FILM CORP. All Rights Reserved.

150

Shoot-out at the chasm!
★ © 1977 20TH CENTURY-FOX FILM CORP. All Rights Reserved.

151

Planning an escape!
★ © 1977 20TH CENTURY-FOX FILM CORP. All Rights Reserved.

152

Spirited
Princess Leia!™
★ © 1977 20TH CENTURY-FOX FILM CORP. All Rights Reserved.

153

The fantastic
droid Threepio!™
★ © 1977 20TH CENTURY-FOX FILM CORP. All Rights Reserved.

154

Princess Leia™ comforts Luke!
★ © 1977 20TH CENTURY-FOX FILM CORP. All Rights Reserved

155

The Escape Pod™ is jettisoned!
★ © 1977 20TH CENTURY-FOX FILM CORP. All Rights Reserved

156

R2-D2™ is lifted aboard!
★ © 1977 20TH CENTURY-FOX FILM CORP. All Rights Reserved

157

"Learn about the Force™, Luke!"
★ © 1977 20TH CENTURY-FOX FILM CORP. All Rights Reserved

158

Rebel victory
★ © 1977 20TH CENTURY-FOX FILM CORP. All Rights Reserved

159

Luke Skywalker's™ home
★ © 1977 20TH CENTURY-FOX FILM CORP. All Rights Reserved

160

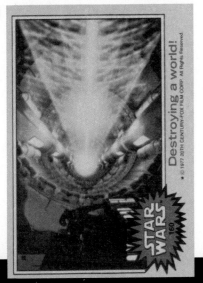

Destroying a world!
★ © 1977 20TH CENTURY-FOX FILM CORP. All Rights Reserved

161

Preparing for the raid!
★ © 1977 20TH CENTURY-FOX FILM CORP. All Rights Reserved

162

Han Solo™ cornered by Greedo!™
★ © 1977 20TH CENTURY-FOX FILM CORP. All Rights Reserved

163

Caught in the tractor beam!
★ © 1977 20TH CENTURY-FOX FILM CORP. All Rights Reserved

164

Tusken Raiders capture Luke!
★ © 1977 20TH CENTURY-FOX FILM CORP. All Rights Reserved

165

Escaping from stormtroopers!
★ © 1977 20TH CENTURY-FOX FILM CORP. All Rights Reserved

166

A close call for Luke and Princess Leia!™
★ © 1977 20TH CENTURY-FOX FILM CORP. All Rights Reserved

167

Surrounded by Lord Vader's™ soldiers!
★ © 1977 20TH CENTURY-FOX FILM CORP. All Rights Reserved

168

Hunting the fugitives
★ © 1977 20TH CENTURY-FOX FILM CORP. All Rights Reserved

169

Meeting at the Death Star!™
★ © 1977 20TH CENTURY-FOX FILM CORP. All Rights Reserved

170

Luke and the princess. . .trapped!
★ © 1977 20TH CENTURY-FOX FILM CORP. All Rights Reserved

171

"The walls are moving!"
★ © 1977 20TH CENTURY-FOX FILM CORP. All Rights Reserved

172

Droids in the Escape Pod™
★ © 1977 20TH CENTURY-FOX FILM CORP. All Rights Reserved

173

The stormtroopers
★ © 1977 20TH CENTURY-FOX FILM CORP. All Rights Reserved

174

Solo aims for trouble!
★ © 1977 20TH CENTURY-FOX FILM CORP. All Rights Reserved

175

A closer look at a "Jawa"™
★ © 1977 20TH CENTURY-FOX FILM CORP. All Rights Reserved.

176

Luke Skywalker's™ dream
★ © 1977 20TH CENTURY-FOX FILM CORP. All Rights Reserved

177

Solo swings into action!
★ © 1977 20TH CENTURY-FOX FILM CORP. All Rights Reserved

178

The Star Warriors!
★ © 1977 20TH CENTURY-FOX FILM CORP. All Rights Reserved

179

Stormtroopers search the spaceport!
★ © 1977 20TH CENTURY-FOX FILM CORP. All Rights Reserved

180

Princess Leia™ honors the victors
★ © 1977 20TH CENTURY-FOX FILM CORP. All Rights Reserved.

181

Peter Cushing as
Grand Moff Tarkin™
★ © 1977 20TH CENTURY-FOX FILM CORP. All Rights Reserved.

182

Deadly blasters!
★ © 1977 20TH CENTURY-FOX FILM CORP. All Rights Reserved.

183

Dave Prowse as
Darth Vader™
★ © 1977 20TH CENTURY-FOX FILM CORP. All Rights Reserved.

184

Luke and his uncle
★ © 1977 20TH CENTURY-FOX FILM CORP. All Rights Reserved.

185

Luke on Tatooine
★ © 1977 20TH CENTURY-FOX FILM CORP. All Rights Reserved.

186

The Jawas™
★ © 1977 20TH CENTURY-FOX FILM CORP. All Rights Reserved.

187

Threepio™
and friend
★ © 1977 20TH CENTURY-FOX FILM CORP. All Rights Reserved.

188

Starship under fire!
★ © 1977 20TH CENTURY-FOX FILM CORP. All Rights Reserved.

189

Mark Hamill as Luke
★ © 1977 20TH CENTURY-FOX FILM CORP. All Rights Reserved.

190

Carrie Fisher
as Princess Leia™

★ © 1977 20TH CENTURY-FOX FILM CORP. All Rights Reserved.

191

Life on the desert world
★ © 1977 20TH CENTURY-FOX FILM CORP. All Rights Reserved.

192

Liberated
Princess!

★ © 1977 20TH CENTURY-FOX FILM CORP. All Rights Reserved.

193

Luke's uncle buys Threepio!™
★ © 1977 20TH CENTURY-FOX FILM CORP. All Rights Reserved.

194

Stormtroopers attack!
★ © 1977 20TH CENTURY-FOX FILM CORP. All Rights Reserved.

195

Alec Guinness™
as Ben Kenobi™

★ © 1977 20TH CENTURY-FOX FILM CORP. All Rights Reserved.

196

Lord
Darth Vader™

★ © 1977 20TH CENTURY-FOX FILM CORP. All Rights Reserved.

197

Leia blasts a stormtrooper!
★ © 1977 20TH CENTURY-FOX FILM CORP. All Rights Reserved.

198

Luke decides to leave Tatooine!
★ © 1977 20TH CENTURY-FOX FILM CORP. All Rights Reserved.

199

The star warriors aim for action!

★ ★ ©1977 20TH CENTURY-FOX FILM CORP. All Rights Reserved.

200

C-3PO™ searches for his counterpart.

★ ★ ©1977 20TH CENTURY-FOX FILM CORP. All Rights Reserved.

201

Raid at Mos Eisley™.

★ ★ ©1977 20TH CENTURY-FOX FILM CORP. All Rights Reserved.

202

Inquiring about Obi-Wan Kenobi™.

★ ★ ©1977 20TH CENTURY-FOX FILM CORP. All Rights Reserved.

203

A band of Jawas™.

★ ★ ©1977 20TH CENTURY-FOX FILM CORP. All Rights Reserved.

204

Stalking the corridors of Death Star™.

★ ★ ©1977 20TH CENTURY-FOX FILM CORP. All Rights Reserved.

205

Desperate moments for our heroes!

★ ★ ©1977 20TH CENTURY-FOX FILM CORP. All Rights Reserved.

206

Searching for the missing droid.

★ ★ ©1977 20TH CENTURY-FOX FILM CORP. All Rights Reserved.

207

C-3PO™ (Anthony Daniels)

★ ★ ©1977 20TH CENTURY-FOX FILM CORP. All Rights Reserved.

208

Luke Skywalker™ on the desert planet

209

The Rebel Troops

210

Princess Leia blasts the enemy

211

A proud moment for Han and Luke

212

A stormtrooper is blasted!

213

Monitoring the battle

214

Luke and Leia shortly before the raid

215

Han bows out of the battle

216

Han and Leia quarrel about the escape plan

217

STAR WARS
217
The Dark Lord of the Sith™
★★ © 1977 20TH CENTURY-FOX FILM CORP. All Rights Reserved.

218

Luke Skywalker's home... destroyed!
★★ © 1977 20TH CENTURY-FOX FILM CORP. All Rights Reserved.
STAR WARS 218

219

The swing to freedom!
★★ © 1977 20TH CENTURY-FOX FILM CORP. All Rights Reserved.
STAR WARS 219

220

"I'm going to regret this!"
★★ © 1977 20TH CENTURY-FOX FILM CORP. All Rights Reserved.
STAR WARS 220

221

STAR WARS 221
Princess Leia (Carrie Fisher)™
★★ © 1977 20TH CENTURY-FOX FILM CORP. All Rights Reserved.

222

Evacuate... in our moment of triumph?
★★ © 1977 20TH CENTURY-FOX FILM CORP. All Rights Reserved.
STAR WARS 222

223

Han Solo covers his friends
★★ © 1977 20TH CENTURY-FOX FILM CORP. All Rights Reserved.
STAR WARS 223

224

Luke's secret yen for action!
★★ © 1977 20TH CENTURY-FOX FILM CORP. All Rights Reserved.
STAR WARS 224

225

STAR WARS 225
Aunt Beru Lars™ (Shelagh Fraser)
★★ © 1977 20TH CENTURY-FOX FILM CORP. All Rights Reserved.

226

227

228

229

230

231

231

233

234

235

236

237

238

239

240

241

242

243

244

Waiting at Mos Eisley™
**© 1977 20TH CENTURY-FOX FILM CORP. All Rights Reserved.

245

Member of the evil Empire™
**© 1977 20TH CENTURY-FOX FILM CORP. All Rights Reserved.

246

Stormtrooper—
tool of the Empire
**© 1977 20TH CENTURY-FOX FILM CORP. All Rights Reserved.

247

Soldier
of evil!
**© 1977 20TH CENTURY-FOX FILM CORP. All Rights Reserved.

248

Luke suspects the
worst about his family
**© 1977 20TH CENTURY-FOX FILM CORP. All Rights Reserved.

249

Ben Kenobi™
(Alec Guinness)
**© 1977 20TH CENTURY-FOX FILM CORP. All Rights Reserved.

250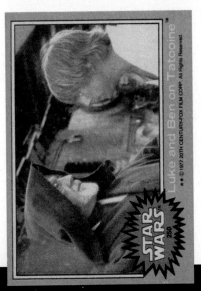

Luke and Ben on Tatooine™
**© 1977 20TH CENTURY-FOX FILM CORP. All Rights Reserved.

251

An overjoyed
Han Solo™!
**© 1977 20TH CENTURY-FOX FILM CORP. All Rights Reserved.

252

The honored heroes!
**© 1977 20TH CENTURY-FOX FILM CORP. All Rights Reserved.

253

R2-D2™
(Kenny Baker)
★★ ©1977 20TH CENTURY-FOX FILM CORP. All Rights Reserved.

254

Darth Vader™
(David Prowse)
★★ ©1977 20TH CENTURY-FOX FILM CORP. All Rights Reserved.

255

Luke poses
with his weapon
★★ ©1977 20TH CENTURY-FOX FILM CORP. All Rights Reserved.

256

The marvelous droid
See-Threepio™!
★★ ©1977 20TH CENTURY-FOX FILM CORP. All Rights Reserved.

257

A pair
of Jawas™
★★ ©1977 20TH CENTURY-FOX FILM CORP. All Rights Reserved.

258

Fighting
impossible odds!
★★ ©1977 20TH CENTURY-FOX FILM CORP. All Rights Reserved.

259

Challenging
the evil Empire!
★★ ©1977 20TH CENTURY-FOX FILM CORP. All Rights Reserved.

260

Han Solo™
(Harrison Ford)
★★ ©1977 20TH CENTURY-FOX FILM CORP. All Rights Reserved.

261

Fury of the Tusken Raider™
★★ ©1977 20TH CENTURY-FOX FILM CORP. All Rights Reserved.

262

Creature of Tatooine™
★ ★ © 1977 20TH CENTURY-FOX FILM CORP. All Rights Reserved.

263

The courage of Luke Skywalker™
★ ★ © 1977 20TH CENTURY-FOX FILM CORP. All Rights Reserved.

264

Star pilot Luke Skywalker!™
★ ★ © 1977 20TH CENTURY-FOX FILM CORP. All Rights Reserved.

265

Anxious moments for the Rebels™
★ © 1977 20TH CENTURY-FOX FILM CORP. All Rights Reserved.

266

Threepio™ and Leia monitor the battle
★ © 1977 20TH CENTURY-FOX FILM CORP. All Rights Reserved.

267

No-nonsense privateer Han Solo™!
★ © 1977 20TH CENTURY-FOX FILM CORP. All Rights Reserved.

268

Ben prepares to turn off the tractor beam
★ © 1977 20TH CENTURY-FOX FILM CORP. All Rights Reserved.

269

Droids on the run!
★ © 1977 20TH CENTURY-FOX FILM CORP. All Rights Reserved.

270

Luke Skywalker™: farmboy-turned-warrior!
★ © 1977 20TH CENTURY-FOX FILM CORP. All Rights Reserved.

271

"Do you think they'll melt us down, Artoo™?"
★ © 1977 20TH CENTURY-FOX FILM CORP. All Rights Reserved.

272

Corridors of the Death Star™
★ © 1977 20TH CENTURY-FOX FILM CORP. All Rights Reserved.

273

"This is all your fault, Artoo™!"
★ © 1977 20TH CENTURY-FOX FILM CORP. All Rights Reserved.

274

Droids trick the stormtroopers!
★ © 1977 20TH CENTURY-FOX FILM CORP. All Rights Reserved.

275

Guarding the Millennium Falcon™
★ © 1977 20TH CENTURY-FOX FILM CORP. All Rights Reserved.

276

It's not wise to upset a Wookiee™!
★ © 1977 20TH CENTURY-FOX FILM CORP. All Rights Reserved.

277

Bizarre inhabitants of the cantina!
★ © 1977 20TH CENTURY-FOX FILM CORP. All Rights Reserved.

278

A narrow escape!
★ © 1977 20TH CENTURY-FOX FILM CORP. All Rights Reserved.

279

Awaiting the Imperial attack
★ © 1977 20TH CENTURY-FOX FILM CORP. All Rights Reserved.

280

"Remember Luke, The Force" will be with you."
★ © 1977 20TH CENTURY-FOX FILM CORP. All Rights Reserved.

281

A monstrous thirst!
★ © 1977 20TH CENTURY-FOX FILM CORP. All Rights Reserved.

282

"Hurry up, Luke—we're gonna have company!"
★ © 1977 20TH CENTURY-FOX FILM CORP. All Rights Reserved.

283

The Cantina musicians
★ © 1977 20TH CENTURY-FOX FILM CORP. All Rights Reserved.

284

Distracted by Solo's assault
★ © 1977 20TH CENTURY-FOX FILM CORP. All Rights Reserved.

285

Spiffed-up for the Awards Ceremony!
★ © 1977 20TH CENTURY-FOX FILM CORP. All Rights Reserved.

286

Cantina denizens!
★ © 1977 20TH CENTURY-FOX FILM CORP. All Rights Reserved.

287

Han and Chewie™ ready for action!
★ © 1977 20TH CENTURY-FOX FILM CORP. All Rights Reserved.

288

Blasting the enemy!
★ © 1977 20TH CENTURY-FOX FILM CORP. All Rights Reserved.

289

The Rebel Fighters™ take off!
★ ©1977 20TH CENTURY-FOX FILM CORP. All Rights Reserved.

290

Chewie™ aims for danger!
★ ©1977 20TH CENTURY-FOX FILM CORP. All Rights Reserved.

291

Lord Vader™ senses The Force™
★ ©1977 20TH CENTURY-FOX FILM CORP. All Rights Reserved.

292

The stormtroopers assemble
★ ©1977 20TH CENTURY-FOX FILM CORP. All Rights Reserved.

293

A friendly chat among alien friends!
★ ©1977 20TH CENTURY-FOX FILM CORP. All Rights Reserved.

294

Droids make their way to the Escape Pod™
★ ©1977 20TH CENTURY-FOX FILM CORP. All Rights Reserved.

295

Han and the Rebel Pilots™
★ ©1977 20TH CENTURY-FOX FILM CORP. All Rights Reserved.

296

Artoo-Detoo™ is abducted by Jawas™!
★ ©1977 20TH CENTURY-FOX FILM CORP. All Rights Reserved.

297

Inside the Sandcrawler™
★ ©1977 20TH CENTURY-FOX FILM CORP. All Rights Reserved.

298

Chewie™ gets riled!

★ © 1977 20TH CENTURY-FOX FILM CORP. All Rights Reserved.

299

Leia wishes Luke good luck!

★ © 1977 20TH CENTURY-FOX FILM CORP. All Rights Reserved.

300

A crucial moment for Luke Skywalker™

★ © 1977 20TH CENTURY-FOX FILM CORP. All Rights Reserved.

301

Luke, the Star Warrior!

★ © 1977 20TH CENTURY-FOX FILM CORP. All Rights Reserved.

302

Threepio™ and Artoo™

★ © 1977 20TH CENTURY-FOX FILM CORP. All Rights Reserved.

303

Various droids collected by the Jawas™

★ © 1977 20TH CENTURY-FOX FILM CORP. All Rights Reserved.

304

The Jawas™ ready their new merchandise

★ © 1977 20TH CENTURY-FOX FILM CORP. All Rights Reserved.

305

Director George Lucas and "Greedo"

★ © 1977 20TH CENTURY-FOX FILM CORP. All Rights Reserved.

306

Technicians ready C-3PO™ for the cameras

★ © 1977 20TH CENTURY-FOX FILM CORP. All Rights Reserved.

307

A touch-up for Chewbacca™!
★ © 1977 20TH CENTURY-FOX FILM CORP. All Rights Reserved.

308

Directing the Cantina creatures
★ © 1977 20TH CENTURY-FOX FILM CORP. All Rights Reserved.

309

The birthday celebration for Sir Alec Guinness
★ © 1977 20TH CENTURY-FOX FILM CORP. All Rights Reserved.

310

Filming the Awards Ceremony
★ © 1977 20TH CENTURY-FOX FILM CORP. All Rights Reserved.

311

The model builders proudly display their work
★ © 1977 20TH CENTURY-FOX FILM CORP. All Rights Reserved.

312

Using the "blue screen" process for X-wings™
★ © 1977 20TH CENTURY-FOX FILM CORP. All Rights Reserved.

313

The birth of a droid
★ © 1977 20TH CENTURY-FOX FILM CORP. All Rights Reserved.

314

Shooting in Tunisia
★ © 1977 20TH CENTURY-FOX FILM CORP. All Rights Reserved.

315

Inside the Millennium Falcon™
★ © 1977 20TH CENTURY-FOX FILM CORP. All Rights Reserved.

316

Photographing the
miniature explosions

★ © 1977 20TH CENTURY-FOX FILM CORP. All Rights Reserved.

317

Filming explosions on the Death Star™
★ © 1977 20TH CENTURY-FOX FILM CORP. All Rights Reserved.

318

"Make-up" for the Bantha™
★ © 1977 20TH CENTURY-FOX FILM CORP. All Rights Reserved.

319

Dave Prowse and Alec Guinness rehearse
★ © 1977 20TH CENTURY-FOX FILM CORP. All Rights Reserved.

320

Flight of
the Falcon

★ © 1977 20TH CENTURY-FOX FILM CORP. All Rights Reserved.

321

George Lucas directs his counterpart "Luke"
★ © 1977 20TH CENTURY-FOX FILM CORP. All Rights Reserved.

322

Constructing the Star Destroyer™
★ © 1977 20TH CENTURY-FOX FILM CORP. All Rights Reserved.

323

Aboard the Millennium Falcon™
★ © 1977 20TH CENTURY-FOX FILM CORP. All Rights Reserved.

324

Chewie™ takes a
breather between scenes

★ © 1977 20TH CENTURY-FOX FILM CORP. All Rights Reserved.

307

The princess gets the brush!
© 1977 20TH CENTURY-FOX FILM CORP. · All Rights Reserved.

326

Animating the "chessboard" creatures
© 1977 20TH CENTURY-FOX FILM CORP. · All Rights Reserved.

327

Filming the Sandcrawler™
© 1977 20TH CENTURY-FOX FILM CORP. · All Rights Reserved.

328

X-wings™ positioned for the cameras
© 1977 20TH CENTURY-FOX FILM CORP. · All Rights Reserved.

329

Sir Alec Guinness and George Lucas
© 1977 20TH CENTURY-FOX FILM CORP. · All Rights Reserved.

330

Filming Luke and Threepio™ in Tunisia
© 1977 20TH CENTURY-FOX FILM CORP. · All Rights Reserved.

WHAT'S LISTED?

Products in the price guide typically:

■ Are produced by licensed manufacturers

■ Are widely available

■ Have market activity on single items

WHAT THE COLUMNS MEAN

The LO and HI columns reflect current retail selling ranges. The HI column on the right generally represents the full retail selling price. The LO column on the left generally represents the lowest price one would expect to find with extensive shopping

CONDITION

Prices in this issue reflect the highest raw condition (i.e. not professionally graded by a third party) of the card commonly found at shows, shops, online, and right out of the pack for brand new releases. This generally means NrMint to Mint condition. Action figure prices are based on Mint condition. Action figures that are loose (out-of-package) are generally sold for 50 percent of the listed price, but may list for less/more depending on popularity, condition, completeness, and market sales.

CURRENCY

This price guide is intended to reflect the entire North American market. While not all the cards/figures are produced in the United States, they will reflect the market value in U.S. dollars.

GLOSSARY/LEGEND

Our glossary defines terms most frequently used in the action figure/non-sports card collecting hobby. Some of these terms are common to other types of collecting. Some terms may have several meanings depending on the use and context.

ALB - Album exclusive card. This indicates that a card was only available in a collector album or binder that was devoted to a certain product.

AU - Certified autograph

BB - Box bottom - A card or panel of cards on the bottom of a trading card box.

BI - Box incentive

BN - Barnes & Noble exclusive

BT - Box topper - A card, either regulation or jumbo-sized, that is inserted in the top of a box of trading cards.

C - Common card

CI - Case-Incentive or Case Insert - A unique card that is offered as an incentive to purchase a case (or cases) of trading cards.

COA - Certificate of Authenticity - A certificate issued by the manufacturer to insure a product's authenticity.

COR - Corrected version of an error (ERR) card

CT - Case-topper exclusive card

D23 - Disney D23 Convention

ECCC - Emerald City Comic Con

EE - Entertainment Earth exclusive - An exclusive that was offered for sale on Entertainment Earth's website.

EL - Extremely limited

ERR - Error card - A card with erroneous information, spelling, or depiction on either side of the card, most of which are not corrected by the manufacturer.

EXCH - Exchange card

FACT - Factory set exclusive

FLK - Flocked variant - This description applies exclusively to Funko products.

FOIL - holofoil

GCE - Galactic Convention Exclusive - This description applies specifically to Funko products.

GEN - General distribution - This term most usually applies to promotional cards.

GITD - Glow-in-the-Dark variant - This description usually applies to Funko products.

GS - GameStop exclusive

HOLO - hologram

HT - Hot Topic exclusive

L - Limited

LE - Limited Edition

LS - Limited Series

MEM - Memorabilia card

MET - Metallic variant - This describes a metallic version of a Funko product.

NNO - Unnumbered card

NSU - Non-Sports Update exclusive card

NYCC - New York Comic Con

OPC - O-Pee-Chee (a Canadian subsidiary of Topps)

R - Rare card

RED - Redemption card

SDCC - San Diego Comic Con

SI - Set-Incentive

SP - Single or Short Print - A short print is a card that was printed in less quantity compared to the other cards in the same series.

SR - Super Rare card

SWC - Star Wars Celebration

TW - Toy Wars exclusive

U - Uncommon card

UER - Uncorrected error

UNC - Uncut sheet or panel

UR - Ultra Rare card

VAR - Variation card - One of two or more cards from the same series, with the same card number, that differ from one another in some way. This sometimes occurs when the manufacturer notices an error in one or more of the cards, corrects the mistake, and then resumes the printing process. In some cases, one of the variations may be relatively scarce.

VAULT - This description applies specifically to Funko products and indicates a figurine that has been re-released by the company.

VL - Very Limited

VR - Very Rare card

WG - Walgreen's exclusive

WM - Walmart exclusive

As with any publication, we appreciate reader feedback. While there are many listings, not all collectibles may be priced due to market constraints. If you have any questions, concerns, or suggestions, please contact us at: nonsports@beckett.com

Action Figures and Figurines

PRICE GUIDE

VINTAGE

1977-78 Star Wars 12-Backs A

1 Ben Kenobi grey hair	1250.00	2500.00
2 Ben Kenobi white hair	1250.00	2500.00
3 Ben Kenobi (w/double telescoping lightsaber)	4000.00	8000.00
4 C-3PO	500.00	1000.00
5 Chewbacca	1000.00	2000.00
6 Darth Vader	1750.00	3500.00
7 Darth Vader (w/double telescoping lightsaber)	5000.00	8500.00
8 Death Squad Commander	450.00	900.00
10 Han Solo (small head)	1500.00	3000.00
12 Jawa (plastic cape)	5000.00	8500.00
13 Luke Skywalker (blond hair)	1500.00	3000.00
14 Luke Skywalker/telescoping lightsaber	6000.00	10000.00
15 Princess Leia	1500.00	3000.00
16 R2-D2	1000.00	2000.00
17 Stormtrooper	500.00	1000.00

1977-78 Star Wars 12-Backs B

1 Ben Kenobi (grey hair)	1000.00	2000.00
2 Ben Kenobi (white hair)	1000.00	2000.00
4 C-3PO	400.00	750.00
5 Chewbacca	800.00	1500.00
6 Darth Vader	1400.00	2800.00
10 Han Solo (small head)	1200.00	2250.00
11 Jawa	625.00	1250.00
13 Luke Skywalker (w/blond hair)	1000.00	2000.00
16 R2-D2	625.00	1250.00
17 Stormtrooper	500.00	850.00
18 Tusken Raider	500.00	850.00

1977-78 Star Wars 12-Backs C

4 C-3PO	400.00	750.00
5 Chewbacca	625.00	1250.00
6 Darth Vader	1000.00	2000.00
8 Death Squad Commander	450.00	850.00
9 Han Solo (large head)	850.00	1700.00
11 Jawa	600.00	1200.00
13 Luke Skywalker (blond hair)	750.00	1500.00
14 Luke Skywalker (w/telescoping lightsaber)	4000.00	8000.00
15 Princess Leia	500.00	1000.00
16 R2-D2	500.00	1000.00
17 Stormtrooper	400.00	750.00
18 Tusken Raider	400.00	750.00

1977-78 Star Wars 12-Backs D

4 C-3PO	400.00	750.00
5 Chewbacca	500.00	1000.00
13 Luke Skywalker (blond hair)	500.00	1000.00
15 Princess Leia	500.00	1000.00
16 R2-D2	500.00	1000.00

1977-78 Star Wars 12-Backs E

16 R2-D2	350.00	850.00

1977-78 Star Wars 20-Backs A

1 Ben Kenobi (white hair)	75.00	150.00
2 C-3PO	50.00	100.00
3 Chewbacca	60.00	120.00
5 Death Squad Commander	60.00	120.00
9 Han Solo (large head)	200.00	350.00
10 Jawa	75.00	150.00

13	Princess Leia	125.00	225.00
18	Stormtrooper	50.00	100.00
19	Tusken Raider	60.00	120.00

1977-78 Star Wars 20-Backs B

5	Chewbacca	60.00	120.00
17	Stormtrooper	50.00	100.00
19	Death Star Droid	75.00	150.00
20	Greedo	60.00	120.00
21	Hammerhead	100.00	200.00
22	Luke X-Wing Pilot	125.00	250.00
23	Power Droid	50.00	100.00
24	R5-D4	75.00	150.00
25	Snaggletooth (red)	60.00	120.00
26	Walrus Man	60.00	120.00

1977-78 Star Wars 20-Backs C

5	Chewbacca	60.00	120.00
8	Death Squad Commander	60.00	120.00
11	Jawa	75.00	150.00
17	Stormtrooper	50.00	100.00
21	Hammerhead	100.00	200.00
22	Luke X-Wing Pilot	125.00	250.00

1977-78 Star Wars 20-Backs D

11	Jawa	75.00	150.00
19	Death Star Droid	75.00	150.00
22	Luke X-Wing Pilot	125.00	250.00
24	R5-D4	75.00	150.00

1977-78 Star Wars 20-Backs E

2	Ben Kenobi (white hair)	75.00	150.00
5	Chewbacca	60.00	120.00
6	Darth Vader	100.00	200.00
8	Death Squad Commander	60.00	120.00
11	Jawa	75.00	150.00
13	Luke Skywalker (blond hair)	150.00	300.00
15	Princess Leia	125.00	225.00
17	Stormtrooper	50.00	100.00
18	Tusken Raider	60.00	120.00
20	Greedo	60.00	120.00
21	Hammerhead	100.00	200.00
22	Luke X-Wing Pilot	125.00	250.00
23	Power Droid	50.00	100.00
24	R5-D4	75.00	150.00
25	Snaggletooth (red)	60.00	120.00
26	Walrus Man	60.00	120.00

1977-78 Star Wars 20-Backs F

| 6 | Darth Vader | 100.00 | 200.00 |
| 15 | Princess Leia | 125.00 | 225.00 |

1977-78 Star Wars 20-Backs G

| 8 | Death Squad Commander | 60.00 | 120.00 |
| 9 | Han Solo (large head) | 200.00 | 350.00 |

11	Jawa	75.00	150.00
13	Luke Skywalker (blond hair)	150.00	300.00
18	Tusken Raider	60.00	120.00

1977-78 Star Wars 20-Backs H

| 18 | Tusken Raider | 60.00 | 120.00 |

1977-78 Star Wars 20-Backs I

| 11 | Jawa | 80.00 | 150.00 |

1977-78 Star Wars 20-Backs J

11	Jawa	80.00	150.00
17	Stormtrooper	50.00	100.00
26	Walrus Man	60.00	120.00

1977-78 Star Wars 20-Backs K

11	Jawa	75.00	150.00
17	Stormtrooper	50.00	100.00
18	Tusken Raider	60.00	120.00

1977-78 Star Wars 21-Backs A1

2	Ben Kenobi (white hair)	75.00	150.00
6	Darth Vader	100.00	200.00
9	Han Solo (large head)	350.00	350.00
11	Jawa	75.00	150.00

1977-78 Star Wars 21-Backs A2

13	Luke Skywalker (blond hair)	150.00	300.00
16	R2-D2	50.00	100.00
20	Greedo	60.00	120.00
21	Hammerhead	100.00	200.00
22	Luke X-Wing Pilot	125.00	250.00
23	Power Droid	50.00	100.00
24	R5-D4	75.00	150.00
25	Snaggletooth (red)	60.00	120.00
26	Walrus Man	60.00	120.00

1977-78 Star Wars 21-Backs B

4 C-3PO	50.00	100.00
6 Darth Vader	100.00	200.00
8 Death Squad Commander	60.00	120.00
9 Han Solo (large head)	200.00	350.00
13 Luke Skywalker (blond hair)	150.00	300.00
15 Princess Leia	125.00	225.00
16 R2-D2	50.00	100.00
18 Tusken Raider	60.00	120.00
20 Greedo	60.00	120.00
21 Hammerhead	100.00	200.00
22 Luke X-Wing Pilot	125.00	250.00
23 Power Droid	50.00	100.00
24 R5-D4	75.00	150.00
25 Snaggletooth (red)	60.00	120.00
26 Walrus Man	60.00	120.00
27 Boba Fett	3000.00	5000.00

1977-78 Star Wars 21-Backs C

2 Ben Kenobi (white hair)	75.00	150.00
4 C-3PO	50.00	100.00
5 Chewbacca	60.00	120.00
6 Darth Vader	100.00	200.00
8 Death Squad Commander	60.00	120.00
9 Han Solo (large head)	200.00	350.00
13 Luke Skywalker (blond hair)	150.00	300.00
15 Princess Leia	125.00	225.00
16 R2-D2	50.00	100.00
20 Greedo	60.00	120.00
22 Luke X-Wing Pilot	125.00	250.00
23 Power Droid	50.00	100.00
25 Snaggletooth (red)	60.00	120.00
26 Walrus Man	60.00	120.00

1977-78 Star Wars 21-Backs D

13 Luke Skywalker (blond hair)	60.00	300.00

1977-78 Star Wars 21-Backs E4

26 Walrus Man	60.00	120.00

1977-78 Star Wars 21-Backs E5

26 Walrus Man	60.00	120.00

1977-78 Star Wars 21-Backs F

26 Walrus Man	60.00	120.00

1977-78 Star Wars (loose)

1a Ben Kenobi (grey hair)	20.00	50.00
1b Ben Kenobi (white hair)	20.00	50.00
2 Boba Fett	25.00	60.00
3 C-3PO	12.00	30.00
4 Chewbacca	12.00	30.00
5 Darth Vader	20.00	50.00
6 Death Squad Commander	10.00	25.00
7 Death Star Droid	10.00	25.00
8 Greedo	12.00	30.00
9 Hammerhead	12.00	30.00
10a Han Solo (large head)	20.00	50.00
10b Han Solo (small head)	20.00	50.00
11 Jawa	15.00	40.00
12a Luke Skywalker (blond hair)	20.00	50.00
12b Luke Skywalker (brown hair)	20.00	50.00
13 Luke Skywalker X-wing	15.00	40.00
14 Power Droid	10.00	25.00
15 Princess Leia	15.00	40.00
16 R2-D2	12.00	30.00
17 R5-D4	10.00	25.00
18a Snaggletooth blue	75.00	350.00
(found in cantina playset)		
18b Snaggletooth (red)	10.00	25.00
19 Stormtrooper	10.00	25.00
20 Tusken Raider	10.00	25.00
21 Walrus Man	10.00	25.00

1978 Star Wars Accessories

1 1977 Early Bird Package w/figures Chewbacca, Leia, Luke, R2-D2	1750.00	3000.00
2 Mini Collector's Case	120.00	250.00

1978 Star Wars Accessories (loose)

10 Mini Collector's Case	15.00	30.00

1978 Star Wars Playsets

1 Cantina Adventure Set/Greedo	400.00	800.00
Snaggletooth blue/Hammerhead		
Walrusman		
2 Creature Cantina Action	300.00	600.00
3 Death Star Space Station	600.00	1200.00
4 Droid Factory	200.00	400.00
5 Jawa Sandcrawler (radio controlled)	1200.00	3000.00
6 Land of the Jawas	150.00	300.00

1978 Star Wars Playsets (loose)

1 Cantina Adventure Set/Greedo	50.00	100.00
Snaggletooth blue/Hammerhead		
Walrusman		
2 Creature Cantina Action		
3 Death Star Space Station	75.00	150.00
4 Droid Factory	30.00	60.00
5 Jawa Sandcrawler (radio controlled)		
6 Land of the Jawas	30.00	60.00

1978 Star Wars Vehicles

1 Imperial Troop Transporter	200.00	400.00
2 Land Speeder	125.00	250.00
3 Millenium Falcon	700.00	1200.00
4 Patrol Dewback	125.00	250.00
5 Sonic Controlled Land Speeder		600.00
6 TIE Fighter	75.00	150.00
7 TIE Fighter Darth Vader	150.00	300.00
8 X-Wing Fighter	100.00	200.00

1978 Star Wars Vehicles (loose)

1 Imperial Troop Transporter	15.00	30.00
2 Land Speeder	15.00	30.00
3 Millenium Falcon	75.00	150.00
4 Patrol Dewback	25.00	50.00
5 Sonic Controlled Land Speeder	100.00	200.00
6 TIE Fighter	25.00	50.00
7 TIE Fighter Darth Vader	30.00	60.00
8 X-Wing Fighter	30.00	60.00

1979-80 Star Wars 12-inch

1 Ben Kenobi	125.00	225.00
2 Boba Fett	300.00	600.00
3 C-3PO	125.00	250.00
4 Chewbacca	100.00	200.00
5 Darth Vader	150.00	300.00
6 Han Solo	125.00	250.00
7 IG-88	600.00	1200.00
8 Jawa	100.00	200.00
9 Luke Skywalker	125.00	250.00
10 Princess Leia	125.00	250.00
11 R2-D2	100.00	200.00
12 Stormtrooper	200.00	350.00

1979-80 Star Wars 12-inch (loose)

1 Ben Kenobi	50.00	100.00
2 Boba Fett	150.00	300.00
3 C-3PO	20.00	40.00
4 Chewbacca	30.00	60.00
5 Darth Vader	50.00	100.00
6 Han Solo	60.00	120.00
7 IG-88	150.00	300.00
8 Jawa	25.00	50.00
9 Luke Skywalker	30.00	60.00
10 Princess Leia	30.00	60.00
11 R2-D2	25.00	50.00
12 Stormtrooper	25.00	50.00

1977-78 Star Wars Palitoy 12-Backs A

1 Artoo-Detoo (R2-D2)
2 Ben (Obi-Wan) Kenobi (White Hair)
3 Chewbacca
4 Darth Vader
5 Death Squad Commander
6 Han Solo (Large Head)
7 Han Solo (Small Head)
8 Luke Skywalker (Blond Hair)
9 Princess Leia Organa
10 Sand People
11 See-Threepio (C-3PO)
12 Stormtrooper

1977-78 Star Wars Palitoy 12-Backs B

1 Artoo-Detoo (R2-D2)
2 Ben Kenobi (White Hair)
3 Chewbacca
4 Darth Vader
5 Death Squad Commander
6 Jawa (Cloth Cape)
7 Jawa (Vinyl Cape)
8 Luke Skywalker (Blond Hair)
9 Princess Leia Organa
10 Sand People
11 See-Threepio (C-3PO)
12 Stormtrooper

1977-78 Star Wars Palitoy 20-Backs

1 Death Star Droid
2 Greedo
3 Hammerhead
4 Luke Skywalker X-wing
5 Power Droid
6 R5-D4
7 Snaggletooth
8 Walrus Man

1980-82 Star Wars Empire Strikes Back 21-Backs
G

5 Ben Kenobi	50.00	100.00
8 Boba Fett	2750.00	5500.00
10 C-3PO	60.00	120.00
12 Chewbacca	50.00	100.00
14 Darth Vader	100.00	200.00
15 Death Squad Commander	150.00	300.00
16 Death Star Droid	50.00	100.00
19 Greedo	50.00	100.00
20 Hammerhead	50.00	100.00
21 Han Solo (Large Head)	60.00	120.00
29 Jawa	40.00	80.00
37 Luke Skywalker (Blond Hair)	100.00	200.00
39 Luke X-Wing Pilot	50.00	100.00
40 Power Droid	60.00	120.00
41 Princess Leia	60.00	120.00
46 R2-D2	60.00	120.00
48 R5-D4		
51 Sand People	50.00	100.00
52 Snaggletooth (Red)	40.00	80.00
54 Stormtrooper	50.00	100.00
56 Walrus Man	50.00	100.00

1980-82 Star Wars Empire Strikes Back 21-Backs
H1

5 Ben Kenobi	50.00	100.00
39 Luke X-Wing Pilot	50.00	100.00

1980-82 Star Wars Empire Strikes Back 21-Backs
H2

56 Walrus Man	50.00	100.00

1980-82 Star Wars Empire Strikes Back 21-Backs
I

8 Boba Fett	2250.00	4500.00
19 Greedo	50.00	100.00
20 Hammerhead	50.00	100.00

1980-82 Star Wars Empire Strikes Back 31-Backs
A

5 Ben Kenobi	225.00	450.00
7 Bespin Security Guard (White)	150.00	300.00
8 Boba Fett	1500.00	3000.00
9 Bossk	350.00	675.00
12 Chewbacca	350.00	675.00
18 FX-7	300.00	575.00
19 Greedo	275.00	550.00
21 Han Solo (Large Head)	325.00	650.00
22 Han Solo (Small Head)	325.00	650.00
24 Han Solo Hoth	275.00	550.00
25 IG-88	300.00	600.00
27 Imperial Stormtrooper Hoth	225.00	450.00
29 Jawa	225.00	450.00
39 Luke X-Wing Pilot	250.00	475.00
40 Power Droid	225.00	450.00
46 R2-D2	225.00	450.00
48 R5-D4	225.00	450.00
52 Snaggletooth (Red)	200.00	400.00
53 Star Destroyer Commander	200.00	400.00
54 Stormtrooper	175.00	375.00

1980-82 Star Wars Empire Strikes Back 31-Backs
B

10 C-3PO	60.00	120.00
14 Darth Vader	100.00	200.00
16 Death Star Droid	50.00	100.00
20 Hammerhead	50.00	100.00
31 Lando Calrissian (Without Teeth)	40.00	80.00
34 Luke Bespin (Blond Hair/Walking)	100.00	200.00
37 Luke Skywalker (Blond Hair)	100.00	200.00
41 Princess Leia	60.00	120.00
42 Princess Leia Bespin (Flesh Neck)	60.00	120.00
50 Rebel Soldier Hoth	30.00	60.00

51	Sand People	50.00	100.00
54	Stormtrooper	50.00	100.00
56	Walrus Man	50.00	100.00

1980-82 Star Wars Empire Strikes Back 31-Backs
C

48	R5-D4	125.00	300.00

1980-82 Star Wars Empire Strikes Back 32-Backs
A

7	Bespin Security Guard (White)	30.00	60.00
8	Boba Fett	1500.00	3000.00
10	C-3PO	60.00	120.00
12	Chewbacca	50.00	100.00
18	FX-7	50.00	100.00
24	Han Solo Hoth	50.00	100.00
25	IG-88	60.00	120.00
37	Luke Skywalker (Blond Hair)	100.00	200.00
41	Princess Leia	60.00	120.00
50	Rebel Soldier Hoth	30.00	60.00
54	Stormtrooper	50.00	100.00
56	Walrus Man	50.00	100.00

1980-82 Star Wars Empire Strikes Back 32-Backs
B

5	Ben Kenobi	50.00	100.00
9	Bossk	200.00	350.00
14	Darth Vader	100.00	200.00
19	Greedo	50.00	100.00
21	Han Solo (Large Head)	60.00	120.00
27	Imperial Stormtrooper Hoth	60.00	120.00
31	Lando Calrissian (Without Teeth)	40.00	80.00
33	Luke Bespin (Blond Hair/Gun Drawn)	100.00	200.00
39	Luke X-Wing Pilot	50.00	100.00
42	Princess Leia Bespin (Flesh Neck)	60.00	120.00
46	R2-D2	60.00	120.00
53	Star Destroyer Commander	150.00	300.00
58	Yoda (Orange Snake)	75.00	150.00

1980-82 Star Wars Empire Strikes Back 32-Backs
C

7	Bespin Security Guard (White)	30.00	60.00
27	Imperial Stormtrooper Hoth	60.00	120.00

1980-82 Star Wars Empire Strikes Back 41-Backs
A

1	2-1B	30.00	60.00
2	4-LOM	75.00	150.00
3	AT-AT Commander	30.00	60.00
4	AT-AT Driver	40.00	80.00
5	Ben Kenobi	50.00	100.00
6	Bespin Security Guard (Black)	30.00	60.00
7	Bespin Security Guard (White)	30.00	60.00
8	Boba Fett	800.00	1700.00
9	Bossk	50.00	100.00
10	C-3PO	60.00	120.00
11	C-3PO (Removable Limbs)	60.00	120.00
12	Chewbacca	50.00	100.00
13	Cloud Car Pilot	40.00	80.00
14	Darth Vader	100.00	200.00
16	Death Star Droid	50.00	100.00
17	Dengar	60.00	120.00
18	FX-7	50.00	100.00
19	Greedo	50.00	100.00
20	Hammerhead	50.00	100.00
21	Han Solo (Large Head)	60.00	120.00
22	Han Solo (Small Head)	60.00	120.00
23	Han Solo Bespin	60.00	120.00
24	Han Solo Hoth	50.00	100.00
25	IG-88	60.00	120.00
26	Imperial Commander	30.00	60.00
27	Imperial Stormtrooper Hoth	60.00	120.00
28	Imperial TIE Fighter Pilot	50.00	100.00
29	Jawa	40.00	80.00
30	Lando Calrissian (With Teeth)	40.00	80.00
31	Lando Calrissian (Without Teeth)	40.00	80.00
32	Lobot	40.00	80.00
33	Luke Bespin (Blond Hair/Gun Drawn)	100.00	200.00
35	Luke Bespin (Brown Hair/Gun Drawn)	100.00	200.00
36	Luke Hoth	50.00	100.00
37	Luke Skywalker (Blond Hair)	50.00	100.00
39	Luke X-Wing Pilot	50.00	100.00
40	Power Droid	60.00	120.00
41	Princess Leia	60.00	120.00
45	Princess Leia Hoth	60.00	120.00
46	R2-D2	60.00	120.00
47	R2-D2 (Sensorscope)	75.00	150.00
48	R5-D4	50.00	100.00
49	Rebel Commander	40.00	80.00
50	Rebel Soldier Hoth	30.00	60.00
51	Sand People	50.00	100.00
52	Snaggletooth (Red)	40.00	80.00
53	Star Destroyer Commander	150.00	300.00
54	Stormtrooper	50.00	100.00
56	Walrus Man	50.00	100.00
58	Yoda (Orange Snake)	75.00	150.00
59	Zuckuss	50.00	100.00

1980-82 Star Wars Empire Strikes Back 41-Backs
B

1	2-1B	30.00	60.00
8	Boba Fett	500.00	1000.00
9	Bossk	50.00	100.00
10	C-3PO	60.00	120.00
18	FX-7	50.00	100.00
21	Han Solo (Large Head)	60.00	120.00
32	Lobot	40.00	80.00
33	Luke Bespin (Blond Hair/Gun Drawn)	100.00	200.00
39	Luke X-Wing Pilot	50.00	100.00
50	Rebel Soldier Hoth	30.00	60.00
54	Stormtrooper	50.00	100.00
57	Yoda (Brown Snake)	300.00	600.00
58	Yoda (Orange Snake)	75.00	150.00

1980-82 Star Wars Empire Strikes Back 41-Backs
C

4	AT-AT Driver	40.00	80.00
7	Bespin Security Guard (White)	30.00	60.00
12	Chewbacca	50.00	100.00
24	Han Solo Hoth	50.00	100.00
25	IG-88	60.00	120.00
26	Imperial Commander	30.00	60.00
29	Jawa	40.00	80.00
37	Luke Skywalker (Blond Hair)	100.00	200.00
41	Princess Leia	60.00	120.00
49	Rebel Commander	40.00	80.00
55	Ugnaught	30.00	60.00
56	Walrus Man	50.00	100.00

1980-82 Star Wars Empire Strikes Back 41-Backs
D

1	2-1B	30.00	60.00
8	Boba Fett	900.00	1800.00
18	FX-7	50.00	100.00
21	Han Solo (Large Head)	60.00	120.00
23	Han Solo Bespin	60.00	120.00
27	Imperial Stormtrooper Hoth	60.00	120.00
30	Lando Calrissian (With Teeth)	40.00	80.00
32	Lobot	40.00	80.00
35	Luke Bespin (Brown Hair/Gun Drawn)	100.00	200.00
39	Luke X-Wing Pilot	50.00	100.00
44	Princess Leia Bespin (Neck Painted/Front)	60.00	120.00
45	Princess Leia Hoth	60.00	120.00
50	Rebel Soldier Hoth	30.00	60.00
54	Stormtrooper	50.00	100.00
57	Yoda (Brown Snake)	100.00	200.00
58	Yoda (Orange Snake)	75.00	150.00

1980-82 Star Wars Empire Strikes Back 41-Backs
E

4	AT-AT Driver	40.00	80.00
7	Bespin Security Guard (White)	30.00	60.00
10	C-3PO	60.00	120.00
12	Chewbacca	50.00	100.00
17	Dengar	60.00	120.00
19	Greedo	50.00	100.00
24	Han Solo Hoth	50.00	100.00
25	IG-88	60.00	120.00
26	Imperial Commander	30.00	60.00
27	Imperial Stormtrooper Hoth	60.00	120.00
29	Jawa	40.00	80.00
37	Luke Skywalker (Blond Hair)	100.00	200.00
38	Luke Skywalker (Brown Hair)	125.00	250.00
41	Princess Leia	60.00	120.00
49	Rebel Commander	40.00	80.00
50	Rebel Soldier Hoth	30.00	60.00
51	Sand People	50.00	100.00
52	Snaggletooth (Red)	40.00	80.00
53	Star Destroyer Commander	150.00	300.00
55	Ugnaught	30.00	60.00
56	Walrus Man	50.00	100.00

1980-82 Star Wars Empire Strikes Back 45-Backs
A

1	2-1B	30.00	60.00
2	4-LOM	75.00	150.00
3	AT-AT Commander	30.00	60.00
5	Ben Kenobi	50.00	100.00
6	Bespin Security Guard (Black)	30.00	60.00
7	Bespin Security Guard (White)	30.00	60.00
9	Bossk	50.00	100.00
10	C-3PO	60.00	120.00
12	Chewbacca	50.00	100.00
13	Cloud Car Pilot	40.00	80.00

14	Darth Vader	100.00	200.00
15	Death Squad Commander	150.00	300.00
16	Death Star Droid	50.00	100.00
19	Greedo	50.00	100.00
20	Hammerhead	50.00	100.00
21	Han Solo (Large Head)	60.00	120.00
22	Han Solo (Small Head)	60.00	120.00
23	Han Solo Bespin	60.00	120.00
24	Han Solo Hoth	50.00	100.00
26	Imperial Commander	30.00	60.00
27	Imperial Stormtrooper Hoth	60.00	120.00
28	Imperial TIE Fighter Pilot	50.00	100.00
29	Jawa	40.00	80.00
30	Lando Calrissian (With Teeth)	40.00	80.00
32	Lobot	40.00	80.00
34	Luke Bespin (Blond Hair/Walking)	100.00	200.00
35	Luke Bespin (Brown Hair/Gun Drawn)	100.00	200.00
36	Luke Hoth	50.00	100.00
38	Luke Skywalker (Brown Hair)	100.00	200.00
39	Luke X-Wing Pilot	50.00	100.00
41	Princess Leia	60.00	120.00
42	Princess Leia Bespin (Flesh Neck)	200.00	350.00
44	Princess Leia Bespin (Neck Painted/Front)	200.00	350.00
45	Princess Leia Hoth	60.00	120.00
46	R2-D2	60.00	120.00
47	R2-D2 (Sensorscope)	75.00	150.00
48	R5-D4		
49	Rebel Commander	40.00	80.00
50	Rebel Soldier Hoth	30.00	60.00
51	Sand People	50.00	100.00
52	Snaggletooth (Red)	40.00	80.00
53	Star Destroyer Commander	150.00	300.00
54	Stormtrooper	50.00	100.00
55	Ugnaught	30.00	60.00
56	Walrus Man	50.00	100.00
57	Yoda (Brown Snake)	100.00	200.00
59	Zuckuss	50.00	100.00

1980-82 Star Wars Empire Strikes Back 45-Backs
B

3	AT-AT Commander	30.00	60.00
6	Bespin Security Guard (Black)	30.00	60.00
14	Darth Vader	100.00	200.00
27	Imperial Stormtrooper Hoth	60.00	120.00
50	Rebel Soldier Hoth	30.00	60.00

1980-82 Star Wars Empire Strikes Back 47-Backs
A

1	2-1B	30.00	60.00
2	4-LOM	75.00	150.00
3	AT-AT Commander	30.00	60.00
4	AT-AT Driver	40.00	80.00
5	Ben Kenobi	50.00	100.00

6	Bespin Security Guard (Black)	30.00	60.00
7	Bespin Security Guard (White)	30.00	60.00
8	Boba Fett	600.00	1200.00
9	Bossk	50.00	100.00
11	C-3PO (Removable Limbs)	60.00	120.00
12	Chewbacca	50.00	100.00
13	Cloud Car Pilot	40.00	80.00
14	Darth Vader	100.00	200.00
15	Death Squad Commander	150.00	300.00
16	Death Star Droid	50.00	100.00
17	Dengar	60.00	120.00
18	FX-7	50.00	100.00
19	Greedo	50.00	100.00
20	Hammerhead	50.00	100.00
21	Han Solo (Large Head)	60.00	120.00
23	Han Solo Bespin	60.00	120.00
24	Han Solo Hoth	50.00	100.00
25	IG-88	60.00	120.00
26	Imperial Commander	30.00	60.00
27	Imperial Stormtrooper Hoth	60.00	120.00
28	Imperial TIE Fighter Pilot	50.00	100.00
29	Jawa	40.00	80.00
30	Lando Calrissian (With Teeth)	40.00	80.00
32	Lobot	40.00	80.00
35	Luke Bespin (Brown Hair/Gun Drawn)	125.00	250.00
36	Luke Hoth	50.00	100.00
37	Luke Skywalker (Blond Hair)	100.00	200.00
38	Luke Skywalker (Brown Hair)	125.00	250.00
39	Luke X-Wing Pilot	50.00	100.00
40	Power Droid	60.00	120.00
41	Princess Leia	60.00	120.00
44	Princess Leia Bespin (Neck Painted/Front)		
45	Princess Leia Hoth	60.00	120.00
47	R2-D2 (Sensorscope)	75.00	150.00
48	R5-D4		
49	Rebel Commander	40.00	80.00
50	Rebel Soldier Hoth	30.00	60.00
51	Sand People	50.00	100.00
52	Snaggletooth (Red)	40.00	80.00
53	Star Destroyer Commander	150.00	300.00
54	Stormtrooper	50.00	100.00
55	Ugnaught	30.00	60.00
56	Walrus Man	50.00	100.00
57	Yoda (Brown Snake)	100.00	200.00
58	Yoda (Orange Snake)	75.00	150.00

1980-82 Star Wars Empire Strikes Back 48-Backs
A

1	2-1B	30.00	60.00
3	AT-AT Commander	30.00	60.00
5	Ben Kenobi	50.00	100.00
6	Bespin Security Guard (Black)	30.00	60.00
7	Bespin Security Guard (White)	30.00	60.00
11	C-3PO (Removable Limbs)	60.00	120.00
12	Chewbacca	50.00	100.00
13	Cloud Car Pilot	40.00	80.00
24	Han Solo Hoth	50.00	100.00
26	Imperial Commander	30.00	60.00
27	Imperial Stormtrooper Hoth	60.00	120.00
28	Imperial TIE Fighter Pilot	50.00	100.00
36	Luke Hoth	50.00	100.00
39	Luke X-Wing Pilot	50.00	100.00
45	Princess Leia Hoth	60.00	120.00
47	R2-D2 (Sensorscope)	75.00	150.00
49	Rebel Commander	40.00	80.00
51	Sand People	50.00	100.00
52	Snaggletooth (Red)	40.00	80.00
54	Stormtrooper	50.00	100.00
59	Zuckuss	50.00	100.00

1980-82 Star Wars Empire Strikes Back 48-Backs B

2 4-LOM	75.00	150.00
5 Ben Kenobi	50.00	100.00
6 Bespin Security Guard (Black)	30.00	60.00
7 Bespin Security Guard (White)	30.00	60.00
9 Bossk	50.00	100.00
11 C-3PO (Removable Limbs)	60.00	120.00
14 Darth Vader	100.00	200.00
17 Dengar	60.00	120.00
18 FX-7	50.00	100.00
26 Imperial Commander	30.00	60.00
27 Imperial Stormtrooper Hoth	60.00	120.00
28 Imperial TIE Fighter Pilot	50.00	100.00
30 Lando Calrissian (With Teeth)	40.00	80.00
33 Luke Bespin (Blond Hair/Gun Drawn)	100.00	200.00
35 Luke Bespin (Brown Hair/Gun Drawn)	125.00	250.00
39 Luke X-Wing Pilot	50.00	100.00
49 Rebel Commander	40.00	80.00
50 Rebel Soldier Hoth	40.00	80.00
54 Stormtrooper	50.00	100.00
55 Ugnaught	30.00	60.00
57 Yoda (Brown Snake)	100.00	200.00
59 Zuckuss	50.00	100.00

1980-82 Star Wars Empire Strikes Back 48-Backs C

1 2-1B	25.00	60.00
2 4-LOM	80.00	150.00
3 AT-AT Commander	25.00	60.00
4 AT-AT Driver	30.00	80.00
5 Ben Kenobi	50.00	100.00
6 Bespin Security Guard (Black)	25.00	60.00
8 Boba Fett	225.00	450.00
9 Bossk	50.00	100.00
11 C-3PO (Removable Limbs)	60.00	120.00
12 Chewbacca	50.00	100.00
13 Cloud Car Pilot	40.00	80.00
14 Darth Vader	100.00	200.00
18 FX-7	50.00	100.00
23 Han Solo Bespin	60.00	120.00
24 Han Solo Hoth	50.00	100.00
25 IG-88	60.00	120.00
26 Imperial Commander	30.00	60.00
28 Imperial TIE Fighter Pilot	50.00	100.00
29 Jawa	40.00	80.00
30 Lando Calrissian (With Teeth)	40.00	80.00
32 Lobot	40.00	80.00
35 Luke Bespin (Brown Hair/Gun Drawn)	100.00	200.00
36 Luke Hoth	50.00	100.00
39 Luke X-Wing Pilot	50.00	100.00
49 Rebel Commander	40.00	80.00
50 Rebel Soldier Hoth	30.00	60.00
51 Sand People	50.00	100.00
52 Snaggletooth (Red)	40.00	80.00
53 Star Destroyer Commander	150.00	300.00
54 Stormtrooper	50.00	100.00
55 Ugnaught	30.00	60.00
57 Yoda (Brown Snake)	100.00	200.00
59 Zuckuss	50.00	100.00

1980-82 Star Wars Empire Strikes Back (loose)

1 2-1B	6.00	12.00
2 4-LOM	12.50	25.00
3 AT-AT Commander	6.00	12.00
4 AT-AT Driver	7.50	15.00
5a Ben Kenobi (grey hair)	10.00	20.00
5b Ben Kenobi (white hair)	10.00	20.00
6a Bespin guard (black)	6.00	12.00
6b Bespin guard (white)	6.00	12.00
7 Boba Fett	25.00	50.00

8 Bossk	7.50	15.00
9 C-3PO	7.50	15.00
10 C-3PO (removable limbs)	7.50	15.00
11 Chewbacca	6.00	12.00
12 Cloud Car Pilot	6.00	12.00
13 Darth Vader	10.00	20.00
14 Death Squad Commander	10.00	20.00
15 Death Star Droid	6.00	12.00
16 Dengar	6.00	12.00
17 FX-7	6.00	12.00
18 Greedo	6.00	12.00
19 Hammerhead	6.00	12.00
20 Han Solo (Bespin)	7.50	15.00
21 Han Solo (Hoth gear)	6.00	12.00
22 Han Solo (large head)	6.00	12.00
23 Han Solo (small head)	6.00	12.00
24 IG-88	7.50	15.00
25 Imperial Commander	6.00	12.00
26 Imperial Stormtrooper	7.50	15.00
27 Jawa	6.00	12.00
28 Lando Calrissian	6.00	12.00
29 Lando Calrrissian (no teeth)	6.00	12.00
30 Lobot	7.50	15.00
31a Luke Skywalker	10.00	20.00
(Bespin yellow hair tan legs)		
31b Luke Skywalker		
(Bespin yellow hair brown legs)		
31c Luke Skywalker	10.00	20.00
(Bespin brown hair)		
31d Luke Skywalker	12.50	20.00
(Bespin white shirt blond hair)		
31e Luke Skywalker	12.50	25.00
(Bespin white shirt brown hair)		
32 Luke Skywalker (Hoth gear)	6.00	12.00
33 Luke Skywalker X-wing	6.00	12.00
34 Power Droid	7.50	15.00
35a Princess Leia Organa	7.50	15.00
(Bespin flesh neck)		
35b Princess Leia Organa	7.50	15.00
(Bespin turtle neck)		
35c Princess Leia Organa		
(Bespin gold/green neck)		
36 Leia Organa (Hoth gear)	7.50	15.00
37a R2-D2	7.50	15.00
37b R2-D2 (sensorscope)	7.50	15.00
38 R5-D4		
39 Rebel Commander	6.00	12.00
40 Rebel Soldier (Hoth gear)	6.00	12.00
41 Snaggletooth (red)	6.00	12.00
42 Stormtrooper	6.00	12.00
43 TIE Fighter Pilot	6.00	12.00
44 Tusken Raider	6.00	12.00
45 Ugnaught		12.00
46 Walrusman	6.00	12.00
48a Yoda (brown snake)	7.50	15.00
48b Yoda (orange snake)	7.50	15.00
49 Zuckuss	6.00	12.00

1980-82 Star Wars Empire Strikes Back Accessories

1 Darth Vader Case	200.00	350.00
2 Darth Vader Case/Boba Fett/IG88	200.00	400.00
3 Mini Collector's Case	125.00	225.00

1980-82 Star Wars Empire Strikes Back Accessories (loose)

1 Darth Vader Case	15.00	30.00
2 Mini Collector's Case	15.00	30.00

1980-82 Star Wars Empire Strikes Back Playsets

1 Cloud City	200.00	400.00
2 Dagobah	125.00	250.00
3 Darth Vader/ Star Destroyer	125.00	250.00
4 Droid Factory	200.00	350.00
5 Hoth Ice Planet	75.00	150.00
6 Imperial Attack Base	125.00	225.00
7 Land of the Jawas	100.00	200.00
8 Rebel Command Center	100.00	200.00
9 Turret and Probot	40.00	80.00

1980-82 Star Wars Empire Strikes Back Playsets (loose)

1 Cloud City	30.00	60.00
2 Dagobah	25.00	50.00
3 Darth Vader/ Star Destroyer	25.00	50.00
4 Droid Factory	30.00	60.00
5 Hoth Ice Planet	20.00	40.00

6 Imperial Attack Base	30.00	60.00
7 Land of the Jawas	30.00	60.00
8 Rebel Command Center	30.00	60.00
9 Turret and Probot	12.50	25.00

1980-82 Star Wars Empire Strikes Back Vehicles

1 AT-AT	150.00	300.00
2 Imperial Cruiser	100.00	200.00
3 Imperial Transport	100.00	200.00
4 Millenium Falcon	250.00	500.00
5 Patrol Dewback	100.00	200.00
6 Rebel Transport	100.00	200.00
7 Scout Walker	75.00	150.00
8 Slave 1	100.00	200.00
9a Snowspeeder (blue box)	60.00	120.00
9b Snowspeeder (pink box)	75.00	150.00
10 Tauntaun	50.00	100.00
11 Tauntaun (split belly)	60.00	120.00
12 TIE Fighter	75.00	150.00
13 Twin Pod Cloud Car	40.00	80.00
14 Wampa	150.00	300.00
15a X-Wing Fighter (battle damage red photo background box)	100.00	200.00
15b X-Wing Fighter (battle damage landscape photo background box)	100.00	200.00

1980-82 Star Wars Empire Strikes Back Vehicles (loose)

1 AT-AT	40.00	80.00
2 Imperial Cruiser	15.00	30.00
3 Imperial Transport	15.00	30.00
4 Millenium Falcon	50.00	100.00
5 Patrol Dewback	25.00	50.00
6 Rebel Transport	15.00	30.00
7 Scout Walker	15.00	30.00
8 Slave 1	60.00	125.00
9 Snowspeeder	15.00	30.00
10 Tauntaun	20.00	40.00
11 Tauntaun split belly	25.00	50.00
12 TIE Fighter	25.00	50.00
13 Twin Pod Cloud Car	20.00	40.00
14 Wampa	25.00	60.00
15 X-Wing Fighter	30.00	60.00

1980 Star Wars Empire Strikes Back Micro Set

1 Bespin Control Room/Darth Vader	30.00	60.00
Darth Vader lightsaber/Luke Skywalker		
2 Bespin Freeze Chamber/Boba Fett	75.00	150.00
Darth Vader/Han Solo in cuffs/Han Solo		
3 Bespin Gantry/Darth Vader	40.00	80.00
Darth Vader lightsaber/Luke Skywalker		
4 Bespin World/Boba Fett/Darth Vader	100.00	200.00
Darth Vader lightsaber/Han Solo carbonite		
5 Death Star Compactor/Ben Kenobi	125.00	225.00
Darth Vader lightsaber/Han Solo stormtrooper		
6 Death Star Escape/Chewbacca	40.00	80.00
Darth Vader/Luke Skywalker		
Princess Leia		
7 Death Star World/Ben Kenobi	125.00	225.00
Chewbacca/Darth Vader		
Darth Vader lightsaber/Han Solo		
Luke Skywalker/Luke Skywalker stormtrooper		
Princess Leia/Princess Leia holding gun		
Stormtrooper kneeling/Stormtrooper walking		
Stormtrooper firing/Stormtrooper firing u		
8 Hoth Generator Attack/AT-AT	30.00	60.00
AT-AT Operator/Darth Vader unpainted		
Rebel		
9 Hoth Ion Cannon/Rebel on Tauntaun	50.00	100.00
Rebel crouching/Rebel laying		
10 Hoth Turret Defense	40.00	80.00
Rebel on Tauntaun blaster		
Rebel crouching		
11 Hoth Wampa Cave/Chewbacca	30.00	60.00
Han Solo/Luke Skywalker hanging		
Probot/Wampa		
12 Hoth World/Hot Wampa Cave	100.00	200.00
Hoth Ion Cannon/Hoth Generator Attack		
13 Imperial TIE Fighter	50.00	100.00
TIE Fighter Pilot		
14 Millenium Falcon/C-3PO	150.00	300.00
Chewbacca with wrench/Lando Calrissian		
Luke Skywalker		
15 Snowspeeder	75.00	150.00
X-Wing Pilot sitting		
X-Wing Pilot crouching		
16 X-Wing/X-Wing Pilot	75.00	150.00

1980 Star Wars Empire Strikes Back Micro Set (loose)

1 Bespin Control Room	7.50	15.00
2 Bespin Freeze Chamber	12.50	25.00
3 Bespin Gantry	7.50	15.00
4 Bespin World	12.50	25.00
5 Death Star Compactor	12.50	25.00
6 Death Star Escape	7.50	15.00
7 Death Star World	12.50	25.00
8 Hoth Generator Attack	7.50	15.00
9 Hoth Ion Cannon	10.00	20.00
10 Hoth Turret Defense	6.00	12.00
11 Hoth Wampa Cave	7.50	15.00
12 Hoth World	12.50	25.00
13 Imperial Tie Fighter	6.00	12.00
14 Millenium Falcon	12.50	25.00
15 Snowspeeder	6.00	12.00
16 X-Wing	7.50	15.00
17 AT-AT	6.00	12.00
18 AT-AT Operator	.75	2.00
19 Ben Kenobi	1.50	4.00
20 Boba Fett	.75	2.00
21 C-3PO	.75	2.00
22 Chewbacca	.75	2.00
23 Chewbacca (with wrench)	.75	2.00
24 Darth Vader	1.25	3.00
25 Darth Vader (lightsaber)	1.25	3.00
26 Darth Vader (unpainted)	1.25	3.00
27 Han Solo	1.25	3.00
28 Han Solo (carbonite)	1.25	3.00

29 Han Solo (in cuffs)	1.25	3.00
30 Han Solo (stormtrooper)	1.25	3.00
31 Lando Calrissian	.75	2.00
32 Lobot	.75	2.00
33 Luke Skywalker	1.25	3.00
34 Luke Skywalker (hanging)	1.25	3.00
35 Luke Skywalker (lightsaber)	1.25	3.00
36 Luke Skywalker (stormtrooper)	1.25	3.00
37 Princess Leia	1.25	3.00
38 Princess Leia (holding gun)	1.25	3.00
39 Probot	.75	2.00
40 Rebel (crouching)	.75	2.00
41 Rebel (gun at side/unpainted)	.75	2.00
42 Rebel (gun on hip/unpainted)	.75	2.00
43 Rebel (gun on sholder/unpainted)	.75	2.00
44 Rebel (gun on sholder)	.75	2.00
45 Rebel (laying)	.75	2.00
46 Rebel (laying unpainted)	.75	2.00
47 Rebel (on Tauntaun)	.75	2.00
48 Rebel (on Tauntaun w/blaster)	.75	2.00
49 Rebel (w/blaster at side)	.75	2.00
50 Rebel (w/blaster brown)	.75	2.00
51 Rebel (w/blaster white)	.75	2.00
52 Stormtrooper	.75	2.00
53 Stormtrooper (firing)	.75	2.00
54 Stormtrooper (kneeling)	.75	2.00
55 Stormtrooper (on gun)	.75	2.00
56 Stormtrooper (walking)	.75	2.00
57 TIE Fighter Pilot	.75	2.00
58 Turret Operator	.75	2.00
59 Wampa	1.00	2.50
60 X-Wing Pilot	.75	2.00
61 X-Wing Pilot (crouching)	.75	2.00
62 X-Wing Pilot (sitting)	.75	2.00

1980 Star Wars Empire Strikes Back Mini Rigs

1 CAP-2	10.00	20.00
2 INT-4	20.00	40.00
3 MLC-3	12.50	25.00
4 MTV-7	20.00	40.00
5 PDT-8	15.00	30.00
6 Tripod Laser Canon	20.00	40.00

1980 Star Wars Empire Strikes Back Mini Rigs (loose)

1 CAP-2	5.00	10.00
2 INT-4	7.50	15.00
3 MLC-3	5.00	10.00
4 MTV-7	6.00	12.00
5 PDT-8	7.50	15.00
6 Tripod Laser Canon	7.50	15.00

1980-82 Star Wars Empire Strikes Back Palitoy 30-Backs A

1 Bespin Security Guard (White)
2 Bossk (Bounty Hunter)
3 FX-7 (Medical Droid)
4 Han Solo (Hoth Outfit)
5 IG-88 (Bounty Hunter)
6 Imperial Stormtrooper (Hoth Battle Gear)
7 Lando Calrissian (Without Teeth)
8 Leia Organa (Bespin Gown, Flesh Neck)
9 Luke Skywalker (Bespin Fatigues, Blond Hair)
10 Rebel Soldier (Hoth Battle Gear)

1980-82 Star Wars Empire Strikes Back Palitoy 30-Backs B

1 2-1B
2 Artoo-Detoo (R2-D2)

3 AT-AT Driver
4 Ben (Obi-Wan) Kenobi (White Hair)
5 Bespin Security Guard (White)
6 Boba Fett
7 Bossk (Bounty Hunter)
8 Chewbacca
9 Darth Vader
10 Death Squad Commander
11 Death Star Droid
12 FX-7 (Medical Droid)
13 Hammerhead
14 Han Solo (Bespin Outfit)
15 Han Solo (Hoth Outfit)
16 Han Solo (Large Head)
17 IG-88 (Bounty Hunter)
18 Imperial Commander
19 Imperial Stormtrooper (Hoth Battle Gear)
20 Jawa (Cloth Cape)
21 Lando Calrissian (Without Teeth)
22 Leia (Hoth Outfit)
23 Leia Organa (Bespin Gown, Flesh Neck)
24 Leia Organa (Bespin Gown, Turtle Neck)
25 Lobot
26 Luke Skywalker (Bespin Fatigues, Blond Hair)
27 Luke Skywalker (Bespin Fatigues, Brown Hair)
28 Luke Skywalker (Blond Hair)
29 Luke Skywalker (X-Wing Pilot)
30 Power Droid
31 Princess Leia Organa
32 R5-D4
33 Rebel Commander
34 Rebel Soldier (Hoth Battle Gear)
35 See-Threepio (C-3PO)
36 Stormtrooper
37 Ugnaught
38 Walrus Man
39 Yoda (Brown Snake)

1980-82 Star Wars Empire Strikes Back Palitoy 41-Backs A

1 2-1B
2 AT-AT Driver
3 Bespin Security Guard (White)
4 Chewbacca
5 Death Squad Commander
6 Death Star Droid
7 Greedo
8 Han Solo (Hoth Outfit)
9 IG-88 (Bounty Hunter)
10 Imperial Commander
11 Imperial Stormtrooper (Hoth Battle Gear)
12 Jawa (Cloth Cape)
13 Luke Skywalker (Blond Hair)
14 Princess Leia Organa
15 Rebel Commander
16 Sand People
17 See-Threepio (C-3PO)
18 Ugnaught

1980-82 Star Wars Empire Strikes Back Palitoy 41-Backs B

1 2-1B
2 Artoo-Detoo (R2-D2)
3 Ben (Obi-Wan) Kenobi (Grey Hair)
4 Ben (Obi-Wan) Kenobi (White Hair)
5 Boba Fett
6 Bossk (Bounty Hunter)
7 Darth Vader
8 Dengar
9 FX-7 (Medical Droid)
10 Han Solo (Bespin Outfit)

11 Han Solo (Large Head)
12 Lando Calrissian (With Teeth)
13 Leia (Hoth Outfit)
14 Leia Organa (Bespin Gown, Turtle Neck)
15 Lobot
16 Luke Skywalker (Bespin Fatigues, Blond Hair)
17 Luke Skywalker (Bespin Fatigues, Brown Hair)
18 Luke Skywalker (X-Wing Pilot)
19 Power Droid
20 R5-D4
21 Rebel Soldier (Hoth Battle Gear)
22 Stormtrooper
23 Yoda (Brown Snake)

1980-82 Star Wars Empire Strikes Back Palitoy 41-Backs C

1 Artoo-Detoo (R2-D2)
2 Boba Fett
3 Han Solo (Bespin Outfit)
4 Lando Calrissian (With Teeth)
5 Leia (Hoth Outfit)
6 Leia Organa (Bespin Gown, Turtle Neck)
7 Luke Skywalker (X-Wing Pilot)
8 Power Droid
9 Stormtrooper

1980-82 Star Wars Empire Strikes Back Palitoy 45-Backs A

1 4-LOM
2 Ben (Obi-Wan) Kenobi (Grey Hair)
3 Ben (Obi-Wan) Kenobi (White Hair)
4 Han Solo (Bespin Outfit)
5 Imperial TIE Fighter Pilot
6 Luke Skywalker (Bespin Fatigues, Blond Hair)
7 Luke Skywalker (Bespin Fatigues, Brown Hair)
8 R5-D4
9 Sand People

1980-82 Star Wars Empire Strikes Back Palitoy 45-Backs B

1 (Twin-Pod) Cloud Car Pilot
2 2-1B
3 4-LOM
4 Artoo-Detoo (R2-D2) (With Sensorscope)
5 AT-AT Commander
6 AT-AT Driver
7 Ben (Obi-Wan) Kenobi (Grey Hair)
8 Ben (Obi-Wan) Kenobi (White Hair)
9 Bespin Security Guard (Black)
10 Bespin Security Guard (White)
11 Boba Fett
12 Bossk (Bounty Hunter)
13 C-3PO (Removeable Limbs)
14 Chewbacca
15 Darth Vader
16 Death Squad Commander
17 Death Star Droid
18 FX-7 (Medical Droid)
19 Greedo
20 Hammerhead
21 Han Solo (Bespin Outfit)
22 Han Solo (Hoth Outfit)
23 Han Solo (Large Head)
24 IG-88 (Bounty Hunter)
25 Imperial Commander
26 Imperial Stormtrooper (Hoth Battle Gear)
27 Imperial TIE Fighter Pilot
28 Jawa (Cloth Cape)
29 Lando Calrissian (With Teeth)
30 Leia (Hoth Outfit)

31 Leia Organa (Bespin Gown, Turtle Neck)
32 Luke Skywalker (Bespin Fatigues, Blond Hair)
33 Luke Skywalker (Blond Hair)
34 Luke Skywalker (Hoth Battle Gear)
35 Luke Skywalker (X-Wing Pilot)
36 Power Droid
37 Princess Leia Organa
38 R5-D4
39 Rebel Commander
40 Sand People
41 Snaggletooth
42 Stormtrooper
43 Walrus Man
44 Yoda (Brown Snake)

1983 Star Wars Return of the Jedi 48-Backs D

1 2-1B	40.00	80.00
2 4-LOM	40.00	80.00
5 AT-AT Commander	25.00	50.00
6 AT-AT Driver	40.00	80.00
8 Ben Kenobi	30.00	60.00
10 Bespin Security Guard (black)	30.00	60.00
11 Bespin Security Guard (white)	30.00	60.00
14 Boba Fett	300.00	700.00
16 Bossk	40.00	80.00
18 C-3PO (removable limbs)	40.00	80.00
19 Chewbacca	40.00	80.00
22 Cloud Car Pilot	30.00	60.00
23 Darth Vader	60.00	120.00
25 Death Star Droid	30.00	60.00
26 Dengar	30.00	60.00
28 FX-7	30.00	60.00
31 Greedo	40.00	80.00
32 Hammerhead	25.00	50.00
33 Han Solo (large head)	100.00	200.00
35 Han Solo (Bespin)	60.00	120.00
36 Han Solo (Hoth gear)	60.00	120.00
38 IG-88	20.00	40.00
39 Imperial Commander	40.00	80.00
40 Imperial Stormtrooper Hoth	40.00	80.00
41 Imperial TIE Fighter Pilot	50.00	100.00
42 Jawa	50.00	100.00
46 Lando Calrissian (with teeth)	30.00	60.00
47 Lobot	30.00	60.00
49 Luke Bespin (brown hair gun drawn)	150.00	300.00
50 Luke Hoth	60.00	120.00
55 Luke Skywalker (brown hair)		
56 Luke X-Wing Pilot	100.00	200.00
61 Power Droid	50.00	100.00
62 Princess Leia	450.00	800.00
63 Princess Leia (Bespin neck painted front)		
66 Princess Leia (Hoth)	125.00	250.00
68 R2-D2 (sensorscope)	40.00	80.00
69 R5-D4	50.00	100.00
71 Rebel Commander	40.00	80.00
75 Sand People	40.00	80.00
76 Snaggletooth (red)	50.00	100.00
78 Star Destroyer Commander		
79 Stormtrooper	50.00	100.00
82 Ugnaught	40.00	80.00
83 Walrus Man	30.00	60.00
86 Yoda (brown snake)	60.00	120.00
88 Zuckuss	20.00	40.00

1983 Star Wars Return of the Jedi 65-Backs A

2	4-LOM	40.00	80.00
4	Admiral Ackbar	25.00	50.00
6	AT-AT Driver	40.00	80.00
8	Ben Kenobi	30.00	60.00
10	Bespin Security Guard (black)	30.00	60.00
12	Bib Fortuna	25.00	50.00
13	Biker Scout	30.00	60.00
14	Boba Fett	250.00	500.00
18	C-3PO (removable limbs)	40.00	80.00
19	Chewbacca	40.00	80.00
21	Chief Chirpa	20.00	40.00
22	Cloud Car Pilot	30.00	60.00
23	Darth Vader	60.00	120.00
25	Death Star Droid	30.00	60.00
26	Dengar	30.00	60.00
27	Emperor's Royal Guard	40.00	80.00
29	Gamorrean Guard	25.00	50.00
30	General Madine	20.00	40.00
33	Han Solo (large head)	100.00	200.00
41	Imperial TIE Fighter Pilot	50.00	100.00
42	Jawa	50.00	100.00
43	Klaatu	20.00	40.00
45	Lando Calrisian (skiff)	25.00	50.00
48	Logray	20.00	40.00
50	Luke Hoth	60.00	120.00
51	Luke Jedi Knight (blue lightsaber)	75.00	150.00
52	Luke Jedi Knight (green lightsaber)	75.00	150.00
56	Luke X-Wing Pilot	100.00	200.00
58	Nien Nunb	25.00	50.00
64	Princess Leia (Boushh)	40.00	80.00
68	R2-D2 (sensorscope)	40.00	80.00
72	Rebel Commando	20.00	40.00
74	Ree-Yees	20.00	40.00
77	Squid Head	20.00	40.00
79	Stormtrooper	50.00	100.00
84	Weequay	20.00	40.00
86	Yoda (brown snake)	60.00	120.00
87	Yoda (brown snake/new image)	60.00	120.00
88	Zuckuss	20.00	40.00

1983 Star Wars Return of the Jedi 65-Backs B

1	2-1B	40.00	80.00
2	4-LOM	40.00	80.00
4	Admiral Ackbar	25.00	50.00
5	AT-AT Commander	25.00	50.00
6	AT-AT Driver	40.00	80.00
8	Ben Kenobi	30.00	60.00
10	Bespin Security Guard (black)	30.00	60.00
12	Bib Fortuna	25.00	50.00
13	Biker Scout	30.00	60.00
16	Bossk	40.00	80.00
18	C-3PO (removable limbs)	40.00	80.00

19	Chewbacca	40.00	80.00
21	Chief Chirpa	20.00	40.00
22	Cloud Car Pilot	30.00	60.00
23	Darth Vader	60.00	120.00
24	Darth Vader (new image)	60.00	120.00
25	Death Star Droid	30.00	60.00
27	Emperor's Royal Guard	40.00	80.00
29	Gamorrean Guard	25.00	50.00
30	General Madine	20.00	40.00
33	Han Solo (large head)	100.00	200.00
35	Han Solo (Bespin)	60.00	120.00
36	Han Solo (Hoth gear)	60.00	120.00
38	IG-88	20.00	40.00
39	Imperial Commander	40.00	80.00
40	Imperial Stormtrooper Hoth	40.00	80.00
41	Imperial TIE Fighter Pilot	50.00	100.00
42	Jawa		
43	Klaatu	20.00	40.00
45	Lando Calrisian (skiff)	25.00	50.00
46	Lando Calrissian (with teeth)	30.00	60.00
48	Logray	20.00	40.00
51	Luke Jedi Knight (blue lightsaber)	75.00	150.00
53	Luke Skywalker (blond hair)	100.00	200.00
56	Luke X-Wing Pilot	100.00	200.00
58	Nien Nunb	25.00	50.00
61	Power Droid	50.00	100.00
63	Princess Leia (Bespin neck painted/front picture)		
64	Princess Leia (Boushh)	40.00	80.00
66	Princess Leia (Hoth gear)	125.00	250.00
68	R2-D2 (sensorscope)	40.00	80.00
69	R5-D4	50.00	100.00
71	Rebel Commander	30.00	60.00
72	Rebel Commando	20.00	40.00
73	Rebel Soldier Hoth	50.00	100.00
74	Ree-Yees	20.00	40.00
75	Sand People	40.00	80.00
77	Squid Head	20.00	40.00
78	Star Destroyer Commander		
79	Stormtrooper	50.00	100.00
82	Ugnaught	40.00	80.00
84	Weequay	20.00	40.00
86	Yoda (brown snake)	60.00	120.00
88	Zuckuss	20.00	40.00

1983 Star Wars Return of the Jedi 65-Backs C

2	4-LOM	40.00	80.00
4	Admiral Ackbar	25.00	50.00
9	Ben Kenobi (new image)	30.00	60.00
12	Bib Fortuna	25.00	50.00
13	Biker Scout	40.00	80.00
15	Boba Fett (new image)	350.00	700.00
18	C-3PO (removable limbs)	40.00	80.00
20	Chewbacca (new image)	40.00	80.00
21	Chief Chirpa	20.00	40.00

1983 Star Wars Return of the Jedi 65-Backs D

23	Darth Vader	60.00	120.00
24	Darth Vader (new image)	60.00	120.00
27	Emperor's Royal Guard	40.00	80.00
29	Gamorrean Guard	25.00	50.00
30	General Madine	20.00	40.00
34	Han Solo (large head/new image)	100.00	200.00
41	Imperial TIE Fighter Pilot	40.00	80.00
42	Jawa	50.00	100.00
43	Klaatu	20.00	40.00
44	Klaatu (skiff)		
45	Lando Calrisian (skiff)	25.00	50.00
48	Logray	20.00	40.00
51	Luke Jedi Knight (blue lightsaber)	75.00	150.00
52	Luke Jedi Knight (green lightsaber)	75.00	150.00
58	Nien Nunb	25.00	50.00
64	Princess Leia (Boushh)	40.00	80.00
68	R2-D2 (sensorscope)	40.00	80.00
72	Rebel Commando	20.00	40.00
74	Ree-Yees	20.00	40.00
77	Squid Head	20.00	40.00
79	Stormtrooper	50.00	100.00
84	Weequay	20.00	40.00
87	Yoda (brown snake/new image)	60.00	120.00
88	Zuckuss	20.00	40.00

1983 Star Wars Return of the Jedi 65-Backs D

1	2-1B	40.00	80.00
4	Admiral Ackbar	25.00	50.00
13	Biker Scout	40.00	80.00
19	Chewbacca	40.00	80.00
21	Chief Chirpa	20.00	40.00
24	Darth Vader (new image)	60.00	120.00
29	Gamorrean Guard	25.00	50.00

1983 Star Wars Return of the Jedi 65-Backs E

30	General Madine	20.00	40.00

1983 Star Wars Return of the Jedi 77-Backs A

1	2-1B	40.00	80.00
2	4-LOM	40.00	80.00
3	8D8	25.00	50.00
4	Admiral Ackbar	25.00	50.00
5	AT-AT Commander	25.00	50.00
6	AT-AT Driver	40.00	80.00
7	AT-ST Driver	20.00	40.00
9	Ben Kenobi (new image)	30.00	60.00
10	Bespin Security Guard (black)	30.00	60.00
11	Bespin Security Guard (white)	30.00	60.00
12	Bib Fortuna	25.00	50.00
13	Biker Scout	40.00	80.00
15	Boba Fett (new image)	350.00	700.00
16	Bossk	40.00	80.00

17	B-Wing Pilot	20.00	40.00
18	C-3PO (removable limbs)	40.00	80.00
20	Chewbacca (new image)	40.00	80.00
21	Chief Chirpa	20.00	40.00
22	Cloud Car Pilot	30.00	60.00
24	Darth Vader (new image)	60.00	120.00
25	Death Star Droid	30.00	60.00
26	Dengar	30.00	60.00
27	Emperor's Royal Guard	40.00	80.00
28	FX-7	30.00	60.00
29	Gamorrean Guard	25.00	50.00
30	General Madine	20.00	40.00
31	Greedo	40.00	80.00
32	Hammerhead	25.00	50.00
34	Han Solo (large head/new image)	100.00	200.00
35	Han Solo (Bespin)	60.00	120.00
36	Han Solo (Hoth gear)	60.00	120.00
37	Han Solo (trench coat)	30.00	60.00
38	IG-88	20.00	40.00
39	Imperial Commander	40.00	80.00
40	Imperial Stormtrooper Hoth	40.00	80.00
41	Imperial TIE Fighter Pilot	50.00	100.00
42	Jawa	50.00	100.00
43	Klaatu	20.00	40.00
44	Klaatu (skiff)	20.00	40.00
45	Lando Calrisian (skiff)	25.00	50.00
46	Lando Calrissian (with teeth)	30.00	60.00
47	Lobot	30.00	60.00
48	Logray	20.00	40.00
49	Luke Bespin (brown hair gun drawn)	150.00	300.00
50	Luke Hoth	60.00	120.00
52	Luke Jedi Knight (green lightsaber)	75.00	150.00
54	Luke Skywalker (blond hair gunner	350.00	600.00
56	Luke X-Wing Pilot	100.00	200.00
58	Nien Nunb	25.00	50.00
59	Nikto	20.00	40.00
61	Power Droid	50.00	100.00
62	Princess Leia	450.00	800.00
63	Princess Leia (Bespin neck painted/front picture)		
64	Princess Leia (Boushh)	40.00	80.00
65	Princess Leia (poncho)	40.00	80.00
66	Princess Leia (Hoth gear)	125.00	250.00
67	Prune Face	20.00	40.00
68	R2-D2 (sensorscope)	40.00	80.00
69	R5-D4	50.00	100.00
70	Rancor Keeper	20.00	40.00
71	Rebel Commander	30.00	60.00
72	Rebel Commando	20.00	40.00
73	Rebel Soldier Hoth	50.00	100.00
74	Ree-Yees	20.00	40.00
75	Sand People	40.00	80.00
76	Snaggletooth (red)	50.00	100.00
77	Squid Head	20.00	40.00
78	Star Destroyer Commander		
79	Stormtrooper	50.00	100.00
80	Teebo	20.00	40.00
81	The Emperor	40.00	80.00
82	Ugnaught	40.00	80.00
83	Walrus Man	30.00	60.00
84	Weequay	20.00	40.00
85	Wicket	40.00	80.00
87	Yoda (brown snake/new image)	60.00	120.00
88	Zuckuss	20.00	40.00

1983 Star Wars Return of the Jedi 77-Backs B

1	2-1B	25.00	50.00
5	AT-AT Commander		
7	AT-ST Driver	20.00	40.00
10	Bespin Security Guard (black)	30.00	60.00
11	Bespin Security Guard (white)	30.00	60.00
13	Biker Scout	30.00	60.00
21	Chief Chirpa	20.00	40.00
24	Darth Vader (new image)	60.00	120.00

26	Dengar	30.00	60.00
28	FX-7	30.00	60.00
29	Gamorrean Guard	25.00	50.00
30	General Madine	20.00	40.00
32	Hammerhead	25.00	50.00
34	Han Solo (large head/new image)	100.00	200.00
37	Han Solo (trench coat)	30.00	60.00
41	Imperial TIE Fighter Pilot	40.00	80.00
43	Klaatu	20.00	40.00
49	Luke Bespin (brown hair/gun drawn)	150.00	300.00
56	Luke X-Wing Pilot	100.00	200.00
59	Nikto	20.00	40.00
61	Power Droid	50.00	100.00
65	Princess Leia (poncho)	40.00	80.00
66	Princess Leia (Hoth gear)	125.00	250.00
67	Prune Face	20.00	40.00
70	Rancor Keeper	20.00	40.00
73	Rebel Soldier Hoth	50.00	100.00
74	Ree-Yees	20.00	40.00
76	Snaggletooth (red)		
77	Squid Head	20.00	40.00
79	Stormtrooper	50.00	100.00
80	Teebo	20.00	40.00
82	Ugnaught	40.00	80.00
84	Weequay	20.00	40.00

1983 Star Wars Return of the Jedi 79-Backs A

3	8D8	25.00	50.00
6	AT-AT Driver	40.00	80.00
7	AT-ST Driver	20.00	40.00
9	Ben Kenobi (new image)	30.00	60.00
15	Boba Fett (new image)	275.00	500.00
17	B-Wing Pilot	20.00	40.00
18	C-3PO (removable limbs)	40.00	80.00
24	Darth Vader (new image)	60.00	120.00
27	Emperor's Royal Guard	40.00	80.00
29	Gamorrean Guard	25.00	50.00
31	Greedo	40.00	80.00
37	Han Solo Trench Coat	30.00	60.00
41	Imperial TIE Fighter Pilot	40.00	80.00
42	Jawa	50.00	100.00
43	Klaatu	20.00	40.00
44	Klaatu (skiff)	20.00	40.00
45	Lando Calrisian (skiff)	25.00	50.00
46	Lando Calrissian (with teeth)	30.00	60.00
52	Luke Jedi Knight (green lightsaber)	75.00	150.00
59	Nikto	20.00	40.00
64	Princess Leia (Boushh)	40.00	80.00
65	Princess Leia (poncho)	40.00	80.00
67	Prune Face	20.00	40.00
70	Rancor Keeper	20.00	40.00
74	Ree-Yees	20.00	40.00
76	Snaggletooth (red)	50.00	100.00
79	Stormtrooper	50.00	100.00
80	Teebo	20.00	40.00
81	The Emperor	40.00	80.00
82	Ugnaught	40.00	80.00
83	Walrus Man	30.00	60.00
85	Wicket	40.00	80.00
87	Yoda (brown snake/new image)	60.00	120.00
88	Zuckuss	20.00	40.00

1983 Star Wars Return of the Jedi 79-Backs B

3	8D8	25.00	50.00
7	AT-ST Driver	20.00	40.00
12	Bib Fortuna	25.00	50.00
17	B-Wing Pilot	20.00	40.00
20	Chewbacca (new image)	40.00	80.00
21	Chief Chirpa	20.00	40.00
24	Darth Vader (new image)	60.00	120.00
27	Emperor's Royal Guard	40.00	80.00
29	Gamorrean Guard	25.00	50.00
35	Han Solo Bespin	60.00	120.00
43	Klaatu	20.00	40.00
44	Klaatu (skiff)		
45	Lando Calrisian (skiff)	25.00	50.00
48	Logray	20.00	40.00
52	Luke Jedi Knight (green lightsaber)	75.00	150.00
56	Luke X-Wing Pilot	100.00	200.00
64	Princess Leia (Boushh)	40.00	80.00
65	Princess Leia (poncho)	40.00	80.00
69	R5-D4	50.00	100.00
70	Rancor Keeper	20.00	40.00
72	Rebel Commando	20.00	40.00
74	Ree-Yees	20.00	40.00
80	Teebo	20.00	40.00
81	The Emperor	40.00	80.00
84	Weequay	20.00	40.00
85	Wicket	40.00	80.00

1983 Star Wars Return of the Jedi 79-Backs C

57	Lumat	40.00	80.00
60	Paploo	40.00	80.00

1983 Star Wars Return of the Jedi (loose)

1	2-1B	6.00	12.00
2	4-LOM	12.50	25.00
3	8D8	6.00	12.00
4	Admiral Ackbar	6.00	12.00
5	Amanaman	60.00	125.00
6	AT-AT Commander	6.00	12.00
7	AT-AT Driver	7.50	15.00
8	AT-ST Driver	6.00	12.00
9	Barada	25.00	60.00
10	Ben Kenobi (blue saber)	10.00	20.00
11	Ben Kenobi (gray hair)	10.00	20.00
12	Ben Kenobi (white hair)	10.00	20.00
13	Bespin Guard (black)	6.00	12.00
14	Bespin Guard (white)	6.00	12.00
15	Bib Fortuna	5.00	10.00
16	Biker Scout (long mask)	5.00	10.00
17	Biker Scout (short mask)	7.50	15.00
18	Boba Fett	25.00	50.00
19	Bossk	7.50	15.00

20	B-Wing Pilot	5.00	10.00
21	C-3PO (removable limbs)	7.50	15.00
22	Chewbacca	6.00	12.00
23	Chief Chirpa	5.00	10.00
24	Cloud Car Pilot	6.00	12.00
25	Darth Vader	10.00	20.00
26	Death Squad Commander	10.00	20.00
27	Death Star Droid	6.00	12.00
28	Dengar	6.00	12.00
29	Dengar (white face)	7.50	15.00
30	Droopy McCool	5.00	10.00
31	Emperor	7.50	15.00
32	Emperors Royal Guard	6.00	12.00
33	FX-7	6.00	12.00
34	Gamorrean Guard	5.00	10.00
35	General Madine	5.00	10.00
36	Greedo	6.00	12.00
37	Hammerhead	6.00	12.00
38	Han Solo	7.50	15.00
39	Han Solo (Bespin)	6.00	12.00
40	Han Solo (carbonite)	80.00	150.00
41	Han Solo (Hoth gear)	6.00	12.00
42	Han Solo (trench coat)	6.00	12.00
43	IG-88	7.50	15.00
44	Imperial Commander	6.00	12.00
45	Imperial Dignitary	20.00	40.00
46	Imperial Gunner	20.00	40.00
47	Imperial Stormtrooper	7.50	15.00
48	Imperial TIE Fighter Pilot	6.00	12.00
49	Jawa	6.00	12.00
50	Klaatu	5.00	10.00
51	Klaatu (skiff)	5.00	10.00
52	Lando Calrissian	6.00	12.00
53	Lando Calrissian (skiff)	6.00	12.00
54	Lobot	7.50	15.00
55	Logray	5.00	10.00
56	Luke Skywalker	10.00	20.00
57	Luke Skywalker bespin brown hair	10.00	20.00
58	Luke Skywalker bespin white shirt blond hair	10.00	20.00
59	Luke Skywalker bespin white shirt brown hair	12.50	25.00
60	Luke Skywalker bespin yellow hair brown legs		
61	Luke Skywalker bespin yellow hair tan legs	10.00	20.00
62	Luke Skywalker (Hoth gear)	6.00	12.00
63	Luke Skywalker (stormtrooper)	5.00	10.00
64	Luke Skywalker Jedi Knight (blue lightsaber)	6.00	12.00
65	Luke Skywalker Jedi Knight(green lightsaber)	10.00	20.00
66	Luke Skywalker X-wing	50.00	100.00
67	Lumat	10.00	20.00
68	Max Rebo	5.00	10.00
69	Nien Nunb	5.00	10.00
70	Nikto	5.00	10.00
71	Paploo	5.00	10.00
72	Power Droid	5.00	10.00
73	Princess Leia Organa	5.00	10.00
74	Princess Leia Organa bespin flesh neck	10.00	20.00
75	Princess Leia Organa bespin gold neck sometimes looks green	7.50	15.00
76	Princess Leia Organa bespin turtle neck	7.50	15.00
77	Princess Leia Organa (Boushh)		
78	Princess Leia Organa (Hoth gear)	7.50	15.00
79	Princess Leia Organa (poncho)	7.50	15.00

80	Prune Face	7.50	15.00
81	R2-D2 sensorscope	5.00	10.00
82	R5-D4	7.50	15.00
83	Rancor	7.50	15.00
84	Rancor Keeper	20.00	40.00
85	Rebel Commander	5.00	10.00
86	Rebel Commando	5.00	10.00
87	Rebel Soldier (Hoth gear)	5.00	10.00
88	Ree-Yees	6.00	12.00
89	Romba	5.00	10.00
90	Sand People		
91	Snaggletooth (red)	6.00	12.00
92	Snowtrooper	6.00	12.00
93	Squid Head	15.00	30.00
94	Stormtrooper	5.00	10.00
95	Sy Snootles	6.00	12.00
96	Teebo	5.00	10.00
97	Ugnaught	5.00	10.00
98	Walrusman	5.00	10.00
99	Weequay	6.00	12.00
100	Wicket	5.00	10.00
101	Yoda (brown snake)	7.50	15.00
102	Zuckuss	6.00	12.00

1983 Star Wars Return of the Jedi Accessories

1	C-3PO Case	30.00	60.00
2	Chewy Strap	25.00	50.00
3	Darth Vader Case	75.00	150.00
4	Jedi Vinyl Case	100.00	200.00
5	Laser Rifle Case	40.00	80.00

1983 Star Wars Return of the Jedi Accessories (loose)

1	C-3PO Case	15.00	30.00
2	Chewy Strap	15.00	30.00
3	Darth Vader Case	15.00	30.00
4	Jedi Vinyl Case	15.00	30.00
5	Laser Rifle Case	15.00	30.00

1983 Star Wars Return of the Jedi Playsets

1	Ewok Village	100.00	200.00
2	Jabba The Hutt	30.00	60.00
	Salacious Crumb		
3	Jabba The Hutt Dungeon	75.00	150.00
	Klaatu/Nikto/8D8		
4	Jabba The Hutt Dungeon	300.00	650.00
	EV-9D9/Amanaman/Barada		

1983 Star Wars Return of the Jedi Playsets (loose)

1	Ewok Village	30.00	60.00
2	Jabba The Hutt	15.00	30.00
3	Jabba The Hutt Dungeon	20.00	40.00

1983 Star Wars Return of the Jedi Vehicles

1	AT-AT	150.00	300.00
2	B-Wing Fighter	75.00	150.00
3	Ewok Assault Catapult	25.00	50.00
4	Ewok Glider	30.00	60.00
5	Imperial Shuttle	250.00	500.00
6	Millenium Falcon	125.00	250.00
7	Rancor	150.00	300.00
8	Scout Walker	50.00	100.00
9	Speeder Bike	20.00	40.00
10	Sy Snootles and the Rebo Band (w/Sy Snootles/Droopy McCool/Max Rebo)	120.00	250.00
11	TIE Fighter (battle damage)	40.00	80.00
12	TIE Interceptor	60.00	120.00
13	X-Wing (battle damage)	75.00	150.00
14	Y-Wing	75.00	150.00

1983 Star Wars Return of the Jedi Vehicles (loose)

1	AT-AT	40.00	80.00
2	B-Wing Fighter	30.00	60.00
3	Droopy McCool	12.00	30.00
4	Ewok Assault Catapult	15.00	30.00
5	Ewok Glider	15.00	30.00
6	Imperial Shuttle	30.00	60.00
7	Max Rebo	8.00	20.00

8	Millenium Falcon	50.00	100.00
9	Rancor	30.00	80.00
10	Scout Walker	15.00	30.00
11	Speeder Bike	7.50	15.00
12	Sy Snootles	10.00	25.00
13	TIE Fighter (battle damage)	20.00	40.00
14	TIE Interceptor	20.00	40.00
15	X-Wing (battle damage)	30.00	60.00
16	Y-Wing	30.00	60.00

1983 Star Wars Return of the Jedi Palitoy 45-Backs C

1 (Twin-Pod) Cloud Car Pilot
2 2-1B
3 4-LOM
4 Artoo-Detoo (R2-D2) (With Sensorscope)
5 AT-AT Commander
6 AT-AT Driver
7 Ben (Obi-Wan) Kenobi (Grey Hair)
8 Ben (Obi-Wan) Kenobi (White Hair)
9 Bespin Security Guard (Black)
10 Bespin Security Guard (White)
11 Boba Fett
12 Boba Fett (Light Blue Painted Knee)
13 Boba Fett (Light Blue Unpainted Knee)
14 Bossk (Bounty Hunter)
15 C-3PO (Removeable Limbs)
16 Chewbacca
17 Darth Vader
18 Death Squad Commander
19 Death Star Droid
20 Dengar
21 FX-7 (Medical Droid)
22 Greedo
23 Hammerhead
24 Han Solo (Bespin Outfit)
25 Han Solo (Hoth Outfit)
26 Han Solo (Large Head)
27 IG-88 (Bounty Hunter)
28 Imperial Commander
29 Imperial Stormtrooper (Hoth Battle Gear)
30 Jawa (Cloth Cape)
31 Lando Calrisian (With Teeth)
32 Leia (Hoth Outfit)
33 Leia Organa (Bespin Gown, Turtle Neck)
34 Lobot
35 Luke Skywalker (Bespin Fatigues, Blond Hair)
36 Luke Skywalker (Bespin Fatigues, Brown Hair)
37 Luke Skywalker (Blond Hair)
38 Luke Skywalker (Brown Hair)
39 Luke Skywalker (Hoth Battle Gear)
40 Luke Skywalker (X-Wing Pilot)
41 Power Droid
42 Princess Leia Organa
43 R5-D4
44 Rebel Commander
45 Sand People
46 Snaggletooth
47 Stormtrooper
48 Ugnaught
49 Walrus Man
50 Yoda (Brown Snake)
51 Zuckuss

1983 Star Wars Return of the Jedi Palitoy 65-Backs A

1 Bib Fortuna
2 Chief Chirpa
3 Klaatu
4 Lando Calrissian (Skiff Guard Disguise)
5 Luke Skywalker (Jedi Knight Outfit, Green saber)
6 Princess Leia Organa (Boushh Disguise)
7 Rebel Commando
8 Ree-Yees
9 Squid Head
10 Weequay

1983 Star Wars Return of the Jedi Palitoy 65-Backs B

1 Admiral Ackbar
2 Bib Fortuna
3 Biker Scout
4 Chief Chirpa
5 Emporer's Royal Guard
6 Gamorrean Guard
7 General Madine
8 Klaatu
9 Lando Calrissian (Skiff Guard Disguise)
10 Lobray (Ewok Medicine Man)
11 Luke Skywalker (Jedi Knight Outfit, Blue Saber)
12 Luke Skywalker (Jedi Knight Outfit, Green saber)
13 Princess Leia Organa (Boushh Disguise)
14 Rebel Commando
15 Ree-Yees
16 Squid Head
17 Weequay

1983 Star Wars Return of the Jedi Palitoy 65-Backs C

1 Admiral Ackbar
2 Bib Fortuna
3 Biker Scout
4 Chief Chirpa
5 Emporer's Royal Guard
6 Gamorrean Guard
7 General Madine
8 Klaatu
9 Lando Calrissian (Skiff Guard Disguise)
10 Logray (Ewok Medicine Man)
11 Luke Skywalker (Jedi Knight Outfit, Blue Saber)
12 Luke Skywalker (Jedi Knight Outfit, Green saber)
13 Princess Leia Organa (Boushh Disguise)
14 Rebel Commando
15 Ree-Yees
16 Squid Head
17 Weequay

1983 Star Wars Return of the Jedi Palitoy 65-Backs D

1 4-LOM
2 Artoo-Detoo (R2-D2) (With Sensorscope)
3 AT-AT Commander
4 AT-AT Driver
5 Ben (Obi-Wan) Kenobi (Grey Hair)
6 Ben (Obi-Wan) Kenobi (White Hair)
7 Boba Fett
8 Boba Fett (Light Blue)
9 C-3PO (Removable Limbs)
10 Chewbacca
11 Darth Vader
12 Death Squad Commander
13 Death Star Droid
14 Han Solo (Bespin Outfit)
15 Han Solo (Hoth Outfit)
16 Han Solo (Large Head)
17 Imperial Commander
18 Imperial Stormtrooper (Hoth Battle Gear)
19 Jawa (Cloth Cape)
20 Leia (Hoth Outfit)
21 Luke Skywalker (Bespin Fatigues, Blond Hair)
22 Luke Skywalker (Blond Hair)
23 Luke Skywalker (Brown Hair)
24 Luke Skywalker (Hoth Battle Gear)
25 Luke Skywalker (X-Wing Pilot)
26 Power Droid
27 Princess Leia Organa
28 R5-D4
29 Sand People
30 Stormtrooper
31 Walrus Man
32 Yoda (Brown Snake)

1983 Star Wars Return of the Jedi Palitoy 70-Backs A

1 (Twin-Pod) Cloud Car Pilot
2 Bespin Security Guard (Black)
3 Bespin Security Guard (White)
4 Greedo
5 Hammerhead
6 Snaggletooth

1983 Star Wars Return of the Jedi Palitoy 70-Backs B

1 2-1B
2 8D8
3 Admiral Ackbar
4 Artoo-Detoo (R2-D2) (With Sensorscope)
5 AT-AT Commander
6 AT-AT Driver
7 AT-ST Driver
8 Bib Fortuna
9 Biker Scout
10 Boba Fett
11 Boba Fett (Light Blue Unpainted Knee)
12 Bossk (Bounty Hunter)
13 B-Wing Pilot
14 C-3PO (Removable Limbs)
15 Chewbacca

16 Chief Chirpa
17 Darth Vader
18 Death Star Droid
19 Dengar
20 Emporer's Royal Guard
21 FX-7 (Medical Droid)
22 Gamorrean Guard
23 General Madine
24 Han Solo (Bespin Outifit)
25 Han Solo (Hoth Outfit)
26 Han Solo (In Trench Coat)
27 IG-88 (Bounty Hunter)
28 Imperial Commander
29 Imperial Stormtrooper (Hoth Battle Gear)
30 Imperial TIE Fighter Pilot
31 Klaatu
32 Klaatu (Skiff Guard Outfit)
33 Lando Calrissian (Skiff Guard Disguise)
34 Lando Calrissian (With Teeth)
35 Leia (Hoth Outfit)
36 Leia Organa (Bespin Gown, Turtle Neck)
37 Lobot
38 Logray (Ewok Medicine Man)
39 Luke Skywalker (Bespin Fatigues, Blond Hair)
40 Luke Skywalker (Bespin Fatigues, Brown Hair)
41 Luke Skywalker (Hoth Battle Gear)
42 Luke Skywalker (Jedi Knight Outfit, Blue Saber)
43 Luke Skywalker (Jedi Knight Outfit, Green saber)
44 Nien Nunb
45 Nikto
46 Princess Leia Organa
47 Princess Leia Organa (Boushh Disguise)
48 Princess Leia Organa (In Combat Poncho)
49 Prune Face
50 R5-D4
51 Rancor Keeper
52 Rebel Commander
53 Rebel Commando
54 Ree-Yees
55 Sand People
56 Squid Head
57 Stormtrooper
58 Teebo
59 The Emporer
60 Ugnaught
61 Weequay
62 Wicket W. Warrick
63 Yoda (Brown Snake)
64 Yoda (Green Snake)
65 Yoda (Orange Snake)
66 Zuckuss

1983 Star Wars Return of the Jedi Palitoy 70-Backs C

1 8D8
2 Artoo-Detoo (R2-D2) (With Sensorscope)
3 AT-ST Driver
4 C-3PO (Removeable Limbs)
5 Chewbacca
6 Death Star Droid
7 FX-7 (Medical Droid)
8 Klaatu (Skiff Guard Outfit)
9 Lando Calrissian (Skiff Guard Disguise)
10 Leia Organa (Bespin Gown, Turtle Neck)
11 Lobot
12 Luke Skywalker (Jedi Knight Outfit, Green saber)
13 Nikto
14 R5-D4
15 Rancor Keeper

16 Rebel Commander
17 Sand People
18 Stormtrooper
19 Teebo
20 Ugnaught

1983 Star Wars Return of the Jedi Palitoy 70-Backs D

1 Amanaman
2 Anakin Skywalker
3 Artoo-Detoo (R2-D2) with pop-up Lightsabre
4 A-Wing Pilot
5 Barada
6 EV-9D9
7 Han Solo (in Carbonite Chamber)
8 Imperial Dignatary
9 Imperial Gunner
10 Lando Calrissian (General Pilot)
11 Luke Skywalker (Imperial Stormtrooper Outfit)
12 Luke Skywalker (in Battle Poncho)
13 Romba
14 Warok
15 Yak Face

1983 Star Wars Return of the Jedi Tri-Logo

1 2-1B	30.00	60.00
2 8D8	30.00	60.00
3 A-Wing Pilot	40.00	80.00
4 Admiral Ackbar	20.00	40.00
5 Amanaman	100.00	200.00
6 Anakin Skywalker	25.00	50.00
7 AT-AT Commander	20.00	40.00
8 AT-ST Driver	30.00	60.00
9 B-Wing Pilot	20.00	40.00
10 Barada	40.00	80.00
11 Ben Kenobi (blue lightsaber)	60.00	120.00
12 Bespin Guard (black/ tri-logo back only)	150.00	300.00
13 Bespin Guard (white/ tri-logo back only)	250.00	500.00
14 Bib Fortuna	15.00	30.00
15 Biker Scout (long mask)	30.00	60.00
16 Boba Fett	350.00	700.00
17 Bossk	40.00	80.00
18 C-3PO (removable limbs)	40.00	80.00
19 Chewbacca	40.00	80.00
20 Darth Vader	75.00	150.00
21 Death Star Droid	40.00	80.00
22 Dengar	25.00	50.00
23 Emperor	30.00	60.00
24 Emperors Royal Guard	150.00	300.00

25 FX-7	30.00	60.00
26 Gamorrean Guard	30.00	60.00
27 General Madine	60.00	120.00
28 Greedo (tri-logo back only)	60.00	120.00
29 Hammerhead (tri-logo back only)	40.00	80.00
30 Han Solo	75.00	150.00
31 Han Solo (carbonite)	250.00	500.00
32 IG-88	100.00	200.00
33 Imperial Commander	50.00	100.00
34 Imperial Dignitary	125.00	250.00
35 Imperial Gunner	125.00	250.00
36 Jawa	500.00	1000.00
37 Klaatu	15.00	30.00
38 Klaatu (skiff)	25.00	50.00
39 Lando Calrissian	40.00	80.00
40 Lando Calrissian (skiff)	30.00	60.00
41 Lobot	30.00	60.00
42 Luke Skywalker (Bespin)	200.00	400.00
43 Luke Skywalker (gunner card)	125.00	250.00
44 Luke Skywalker (Hoth gear)	200.00	400.00
45 Luke Skywalker Jedi Knight	40.00	80.00
46 Luke Skywalker (stormtrooper)	150.00	300.00
47 Luke Skywalker (poncho)	30.00	60.00
48 Luke Skywalker X-wing	100.00	200.00
49 Lumat	30.00	60.00
50 Nien Nunb	50.00	100.00
51 Nikto	15.00	30.00
52 Paploo	15.00	30.00
53 Princess Leia Organa	60.00	120.00
54 Princess Leia Organa (Bespin turtle neck)	60.00	120.00
55 Princess Leia Organa (Boushh)	75.00	150.00
56 Princess Leia Organa (poncho)	50.00	100.00
57 Prune Face	25.00	50.00
58a R2-D2 (sensorscope/blue background card)	20.00	40.00
58b R2-D2 (sensorscope/sparks card)	75.00	120.00
59 R5-D4	30.00	60.00
60 Rancor	20.00	40.00
61 Rebel Soldier (Hoth gear)	40.00	80.00
62 Ree-Yees	20.00	40.00
63 Romba	30.00	60.00
64 Snowtrooper	30.00	60.00
65 Squid Head	25.00	50.00
66 Stormtrooper	100.00	200.00
67 TIE Fighter Pilot	30.00	60.00
68 Ugnaught	30.00	60.00
69 Warok	50.00	100.00
70 Wicket	40.00	80.00
71 Yak Face	1200.00	2500.00
72a Yoda (brown snake)	50.00	100.00
72b Yoda (orange snake)	500.00	900.00

1985 Star Wars Droids Cartoon

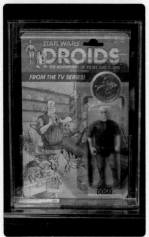

1	A-Wing Pilot	250.00	500.00
2	Boba Fett	1200.00	2500.00
3	C-3PO	250.00	500.00
4	Jann Tosh	30.00	60.00
5	Jord Dusat	30.00	60.00
6	Kea Moll	30.00	60.00
7	Kez-Iban	30.00	60.00
8	R2-D2	250.00	500.00
9	Sise Fromm	150.00	300.00
10	Thall Joben	30.00	60.00
11	Tig Fromm	75.00	150.00
12	Uncle Gundy	30.00	60.00

1985 Star Wars Droids Cartoon (loose)

1	A-Wing Pilot	40.00	80.00
2	Boba Fett	125.00	225.00
3	C-3PO	40.00	80.00
4	Jann Tosh	15.00	30.00
5	Jord Dusat	15.00	30.00
6	Kea Moll	15.00	30.00
7	Kez-Iban	15.00	30.00
8	R2-D2	40.00	80.00
9	Sise Fromm	60.00	120.00
10	Thall Joben	15.00	30.00
11	Tig Fromm	40.00	80.00
12	Uncle Gundy	15.00	30.00

1985 Star Wars Droids Cartoon Coins (loose)

1	A-Wing Pilot	4.00	10.00
2	Boba Fett	12.50	25.00
3	C-3PO	4.00	10.00
4	Jann Tosh	4.00	10.00
5	Jord Dusat	4.00	10.00
6	Kea Moll	4.00	10.00
7	Kez-Iban	4.00	10.00
8	R2-D2	5.00	12.00
9	Sise Fromm	4.00	10.00
10	Thall Joben	4.00	10.00
11	Tig Fromm	4.00	10.00
12	Uncle Gundy	4.00	10.00

1985 Star Wars Droids Cartoon Vehicles

1	A-Wing Fighter	50.00	100.00
2	ATL Interceptor	50.00	100.00
3	Sidegunner	30.00	60.00

1985 Star Wars Droids Cartoon Vehicles (loose)

1	A-Wing Fighter	25.00	50.00
2	ATL Interceptor	25.00	50.00
3	Sidegunner	15.00	30.00

1988 Star Wars Droids Cartoon Glasslite

1	C-3PO
2	Jord Dusat
3	Kea Moll
4	Kez Iban
5	R2-D2
6	Thall Joben
7	Vlix

1988 Star Wars Droids Cartoon Glasslite Vehicles

1	Interceptor
2	Side Gunner

1985 Star Wars Ewoks Cartoons

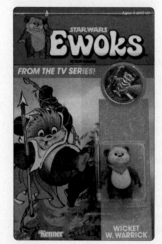

1	Dulok Scout	25.00	50.00
2	Dulok Shaman	30.00	60.00
3	King Gorneesh	20.00	40.00
4	Lady Gorneesh	25.00	50.00
5	Logray	40.00	80.00
6	Wicket	50.00	100.00

1985 Star Wars Ewoks Cartoons (loose)

1	Dulok Scout	12.50	25.00
2	Dulok Shaman	15.00	30.00
3	King Gorneesh	10.00	20.00
4	Lady Gorneesh	12.50	25.00
5	Logray	20.00	40.00
6	Wicket	25.00	50.00

1985 Star Wars Ewoks Cartoons Coins (loose)

1	Dulok Scout	4.00	10.00
2	Dulok Shaman	4.00	10.00
3	King Gorneesh	4.00	10.00
4	Lady Gorneesh	4.00	10.00
5	Logray	5.00	12.00
60	Wicket	5.00	12.00

1985 Star Wars Power of the Force

1	A-Wing Pilot	50.00	100.00
2	Amanaman	150.00	300.00
3	Anakin Skywalker		
4	AT-AT Driver		
5	AT-ST Driver	50.00	100.00
6	B-Wing Pilot	25.00	50.00
7	Barada	100.00	250.00
8	Ben Kenobi (blue saber)	60.00	120.00
9	Biker Scout	75.00	150.00
10	C-3PO (removable limbs)	50.00	100.00
11	Chewbacca	50.00	100.00
12	Darth Vader	100.00	200.00
13	Emperor	40.00	80.00
14	EV-9D9	175.00	350.00
15	Gamorrean Guard	200.00	400.00
16	Han Solo (carbonite)	150.00	400.00
17	Han Solo (trench coat)	400.00	700.00
18	Imperial Dignitary	50.00	100.00
19	Imperial Gunner	50.00	100.00
20	Jawa	50.00	100.00
21	Lando Calrissian	60.00	120.00
22	Luke Skywalker (Hoth gear)		
23	Luke Skywalker (Jedi)	75.00	150.00
24	Luke Skywalker (poncho)	60.00	120.00
25	Luke Skywalker (stormtrooper)	125.00	250.00
26	Luke Skywalker X-wing	60.00	120.00
27	Lumat	40.00	80.00
28	Nikto	1000.00	1500.00
29	Paploo	40.00	80.00
30	Princess Leia (poncho)	40.00	80.00
31	R2-D2 (lightsaber)	200.00	400.00
32	Romba	40.00	80.00
33	Stormtrooper	100.00	200.00
34	Teebo	60.00	120.00
35	TIE Fighter Pilot		

36 Ugnaught		
37 Warok	50.00	100.00
38 Wicket	40.00	80.00
39 Yak Face	3000.00	7000.00
40 Yoda (brown snake)	300.00	600.00

1985 Star Wars Power of the Force (loose)

1 A-Wing Pilot	25.00	50.00
2 Amanaman	40.00	80.00
3 Anakin Skywalker	15.00	30.00
4 AT-AT Driver		
5 AT-ST Driver	10.00	20.00
6 B-Wing Pilot	10.00	20.00
7 Barada	20.00	40.00
8 Ben Kenobi (blue saber)	20.00	40.00
9 Biker Scout	20.00	40.00
10 C-3PO (removable limbs)	10.00	20.00
11 Chewbacca	20.00	40.00
12 Darth Vader	20.00	40.00
13 Emperor	15.00	30.00
14 EV-9D9	25.00	50.00
15 Gamorrean Guard	50.00	100.00
16 Han Solo (carbonite)	100.00	200.00
17 Han Solo (trench coat)	125.00	225.00
18 Imperial Dignitary	30.00	60.00
19 Imperial Gunner	50.00	100.00
20 Jawa	20.00	40.00
21 Lando Calrissian	25.00	50.00
22 Luke Skywalker (Hoth gear)	25.00	50.00
23 Luke Skywalker (Jedi)	25.00	50.00
24 Luke Skywalker (poncho)	25.00	50.00
25 Luke Skywalker (stormtrooper)	40.00	80.00
26 Luke Skywalker X-wing	25.00	50.00
27 Lumat	15.00	30.00
28 Nikto		
29 Paploo	12.50	25.00
30 Princess Leia (poncho)	20.00	40.00
31 R2-D2 (lightsaber)	100.00	200.00
32 Romba	15.00	30.00
33 Stormtrooper	30.00	60.00
34 Teebo	12.50	25.00
35 TIE Fighter Pilot		
36 Ugnaught		
37 Warok	20.00	40.00
38 Wicket	20.00	40.00
39 Yak Face	350.00	700.00
40 Yoda (brown snake)	75.00	150.00

1985 Star Wars Power of the Force Coins (loose)

1 A-Wing Pilot	6.00	12.00
2 Amanaman	6.00	12.00
3 Anakin Skywalker	20.00	40.00
4 AT-AT Driver		
5 AT-ST Driver	5.00	10.00
6 B-Wing Pilot	5.00	10.00
7 Barada	7.50	15.00
8 Ben Kenobi (blue saber)	7.50	15.00
9 Biker Scout	7.50	15.00
10 C-3PO (removable limbs)	6.00	12.00
11 Chewbacca	7.50	15.00
12 Darth Vader	10.00	20.00
13 Emperor	7.50	15.00
14 EV-9D9	7.50	15.00
15 Gamorrean Guard	10.00	20.00
16 Han Solo (carbonite)	10.00	20.00
17 Han Solo (trench coat)	15.00	30.00
18 Imperial Dignitary	7.50	15.00
19 Imperial Gunner	5.00	10.00

20 Jawa	10.00	20.00
21 Lando Calrissian	6.00	12.00
22 Luke Skywalker (Hoth gear)	10.00	20.00
23 Luke Skywalker (Jedi)	10.00	20.00
24 Luke Skywalker (poncho)	10.00	20.00
25 Luke Skywalker (stormtrooper)	15.00	30.00
26 Luke Skywalker X-wing	10.00	20.00
27 Lumat	5.00	10.00
28 Nikto		
29 Paploo	5.00	10.00
30 Princess Leia (poncho)	7.50	15.00
31 R2-D2 (lightsaber)	7.50	15.00
32 Romba	5.00	10.00
33 Stormtrooper	10.00	20.00
34 Teebo	5.00	10.00
35 TIE Fighter Pilot		
36 Ugnaught		
37 Warok	6.00	12.00
38 Wicket	10.00	20.00
39 Yak Face	150.00	300.00
40 Yoda (brown snake)	20.00	40.00

1985 Star Wars Power of the Force Vehicles

1 Ewok Battle Wagon	125.00	250.00
2 Imperial Sniper Vehicle	75.00	150.00
3 Sand Skimmer	75.00	150.00
4 Security Scout	75.00	150.00
5 Tattoine Skiff	200.00	400.00

1985 Star Wars Power of the Force Vehicles (loose)

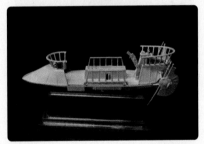

1 Ewok Battle Wagon	50.00	100.00
2 Imperial Sniper Vehicle	30.00	60.00
3 Sand Skimmer	30.00	60.00
4 Security Scout	30.00	60.00
5 Tattoine Skiff	100.00	200.00

1988 Star Wars Power of the Force Glasslite

1 C-3PO	
2 Chewbacca	
3 Darth Vader	
4 Han Solo	
5 Luke Skywalker	
6 Princess Leia	
7 R2-D2	
8 Snowtrooper	
9 Stormtrooper	

1988 Star Wars Power of the Force Glasslite Vehicles

1 TIE Fighter
2 X-Wing Fighter

1988 Star Wars Uzay Savascilari Turkish Bootlegs

1a Stormtroper (Asker)(single arm band)
1b Stormtroper (Asker)(double arm band)
2 Imperial Stormtroper (Imperatorlugun Askeri)
3a AT-Driver (Surucu)(gold rocks on card)
3b AT-Driver (Surucu)(silver rocks on card)
4a Darth Vader (Kara Lider)(no dot on chest)
4b Darth Vader (Kara Lider)(dot on chest)
5a Chewbacca (Aslan Adam)(space background)
5b Chewbacca (Aslan Adam)(profile shot)
6a T E Fighter Pilot (Savas Polotu)(black boots)
6b T E Fighter Pilot (Savas Polotu)(unpainted boots)
7a See Threep (CPO)(no text on front)
7b See Threep (CPO)(text on front)
8 Death Star Droid
9 Blue Stars
10a Emperor's Royal Guard (dark red cape)
10b Emperor's Royal Guard (light red cape)
10c Emperor's Royal Guard (no cape)
11a Imperial Gunner (tan background)
11b Imperial Gunner (green background)
12a Arfive Defour (R2-D4)
12b Arfive Defour (R2-D4)(printing error)
13 Head Man
14a Artoo Detoo (R2-D2)(white scope)
14b Artoo Detoo (R2-D2)(gray scope)

1988 Star Wars Uzay Savascilari Turkish Bootlegs Vehicles

1 MTV-7
2 MLC-3

ACTION FIGURES AND FIGURINES PRICE GUIDE

2007-08 Star Wars 30th Anniversary Collection

1 Darth Vader (w/30th Anniversary coin album)	10.00	25.00
2 Galactic Marine	4.00	8.00
3 Mustafar Lava Miner	4.00	8.00
4 R2-D2	4.00	8.00
5 Obi-Wan Kenobi	4.00	8.00
6 Mace Windu	6.00	12.00
7 Airborne Trooper	4.00	8.00
8 Super Battle Droid	4.00	8.00
9 Concept Stormtrooper (McQuarrie Signature Series)	4.00	8.00
10 Rebel Honor Guard (Yavin)	4.00	8.00
11 Han Solo (smuggler)	4.00	8.00
12 Luke Skywalker (Yavin ceremony)	4.00	8.00
13 Death Star Trooper	5.00	10.00
14 Biggs Darklighter (Rebel pilot)	4.00	8.00
15 Concept Boba Fett (McQuarrie Signature Series)	12.00	25.00
16 Darth Vader (removable helmet)	4.00	8.00
17 Biggs Darklighter (academy gear)	4.00	8.00
18 Luke Skywalker (moisture farmer)	8.00	15.00
19 Jawa & LIN Droid (Tatooine scavenger)	4.00	8.00
20 Imperial Stormtrooper (Galactic Empire)	4.00	8.00
21 Concept Chewbacca (McQuarrie Signature Series)	6.00	12.00
22 M'liyoom Onith (Hementhe)	5.00	10.00
23 Elis Helrot (Givin)	5.00	10.00
24 Boba Fett (animated debut)	6.00	12.00
25 Luke Skywalker (Jedi Knight)	4.00	8.00
26 CZ-4 (CZ-Series droid)	4.00	8.00
27 Umpass-Stay (Klatooinian)	4.00	8.00
28 Concept Darth Vader (McQuarrie Signature Series)	8.00	15.00
29 Hermi Odle (Baragwin)	12.00	25.00
30 C-3PO & Salacious Crumb (Jabba's Servants)	10.00	20.00
31 Roron Corobb (Jedi Knight)	6.00	12.00
32 Yoda & Kybuck (Jedi Master)	4.00	8.00
33 Anakin Skywalker (Jedi Knight)	4.00	8.00
34 Darth Revan (Sith Lord)	30.00	60.00
35 Darth Malak (Sith Lord)	15.00	30.00
36 Pre-Cyborg Grievous	20.00	40.00
(Kaleesh warlord Qymaen jai Sheelal)		
37 Concept Starkiller Hero (McQuarrie Signature Series)	4.00	8.00
38 Han Solo (w/torture rack)	10.00	20.00
39 Lando Calrissian (smuggler)	4.00	8.00
40 General McQuarrie (Rebel officer)	4.00	8.00
41 4-LOM (bounty hunter)	4.00	8.00
42 Concept Snowtrooper (McQuarrie Signature Series)	4.00	8.00
43 Romba & Graak (Ewok warriors)	12.00	25.00
44 Tycho Celchu (A-Wing pilot)	4.00	8.00
45 Anakin Skywalker (Jedi Spirit)	10.00	20.00
46 R2-D2 (w/cargo net)	4.00	8.00
47 Concept Han Solo (McQuarrie Signature Series)	12.00	25.00
48 Darth Vader (hologram)	4.00	8.00
49a Clone Trooper (7th Legion Trooper)	4.00	8.00
49b Clone Trooper (Revenge of the Sith stand/no coin)	4.00	8.00
50a Clone Trooper (Hawkbat Batallion)	8.00	15.00
50b Clone Trooper (Hawkbat Batallion	4.00	8.00
Revenge of the Sith stand/no coin)		
51a R2-B1 (astromech droid)	4.00	8.00
51b R2-B1 (Revenge of the Sith stand/no coin)	4.00	8.00
52 Naboo Soldier (Royal Naboo Army)	6.00	12.00
53a Rebel Vanguard Trooper (Star Wars: Battlefront)	4.00	8.00
53b Rebel Vanguard Trooper (Expanded Universe stand/no coin)	4.00	8.00
54 Pax Bonkik (Rodian podracer mechanic)	4.00	8.00
55 Clone Trooper (training fatigues)	8.00	15.00
56a Padme Amidala (Naboo Senator)	4.00	8.00
56b Padme Amidala (Attack of the Clones stand/no coin)	4.00	8.00
57a Jango Fett (bounty hunter)	4.00	8.00
57b Jango Fett (Attack of the Clones stand/no coin)	10.00	20.00
58a Voolvif Monn (Jedi Master)	4.00	8.00
58b Voolvif Monn (Expanded Universe stand/no coin)	4.00	8.00
59 Destroyer Droid (droideka)	4.00	8.00
60 Concept Rebel Trooper (McQuarrie Signature Series)	4.00	8.00

2007-08 Star Wars 30th Anniversary Collection Battle Packs

1 Battle of Geonosis (Jango Fett/Obi-Wan	20.00	40.00
Kenobi/Count Dooku/Aayla Secura)		
2 Battle on Mygeeto (Galactic Marine/Ki-Adi Mundi	30.00	60.00
Clone Commander Bacara/Super Battle Droid/Tri-Droid)		
3 Betrayal at Bespin (Boba Fett/Chewbacca	20.00	40.00
Darth Vader/Han Solo/Princess Leia)		
4 Capture of Tantive IV (Darth Vader	15.00	30.00
2 Rebel Troopers/2 Stormtroopers)		
5 Clone Attack on Coruscant	25.00	50.00
(Clone Trooper Commander/4 Clone Troopers)		
6 Droid Factory Capture (C-3PO with droid head	20.00	40.00
R2-D2/Jango Fett/Anakin/Destroyer Droid)		
7 Hoth Patrol (Luke Skywalker/Tauntaun/Wampa)	20.00	40.00
8 Jedi vs. Sith (Yoda/Anakin Skywalker	10.00	20.00
Asajj Ventress/General Grievous/Obi-Wan)		
9 Jedi vs. Sidious (Darth Sidious/Kit Fisto	10.00	20.00
Mace Windu/Saesee-Tiin/Agen Kolar)		
10 Jedi Training on Dagobah (Yoda/R2-D2	10.00	20.00
Luke Skywalker/Spirit of Obi-Wan/Darth Vader)		
11 The Hunt for Grievous (Captain Fordo	30.00	60.00
Clone Trooper Gunner/3 Clone Troopers)		

2007-08 Star Wars 30th Anniversary Collection Battle Packs Exclusives

1 Ambush on Ilum	30.00	60.00
(R2-D2/C-3PO/Padme/Chameleon Droids)		
(2007 Target Exclusive)		
2 ARC-170 Elite Squad	60.00	120.00
(Astromech Droid/2 Clone pilots/2 Clone Troopers)		
(2007 Target Exclusive)		
3 Arena Encounter	100.00	200.00
(Anakin Skywalker/Padme Amidala/Obi-Wan/Creatures)		
(2007 Toys R Us Exclusive)		
4 AT-RT Assault Squad	25.00	50.00
(2 AT-RT's/2 AT-RT Drivers/Clone Commander)		
(2007 Target Exclusive)		
5 Attack on Kashyyyk	20.00	40.00
(Darth Vader/2 Stormtroopers/2 Wookiee warriors)		
(2008 Target Exclusive)		
6 Bantha with Tusken Raiders	30.00	60.00
(brown - Bantha/2 Tusken Raiders/Tusken female)		
(2007 Toys R Us Exclusive)		
7 Bantha with Tusken Raiders	50.00	100.00
(tan - Bantha/2 Tusken Raiders/Tusken female)		
(2007 Toys R Us Exclusive)		
8 Battle Rancor	60.00	120.00
(w/Felucian warrior)		
(2008 Target Exclusive)		
9 Betrayal on Felucia	20.00	40.00
(Aayla Secura/4 Clone Troopers yellow)		
(2007 Target Exclusive)		
10 STAP Attack	25.00	50.00
(2 Battle Droids/Super Battle Droid/2 STAP's)		
(2008 Toys R Us Exclusive)		
11 Treachery on Saleucami	20.00	40.00
(Commander Neyo/Clone Trooper red/2 BARC Speeder Bikes)		
(2007 Walmart Exclusive)		

2007-08 Star Wars 30th Anniversary Collection Comic Packs

1 Carnor Jax & Kir Kanos		
(2006 Internet Exclusive)		
2 Darth Vader & Rebel Officer		
3 Governor Tarkin & Stormtrooper		
4 Chewbacca & Han Solo		
5 Quinlan Vos & Vilmarh Grahrk		
6 Luke Skywalker & R2-D2		
7 Obi-Wan Kenobi & ARC Trooper		
8 A'sharad Hett & The Dark Woman	20.00	40.00
9 Leia Organa & Darth Vader		
10 Mara Jade & Luke Skywalker	20.00	40.00
11 Anakin Skywalker & Assassin Droid		
12 Baron Soontir Fel & Derek Hobbie Klivian		
13 Koffi Arana & Bultar Swan		
14 Lt. Jundland & Deena Shan		
15 Mouse & Basso		
16 Clone Commando & Super Battle Droid	20.00	40.00
NNO Obi-Wan Kenobi & Bail Organa		
(2007 Walmart Exclusive)		
NNO Boba Fett & RA-7 Droid (Wal-Mart Exclusive)	12.00	25.00
NNO Commander Keller & Galactic Marine		
(2007 Walmart Exclusive)		
NNO Count Dooku & Anakin Skywalker		
NNO Kashyyyk Trooper & Wookiee Warrior		
NNO Lando Calrissian & Stormtrooper		

2007-08 Star Wars 30th Anniversary Collection
Commemorative Tins

1 Episode I (Darth Maul/Anakin Skywalker		
Qui-Gon Ginn/R2-D9)		
2 Episode II (Clone Trooper blue		
Anakin Skywalker/Count Dooku/Boba Fett)		
3 Episode III (Yoda/Mace Windu		
Anakin Skywalker/Clone Trooper yellow shins)		
4 Episode IV (Stormtrooper black shoulders	20.00	40.00
Princess Leia/Darth Vader/C-3PO)		
5 Episode V (Snowtrooper/Luke Skywalker hoth		
Han Solo hoth/Chewbacca hoth)		
6 Episode VI (Bike Trooper/Darth Vader		
Princess Leia endor/Rebel Trooper)		
7 The Modal Nodes Cantina Band	25.00	50.00
8 Episode II		
(Mace Windu/Sora Bulq/Oppo Rancisis/Zam Wesell)		
(2007 K-Mart Exclusive)		
9 Episode III		
(Commander Cody/Anakin/General Grievous/Clone Pilot)		
(2007 K-Mart Exclusive)		
10 Episode VI		
(Darth Vader/R5-J2/Biker Scout/Death Star Gunner)		
(2007 K-Mart Exclusive)		

2007-08 Star Wars 30th Anniversary
Collection Evolutions

1 Anakin Skywalker to Darth Vader	20.00	40.00
2 Clone Trooper to Stormtrooper	20.00	40.00
3 The Sith		
4 The Fett Legacy	25.00	50.00
5 The Jedi Legacy	20.00	40.00
6 The Sith Legacy		
7 Vader's Secret Apprentice/Secret Apprentice/Sith Lord/Jedi Knight	30.00	75.00

2007-08 Star Wars 30th Anniversary Collection
Exclusives

1 Cantina Band Member	20.00	40.00
(2007 Disney Weekends Exclusive)		
2 Concept General Grievous	15.00	30.00
(2007 SWS Exclusive)		
3 Concept Luke Skywalker (McQuarrie Signature Series)	15.00	30.00
(2007 C4 & CE Exclusive)		
4 Concept Obi-Wan & Yoda (McQuarrie Signature Series)	20.00	40.00
(2007 SDCC Exclusive)		
5 Concept R2-D2 & C-3PO (McQuarrie Signature Series)	12.00	25.00
(2007 C4 & CE Exclusive)		
6 Darth Vader & Incinerator Troopers (The Force Unleashed)	25.00	50.00
(2008 Walmart Exclusive)		
7 Emperor Palpatine & Shadow Stormtroopers (The Force Unleashed)		
(2008 Walmart Exclusive)		
8 R2-KT	30.00	60.00
(2007 Shared Exclusive)		
9 Shadow Scout Trooper & Speeder Bike	15.00	30.00
(2007 SDCC Exclusive)		
10 Shadow Troopers 2-Pack		
(2008 Jedi-Con Exclusive)		
11 Star Wars Collector Coin		
(2007 Toy Fair Exclusive)		
12 Stormtrooper Commander	25.00	50.00
(2008 GameStop Exclusive)		

2007-08 Star Wars 30th Anniversary Collection
Force Unleashed

9 Imperial EVO Trooper	8.00	15.00
10 Imperial Jumptrooper	10.00	20.00
11a Maris Brood (flesh)	15.00	30.00
11b Maris Brood (white)	10.00	20.00
12 Darth Vader (battle-damaged)	10.00	20.00
13 Rahm Kota	20.00	40.00
14 Emperor's Shadow Guard	20.00	40.00
15 Juno Eclipse	10.00	20.00

2007-08 Star Wars 30th Anniversary Collection
Multi-Packs

1 Clone Pack (Battlefront II)		
(2007 Shared Exclusive)		
2 Droid Pack (Battlefront II)	25.00	50.00
(2007 Shared Exclusive)		
3 Clones & Commanders Gift Pack	20.00	40.00
(Toys R Us Exclusive)		
4 I Am Your Father's Day Gift Pack (2007 Walmart Exclusive)		
5 The Max Rebo Band Jabba's Palace Entertainers	30.00	60.00
(2007 Walmart Exclusive)		
6 The Max Rebo Band Jabba's Palace Musicians	40.00	80.00
(2007 Walmart Exclusive)		
7 Republic Elite Forces Mandalorians & Clone Troopers		
(2007 Entertainment Earth Exclusive)		
8 Republic Elite Forces Mandalorians & Omega Squad	75.00	150.00
(2007 Entertainment Earth Exclusive)		

2007-08 Star Wars 30th Anniversary Collection
Revenge of the Sith

1 Obi-Wan Kenobi	6.00	12.00
2 Darth Vader	10.00	20.00
3 Clone Commander (green)	5.00	10.00
4 Kashyyyk Trooper	8.00	15.00
5 Tri-Droid	8.00	15.00
6 2-1B Surgical Droid	6.00	12.00
7 Po Nudo	8.00	15.00
8 Mustafar Panning Droid	6.00	12.00

2007-08 Star Wars 30th Anniversary Collection
Saga Legends

1 501st Legion Trooper	8.00	15.00
2 Boba Fett	15.00	30.00
3 C-3PO (w/battle droid head)	6.00	12.00
4 Chewbacca	6.00	12.00
5 Clone Trooper (AOTC)	8.00	15.00
6 Clone Trooper (ROTS)	6.00	12.00
7 Darth Maul	8.00	15.00
8 Darth Vader	8.00	15.00
9 Darth Vader (as Anakin Skywalker)	8.00	15.00

10	Destroyer Droid	6.00	12.00
11	General Grievous	12.00	25.00
12	Obi-Wan Kenobi	6.00	12.00
13	Princess Leia (Boushh disguise)	8.00	15.00
14	R2-D2 (electronic)	10.00	20.00
15	Saesee Tiin	8.00	15.00
16	Shock Trooper	10.00	20.00
17	Yoda	8.00	15.00

2007-08 Star Wars 30th Anniversary Collection
Saga Legends Battle Droid 2-Packs

1	Battle Droids 2-Pack I (tan infantry & commander)	8.00	15.00
2	Battle Droids 2-Pack II (maroon blaster and lightsaber damage)	8.00	15.00
3	Battle Droids 2-Pack III (tan blaster and lightsaber damage)	8.00	15.00
4	Battle Droids 2-Pack IV (tan dirty & clean)	8.00	15.00

2007-08 Star Wars 30th Anniversary Collection
Saga Legends Fan's Choice (2007)

1	Biker Scout	8.00	15.00
2	Biker Scout (w/Clone Wars sticker)		
3	Clone Commander (Coruscant)	12.00	25.00
4	Clone Trooper Officer (red)	8.00	15.00
5	Clone Trooper Officer (yellow)	8.00	15.00
6	Clone Trooper Officer (green)	10.00	20.00
7	Clone Trooper Officer (blue)	6.00	12.00
8	Dark Trooper (Fan's Choice Figure #1)	12.00	25.00
9	Imperial Officer (brown hair)	6.00	12.00
10	Imperial Officer (blonde hair)	8.00	15.00
11	Imperial Officer (red hair)		
12	Pit Droids 2-Pack (white)		
13	Pit Droids 2-Pack (brown)		
14	Pit Droids 2-Pack (orange)	12.00	25.00
15	R4-I9	10.00	20.00
16	RA-7	6.00	12.00
17	Sandtrooper (dirty; tan shoulder)	8.00	15.00
18	Sandtrooper (dirty; orange shoulder)	10.00	20.00
19	Sandtrooper (clean; black shoulder)	25.00	50.00
20	Sandtrooper (clean; white shoulder)	12.00	25.00
21	Sandtrooper (dirty; red shoulder)		
22	TC-14	10.00	20.00

2007-08 Star Wars 30th Anniversary Collection
Saga Legends Fan's Choice (2008)

1	501st Legion Trooper		
2	Commander Neyo	10.00	20.00
3	Covert Ops Clone Trooper (gold coin)	10.00	20.00
4	Pit Droids 2-Pack (white)	8.00	15.00
5	Pit Droids 2-Pack (maroon)	8.00	15.00
6	Pit Droids 2-Pack (orange)	8.00	15.00
7	Shadow Stormtrooper	12.00	25.00
8	Utapau Shadow Trooper	12.00	25.00
9	Zev Senesca	8.00	15.00

2007-08 Star Wars 30th Anniversary Collection
Silver Coins

1a	Darth Vader
1b	30th Anniversary Coin Album
2	Galactic Marine
3	Mustafar Lava Miner
4	R2-D2
5	Obi-Wan Kenobi
6	Mace Windu
7	Airborne Trooper
8	Super Battle Droid
9	Concept Stormtrooper (McQuarrie Signature Series)
10	Rebel Honor Guard
11	Han Solo
12	Luke Skywalker ceremony
13	Death Star Trooper
14	Biggs Darklighter
15	Concept Boba Fett (McQuarrie Signature Series)
16	Darth Vader
17	Biggs Darklighter
18	Luke Skywalker tatooine
19	Jawa & Lin Droid
20	Imperial Stormtrooper
21	Concept Chewbacca (McQuarrie Signature Series)
22	M'liyoom Onith
23	Elis Helrot
24	Boba Fett
25	Luke Skywalker
26	CZ-4
27	Umpass-Stay
28	Concept Darth Vader (McQuarrie Signature Series)
29	Hermi Odle
30	C-3PO & Salacious Crumb
31	Roron Corobb
32	Yoda & Kybuck
33	Anakin Skywalker
34	Darth Revan
35	Darth Malak
36	Pre-Cyborg Grievous
37	Concept Starkiller Hero
38	Han Solo
39	Lando Calrissian
40	General McQuarrie
41	4-LOM
42	Concept Snowtrooper (McQuarrie Signature Series)
43	Romba & Graak
44	Tycho Celchu
45	Anakin Skywalker (Jedi Spirit)
46	R2-D2
47	Concept Han Solo (McQuarrie Signature Series)
48	Darth Vader (hologram)
49	Clone Trooper (7th Legion Trooper)
50	Clone Trooper (Hawkbat Batallion)
51	R2-B1
52	Naboo Soldier
53	Rebel Vanguard Trooper
54	Pax Bonkin
55	Clone Trooper (training fatigues)
56	Padme Amidala
57	Jango Fett
58	Voolvif Monn
59	Destroyer Droid
60	Concept Rebel Trooper (McQuarrie Signature Series)

2007-08 Star Wars 30th Anniversary Collection
Ultimate Galactic Hunt

1	Airborne Trooper	12.00	25.00
2	Biggs Darklighter (Rebel pilot)	7.50	15.00
3	Boba Fett (animated debut)	12.00	25.00
4	Concept Boba Fett (McQuarrie Signature Series)	20.00	40.00
5	Concept Chewbacca (McQuarrie Signature Series)	15.00	30.00
6	Concept Stormtrooper (McQuarrie Signature Series)	12.00	25.00
7	Darth Vader (Sith Lord)	10.00	20.00
8	Galactic Marine	10.00	20.00
9	Han Solo (smuggler)	7.50	15.00
10	Luke Skywalker (Yavin ceremony)	6.00	12.00
11	Mace Windu	7.50	15.00
12	R2-D2	6.00	12.00

2007-08 Star Wars 30th Anniversary Collection
Ultimate Galactic Hunt Gold Coins

1 Airborne Trooper	6.00	12.00
2 Biggs Darklighter	4.00	8.00
3 Boba Fett	6.00	12.00
4 Concept Boba Fett (McQuarrie Signature Series)	10.00	20.00
5 Concept Chewbacca (McQuarrie Signature Series)	7.50	15.00
6 Concept Stormtrooper (McQuarrie Signature Series)	6.00	12.00
7 Darth Vader	5.00	10.00
8 Galactic Marine	5.00	10.00
9 Han Solo	4.00	8.00
10 Luke Skywalker	3.00	6.00
11 Mace Windu	4.00	8.00
12 R2-D2	3.00	6.00

2007-08 Star Wars 30th Anniversary Collection Vehicles

1 Aayla Secura's Jedi Starfighter	20.00	40.00
2 ARC-170 Fighter (Clone Wars)	50.00	100.00
3 AT-AP Walker	20.00	40.00
4 Anakin Skywalker's Jedi Starfighter (Coruscant)	20.00	40.00
5 Anakin Skywalker's Jedi Starfighter (Mustafar)	20.00	40.00
6 Darth Vader's Sith Starfighter	40.00	80.00
7 Darth Vader's TIE Advanced Starfighter	30.00	60.00
8 General Grievous' Starfighter	25.00	50.00
9 Hailfire Droid	25.00	50.00
10 Mace Windu's Jedi Starfighter	15.00	30.00
11 Obi-Wan's Jedi Starfighter (Coruscant)	25.00	50.00
12 Obi-Wan's Jedi Starfighter (Utapau)	25.00	50.00
13 Saesee Tiin's Jedi Starfighter	20.00	40.00
14 Sith Infiltrator	25.00	50.00
15 TIE Fighter	15.00	30.00
16 Trade Federation Armored Assault Tank (AAT)	20.00	40.00
17 V-Wing Starfighter/ spring-open wings	50.00	100.00

2007-08 Star Wars 30th Anniversary Collection Vehicles Exclusives

1 Elite TIE Inteceptor/181st Squadron TIE Pilot	75.00	150.00
(Toys R Us exclusive)		
2 Obi-Wan's Jedi Starfighter (w/hyperspace ring)	25.00	50.00
(2007 Toys R Us Exclusive)		
3 TIE Bomber (w/TIE Bomber Pilot)	30.00	75.00
(2007 Target Exclusive)		
4 TIE Fighter (w/TIE Pilot/opening cockpit and ejecting wing panels)	25.00	50.00
(2007 Toys R Us Exclusive)		
5 Y-Wing Fighter (w/Lt. Lepira & R5-F7)	75.00	150.00
(2007 Toys R Us Exclusive)		

2017 Star Wars 40th Anniversary Black Series 6-Inch

NNO Artoo Detoo	30.00	60.00
NNO Ben (Obi-Wan) Kenobi	15.00	30.00
NNO Chewbacca	25.00	50.00
NNO Darth Vader Legacy Pack	30.00	60.00
NNO Death Squad Commander	15.00	30.00
NNO Han Solo	25.00	50.00

NNO Jawa	20.00	40.00
NNO Luke Skywalker	20.00	40.00
NNO Luke Skywalker X-Wing Pilot	175.00	350.00
(Celebration Orlando Exclusive)		
NNO Princess Leia Organa	15.00	30.00
NNO R5-D4	25.00	50.00
(GameStop Exclusive)		
NNO Sand People	30.00	60.00
NNO See Threepio	25.00	50.00
NNO Stormtrooper	30.00	60.00

2017 Star Wars 40th Anniversary Black Series Titanium Series 3.75-Inch

1 Darth Vader	20.00	40.00
2 Obi-Wan Kenobi	12.00	25.00
3 Luke Skywalker	12.00	25.00
4 Princess Leia Organa	12.00	25.00
5 Han Solo	15.00	30.00

1998-99 Star Wars Action Collection

1 AT-AT Driver	15.00	30.00
2 Barquin D'an	10.00	20.00
3 Chewbacca in Chains	15.00	30.00
4 Emperor Palpatine	12.00	25.00
5 Grand Moff Tarkin	12.00	25.00
6 Greedo	15.00	30.00
7 Han Solo (carbonite)	15.00	30.00
(Target Exclusive)		
8 Han Solo (Hoth)	15.00	30.00
9 Jawa	10.00	20.00
10 Luke Skywalker (ceremonial dress)		
11 Luke Skywalker (Hoth)	15.00	30.00
12 Luke Skywalker (Jedi Knight)	12.00	25.00
13 Princess Leia (Hoth)	12.00	25.00
(Service Merchandise Exclusive)		
14 R2-D2	20.00	40.00
15 R2-D2 (detachable utility arms)	20.00	40.00
16 R5-D4	15.00	30.00
(Walmart Exclusive)		
17 Sandtrooper (w/droid)	8.00	15.00
18 Snowtrooper	12.00	25.00
19 Snowtrooper (blue variant)		
20 Wicket	20.00	40.00

(Walmart Exclusive)		
21 Yoda	20.00	40.00

1998-99 Star Wars Action Collection Electronic

1 Boba Fett	25.00	50.00
(KB Toys Exclusive)		
2 Darth Vader	20.00	40.00

1998-99 Star Wars Action Collection Multi-Packs

1 C-3PO and R2-D2 2-Pack	40.00	80.00
2 Emperor Palpatine and Royal Guard 2-Pack	20.00	40.00
3 Wedge Antilles and Biggs Darklighter 2-Pack	25.00	50.00
(FAO Schwarz Exclusive)		
4 Luke (Tatooine)/Leia (Boushh)/Han (Bespin) 3-Pack	40.00	80.00
(KB Toys Exclusive)		
5 Luke/Han/Snowtrooper/AT-AT Driver Hoth 4-Pack	60.00	120.00
(JC Penney Exclusive)		

1993 Star Wars Bend Ems

1 Admiral Ackbar	7.50	15.00
2 Ben Kenobi	10.00	20.00
3 Bib Fortuna	7.50	15.00
4 Boba Fett	15.00	30.00
5 C-3PO	10.00	20.00
6 Chewbacca	7.50	15.00
7 Darth Vader	12.50	25.00
8 Emperor	10.00	20.00
9 Emperor's Royal Guard	7.50	15.00
10 Gamorrean Guard	7.50	15.00
11 Han Solo	10.00	20.00
12 Lando Calrissian	7.50	15.00
13 Leia Organa	10.00	20.00
14 Luke Skywalker	10.00	20.00
15 Luke Skywalker X-wing	10.00	20.00

16 R2-D2	7.50	15.00
17 Stormtrooper	7.50	15.00
18 Tusken Raider	7.50	15.00
19 Wicket	7.50	15.00
20 Yoda	7.50	15.00
21 4-Piece A New Hope	20.00	40.00
(Chewbacca/Luke Skywalker/R2-D2/Tusken Raider)		
22 4-Piece Empire Strikes Back	20.00	40.00
(Han Solo/Darth Vader/Yoda/Lando Calrissian)		
23 4-Piece Return of the Jedi	25.00	50.00
(Admiral Ackbar/Boba Fett/Wicket/Bib Fortuna)		
24 4-Piece Gift Set 1	20.00	40.00
(Ben Kenobi/Leia Organa/Han Solo/C-3PO)		
25 4-Piece Gift Set 2	20.00	40.00
(Storm Trooper/Wicket/Yoda/Chewbacca)		
26 4-Piece Gift Set 3	20.00	40.00
(Storm Trooper/R2-D2/C-3PO/Darth Vader)		
27 4-Piece Gift Set 4	20.00	40.00
(Emperor/C-3PO/Luke Skywalker/Darth Vader)		
28 6-Piece Gift Set 1	25.00	50.00
(Darth Vader/Stormtrooper/Luke Skywalker/R2-D2/C-3PO		
29 6-Piece Gift Set 2	25.00	50.00
(Stormtrooper/Darth Vader/Emperor's Royal Guard		
Admiral Ackbar/Lando Calrissian/Chewbacca)		
30 8-Piece Gift Set	25.00	50.00
(Darth Vader/Luke Skywalker/C-3PO/Emperor		
Stormtrooper/R2-D2/Princess Leia/Ewok)		
31 10-Piece Gift Set	30.00	60.00
(R2-D2/Stormtrooper/Darth Vader/Admiral Ackbar		
Chewbacca/Han Solo/Princess Leia/Luke Skywalker		
Bib Fortuna/Emperor's Royal Guard)		

1993 Star Wars Bend Ems (loose)

1 Admiral Ackbar	4.00	10.00
2 Ben Kenobi	5.00	12.00
3 Bib Fortuna	4.00	10.00
4 Boba Fett	8.00	20.00
5 C-3PO	5.00	12.00
6 Chewbacca	4.00	10.00
7 Darth Vader	6.00	15.00
8 Emperor	5.00	12.00
9 Emperor's Royal Guard	4.00	10.00
10 Gamorrean Guard	4.00	10.00
11 Han Solo	5.00	12.00
12 Lando Calrissian	4.00	10.00
13 Leia Organa	5.00	12.00
14 Luke Skywalker	5.00	12.00
15 Luke Skywalker X-wing	5.00	12.00
16 R2-D2	4.00	10.00
17 Stormtrooper	4.00	10.00
18 Tusken Raider	4.00	10.00
19 Wicket	4.00	10.00
20 Yoda	4.00	10.00

2014-15 Star Wars Black Series 3.75-Inch Blue

1 R5-G19	10.00	20.00
2A Luke Skywalker Hoth	8.00	15.00

(incorrect elbow pegs)		
2B Luke Skywalker Hoth	8.00	15.00
(correct elbow pegs)		
3 Darth Vader	8.00	15.00
(Revenge Of The Sith)		
4 Darth Malgus	20.00	40.00
5 Starkiller	20.00	40.00
(Galen Marek)		
6 Yoda	12.00	25.00
(pack forward)		
7 Darth Vader	12.00	25.00
(Dagobah Test)		
8 Stormtrooper	10.00	20.00
9 Captain Rex	8.00	15.00
10 Jon Dutch Vander	10.00	20.00
11 Chewbacca	8.00	15.00
12 Clone Commander Wolffe	10.00	20.00
13 Clone Commander Doom	6.00	12.00
14 Imperial Navy Commander	10.00	20.00
15 Commander Thorn	12.00	25.00
16 C-3PO	12.00	25.00
17 Princess Leia Organa	10.00	20.00
(Boushh)		
18 Mosep Binneed	10.00	20.00
19 Han Solo	20.00	40.00
(with Carbonite Block)		
20 Jawas	8.00	15.00

2014-15 Star Wars Black Series 3.75-Inch Blue Exclusives

1 Battle on Endor 8-Pack	80.00	150.00
(Toys R Us Exclusive)		
2 Jabba's Rancor Pit	100.00	200.00
(Toys R Us Exclusive)		

2013-14 Star Wars Black Series 3.75-Inch Orange

1 Padme Amidala	25.00	50.00
2 Clone Trooper Sergeant	6.00	12.00
3A Anakin Skywalker	10.00	20.00
(dark brown hair)		
3B Anakin Skywalker	10.00	20.00
(light brown hair)		
4 Biggs Darklighter	6.00	12.00

5A Luke Skywalker	8.00	15.00
(short medal strap)		
5B Luke Skywalker	8.00	15.00
(long medal strap)		
6 Darth Vader	8.00	15.00
7 Biker Scout	6.00	12.00
8 Clone Pilot	6.00	12.00
9 R2-D2	15.00	30.00
10 Pablo-Jill	20.00	40.00
11 Luminara Unduli	6.00	12.00
12A 41st Elite Corps Clone Trooper		
(incorrect markings)		
12B 41st Elite Corps Clone Trooper	6.00	12.00
(correct markings)		
13 Stormtrooper	8.00	15.00
14 Mara Jade	15.00	30.00
15 Merumeru	10.00	20.00
16 Clone Commander Neyo	10.00	20.00
17 Vizam	8.00	15.00
18 Darth Plageuis		
19 Mace Windu	12.00	25.00
20 Bastila Shan	20.00	40.00
21 Luke Skywalker	8.00	15.00
22 Yoda	10.00	20.00
23 Toryn Farr	10.00	20.00
24 Snowtrooper Commander	8.00	15.00
25 Dak Ralter	10.00	20.00
26 Darth Vader	15.00	30.00
27 Jabba's Skiff Guard	25.00	50.00
28 Ree-Yees	20.00	40.00
29 Wedge Antilles	8.00	15.00

2013-14 Star Wars Black Series 3.75-Inch Orange Exclusives

1 Luke Skywalker Hoth Battle Gear	6.00	12.00
2 R5-D4		

2015-16 Star Wars Black Series 3.75-Inch Red

NNO Admiral Ackbar		
NNO Ahsoka Tano		
NNO Captain Cassian Andor		
(Walmart Exclusive)		
NNO Captain Phasma		
NNO Chewbacca		
NNO Darth Vader		
NNO Emperor's Royal Guard		
NNO Finn (Jakku)	10.00	20.00
NNO First Order Stormtrooper	6.00	12.00
NNO Han Solo		
NNO Han Solo (Starkiller Base)		
NNO Imperial Death Trooper		
(Walmart Exclusive)		
NNO Kylo Ren		
NNO Lando Calrissian		
NNO Luke Skywalker		
NNO Poe Dameron	6.00	12.00
NNO Princess Leia Organa	8.00	15.00
NNO Princess Leia Organa (D'Qar Gown)		

NNO Rey (Jakku)	10.00	20.00
NNO Scarif Stormtrooper Squad Leader		
NNO Sergeant Jyn Erso		

2015-16 Star Wars Black Series 3.75-Inch Red Vehicles

1 Special Forces TIE Fighter and Pilot Elite	120.00	250.00

2014-15 Star Wars Black Series 6-Inch Blue

1 Sandtrooper	15.00	30.00
Black Pauldron		
2 Darth Vader	12.00	25.00
Episode VI		
3 Luke Skywalker	25.00	50.00
Episode VI		
4 Chewbacca	20.00	40.00
5 TIE Pilot	15.00	30.00
6 Yoda	25.00	50.00
7 Clone Trooper Sergeant	12.00	25.00
8 Obi-Wan Kenobi	10.00	20.00
Reissue		
9 Han Solo Stormtrooper	12.00	25.00
10 Bossk	20.00	40.00
11 Luke Skywalker	12.00	25.00
Stormtrooper		
12 Emperor Palpatine	15.00	30.00
13 Clone Trooper Captain	12.00	25.00
14 IG-88	20.00	40.00
15 Princess Leia	30.00	60.00
16 Clone Commander Cody	12.00	25.00

2014-15 Star Wars Black Series 6-Inch Blue Deluxe

1 Han Solo (w/Tauntaun)	25.00	50.00
2 Jabba the Hutt	25.00	50.00
3 Luke Skywalker (w/Wampa)	20.00	40.00
4 Scout Trooper (w/Speeder Bike)	20.00	40.00

2013-17 Star Wars Black Series 6-Inch Exclusives

1 Admiral Ackbar & First Order Officer 2-Pack		
(2017 Toys R Us Exclusive)		
2 Astromech 3-Pack	50.00	100.00
(2016 Toys R Us Exclusive)		
3 Boba Fett (Prototype Armor)	25.00	50.00
(2014 Walgreens Exclusive)		
4 Boba Fett and Han Solo in Carbonite	200.00	400.00
(2013 SDCC Exclusive)		
5 C-3PO	20.00	40.00
(2016 Walgreens Exclusive)		
6 Cantina Showdown	50.00	100.00
(2014 Toys R Us Exclusive)		
7 Darth Vader Emperor's Wrath	15.00	30.00
(2015 Walgreen's Exclusive)		
8 First Order Snowtrooper Officer	15.00	30.00
(2015 Toys R Us Exclusive)		
9 First Order Stormtrooper Officer	30.00	75.00
(2015 SDCC Exclusive)		
10 Imperial Forces 4-Pack	50.00	100.00
(2015 Entertainment Earth Exclusive)		
11 Imperial Hovertank Pilot	15.00	30.00
(2016 Toys R Us Exclusive)		
12 Imperial Shadow Squadron	100.00	175.00
(2014 Target Exclusive)		
13 Imperial Shock Trooper	30.00	60.00
(2015 Walmart Exclusive)		
14 Jabba's Throne Room	100.00	200.00
(2014 SDCC Exclusive)		
15 Kylo Ren (unmasked)	50.00	100.00
(2016 Celebration/SDCC Exclusive)		
16 Kylo Ren	25.00	50.00
(2015 Kmart Exclusive)		
17 Obi-Wan Kenobi	50.00	100.00
(2016 SDCC Exclusive)		
18 Phase II Clone Trooper 4-Pack	50.00	100.00
(2016 Entertainment Earth Exclusive)		
19 Poe Dameron and Riot Control Stormtrooper	30.00	60.00
(2015 Target Exclusive)		
20 Resistance Tech Rose		
(2017 Walmart Exclusive)		
21 Rey (Jedi Training) & Luke Skywalker (Jedi Master) 2-Pack		
(2017 SDCC Exclusive)		
22 Rey (Starkiller Base)	15.00	30.00
(2016 Kmart Exclusive)		
23 Rogue One 3-Pack	30.00	75.00
Imperial Death Trooper/Captain Cassian Andor/Sergeant Jyn Erso (Jedha)		
(2016 Target Exclusive)		
24 Scarif Stormtrooper	20.00	40.00
(2016 Walmart Exclusive)		
25 Sergeant Jyn Erso (Eadu)	10.00	20.00
(2016 Kmart Exclusive)		
26 Sergeant Jyn Erso	60.00	120.00
(2016 SDCC Exclusive)		
27 Stormtrooper Evolution 4-Pack	50.00	100.00
(Amazon Exclusive)		
28 Supreme Leader Snoke (Throne Room)		
(2017 GameStop Exclusive)		

2013-14 Star Wars Black Series 6-Inch Orange

1 Luke Skywalker X-Wing Pilot	50.00	100.00
2 Darth Maul	25.00	50.00
3 Sandtrooper	20.00	40.00
4 R2-D2	40.00	80.00
5 Princess Leia Organa (Slave attire)	40.00	80.00
6 Boba Fett	40.00	80.00
7 Greedo	20.00	40.00
8 Han Solo	20.00	40.00
9 Stormtrooper	12.00	25.00
10 Obi-Wan Kenobi	20.00	40.00
Episode II		
11 Luke Skywalker Bespin Gear	30.00	60.00
12 Anakin Skywalker	40.00	80.00
Episode III		
13 Clone Trooper	12.00	25.00
Episode II		

2015-17 Star Wars Black Series 6-Inch Red

1A Finn Jakku	12.00	25.00
(Glossy Head)		
1B Finn Jakku	12.00	25.00
(Matte Head)		
2A Rey and BB-8	12.00	25.00
(Clean)		
2B Rey and BB-8	12.00	25.00
(Dirty)		
3 Kylo Ren	10.00	20.00
4 First Order Stormtrooper	10.00	20.00
5 Chewbacca	10.00	20.00
6 Captain Phasma	12.00	25.00
7 Poe Dameron	10.00	20.00
8 Guavian Enforcer	12.00	25.00
9A Constable Zuvio		
(green helmet)		
9B Constable Zuvio		
(brown helmet)		
10A Resistance Soldier	20.00	40.00
(green helmet)		
10B Resistance Soldier	10.00	20.00
(brown helmet)		

11 First Order TIE Fighter Pilot	10.00	20.00
12 First Order Snowtrooper	12.00	25.00
13 First Order General Hux	15.00	30.00
14 X-Wing Pilot Asty	15.00	30.00
15 Jango Fett	10.00	20.00
16 First Order Flametrooper	10.00	20.00
17 Finn (FN-2187)	20.00	40.00
18 Han Solo	12.00	25.00
19 Kanan Jarrus		
20 Ahsoka Tano	20.00	40.00
21 Luke Skywalker	10.00	20.00
22 Sergeant Jyn Erso (Jedha)		
23 Captain Cassian Andor (Eadu)		
24 K-2SO		
25 Imperial Death Trooper		
26 Kylo Ren (unmasked)		
27 Director Krennic		
28 Scarif Stormtrooper Squad Leader		
29 C-3PO (Resistance Base)		
30 Princess Leia Organa		
31 AT-AT Pilot/AT-AT Driver		
32 Obi-Wan Kenobi		
33 Sabine Wren		
34 Darth Revan		
35 Snowtrooper		
36 Chirrut Imwe		
37 Baze Malbus		
38 Imperial Royal Guard		
39 Lando Calrissian		
40 Qui-Gon Jinn		
41 Tusken Raider		
42 Hera Syndulla		
43 Darth Vader		
44 Rey (Jedi Training)		
45 Kylo Ren		
46 Luke Skywalker (Jedi Master)		
47 Grand Admiral Thrawn		
48 Stormtrooper		
49 Maz Kanata		
50 Elite Praetorian Guard		
51 Finn (First Order Disguise)		
52 General Leia Organa		
53 Poe Dameron		
56 Jaina Solo		

2017 Star Wars Black Series Centerpiece

NNO Darth Vader	
NNO Luke Skywalker	

2013-16 Star Wars Black Series Vehicles

1 Millennium Falcon	10.00	20.00
2 Resistance X-Wing	8.00	15.00
3A Kylo Ren's Command Shuttle	6.00	12.00
3B Kylo Ren Command Shuttle (black)	6.00	12.00
4 First Order Special Forces Tie Fighter	6.00	12.00
5 Rey's Speeder (Jakku)	10.00	20.00
6 First Order Star Destroyer	8.00	15.00
7 X-Wing	12.00	25.00
8 Y-Wing	15.00	30.00
9 Luke Skywalker Landspeeder	10.00	20.00
10 Slave I	12.00	25.00
11 First Order Snowspeeder	5.00	10.00
12 Poe's X-Wing Fighter	5.00	10.00
13 First Order Tie Fighter	4.00	8.00
14 First Order Transporter	4.00	8.00
15 Tie Advanced	5.00	10.00
16 B-Wing	12.00	25.00
17 Snowspeeder	8.00	15.00
18 AT-AT	30.00	60.00
19 Jakku Landspeeder	8.00	15.00
20 A-Wing	15.00	30.00
21 Sith Infiltrator	8.00	15.00
22 Anakin Skywalker's Jedi Starfighter	12.00	30.00
23 Republic Gunship	12.00	25.00
24 Star Destroyer	6.00	12.00
25 Imperial Shuttle	30.00	60.00
26 The Ghost	6.00	12.00
27 Jango Fett's Slave I	8.00	15.00
28 Inquisitor's Tie Advanced Prototype	6.00	12.00
29 Rebel U-Wing Fighter	8.00	15.00
30 TIE Striker	8.00	15.00
31 Imperial Cargo Shuttle SW-0608	8.00	15.00

2003-05 Star Wars Clone Wars

42 Anakin Skywalker	6.00	12.00
43a ARC Trooper (blue)	5.00	10.00
43b ARC Trooper (blue w/gray shoulder pad and thick blue chin paint)	5.00	10.00
43c ARC Trooper (red)	5.00	10.00

44 Yoda	5.00	10.00
45 Obi-Wan Kenobi (General of The Republic Army)	4.00	8.00
46 Durge Commander of the Seperatist Forces	10.00	20.00
47 Asajj Ventress (Sith Apprentice)	5.00	10.00
48 Mace Windu (General of the Republic Army)	5.00	10.00
49 Kit Fisto	8.00	15.00
50a Clone Trooper (facing left)	8.00	15.00
50b Clone Trooper (facing right)	4.00	8.00
51 Saesee Tiin	8.00	15.00

2003-05 Star Wars Clone Wars Deluxe

1 Clone Trooper (w/speeder bike)	8.00	15.00
2 Spider Droid	6.00	12.00
3 Durge (w/swoop bike)	15.00	30.00

2003-05 Star Wars Clone Wars Multipacks

1 Clone Trooper Army	8.00	15.00
2 Clone Trooper Army (w/blue lieutenant)	10.00	20.00
3 Clone Trooper Army (w/green sergeant)	8.00	15.00
4 Clone Trooper Army (w/red captain)	8.00	15.00
5 Clone Trooper Army (w/yellow commander)	8.00	15.00
6 Droid Army	6.00	12.00
7 Jedi Knight Army	6.00	12.00

2003-05 Star Wars Clone Wars Value Packs

1 Anakin Skywalker/Clone Trooper (blue)	5.00	10.00
2 ARC Trooper/Clone Trooper	10.00	20.00
3 Yoda/Clone Trooper (yellow)	5.00	10.00

2003-05 Star Wars Clone Wars Vehicles

1	Anakin Skywalker's Jedi Starfighter	25.00	50.00
2	Armored Assault/ Tank (AAT)	75.00	150.00
3	Command Gunship	30.00	75.00
4	Geonosian Starfighter	15.00	30.00
5	Hailfire Droid	12.00	25.00
6	Jedi Starfighter	15.00	30.00

2003-05 Star Wars Clone Wars Animated Series

1	Anakin Skywalker		
2	Anakin Skywalker (no sleeves torn pants)	5.00	12.00
3	ARC Trooper		
4	Asajj Ventress		
5	Clone Trooper	5.00	10.00
6	Clone Trooper (blue)	12.00	30.00
7	Clone Trooper (red)		
8	Clone Trooper (yellow)	6.00	12.00
9	Count Dooku	5.00	10.00
10	Durge	5.00	10.00
11	General Grievous		
12	Mace Windu	5.00	10.00
13	Obi-Wan Kenobi		
14	Yoda		

2003-05 Star Wars Clone Wars Animated Series Commemorative DVD Collection

1	Volume 1 Jedi Force		
	(Anakin Skywalker/ARC Trooper/Obi-Wan Kenobi)		
2	Volume 1 Sith Attack	12.00	25.00
	(Asojj Ventress/Durge/General Grievous)		
3	Volume 2 (Anakin Skywalker tattoo		
	Clone Trooper/Saesee Tiin)		
4	Volume 2 (Clone Commander Cody		
	General Grievous/Obi-Wan Kenobi)		

2003-05 Star Wars Clone Wars Animated Series Maquettes

1	ARC Trooper Captain		
2	Anakin Skywalker		
3	Asajj Ventress		
4	Bariss Offee & Luminara Unduli		
5	General Grievous		
6	Obi-Wan Kenobi		
7	Padme Amidala		
8	Yoda		

2008-13 Star Wars The Clone Wars Battle Packs

1	Ambush at Abregado	15.00	30.00
2	Ambush on the Vulture's Claw	30.00	75.00
3	Anti-Hailfire Droid Squad	20.00	40.00
4	ARC Troopers		
5	Army of the Republic		
6	Assault on Ryloth	30.00	60.00
7	Assault on Geonosis	15.00	30.00
8	AT-TE Assault Squad	20.00	40.00
9	Battle of Orto Plutonia	12.00	25.00
10	B'omarr Monastery Assault		
11	Cad Bane's Escape		
12	Capture of the Droids		
13	Clone Troopers & Droids	20.00	40.00
14	Defend Kamino	60.00	120.00
15	Holocron Heist		
16	Hunt for Grievous	25.00	50.00
17	Jabba's Palace	12.00	25.00
18	Jedi Showdown	20.00	40.00
19	Mandalorian Warriors	100.00	200.00
20	Republic Troopers	20.00	40.00
21	Rishi Moon Outpost Attack	30.00	75.00
22	Speeder Bike Recon	15.00	30.00
23	Stop the Zillo Beast	20.00	40.00

2008-13 Star Wars The Clone Wars Battle Packs Exclusives

1	Assassin Spider Droid & Clones		
	(Toys R Us Exclusive)		
2	Battle of Christophsis (ultimate)	60.00	120.00
	(2008 Target Exclusive)		
3	Darth Maul Returns	25.00	50.00
	(2012 Target Exclusive)		
4	Hidden Enemy (w/DVD)	30.00	75.00
	(2010 Target Exclusive)		
5	Hostage Crisis (w/DVD)		
	(Target Exclusive)		

6	Obi-Wan & 212th Attack Battalion	30.00	75.00
	(2008 Target Exclusive)		
7	Rise of Boba Fett (ultimate)	75.00	150.00
	(2010 Toys R Us Exclusive)		
8	Yoda & Coruscant Guard		
	(2008 Target Exclusive)		

2008-13 Star Wars The Clone Wars Blue and Black

CW1	Captain Rex		
CW2	Obi-Wan Kenobi	8.00	15.00
CW3	Clone Commander Cody		
CW4	Destroyer Droid		
CW5	Yoda		
CW6	Count Dooku		
CW7	Anakin Skywalker		
CW8	Pre Vizsla		
CW9	Mandalorian Police Officer		
CW10	General Grievous		
CW11	Aurra Sing		
CW12	Captain Rex (cold weather gear)		
CW13	Cad Bane		
CW14	Clone Pilot Odd Ball		
CW15	Asajj Ventress		
CW16	Super Battle Droid		
CW17	Ahsoka Tano		
CW18	ARF Trooper		
CW19	Battle Droid		
CW20	Mace Windu		
CW21	Commander Gree		
CW22	Battle Droid Commander		
CW23	Kit Fisto		
CW24	ARF Trooper (jungle deco)		
CW25	Ki-Adi-Mundi		
CW26	Clone Trooper (flamethrower)		
CW27	R2-D2	8.00	15.00
CW28	Clone Pilot Goji		
CW29	Mandalorian Warrior		
CW30	R4-P17		
CW31	Shaak Ti		
CW32	Boba Fett		
CW33	Embo		
CW34	Undead Geonosian		
CW35	Clone Trooper Draa		
CW36	Quinlan Vos		
CW37	Cato Parasiti		
CW38	Clone Commander Jet		
CW39	Hondo Ohnaka		
CW40	Obi-Wan Kenobi (new outfit)		
CW41	Clone Trooper Hevy (training armor)		
CW42	Cad Bane (w/TODO-360)		
CW43	R7-A7		
CW44	Ahsoka (new outfit)		
CW45	Anakin Skywalker (new outfit)		
CW46	Aqua Battle Droid		
CW47	El-Les		
CW48	Clone Commander Wolffe		

CW49 Riot Control Clone Trooper

CW50 Barriss Offee

CW51 Eeth Koth

CW52 Clone Commander Colt   30.00   75.00

CW53 Plo Koon (cold weather gear)

CW54 Saesee Tin

CW55 Savage Opress (shirtless)

CW56 ARF Trooper (Kamino)

CW57 Stealth Ops Clone Trooper

CW58 Even Piell

CW59 Savage Opress (armored apprentice)

CW60 Kit Fisto (cold weather gear)

CW61 Seripas

CW62 Captain Rex (jet propulsion pack)   30.00   60.00

CW63 Chewbacca

CW64 R7-D4 (Plo Koon's astromech droid)

CW65 Jar Jar Binks

2008-13 Star Wars The Clone Wars Blue and White

1 Anakin Skywalker

2 Obi-Wan Kenobi

3 Yoda

4 Captain Rex

5 Clone Trooper

6 General Grievous

7 Battle Droid

8 R2-D2

9 Ahsoka Tano

10 Clone Commander Cody

11 Clone Pilot Odd Ball

12 Super Battle Droid

13 Count Dooku

14 Plo Koon

15 Asajj Ventress

16 C-3PO

17 Destroyer Droid

18 IG-86 Assassin Droid

19 Clone Trooper (212th Attack Battalion)

20 Padme Amidala (diplomat)

21 Clone Trooper (space gear)

22 Magnaguard

23 R3-S6 (Goldie)

24 Jar Jar Binks

25 Rocket Battle Droid

26 Clone Trooper (41st Elite Corps)

27 Kit Fisto

2008-13 Star Wars The Clone Wars Darth Maul Pack

CW1 Anakin Skywalker (new sculpt)

CW2 Clone Trooper (Phase II armor)

CW3 Savage Opress (shirtless)

CW4 Cad Bane

CW5 Yoda

CW6 Plo Koon (cold weather gear)

CW7 Clone Commander Cody (jet propulsion pack)

CW8 Mace Windu

CW9 Chewbacca

CW10 Aqua Battle Droid

CW11 Republic Commando Boss

CW12 Obi-Wan Kenobi

CW13 Captain Rex (Phase II)

CW14 Aayla Secura

CW15 Ahsoka Tano (scuba gear)

CW16 Training Super Battle Droid

CW17 Clone Commander Wolffe (Phase II)

CW18 Clone Commander Fox (Phase II)

2008-13 Star Wars The Clone Wars Deluxe Figures and Vehicles

1 212th Battalion Clone Troopers & Jet Backpacks

2 Armored Scout Tank (w/Battle Droid)

3 Armored Scout Tank (w/Tactical Droid)

4 AT-RT (w/ARF Trooper)

5 AT-RT (w/ARF Trooper Boil)

6 Attack Cycle (w/General Grievous)

7 Attack Recon Fighter (w/Anakin Skywalker)

8 BARC Speeder (w/Commander Cody)

9 BARC Speeder (w/Clone Trooper)

10 BARC Speeder Bike (w/Clone Trooper Jesse)

11 BARC Speeder Bike (w/Obi-Wan Kenobi)

12 Can-Cell (w/Anakin Skywalker)

13 Crab Droid

14 Desert Skiff (w/Anakin Skywalker)

15 Freeco Speeder (w/Clone Trooper)

16 Freeco Speeder (w/Obi-Wan Kenobi)

17 Mandalorian Speeder (w/Mandalorian Warrior)

18 Naboo Star Skiff (w/Anakin Skywalker)

19 Pirate Speeder Bike (w/Cad Bane)

20 Republic Assault Submarine with Scuba Clone Trooper

21 Republic Attack Dropship with Clone Pilot

22 Republic Scout Speeder with ARF Trooper

23 Separatist Droid Speeder with Battle Droid

24 Speeder Bike with Castas

25 Speeder Bike with Count Dooku

26 Speeder Bike with Plo Koon

27 Turbo Tank Support Squad

28 Y-Wing Scout Bomber with Clone Trooper Pilot

2008-13 Star Wars The Clone Wars Deluxe Figures and Vehicles Exclusives

1 AT-RT with ARF Trooper

(Walmart Exclusive)

2 BARC Speeder with Clone Trooper Buzz

(Walmart Exclusive)

3 Separatist Speeder with Geonosian Warrior

(2011 Toys R Us Exclusive)

4 STAP with Battle Droid

(2010 Toys R Us Exclusive)

2008-13 Star Wars The Clone Wars Exclusives

1 Captain Rex

(2008 Sneak Preview Mailaway Exclusive)

2 Clone Captain Lock

(2011 K-Mart Exclusive)

3 Clone Trooper: 501st Legion

(2008 Wal-Mart Exclusive)

4 Clone Trooper: Senate Security

(2008 SDCC Exclusive)

5 Commander Fox

(2008 Target Exclusive)

6 Commander Ponds

(2009 Toys R Us Exclusive)

7 General Grievous: Holographic

(2008 Toys R Us Exclusive)

8 Kul Teska

(2010 Toys R Us Exclusive)

9 Nahdar Vebb

(2009 Mailaway Exclusive)

10 Nikto Skiff Guard Puko Naga

(2010 Toys R Us Exclusive)

11 Sgt. Bric & Galactic Battle Mat

(2010 Mailaway Exclusive)

12 Stealth Operation Clone Trooper: Commander Blackout

(2011 Toys R Us Exclusive)

2008-13 Star Wars The Clone Wars Red and White

CW1 General Grievous
CW2 Clone Trooper (space gear)
CW3 Rocket Battle Droid
CW4 Clone Trooper (41st Elite Corps)
CW5 Kit Fisto
CW6 Mace Windu
CW7 Admiral Yularen
CW8 Jawas
CW9 Commander Gree
CW10 ARF Trooper
CW11 Heavy Assault Super Battle Droid
CW12 Obi-Wan Kenobi (space suit)
CW13 4A-7
CW14 Yoda
CW15 Whorm Loathsom
CW16 Commando Droid
CW17 Clone Trooper Echo
CW18 Anakin Skywalker
CW19 Obi-Wan Kenobi
CW20 Clone Trooper Denal
CW21 Anakin Skywalker (space suit)
CW22 Cad Bane
CW23 Ahsoka Tano (space suit)
CW24 Captain Rex
CW25 R2-D2
CW26 Ahsoka Tano
CW27 Count Dooku
CW28 Commander Cody
CW29 Destroyer Droid
CW30 Luminara Unduli
CW31 Captain Argyus
CW32 Clone Commander Thire
CW33 Battle Droid (AAT Driver)
CW34 Matchstick
CW35 Padme Amidala (adventurer suit)
CW36 Clone Tank Gunner
CW37 Ziro's Assassin Droid
CW38 Clone Trooper Jek
CW39 Commander Bly
CW40 Aayla Secura
CW41 Hondo Ohnaka
CW42 Anakin Skywalker (cold weather gear)
CW43 Thi-Sen
CW44 Clone Commander Stone
CW45 Darth Sidious
CW46 Commander TX-20
CW47 Firefighter Droid
CW48 Obi-Wan Kenobi (cold weather gear)
CW49 Magnaguard (w/cape)
CW50 Captain Rex (cold assault gear)

2008-13 Star Wars The Clone Wars Vehicles

1	Ahsoka Tano's Delta Starfighter		
1	AT-AP Walker		
2	AT-TE (All Terrain Tactical Enforcer)		
2	Anakin's Delta Starfighter	8.00	15.00
3	Anakin's Modified Jedi Starfighter	15.00	40.00
3	Clone Turbo Tank		
4	Corporate Alliance Tank Droid		
4	ARC-170 Starfighter (Imperial Shadow Squadron)		
5	Droid Tri-Fighter		
6	General Grievous' Starfighter		
7	Hailfire Droid (Remote Control)		
8	Homing Spider Droid		
9	Hyena Bomber		
10	Jedi Turbo Speeder		
11	MagnaGuard Fighter		
12	Mandalorian Assault Gunship		
13	Obi-Wan's Jedi Starfighter (Utapau)		
14	Obi-Wan Kenobi's Delta Starfighter		
15	Plo Koon's Delta Starfighter		
16	Republic Attack Shuttle		
17	Republic AV-7 Mobile Cannon		
18	Republic Fighter Tank		
19	Republic Fighter Tank (blue deco)		
20	Republic Fighter Tank (green deco)		
21	Republic Fighter Tank (Remote Control)		
22	Republic Swamp Speeder		
23	Separatist Droid Gunship		
24	V-19 Torrent Starfighter		
25	V-Wing Starfighter		
26	Vulture Droid		
27	Trade Federation Armored Assault Tank (AAT)		
28	Trade Federation Armored Assault Tank (AAT - brown/blue)		
29	Xanadu Blood		
30	Y-Wing Bomber		

2008-13 Star Wars The Clone Wars Vehicles Exclusives

1 ARC-170 Starfighter (flaming wampa)
(Toys R Us Exclusive)
2 Hailfire Droid & General Grievous
(Toys R Us Exclusive)
3 Kit Fisto's Delta Starfighter
(Walmart Exclusive)
4 Octuptarra Droid
(Walmart Exclusive)
5 Republic Gunship (crumb bomber)
(Toys R Us Exclusive)
6 Republic Gunship (Lucky Lekku)
(Walmart Exclusive)
7 V-Wing Starfighter & V-Wing Pilot
(Toys R Us Exclusive)
8 V-Wing Starfighter (Imperial)
(Toys R Us Exclusive)

2008-13 Star Wars The Clone Wars Yoda Pack

CW1 Obi-Wan Kenobi
CW2 Savage Opress (armoured apprentice)
CW3 Anakin Skywalker
CW4 Captain Rex
CW5 R2-D2
CW6 501st Legion Clone Trooper
CW7 Clone Commander Cody (jet propulsion pack)
CW8 Darth Maul
CW9 Battle Droid

1996-99 Star Wars Collector Series

1	Admiral Ackbar	20.00	40.00
2	AT-AT Driver	15.00	30.00
3	Boba Fett	25.00	50.00
4	C-3PO	20.00	40.00
5	Cantina Band - Doikk Na'ts (w/Fizzz)	12.00	25.00
	(Walmart Exclusive)		
6	Cantina Band - Figrin D'an (w/Kloo Horn)	10.00	20.00
	(Walmart Exclusive)		
7	Cantina Band - Ickabel (w/fanfar)	12.00	25.00
	(Walmart Exclusive)		
8	Cantina Band - Nalan (w/Bandfill)	10.00	20.00
	(Walmart Exclusive)		
9	Cantina Band - Tech (w/Omni Box)	12.00	25.00
	(Walmart Exclusive)		
10	Cantina Band - Tedn (w/fanfar)	10.00	20.00
	(Walmart Exclusive)		
11	Chewbacca	20.00	40.00
12	Darth Vader	15.00	30.00
13	Greedo	15.00	30.00
	(JC Penney Exclusive)		
14	Han Solo	15.00	30.00
15	Lando Calrissian	12.00	25.00
16	Luke Skywalker	15.00	30.00
17	Luke Skywalker (Bespin)	12.00	25.00
18	Luke Skywalker (X-Wing Pilot)	20.00	40.00
19	Obi-Wan Kenobi	15.00	30.00
20	Princess Leia	15.00	30.00
21	Sandtrooper	15.00	30.00
22	Stormtrooper	15.00	30.00
23	TIE Fighter Pilot	20.00	40.00

24 Tusken Raider (blaster and binoculars)	12.00	25.00
25 Tusken Raider (gaderffii stick)	12.00	25.00

1996-99 Star Wars Collector Series 2-Packs

1 Grand Moff Tarkin and Imperial Gunner	25.00	50.00
(FAO Schwarz Exclusive)		
2 Han Solo and Luke Skywalker (stormtrooper gear)	30.00	60.00
(KB Toys Exclusive)		
3 Han Solo and Tauntaun	30.00	60.00
4 Luke Hoth and Wampa	25.00	50.00
5 Luke Jedi and Bib Fortuna	25.00	50.00
(FAO Schwarz Exclusive)		
6 Obi-Wan Kenobi vs. Darth Vader (electronic)	25.00	50.00
(JC Penney/KB Toys Exclusive)		
7 Princess Leia and R2-D2 (Jabba's prisoners)		
(FAO Schwarz/KB Toys Exclusive)		

1996-99 Star Wars Collector Series European Exclusives

1 Han Solo (drawing action)	12.00	25.00
2 Luke Skywalker (drawing action)		

1996-99 Star Wars Collector Series Masterpiece Edition

1 Anakin Skywalker/Story of Darth Vader	10.00	20.00
2 Aurra Sing/Dawn of the Bounty Hunters	12.00	25.00
3 C-3PO/Tales of the Golden Droid	20.00	40.00

2006 Star Wars Customs

1 Boba Fett's/ Outlaw Chopper
2 Darth Vader's/ Imperial Chopper
3 Luke Skywalker's/ Rebel Chopper

2006 Star Wars Customs International

1 Boba Fett's/ Outlaw Chopper
2 Darth Vader's/ Imperial Chopper
3 Luke Skywalker's/ Rebel Chopper

2008-10 Star Wars Diamond Select

1 Anakin Skywalker	25.00	50.00
2 Darth Maul	30.00	75.00
3 Emperor Palpatine	25.00	50.00
4 Luke Skywalker Jedi Knight	60.00	120.00
5 Mace Windu	30.00	60.00
6 Obi-Wan Kenobi (ROTS)	30.00	60.00

2012-13 Star Wars Discover the Force

1 Aurra Sing	8.00	15.00
2 Darth Maul	8.00	15.00
3 Destroyer Droid	6.00	12.00
4 G8-R3	12.00	25.00
5 Gungan Warrior	8.00	15.00
6 Mawhonic	6.00	12.00
7 Obi-Wan Kenobi	8.00	15.00
8 Qui-Gon Jinn	6.00	12.00
9 Ric Olie	6.00	12.00
10 Naboo Pilot	5.00	10.00
11 Tusken Raider	5.00	10.00
12 Yoda	8.00	15.00

2012-13 Star Wars Discover the Force Battle Packs

1 Mos Espa Arena	20.00	40.00
(C-3PO/Anakin/Sebulba/2 Pit Droids)		
2 Royal Starship Droids		
(R2-B1/R2-R9/R2-D2/R2-N3)		

2012-13 Star Wars Discover the Force Vehicles-Creatures

1 Dewback	25.00	50.00
2 Vulture Droid		

2015-17 Star Wars Disney Parks Droid Factory

NNO BB-8	
NNO C1-10P Chopper	
NNO R2-B00	
(2016 Halloween Exclusive)	
NNO R2-D60	
(2015 Disneyland 60th Anniversary Exclusive)	
NNO R2-H15	
(2015 Holiday Exclusive)	
NNO R2-H16	
(2016 Holiday Exclusive)	
NNO R3-B0017	
(2017 Halloween Exclusive)	
NNO R-3D0	
NNO R3-H17	
(2017 Holiday Exclusive)	
NNO R5-M4	
(2016 May 4th Exclusive)	

2015-17 Star Wars Disney Parks Droid Factory Multipacks

NNO Artoo Detoo (R2-D2)/See-Threepio (C-3PO)	
(2017 40th Anniversary Exclusive)	
NNO BB-8/2BB-2/BB-4/BB-9E	
NNO C2-B5/R2-BHD/R3-M2/R5-SK1	
NNO R4-X2/Y5-X2	
NNO R5-013/R2-C2/R5-S9/R5-P8	

2015 Star Wars Elite Series

NNO Anakin Skywalker	25.00	50.00
NNO Boba Fett (w/cape)	20.00	40.00
NNO Boba Fett (w/o cape)	75.00	150.00
NNO Darth Maul	30.00	60.00
NNO Darth Vader	20.00	40.00
NNO General Grievous	30.00	75.00
NNO Prototype Boba Fett	30.00	75.00
NNO Stormtrooper	15.00	30.00

2016-17 Star Wars Elite Series 11-Inch

NNO Darth Vader	
NNO Death Trooper	
NNO Jyn Erso	
NNO Kylo Ren	
NNO Director Orson Krennic	
NNO Princess Leia Organa	
NNO Rey	

2015-17 Star Wars Elite Series Multipacks and Exclusives

NNO 8-Piece Gift Set	500.00	750.00
Darth Maul/Anakin/Grievous/Stormtrooper		
Vader/C-3PO/R2-D2/Boba Fett)		
(2016 D23 Exclusive)		
NNO Deluxe Gift Set	60.00	120.00
Stormtrooper/Phasma/Kylo Ren/Finn/Flametrooper		
NNO Droid Gift Pack	30.00	75.00
BB-8, C-3PO, R2-D2		
NNO Han Solo & Luke Skywalker w/blond hair (Stormtrooper Disguise)	60.00	120.00
NNO Han Solo & Luke Skywalker w/brown hair (Stormtrooper Disguise)		
NNO Princess Leia & Darth Vader/1000*	75.00	150.00
(2017 D23 Exclusive)		

1999-00 Star Wars Episode I 2-Packs

1 Darth Maul and Sith Infiltrator	8.00	15.00
2 Final Jedi Duel (Qui-Gon Jinn/Darth Maul break apart)	20.00	50.00

1999-00 Star Wars Episode I Accessory Sets

1 Flash Cannon	8.00	15.00
2 Gungan Catapult	10.00	20.00
3 Hyperdrive Repair Kit	25.00	50.00
4 Naboo Accessory Set	8.00	15.00
5 Pod Race Fuel Station	8.00	15.00
6 Rappel Line Attach	12.00	25.00
7 Sith Accessory Set	8.00	15.00
8 Tatooine Accessory Set	8.00	15.00
9 Tatooine Disguise Set	12.00	25.00
10 Underwater Accessory Set	8.00	15.00

1999-00 Star Wars Episode I Action Collection 12-Inch

1 Anakin Skywalker (fully poseable)	10.00	20.00
2 Anakin Skywalker (w/Theed Hangar Droid)	20.00	40.00
3 Battle Droid (w/blaster rifle)	15.00	30.00
4 Battle Droid Commander(#(w/electrobinoculars)	10.00	20.00
5 Boss Nass	15.00	30.00
6 Chancellor Valorum & Coruscant Guard	20.00	40.00
7 Darth Maul (w/lightsaber)	12.00	25.00
8 Darth Maul & Sith Speeder	20.00	40.00
(Walmart Exclusive)		
9 Jar Jar Binks (fully poseable)	12.00	25.00
10 Mace Windu (w/lightsaber)	15.00	30.00
11 Obi-Wan Kenobi (w/lightsaber)	12.00	25.00
12 Pit Droids (fully poseable)	12.00	20.00
13 Qui-Gon Jinn (w/lightsaber)	15.00	30.00
14 Qui-Gon Jinn (Tatooine)	10.00	20.00
15 R2-A6 (metalized dome)	20.00	40.00
16 Sebulba (w/Chubas)	12.00	25.00
17 Watto (w/data pad)	10.00	20.00

1999-00 Star Wars Episode I Battle Bags

1 Sea Creatures I	6.00	12.00
2 Sea Creatures II	6.00	12.00
3 Swamp Creatures I	6.00	12.00
4 Swamp Creatures II	6.00	12.00

1999-00 Star Wars Episode I Bonus Battle Droid 2-Packs

NNO Anakin Skywalker (Naboo)/Battle Droid (tan clean)		
NNO Anakin Skywalker (Tatooine)/Battle Droid (tan clean)		
NNO Battle Droid (tan clean)/Battle Droid (tan clean)		
NNO Battle Droid (tan clean)/Battle Droid (gold/dirty)		
NNO Battle Droid (tan clean)/Battle Droid (tan/blast on chest)		
NNO Battle Droid (tan clean)/Battle Droid (tan/slash on chest/burn marks)		
NNO C-3PO/Battle Droid (tan clean)		
NNO Captain Panaka/Battle Droid (tan clean)		
NNO Darth Maul (Jedi duel)/Battle Droid (tan clean)		
NNO Darth Maul (Tatooine)/Battle Droid (tan clean)	8.00	15.00
NNO Darth Sidious/Battle Droid (tan clean)		
NNO Destroyer Droid/Battle Droid (tan clean)		
NNO Jar Jar Binks/Battle Droid (tan clean)		
NNO Naboo Royal Security/Battle Droid (tan clean)		
NNO Nute Gunray/Battle Droid (tan clean)		
NNO Obi-Wan Kenobi (Jedi duel)/Battle Droid (tan clean)	6.00	12.00
NNO Obi-Wan Kenobi (Jedi Knight)/Battle Droid (tan clean)	6.00	12.00
NNO Padme Naberrie/Battle Droid (tan clean)		
NNO Queen Amidala (Naboo)/Battle Droid (tan clean)	6.00	12.00
NNO Queen Amidala (red senate gown)/Battle Droid (tan clean)		
NNO Qui-Gon Jinn/Battle Droid (tan clean)		
NNO Qui-Gon Jinn (Jedi Master)/Battle Droid (tan clean)		
NNO R2-D2/Battle Droid (tan clean)		
NNO Ric Olie/Battle Droid (tan clean)		
NNO Rune Haako/Battle Droid (tan clean)		
NNO Senator Palpatine/Battle Droid (tan clean)		
NNO Watto/Battle Droid (tan clean)	20.00	40.00
NNO Yoda/Battle Droid (tan clean)		

1999-00 Star Wars Episode I Bonus Pit Droid 2-Packs

NNO Anakin Skywalker (Tatooine)/Pit Droid (maroon)		
NNO Anakin Skywalker (Tatooine)/Pit Droid (orange)		
NNO Anakin Skywalker (Tatooine)/Pit Droid (white)		
NNO Darth Maul (Jedi duel)/Pit Droid (maroon)		
NNO Darth Maul (Jedi duel)/Pit Droid (orange)		
NNO Darth Maul (Jedi duel)/Pit Droid (white)		
NNO Darth Sidius (hologram)/Pit Droid (maroon)		
NNO Darth Sidius (hologram)/Pit Droid (orange)		
NNO Darth Sidius (hologram)/Pit Droid (white)		
NNO Naboo Royal Guard/Pit Droid (maroon)		
NNO Naboo Royal Guard/Pit Droid (orange)		
NNO Naboo Royal Guard/Pit Droid (white)		
NNO Obi-Wan Kenobi (Jedi Knight)/Pit Droid (maroon)		
NNO Obi-Wan Kenobi (Jedi Knight)/Pit Droid (orange)		
NNO Obi-Wan Kenobi (Jedi Knight)/Pit Droid (white)		

1999-00 Star Wars Episode I CommTech Cinema Scenes

1 Mos Espa Encounter (Sebulba/Jar Jar Binks/Anakin Skywalker)	12.00	25.00
2 Tatooine Showdown (Darth Maul/Qui-Gon Jinn Tatooine Anakin Skywalker Tatooine)	8.00	20.00
3 Watto's Box (Watto/Graxol Kelvyyn/Shakka)	25.00	50.00

1999-00 Star Wars Episode I CommTech Collection 1

1a Anakin Skywalker Naboo (new sticker)	6.00	12.00
1b Anakin Skywalker Naboo (no new sticker)	12.00	25.00
2a Anakin Skywalker Naboo pilot (new sticker)	6.00	12.00
2b Anakin Skywalker Naboo pilot (no new sticker)	3.00	6.00
3a Anakin Skywalker Tatooine (.00)	10.00	20.00
3b Anakin Skywalker Tatooine (.0100)	3.00	6.00
3c Anakin Skywalker Tatooine (.01 innovision back)	3.00	6.00
4a Battle Droid (tan clean .00)	5.00	10.00
4b Battle Droid (tan clean .01)	5.00	10.00
4c Battle Droid (tan clean .02 innovision back)	5.00	10.00
5a Battle Droid (tan slash on chest w/burn marks .00)	8.00	15.00
5b Battle Droid (tan slash on chest w/burn marks .01)	4.00	8.00
5c Battle Droid (tan slash on chest w/burn marks .02 innovision back)	3.00	6.00
6a Battle Droid (tan blast on chest .00)	4.00	8.00
6b Battle Droid (tan blast on chest .01)	3.00	6.00
6c Battle Droid (tan blast on chest .02 innovision back)	6.00	12.00
7a Battle Droid (gold/dirty .00)	3.00	6.00
7b Battle Droid (gold/dirty .01)	3.00	6.00
7c Battle Droid (gold/dirty .02 innovision back)	3.00	6.00
8a Darth Maul Jedi duel (.00)	8.00	15.00
8b Darth Maul Jedi duel (.01/ innovision back)	3.00	6.00
8c Darth Maul Jedi duel (.02)	5.00	10.00
8d Darth Maul Jedi duel	4.00	8.00
(.0000 large eyes different face more red paint on)		
8e Darth Maul Jedi duel (white strip on package card instead of yellow)	3.00	6.00
9a Darth Maul Sith Lord (new sticker)	5.00	10.00
9b Darth Maul Sith Lord (no new sticker)	5.00	10.00
10a Darth Maul Tatooine (new sticker)	4.00	8.00
10b Darth Maul Tatooine (new sticker/hologram chip sticker)	3.00	6.00

10c	Darth Maul Tatooine (no new sticker)	3.00	6.00
10d	Darth Maul Tatooine (no new sticker/hologram chip sticker)	3.00	6.00
10e	Darth Maul Sith Lord (new sticker/white strip on package card)	3.00	6.00
11a	Destroyer Droid battle damaged (new sticker)	5.00	10.00
11b	Destroyer Droid battle damaged (no new sticker)	3.00	6.00
12a	Jar Jar Binks (.00 large package photo)	12.00	25.00
12b	Jar Jar Binks (.0100 small package photo)	3.00	6.00
12c	Jar Jar Binks (.0200/ innovision back)	3.00	6.00
13	Jar Jar Binks (Naboo swamp)	4.00	8.00
14a	Obi-Wan Kenobi Jedi duel (.00)	4.00	8.00
14b	Obi-Wan Kenobi Jedi duel (.0100)	3.00	6.00
15a	Obi-Wan Kenobi Jedi Knight (new sticker)	4.00	8.00
15b	Obi-Wan Kenobi Jedi Knight (no new sticker)	3.00	6.00
16a	Obi-Wan Kenobi Naboo (new sticker)	6.00	12.00
16b	Obi-Wan Kenobi Naboo (no new sticker)	3.00	6.00
17a	Padme Naberrie (.00)	10.00	20.00
17b	Padme Naberrie (.0100 innovision back)	3.00	6.00
18a	Queen Amidala Coruscant (new sticker)	4.00	8.00
18b	Queen Amidala Coruscant (no new sticker)	4.00	8.00
19a	Queen Amidala Naboo (.00)	3.00	6.00
19b	Queen Amidala Naboo (.0100 innovision back)	6.00	12.00
20a	Qui-Gon Jinn (.00)	6.00	12.00
20b	Qui-Gon Jinn (.0100 innovision back)	4.00	8.00
21a	Qui-Gon Jinn Jedi Master (new sticker)	3.00	6.00
21b	Qui-Gon Jinn Jedi Master (no new sticker)	3.00	6.00
22a	Qui-Gon Jinn Naboo (new sticker)	5.00	10.00
22b	Qui-Gon Jinn Naboo (no new sticker)	3.00	6.00

1999-00 Star Wars Episode I CommTech Collection 2

1a	C-3PO (.00)	5.00	10.00
1b	C-3PO (.01 innovision back)	20.00	40.00
2a	Captain Panaka (wrong chip line on back they need her to sign a treaty)	5.00	10.00
2b	Captain Panaka (correct chip line on back this battle I do not think)	5.00	10.00
3a	Darth Sidious (.00)	5.00	10.00
3b	Darth Sidious (.01/innovision back)	3.00	6.00
4	Darth Sidious (holograph)	15.00	30.00
5a	Destroyer Droid (new sticker)	6.00	12.00
5b	Destroyer Droid (no new sticker)	4.00	8.00
6a	Naboo Royal Guard	8.00	15.00
6b	Naboo Royal Security	3.00	6.00
7a	Nute Gunray (new sticker)	5.00	10.00
7b	Nute Gunray (no new sticker)	8.00	15.00
8a	R2-B1 (.0000/Astromech back/no space)	8.00	15.00
8b	R2-B1 (.0100/Astromech back/space)	8.00	15.00
9a	R2-D2 (large packing bubble/new sticker)	6.00	12.00
9b	R2-D2 (small packing bubble)	6.00	12.00
10	Pit Droids	5.00	10.00
11	Queen Amidala (battle)	6.00	12.00
12a	Ric Olie (.00)	3.00	6.00
12b	Ric Olie (.0100/innovision back)	3.00	6.00
13a	Rune Haako (new sticker)	4.00	8.00
13b	Rune Haako (no new sticker)	3.00	6.00
14a	Senator Palpatine (.00)	3.00	6.00
14b	Senator Palpatine (.0100/innovision back)	3.00	6.00
15	Sio Bibble	10.00	20.00
16a	Watto (.00)	3.00	6.00

16b	Watto (.0100 innovision back)	3.00	6.00
17a	Yoda (episode 1 on front)	3.00	6.00
17b	Yoda (no episode 1 on front)	5.00	10.00

1999-00 Star Wars Episode I CommTech Collection 3

1	Adi Gallia	4.00	8.00
2a	Boss Nass (.00)	3.00	6.00
2b	Boss Nass (.01/innovision back)	3.00	6.00
3a	Captain Tarpals (.00)	5.00	10.00
3b	Captain Tarpals (.01)	3.00	6.00
4a	Chancellor Valorum (.00/warning)	3.00	6.00
4b	Chancellor Valorum (.00/no warning)	3.00	6.00
4c	Chancellor Valorum (.01/no warning)	3.00	6.00
4d	Chancellor Valorum (.02/no warning)	3.00	6.00
5a	Gasgano with Pit Droid (.0100)	5.00	10.00
5b	Gasgano with Pit Droid (.0200)	3.00	6.00
6a	Ki-Adi-Mundi (.0000)	3.00	6.00
6b	Ki-Adi-Mundi (.0100/innovision back)	3.00	6.00
7a	Mace Windu (.0000)	3.00	6.00
7b	Mace Windu (.0100/innovision back)	3.00	6.00
8a	Ody Mandrell and Otoga (222 Pit Droid	3.00	6.00
8b	Ody Mandrell and Otoga (222 Pit Droid/hologram chip sticker)	3.00	6.00
9a	OOM-9 (binoculars in package)	3.00	6.00
9b	OOM-9 (binoculars in package/hologram chip sticker)	3.00	6.00
9c	OOM-9 (binoculars in right hand)	3.00	6.00
9d	OOM-9 (binoculars in left hand/hologram chip sticker)	5.00	10.00
10	TC-14 Protocol Droid	8.00	15.00

1999-00 Star Wars Episode I CommTech Figure Collector 2-Packs

1	Anakin Skywalker naboo/Obi-Wan Kenobi naboo	12.00	25.00
2	Battle Droid (tan blast on chest)/Darth Maul Tatooine		
3	Battle Droid (tan slash on chest w/burn marks)/Darth Maul Tatooine		
4	Darth Maul Jedi duel/Anakin Skywalker Tatooine	10.00	20.00
5	Jar Jar Binks/Qui-Gon Jinn	6.00	12.00
6	Padme Naberrie/Obi-Wan Kenobi Jedi Knight		
7	Queen Amidala Naboo/Qui-Gon Jinn Jedi Knight		

1999-00 Star Wars Episode I Creature 2-Packs

1	Ammo Wagon and Falumpaset	20.00	40.00
2	Eopie (w/Qui-Gon Jinn)		
3	Fambaa (w/Gungan warrior)	50.00	100.00
4	Jabba the Hut (w/two-headed announcer)	10.00	20.00
5	Kaadu and Jar Jar Binks	10.00	20.00
6	Opee and Qui-Gon Jinn	10.00	20.00

1999-00 Star Wars Episode I Deluxe

1	Darth Maul	3.00	6.00
2	Obi-Wan Kenobi	3.00	6.00
3	Qui-Gon Jinn	5.00	10.00

1999-00 Star Wars Episode I Electronic Talking 12-Inch

1	C-3PO	15.00	30.00
2	Darth Maul	10.00	20.00
3	Jar Jar Binks	15.00	30.00
4	Qui-Gon Jinn	12.00	25.00
5	TC-14	20.00	40.00

1999-00 Star Wars Episode I Epic Force

1	Darth Maul	8.00	15.00
2	Obi-Wan Kenobi	10.00	20.00
3	Qui-Gon Jinn	8.00	15.00

1999-00 Star Wars Episode I Invasion Force

1 Armored Scout Tank (w/Battle Droid tan clean)		6.00	12.00
2 Gungan Assault Cannon (w/Jar Jar Binks)		6.00	12.00
3 Gungan Scout Sub (w/Obi-Wan Kenobi Naboo water)		8.00	15.00
4 Sith Attack Speeder (w/Darth Maul Tatooine)		10.00	20.00

1999-00 Star Wars Episode I Jabba Glob

1 Jabba the Hutt		10.00	20.00

1999-00 Star Wars Episode I Light-Up

1 Darth Maul hologram/ Wal-Mart exclusive			
2 Qui-Gon Jinn Hologram		10.00	20.00
(Walmart Exclusive)			

1999-00 Star Wars Episode I Playsets

1 R2-D2 Carryall		12.00	25.00
2 Theed Generator Complex (w/Battle Droid)		12.00	25.00
3 Theed Hangar Power Spin Qui-Gon Jinn/Battle Droid break up	25.00	50.00

1999-00 Star Wars Episode I Portrait Edition 12-Inch

1 Princess Leia (ceremonial dress)		20.00	40.00
2 Queen Amidala (black travel gown)		12.00	25.00
3 Queen Amidala (return to Naboo)		15.00	30.00
4 Queen Amidala (Senate gown)		15.00	30.00
5 Return to Naboo 2-Pack/Padme/Qui Gon Ginn			

1999-00 Star Wars Episode I Vehicles

ARMORED SCOUT TANK with BATTLE DROID

1 Anakin's Podracer		20.00	40.00
2 Flash Speeder		15.00	30.00
3 Naboo Fighter		15.00	30.00
4 Naboo Royal Starship		100.00	200.00
5 Sith Speeder (w/Darth Maul Jedi duel)		8.00	15.00
6 Stap and Battle Droid (burn marks on arms and legs)		8.00	15.00
7 Sebulba's Podracer (w/Sebulba podrace gear)		15.00	30.00
8 Trade Federation Droid Fighters		15.00	30.00
9 Trade Federation Tank		20.00	40.00

2015-16 Star Wars The Force Awakens 12-Inch

1 BB-8			
2 Chewbacca		20.00	40.00
3 Darth Vader		12.00	25.00
4 Fifth Brother Inquisitor			
5 Finn (Jakku)		10.00	20.00
6 First Order Flametrooper		10.00	20.00
7 First Order Stormtrooper		8.00	15.00
8 First Order TIE Fighter Pilot		8.00	15.00
9 Kylo Ren		8.00	15.00
10 R2-D2			
11 Rey (Jakku)		10.00	20.00

2015-16 Star Wars The Force Awakens 12-Inch Vehicles

NNO Assault Walker (w/Riot Control Stormtrooper)	12.00	25.00
NNO Speeder Bike (w/Poe Dameron)		12.00	25.00

2015-16 Star Wars The Force Awakens Armor Up 1

1 Boba Fett		6.00	15.00
2 Captain Phasma (Epic Battles)			
(Toys R Us Exclusive)			
3 Chewbacca		5.00	12.00
4 Finn (Jakku)			
5 Finn (Starkiller Base)		6.00	12.00
6 First Order Flametrooper		6.00	15.00
7 First Order Stormtrooper		6.00	15.00
8 First Order TIE Fighter Pilot			
9 Kylo Ren		5.00	10.00
10 Luke Skywalker		6.00	15.00
11 Poe Dameron		6.00	15.00
12 Poe Dameron (Epic Battles)			
(Toys R Us Exclusive)			

2015-16 Star Wars The Force Awakens Armor Up 1 (loose)

1 Boba Fett			
2 Captain Phasma (Epic Battles)			
Toys R Us Exclusive			
3 Chewbacca			
4 Finn (Jakku)			
5 Finn (Starkiller Base)			
6 First Order Flametrooper			
7 First Order Stormtrooper			
8 First Order TIE Fighter Pilot			
9 Kylo Ren			
10 Luke Skywalker			

11 Poe Dameron			
12 Poe Dameron (Epic Battles)			
(Toys R Us Exclusive)			

2015-16 Star Wars The Force Awakens Build-a-Weapon Collection

NNO Admiral Ackbar			
NNO Captain Phasma		6.00	15.00
NNO Captain Rex			
NNO Constable Zuvio		5.00	12.00
NNO Darth Maul			
NNO Darth Vader		5.00	12.00
NNO Ezra Bridger			
NNO Fifth Brother			
NNO Finn (FN-2187)			
NNO Finn (Jakku)		6.00	15.00
NNO First Order Flametrooper		5.00	12.00
NNO First Order Snowtrooper			
NNO First Order Stormtrooper (running image)		5.00	12.00
NNO First Order Stormtrooper (shooting blaster image)		
NNO First Order Stormtrooper Squad Leader			
NNO First Order TIE Fighter Pilot			
NNO General Hux			
NNO Goss Toowers			
NNO Guavian Enforcer			
NNO Han Solo			
NNO Hassk Thug			
NNO Inquisitor			
NNO Kanan Jarrus			
NNO Kanan Jarrus (stormtrooper disguise)			
NNO Kylo Ren (Force grip image)		6.00	15.00
NNO Kylo Ren (lightsaber image)			
NNO Kylo Ren Unmasked			
NNO Luke Skywalker (Episode V)		5.00	12.00
NNO Nien Nunb			
NNO Poe Dameron		5.00	12.00
NNO Princess Leia			
NNO PZ-4CO			
NNO Resistance Trooper		5.00	12.00
NNO Rey (Resistance fatigues)			
NNO Rey (Starkiller Base)		6.00	15.00
NNO Sabine Wren			
NNO Sarco Plank			
NNO Seventh Sister			
NNO Tasu Leech			
NNO Unkar Plutt			
NNO X-Wing Pilot Asty			

2015-16 Star Wars The Force Awakens Elite Series

NNO C-3PO		20.00	40.00
NNO Captain Phasma		10.00	20.00
NNO Finn		12.00	25.00
NNO Finn (w/lightsaber)			
NNO Flametrooper		12.00	25.00
NNO FN-2187 (Finn)			
NNO Han Solo			
NNO Kylo Ren		10.00	20.00
NNO Kylo Ren (unmasked)		12.00	25.00
NNO Poe Dameron		10.00	20.00
NNO R2-D2		20.00	40.00
NNO Rey and BB-8		12.00	25.00
NNO Rey and BB-8 (w/lightsaber)		15.00	30.00
NNO Stormtrooper		10.00	20.00
NNO Stormtrooper (squad leader)			
NNO Stormtrooper (w/riot gear)			
NNO Stormtrooper Officer			
NNO TIE Fighter Pilot			

2015-16 Star Wars The Force Awakens Multi-Packs

1 BB-8, Unkar's Thug, Jakku Scavenger 3-Pack	8.00	15.00
2 Forest Mission 5-Pack	20.00	40.00
BB-8, Kylo Ren, Chewbacca, Stormtrooper, Resistance Trooper		
(Amazon Exclusive)		
3 Takodana Encounter 4-Pack	12.00	25.00
Maz Kanata, Rey, Finn, BB-8		
4 Troop Builder 7-Pack	30.00	60.00
(Kohl's Exclusive)		

2015-16 Star Wars The Force Awakens 2-Packs

NNO Anakin Skywalker & Yoda	12.00	25.00
NNO Clone Commander Cody & Obi-Wan Kenobi	8.00	15.00
NNO Darth Vader & Ahsoka Tano	12.00	25.00
NNO First Order Snowtrooper Officer & Snap Wexley	8.00	15.00
NNO Garazeb Orrelios & C1-10P Chopper	8.00	20.00
NNO Han Solo & Princess Leia	8.00	15.00
NNO R2-D2 & C-3PO	10.00	20.00
NNO Sidon Ithano & First Mate Quiggold	6.00	12.00

2015-16 Star Wars The Force Awakens Vehicles

1 Assault Walker (w/Stormtrooper Sergeant)
2 Battle Action Millennium Falcon (w/Finn, BB-8, Chewbacca)
3 Desert Assault Walker (w/Stormtrooper Officer)
(2015 Entertainment Earth Exclusive)
4 Desert Landspeeder (w/Jakku Finn)
5 Elite Speeder Bike (w/Special Edition Stormtrooper)
6 First Order Snowspeeder (w/Snowspeeder Officer)
7 First Order Special Forces TIE Fighter (w/TIE Fighter Pilot)
8 Poe Dameron's Black Squadron X-Wing (w/Poe Dameron)
9 Rey's Speeder (w/Special Edition Rey)

10 Slave I (w/Boba Fett)
11 Y-Wing Scout Bomber (w/Kanan Jarrus)

2015-16 Star Wars The Force Awakens Vehicles (loose)

1 Assault Walker
2 Battle Action Millennium Falcon
3 Desert Assault Walker
(2015 Entertainment Earth Exclusive)
4 Desert Landspeeder
5 Elite Speeder Bike
6 First Order Snowspeeder
7 First Order Special Forces TIE Fighter
8 Poe Dameron's Black Squadron X-Wing
9 Rey's Speeder
10 Slave I
11 Y-Wing Scout Bomber

2015-16 Star Wars The Force Awakens Vehicles Figures (loose)

1 BB-8
2 Boba Fett
3 Chewbacca
4 Finn
5 Finn (Jakku)
6 Kanan Jarrus
7 Poe Dameron
8 Snowspeeder Officer
9 Special Edition Rey (Jakku)
10 Special Edition Stormtrooper
11 Stormtrooper Officer
12 Stormtrooper Sergeant
13 TIE Fighter Pilot

2005 Star Wars Force Battlers

1 Anakin Skywalker		
2 Chewbacca		
3 Clone Trooper		
4 Darth Vader/ slashing attack		
5 Darth Vader/ missile-launching/ glider cape		
6 Emperor Palpatine		
7 General Grievous		
8 Han Solo		
9 Luke Skywalker	12.00	25.00
10 Mace Windu	8.00	15.00
11 Obi-Wan Kenobi		
12 Yoda		

2006 Star Wars Force Battlers

1 Chewbacca
2 General Grievous
3 Jango Fett
4 Obi-Wan Kenobi

2006 Star Wars Force Battlers International

10 Darth Vader/ with missile-launching/ glider cape
20 Emperor Palpatine

2004-10 Star Wars Galactic Heroes

1 4-LOM/Bossk	8.00	15.00
2 Ahsoka Tano/Captain Rex	15.00	30.00
3 Ahsoka Tano/R3-S6 Goldie	8.00	15.00
4 Anakin Skywalker/Clone Trooper (white)	6.00	12.00
5 Anakin Skywalker/Clone Trooper (blue)	6.00	12.00
6 Anakin Skywalker/Count Dooku	6.00	12.00
7 Anakin Skywalker/STAP		
8 Asajj Ventress/Count Dooku	12.00	25.00
9 AT-AT Commander/AT-AT Driver	8.00	15.00
10 Battle Droid/Clone Trooper	6.00	12.00
11 C-3PO/Chewbacca	8.00	15.00
12 Chewbacca/Clone Trooper	6.00	12.00
13 Chewbacca/Death Star Droid/Mouse Droid	8.00	15.00
14 Chewbacca/Disassembled C-3PO	10.00	20.00
15 Clone Trooper/Dwarf Spider Droid	8.00	15.00
16 Clone Trooper/Mace Windu	8.00	15.00
17 Commander Bly/Aayla Secura	12.00	25.00
18 Dark Side Anakin/Clone Trooper	8.00	12.00
19 Darth Maul/Sith Speeder	8.00	15.00
20 Darth Vader/Holographic Emperor Palpatine		
21 Death Star Trooper/Imperial Officer	6.00	12.00
22 Dengar/Boba Fett	12.00	25.00
23 Duros/Garindan		
24 Emperor Palpatine/Shock Trooper		
25 Emperor Palpatine/Yoda	6.00	15.00
26 Figrin D'an/Hammerhead	6.00	12.00
27 Grand Moff Tarkin/Imperial Officer	5.00	10.00
28 Greedo/Han Solo	15.00	30.00
29 Han Solo/Logray	8.00	15.00
30 IG-86/Clone Commander Thire		
31 IG-88/Zuckuss	6.00	12.00
32 Jango Fett/Obi-Wan Kenobi	8.00	15.00
33 Jar Jar Binks/Destroyer Droid		
34 Jawa/Tusken Raider	6.00	12.00
35 Ki-Adi-Mundi/Commander Bacara		
36 Kit Fisto/General Grievous	8.00	15.00
37 Kit Fisto/Mace Windu	10.00	20.00
38 Luke Skywalker (w/Yoda)/Spirit of Obi-Wan	6.00	12.00
39 Luke Skywalker Stormtrooper/Han Solo Stormtrooper	10.00	20.00
40 Luke Skywalker/Darth Vader	8.00	15.00
41 Luke Skywalker/Gamorrean Guard	6.00	12.00
42 Luke Skywalker/Han Solo		
43 Luke Skywalker/Lando Calrissian	6.00	12.00
44 Luke Skywalker/R2-D2	6.00	12.00
45 Luke Skywalker/Speeder	15.00	30.00
46 Nien Nunb/Admiral Ackbar	10.00	20.00
47 Obi-Wan Kenobi/Clone Commander Cody		
48 Obi-Wan Kenobi/Clone Trooper (blue Star Wars logo)		
49 Obi-Wan Kenobi/Clone Trooper (red Star Wars logo)		
50 Obi-Wan Kenobi/Darth Maul	8.00	15.00
51 Obi-Wan Kenobi/Darth Vader	6.00	12.00
52 Obi-Wan Kenobi/Durge	6.00	12.00
53 Obi-Wan Kenobi/General Grievous		
54 Padme Amidala/Anakin Skywalker	12.00	25.00
55 Padme Amidala/Clone Trooper		

56 Padme Amidala/Jar Jar Binks
57 Plo Koon/Captain Jag
58 Ponda Baba/Snaggletooth
59 Princess Leia (Endor general)/Rebel Commando (Battle of Endor)
60 Princess Leia Boushh/Han Solo
61 Princess Leia/Darth Vader
62 Princess Leia/Han Solo   12.00   25.00
63 R2-D2 (serving tray)/Princess Leia (slave)
64 R2-D2/Jawas
65 Royal Guard/Imperial Gunner
66 Saesee Tiin/Agen Kolar
67 Sandtrooper/Obi-Wan Kenobi
68 Scout Trooper/Speeder Bike   6.00   12.00
69 Shaak Ti/Magna Guard
70 Skiff Guard/Lando Calrissian   8.00   15.00
71 Snowtrooper/Rebel Trooper
72 Stormtrooper/Rebel Trooper
73 Super Battle Droid/Luminara Unduli
74 Super Battle Droid/R2-D2
75 Tarfful/Commander Gree
76 Wedge/TIE Pilot
77 Weequay/Barada
78 Yoda/Clone Trooper
79 Yoda/Kashyyyk Trooper

2004-10 Star Wars Galactic Heroes Backpack Heroes

1 Boba Fett
2 Darth Tater
3 Darth Vader
4 Han Solo
5 Luke Skywalker
6 Yoda

2004-10 Star Wars Galactic Heroes Cinema Scenes

1 Assault on Ryloth
2 Assault on the Death Star
3 Assault on the Death Star 2
4 Battle of Geonosis
5 Battle of Hoth
6 Battle of Naboo
7 Battle of Kashyyyk
8 Battle of Mustafar
9 Cantina Band
10 Cantina Encounter
11 Death Star Escape
12 Endor Attack
13 Endor Celebration
14 Escape from Mos Eisley
15 Geonosis Battle Arena
16 Hoth Snowspeeder Assault

17 Jabba's Palace
18 Jabba's Sail Barge
19 Jabba's Skiff The Pit of Carkoon
20 Jedi Starfighter
21 Jedi vs. Sith
22 Kamino Showdown
23 Millennium Falcon
24 Purchase of the Droids
25 Rancor Pit
26 Shadow Squadron Y-Wing
27 Slave I and Boba Fett
28 Speeder Bike Chase
29 Vader's Bounty Hunters
30 Vader's TIE Fighter (w/Darth Vader)
31 X-Wing Dagobah Landing

2004-10 Star Wars Galactic Heroes Exclusives

1 Scout Trooper
(2004 SDCC Exclusive)
2 Yoda/R2-D2
(2004 Burger King Exclusive)

2004-10 Star Wars Galactic Heroes Singles

1 Anakin Skywalker
2 Battle Droid
3 Boba Fett
4 Bossk
5 C-3PO
6 Chewbacca
7 Clone Trooper
8 Darth Maul
9 Darth Vader
10 Han Solo
11 Luke Skywalker
12 Obi-Wan Kenobi
13 R2-D2

2004-10 Star Wars Galactic Heroes Stocking Stuffers

1 Darth Vader/Boba Fett/Stormtrooper
2 Han Solo/Chewbacca/C-3PO
3 Luke Skywalker/Yoda/R2-D2
4 Obi-Wan Kenobi/Anakin Skywalker/Shock Trooper

2004-10 Star Wars Galactic Heroes Vehicles

1 Anakin's Delta Starfighter
2 Landspeeder
3 Millennium Falcon
4 Obi-Wan's Starfighter
5 Snowspeeder
6 X-Wing Fighter
7 X-Wing Racer

2015 Star Wars Hero Mashers

NNO Boba Fett
NNO Bossk
NNO Darth Vader
NNO General Grievous
NNO Jar Jar Binks
NNO Kanan Jarrus
NNO Zeb Orrelios

2015 Star Wars Hero Mashers Deluxe

NNO Anakin Skywalker with Speeder Bike
NNO Darth Maul with Sith Speeder Bike
NNO Han Solo vs. Boba Fett
NNO Luke Skywalker vs. Darth Vader
NNO Yoda vs. Emperor Palpatine

2004-05 Star Wars Jedi Force Blue

1 Anakin Skywalker (w/Jedi Pod)
2 Anakin Skywalker (w/rescue glider)
3 C-3PO/R2-D2
4 Chewbacca (w/Wookiee Action Tool)
5 Chewbacca (w/Wookiee Scout Flyer)
6 Darth Vader (w/Imperial Claw Droid)
7 Han Solo (w/Jet Bike)
8 Luke Skywalker (w/Jedi Jet Pack)
9 Luke Skywalker (w/Speeder Bike)
10 Luke Skywalker (w/Speeder Board)
11 Luke's X-Wing
12 Mace Windu (w/Jedi Grappling Hook)
13 Obi-Wan Kenobi (w/Boga)
14 Yoda (w/Swamp Stomper)

2004-05 Star Wars Jedi Force White

1 Anakin Skywalker/Jar Jar Binks
2 Anakin Skywalker's Jedi Starfighter (w/R2-D2)
3 BARC Speeder Bike (w/Anakin Skywalker)
4 C-3PO/R2-D2
5 Darth Vader/Stormtrooper
6 Freeco Bike (w/Obi-Wan Kenobi)
7 Han Solo/Chewbacca
8 Landspeeder (w/Luke Skywalker)
9 Millennium Falcon (w/Han Solo/Chewbacca)
10 Obi-Wan Kenobi/Commander Cody
11 Snowspeeder (w/Luke Skywalker/Han Solo)
12 Yoda/Luke Skywalker

2017 Star Wars The Last Jedi Big Figs

NNO Captain Phasma
NNO Elite Praetorian Guard
NNO First Order Executioner
NNO First Order Stormtrooper
NNO Kylo Ren
NNO Poe Dameron
NNO Rey

2017 Star Wars The Last Jedi Elite Series

NNO Elite Praetorian Guard		30.00	60.00
NNO First Order Judicial		30.00	60.00
NNO Kylo Ren		15.00	30.00
NNO Luke Skywalker		30.00	75.00
NNO R2-D2		20.00	40.00
NNO Rey		20.00	40.00

2017 Star Wars The Last Jedi Force Link

NNO C-3PO
NNO Chewbacca (w/porg)
NNO Finn (Resistance Fighter)
NNO First Order Stormtrooper
NNO General Hux
NNO Luke Skywalker (Jedi Master)
NNO Kylo Ren
NNO Poe Dameron (Resistance Pilot)

NNO Resistance Gunner Paige
NNO Resistance Gunner Rose
NNO Rey (Jedi Training)
NNO Obi-Wan Kenobi
NNO Yoda
NNO R2-D2
NNO DJ (Canto Bight)
NNO General Leia Organa
NNO Jyn Erso (Jedha)
NNO Luke Skywalker (Jedi Exile)
NNO Rey (Island Journey)

2017 Star Wars The Last Jedi Force Link 2-Packs

NNO Bala-Tik & Rathtar
NNO Darth Vader & Imperial Probe Droid
NNO Han Solo & Boba Fett
NNO Rey (Jedi Training) & Elite Praetorian Guard

2017 Star Wars The Last Jedi Force Link Multipacks

NNO Emperor Palpatine/Luke Skywalker/Emperor's Royal Guard 3-Pack
(Target Exclusive)
NNO Luke Skywalker/Resistance Tech Rose
Rey (Jedi Training)/First Order Stormtrooper 4-Pack

2017 Star Wars The Last Jedi Force Link Sets

NNO BB-8 2-in-1 Mega Playset
NNO Starter Set (w/Kylo Ren)

2017 Star Wars The Last Jedi Force Link Vehicles

NNO Canto Bight Police Speeder (w/Canto Bight Police)
NNO Kylo Ren's TIE Silencer (w/Kylo Ren)
NNO Resistance A-Wing Fighter (w/Resistance Pilot Tallie)
NNO Resistance Ski Speeder (w/Captain Poe Dameron)
NNO TIE Fighter (w/TIE Fighter Pilot)

2017 Star Wars The Last Jedi S.H. Figuarts

NNO Captain Phasma
NNO Elite Praetorian Guard (w/dual blades)
NNO Elite Praetorian Guard (w/single blade)
NNO Elite Praetorian Guard (w/whip staff)
NNO First Order Executioner
NNO First Order Stormtrooper
NNO Kylo Ren
NNO Rey

2008-10 Star Wars The Legacy Collection Battle Packs

1 Battle at the Sarlaac Pit (ultimate)	50.00	100.00
(2008 Target Exclusive)		
2 Battle of Endor		
3 Birth of Darth Vader	20.00	40.00
4 Clone Attack on Coruscant	12.00	25.00
5 Disturbance at Lars Homestead	75.00	150.00
(2008 Toys R Us Exclusive)		
6 Duel on Mustafar		
7 Gelagrub Patrol	15.00	30.00
8 Geonosis Assault	50.00	100.00
9 Hoth Recon Patrol	30.00	60.00
10 Hoth Speeder Bike Patrol	25.00	50.00
11 Jedi Training on Dagobah		
12 Jedi vs. Darth Sidious	15.00	30.00
13 Kamino Conflict		
14 Resurgence of the Jedi	20.00	40.00
15 Scramble on Yavin	100.00	175.00

16	Shield Generator Assault	25.00	50.00
17	Tatooine Desert Ambush		
18	Training on the Falcon	30.00	75.00

2008-10 Star Wars The Legacy Collection Build-A-Droid Wave 1

BD1a	Han Solo/ with R4-D6 left leg	6.00	12.00
BD1b	Han Solo/ with R4-D6 left leg/ first day of issue sticker		
BD2a	Luke Skywalker/ with R4-D6 right leg		
BD2b	Luke Skywalker/ with R5-A2 head/ and center leg		
BD2c	Luke Skywalker/ with R4-D6 right leg/ first day of issue sticker		
BD3a	Chewbacca/ with R4-D6 head/ and center leg		
BD3b	Chewbacca/ with R4-D6 head/ and center leg/ first day of issue sticker		
BD4a	Leektar/Nippet/ with R4-D6 torso		
BD4b	Leektar/Nippet/ with R4-D6 torso/ first day of issue sticker		
BD5a	Ak-Rev/ with R7-Z0 leg		
BD5b	Ak-Rev/ with R7-Z0 left leg/ first day of issue sticker	6.00	12.00
BD6a	Yarna D'Al'Gargan/ with R7-Z0 right leg	8.00	15.00
BD6b	Yarna D'Al'Gargan/ with R7-Z0 right leg/ first day of issue sticker	6.00	12.00
BD7a	Bane Malar/ with R7-Z0 torso		
BD7b	Bane Malar/ with R7-Z0 torso/ first day of issue sticker		
BD8a	Darth Vader/ multi-piece helmet/ with R7-Z0 head		
BD8b	Darth Vader/ multi-piece helmet/ with R7-Z0 head/ first day of issue sti		
BD8c	Darth Vader/ multi-piece helmet/ with MB-RA-7 head		

2008-10 Star Wars The Legacy Collection Build-A-Droid Wave 2

BD9	Obi-Wan Kenobi general/ with R4-J1 left leg	10.00	20.00
BD10	Clone Scuba Trooper/ with R4-J1 head/ and center leg		
BD11	Saesee Tiin general/ with R7-T1 right leg		
BD12	Padme Amidala snow/ with R7-T1 left leg		
BD13	IG Lancer Droid/ with R4-J1 torso		
BD14	Mon Calimari Warrior/ with R7-T1 Torso	8.00	15.00
BD15	Quarren Soldier/ with R7-T1 head/ and center leg		
BD16	Clone Trooper blue/ with cannon/with R4-J1 right leg		

2008-10 Star Wars The Legacy Collection Build-A-Droid Wave 3

BD17a	Clone Trooper coruscant/ landing platform/ with RD6-RA7 torso	10.00	20.00
BD17b	Clone Trooper coruscant/ landing platform/ with MB-RA-7 right arm		
BD18a	Jodo Kast/ with RD6-RA7 head	10.00	20.00
BD18b	Jodo Kast/ with MB-RA-7 left arm		
BD19	Yaddle/Evan Piell/ with RD6-RA7 right leg	15.00	30.00
BD20a	Saleucami Trooper/ with 5D6-RA7 left leg		
BD20b	Saleucami Trooper/ with MB-RA-7 right leg		
BD21	Count Dooku/ holographic transmission/ with RD6-RA7 right arm		
BD22	Imperial Engineer/ with RD6-RA7 left arm		

2008-10 Star Wars The Legacy Collection Build-A-Droid Wave 4

BD23	Stass Allie/ with MB-RA-7 left arm	12.00	25.00
BD24a	Commander Faie/ with MB-RA-7 torso	10.00	20.00
BD24b	Commander Faie/ with R5-A2 left leg	10.00	20.00
BD25a	General Grievous/ with MB-RA-7 head	12.00	25.00
BD25b	General Grievous/ with R5-A2 right leg		
BD26a	Bail Organa/ light skin/ with MB-RA-7 left arm		
BD26b	Bail Organa/ dark skin/ with MB-RA-7 left arm		
BD27a	Breha Organa/ light skin/ with MB-RA-7 left leg		
BD27b	Breha Organa/ dark skin/ with MB-RA-7 left leg		
BD28	FX-6/ with MB-RA-7 right leg	10.00	20.00
BD29	Clone Trooper 327th Star/ Corps yellow shoulder/ with MB-RA-7 torso		
BD29a	Clone Trooper 327th Star/ Corps yellow shoulder/ with R5-A2 torso		
BD29b	Clone Trooper 327th Star/ Corps yellow shoulder/ with MB-RA-7 torso		
BD29c	Clone Trooper 327th Star/ Corps yellow shoulder/ with R5-A2 torso		

2008-10 Star Wars The Legacy Collection Build-A-Droid (loose)

1	R4-D6	10.00	20.00
2	R7-Z0		
3	R4-J1	6.00	12.00
4	R7-T1	12.00	25.00
5	5D6-RA7	8.00	15.00
6	MB-RA7	6.00	12.00
7	R2-L3	6.00	12.00
8	R5-A2	12.00	25.00
9a	U-3PO (champagne deco)	15.00	30.00
9b	U-3PO (silver deco)	10.00	20.00
10	HK-47	30.00	75.00
11	L8-L9	12.00	25.00
12	R3-M3	15.00	30.00
13	R5-C7	12.00	25.00
14	R3-A2	10.00	20.00
15	R4-P44	12.00	25.00
16	YVH-1	12.00	25.00
17	HK-50	8.00	15.00
18	BG-J38	50.00	100.00

2008-10 Star Wars The Legacy Collection Comic Packs Blue and White

1 Asajj Ventress and Tol Skorr
2 Anakin Skywalker and Durge
3 Anakin Skywalker and Assassin Droid
4 Darth Talon and Cade Skywalker
5 Antares Draco and Ganner Krieg
6 Fenn Shysa and Dengar
7 Princess Leia and Tobbi Dala
8 Leia Organa and Prince Xizor
9 Grand Admiral Thrawn and Talon Karrde
10 Darth Vader and Grand Moff Trachta
11 Darth Vader and Princess Leia
12 Clone Emperor and Luke Skywalker
13 Quinlan Vos and Commander Faie
14 Wedge Antilles and Borsk Fey'lya
15 Luke Skywalker and Deena Shan
16 Ki-Adi-Mundi and Sharad Hett

2008-10 Star Wars The Legacy Collection Comic Packs Blue and White Exclusives

NNO	Ibtisam and Nrin Vakil	25.00	50.00
	(2008 Walmart Exclusive)		
NNO	Janek Sunber and Amanin	15.00	30.00
	(2008 Walmart Exclusive)		
NNO	Machook/Keoulkeech/Kettch	30.00	60.00
	(2008 Walmart Exclusive)		

2008-10 Star Wars The Legacy Collection Comic Packs Red and White

1 Darth Vader and Rebel Officer
2 Chewbacca and Han Solo
3 Yuuzhan Vong and Kyle Katarn
4 Wedge Antilles and Borsk Fey'lya
5 Luke Skywalker and Deena Shan
6 Ki-Adi-Mundi and Sharad Hett
7 Lumiya and Luke Skywalker
8 Darth Krayt and Sigel Dare
9 Clone Trooper and Clone Commander
10 Clone Trooper Lieutenant and Clone Trooper
11 Ulic Qel-Droma and Exar Kun
12 T'ra Saa and Tholme
13 Stormtrooper and Blackhole Hologram

2008-10 Star Wars The Legacy Collection Comic Packs Red and White Exclusives

NNO Baron Soontir Fel and Ysanne Isard (X-Wing Rogue Squadron)
(2010 Entertainment Earth Exclusive)
NNO Deliah Blue and Darth Nihl (Legacy)
(2010 Entertainment Earth Exclusive)
NNO IG-97 and Rom Mohc
(2009 Walmart Exclusive)
NNO Jarael and Rohlan Dyre (Knights of the Old Republic)
(2010 Entertainment Earth Exclusive)
NNO Montross and Jaster Mareel (Jango Fett Open Seasons)
(2010 Entertainment Earth Exclusive)
NNO Plourr Ilo and Dllr Nep
(2009 Online Exclusive)
NNO Storm Commando and General Weir
(2009 Walmart Exclusive)

2008-10 Star Wars The Legacy Collection Creatures

1 Dewback (w/Imperial sandtrooper)   25.00   50.00
(2009 Walmart Exclusive)
2 Jabba's Rancor (w/Luke Skywalker)   60.00   120.00
(2008 Target Exclusive)

2008-10 Star Wars The Legacy Collection Evolutions

1 Clone Commandos   50.00   100.00
(2009 Walmart Exclusive)
2 Imperial Pilot Legacy I   15.00   30.00
3 Imperial Pilot Legacy II   15.00   30.00
(2009 Walmart Exclusive)
4 Rebel Pilot Legacy I   15.00   40.00
5 Rebel Pilot Legacy II   25.00   50.00
6 Rebel Pilot Legacy III   30.00   75.00
(2009 Walmart Exclusive)
7 The Fett Legacy   15.00   40.00
8 The Jedi Legacy
9 The Padme Amidala Legacy   12.00   25.00
10 The Sith Legacy   60.00   120.00
11 Vader's Secret Apprentice   30.00   60.00

2008-10 Star Wars The Legacy Collection Geonosis Battle Arena 2009 Edition

1 Coleman Trebor Vs. Jango Fett
2 Kit Fisto Vs. Geonosis Warrior
3 Mace Windu Vs. Battle Droid Commander
4 Joclad Danva Vs. Battle Droid
5 Roth Del Masona Vs. Super Battle Droid
6 Yoda Vs. Destroyer Droid

2008-10 Star Wars The Legacy Collection Geonosis Battle Arena 2010 Edition

1. Obi-Wan Kenobi & Super Battle Droid
2. Rodian Jedi & Battle Droid
3. Anakin Skywalker & Droideka
4. Shaak Ti & Geonosian Warrior
5. Nicanas Tassu & Count Dooku
6. C-3PO & R2-D2

2008-10 Star Wars The Legacy Collection Greatest Hits 2008

GH1 Commander Gree   6.00   12.00
GH2 Kashyyyk Trooper   6.00   12.00
GH3 Darth Vader (Battle Damage)   10.00   20.00
GH4 Imperial EVO Trooper   6.00   12.00

2008-10 Star Wars The Legacy Collection Saga Legends Blue and White

SL1 R2-D2 (electronic)
SL2 Yoda and Kybuck
SL3 Darth Vader (Anakin Skywalker)
SL4 Obi-Wan Kenobi
SL5 Clone Trooper (AOTC)
SL6 C-3PO
SL7 General Grievous
SL8 Mace Windu
SL9 Plo Koon
SL10 Super Battle Droid
SL11 Destroyer Droid
SL13 Darth Vader
SL14 Darth Maul
SL15 Jango Fett
SL16 501st Legion Trooper
SL17 Shock Trooper
SL18 BARC Trooper
SL19 ARC Trooper
SL21 Sandtrooper
SL22 Luke Skywalker (X-Wing pilot)
SL23 ARC trooper Commander (red)
SL24 Tri-Droid
SL25 Snowtrooper
SL26 Saesee Tiin
SL27 Clone Trooper (ROTS)
SL12a Clone Trooper Officer (red)
SL12b Clone Trooper Officer (yellow)

SL12c Clone Trooper Officer (blue)
SL12d Clone Trooper Officer (green)
SL20a Battle Droids (tan)
SL20b Battle Droids (brown)

2008-10 Star Wars The Legacy Collection Saga Legends Red and White

SL1 R2-D2 (electronic)
SL2 Darth Vader (Anakin Skywalker)
SL3 Obi-Wan Kenobi
SL4 Clone Trooper (Episode II)
SL5 Super Battle Droid
SL6 Darth Vader
SL7 Darth Maul
SL8 501st Legion Trooper
SL9 Yoda
SL10 Sandtrooper
SL11 Saesee Tiin
SL12 Clone Trooper (Episode III)
SL13 Plo Koon
SL14 Shocktrooper
SL15a Chewbacca I
SL15b Chewbacca II
SL16 Han Solo
SL17 Luke Skywalker

2008-10 Star Wars The Legacy Collection Vehicles

1 AT-ST   30.00   75.00
(2009 Walmart Exclusive)
2 Dagger Squadron B-Wing Fighter   50.00   100.00
(2008 Toys R Us Exclusive)
3 Darth Vader's TIE Advanced x1 Starfighter 15.00   30.00
4 Green Leader's A-Wing Fighter   50.00   100.00
(2008 Walmart Exclusive)
5 Millennium Falcon   300.00   600.00
6 Speeder Bike (w/biker scout)   25.00   50.00
(Toys R Us Exclusive)
7 TIE Fighter
8 TIE Fighter Pirate
(PX Previews Exclusive)
9 TIE Fighter Shadows of the Empire 150.00   300.00
(2009 Target Exclusive)
10 TIE Interceptor   30.00   60.00
(2009 Toys R Us Exclusive)
11 Wedge Antilles' X-Wing Starfighter 120.00   200.00
(2009 Target Exclusive)

2008-09 Star Wars Mighty Muggs

NNO	Anakin Skywalker		
NNO	Asajj Ventress		
NNO	Boba Fett	8.00	15.00
NNO	C-3PO	8.00	15.00
NNO	Captain Rex	6.00	12.00
NNO	Chewbacca	8.00	15.00
NNO	Commander Cody	12.00	25.00
NNO	Count Dooku	6.00	12.00
NNO	Darth Maul	6.00	12.00
NNO	Darth Maul (shirtless)	6.00	12.00
NNO	Darth Revan	10.00	20.00
NNO	Darth Vader	8.00	15.00
NNO	Darth Vader (unmasked)		
NNO	Emperor	5.00	10.00
NNO	Gamorrean Guard	5.00	10.00
NNO	General Grievous	12.00	25.00
NNO	Grand Moff Tarkin		
NNO	Han Solo	8.00	15.00
NNO	Han Solo (Hoth)	10.00	20.00
NNO	Jango Fett	6.00	12.00
NNO	Lando Calrissian	8.00	15.00
NNO	Luke (Bespin)	8.00	15.00
NNO	Luke Skywalker	8.00	15.00
NNO	Luke Skywalker (Hoth)	8.00	15.00
NNO	Mace Windu		
NNO	Obi-Wan Kenobi (old)	6.00	12.00
NNO	Obi-Wan Kenobi (young)		
NNO	Plo Koon		
NNO	Princess Leia		
NNO	Qui-Gon Jinn	8.00	15.00
NNO	Royal Guard		
NNO	Stormtrooper	6.00	12.00
NNO	Wampa	5.00	10.00
NNO	Wicket	5.00	10.00
NNO	Yoda	8.00	15.00

2008-09 Star Wars Mighty Muggs Exclusives

1 Admiral Ackbar

	(2008 PX Previews Exclusive)		
2	Biggs Darklighter		
	(2009 Target Exclusive)		
3	Bossk		
	(2009 Target Exclusive)		
4	Commander Gree		
	(2008 SDCC Exclusive)		
5	Shadow Trooper		
	(2008 PX Previews Exclusive)		
6	Shock Trooper	8.00	15.00
	(2009 Target Exclusive)		
7	Snowtrooper	8.00	15.00
	(2009 Target Exclusive)		
8	Teebo		
	(2009 Target Exclusive)		

2012 Star Wars Movie Heroes

MH1	Shock Trooper
MH2	Super Battle Droid
MH3	R2-D2
MH4	Battle Droid (repaint)
MH5	Battle Droid (variant)
MH6	Darth Maul (repaint)
MH7	Darth Vader
MH8	General Grievous
MH9	Obi-Wan Kenobi
MH10	Yoda
MH11	Qui-Gon Jinn
MH12	Clone Trooper (with Jetpack)
MH13	Destroyer Droid
MH14	Jar Jar Binks
MH15	Anakin Skywalker
MH16	Darth Maul (Spinning Action)
MH17	Obi-Wan Kenobi (Light-Up Lightsaber)
MH18	Padme Amidala
MH19	Qui-Gon Jinn (Light-Up Lightsaber)
MH20	Anakin Skywalker (Light-Up Lightsaber)
MH21	Darth Vader (Light-Up Lightsaber)
MH22	Luke Skywalker (zipline backpack)
MH23	Battle Droid (The Phantom Menace)(exploding action)
MH24	Sandtrooper (Light-Up Weapon)
MH25	Boba Fett (zipline jetpack)

2012 Star Wars Movie Heroes Battle Packs

1 Bespin Battle
2 Duel on Naboo
3 Ewok Pack
4 Geonosis Arena Battle

---

5 Rebel Heroes
6 Rebel Pilots
7 Republic Troopers

2012 Star Wars Movie Heroes Exclusives

1 Darth Maul Returns
2 Podracer Pilots
(Toys R Us Exclusive)

2012 Star Wars Movie Heroes Vehicles

1	Anakin Skywalker's Jedi Starfighter (The Clone Wars)		
2	Anakin Skywalker's Podracer		
3	Attack Recon Fighter with Anakin Skywalker		
4	BARC Speeder with Clone Trooper		
5	Naboo Royal Fighter with Obi-Wan Kenobi		
6	Naboo Starfighter	60.00	120.00
7	Republic Assault Submarine with Scuba Clone Trooper		
8	Republic Attack Dropship with Clone Pilot		
9	Sebulba's Podracer		
10	Sith Infiltrator		
11	Sith Speeder with Darth Maul		
12	Speeder Bike with Scout and Cannon		
	(Toys R Us Exclusive)		
13	STAP with Battle Droid		
14	Trade Federation AAT (Armored Assault Tank)		

2005 Star Wars M&M's Chocolate Mpire

1	Chewbacca/Mace Windu	6.00	12.00
2	Clone Trooper/Darth Vader	6.00	12.00
3	Count Dooku/Darth Maul	12.00	25.00
4	Emperor Palpatine/Anakin Skywalker	12.00	25.00
5	General Grievous/Obi-Wan Kenobi	8.00	15.00
6	Han Solo/Boba Fett	10.00	20.00
7	Luke Skywalker/Princess Leia	8.00	15.00
8	Queen Amidala/R2-D2/C-3PO	8.00	15.00

2007 Star Wars Order 66 Target Exclusives

1	Emperor Palpatine/Commander Thire	12.00	25.00
2	Mace Windu/Galactic Marine	10.00	20.00
3	Darth Vader/Commander Bow	12.00	25.00
4	Obi-Wan Kenobi/AT-RT Driver		
5	Anakin Skywalker/Airborne Trooper	12.00	25.00
6	Yoda/Kashyyyk Trooper	10.00	20.00

2008 Star Wars Order 66 Target Exclusives

1	Obi-Wan Kenobi/ARC Trooper Commander	12.00	25.00
2	Anakin Skywalker/ARC Trooper	10.00	20.00
3	Tsui Choi/BARC Trooper	15.00	30.00
4	Emperor Palpatine/Commander VIll	12.00	25.00
5	Luminara Unduli/AT-RT Driver	10.00	20.00
6	Master Sev/ARC Trooper	15.00	30.00

2004-05 Star Wars The Original Trilogy Collection

1	Luke Skywalker (Dagobah training)	6.00	12.00
2	Yoda (Dagobah training)	3.00	6.00
3	Spirit Obi-Wan Kenobi	8.00	15.00
4	R2-D2 (Dagobah training)	6.00	12.00
5	Luke Skywalker (X-Wing pilot)	8.00	15.00
6	Luke Skywalker (Jedi Knight)	8.00	15.00

7	Han Solo (Mos Eisley escape)	3.00	6.00
8	Chewbacca (Hoth escape)	6.00	12.00
9	Princess Leia	10.00	20.00
10	Darth Vader (throne room)	8.00	15.00
11	Scout Trooper	6.00	12.00
12	R2-D2	8.00	15.00
13	C-3PO	8.00	15.00
14	Boba Fett	12.00	25.00
15	Obi-Wan Kenobi	12.00	25.00
16	Stormtrooper (Death Star attack)	8.00	15.00
17	Wicket	3.00	6.00
18	Princess Leia (Cloud City)	8.00	15.00
19	Cloud Car Pilot	3.00	6.00
20	Lobot	3.00	6.00
21	TIE Fighter Pilot	8.00	15.00
22	Greedo	6.00	12.00
23	Tusken Raider	10.00	20.00
24	Jawas	3.00	6.00
25	Snowtrooper	6.00	12.00
26	Luke Skywalker (Bespin)	8.00	15.00
27	IG-88	12.00	25.00
28	Bossk	6.00	12.00
29	Darth Vader (Hoth)	10.00	20.00
30	Gamorrean Guard	10.00	20.00
31	Bib Fortuna	3.00	6.00
32	Darth Vader	3.00	6.00
33	Lando Calrissian (skiff guard)	6.00	12.00
34	Princess Leia (sail barge)	15.00	30.00
35	Han Solo (AT-ST driver uniform)	3.00	6.00
36	General Madine	3.00	6.00
37	Lando Calrissian (General)	8.00	15.00
38a	Imperial Trooper (white)	3.00	6.00
38b	Imperial Trooper (gray)	3.00	6.00

2004-05 Star Wars The Original Trilogy Collection 12-Inch

1	Boba Fett	30.00	60.00
2	Chewbacca	20.00	40.00
3	Luke Skywalker	20.00	40.00
4	Stormtrooper	15.00	30.00

2004-05 Star Wars The Original Trilogy Collection Cards

1	Pablo-Jill/ genosis arena	
2	Yarua (Coruscant Senate)	
3	Sly Moore (Coruscant Senate)	

4	Queen Amidala (celebration ceremony)	
5	Rabe (Queen's chambers)	
6	Feltipern Trevagg (cantina encounter)	
7	Myo (cantina encounter)	
8	Dannik Jerrico (cantina encounter)	
9	Luke Skywalker (Dagobah training)	
10	Darth Vader (Death Star hangar)	
11	Stormtrooper (Death Star attack)	
12	Sandtrooper (Tatooine search)	
13	Scout Trooper (Endor raid)	
14	Han Solo (Mos Eisley escape)	
15	Chewbacca (Hoth escape)	
16	Yoda (Dagobah training)	

2004-05 Star Wars The Original Trilogy Collection DVD Collection

1	A New Hope	6.00	12.00
2	Empire Strikes Back	10.00	20.00
3	Return of the Jedi	8.00	15.00

2004-05 Star Wars The Original Trilogy Collection Exclusives

1	Darth Vader (silver)	10.00	20.00
	(2004 Toys R Us Exclusive)		
2	Emperor Palpatine (executor transmission)		
	(2004 StarWarsShop.com Exclusive)		
3	Holiday Darth Vader	30.00	60.00
	(2005 StarWarsShop.com Exclusive)		
4	Holographic Princess Leia	12.00	25.00
	(2005 SDCC Exclusive)		
5	Holiday Edition Jawas	15.00	30.00
	(2004 Entertainment Earth Exclusive)		
6	Luke Skywalker's Encounter with Yoda		
	(2004 Encuentros Mexico Exclusive)		
7	Wedge Antilles		
	(2005 Internet Exclusive)		

2004-05 Star Wars The Original Trilogy Collection Multipacks

1	Clone Trooper/Troop Builder 4-Pack	25.00	50.00
	Clone Trooper/Clone Trooper/Clone Tr		
2	Clone Trooper Builder 4-Pack (white w/battle damage)	20.00	40.00
3	Clone Trooper Builder 4-Pack (colored)		

4 Clone Trooper Builder 4-Pack (colored w/battle damage) 20.00 40.00
5 Endor Ambush (Han Solo/Logray/Rebel Trooper/Wicket/Speeder) 12.00 25.00
6 Naboo Final Combat (Battle Droid tan
Gungan Soldier/Captain Tarpals/Kaad) 20.00 40.00

2004-05 Star Wars The Original Trilogy Collection Screen Scenes

1 Mos Eisley Cantina I/Dr. Evanzan/Wuher/Kitik Keed'kak 30.00 60.00
2 Mos Eisley Cantina II (Obi-Wan Kenobi/Ponda Baba/Zutton 30.00 60.00
3 Jedi High Council I (Qui-Gon Jinn/Ki-Adi Mundi/Yoda)
4 Jedi High Council II (Plo Koon/Obi-Wan Kenobi/Eeth Koth)
5 Jedi High Council III (Anakin Skywalker/Saesee Tiin/Adi Gallia)
6 Jedi High Council IV (Shaak Ti/Agen Kolar/Stass Alli)

2004-05 Star Wars The Original Trilogy Collection Transitional

1 Pablo-Jill (Geonosis Arena) 6.00 12.00
2 Yarua (Wookiee Senator) 10.00 20.00
3 Sly Moore 5.00 10.00
4 Queen Amidala (Naboo Celebration) 5.00 10.00
5 Rabe (Royal Handmaiden) 4.00
6 Feltipern Trevagg (Cantina) 8.00 15.00
7 Myo (Cantina) 8.00 15.00
8 Dannik Jerriko (Cantina Encounter) 8.00 15.00
9 Luke Skywalker (Dagobah Training)
10 Darth Vader (Death Star Hangar) 15.00 30.00
11 Stormtrooper (Death Star Attack)
12 Sandtrooper (Tatooine Search)
13 Scout Trooper (Endor Raid)
14 Han Solo (Mos Eisley Escape)
15 Chewbacca (Hoth Escape) 12.00 25.00
16 Yoda (Dagobah Training)

2004-05 Star Wars The Original Trilogy Collection Vehicles

1 Darth Vader's TIE Fighter 30.00 75.00
2 Millennium Falcon
3 Millennium Falcon (w/Chewbacca/Han/Luke/Obi-Wan/C-3PO/R2-D2)
(2004 Sam's Club Exclusive)
4 Sandcrawler (w/RA-7 and Jawas) 100.00 200.00
5 Slave I (w/Boba Fett in tan cape) 75.00 150.00
6 TIE Fighter 30.00 75.00
7 TIE Fighter & X-Wing Fighter 30.00 75.00
8 X-Wing Fighter
9 Y-Wing Fighter (w/pilot)

2004-05 Star Wars The Original Trilogy Collection Vintage

1 Boba Fett (ROTJ) 15.00 30.00
2 C-3PO (ESB) 6.00 12.00
3 Chewbacca (ROTJ) 12.00 25.00
4 Darth Vader (ESB) 8.00 15.00
5 Han Solo (SW) 6.00 12.00
6 Lando Calrissian (ESB) 12.00 25.00
7 Luke Skywalker (SW) 6.00 12.00

8 Obi-Wan Kenobi (SW) 5.00 10.00
9 Princess Leia Organa (SW) 5.00 10.00
10 R2-D2 (ROTJ) 15.00 30.00
11 Stormtrooper (ROTJ) 8.00 15.00
12 Yoda ESB 6.00 12.00

2000-02 Star Wars Power of the Jedi Action Collection 12-Inch

1 4-LOM 12.00 25.00
2 Bossk 15.00 30.00
3 Captain Tarpals (w/Kaadu) 20.00 40.00
4 Death Star Droid 15.00 30.00
5 Death Star Trooper 20.00 40.00
6 Han Solo Stormtrooper 15.00 30.00
7 IG-88 8.00 15.00
8 Luke Skywalker & Yoda 20.00 40.00
9 Luke Skywalker (100th figure) 30.00 60.00
10 Luke Skywalker (w/speeder bike) 40.00 80.00

2000-02 Star Wars Power of the Jedi Attack of the Clones Sneak Preview

1 Clone Trooper 4.00 8.00
2 Jango Fett 5.00 10.00
3 R3-T7 6.00 12.00
4 Zam Wesell 4.00 8.00

2000-02 Star Wars Power of the Jedi Collection 1

1 Anakin Skywalker (mechanic) 8.00 15.00
2 Aurra Sing (bounty hunter) 6.00 12.00
3 Battle Droid (boomer damage) 4.00 8.00
4 Ben Obi Wan Kenobi (Jedi Knight) 5.00 10.00
5 Chewbacca (Millennium Falcon mechanic) 10.00 20.00
6 Darth Maul (final duel) 6.00 12.00
7 Darth Maul (Sith Apprentice) 5.00 10.00
8 Darth Vader (Dagobah) 8.00 15.00
9 Darth Vader (Emperor's wrath) 5.00 10.00
10 Han Solo (Bespin capture) 4.00 8.00
11 Han Solo (Death Star escape) 6.00 12.00
12 Leia Organa (general) 5.00 10.00
13 Luke Skywalker (X-Wing Pilot) 4.00 8.00
14 Obi-Wan Kenobi (cold weather gear) 4.00 8.00
15 Obi-Wan Kenobi (Jedi) 4.00 8.00
16 Qui-Gon Jinn (Jedi training gear) 8.00 15.00
17 Qui-Gon Jinn (Mos Espa disguise) 4.00 8.00
18 R2-D2 (Naboo escape) 5.00 10.00
19 Sandtrooper (Tatooine patrol) 6.00 12.00

2000-02 Star Wars Power of the Jedi Collection 2

1 Battle Droid (security) 4.00 8.00
2 Bespin Guard (cloud city security) 4.00 8.00
3 BoShek 8.00 15.00
4 Boss Nass (Gungan sacred place) 4.00 8.00
5 Chewbacca (Dejarik Champion) 10.00 20.00
6 Coruscant Guard 5.00 10.00
7 Eeth Koth (Jedi Master) 6.00 12.00
8 Ellorrs Madak (Fan's Choice Figure #1) 5.00 10.00
9 Fode and Beed (pod race announcers) 4.00 8.00
10 FX-7 (medical droid) 10.00 20.00
11 Gungan Warrior 4.00 8.00
12 IG-88 (bounty hunter) 12.00 25.00
13 Imperial Officer 4.00 8.00
14 Jar Jar Binks (Tatooine) 4.00 8.00
15 Jek Porkins (X-Wing pilot) 10.00 20.00
16 K-3PO (Echo Base protocol droid) 6.00 12.00
17 Ketwol 4.00 8.00
18 Lando Calrissian (Bespin escape) 6.00 12.00
19 Leia Organa (Bespin escape) 8.00 15.00
20 Mas Amedda 5.00 10.00
21 Mon Calamari (officer) 8.00 15.00

22 Obi-Wan Kenobi (Jedi training gear) 4.00 8.00
23 Plo Koon (Jedi Master) 4.00 8.00
24 Queen Amidala (royal decoy) 6.00 12.00
25 Queen Amidala (Theed invasion) 6.00 12.00
26 R4-M9 8.00 15.00
27 R2-Q5 (Imperial astromech droid) 8.00 15.00
28 Rebel Trooper (Tantive IV defender) 4.00 8.00
29 Sabe (Queen's decoy) 5.00 10.00
30 Saesee Tiin (Jedi Master) 4.00 8.00
31 Scout Trooper (Imperial patrol) 6.00 12.00
32 Sebulba (Boonta Eve Challenge) 5.00 10.00
33 Shmi Skywalker 5.00 10.00
34 Teebo 6.00 12.00
35 Tessek 5.00 10.00
36 Tusken Raider (desert sniper) 6.00 12.00
37 Zutton (Snaggletooth) 5.00 10.00

2000-02 Star Wars Power of the Jedi Deluxe

1 Amanaman (w/Salacious Crumb) 10.00 20.00
(Fan's Choice Figure #2)
2 Darth Maul (w/Sith Attack Droid) 8.00 15.00
3 Luke Skywalker (in Echo Base Bacta Tank) 10.00 20.00
4 Princess Leia (Jabba's prisoner w/sail barge cannon) 8.00 15.00

2000-02 Star Wars Power of the Jedi Masters of the Darkside

1 Darth Vader and Darth Maul 6.00 30.00

2000-02 Star Wars Power of the Jedi Mega Action

1 Darth Maul 12.00 25.00
2 Destroyer Droid 20.00 40.00
3 Obi-Wan Kenobi 12.00 25.00

2000-02 Star Wars Power of the Jedi Playsets

1 Carbon Freezing Chamber (w/Bespin guard) 40.00 80.00

2000-02 Star Wars Power of the Jedi Special Edition

1 Boba Fett (300th figure) 15.00 30.00
2 Rorworr (Wookiee scout) 5.00 10.00

2000-02 Star Wars Power of the Jedi Vehicles

1 B-Wing Fighter (w/Sullustan pilot) 40.00 80.00
2 Imperial AT-ST & Speeder Bike (w/Paploo) 25.00 50.00
3 Luke Skywalker's Snowspeeder (w/Dack Ralter) 40.00 80.00
4 TIE Bomber 25.00 50.00
5 TIE Interceptor (w/Imperial pilot) 30.00 60.00

1995-00 Star Wars Power of the Force 3-Packs

1 Lando/Chewbacca/Han Solo
2 Lando/Luke Dagobah/TIE Fighter Pilot
3 Luke Jedi/AT-ST Driver/Leia Boushh
4 Luke Stormtrooper/Tusken Raider/Ben Kenobi
5 Luke/Ben Kenobi/Darth Vader
6 Stormtrooper/R2-D2/C-3PO

1995-00 Star Wars Power of the Force Accessories

1	Escape the Death Star Action Figure Game	10.00	20.00
2	Millennium Falcon Carrying Case (w/Imperial Scanning Trooper)	20.00	40.00
3	Millennium Falcon Carrying Case (w/Wedge)	15.00	30.00
4	Power of the Force Carrying Case	6.00	12.00
5	Talking C-3PO Carrying Case	25.00	50.00

1995-00 Star Wars Power of the Force Cinema Scenes

1	Cantina Aliens	10.00	20.00
2a	Cantina Showdown (.00)	6.00	12.00
2b	Cantina Showdown (.01)	6.00	12.00
3a	Death Star Escape (.00)	12.00	25.00
3b	Death Star Escape (.01)	12.00	25.00
4a	Final Jedi Duel (.00)	10.00	20.00
4b	Final Jedi Duel (.01)	10.00	20.00
5	Jabba the Hutt's Dancers	10.00	20.00
6	Jabba's Skiff Guards	10.00	20.00
7	Jedi Spirits	10.00	20.00
8	Mynock Hunt	15.00	30.00
9	Purchase of the Droids	8.00	15.00
10	Rebel Pilots	10.00	20.00

1995-00 Star Wars Power of the Force Comm-Tech

1	Admiral Motti	20.00	40.00
2a	Darth Vader (holographic chip)	8.00	15.00
2b	Darth Vader (white chip)	8.00	15.00
3	Greedo	6.00	12.00
4	Han Solo	6.00	12.00
5a	Jawa (w/Gonk Droid holographic chip)	8.00	15.00
5b	Jawa (w/Gonk Droid white chip)	8.00	15.00

6	Luke Skywalker (w/T16 Skyhopper)	6.00	12.00
7	Princess Leia	8.00	15.00
8	R2-D2 (w/Princess Leia)	12.00	25.00
9	Stormtrooper	8.00	15.00
10a	Wuher (no sticker)	8.00	15.00
	(2000 Fan Club Exclusive)		
10b	Wuher (sticker)	6.00	12.00
	(2000 Fan Club Exclusive)		

1995-00 Star Wars Power of the Force Complete Galaxy

1	Dagobah (w/Yoda)	8.00	15.00
2	Death Star (w/Darth Vader)	12.00	25.00
3a	Endor (w/Ewok) (.00)	15.00	30.00
3b	Endor (w/Ewok) (.01)	15.00	30.00
4	Tatooine (w/Luke)	10.00	20.00

1995-00 Star Wars Power of the Force Creatures

1	Bantha & Tusken Raider	30.00	60.00
2	Dewback & Sandtrooper	20.00	40.00
3a	Jabba the Hutt & Han Solo (Han on left)		
3b	Jabba the Hutt & Han Solo (Han on right)	15.00	30.00
4	Rancor & Luke Skywalker	30.00	60.00
5	Ronto & Jawa	12.00	25.00
6	Tauntaun & Han Solo	25.00	50.00
7	Tauntaun & Luke Skywalker	12.00	25.00
8	Wampa & Luke Skywalker	25.00	50.00

1995-00 Star Wars Power of the Force Deluxe

NNO	Boba Fett (photon torpedo)	8.00	15.00
NNO	Boba Fett (proton torpedo)	10.00	20.00
NNO	Han Solo (Smuggler's Flight)	6.00	12.00
NNO	Hoth Rebel Soldier	8.00	15.00
NNO	Luke Skywalker (Desert Sport Skiff)	25.00	50.00
NNO	Probe Droid (printed warning/green cardback)	6.00	12.00
NNO	Probe Droid (printed warning/red cardback)	6.00	12.00
NNO	Probe Droid (warning sticker/red cardback)	6.00	12.00
NNO	Snowtrooper (Tripod Cannon)	6.00	12.00
NNO	Stormtrooper (Crowd Control)(no sticker)	5.00	10.00
NNO	Stormtrooper (Crowd Control)(warning sticker)	5.00	10.00

1995-00 Star Wars Power of the Force Epic Force

1	Bespin Luke Skywalker	5.00	12.00
2	Boba Fett	5.00	12.00
3	C-3PO	8.00	15.00
4	Chewbacca	5.00	12.00
5	Darth Vader	5.00	12.00
6	Han Solo	5.00	12.00
7	Obi-Wan Kenobi	5.00	12.00
8	Princess Leia	4.00	8.00
9	Stormtrooper	4.00	8.00

1995-00 Star Wars Power of the Force Exclusives

1a	B-Omarr Monk (.00)	12.00	25.00
	(1997 Online Exclusive)		
1b	B-Omarr Monk (.01)	12.00	25.00
	(1997 Online Exclusive)		
2	C-3PO (greenish tint)		
	(Japanese Exclusive)		
3	Cantina Band Member	6.00	15.00
	(1997 Fan Club Exclusive)		
4	Han Solo (w/Tauntaun)	15.00	30.00
	(1997 Toys R Us Exclusive)		
5	Han Solo Stormtrooper	8.00	15.00
	(Kellogg's Mail Order Exclusive)		
6	Kabe and Muftak	10.00	20.00
	(1998 Online Exclusive)		
7	Luke Skywalker Jedi Knight	10.00	20.00
	(Theater Edition Exclusive)		
8	Oola & Salacious Crumb	12.00	25.00
	(1998 Fan Club Exclusive)		
9	Spirit of Obi-Wan Kenobi	8.00	15.00
	(Frito-Lay Mail Order Exclusive)		
10	Spirit of Obi-Wan		
	(UK Special Edition Exclusive)		

1995-00 Star Wars Power of the Force Expanded Universe Vehicles

1	Airspeeder (w/pilot)	20.00	40.00
2	Cloud Car (w/pilot)	10.00	20.00
3	Rebel Speeder Bike (w/pilot)	12.00	25.00

1995-00 Star Wars Power of the Force Flashback

1 Anakin Skywalker	6.00	12.00
2 Aunt Beru	5.00	10.00
3 C-3PO (removable arm)	5.00	10.00
4 Darth Vader	8.00	15.00
5 Emperor Palpatine	8.00	15.00
6 Hoth Chewbacca	8.00	15.00
7 Luke Skywalker	6.00	12.00
8 Obi-Wan Kenobi	5.00	10.00
9 Princess Leia (ceremonial dress)	6.00	12.00
10a R2-D2 (pop-up lightsaber)(forward position)	6.00	12.00
10b R2-D2 (pop-up lightsaber)(slanted)	4.00	8.00
11 Yoda	10.00	20.00

1995-00 Star Wars Power of the Force Freeze Frame Collection 1

1 C-3PO (removable limbs)	10.00	20.00
2a Endor Rebel Commando (.00)		
2b Endor Rebel Commando (.01)		
3 Garindan (long snoot)	8.00	15.00
4 Han Solo		
5 Han Solo (Bespin)	6.00	12.00
6a Han Solo (carbonite)(.04)	8.00	15.00
6b Han Solo (carbonite)(.05)	8.00	15.00
7a Han Solo (Endor)(.01)	5.00	10.00
7b Han Solo (Endor)(.02)	5.00	10.00
8a Hoth Rebel Soldier (.02)	6.00	12.00
8b Hoth Rebel Soldier (.03)	6.00	12.00
9a Lando Calrissian (General)(.00)	5.00	10.00
9b Lando Calrissian (General)(.01)	5.00	10.00
10a Lando Calrissian (Skiff guard)(.01)	5.00	10.00
10b Lando Calrissian (Skiff guard)(.02)	5.00	10.00
11 Lobot	3.00	6.00
12a Luke Skywalker (Bespin)(w/gold buckle)(.00)	6.00	12.00
12b Luke Skywalker (Bespin)(w/gold buckle)(.01)	6.00	12.00
12c Luke Skywalker (Bespin)(w/silver buckle)(.00)	6.00	12.00
12d Luke Skywalker (Bespin)(w/silver buckle)(.01)	6.00	12.00
13 Luke Skywalker (blast shield helmet)	8.00	15.00
14 Luke Skywalker (ceremonial)	5.00	10.00
15a Luke Skywalker (stormtrooper disguise)(.03)	5.00	10.00
15b Luke Skywalker (stormtrooper disguise)(.04)	5.00	10.00
16 Mon Mothma	6.00	12.00
17a Obi-Wan Kenobi (.03)	5.00	10.00
17b Obi-Wan Kenobi (.04)		
18 Orrimaarko (Prune Face)	4.00	8.00
19 Princess Leia Organa (Ewok celebration)	5.00	10.00
20a Princess Leia Organa (Jabba's prisoner)(.01)	8.00	15.00
20b Princess Leia Organa (Jabba's prisoner)(.02)	8.00	15.00
21 Princess Leia Organa (new likeness)		
22a R2-D2 (Death Star slide)	6.00	12.00

22b R2-D2 (Imperial slide)	6.00	12.00
23a Rebel Fleet Trooper (.01)	5.00	10.00
23b Rebel Fleet Trooper (.02)	5.00	10.00
23c Rebel Fleet Trooper (w/sticker)(.01)	5.00	10.00

1995-00 Star Wars Power of the Force Freeze Frame Collection 2

1 8D8	6.00	12.00
2a Admiral Ackbar (comlink wrist blaster)	6.00	12.00
2b Admiral Ackbar (wrist blaster)	6.00	12.00
3 Biggs Darklighter	4.00	8.00
4 EV-9D9	5.00	10.00
5 Ewoks Wicket & Logray	10.00	20.00
6 Gamorrean Guard	6.00	12.00
7a Han Solo (Bespin)(.02)	6.00	12.00
7b Han Solo (Bespin)(.03)	6.00	12.00
8 Lak Sivrak	6.00	12.00
9 Malakili (Rancor Keeper)	5.00	10.00
10 Nien Nunb	5.00	10.00
11 Saelt-Marae (Yak Face)	5.00	10.00
12 Ugnaughts	6.00	12.00

1995-00 Star Wars Power of the Force Freeze Frame Collection 3

1 AT-AT Driver	10.00	20.00
(1998 Fan Club Exclusive)		
2 Boba Fett	6.00	15.00
3a Captain Piett (baton sticker)	5.00	10.00
3b Captain Piett (pistol sticker)	5.00	10.00
4 Darth Vader	6.00	12.00
5 Darth Vader (removable helmet)	8.00	15.00
6 Death Star Droid (w/mouse droid)	8.00	15.00
7 Death Star Trooper	12.00	25.00
8 Emperor Palpatine	8.00	15.00
9 Emperor's Royal Guard	8.00	15.00
10 Grand Moff Tarkin	6.00	12.00
11a Ishi Tib (brown pouch)	5.00	10.00
11b Ishi Tib (gray pouch)	5.00	10.00
12 Pote Snitkin	12.00	25.00
(1999 Internet Exclusive)		
13 Princess Leia Organa (Hoth)	8.00	15.00
(1999 Fan Club Exclusive)		
14 Ree-Yees	6.00	12.00
15 Sandtrooper		
16 Snowtrooper	5.00	10.00
17 Stormtrooper	5.00	10.00
18 TIE Fighter Pilot		
19 Weequay		
20 Zuckuss	4.00	8.00

1995-00 Star Wars Power of the Force Green Collection 1

1a Bib Fortuna (hologram)	6.00	12.00
1b Bib Fortuna (photo)	6.00	12.00
2 Boba Fett (hologram)	15.00	30.00
3 C-3PO (hologram)	8.00	15.00
4a Chewbacca	10.00	20.00
4b Chewbacca (hologram)	4.00	8.00
5a Darth Vader	6.00	12.00
5b Darth Vader (hologram)	8.00	15.00
6a Death Star Gunner	6.00	12.00
6b Death Star Gunner (hologram)	6.00	12.00
7a Emperor Palpatine	6.00	12.00
7b Emperor Palpatine (hologram)	6.00	12.00
8 Garindan (long snoot)	4.00	8.00
9a Greedo	6.00	12.00
9b Greedo (hologram)	6.00	12.00
10a Han Solo	5.00	10.00
10b Han Solo (hologram)	6.00	12.00
11a Han Solo (Bespin)	6.00	12.00
11b Han Solo (Bespin)(hologram)	6.00	12.00
12a Han Solo (carbonite stand-up bubble)	8.00	15.00
12b Han Solo (carbonite stand-up bubble)(hologram)	8.00	15.00
13a Han Solo (Endor blue pants)	8.00	15.00
13b Han Solo (Endor blue pants)(hologram)	8.00	15.00
13c Han Solo (Endor brown pants)	10.00	20.00
14 Hoth Rebel Soldier (hologram)	5.00	10.00
15 Lando Calrissian	20.00	40.00
16 Lando Calrissian (Skiff guard)(hologram)	6.00	12.00
17a Luke Skywalker (ceremonial)	5.00	10.00
17b Luke Skywalker (ceremonial)(hologram)	5.00	10.00
18 Luke Skywalker (Hoth)(hologram)	5.00	10.00
19a Luke Skywalker (Jedi Knight)	6.00	12.00
19b Luke Skywalker (Jedi Knight)(hologram)	6.00	12.00
20 Luke Skywalker (stormtrooper disguise)(hologram)	6.00	12.00
21 Luke Skywalker (X-Wing pilot)(hologram)	8.00	15.00
22a Obi-Wan Kenobi (hologram)	5.00	10.00
22b Obi-Wan Kenobi (photo)	5.00	10.00
23a Princess Leia Organa (Jabba's prisoner)	5.00	10.00
23b Princess Leia Organa (Jabba's prisoner) (hologram)	5.00	10.00
24a Princess Leia Organa (photo)		
24b Princess Leia Organa (three-ring belt)	10.00	20.00
24c Princess Leia Organa (two-ring belt)(hologram)	8.00	15.00
25 R2-D2	10.00	20.00
26 Rebel Fleet Trooper (hologram)	5.00	10.00
27a Sandtrooper	8.00	15.00
27b Sandtrooper (hologram)	8.00	15.00
28a Yoda	6.00	12.00
28b Yoda (hologram)	6.00	12.00

1995-00 Star Wars Power of the Force Green Collection 2

1a	2-1B (.00)	5.00	10.00
1b	2-1B (.00)(hologram)	6.00	12.00
1c	2-1B (.01)	4.00	8.00
1d	2-1B (.01)(hologram)	6.00	12.00
2a	4-LOM	6.00	12.00
2b	4-LOM (hologram)	6.00	12.00
3	Admiral Ackbar	4.00	8.00
4a	ASP-7 (hologram)	5.00	10.00
4b	ASP-7 (photo)	5.00	10.00
5a	AT-ST Driver		
5b	AT-ST Driver (hologram)		
6a	Bib Fortuna (hologram/stand-up bubble)		
6b	Bib Fortuna (hologram/straight bubble)		
7a	Bossk (.00)(hologram)		
7b	Bossk (.00)(photo)	4.00	8.00
7c	Bossk (.01)(photo)		
8	Clone Emperor Palpatine (Expanded Universe)	8.00	15.00
9	Darktrooper (Expanded Universe)	10.00	20.00
10a	Dengar (hologram)		
10b	Dengar (photo)		
11a	EV-9D9 (hologram)		
11b	EV-9D9 (photo)		
12	Gamorrean Guard (hologram)		
13	Grand Admiral Thrawn (Expanded Universe)	20.00	40.00
14a	Grand Moff Tarkin		
14b	Grand Moff Tarkin (hologram)		
15a	Han Solo (carbonite)		
15b	Han Solo (carbonite)(hologram)		
16a	Hoth Rebel Soldier		
16b	Hoth Rebel Soldier (hologram)		
17	Imperial Sentinel (Expanded Universe)	10.00	20.00
18a	Jawas		
18b	Jawas (hologram)		
18c	Jawas (new bubble)		
18d	Jawas (new bubble)(hologram)		
19	Kyle Katarn (Expanded Universe)	10.00	20.00
20a	Luke Skywalker (ceremonial)(hologram)		
20b	Luke Skywalker (ceremonial/different head)		
21	Luke Skywalker (Expanded Universe)	10.00	20.00
22a	Luke Skywalker (Hoth)		
22b	Luke Skywalker (Hoth)(hologram)		
23a	Luke Skywalker (Jedi Knight)	6.00	12.00
23b	Luke Skywalker (Jedi Knight)(hologram)		
24a	Luke Skywalker (stormtrooper disguise)		
24b	Luke Skywalker (stormtrooper disguise)(hologram)		
25	Malakili (Rancor Keeper)(hologram)		
26	Mara Jade (Expanded Universe)	15.00	30.00
27a	Momaw Nadon (Hammerhead)		
27b	Momaw Nadon (Hammerhead)(hologram)		
28	Nien Nunb (hologram)		
29a	Ponda Baba (black beard) (hologram)		
29b	Ponda Baba (gray beard) (hologram)		
30	Princess Leia (Expanded Universe)	8.00	15.00
31a	R5-D4 (no warning sticker/L-latch)		
31b	R5-D4 (no warning sticker/L-latch)(hologram)		
31c	R5-D4 (no warning sticker/straight latch)		
31d	R5-D4 (no warning sticker/straight latch)(hologram)		
31e	R5-D4 (warning sticker/L-latch)		
31f	R5-D4 (warning sticker/L-latch)(hologram)		
31g	R5-D4 (warning sticker/straight latch)		
31h	R5-D4 (warning sticker/straight latch)(hologram)		
32a	Rebel Fleet Trooper		
32b	Rebel Fleet Trooper (hologram)		
33	Saelt-Marae (Yak Face)(hologram)		
34	Spacetrooper (Expanded Universe)	8.00	15.00
35	TIE Fighter Pilot (hologram)		
36	Tusken Raider (hologram)	4.00	8.00
37	Weequay		
38a	Yoda		
38b	Yoda (hologram)		

1995-00 Star Wars Power of the Force Green Collection 3

1	AT-ST Driver	5.00	10.00
2	AT-ST Driver (hologram)	5.00	10.00
3	Boba Fett (hologram)	12.00	25.00
4	Darth Vader (hologram)	4.00	8.00
5a	Death Star Gunner	5.00	10.00
5b	Death Star Gunner (hologram)	5.00	10.00
6	Emperor Palpatine (hologram)	4.00	8.00
7a	Emperor's Royal Guard	6.00	12.00
7b	Emperor's Royal Guard (hologram)	6.00	12.00
8a	Garindan (long snoot)(hologram)	4.00	8.00
8b	Garindan (long snoot)(photo)	4.00	8.00
9	Grand Moff Tarkin	4.00	8.00
10a	Ponda Baba (black beard)	5.00	10.00
10b	Ponda Baba (gray beard)	50.00	100.00
11a	Sandtrooper	5.00	10.00
11b	Sandtrooper (hologram)	5.00	10.00
12a	Snowtrooper		
12b	Snowtrooper (hologram)		
13a	Stormtrooper	5.00	10.00
13b	Stormtrooper (holosticker)	5.00	10.00
14	TIE Fighter Pilot (hologram)	6.00	12.00
15	Weequay (hologram)	4.00	8.00

1995-00 Star Wars Power of the Force Gunner Stations

1a	Gunner Station (Millennium Falcon w/Han Solo)(.00)	6.00	12.00
1b	Gunner Station (Millennium Falcon w/Han Solo)(.01)	6.00	12.00
2a	Gunner Station (Millennium Falcon w/Luke Skywalker)(.00)	6.00	12.00
2b	Gunner Station (Millennium Falcon w/Luke Skywalker)(.01)	6.00	12.00
3	Gunner Station (TIE Fighter w/Darth Vader)	8.00	15.00

1995-00 Star Wars Power of the Force Max Rebo Band Pairs

1a	Droopy McCool & Barquin D'an (CGI Sy Snootles on back) (1998 Walmart Exclusive)	12.00	25.00
1b	Droopy McCool & Barquin D'an (puppet Sy Snootles on back) (1998 Walmart Exclusive)	8.00	15.00
2	Max Rebo & Doda Bodonawieedo	15.00	30.00
3a	Sy Snootles & Joh Yowza (CGI Sy Snootles on back) (1998 Walmart Exclusive)	12.00	25.00
3b	Sy Snootles & Joh Yowza (puppet Sy Snootles on back) (1998 Walmart Exclusive)	8.00	15.00

1995-00 Star Wars Power of the Force Millennium Mint

1	C-3PO	5.00	12.00
2a	Chewbacca (.00) (1998 Toys R Us Exclusive)	6.00	12.00
2b	Chewbacca (.01/new insert) (1998 Toys R Us Exclusive)	6.00	12.00
3	Emperor Palpatine (1998 Toys R Us Exclusive)	5.00	12.00
4a	Han Solo (Bespin)(.00) (1998 Toys R Us Exclusive)	6.00	12.00
4b	Han Solo (Bespin)(.01/new insert) (1998 Toys R Us Exclusive)	12.00	25.00
5a	Luke Skywalker (Endor gear)(.00) (1998 Toys R Us Exclusive)	10.00	20.00
5b	Luke Skywalker (Endor gear)(.01) (1998 Toys R Us Exclusive)	8.00	15.00
6a	Princess Leia (Endor gear)(.00) (1998 Toys R Us Exclusive)	12.00	25.00
6b	Princess Leia (Endor gear)(.01) (1998 Toys R Us Exclusive)	10.00	20.00
7a	Snowtrooper (.00) (1998 Toys R Us Exclusive)	6.00	12.00
7b	Snowtrooper (.01) (1998 Toys R Us Exclusive)	8.00	15.00

1995-00 Star Wars Power of the Force Orange

1	Chewbacca	6.00	12.00
2a	Darth Vader (long saber)	8.00	15.00
2b	Darth Vader (short saber/long tray)		
2c	Darth Vader (short saber/short tray)		
3	Han Solo		
4a	Stormtrooper	4.00	8.00
4b	Stormtrooper (holosticker)	6.00	12.00

1995-00 Star Wars Power of the Force Playsets

1a	Cantina Pop-Up Diorama (w/sandtrooper)	12.00	25.00
	(Retail Store Version - 25" sticker correction)		
1b	Cantina Pop-Up Diorama (w/sandtrooper)	15.00	30.00
	(Retail Store Version - 25" wide description)		
1c	Cantina Pop-Up Diorama (w/sandtrooper)		
	(Retail Store Version - 26" wide description)		
2	Cantina Pop-Up Diorama		
	(1997 Mail Order Exclusive)		
3	Death Star Escape	10.00	20.00
4	Detention Block Rescue		
5a	Endor Attack (no warning sticker)		
5b	Endor Attack (warning sticker)		
6a	Hoth Battle (no warning sticker)		
6b	Hoth Battle (warning sticker)		
7a	Jabba's Palace (w/Han Solo)(podrace arena bio card)		
7b	Jabba's Palace (w/Han Solo)(podracer bio card)	15.00	30.00
8	Millennium Falcon Cockpit	20.00	40.00
	(PC Explorer Game)		

1995-00 Star Wars Power of the Force Power F/X

1	Ben (Obi-Wan) Kenobi	5.00	10.00
2	Darth Vader	5.00	10.00
3a	Emperor Palpatine (.00)	5.00	10.00
3b	Emperor Palpatine (.01)	4.00	8.00
4	Luke Skywalker	6.00	12.00
5a	R2-D2 (.00)	4.00	8.00
5b	R2-D2 (.01)	4.00	8.00
5c	R2-D2 (.02)	4.00	8.00
5d	R2-D2 (.103)	4.00	8.00

1995-00 Star Wars Power of the Force Princess Leia Collection

1a	Princess Leia & Han Solo (gold border)	4.00	8.00
1b	Princess Leia & Han Solo (gray border)	10.00	20.00
2a	Princess Leia & Luke Skywalker (gold border)	8.00	15.00
2b	Princess Leia & Luke Skywalker (gray border)	10.00	20.00
3a	Princess Leia & R2-D2 (gold border)	25.00	50.00
3b	Princess Leia & R2-D2 (gray border)	10.00	20.00
4a	Princess Leia & Wicket (gold border)	4.00	8.00
4b	Princess Leia & Wicket (gray border)	10.00	20.00

1995-00 Star Wars Power of the Force Red

1a	Boba Fett (full circle)	8.00	15.00
1b	Boba Fett (half circle)	25.00	50.00
1c	Boba Fett (no circle)	12.00	25.00
2	C-3PO (.00)	6.00	12.00
3	Death Star Gunner	10.00	20.00
4	Greedo	5.00	10.00
5a	Han Solo (carbonite block)	6.00	12.00
5b	Han Solo (carbonite freezing chamber)	6.00	12.00
6a	Han Solo (Hoth - closed hand)	6.00	12.00
6b	Han Solo (Hoth - open hand)	4.00	8.00
7	Jawas	12.00	25.00
8	Lando Calrissian	3.00	6.00
9a	Luke Skywalker (Dagobah - long saber)	6.00	12.00
9b	Luke Skywalker (Dagobah - short saber/long tray)		
9c	Luke Skywalker (Dagobah - short saber/short tray)		
10a	Luke Skywalker (Jedi Knight - black vest)	6.00	12.00
10b	Luke Skywalker (Jedi Knight - brown vest)	8.00	15.00
11a	Luke Skywalker (long saber)	8.00	15.00
11b	Luke Skywalker (short saber/long tray)	5.00	10.00
11c	Luke Skywalker (short saber/short tray)	6.00	12.00
12a	Luke Skywalker (stormtrooper disguise)	8.00	15.00
12b	Luke Skywalker (stormtrooper disguise)(hologram)		
13a	Luke Skywalker (X-Wing pilot - long saber)	10.00	20.00
13b	Luke Skywalker (X-Wing pilot - short saber/long tray)		
13c	Luke Skywalker (X-Wing pilot - short saber/short tray)		
14	Momaw Nadon (Hammerhead) (warning sticker)	4.00	8.00
15a	Obi-Wan Kenobi (hologram)	5.00	10.00
15b	Obi-Wan Kenobi (short saber/long tray)	5.00	10.00
15c	Obi-Wan Kenobi (short saber/short tray)	4.00	8.00
15d	Obi-Wan Kenobi (long saber)	4.00	8.00
15e	Obi-Wan Kenobi (photo)		
16a	Princess Leia Organa (2-band belt)	6.00	12.00
16b	Princess Leia Organa (3-band belt)		
16c	Princess Leia Organa (hologram)		
17a	R2-D2	8.00	15.00
17b	R2-D2 (hologram)		
18a	R5-D4 (no warning sticker/straight latch)		
18b	R5-D4 (warning sticker/straight latch)		
19	Sandtrooper		
20a	TIE Fighter Pilot (printed warning)	4.00	8.00
20b	TIE Fighter Pilot (SOTE)		
20c	TIE Fighter Pilot (warning sticker)		
21a	Tusken Raider (closed left hand)		
21b	Tusken Raider (open left hand)		
22a	Yoda (.00)	6.00	12.00
22b	Yoda (.00)(hologram)		
22c	Yoda (.01)		

2014-15 Star Wars Rebels Hero Series

1	Agent Kallus	12.00	25.00
2	Clone Trooper	6.00	12.00
3	Darth Vader		
4	Ezra Bridger	10.00	20.00
5	Garazeb Orrelios	15.00	30.00
6	Heroes and Villains	20.00	50.00
	(2014 Target Exclusive)		
7	Kanan Jarrus	12.00	25.00
8	Luke Skywalker	12.00	25.00
9	Stormtrooper	10.00	20.00
10	The Inquisitor	8.00	15.00

2014-15 Star Wars Rebels Mission Series

MS1	Garazeb Orrelios/Stormtrooper	8.00	15.00
MS2	R2-D2/C-3PO	15.00	30.00
MS3	Luke Skywalker/Darth Vader	10.00	20.00
MS4	Darth Sidious/Yoda	12.00	25.00
MS5	Boba Fett/Stormtrooper	12.00	25.00
MS7	Wullffwarro/Wookiee Warrior	8.00	15.00
MS8	Sabine Wren/Stormtrooper	20.00	40.00
MS9	Cikatro Vizago/IG-RM	10.00	20.00
MS10	Wicket/Biker Scout	8.00	15.00
MS11	Bossk/IG-88	10.00	20.00
MS15	Luke Skywalker/Han Solo	12.00	25.00
MS16	R2-D2/Yoda	15.00	30.00
MS17	TIE Pilot/Stormtrooper	8.00	15.00
MS18	Ezra Bridger/Kanan Jarrus	8.00	15.00
MS19	Stormtrooper Commander/Hera Syndulla	12.00	25.00
MS20	Princess Leia/Luke Skywalker Stormtrooper	10.00	20.00

2014-15 Star Wars Rebels Saga Legends

SL1 Stormtrooper		
SL2 Ezra Bridger	8.00	15.00
SL3 The Inquisitor		
SL4 Kanan Jarrus	6.00	12.00
SL5 Agent Kallus	12.00	30.00
SL6 C1-10P (Chopper)	12.00	30.00
SL7 Jango Fett	6.00	12.00
SL8 Clone Trooper	6.00	12.00
SL9 Darth Vader	10.00	20.00
SL10 Luke Skywalker (Jedi Knight)	8.00	15.00
SL11 Obi-Wan Kenobi		
SL12 Snowtrooper		
SL13 TIE Pilot		
SL14 AT-DP Driver	20.00	40.00
SL15 Clone Commander Gree	6.00	12.00
SL16 Plo Koon		
SL17 Jedi Temple Guard	30.00	75.00
SL18 AT-AT Driver	6.00	12.00
SL22 Luke Skywalker (X-Wing Pilot)	8.00	15.00
SL23 Lando Calrissian	8.00	15.00
SL24 Han Solo	8.00	15.00
SL25 Luke Skywalker (Endor)	8.00	15.00
SL26 Commander Bly	6.00	12.00
SL27 Han Solo (Endor)	8.00	15.00
SL28 Princess Leia (Endor)		

2005 Star Wars Revenge of the Sith

III1 Obi-Wan Kenobi (slashing attack)	8.00	15.00
III2 Anakin Skywalker (slashing attack straight saber red)	6.00	12.00
III2a Anakin Skywalker (slashing attack bent saber red)	4.00	8.00
III2b Anakin Skywalker (slashing attack bent saber pink)	4.00	8.00
III3 Yoda (firing cannon)	4.00	8.00
III4 Super Battle Droid (firing arm blaster)	10.00	20.00
III5 Chewbacca (Wookiee rage)	8.00	15.00
III6a Clone Trooper (white - quick draw attack)	6.00	12.00
III6b Clone Trooper (red - quick draw attack)	6.00	12.00
III7 R2-D2 (droid attack)	5.00	10.00
III8 Grievous's Bodyguard (battle attack)	4.00	8.00
III9 General Grievous (four lightsaber attack)	4.00	8.00

III10 Mace Windu (Force combat)	6.00	12.00
III11 Darth Vader (lightsaber attack)	4.00	8.00
III12 Emperor Palpatine (firing Force lightning)	5.00	10.00
III13 Count Dooku (Sith Lord)	5.00	10.00
III14 Chancellor Palpatine (supreme chancellor)	4.00	8.00
III15 Bail Organa (Republic Senator)	5.00	10.00
III16 Plo Koon (Jedi Master)	4.00	8.00
III17 Battle Droid (separatist army)	5.00	10.00
III18 C-3PO (protocal droid)	4.00	8.00
III19 Padme republic senator	10.00	20.00
III20 Agen Kolar (Jedi Master)	6.00	12.00
III21 Shaak Ti (Jedi Master)	10.00	20.00
III22 Kit Fisto (Jedi Master)	6.00	12.00
III23a Royal Guard (blue - senate security)	6.00	12.00
III23b Royal Guard (red - senate security)	8.00	15.00
III24 Mon Mothma (Republic Senator)	6.00	12.00
III25 Tarfful (firing bowcaster)	4.00	8.00
III26 Yoda (spinning attack)	6.00	12.00
III27 Obi-Wan Kenobi (Jedi kick)	4.00	8.00
III28 Anakin Skywalker (slashing attack)	8.00	15.00
III29 Ki-Adi-Mundi (Jedi Master)	5.00	10.00
III30 Saesee Tiin (Jedi Master)	5.00	10.00
III31 Luminara Unduli (Jedi Master)	6.00	12.00
III32 Aayla Secura (Jedi Knight)	8.00	15.00
III33a Clone Commander (red - battle gear)	8.00	15.00
III33b Clone Commander (green - battle gear)	8.00	15.00
III34a Clone Pilot (firing cannon)	5.00	10.00
III34b Clone Pilot (black - firing cannon)	5.00	10.00
III35a Palpatine (red lightsaber - lightsaber attack)	6.00	12.00
III35b Palpatine (blue lightsaber - lightsaber attack)	6.00	12.00
III36 General Grievous (exploding body)	10.00	20.00
III37 Vader's Medical Droid (chopper droid)	4.00	8.00
III38 AT-TE Tank Gunner (clone army)	6.00	12.00
III39 Polis Massan (medic droid)	4.00	8.00
III40 Mas Amedda (Republic Senator)	5.00	10.00
III41 Clone Trooper (white - super articulation)	5.00	10.00
III42 Neimoidian Warrior (Neimoidian weapon attack)	4.00	8.00
III43a Warrior Wookie (dark - wookie battle bash)	4.00	8.00
III43b Warrior Wookie (light - wookie battle bash)	12.00	25.00
III44 Destroyer Droid (firing arm blaster)	8.00	15.00
III45 Tarkin (Governor)	4.00	8.00
III46 Ask Aak (Senator)	6.00	12.00
III47 Meena Tills (Senator)	4.00	8.00
III48 R2-D2 (try me electronic)	6.00	12.00
III49 Commander Bacara (quick-draw attack)	5.00	10.00
III50 Anakin Skywalker (battle damaged)	8.00	15.00
III51 Captain Antilles (Senate security)	4.00	8.00
III52 Jett Jukassa (Jedi Padawan)	4.00	8.00
III53 Utapaun Warrior (Utapau security)	5.00	10.00
III54 AT-RT Driver (missile-firing blaster)	12.00	25.00
III55 Obi-Wan Kenobi (w/pilot gear)	8.00	15.00
III56 Mustafar Sentury (spinning energy bolt)	5.00	10.00
III57 Commander Bly (battle gear)	8.00	15.00
III58 Wookie Commando (Kashyyyk battle gear)	6.00	12.00
III59 Commander Gree (battle gear)	10.00	20.00
III60 Grievous's Bodyguard (battle attack)	6.00	12.00
III61 Passel Argente (separatist leader)	6.00	12.00
III62 Cat Miin (separatist)	4.00	8.00
III63 Neimoidian Commander (separatist bodyguard)	4.00	8.00
III64 R4-P17 (rolling action)	8.00	15.00
III65 Tactical Ops Trooper (Vader's legion)	6.00	12.00
III66 Plo Koon (Jedi hologram transmission)	8.00	15.00
III67 Aayla Secura (Jedi hologram transmission)	5.00	10.00
III68 Wookiee Heavy Gunner (blast attack)	5.00	10.00

2005 Star Wars Revenge of the Sith 12-Inch

1 Anakin Skywalker/Darth Vader (ultimate villain)	30.00	60.00
2 Barriss Offee	15.00	30.00
3 Chewbacca	20.00	40.00
(2005 KB Toys Exclusive)		
4 Clone Trooper	12.00	25.00
5 Darth Sidious		
6 General Grievous	30.00	60.00
7 Shaak Ti	15.00	30.00

2005 Star Wars Revenge of the Sith Accessories

10 Darth Vader Carrying Case (w/Clone Trooper & Anakin Skywalker)		
20 Darth Vader Carrying Case (w/Darth Vader & Obi-Wan Kenobi)		

2005 Star Wars Revenge of the Sith Battle Arena

1 Bodyguard vs. Obi-Wan (Utapau landing platform)	8.00	15.00
2 Dooku vs Anakin (Trade Federation cruiser)	8.00	15.00
3 Sidius vs. Mace (Chancellor's office)	8.00	15.00

2005 Star Wars Revenge of the Sith Battle Packs

1 Assault on Hoth (General Veers/Probot/3 Snowtroopers)

2 Attack on Coruscant (5 Clone Troopers)

3 Imperial Throne Room (Emperor Palpatine
Imperial Dignitary/2 Royal Guards/Stormtrooper)

4 Jedi Temple Assault (Anakin/Clone Pilot/3 Special Ops Troopers)

5 Jedi vs. Sith (Anakin/Asajj Ventress   20.00   40.00

General Grievous/Obi-Wan/Yoda)

6 Jedi vs. Separatists (Anakin/Darth Maul

Jango Fett/Obi-Wan/Mace Windu)

7 Rebel vs. Empire (Chewbacca/Vader/Han/Luke/Stormtrooper)   20.00   40.00

2005 Star Wars Revenge of the Sith Collectible Cup Figures

1 Boba Fett	12.00	25.00
2 Clone Trooper		
3 Darth Vader	10.00	20.00
4 General Grievous		
5 Han Solo	10.00	20.00
6 Obi-Wan Kenobi	10.00	20.00
7 Princess Leia		
8 Stormtrooper	8.00	15.00
9 Yoda	8.00	15.00

2005 Star Wars Revenge of the Sith Commemorative Episode III DVD Collection

1 Jedi Knights (Anakin Skywalker/Mace Windu/Obi-Wan Kenobi)	10.00	20.00
2 Sith Lords (Emperor Palpatine/Darth Vader/Count Dooku)	10.00	20.00
3 Clone Troopers (3 Clone Troopers)	12.00	25.00

2005 Star Wars Revenge of the Sith Creatures

10 Boga (w/Obi-Wan Kenobi)	20.00	40.00

2005 Star Wars Revenge of the Sith Deluxe

1 Anakin Skywalker (changes to Darth Vader)	15.00	30.00
2 Clone Trooper (firing jet pack)	5.00	10.00
3 Clone Troopers (Build Your Army - 3 white)	8.00	15.00
4 Clone Troopers (Build Your Army - 2 white and 1 red)	10.00	20.00
5 Clone Troopers (Build Your Army - 2 white and 1 green)	8.00	15.00
6 Clone Troopers (Build Your Army - 2 white and 1 blue)	12.00	25.00
7 Crab Droid (moving legs/missile launcher)	12.00	25.00
8 Darth Vader (rebuild Darth Vader)	10.00	20.00
9 Emperor Palpatine (changes to Darth Sidious)	8.00	15.00
10 General Grievous (secret lightsaber attack)	15.00	30.00
11 Obi-Wan Kenobi (Force jump attack - w/super battle droid)	5.00	10.00
12 Spider Droid (firing laser action)	5.00	10.00
13 Stass Allie (exploding action - w/BARC speeder)	5.00	10.00
14 Vulture Droid (blue - firing missile launcher)	6.00	12.00
15 Vulture Droid (brown - firing missile launcher)	10.00	20.00
16 Yoda (fly into battle - w/can-cell)	8.00	15.00

2005 Star Wars Revenge of the Sith Evolutions

1 Anakin Skywalker to Darth Vader	12.00	25.00
2 Clone Trooper (Attack of the Clones	15.00	30.00
Revenge of the Sith/A New Hope)		
3 Clone Trooper (Attack of the Clones	15.00	30.00
Revenge of the Sith - gray/A New Hope - gray)		
4 Sith Lords (Darth Maul/Darth Tyranus/Darth Sidious)	15.00	30.00

2005 Star Wars Revenge of the Sith Exclusives

1 Anakin Skywalker Paris-Mai		
(2005 Star Wars Reunion Convention Exclusive)		
2 Clone Trooper (Neyo logo)		
(2005 Target Exclusive)		
3 Clone Trooper (Sith logo)	12.00	25.00
(2005 Target Exclusive)		
4 Covert Ops Clone Trooper		
(2005 StarWarsShop.com Exclusive)		
5 Darth Vader (Duel at Mustafar)	8.00	15.00
(2005 Target Exclusive)		
6 Darth Vader (lava reflection)	8.00	15.00
(2005 Target Exclusive)		

7 Darth Vader	12.00	25.00
(2005 Celebration III Exclusive)		
8 Holographic Emperor	6.00	12.00
(2005 Toys R Us Exclusive)		
9 Holographic Yoda (Kashyyyk transmission)	6.00	12.00
(2005 Toys R Us Exclusive)		
10 Obi-Wan Kenobi (Duel at Mustafar)	12.00	25.00
(2005 Target Exclusive)		
11 R2-D2 (remote control)		
(2005 Japanese Exclusive)		
12 Utapau Shadow Trooper (super articulation)	10.00	20.00
(2005 Target Exclusive)		

2005 Star Wars Revenge of the Sith Kay Bee Toys Collector Packs

1 Luminara Unduli/Count Dooku/Royal Guard/Kit Fisto	20.00	40.00
Darth Vader/Bail Organa/C-3PO/Ki-Adi-Mundi/Chancellor Palpatine		

2005 Star Wars Revenge of the Sith Playsets

1 Mustafar Final Duel/Anakin		
Skywalker/Obi-Wan Kenobi		
2 Mustafar Final Duel (w/Obi-Wan	40.00	80.00
Darth Vader/4 Clone Troopers)		

2005 Star Wars Revenge of the Sith Promos

1 Anakin Skywalker
2 Darth Vader

2005 Star Wars Revenge of the Sith Sneak Preview

1 General Grievous	8.00	15.00
2 Tion Medon	4.00	8.00
3 Wookie Warrior	4.00	8.00
4 R4-G9	4.00	8.00
NNO Anakin's Jedi Starfighter (vehicle)	15.00	30.00

2005 Star Wars Revenge of the Sith Super Deformed

1 Boba Fett	12.00	25.00
2 C-3PO		
3 Chewbacca		
4 Darth Maul		
5 Darth Vader		
6 R2-D2		
7 Stormtrooper		
8 Yoda		

2005 Star Wars Revenge of the Sith Vehicles

1 Anakin's Jedi Starfighter (w/Anakin)	20.00	40.00
(2005 Toys R Us Exclusive)		
2 ARC-170 Fighter	50.00	100.00
3 ARC-170 Fighter (w/4 Troopers)	75.00	150.00
4 AR-RT/AR-RT Driver		
5 AR-RT/AR-RT Driver (w/Clone Trooper white)		
6 Barc Speeder (w/Barc Trooper & Wookiee warrior)		
7 Barc Speeder (w/Barc Trooper)		
8 Droid Tri-Fighter		
9 Grievous's Wheel Bike (w/General Grievous)	25.00	50.00
10 Millennium Falcon		
11 Obi-Wan's Jedi Starfighter	20.00	40.00
12 Obi-Wan's Jedi Starfighter (w/Obi-Wan)	12.00	25.00
(2005 Toys R Us Exclusive)		
13 Plo Koon's Jedi Starfighter	15.00	30.00
(2005 Target Exclusive)		
14 Republic Gunship	100.00	200.00
15 Wookiee Flyer (w/Wookiee warrior)		

2016 Star Wars Rogue One 2-Packs

NNO Baze Malbus vs. Imperial Stormtrooper	12.00	25.00
NNO Captain Cassian Andor vs. Imperial Stormtrooper		
NNO First Order Snowtrooper Officer vs. Poe Dameron	8.00	15.00
NNO Moroff vs. Scariff Stormtrooper Squad Leader	10.00	20.00
NNO Rebel Commander Pao vs. Imperial Death Trooper	8.00	15.00
NNO Seventh Sister Inquisitor vs. Darth Maul	12.00	25.00

2016 Star Wars Rogue One Big Figs

NNO Imperial Death Trooper	15.00	30.00
NNO Imperial Stormtrooper	15.00	30.00
NNO K-2SO	15.00	30.00
NNO Sergeant Jyn Erso	12.00	25.00

2016 Star Wars Rogue One Build-A-Weapon

NNO Admiral Raddus	10.00	20.00
NNO Bodhi Rook	12.00	25.00
NNO Captain Cassian Andor (Eadu)	8.00	15.00
NNO Chirrut Imwe	8.00	15.00
NNO Darth Vader	8.00	15.00
NNO Director Krennic	6.00	12.00
NNO Fenn Rau	60.00	120.00
NNO Galen Erso	12.00	25.00
NNO Grand Admiral Thrawn	30.00	60.00
NNO Imperial Death Trooper (Specialist Gear)	10.00	20.00
NNO Imperial Ground Crew	6.00	12.00
NNO Imperial Stormtrooper	6.00	12.00
NNO K-2SO	6.00	12.00
NNO Kanan Jarrus (stormtrooper disguise)(Star Wars Rebels)	10.00	20.00
NNO Kylo Ren (The Force Awakens)	8.00	15.00
NNO Lieutenant Sefla	6.00	12.00
NNO Princess Leia Organa (Star Wars Rebels)	6.00	12.00
NNO Rey (Jakku)(The Force Awakens)	6.00	12.00
NNO Sabine Wren (Star Wars Rebels)	6.00	12.00
NNO Sergeant Jyn Erso (Eadu)	6.00	12.00
NNO Sergeant Jyn Erso (Imperial Ground Crew Disguise)	8.00	15.00
NNO Sergeant Jyn Erso (Jedha)	6.00	12.00
NNO Shoretrooper	8.00	15.00

2016 Star Wars Rogue One Elite Series

NNO Baze Malbus	12.00	25.00
NNO Bodhi Rook	10.00	20.00
NNO C2-B5	12.00	25.00
NNO Captain Cassian Andor	8.00	15.00
NNO Chirrut Imwe	8.00	15.00
NNO Imperial Death Trooper	10.00	20.00
NNO K-2SO	10.00	20.00
NNO Sergeant Jyn Erso	10.00	20.00
NNO Stormtrooper		

2016 Star Wars Rogue One Hero Series

NNO Captain Cassian Andor	8.00	15.00
NNO First Order Stormtrooper		
NNO Imperial Death Trooper	8.00	15.00
NNO Sergeant Jyn Erso	8.00	15.00
NNO Shoretrooper		

2016 Star Wars Rogue One Multipacks

NNO Eadu 3-Pack	12.00	25.00
Sergeant Jyn Erso/Captain Cassian Andor/K-2SO		
(Walmart Exclusive)		
NNO Jedha Revolt 4-Pack	15.00	30.00
Edrio Two Tubes/Saw Gerrera/Sergeant Jyn Erso/Imperial Hovertank Pilot		
NNO Scarif 4-Pack	12.00	25.00
Rebel Commando Pao/Moroff/Imperial Death Trooper/Imperial Stormtrooper		
(Kohl's Exclusive)		

2016 Star Wars Rogue One Vehicles

NNO Assault Walker (w/stormtrooper sergeant)(The Force Awakens)	20.00	40.00
NNO A-Wing (w/Hera Syndulla)(Star Wars Rebels)	20.00	40.00
NNO Ezra Bridger's Speeder (w/Ezra Bridger)(Star Wars Rebels)	12.00	25.00
NNO First Order Snowspeeder (w/stormtrooper)(The Force Awakens)		
NNO Imperial AT-ACT Playset (w/Jyn Erso/astromech droid/driver)	75.00	150.00
NNO Imperial Speeder (w/AT-DP pilot)(Star Wars Rebels)	12.00	25.00
NNO Imperial TIE Striker (w/pilot)	20.00	40.00
NNO Imperial TIE Striker (w/pilot)		
(Toys R Us Exclusive)		
NNO Rebel U-Wing Fighter (w/Cassian Andor)	20.00	40.00

2015-16 Star Wars S.H. Figuarts

NNO Battle Droid	30.00	60.00
NNO Captain Phasma	30.00	60.00
NNO Clone Trooper (Phase 1)	25.00	50.00
NNO Darth Maul	50.00	100.00
NNO Darth Vader (w/display stand)	80.00	150.00
NNO First Order Riot Control Stormtrooper	30.00	60.00
NNO First Order Stormtrooper	30.00	60.00

NNO First Order Stormtrooper Heavy Gunner	40.00	80.00
NNO Jango Fett	40.00	80.00
NNO Kylo Ren		
NNO Luke Skywalker (Episode IV)	40.00	80.00
NNO Luke Skywalker (Episode VI)	60.00	120.00
NNO Mace Windu	40.00	80.00
NNO Obi-Wan Kenobi (Episode I)	30.00	60.00
NNO Scout Trooper and Speeder Bike	120.00	200.00
NNO Shadow Trooper	40.00	80.00
NNO Stormtrooper	50.00	100.00

2002-04 Star Wars Saga 12-Inch

1 Anakin Skywalker		
2 Anakin Skywalker (w/slashing lightsaber)	15.00	30.00
3 AT-ST Driver		
4 Biker Scout		
5 Clone Commander	8.00	15.00
6 Clone Trooper (black-and-white)	12.00	25.00
7 Clone Trooper (red-and-white)	12.00	25.00
8 Count Dooku	25.00	50.00
9 Dengar		
10 Ewok 2-Pack (Logray & Keoulkeech)		
11 Gamorrean Guard	25.00	50.00
12 Garindan		
13 Geonosian Warrior	12.00	25.00
14 Han Solo		
15 Imperial Officer		
16 Jango Fett	30.00	75.00
17 Jango Fett (electronic battling)	20.00	40.00
18 Jawas		
19 Ki-Adi-Mundi	20.00	40.00
20 Lando Calrissian (Skiff disguise)	12.00	25.00
21 Luke Skywalker & Tauntaun		
22 Luke Skywalker (w/slashing lightsaber)	25.00	50.00
23 Mace Windu	15.00	30.00
24 Obi-Wan Kenobi	12.00	25.00
25 Obi-Wan Kenobi (electronic battling)	10.00	20.00
26 Obi-Wan Kenobi (Tatooine encounter)	20.00	40.00
27 Padme Amidala	15.00	30.00
28 Plo Koon		
29 Princess Leia (Boushh) & Han Solo (carbonite)	30.00	60.00
30 Princess Leia (w/speeder bike)	30.00	75.00
31 Super Battle Droid	12.00	25.00
32 Yoda (w/hoverchair)		
33 Zam Wesell	12.00	25.00
34 Zuckuss	20.00	40.00

2002-04 Star Wars Saga 12-Inch Character Collectibles

1 Anakin Skywalker		
2 Darth Vader		
3 Jango Fett	30.00	60.00
4 Mace Windu	10.00	20.00

2002-04 Star Wars Saga Accessory Sets

1 Arena Conflict with/Battle Droid brown	12.00	25.00
2 Death Star (w/Death Star trooper and droids)	10.00	20.00
3 Endor Victory (w/scout trooper)	10.00	20.00
4 Hoth Survival (w/Hoth Rebel soldier)	8.00	15.00

2002-04 Star Wars Saga Arena Battle Beasts

1 Acklay	25.00	50.00
2 Reek	15.00	30.00

2002-04 Star Wars Saga Cinema Scenes

1 Death Star Trash Compactor	20.00	40.00
(Chewbacca & Princess Leia)		
2 Death Star Trash Compactor (Luke Skywalker & Han Solo)	25.00	50.00
3 Geonosian War Chamber	12.00	25.00
(Nute Gunray/Passel Argente/Shu Mai)		
4 Geonosian War Chamber	12.00	25.00
(Poggle the Lesser/Count Dooku/San Hill)		
5 Jedi High Council (Mace Windu	20.00	40.00
Oppo Rancisis/Even Piell)		
6 Jedi High Council (Yarael Poof	10.00	20.00
Depa Billaba/Yaddle)		

2002-04 Star Wars Saga Collectible Cup Figures

1 Episode I/Darth Maul	10.00	20.00
2 Episode II	10.00	20.00
Anakin Skywalker		
3 Episode IV	10.00	20.00
Obi-Wan Kenobi		
4 Episode V	10.00	20.00
Luke Skywalker		
5 Episode VI	12.00	25.00
Princess Leia Organa		

2002-04 Star Wars Saga Collection 1 (2002)

1 Anakin Skywalker (outland peasant disguise)	6.00	12.00
2 Padme Amidala (arena escape)	6.00	12.00
3 Obi-Wan Kenobi (Coruscant chase)	6.00	12.00
4 C-3PO (protocol droid)	5.00	10.00
5 Kit Fisto (Jedi Master)	5.00	10.00
6 Super Battle Droid	5.00	10.00
17 Clone Trooper	6.00	12.00
18 Zam Wesell (bounty hunter)	6.00	12.00
22 Anakin Skywalker (hangar duel)	12.00	25.00
23 Yoda (Jedi Master)		
27 Count Dooku (Dark Lord)	6.00	12.00
28 Mace Windu (Geonosian rescue)	8.00	15.00
29 Luke Skywalker (Bespin duel)	8.00	15.00
30 Darth Vader (Bespin duel)	6.00	12.00
31 Jango Fett (final battle)	5.00	10.00
36 Obi-Wan Kenobi (Jedi starfighter)	12.00	25.00
37 Han Solo (Endor bunker)		
38 Chewbacca (Cloud City capture w/C-3PO)	6.00	12.00
40 Djas Puhr (bounty hunter)	6.00	12.00
41 Padme Amidala (Coruscant attack)	6.00	12.00
43 Anakin Skywalker (Tatooine attack)	6.00	12.00
47 Jango Fett (Slave-1 pilot)	5.00	10.00
48 Destroyer Droid (Geonosis battle)		
49 Clone Trooper (Republic gunship pilot)	8.00	15.00
53 Yoda (Jedi High Council)		

2002-04 Star Wars Saga Collection 1 (2003)

1	Obi-Wan Kenobi (acklay battle)	5.00	10.00
2	Mace Windu (arena confrontation)	5.00	10.00
3	Darth Tyranus (Geonosian escape)	8.00	15.00
7	Anakin Skywalker (secret ceremony)	8.00	15.00
8	Boba Fett (The Pit of Carkoon)	8.00	15.00
9	R2-D2 (droid factory)	6.00	12.00
13	Han Solo (Hoth rescue)		
14	Chewbacca (mynock hunt)	5.00	10.00
17	Luke Skywalker (throne room duel)	5.00	10.00
18	Darth Vader (throne room duel)	6.00	12.00
19	Snowtrooper (The Battle of Hoth)	8.00	15.00
20	Jango Fett (Kamino duel)		
21	C-3PO (Tatooine attack)		

2002-04 Star Wars Saga Collection 2 (2002)

7	Boba Fett (Kamino escape)	8.00	15.00
8	Tusken Raider Female (w/Tusken child)	6.00	12.00
9	Captain Typho (Padme's head of security)	5.00	10.00
10	Shaak Ti (Jedi Master)	5.00	10.00
11a	Battle Droid (arena battle tan)	5.00	10.00
11b	Battle Droid (arena battle brown)	12.00	25.00
12	Plo Koon (arena battle)		
13	Jango Fett (Kamino escape)	8.00	15.00
14	R2-D2 (Coruscant sentry)	8.00	15.00
15	Geonosian Warrior	5.00	10.00
16	Dexter Jettster (Coruscant informant)	5.00	10.00
19	Royal Guard (Coruscant security)	6.00	12.00
20	Saesee Tin (Jedi Master)	5.00	10.00
21	Nikto (Jedi Knight)	6.00	12.00
24	Jar Jar Binks (Gungan Senator)	5.00	10.00
25	Taun We (Kamino cloner)	6.00	12.00
26	Luminara Unduli	5.00	10.00
32	Qui-Gon Jinn (Jedi Master)	6.00	12.00
33a	Endor Rebel Soldier (facial hair)		
33a	Endor Rebel Soldier (no facial hair)		
34	Massiff (w/Geonosian handler)	8.00	15.00
35	Orn Free Taa (senator)		
39	Supreme Chancellor Palpatine		
42	Darth Maul (Sith training)	5.00	10.00
44	Ki-Adi-Mundi (Jedi Master)	5.00	10.00
45	Ephant Man (Jabba's head of security)		

46	Teemto Pagalies (pod racer)		
50	Watto (Mos Espa junk dealer)	5.00	10.00
51	Lott Dod (Neimoidian Senator)		
52	Tusken Raider (w/massiff)	6.00	12.00
54	Rebel Trooper (Tantive IV defender)		
55	Imperial Officer		
56	Eeth Koth (Jedi Master)		
57	Teebo		

2002-04 Star Wars Saga Collection 2 (2003)

4	Padme Amidala (droid factory chase)		
5	SP-4 & JN-66 (research droids)	6.00	12.00
6	Tusken Raider (Tatooine camp ambush)	5.00	10.00
10	Lama Su (w/clone child)	10.00	20.00
11	Aayla Secura (Battle of Geonosis)	8.00	15.00
12	Barriss Offee (Luminara Unduli's Padawan)	6.00	12.00
15	Yoda and Chian (Padawan lightsaber training)		
16	Ashla & Jempa (Jedi Padawans)	8.00	15.00
22	Padme Amidala (secret ceremony)	10.00	20.00
23	Wat Tambor (Geonosis war room)	10.00	20.00
24	Coleman Trebor (Battle of Geonosis)		
25	Darth Maul (Theed hangar duel)	8.00	15.00
26	Princess Leia Organa (Imperial captive)	5.00	10.00
27	Han Solo (fight to Alderaan)		
28	WA-7 (Dexter's diner)	8.00	15.00
29	Lt. Dannl Faytonni (Coruscant Outlander club)		
30	The Emperor (throne room)		
31	Luke Skywalker (Tatooine encounter)	5.00	10.00
32	Darth Vader (Death Star clash)	8.00	15.00
33	Bail Organa (Alderaan Senator)	6.00	12.00
34	Stormtrooper (McQuarrie concept)	8.00	15.00
35	Imperial Dignitary Janus Greejatus (Death Star procession)		
36	Padme Amidala (Lars' homestead)	15.00	30.00
37	Achk Med-Beq (Coruscant Outlander club)	6.00	12.00
38	Ayy Vida (Outlander nightclub patron)	10.00	20.00
39	Obi-Wan Kenobi (Outlander nightclub patron)	6.00	12.00
40	Elan Sleazebaggano (Outlander nightclub encounter)	8.00	15.00
41	Imperial Dignitary Kren Blista-Vanee (Death Star procession)		

2002-04 Star Wars Saga Deluxe

1	Anakin Skywalker (w/Force flipping attack)	4.00	8.00
2	Anakin Skywalker (w/lightsaber slashing action)	6.00	12.00
3	C-3PO (w/droid factory assembly line)	4.00	8.00
4	Clone Trooper (w/speeder bike)	6.00	12.00
5	Darth Tyranus (w/Force flipping attack)	4.00	8.00
6	Flying Geonosian (w/sonic blaster and attack pod)	4.00	8.00
7	Jango Fett (Kamino showdown)	4.00	8.00
8	Jango Fett (w/electronic backpack and snap-on armor)	4.00	8.00
9	Mace Windu (w/blast apart droid tan)	4.00	8.00
10	Mace Windu (w/blast apart droid brown)	4.00	8.00
11	Nexu (w/snapping jaw and attack roar)	12.00	25.00
12	Obi-Wan Kenobi (Kamino showdown)	4.00	8.00
13	Obi-Wan Kenobi (w/Force flipping attack)	4.00	8.00
14	Spider Droid (w/rotating turret and firing cannon)	4.00	8.00
15	Super Battle Droid Builder (w/droid factory assembly mold)	4.00	8.00
16	Yoda (w/Force powers)	10.00	20.00

2002-04 Star Wars Saga Exclusives

1	Boba Fett (silver)	15.00	30.00
	(2003 Convention Exclusive)		
2	C-3PO (Santa) & R2-D2 (reindeer)	12.00	25.00
	(2002 Holiday Edition Exclusive)		
3	Clone Trooper (silver)	6.00	12.00
	(2003 Toys R Us Exclusive)		
4	Clone Trooper/Super Battle Droid	12.00	25.00
	(2004 Jedi Con Exclusive)		
5	Commander Jorg Sacul	20.00	40.00
	(2002 Celebration 2 Exclusive)		
6	Darth Vader (silver)	30.00	60.00
	(2002 New York Toy Fair Exclusive)		
7	R2-D2 (silver)	15.00	30.00
	(2002 Toys R Us Silver Anniversary Exclusive)		
8	Sandtrooper (silver)		
	(2004 SDCC Exclusive)		
9	Yoda (Santa)		
	(2003 Holiday Edition Exclusive)		

2002-04 Star Wars Saga Mos Eisley Cantina Bar

1	Dr. Evezan		
2	Greedo	8.00	15.00
3	Kitik Keed'kak		
4	Momaw Nadon		
5	Ponda Baba		
6	Wuher		

2002-04 Star Wars Saga Multipacks

1 Endor Soldiers (w/four soldiers paint may vary slightly)		
2 Imperial Forces (Darth Vader Stormtrooper/AT-ST Driver/R4-I9)	15.00	30.00
3 Jedi Warriors (Obi-Wan Kenobi Saesee Tiin/Plo Koon/Fi-Ek Sirch)	10.00	20.00
4 Light Saber Action Pack (Anakin Skywalker/Count Dooku/Yoda)		
5 Rebel Troopers Builder Set		
6 Sandtroopers Builder Set (orange, black, gray, & white shoulder pad)		
7 Skirmish at Karkoon (Han Solo/Klaatu/Nikto/Barada)	10.00	20.00
8 Stormtroopers Builder Set		
9 The Battle of Hoth (Luke Leia/Chewbacca/R3-A2/Tauntaun)	20.00	40.00
10 Ultimate Bounty (Boba Fett Bossk/IG-88/Aurra Sing w/swoop vehicle)	12.00	25.00
11 Value 4-Pack (Zam Wesell Battle Droid/Kit Fisto/Super Battle Droid)		

2002-04 Star Wars Saga Playsets

1 Geonosian Battle Arena	60.00	120.00

2002-04 Star Wars Saga Playskool

1 Arena Adventure	12.00	25.00
2 Duel with Darth Maul	25.00	50.00
3 Fast through the Forest	8.00	15.00
4 Millennium Falcon Adventure	20.00	40.00
5 The Stompin' Wampa		
6 X-Wing Adventure	25.00	50.00

2002-04 Star Wars Saga Re-Issues

1 Anakin Skywalker (hangar duel)	8.00	15.00
2002 Star Wars Saga Collection 1		
2 C-3PO (Death Star escape)		
1997-98 Star Wars Power of the Force Green		
3 Chewbacca (escape from Hoth)		
2000-01 Star Wars Power of the Jedi		
4 Darth Maul (Theed hangar duel)		
2003 Star Wars Saga Collection 2		
5 Darth Vader (Death Star clash)		
2003 Star Wars Saga Collection 2		

6 Han Solo (flight to Alderaan)		
2003 Star Wars Saga Collection 2		
7 Luke Skywalker (Tatooine encounter)		
2003 Star Wars Saga Collection 2		
8 Obi-Wan Kenobi (Coruscant chase)		
2002 Star Wars Saga Collection 1		
9 Princess Leia Organa (Death Star captive)	10.00	20.00
2003 Star Wars Saga Collection 2		
10 R2-D2 (Tatooine mission)		
2000-01 Star Wars Power of the Jedi		
11 Stormtrooper (Death Star chase)	8.00	15.00
1998-99 Star Wars Power of the Force		
12 Yoda (Battle of Geonosis)		
2002 Star Wars Saga Collection 1		

2002-04 Star Wars Saga Ultra With Accessories

1 C-3PO with Escape Pod	12.00	25.00
2 Ewok (w/attack glider)		
3 General Rieekan (w/Hoth tactical screen)	20.00	40.00
4 Jabba's Palace Court Denizens		
5 Jabba the Hutt (w/pipe stand)		
6 Jango Fett (Kamino confrontation)		
7 Obi-Wan Kenobi (Kamino confrontation)	15.00	30.00
8 Wampa (w/Hoth cave)		

2002-04 Star Wars Saga Vehicles

1 Anakin Skywalker's Speeder	10.00	20.00
2 Anakin Skywalker's Swoop Bike (w/Anakin)	20.00	40.00
3 A-Wing Fighter	20.00	40.00
4 Darth Tyranus's Speeder Bike (w/Darth Tyranus)	15.00	30.00
5 Imperial Dogfight TIE Fighter	20.00	40.00
6 Imperial Shuttle	120.00	200.00
7 Jango Fett's Slave 1	25.00	50.00
8 Jedi Starfighter	15.00	30.00
9 Jedi Starfighter (w/Obi-Wan Kenobi)	20.00	40.00
10 Landspeeder (w/Luke Skywalker)	20.00	40.00
11 Luke Skywalker's X-Wing Fighter (w/R2-D2)	60.00	120.00
12 Red Leader's X-Wing Fighter (w/Red Leader)	30.00	60.00
13 Republic Gunship	75.00	150.00
14 TIE Bomber	30.00	75.00
15 Zam Wesell's Speeder	10.00	20.00

2002-04 Star Wars Saga Wave 1 Hoth

1 Hoth Trooper (Hoth evacuation)	8.00	15.00
2 R-3PM (Hoth evacuation)		
3 Luke Skywalker (Hoth attack)		

2002-04 Star Wars Saga Wave 2 Tatooine

4 Luke Skywalker (Jabba's Palace)	6.00	12.00
5 R2-D2 (Jabba's sail barge)	8.00	15.00
6 R1-G4 (Tatooine transaction)		

2002-04 Star Wars Saga Wave 3 Jabba's Palace

7 Lando Calrissian (Jabba's sail barge)	5.00	10.00
8 Rappertunie (Jabba's Palace)		
9 J'Quille (Jabba's sail barge)	12.00	25.00
10 Tanus Spijek		
11 TIE Fighter Pildof		

2002-04 Star Wars Saga Wave 4 Battle of Yavin

12 General Jan Dodonna (Battle of Yavin)		
13 Dutch Vander Gold Leader (Battle of Yavin)		
14 TIE Fighter Pilot (Battle of Yavin)	6.00	12.00
15 Captain Antilles		

2002-04 Star Wars Saga Wave 5 Star Destroyer

16 Admiral Ozzel		
17 Dengar (executor meeting)		
18 Bossk (executor meeting)		

2002-04 Star Wars Saga Wave 6 Battle of Endor

19 Han Solo (Endor strike)		
20 General Madine (Imperial shuttle capture)		
21 Lando Calrissian (Death Star attack)	6.00	12.00

2006-07 Star Wars The Saga Collection

SAGA1 Princess Leia boushh	8.00	15.00
SAGA2 Han Solo carbonite	4.00	8.00
SAGA3 Bib Fortuna	4.00	8.00
SAGA4 Brada skiff	4.00	8.00
SAGA5 Chewbacca/ boushh prisoner	4.00	8.00
SAGA6 Boba Fett	4.00	8.00
SAGA7 General Veers	5.00	10.00
SAGA8 Major Bren Derlin	5.00	10.00
SAGA9 AT-AT Driver	4.00	8.00
SAGA10 R2-D2	4.00	8.00
SAGA11 Snowtrooper	4.00	8.00
SAGA12 General Rieeken	4.00	8.00
SAGA13 Darth Vader	5.00	10.00
SAGA14 Power Droid	4.00	8.00
SAGA15 Sora Bulq	4.00	8.00
SAGA16 Sun Fac	4.00	8.00
SAGA17 C-3PO with/ battle droid head/ droid head on	4.00	8.00
SAGA18 Poggle the Lesser	4.00	8.00
SAGA19 Yoda	4.00	8.00
SAGA20 Jango Fett	4.00	8.00
SAGA21 Scorch	5.00	10.00
SAGA22 Firespeeder Pilot	5.00	10.00
SAGA23 Lushros Dofine	5.00	10.00
SAGA24 Clone Commander Cody/ orange highlights	4.00	8.00
SAGA25 Anakin Skywalker	4.00	8.00
SAGA26 Utapau Clone Trooper	4.00	8.00
SAGA27 Holographic Ki-Adi-Mundi	5.00	10.00
SAGA28 Obi-Wan Kenobi beard	4.00	8.00
SAGA29 Faul Maudama	5.00	10.00
SAGA30 General Grievous	5.00	10.00
SAGA31 Momaw Nadon/ clear cup	5.00	10.00
SAGA32 R5-D4	4.00	8.00
SAGA33 Hem Dazon blue cup	4.00	8.00
SAGA34 Garindan	4.00	8.00
SAGA35 Han Solo	4.00	8.00
SAGA36 Luke Skywalker	4.00	8.00
SAGA37 Sandtrooper	4.00	8.00
SAGA38 Darth Vader bespin/ saber fight	4.00	8.00

SAGA39	Chief Chirpa	4.00	8.00
SAGA40	Moff Jerjerrod	5.00	10.00
SAGA41	Death Star Gunner	4.00	8.00
SAGA42	C-3PO with/ ewok throne/ unpainted knees	6.00	12.00
SAGA43	Emperor Palpatine	4.00	8.00
SAGA44	Luke Skywalker	4.00	8.00
SAGA45	Darth Vader/ shocked by emperor	4.00	8.00
SAGA46	Rebel Trooper/ endor black	4.00	8.00
SAGA47	Obi-Wan Kenobi/ no beard	4.00	8.00
SAGA48	Holographic Darth Maul	4.00	8.00
SAGA49	Rep Been	4.00	8.00
SAGA50	Naboo Soldier yellow	4.00	8.00
SAGA51	Dud Bolt & Mars Guo	4.00	8.00
SAGA52	Gragra	4.00	8.00
SAGA53	Sith Training Darth Maul	4.00	8.00
SAGA54	Chewbacca with/ electronic C-3PO	4.00	8.00
SAGA55	Kit Fisto	4.00	8.00
SAGA56	Holographic Clone/ Commander Cody	5.00	10.00
SAGA57	Clone Trooper/ 442nd Siege Batallion/ green highlights	4.00	8.00
SAGA58	R5-J2	4.00	8.00
SAGA59	Clone Trooper/ Fifth Fleet Security blue stripes on head/ shoulder ches	4.00	8.00
SAGA60	Clone Trooper Sergeant	4.00	8.00
SAGA61	Super Battle Droid	4.00	8.00
SAGA62	Battle Droids/ green and yellow	4.00	8.00
SAGA63	Holographic/ Obi-Wan Kenobi	5.00	10.00
SAGA64	Commander Oppo/ blue highlights/ blue shoulder	4.00	8.00
SAGA65	Elite Corps Clone Commander	4.00	8.00
SAGA66	R4-K5 Darth Vader's/ Astromech Droid	4.00	8.00
SAGA67	Padme Amidala	4.00	8.00
SAGA68	Combat Engineer/ Clone Trooper/ brown highlights	4.00	8.00
SAGA69	Yarael Poof	4.00	8.00
SAGA70	Aurra Sing	4.00	8.00
SAGA71	Kitik Keed'Kak	4.00	8.00
SAGA72	Nabrun Leids & Kabe	4.00	8.00
SAGA73	Labria	4.00	8.00
SAGA74	R4-M6 Mace Windu's/ Astromech Droid	4.00	8.00
SAGA17a	C-3PO with/ battle drod head/ C-3PO head on	4.00	8.00
SAGA31a	Momaw Nadon/ blue cup	5.00	10.00
SAGA33a	Hem Dazon white cup	4.00	8.00
SAGA42a	C-3PO with/ ewok throne/ painted knees	6.00	12.00
SAGA46a	Rebel Trooper/ endor white	4.00	8.00

2006-07 Star Wars The Saga Collection 501st Stormtrooper Exclusive

10 Stormtrooper with/ vader fist banner/ Comicon exclusive

2006-07 Star Wars The Saga Collection Battle Packs

1 Battle Above the Sarlac (Boba Fett
Lando Calrissian skiff/Han Solo carbonite)
2 Jedi Vs Darth Sidious (Darth Sidious
Kit Fisto/Mace Windu/Saesee Tiin)
3 Sith Lord Attack (Obi-Wan Kenobi
Qui-Gon Jinn/Darth Maul/Battle Droid tan)

2006-07 Star Wars The Saga Collection Battle Packs Exclusives

1 Mace Windu's Attack Batallion (Mace Windu
Clone Trooper purple/ with sk)
2 Skirmish in the Senate (Emperor Palpatine

Yoda/Clone Trooper red/Clone)
3 The Hunt for Grievous (Clone Trooper red
Clone Trooper blue/Clone Trooper

2006-07 Star Wars The Saga Collection Commemorative DVD Collection

1 Luke Skywalker/Darth Vader/Obi-Wan Kenobi
2 Han Solo/Chewbacca/Stormtrooper
3 Luke skywalker#Emperor Palpatine/R2-D2/C-3PO

2006-07 Star Wars The Saga Collection Episode III Greatest Battles Collection

1	501st Legion Trooper/ blue with orange feet	4.00	8.00
2	AT-TE Tank Gunner/ gold helmet highlights	4.00	8.00
3	C-3PO	4.00	8.00
4	Count Dooku	4.00	8.00
5	Royal Guard blue	4.00	8.00
6	Padme	4.00	8.00
7	R4-G9	4.00	8.00
8	Kit Fisto	4.00	8.00
9	Wookie Warrior	4.00	8.00
10	R2-D2	4.00	8.00
11	Shock Trooper red	4.00	8.00
12	Obi-Wan Kenobi/ flight helmet	4.00	8.00
13	Emperor Palpatine	4.00	8.00
14a	Clone Commander geen/ with skirt sash	4.00	8.00
14b	Clone Commander red/ with skirt sash	4.00	8.00

2006-07 Star Wars The Saga Collection Episode III Heroes & Villains Collection

1	Darth Vader	4.00	8.00
2	Anakin Skywalker	4.00	8.00
3	Yoda	4.00	8.00
4	Commander Bacara	4.00	8.00
5	Clone Trooper	4.00	8.00
6	Clone Pilot black	4.00	8.00
7	Chewbacca	4.00	8.00
8	Obi-Wan Kenobi	4.00	8.00
9	General Grievous cape	4.00	8.00
10	Mace Windu	4.00	8.00
11	R2-D2	4.00	8.00
12	Destroyer Droid	4.00	8.00
9a	General Grievous/ no cape	4.00	8.00

2006-07 Star Wars The Saga Collection Exclusives

1	501st Stormtrooper	10.00	20.00
	(2006 SDCC Exclusive)		
2	Clone Trooper (Saleucami)		
	(2006 Toys R Us French Exclusive)		
3	Darth Vader		
	(2006 UK Woolworth's Exclusive)		
4	Demise of General Grievous	6.00	12.00
	(2006 Target Exclusive)		
5	Early Bird Certificate Package		
	(2005 Walmart Exclusive)		
6	Early Bird Kit (Luke Skywalker, Princess Leia, Chewbacca, and R2-D2)	30.00	75.00
	(2005 Mailaway Exclusive)		
7	George Lucas Stormtrooper	20.00	40.00
	(2006 Mailaway Exclusive)		
8	Separation of the Twins Leia Organa (w/Bail Organa)	15.00	30.00
	(2005 Walmart Exclusive)		
9	Separation of the Twins Luke Skywalker (w/Obi-Wan Kenobi)	12.00	25.00
	(2005 Walmart Exclusive)		
10	Shadow Stormtrooper	12.00	25.00
	(2006 Starwarsshop.com Exclusive)		

2006-07 Star Wars The Saga Collection International

SAGA1 Princess Leia boushh
SAGA2 Han Solo carbonite
SAGA3 Bib Fortuna
SAGA4 Brada skiff
SAGA5 Chewbacca/ boushh prisoner
SAGA6 Boba Fett

2006-07 Star Wars The Saga Collection Multipacks

1 Droid Pack I/R4-A22/R2-C4/R3-T2/R2-Q2/R3-T6
(2006 Entertainment Earth Exclusive)
2 Droid Pack II/R4-E1/R2-X2/R2-M5/R2-A6/R3-Y2
(2006 Entertainment Earth Exclusive)
3 Episode III Gift Pack/Darth Vader
General Grievous/Obi-Wan Kenobi/R2-D2
  (2006 UK Woolworth's Exclusive)
4 Jedi Knights/Anakin Skywalker
Mace Windu/Obi-Wan Kenobi
  (2005 UK Argos Exclusive)
5 Lucas Collector's Set/Zett Jukassa
Baron Papanoida/Terr Taneel/Chi Eekway
  (2006 Starwarsshop.com Exclusive)
6 Revenge of the Sith Collector's Set
(UK Exclusive)

2006-07 Star Wars The Saga Collection Previews Exclusives

1	Death Star Briefing (Darth Vader	60.00	120.00
	Grand Moff Tarkin/Admiral Motti/General)		
2	The Hunt For the Millenium Falcon	30.00	60.00
	(Darth Vader/Dengar/IG-88/Boba Fett)		
3	Republic Commando Delta Squad		
	(Delta Three-Eight orange/Scoarch blue)		

2006-07 Star Wars The Saga Collection Ultimate Galactic Hunt

1 AT-AT Driver/ empire strikes back stand	6.00	12.00
2 Anakin Skywalker/ revenge of the sith stand	4.00	8.00
3 Boba Fett/ return of the jedi stand	30.00	60.00
4 Commander Cody/ regenge of the sith stand	4.00	8.00
5 Darth Vader/ empire strikes back stand	4.00	8.00
6 General Grievous/ revenge of the sith stand	6.00	12.00
7 Han Solo carbonite/ return of the jedi stand	6.00	12.00
8 Obi-Wan Kenobi/ revenge of the sith stand	4.00	8.00
9 Scorch/ republic commando/ star wars stand	8.00	15.00
10 Snowtrooper/ empire strikes back stand	8.00	15.00

2006-07 Star Wars The Saga Collection Ultimate Galactic Hunt Vehicles

10 Republic Gunship/ Toys R Us exclusive

2006-07 Star Wars The Saga Collection Ultimate Galactic Hunt Vintage

1 Bossk/ bounty hunter ESB		
2 IG-88 (bounty hunter)		
3 Han Solo (Hoth)		
4 Luke Skywalker (Bespin)	10.00	20.00
5 Princess Leia Organa (Endor combat poncho)	10.00	20.00
6 Imperial Stormtrooper (Hoth)		

2006-07 Star Wars The Saga Collection Vehicles

1 Anakin's Jedi Starfighter	20.00	40.00
2 Darth Vader's TIE/ Advanced X1 Starfighter		
3 Droid Tri-Fighter		
4 General Grievous's/ Wheel Bike		
5 Obi-Wan's/ Jedi Starfighter		
6 Mace Windu's/ Jedi Starfighter		

2006-07 Star Wars The Saga Collection Vehicles Exclusives

1 Luke Skywalker's X-Wing (w/Luke Skywalker Dagobah)
(Toys R Us Exclusive)
2 TIE Fighter (w/Tie Fighter Pilot)
(Toys R Us Exclusive)
3 Imperial Shuttle (Royal Guard red/Darth Vader)
(Target Exclusive)

| 4 Kit Fisto's Jedi Starfighter | 20.00 | 40.00 |

(Target Exclusive)
5 Rogue Two Snowspeeder (w/Zev Senesca)

2006-07 Star Wars The Saga Collection Vintage

1 Biker Scout ROTJ	8.00	15.00
2 Greedo SW	6.00	12.00
3 Han Solo cape ROTJ	6.00	12.00
4 Luke Skywalker x-wing SW	10.00	20.00
5 Sand People SW	6.00	12.00

2010 Star Wars Saga Legends

SL1 Bossk	12.00	25.00
SL2 IG-88	10.00	20.00
SL3 Zuckuss	8.00	15.00
SL4 Greedo	8.00	15.00
SL5 Jango Fett	6.00	12.00
SL6a Darth Vader	6.00	12.00
SL6b Darth Vader (unmasked)	8.00	15.00
SL7 Princess Leia Boushh	10.00	20.00
SL8 Darth Maul	6.00	12.00
SL9 General Grievous	10.00	20.00
SL10 Clone Trooper	8.00	15.00
SL11 Darth Vader (Anakin Skywalker)	8.00	15.00
SL12 Obi-Wan Kenobi	6.00	12.00
SL13 Yoda	8.00	15.00
SL14 R2-D2	8.00	15.00
SL15 Shocktrooper	15.00	30.00
SL16 Clone Trooper (Revenge of the Sith)	8.00	15.00
SL17 C-3PO	8.00	15.00
SL18 Chewbacca	8.00	15.00
SL19 501st Legion Trooper	12.00	25.00
SL20 Battle Droid 2-Pack	6.00	12.00
SL21 Luke Skywalker	8.00	15.00
SL22 Han Solo (Hoth)	8.00	15.00
SL23 Snowtrooper	10.00	20.00

2013 Star Wars Saga Legends

SL1 Mace Windu	6.00	12.00
SL2 Clone Trooper		
SL3 Anakin Skywalker	6.00	12.00
SL4 Obi-Wan Kenobi (ROTS)	8.00	15.00

SL5 Super Battle Droid	8.00	15.00
SL6 R4-P17		
SL7 Yoda		
SL8 Shock Trooper		
SL9 Boba Fett		
SL10 Captain Rex		
SL11 Stormtrooper		
SL12 Clone Commander Cody		
SL13 Obi-Wan Kenobi (Clone Wars)		
SL14 Luke Skywalker		
SL15 Darth Maul		
SL16 Snowtrooper		

2013 Star Wars Saga Legends Mission Series

1 Anakin/501st Legion Trooper (Coruscant)
2 Battle Droid/212th Battalion Clone Trooper (Utapau)
3 Battle Droid/Jango Fett (Geonosis)
4 Darth Sidious/Yoda (Senate Duel)
5 Darth Vader/Seeker Droid (Star Destroyer)
6 Han Solo/Chewbacca (Death Star)
7 Luke Skywalker/Darth Vader (Bespin)
8 Obi-Wan Kenobi/Darth Maul (Mandalore)
9 Obi-Wan Kenobi/General Grievous (Utapau)
10 R2-D2/C-3PO (Tantive IV)

2013 Star Wars Saga Legends Multi-Packs

1 Battle of Geonosis I (Jedi Knights)
(2013 Toys R Us Exclusive)
2 Battle of Geonosis II (Jedi Knights)
(2013 Toys R Us Exclusive)
3 The Evolution of Darth Vader
4 The Rise of Darth Vader
(2013 Target Exclusive)

2013 Star Wars Saga Legends Vehicles

1 Obi-Wan's Jedi Starfighter (red)
2 Obi-Wan's Jedi Starfighter (blue)

1996 Star Wars Shadows of the Empire

1 Boba Fett vs IG-88/ with comic book	12.00	25.00
2 Chewbacca/ bounty hunter disguise	8.00	15.00
3 Darth Vader vs Prince Xizor	12.00	25.00
with comic book		
4 Dash Rendar	10.00	20.00

5 Luke Skywalker/ imperial guard	10.00	20.00
6 Prince Xizor	6.00	12.00
7 Princess Leia/ boushh disguise	10.00	20.00

1996 Star Wars Shadows of the Empire (loose)

1 Boba Fett	6.00	12.00
2 Chewbacca bounty/ hunter disguise	5.00	10.00
3 Darth Vader	6.00	12.00
4 Dash Rendar	4.00	8.00
5 Endor Trooper/ found in Vehicles	4.00	8.00
6 IG-88	5.00	10.00
7 Luke Skywalker/ imperial guard	6.00	12.00
8 Prince Xizor	5.00	10.00
9 Princess Leia/ boushh disguise	8.00	15.00
10 Swoop Trooper/ found in Vehicles	4.00	8.00

1996 Star Wars Shadows of the Empire European

1 Chewbacca bounty/ hunter disguise	12.50	25.00
2 Dash Rendar	10.00	20.00
3 Luke Skywalker/ imperial guard	15.00	30.00
4 Princess Leia/ boushh disguise	10.00	20.00
5 Prince Xizor	15.00	30.00

1996 Star Wars Shadows of the Empire Vehicles

1 Boba Fett's Slave I	40.00	80.00
2 Dash Rendar's Outrider	25.00	50.00
3 Swoop with Swoop Trooper	12.00	25.00
4 Speeder Bike/ with Endor Trooper	12.00	25.00

1996 Star Wars Shadows of the Empire Vehicles (loose)

1 Boba Fett's Slave I	25.00	50.00
2 Dash Rendar's Outrider	12.50	25.00
3 Swoop	10.00	20.00
4 Speeder Bike	7.50	15.00

2010-12 Star Wars Sideshow

1 Commander Bacara Base Art	100.00	200.00
2 Tusken Raider		
3 Tusken Raider (Gaffi weapon)	120.00	250.00

2010-12 Star Wars Sideshow 12-Inch

1 Commander Praji	100.00	200.00
2 Grand Admiral Thrawn		
3 Grand Admiral Thrawn (command chair)/750*	800.00	1200.00
4 General Obi-Wan Kenobi Clone Wars	60.00	120.00
5 General Obi-Wan Kenobi Clone Wars (w/Captain Rex hologram)/1500*75.00		150.00

2010-12 Star Wars Sideshow 12-Inch Environments

1 Han Solo in Carbonite/2000*	250.00	400.00
2 Imperial Throne	175.00	350.00
3 Jabba's Throne	500.00	700.00

2010-12 Star Wars Sideshow Action Heroes

1 C-3PO	200.00	350.00
2 R2-D2	100.00	200.00
3 TC-14		

2010-12 Star Wars Sideshow Heroes of the Rebellion

1 Anakin Skywalker Clone Wars		
2 Anakin Skywalker Clone Wars w/Rotta the Hutt)/750*		
3 Han Solo & Luke Skywalker Stormtroopers (SDCC Exclusive)	120.00	250.00
4 Han Solo Bespin	60.00	120.00
5 Han Solo Bespin (w/Mynock)/2000*	50.00	100.00
6 Han Solo Smuggler	75.00	150.00
7 Han Solo Smuggler Cantina Blaster Pistol/1977*		
8 Lando Calrissian		
9 Lando Calrissian (w/Bespin communicator)/750*		
10 Luke Skywalker Episode IV		
11 Luke Skywalker Episode IV (hat and googles)/1977*		
12 Luke Skywalker Rebel Commander	200.00	400.00
13 Luke Skywalker Rebel Commander (missing hand)/1980*	120.00	250.00
14 Luke Skywalker Rebel Hero/600* (30th Anniversary Exclusive)	30.00	75.00
15 Padme Amidala Ilum Mission	30.00	75.00
16 Princess Leia Boushh	75.00	120.00
17 Princess Leia Boushh (Ubese blaster pistol)/2500*	60.00	120.00
18 Princess Leia	50.00	100.00
19 Princess Leia (wrist binders)/1977*		

2010-12 Star Wars Sideshow Jedi Order

1 Aayla Secura (SDCC Exclusive)	120.00	200.00
2 Anakin Skywalker	50.00	100.00
3 Anakin Skywalker (w/holographic Sidious)/1750*	60.00	120.00
4 Ki-Adi-Mundi	50.00	100.00
5 Kit Fisto	50.00	100.00
6 Kit Fisto (w/Battle Droid head)/1250*	60.00	120.00
7 Luke Skywalker Jedi Knight	50.00	100.00
8 Luke Skywalker Jedi Knight (blaster)/1250*	60.00	120.00
9 Mace Windu	50.00	100.00
10 Mace Windu (w/Jango Fett's helmet)/1750*	60.00	120.00
11 Obi-Wan Kenobi	50.00	100.00
12 Obi-Wan Kenobi (blaster)/1750*	60.00	120.00
13 Obi-Wan Kenobi Episode IV	50.00	100.00
14 Obi-Wan Kenobi Episode IV (holographic Leia)/1977*	75.00	150.00
15 Obi-Wan Kenobi Jedi Knight	30.00	75.00
16 Obi-Wan Kenobi Jedi Knight (Kamino dart)/1000*	50.00	100.00
17 Plo Koon		
18 Plo Koon (twin-bladed lightsaber gauntlet)/1500*	60.00	120.00
19 Qui-Gon Jinn	30.00	75.00
20 Qui-Gon Jinn (poncho)/2000*	50.00	100.00

2010-12 Star Wars Sideshow Legendary 40-Inch

1 Darth Maul	

2010-12 Star Wars Sideshow Lords of the Sith

1 Asajj Ventress	120.00	200.00
2 Asajj Ventress (eye paint)/2000*	75.00	150.00
3 Darth Maul	75.00	150.00
4 Darth Maul (damage saber hilt)/LE	500.00	800.00
5 Darth Vader Episode IV		
6 Darth Vader Episode IV (Force choke)/1977*		
7 Darth Vader Sith Apprentice (SDCC Exclusive)		
8 Emperor Palpatine		
9 Emperor Palpatine (angry head)/1000*		
10 Darth Sidious (hologram and mechno-chair)/5000* (SDCC Exclusive)	50.00	100.00
11 Palpatine and Sidious	120.00	250.00
12 Palpatine and Sidious (statue)/2000*	100.00	200.00

2010-12 Star Wars Sideshow Militaries

1 Admiral Piett	120.00	250.00
2 Captain Antilles	100.00	200.00
3 Clone Trooper Episode II Phase 1	100.00	200.00
4 Coruscant Clone Trooper		
5 Coruscant Clone Trooper (41st Elite Corps display base)	100.00	175.00
6 Endor Rebel Commando Sergeant	50.00	100.00
7 Endor Rebel Infantry	50.00	100.00
8 Endor Striker Force Bundle		
9 Imperial Shock Trooper	100.00	200.00
10 Imperial Shock Trooper (display base)/750*	100.00	200.00
11 Nik Sant Endor Rebel Commando Pathfinder	50.00	100.00
12 Rebel Fleet Trooper	120.00	200.00
13 Sandtrooper		
14 Sandtrooper (holding droid piece)/1000*		
15 Sandtrooper Corporal	100.00	175.00
16 Sandtrooper Squad Leader		
17 Stormtrooper	120.00	200.00
18 Stormtrooper (stand)/1500*	100.00	200.00
19 Stormtrooper Commander	100.00	200.00
20 Stormtrooper Commander (base)/1000*	150.00	300.00
21 Utapau Clone Trooper	75.00	150.00
22 Utapau Clone Trooper (Utapau base)/1500*	100.00	175.00

2010-12 Star Wars Sideshow Premium Format

1 Han Solo Carbonite	

2010-12 Star Wars Sideshow Scum and Villainy

1 Bib Fortuna	50.00	100.00
2 Bib Fortuna (ceremonial staff)/2500*	60.00	120.00
3 Boba Fett	150.00	300.00
4 Buboicullaar Creature Pack		
5 Buboicullaar Creature Pack (scratching womp rat)/1500*		
6 Jabba the Hutt	200.00	350.00
7 Jabba the Hutt (cup)	250.00	400.00
8 Salacious Crumb Creature Pack		
9 Salacious Crumb Creature Pack (w/dwarf varacty!)		

2013 Star Wars Titan Heroes 12-Inch

1 Anakin Skywalker
2 Clone Trooper
3 Darth Vader
4 Luke Skywalker
5 Obi-Wan Kenobi

2002-07 Star Wars Unleashed

1 Aayla Secura	15.00	30.00
2 Anakin Skywalker (2005)	15.00	30.00
3 Anakin Skywalker (rage)	12.00	25.00
4 Asajj Ventress	15.00	30.00
5 Aurra Sing	15.00	30.00
6 Boba Fett	25.00	50.00
7 Bossk	15.00	30.00
8 Chewbacca (2004)	10.00	20.00

9 Chewbacca (2006)	15.00	30.00
10 Clone Trooper (red)	15.00	30.00
11 Clone Trooper (white)	12.00	25.00
12 Count Dooku		
13 Darth Maul (fury)	15.00	30.00
14 Darth Sidious	25.00	50.00
15 Darth Tyranus (dissension)	6.00	12.00
16 Darth Vader (2005)	15.00	30.00
17 Darth Vader (power)	12.00	25.00
18 Darth Vader (redemption)	30.00	75.00
19 General Grievous	15.00	30.00
20 General Grievous	20.00	40.00
(2006 Target Exclusive)		
21 Han Solo	20.00	40.00
22 Han Solo Stormtrooper	15.00	30.00
23 IG-88	15.00	30.00
24 Jango and Boba Fett (intensity)	15.00	30.00
25 Luke Skywalker	20.00	40.00
26 Luke Skywalker (snowspeeder pilot)	15.00	30.00
27 Mace Windu (honor)	12.00	25.00
28 Obi-Wan Kenobi (2003)	15.00	30.00
29 Obi-Wan Kenobi (2005)	15.00	30.00
30 Padme Amidala (courage)	30.00	60.00
31 Palpatine vs. Yoda	20.00	40.00
32 Princess Leia	30.00	75.00
33 Shock Trooper	15.00	30.00
34 Stormtrooper	20.00	40.00
35 Tusken Raider	10.00	20.00
36 Yoda	15.00	30.00

2006-08 Star Wars Unleashed Battle Packs

1 Attack on Tantive IV Commanders		
2 Attack on Tantive IV Rebel Blockade Troopers		
3 Attack on Tantive IV Stormtrooper Boarding Party		
4 Battle of Felucia Aayla Secura's 327th Star Corps		
5 Battle of Geonosis The Clone Wars		
6 Battle of Hoth Evacuation at Echo Base		
7 Battle of Hoth Imperial Encounter		
8 Battle of Hoth Imperial Invasion		
9 Battle of Hoth Imperial Stormtroopers		
10 Battle of Hoth Rebel Alliance Troopers		
11 Battle of Hoth Snowspeeder Assault		
12 Battle of Hoth Snowtrooper Battalion		
13 Battle of Hoth Wampa Assault		
14 Battle of Kashyyyk Droid Invasion		
15 Battle of Kashyyyk and Felucia Heroes	30.00	60.00
16 Battle of Kashyyyk Wookiee Warriors	15.00	30.00
17 Battle of Kashyyyk Yoda's Elite Clone Troopers		
18 Battle of Utapau Battle Droids		
19 Battle of Utapau Clone Trooper Attack Battalion		
20 Battle of Utapau Commanders	12.00	25.00
21 Battle of Utapau Utapaun Warriors	10.00	20.00
22 Clone Wars 501st Legion		
23 Clone Wars ARC Troopers		
24 Clone Wars Battle of Mon Calamari		
25 Clone Wars Clone Pilots and AT-TE Gunners		
26 Clone Wars Clone Troopers		
27 Clone Wars Jedi Generals		
28 Clone Wars Jedi Heroes		
29 Clone Wars Jedi vs. Sith		
30 Clone Wars Theed Battle Heroes		
31 Clone Wars Vader's Bounty Hunters		
32 Death Star Encounters Imperial and Rebel Commanders		
33 Death Star Encounters Imperial and Rebel Pilots		
34 Death Star Encounters Imperial Troops		
35 Order 66 A New Empire		
36 Order 66 Jedi Masters		
37 Order 66 Shock Trooper Battalion		
38 Order 66 Vader's 501st Legion		
39 The Force Unleashed Empire		
40 The Force Unleashed Imperial Troopers		
41 The Force Unleashed Unleashed Warriors		
42 Trouble on Tatooine Cantina Encounter		

43 Trouble on Tatooine Jawas and Droids
44 Trouble on Tatooine Sandtrooper Search
45 Trouble on Tatooine The Streets of Mos Eisley
46 Trouble on Tatooine Tusken Raiders
47 Ultimate Battles 187th Legion Troopers
48 Ultimate Battles Battle Droid Factory
49 Ultimate Battles Mygeeto Clone Battalion

2007 Star Wars Unleashed Battle Packs Singles

1 Commander Bly
2 Darth Vader
3 Darth Vader (Anakin Skywalker)
4 Han Solo
5 Luke Skywalker
6 Mace Windu
7 Obi-Wan Kenobi
8 Shock Trooper
9 Stormtrooper

2005-07 Star Wars Unleashed Tubed Packs

1 Anakin Skywalker		
2 ARC Heavy Gunner		
3 Boba Fett		
(2006 Target Exclusive)		
4 Darth Vader	12.00	25.00
(2005 Best Buy Exclusive)		
5 Darth Vader		
(2006 KB Toys Exclusive)		
6 Darth Vader		
(2006 Walmart Exclusive)		
7 Luke Skywalker		
(2006 Walmart Exclusive)		
8 Obi-Wan Kenobi		
9 Shadow Stormtrooper	8.00	15.00

2010-13 Star Wars The Vintage Collection

VC1a Dengar (age warning on left back)
VC1b Dengar (age warning on bottom back)
VC2a Leia (Hoth)(age warning on left back)
VC2b Leia (Hoth)(age warning on bottom back)
VC3a Han Solo (Echo Base)(age warning on left back)
VC3b Han Solo (Echo Base)(age warning on bottom back)
VC3c Han Solo (Echo Base)(FOIL card)
VC4a Luke Skywalker (Bespin)(age warning on left back)
VC4b Luke Skywalker (Bespin)(age warning on bottom back)
VC4c Luke Skywalker (Bespin)(FOIL card)
VC5 AT-AT Commander (age warning on left back)
VC5 AT-AT Commander (age warning on bottom back)
VC6 See-Threepio (C-3PO)(age warning on left back)
VC6 See-Threepio (C-3PO)(age warning on bottom back)
VC7 Dack Ralter
VC8a Darth Vader (age warning on left back)
VC8b Darth Vader (age warning on bottom back)
VC8c Darth Vader (Boba Fett sticker/plus shipping and handling)
VC8d Darth Vader (barcode #54674 sticker)
VC8e Darth Vader (barcode #54674 printed)
VC8f Darth Vader (Revenge of the Jedi)
VC8g Darth Vader (Return of the Jedi)
VC8h Darth Vader (Wave 1 ESB figure back)
VC8i Darth Vader (FOIL card)
VC9aa Boba Fett (age warning on left back)
VC9ab Boba Fett (age warning on bottom back)
VC9ac Boba Fett (black gun barrel)
VC9ad Boba Fett (no warning on card back)
VC9ae Boba Fett (FOIL card)
VC9ba Boba Fett (Revenge of the Jedi)
VC9bb Boba Fett (Return of the Jedi)
VC10a 4-LOM (age warning on left back)
VC10b 4-LOM (age warning on bottom back)
VC11a (Twin-Pod) Cloud Car Pilot (age warning on left back)

VC11b (Twin-Pod) Cloud Car Pilot (age warning on bottom back)
VC12 Darth Sidious
VC12 Darth Sidious (FOIL card)
VC13a Anakin Skywalker (Darth Vader)
(Boba Fett mailway sticker front)
VC13b Anakin Skywalker (Darth Vader)
(Darth Vader title on front and back)
VC13c Anakin Skywalker (Darth Vader)
(Boba Fett sticker/shipping and handling)
VC13d Anakin Skywalker (Darth Vader)(barcode #54885)
VC13e Anakin Skywalker (Darth Vader)(FOIL card)
VC14a Sandtrooper (dim photo front)
VC14b Sandtrooper (bright photo front)
VC14c Sandtrooper (Boba Fett sticker/shipping and handling)
VC14d Sandtrooper (barcode #54573 sticker)
VC14e Sandtrooper (barcode #54573 printed)
VC14e Sandtrooper (FOIL card)
VC15a Clone Trooper (dim photo front)
VC15b Clone Trooper (bright photo front)
VC15c Clone Trooper (Boba Fett sticker/shipping and handling)
VC15d Clone Trooper (barcode #54888 sticker)
VC15e Clone Trooper (barcode #54888 printed)
VC15f Clone Trooper (FOIL card)
VC16a Obi-Wan Kenobi
VC16b Obi-Wan Kenobi (FOIL card)
VC17a General Grievous (Boba Fett sticker on front)
VC17b General Grievous (barcode #54572 sticker)
VC17c General Grievous (barcode #54572 printed)
VC17d General Grievous (FOIL card)
VC18a MagnaGuard
VC18b MagnaGuard (FOIL card)
VC19a Clone Commander Cody (dim photo front)
VC19b Clone Commander Cody (bright photo front)
VC19c Clone Commander Cody (FOIL card)
VC20a Yoda
VC20b Yoda (Boba Fett sticker front)
VC21a Gamorrean Guard (1st Boba Fett rocket sticker)
VC21b Gamorrean Guard (2nd Boba Fett rocket sticker)
VC21c Gamorrean Guard (barcode #54898 sticker)
VC21d Gamorrean Guard (barcode #54898 printed)
VC21e Gamorrean Guard (Darth Maul sticker front)
VC22a Admiral Ackbar (1st Boba Fett rocket sticker)
VC22b Admiral Ackbar (2nd Boba Fett rocket sticker)
VC22c Admiral Ackbar (barcode #54900)
VC22d Admiral Ackbar (barcode #52864)
VC23a Luke Skywalker (Jedi Knight Outfit / Endor Captive)
(1st Boba Fett rocket sticker)
VC23b Luke Skywalker (Jedi Knight Outfit / Endor Captive)
(2nd Boba Fett rocket sticker)
VC23c Luke Skywalker (Jedi Knight Outfit / Endor Captive)
VC23d Luke Skywalker (Jedi Knight Outfit / Endor Captive)
(barcode #54902)
VC23e Luke Skywalker (Jedi Knight Outfit / Endor Captive)
(portrait back)
VC23f Luke Skywalker (Jedi Knight Outfit / Endor Captive)
(no warning on back)
VC23g Luke Skywalker (Jedi Knight Outfit / Endor Captive)
(Revenge of the Jedi)
VC23h Luke Skywalker (Jedi Knight Outfit / Endor Captive)
(barcode #52867)
VC24a Wooof (Klaatu)(1st Boba Fett rocket sticker)
VC24b Wooof (Klaatu)(2nd Boba Fett rocket sticker)
VC24c Wooof (Klaatu)(barcode #54905)
VC24d Wooof (Klaatu)(figures left of backs)
VC25a R2-D2 (w/Pop-Up Lightsaber)
(1st Boba Fett rocket sticker)
VC25b R2-D2 (w/Pop-Up Lightsaber)
(2nd Boba Fett rocket sticker)
VC25c R2-D2 (w/Pop-Up Lightsaber)
(R2-D2 back)
VC25d R2-D2 (w/Pop-Up Lightsaber)
(Revenge of the Jedi)
VC25e R2-D2 (w/Pop-Up Lightsaber)
(no warning on back)

VC26aa Rebel Commando (1st Boba Fett rocket sticker)
VC26ab Rebel Commando (2nd Boba Fett rocket sticker)
VC26ac Rebel Commando (barcode #54907)
VC26ba Rebel Commando (Version II)(Return of the Jedi logo)
VC26bb Rebel Commando (Version II)(Revenge of the Jedi logo)
VC27a Wicket (1st Boba Fett rocket sticker)
VC27b Wicket (2nd Boba Fett rocket sticker)
VC27c Wicket (barcode #54908)
VC27d Wicket (barcode #52900)
VC27e Wicket (no warning on back)
VC28a Wedge Antilles (card image on back)
VC28b Wedge Antilles (film image on back)
VC28ca Wedge Antilles (light violet background)
VC28cb Wedge Antilles (dark blue to violet background)
VC29 Kit Fisto
VC30 Zam Wesell
VC31a Obi-Wan Kenobi (figures left of cardbacks)
VC31b Obi-Wan Kenobi (Prototype Boba Fett sticker)
VC32a Anakin Skywalker (Peasant Disguise)
VC32b Anakin Skywalker (Peasant Disguise)(Boba Fett sticker front)
VC33 Padme Amidala (Peasant Disguise)
VC34a Jango Fett (figures left of cardbacks)
VC34b Jango Fett (no warning on back)
VC34c Jango Fett (Prototype Boba Fett sticker)
VC35 Mace Windu
VC36a Senate Guard (close-up photo front)
VC36b Senate Guard (wide photo front)
VC37 Super Battle Droid
VC38 Clone Trooper (212th Battalion)
VC39 Luke Skywalker (Death Star Escape)
VC40 R5-D4
VC41a Stormtrooper (barcode #62162 sticker)
VC41b Stormtrooper (barcode #62162 printed)
VC41c Stormtrooper (warning sticker on front)
VC41d Stormtrooper (Revenge of the Jedi)
VC41e Stormtrooper (Return of the Jedi)
VC42 Han Solo (Yavin Ceremony)
VC43 Commander Gree (Greatest Hits)
VC44 Luke Skywalker (Dagobah Landing)
VC45 Clone Trooper (Phase I)
VC46 AT-RT Driver
VC47 General Lando Calrissian
VC48 Weequay (Skiff Master)
VC49 Fi-Ek Sirch (Jedi Knight)
VC50 Han Solo (Bespin Outfit)
VC51 Barriss Offee (Jedi Padawan)
VC52 Rebel Fleet Trooper
VC53 Bom Vimdin (Cantina Patron)
VC54 ARC Trooper Commander (Captain Fordo)
VC55 Logray (Ewok Medicine Man)
VC56a Kithaba (Skiff Guard)(black headband)
VC56b Kithaba (Skiff Guard)(red headband)
VC57a Dr. Cornelius Evazan (pink scar)
VC57b Dr. Cornelius Evazan (no pink scar)
VC58 Aayla Secura
VC59 Nom Anor
VC60 Clone Trooper (501st Legion)
VC61 Prototype Armour Boba Fett
(2011 Mailaway Exclusive)
VC62 Han Solo (In Trench Coat)
VC63 B-Wing Pilot (Keyan Farlander)
VC64 Princess Leia (Slave Outfit)
VC65 TIE Fighter Pilot
VC66 Salacious Crumb
(2011 SDCC Exclusive)
VC67 Mouse Droid
(2011 SDCC Exclusive)
VC68 Rebel Soldier (Echo Base Battle Gear)
VC69 Bastila Shan
VC70 Ponda Baba (Walrus Man)
VC71 Mawhonic
VC72 Naboo Pilot
VC73 Aurra Sing
VC74 Gungan Warrior

VC75 Qui-Gon Jinn
VC76 Obi-Wan Kenobi (Jedi Padawan)
VC77 Ratts Tyerell & Pit Droid
VC78 Battle Droid
VC79 Darth Sidious
VC80 Anakin Skywalker (Jedi Padawan)
VC81 Ben Quadinaros & Pit Droid
VC82 Daultay Dofine
VC83 Naboo Royal Guard
VC84 Queen Amidala (Post-Senate)
VC85 Quinlan Vos (Mos Espa)
VC86 Darth Maul
VC87 Luke Skywalker (Lightsaber Construction)
VC88 Princess Leia (Sandstorm Outfit)
VC89 Lando Calrissian (Sandstorm Outfit)
VC90 Colonel Cracken (Millennium Falcon Crew)
VC91 Rebel Pilot (Mon Calamari)
VC92 Anakin Skywalker (The Clone Wars)
VC93 Darth Vader (A New Hope)
VC94 Imperial Navy Commander
VC95 Luke Skywalker (Hoth Outfit)
VC96 Darth Malgus (The Old Republic)
VC97 Clone Pilot Davijaan (Oddball)
VC98 Grand Moff Tarkin
VC99 Nikto (Vintage)
VC100 Galen Marek (The Force Unleashed II)
VC101 Shae Vizsla
VC102 Ahsoka Tano (The Clone Wars)
VC103 Obi-Wan Kenobi (The Clone Wars)
VC104 Lumat
VC105 Emperor's Royal Guard
VC106 Nien Nunb
VC107 Weequay (Hunter)
VC108a Jar Jar Binks
VC108b Jar Jar Binks [Lost Line]
VC109a Clone Trooper Lieutenant
VC109b Clone Trooper Lieutenant [Lost Line]
VC110a Shock Trooper
VC110b Shock Trooper [Lost Line]
VC111a Leia Organa (Bespin)
VC111b Leia Organa (Bespin) [Lost Line]
VC112a Sandtrooper (with Patrol Droid)
VC112b Sandtrooper (with Patrol Droid) [Lost Line]
VC113 Republic Trooper
VC114 Orrimarko
VC115a Darth Vader (Emperor's Wrath)
VC115b Darth Vader (Emperor's Wrath) [Lost Line]

2010-13 Star Wars The Vintage Collection Creatures

1 Luke Skywalker's Tauntaun	30.00	60.00
(Target Exclusive)		

2010-13 Star Wars The Vintage Collection Exclusives

NNO Jocasta Nu	60.00	120.00
(Brian's Toys Exclusive)		
VCP3 Boba Fett (rocket-firing)	30.00	75.00
(Mailaway Exclusive)		
VCP12 4-LOM/Zuckuss 2-Pack	30.00	60.00
(TVC Convention Exclusive)		

2010-13 Star Wars The Vintage Collection Multi-packs

NNO Android 3-Pack	30.00	75.00
C-3PO, R2-D2, Chewbacca		
(Target Exclusive)		
NNO Death Star Scanning Crew	20.00	40.00
(K-Mart Exclusive)		
NNO Droid 3-Pack	12.00	25.00

R5-D4, Death Star Droid, Power Droid		
(Target Exclusive)		
NNO Endor AT-ST Crew 2-Pack	20.00	40.00
(K-Mart Exclusive)		
NNO Ewok Assault Catapult	25.00	50.00
(K-Mart Exclusive)		
NNO Ewok Scouts 2-Pack	15.00	30.00
(K-Mart Exclusive)		
NNO Hero 3-Pack	15.00	30.00
Luke Skywalker, Ben Kenobi, Han Solo		
(Target Exclusive)		
NNO Imperial 3-Pack	20.00	40.00
Imperial Commander, Dengar, AT-AT Driver		
(Target Exclusive)		
NNO Imperial Forces 3-Pack	20.00	40.00
Bossk, IG-88, Snowtrooper		
(Target Exclusive)		
NNO Imperial Scanning Crew	20.00	40.00
(K-Mart Exclusive)		
NNO Lost Line Carbon Freeze Chamber 7-Figure Set	120.00	200.00
(2012 SDCC Exclusive)		
NNO Rebel 3-Pack	20.00	40.00
2-1B, Leia (Hoth), Rebel Commander		
(Target Exclusive)		
NNO Revenge of the Jedi 14-Figure Death Star Set		
(2011 SDCC Exclusive)		
NNO Special Action Figure Set	15.00	30.00
Han Solo (Hoth), Hoth Rebel Trooper, FX-7		
(Target Exclusive)		
NNO Villain 3-Pack 2012	15.00	30.00
Sand People, Boba Fett, Snaggletooth		
(Target Exclusive)		
NNO Villain 3-Pack	20.00	40.00
Stormtrooper, Darth Vader, Death Star Trooper		
(Target Exclusive)		

2010-13 Star Wars The Vintage Collection Vehicles

NNO AT-AP	30.00	75.00
NNO B-Wing Starfighter	75.00	150.00
(K-Mart Exclusive)		
NNO Biggs' Red 3 X-Wing Fighter	100.00	175.00
(Toys R Us Exclusive)		
NNO Imperial AT-AT (ESB)	250.00	400.00
(Toys R Us Exclusive)		
NNO Imperial AT-AT (ROTJ)	200.00	350.00
(Toys R Us Exclusive)		
NNO Imperial TIE Fighter	50.00	100.00
(Target Exclusive)		
NNO Landspeeder	60.00	120.00
(Target Exclusive)		
NNO Millennium Falcon	300.00	500.00
(Toys R Us Exclusive)		
NNO Obi-Wan Kenobi's Jedi Starfighter	50.00	100.00
NNO Rebel Armored Snowspeeder	50.00	100.00
(Target Exclusive)		
NNO Republic Gunship	175.00	300.00
(Toys R Us Exclusive)		
NNO Scout Walker AT-ST	60.00	120.00
(K-Mart Exclusive)		
NNO Slave I	120.00	200.00
(Amazon Exclusive)		
NNO TIE Interceptor		
(Amazon Exclusive)		
NNO V-19 Torrent Starfighter	30.00	75.00
NNO Y-Wing Starfighter	60.00	120.00
(Toys R Us Exclusive)		

2015-17 Funko Pop Vinyl Conan O'Brien SDCC

6	Stormtrooper Conan COCO SDCC	60.00	120.00
10	Jedi Conan COCO SDCC	75.00	150.00

2011-17 Funko Pop Vinyl Freddy Funko

A9A	Clone Trooper/48* SDCC	250.00	500.00
A9B	Cl.Trooper Blue Hair/12* SDCC	1600.00	2100.00
28A	Boba Fett/196* SDCC	500.00	650.00
28B	B.Fett Red Hair/24* SDCC	2500.00	3200.00
46	Kylo Ren/400* FD	250.00	400.00
SE	Poe Dameron/200* FD	550.00	800.00

2011-17 Funko Pop Vinyl Star Wars

1A	Darth Vader	6.00	12.00
1B	Darth Vader MET HT	15.00	30.00
2A	Yoda	6.00	12.00
2B	Yoda Spirit WG ERR	8.00	15.00
2C	Yoda Spirit WG COR	8.00	15.00
2C	Yoda Spirit WG COR Sticker	8.00	15.00
3A	Han Solo V	100.00	175.00
3B	Han Solo VAULT	12.00	25.00
4	Princess Leia	6.00	12.00
5A	Stormtrooper	6.00	12.00
5B	Stormtrooper Red TAR		
6A	Chewbacca	6.00	12.00
6B	Chewbacca FLK/480* SDCC	750.00	1000.00
6C	Chewbacca Hoth GS	12.00	25.00
7A	Greedo V	150.00	300.00
7B	Greedo VAULT	6.00	12.00
8A	Boba Fett	6.00	12.00
8B	Boba Fett Prototype WG ERR	6.00	12.00
8D	Boba Fett Prototype WG COR Sticker	6.00	12.00
8C	Boba Fett Prototype WG COR	6.00	12.00
9	Darth Maul	6.00	12.00
10A	Obi-Wan Kenobi V	75.00	150.00
10B	Obi-Wan VAULT	12.00	25.00

11A	Luke Skywalker Jedi Knight V	25.00	50.00
11B	Jedi Luke Skywalker VAULT	15.00	30.00
12A	Gamorrean Guard V	60.00	120.00
12B	Gamorrean Guard VAULT	6.00	12.00
13A	C-3PO	6.00	12.00
13B	C-3PO Gold Chrome SDCC	15.00	30.00
13C	C-3PO Gold Chrome SCE	15.00	30.00
14	Shadow Trooper/480* SDCC	800.00	1300.00
15	H.Solo Stormtrooper/1000* ECCC	400.00	550.00
16	L.Skywalker Stormtrooper/1000* ECCC	300.00	500.00
17	Luke Skywalker X-Wing	6.00	12.00
18A	Slave Leia V	25.00	50.00
18B	Slave Leia VAULT	15.00	30.00
19A	Tusken Raider V	20.00	40.00
19B	Tusken Raider VAULT	6.00	12.00
20A	Jawa V	30.00	60.00
20B	Jawa VAULT	6.00	12.00
21A	Clone Trooper V	50.00	100.00
21B	Clone Trooper VAULT	6.00	12.00
22	Jabba the Hutt	6.00	12.00
23	Darth Maul HOLO/480* SDCC	1500.00	2000.00
24	Biggs Darklighter/480* SDCC	750.00	1000.00
25	501st Clone Trooper/480* SDCC	450.00	600.00
26A	Wicket the Ewok	6.00	12.00
26B	Wicket the Ewok FLK FT	80.00	150.00
27	Jar Jar Binks V	25.00	50.00
28	Admiral Ackbar V	25.00	50.00
29	Queen Amidala V	60.00	120.00
30	Lando Calrissian V	30.00	60.00
31	R2-D2	6.00	12.00
32	Boba Fett Droids/480* SDCC	450.00	600.00
33A	Darth Vader HOLO GITD DCC	350.00	500.00
33B	Darth Vader HOLO GITD PE	350.00	500.00
34	Luke Skywalker Hoth V	12.00	25.00
35	Bossk V	25.00	50.00
36	The Emperor V	20.00	40.00
37	Hammerhead V	12.00	25.00
38	Biker Scout V	12.00	25.00
39A	6" Wampa V	12.00	25.00
39B	Wampa 6" FLK HT	15.00	30.00
40	Emperor HOLO TW	30.00	60.00
41A	R2-Q5 GCE	15.00	30.00
41B	R2-Q5 SWC	15.00	30.00
42A	Shock Trooper GCE	30.00	60.00
42B	Shock Trooper SWC	30.00	60.00
43A	Unmasked Vader GCE	6.00	12.00
43B	Unmasked Vader SWC	50.00	100.00
44A	R2-R9 GCE	20.00	40.00
44B	R2-R9 SWC	20.00	40.00
45	R2-B1 GS	10.00	20.00
46A	E-3PO GCE	12.00	25.00
46B	E-3PO SWC	12.00	25.00
47	Han Solo Hoth GS	6.00	12.00
48	Figrin D'an GS	6.00	12.00
49	Luke Skywalker Tatooine	6.00	12.00
50	Princess Leia Boussh	6.00	12.00
51A	TIE Fighter Pilot	6.00	12.00
51B	TIE Pilot MET	12.00	25.00
52	Nalan Cheel	6.00	12.00
53	Bib Fortuna	6.00	12.00
54	Leia Boussh Unmasked SDCC	300.00	500.00
55	K-3PO B&N	10.00	20.00
56A	Snowtrooper WG ERR	6.00	12.00
56B	Snowtrooper WG COR	6.00	12.00
56C	Snowtrooper WG COR Sticker	6.00	12.00
57A	Imperial Guard WG ERR	6.00	12.00
57B	Imperial Guard WG COR	6.00	12.00
57C	Imperial Guard WG COR Sticker	6.00	12.00
58A	Rey	6.00	12.00

59	Finn	6.00	12.00
60	Kylo Ren	6.00	12.00
61	BB-8	6.00	12.00
62	Poe Dameron V	6.00	12.00
63A	Chewbacca	6.00	12.00
63B	Chewbacca FLK SB	6.00	12.00
64A	C-3PO	6.00	12.00
64B	C-3PO MET B&N	12.00	25.00
65A	Captain Phasma	6.00	12.00
65B	Captain Phasma Last Jedi Box		
66	First Order Stormtrooper	6.00	12.00
67A	First Order Snowtrooper	6.00	12.00
67B	First Order Snowtrooper Last Jedi Box		
68A	First Order Flametrooper	6.00	12.00
68B	First Order Flametrooper Last Jedi Box		
69	Blue Snaggletooth CH SB	25.00	50.00
70	Red Snaggletooth SB	6.00	12.00
71	Shadow Guard WG	8.00	15.00
72	Poe Dameron No Helmet WM	6.00	12.00
73	Rey w/Goggles HT	6.00	12.00
74	FO Stormtrooper w/Rifle AMZ	6.00	12.00
75	FO Stormtrooper w/Shield WG	6.00	12.00
76	Finn Stormtrooper GS	8.00	15.00
77	Kylo Ren Unhooded TAR	6.00	12.00
78	R2-L3 Dorkside Toys	15.00	30.00
79	Han Solo	6.00	12.00
80	Princess Leia	6.00	12.00
81	Admiral Ackbar	6.00	12.00
82	Nien Nunb	6.00	12.00
83	Sidon Ithano	6.00	12.00
84	Varmik	6.00	12.00
85	Finn w/Lightsaber B&N	6.00	12.00
86	Han Solo Snow Gear LC	6.00	12.00
87	Kylo Ren Unmasked WM	6.00	12.00
88	Nien Nunb w/Helmet GS	6.00	12.00
89	TIE Fighter Pilot SB	6.00	12.00
A90	TIE Fighter Pilot Red Stripe SB CH	15.00	30.00
B90	Luke Ceremony SWC	8.00	15.00
A91	Captain Phasma MET SB	8.00	15.00
B91A	Han Ceremony SWC	6.00	12.00
B91B	Han Ceremony GCE	6.00	12.00
92	AT-AT Driver WG	6.00	12.00
93	Luke Skywalker Bespin	6.00	12.00
94A	Luke Skywalker Bespin SWC	6.00	12.00
94B	Luke Skywalker Bespin GCE	6.00	12.00
95	Ree Yees WG	6.00	12.00
96	Kit Fisto WG	6.00	12.00
97	Plo Koon WG	6.00	12.00
98	Blue Senate Guard SWC	12.00	25.00
99	Old Ben Kenobi SB	10.00	20.00
100	FN-2187 TAR	20.00	40.00

101	4-LOM SWC	15.00	30.00
102	Bobe Fett Action SB	12.00	25.00
103	IG-88 SB	6.00	12.00
104	Rey w/Lightsaber	6.00	12.00
105	Kylo Ren Unmasked Action	6.00	12.00
106	Luke Skywalker Force Awakens	6.00	12.00

107	General Leia	6.00	12.00	170A	Grand Admiral Thrawn SWC	15.00	30.00	220	BB-8 Baseball and Bat Giants	30.00	60.00
108	Maz Kanata	6.00	12.00	170B	Grand Admiral Thrawn GCE	15.00	30.00	221	Tie Fighter w/Tie Pilot	15.00	30.00
109	General Hux	6.00	12.00	171A	442nd Clone Trooper SWC	20.00	40.00	226	Cloud City Duel WG	30.00	60.00
110	Snap Wexley	6.00	12.00	171B	442nd Clone Trooper GCW	20.00	40.00	230A	Dengar NYCC	20.00	40.00
111	FN-2199 V	6.00	12.00	172	Mace Windu WG	8.00	15.00				
112	Guavian	6.00	12.00	173A	Muftak ECCC	15.00	30.00				
113	ME-8D9	6.00	12.00	173B	Muftak SPCE	15.00	30.00				

114	Rey Jedi Temple WG	12.00	25.00	174A	Rey w/Speeder SWC	40.00	80.00			
115A	Han Solo w/Bowcaster SDCC	8.00	15.00	174B	Rey w/Speeder GCE	40.00	80.00			
115B	Han Solo w/Bowcaster SCE	8.00	15.00	175	Luke w/Speeder SB	15.00	30.00			
116A	BB-8 w/Lighter SDCC	10.00	20.00	A176	Darth Vader w/TIE Fighter TAR	30.00	60.00			
116B	BB-8 w/Lighter SCE	10.00	20.00	B176	Commander Cody WG	12.00	25.00	230B	Dengar FCE	20.00	40.00
117	Poe Dameron Jacket/Blaster HT	6.00	12.00	177A	Saw Gerrera w/Hair NYCC	15.00	30.00	NNO	Jango Fett GITD Solutions2Go	25.00	50.00
118	Maz Kanata Goggles Up TAR	6.00	12.00	177B	Saw Gerrera w/Hair FCE	15.00	30.00	NNO	Luke/Wampa SDCC	100.00	175.00
119	Rey X-Wing Helmet GS	8.00	15.00	178A	Jyn Erso w/Helmet NYCC	20.00	40.00	NNO	Dewback	10.00	20.00
120	Poe Dameron X-Wing Jumpsuit FYE	6.00	12.00	178B	Jyn Erso w/Helmet FCE	20.00	40.00		Sandtrooper WM		
121	R2-D2 Jabba's Sail Barge SB	6.00	12.00	179A	K-2SO Action Pose NYCC	20.00	40.00	NNO	Jabba	25.00	50.00
122	Zuckuss TW	10.00	20.00	179B	K-2SO Action Pose FCE	20.00	40.00		Leia		
123	Luke Skywalker (Endor)	6.00	12.00	181	C-3PO Unfinished SB	12.00	25.00		Crumb WM		
124	Dagobah Yoda	6.00	12.00	182A	Snoke GITD SDCC	20.00	40.00	NNO	Rancor	20.00	40.00
A125	Hoth Han Solo w/Tauntaun SB	20.00	40.00	182B	Supreme Leader Snoke GITD SCE	20.00	40.00		Luke		
B125A	Princess Leia Hoth SWC	15.00	30.00	183A	Bodhi Rook SDCC	12.00	25.00		Oola PX		
B125B	Princess Leia Hoth GCE	15.00	30.00	183B	Bodhi Rook SCE	12.00	25.00	NNO	Rogue On 8-Pack	60.00	120.00
126A	Luke Skywalker Hood SWC	30.00	75.00	184B	Tank Trooper SDCC	15.00	30.00	NNO	BB-8 Domed Gold HT BF	15.00	30.00
126B	Luke Skywalker Hood GCE	30.00	75.00	184C	Combat Assault Tank Trooper SCE	15.00	30.00	NNO	Revenge of the Sith 3-Pack WM	20.00	40.00
127A	Garindan SWC	12.00	25.00	185	Young Jyn Erso	6.00	12.00	NNO	Cantina 3-Pack WM	12.00	25.00
127B	Garindan GCE	12.00	25.00	186	Galen Erso	6.00	12.00	NNO	Princess Leia HOLO/R2-D2 SDCC	20.00	40.00
128A	Qui Gon Jinn NYCC	300.00	500.00	187	Weeteef Cyubee	6.00	12.00	NNO	Princess Leia HOLO/R2-D2 SCE	20.00	40.00
128B	Qui Gon Jinn HOLO SWC	30.00	75.00	188A	Death Star Droid Rogue One NYCC	15.00	30.00	NNO	Lobot/Ugnaught/Bespin Guard WM	25.00	50.00
128C	Qui Gon Jinn HOLO GCE	30.00	75.00	188B	Death Star Droid Rogue One FCE	15.00	30.00	NNO	Teebo/Chirpa/Logray WM	30.00	60.00
129	General Grievous WG	15.00	30.00	189	Death Star Droid Black	8.00	15.00	NNO	BB-8 & BB-9E BB	20.00	40.00
130A	Ahsoka HT	12.00	25.00	190	Rey	6.00	12.00	NNO	First Order 3-Pack COST		
130B	Ahsoka GITD Comikaze			191	Finn	6.00	12.00	NNO	Rebel 3-Pack COST		
131	Sabine Masked WG	8.00	15.00	192	Poe Dameron	6.00	12.00	NNO	First Order Four Pack COST	50.00	100.00
132	Kanan	6.00	12.00	193	Luke Skywalker	6.00	12.00	NNO	Rebel Four Pack COST	50.00	100.00
133A	Chopper	6.00	12.00	194	Kylo Ren	6.00	12.00				
133B	Chopper Imperial SWC	6.00	12.00	195A	Chewbacca w/Porg	6.00	12.00				

2015-17 Funko Dorbz

133C	Chopper Imperial GCE	6.00	12.00	195B	Chewbacca w/Porg FLK FYE	12.00	25.00
134	Ezra	6.00	12.00	196	BB-8	8.00	15.00
135	Sabine	6.00	12.00	197	Rose	6.00	12.00
136	Hera	6.00	12.00	198A	Porg	6.00	12.00
137	Zeb	6.00	12.00	198B	Porg Open Mouth CH	15.00	30.00
138	Jyn Erso	6.00	12.00	198C	Porg FLK HT	10.00	20.00
139	Captain Cassian Andor	6.00	12.00	198D	Porg Open Mouth FLK HT	50.00	100.00
140	Chirrut Imwe	6.00	12.00	198E	Porg Wings Open TAR	15.00	30.00
141	Baze Malbus	6.00	12.00	199	Supreme Leader Snoke	6.00	12.00
142	Director Orson Krennic	6.00	12.00	200	Praetorian Guard	6.00	12.00
143	Darth Vader	6.00	12.00				

NNO Greedo/Walrus/Snaggle D23

2015-17 Funko Dorbz Ridez

144	Imperial Death Trooper	6.00	12.00				
145	Scarif Stormtrooper	6.00	12.00				
146	K-2SO	6.00	12.00				
147	C2-B5	6.00	12.00				
148	Jyn Erso Mountain Gear SB	8.00	15.00				
149	Death Trooper Sniper SB	6.00	12.00				
150	Jyn Erso Hooded HT	6.00	12.00				
151	Capt. C.Andor Brown Jacket TAR	6.00	12.00				
152	Jyn Erso Imperial Disguise TAR	6.00	12.00				
153	Saw Gerrera WM	6.00	12.00				
154	Imp. Death Trooper Black MET WM	8.00	15.00				
155	Bistan NYCC	12.00	25.00	201	First Order Executioner	6.00	12.00
156	Scarif Stormtrooper Striped WG	6.00	12.00	202A	BB-9E	6.00	12.00
157	Vader Force Choke GS	8.00	15.00	202B	BB-9E Chrome BL	12.00	25.00
158	Darth Vader Bespin SB	12.00	25.00	203	Kylo Ren w/Helmet TRU	12.00	25.00
159	Grand Moff Tarkin SB	12.00	25.00	205	Rose SS	10.00	20.00
160	Max Rebo SS	6.00	12.00	207	DJ GS	10.00	20.00
161	Rey w/Jacket TAR	8.00	12.00	208	Praetorian Guard w/Swords WG	12.00	25.00
162	Young Anakin	6.00	12.00	209	Praetorian Guard w/Whip WG	12.00	25.00
164	Captain Rex SB	6.00	12.00	211	Resistance BB Unit WM	6.00	12.00
165	Darth Maul Rebels SB	12.00	25.00	212	Medical Droid WG	10.00	20.00
166	The Inquisitor	8.00	15.00	213A	Boba Fett w/Slave I NYCC	30.00	60.00
167	Seventh Sister	6.00	12.00	213B	Boba Fett w/Slave I FCE	30.00	60.00
168	Fifth Brother	6.00	12.00	215	Kylo Ren w/TIE Fighter		
169A	Han Solo SWC	8.00	15.00	218	Princess Leia WM	12.00	25.00
169B	Han Solo GCE	8.00	15.00	219	Wedge Antilles w/Snow Speeder WG		

25 Hoth Han Solo w/Tauntaun D23

2014-16 Funko Fabrikations

2	Yoda	8.00	15.00
3	Boba Fett	6.00	12.00
4	Greedo	6.00	12.00
12	Darth Vader	6.00	12.00
13	Chewbacca	6.00	12.00
26	Wicket Warrick	10.00	20.00
27	Princess Leia	12.00	25.00
29	Stormtrooper	6.00	12.00

2015-17 Funko Hikari Star Wars

NNO	Boba Fett Clear Glitter/750* NYCC	25.00	50.00
NNO	Boba Fett Glitter/1200*	20.00	40.00
NNO	Boba Fett Infrared/1000* SDCC	25.00	50.00
NNO	Boba Fett Infrared/1000* SCE	20.00	40.00
NNO	Boba Fett Midnight/1000* SWC	75.00	150.00
NNO	Boba Fett Prism/750*	60.00	120.00
NNO	Boba Fett Proto/250* FS	50.00	100.00
NNO	Boba Fett/1500*	30.00	60.00
NNO	Bossk MET/1000*	25.00	50.00
NNO	Bossk Planet X/600*	25.00	50.00
NNO	Bossk Prism/500* EE	30.00	60.00
NNO	Bossk Rainbow/550* SLCC	60.00	120.00
NNO	Bossk Starfield/500* NYCC	30.00	60.00
NNO	Bossk/1000*	20.00	40.00
NNO	C-3PO Clear Glitter/750* SLCC	40.00	80.00
NNO	C-3PO Dirty Penny/500* TT	50.00	100.00
NNO	C-3PO Red/750* SLCC	40.00	80.00
NNO	C-3PO Rusty/500* Gemini	40.00	80.00
NNO	C-3PO/1500*	25.00	50.00
NNO	Captain Phasma Alloy/250*	30.00	75.00
NNO	Captain Phasma Blue Steel/400*	40.00	80.00
NNO	Captain Phasma Classic/500*	30.00	75.00
NNO	Captain Phasma Cold Steel/250*	30.00	75.00
NNO	Captain Phasma Meltdown/100* HT	120.00	200.00
NNO	Chopper Mini Black SB	12.00	25.00
NNO	Chopper Mini Clear SB	5.00	10.00
NNO	Chopper Mini Gold SB	5.00	10.00
NNO	Chopper Mini Orange SB	5.00	10.00
NNO	Chopper Mini Red SB	5.00	10.00
NNO	Clone Trooper Dirty Penny/250* EE	30.00	60.00
NNO	Clone Trooper Rusty White/250* GS	60.00	120.00
NNO	Clone Trooper 442 Siege Glitter/100*	80.00	150.00
NNO	Clone Trooper 442 Siege/900*	25.00	50.00
NNO	Clone Trooper 501st Glitter/250*	40.00	80.00
NNO	Clone Trooper 501st/1500* SDCC	40.00	80.00
NNO	Clone Trooper Starfield/1000* SWC	50.00	100.00
NNO	Clone Trooper Utapau Glitter/100* EE	80.00	150.00

NNO	Clone Trooper Utapau/600* EE	25.00	50.00
NNO	Clone Trooper/1500*	30.00	60.00
NNO	Darth Vader Holographic GITD/300* Gemini	30.00	60.00
NNO	Darth Vader Holographic/750*	30.00	60.00
NNO	Darth Vader Infrared/500* EE	50.00	100.00
NNO	Darth Vader Lightning/1500*	25.00	50.00
NNO	Darth Vader Matte Back/1200* SDCC	40.00	80.00
NNO	Darth Vader Starfield/750*Gemini	40.00	80.00
NNO	Darth Vader Mini Black SB	8.00	15.00
NNO	Darth Vader Mini Blue SB	6.00	12.00
NNO	Darth Vader Mini Gold SB	30.00	60.00
NNO	Darth Vader Mini Red SB	6.00	12.00
NNO	Darth Vader Mini Silver SB	6.00	12.00
NNO	Darth Vader/1500*	30.00	60.00
NNO	E-3PO/500*	25.00	50.00
NNO	FO Snowtrooper Ice Storm/500*	30.00	60.00
NNO	FO Snowtrooper Iron Age/250*	40.00	80.00
NNO	FO Snowtrooper/500*	20.00	40.00
NNO	Stormtrooper Inferno/250*	50.00	100.00
NNO	FO Stormtrooper Kiln/400*	30.00	60.00
NNO	FO Stormtrooper Nocturne/400*	30.00	75.00
NNO	FO Stormtrooper Phantasm/250*	30.00	60.00
NNO	FO Stormtrooper/500*	15.00	30.00
NNO	Greedo Mystic Powers/750*	30.00	60.00
NNO	Greedo Platinum/600* NYCC	25.00	50.00
NNO	Greedo Sublime/750*	25.00	50.00
NNO	Greedo Verdigris/500* SWC	50.00	100.00
NNO	Greedo Mini Blue&Clear 2PK GCE	15.00	30.00
NNO	Greedo Mini Blue&Clear 2PK SWC	15.00	30.00
NNO	Greedo Mini Green&Gold 2PK GCE	20.00	40.00
NNO	Greedo Mini Green&Gold 2PK SWC	20.00	40.00
NNO	Greedo Original/2000*	20.00	40.00
NNO	K-3PO/750*	20.00	40.00
NNO	Kylo Ren Alchemy/300*	50.00	100.00
NNO	Kylo Ren Dark Side/500*	50.00	100.00
NNO	Kylo Ren Onyx/150* HT	75.00	150.00
NNO	Kylo Ren Rage/250* HT	60.00	120.00
NNO	Shadow Trooper/1000*	20.00	40.00
NNO	Snowtrooper Celsius/400*	30.00	75.00
NNO	Snowtrooper Galaxy/250*	25.00	50.00
NNO	Stormtrooper Blue MET/1000*	25.00	50.00
NNO	Stormtrooper Cosmic/2000* SDCC LC	25.00	50.00
NNO	Stormtrooper Green/100* ECCC	100.00	200.00
NNO	Stormtrooper Ice/750* SWC	40.00	80.00
NNO	Stormtrooper Prism/750* TT	25.00	50.00
NNO	Stormtrooper Relic/500*	20.00	40.00
NNO	Stormtrooper Rusty Silver/750*	40.00	80.00
NNO	Stormtrooper Starfied/750*	25.00	50.00
NNO	Stormtrooper/1500*	40.00	80.00
NNO	Wampa Bloody/750*	25.00	50.00
NNO	Wampa Glitter/750*	15.00	30.00
NNO	Wampa Grey Skull/250* EE	25.00	50.00
NNO	Wampa Ice/500* Gemini	30.00	60.00
NNO	Wampa Original/1200*	25.00	50.00

2017 Funko MyMoji Star Wars

NNO	Chewbacca (laughing)	2.50	5.00
NNO	Chewbacca (smiling)	2.50	5.00

NNO	Chewbacca (surprised)	2.50	5.00
NNO	Darth Vader (angry)	4.00	8.00
NNO	Darth Vader (sad)	2.50	5.00
NNO	Darth Vader (staring)	2.50	5.00
NNO	Jabba (bored)	2.50	5.00
NNO	Jabba (closed eyes)	2.50	5.00
NNO	Jabba (sad)	2.50	5.00
NNO	Luke Skywalker (big smile)	2.50	5.00
NNO	Luke Skywalker (closed eyes)	2.50	5.00
NNO	Luke Skywalker (sad)	2.50	5.00
NNO	Princess Leia (big smile)	2.50	5.00
NNO	Princess Leia (closed eyes)	2.50	5.00
NNO	Princess Leia (sad)	2.50	5.00
NNO	Wampa (angry)	2.50	5.00
NNO	Wampa (bored)	2.50	5.00
NNO	Wampa (sad)	2.50	5.00
NNO	Wicket (laughing)	2.50	5.00
NNO	Wicket (sad)	2.50	5.00
NNO	Wicket (smiling)	2.50	5.00
NNO	Yoda (closed eyes)	2.50	5.00
NNO	Yoda (curious)	2.50	5.00
NNO	Yoda (smiling)	4.00	8.00

2017 Funko Mystery Minis Star Wars

NNO	C-3PO	2.50	5.00
NNO	Chewbacca	3.00	6.00
NNO	Chewbacca (w/bowcaster)	30.00	60.00
(Walmart Exclusive)			
NNO	Darth Vader (Force Choke)	50.00	100.00
(Hot Topic Exclusive)			
NNO	Darth Vader (Force Lift)	25.00	50.00
NNO	Darth Vader (lightsaber)	25.00	50.00
(GameStop Exclusive)			
NNO	Grand Moff Tarkin	2.50	5.00
NNO	Greedo	4.00	8.00
NNO	Greedo (pistol up)	15.00	30.00
(Hot Topic Exclusive)			
NNO	Hammerhead	4.00	8.00
NNO	Han Solo	4.00	8.00
NNO	Han Solo (stormtrooper)	12.00	25.00
(GameStop Exclusive)			
NNO	Jawa	3.00	6.00
NNO	Luke Skywalker	12.00	25.00
NNO	Luke Skywalker (stormtrooper)	20.00	40.00
(GameStop Exclusive)			
NNO	Obi Wan Kenobi	4.00	8.00
NNO	Obi Wan Kenobi (Force Ghost)	60.00	120.00
(Walmart Exclusive)			
NNO	Ponda Baba	4.00	8.00
NNO	Princess Leia	2.50	5.00
NNO	Shadow Trooper	5.00	10.00
NNO	Snaggletooth	3.00	6.00
NNO	Stormtrooper	3.00	6.00
NNO	TIE Pilot	25.00	50.00
(Hot Topic Exclusive)			
NNO	Tusken Raider	25.00	50.00
(Walmart Exclusive)			

ACTION FIGURES AND FIGURINES PRICE GUIDE

2017 Funko Mystery Minis Star Wars The Last Jedi

COMPLETE SET (24)

NNO	BB-8	2.50	5.00
NNO	BB-9E	5.00	10.00
NNO	C'ai Threnalli	50.00	100.00
(Walgreens Exclusive)			
NNO	Captain Phasma	3.00	6.00
NNO	Chewbacca (w/porg)	5.00	10.00
NNO	DJ	8.00	15.00
NNO	Finn	20.00	40.00
NNO	Finn (First Order uniform)	4.00	8.00
NNO	First Order Executioner	12.00	25.00
(GameStop Exclusive)			
NNO	Kylo Ren	30.00	60.00
NNO	Kylo Ren (unmasked)	30.00	75.00
(Walmart Exclusive)			
NNO	Poe Dameron	4.00	8.00
NNO	Porg	12.00	25.00
NNO	Porg (wings open)	20.00	40.00
(GameStop Exclusive)			
NNO	Praetorian Guard	12.00	25.00
NNO	Praetorian Guard (w/staff)	12.00	25.00
(Walgreens Exclusive)			
NNO	Praetorian Guard (w/whip)	25.00	50.00
(Walmart Exclusive)			
NNO	Princess Leia	8.00	15.00
NNO	Resistance BB Unit	15.00	30.00
NNO	Rey	6.00	12.00
NNO	Rey (cloaked)	8.00	15.00
(GameStop Exclusive)			
NNO	Rose	3.00	6.00
NNO	Supreme Leader Snoke	4.00	8.00
NNO	Supreme Leader Snoke (holographic)	30.00	75.00
(Walgreens Exclusive)			

2015-16 Funko Super Shogun

2	Shadowtrooper SWC	120.00	200.00
3	Boba Fett ROTJ SWC	120.00	200.00
4	Boba Fett ESB	60.00	120.00
5	Boba Fett Proto/400* FS	150.00	250.00

2010 Mighty Beanz Star Wars

1	Luke Skywalker C	
2	Han Solo C	
3	Princess Leia C	
4	Darth Vader C	
5	R2-D2 C	
6	Obi-Wan Kenobi C	
7	Yoda C	
8	Chewbacca C	
9	Jabba the Hutt C	
10	Battle Droid C	
11	C-3PO C	
12	Clone Trooper C	
13	501st Legion Trooper C	
14	Commander Cody C	
15	Stormtrooper C	
16	Admiral Ackbar C	
17	Gamorrean Guard C	
18	Count Dooku C	
19	Boba Fett C	
20	Greedo C	
21	Sandtrooper C	
22	Anakin Skywalker (child) C	
23	Mace Windu C	
24	AT-AT Driver C	
25	General Grievous C	
26	TIE Pilot C	
27	Snowtrooper C	
28	Wicket C	
29	Jawa C	
30	Tusken Raider C	
31	Padme Amidala R	
32	Darth Maul R	
33	Anakin Skywalker R	
34	2-1B R	
35	Han Solo (carbonite) R	
36	Cantina Musician R	
37	Bossk R	
38	Lando Calrissian R	
39	Biggs Darklighter R	
40	Jango Fett R	
41	Bib Fortuna R	
42	IG-88 R	
43	Emperor Palpatine R	
44	Qui-Gon Jinn R	
45	Rancor Keeper R	
46	Max Rebo R	
47	Luke Rebel Pilot R	
48	Sebulba R	
49	Rancor R	
50	Ponda Baba R	
51	Princess Leia UR	
52	Jar Jar Binks UR	
53	Dengar UR	
54	Kit Fisto UR	
55	Ki-Adi-Mundi UR	
56	Jek Porkins UR	
57	Nien Nunb UR	
58	Salacious Crumb UR	
59	Watto UR	
60	Queen Amidala UR	

2017 Vinylmation Eachez Star Wars The Last Jedi

NNO	Praetorian Guard Single Blade	30.00	75.00
NNO	Praetorian Guard Double Blade (chaser)	50.00	100.00
NNO	Praetorian Guard Whip	12.00	25.00

2012-13 Vinylmation Star Wars Disney Characters

NNO	Boba Fett Pete	6.00	12.00
NNO	Chewbacca Goofy	20.00	40.00
(LE 1500)			
NNO	Darth Vader Goofy	8.00	15.00
NNO	Emperor Stitch	25.00	50.00
(LE 2000)			
NNO	Ewok Chip	20.00	40.00
(LE 1500)			
NNO	Ewok Dale	20.00	40.00
(LE 1500)			
NNO	Han Solo Donald	30.00	60.00
(LE 1500)			
NNO	Jedi Mickey	20.00	40.00
(LE 2000)			
NNO	Princess Leia Minnie	10.00	20.00
NNO	Stormtrooper Donald	6.00	12.00
NNO	X-Wing Pilot Luke Mickey	12.00	25.00
NNO	Yoda Stitch	20.00	40.00

2016 Vinylmation Star Wars The Force Awakens Series 2

NNO	Admiral Ackbar	5.00	10.00
NNO	Captain Phasma		
NNO	Ello Asty (w/ helmet)	6.00	12.00
NNO	Ello Asty (helmetless)		
NNO	First Mate Guiggold	4.00	8.00
NNO	First Order Snowtrooper	6.00	12.00
NNO	First Order TIE Fighter Pilot	8.00	15.00
NNO	First Order TIE Fighter Pilot (red mark)		
NNO	Princess Leia	12.00	25.00
NNO	Sidon Ithano	5.00	10.00

2015 Vinylmation Star Wars The Force Awakens Series 1

NNO	BB-8	10.00	20.00
NNO	C-3PO	4.00	8.00
NNO	Finn (leather jacket)	5.00	10.00
NNO	Finn (stormtrooper)		
NNO	First Order Stormtrooper	12.00	25.00
NNO	Han Solo (chaser)	15.00	30.00
NNO	Kylo Ren	10.00	20.00
NNO	Poe Dameron	4.00	8.00
NNO	Rey		
NNO	Rey (desert wear)	30.00	75.00

2016 Vinylmation Star Wars Rogue One

NNO	Admiral Raddus	8.00	15.00
NNO	Baze Malbus	6.00	12.00
NNO	Bistan	4.00	8.00
NNO	C2-B5	6.00	12.00
NNO	Cassian Andor	8.00	15.00
NNO	Chirrut Imwe	8.00	15.00
NNO	Director Orson Krennic	6.00	12.00

NNO	Imperial Death Trooper (w/o shoulder pad)	8.00	15.00
NNO	Imperial Death Trooper (w/ shoulder pad)	30.00	75.00
NNO	Jyn Erso (w/o helm)	8.00	15.00
NNO	Jyn Erso (w/ helm)	60.00	120.00
NNO	K-2SO	10.00	20.00
NNO	Rebel Commando Pao	8.00	15.00
NNO	Saw Gererra	12.00	25.00

2011 Vinylmation Star Wars Series 1

NNO	Boba Fett	12.00	25.00
NNO	C-3PO	8.00	15.00
NNO	Chewbacca	6.00	12.00
NNO	Darth Vader	10.00	20.00
NNO	Han Solo	12.00	25.00
NNO	Lando	10.00	20.00
NNO	Leia	6.00	12.00
NNO	Luke	6.00	12.00
NNO	Obi-Wan Kenobi Ghost	30.00	60.00
NNO	Obi-Wan Kenobi	8.00	15.00
	(chaser)		
NNO	R2-D2	6.00	12.00
NNO	Stormtrooper	8.00	15.00
NNO	Yoda	8.00	15.00

2012 Vinylmation Star Wars Series 2

NNO	Darth Vader	20.00	40.00
NNO	Garindan	25.00	50.00
	(chaser)		
NNO	Grand Moff Tarkin	6.00	12.00
NNO	Greedo	6.00	12.00
NNO	Han Solo	6.00	12.00
NNO	Hologram Princess Leia	30.00	60.00
	(LE 2500) Celebration VI Exclusive		
NNO	Jawa	15.00	30.00
	(LE 2000)		
NNO	Luke Skywalker	8.00	15.00
NNO	Muftak	6.00	12.00
NNO	Obi-Wan Kenobi	8.00	15.00
NNO	Ponda Baba	6.00	12.00
NNO	Princess Leia	8.00	15.00

NNO	R5-D4		
	(LE 2000)		
NNO	Tusken Raider	8.00	15.00
NNO	Wedge Antilles	6.00	12.00

2013 Vinylmation Star Wars Series 3

NNO	Admiral Ackbar	10.00	20.00
NNO	Bib Fortuna	6.00	12.00
NNO	Biker Scout	8.00	15.00
NNO	Emperor Palpatine	30.00	60.00
	(chaser)		
NNO	Emperor's Royal Guard	10.00	20.00
NNO	Gamorrean Guard	6.00	12.00
NNO	Helmetless Princess Leia in Boushh Disguise		
	(variant)		
NNO	Lando Calrissian Skiff Guard Disguise	8.00	15.00
NNO	Logray	10.00	20.00
NNO	Luke Skywalker Jedi	8.00	15.00
NNO	Nien Nunb	6.00	12.00
NNO	Princess Leia in Boushh Disguise	15.00	30.00
NNO	Wicket	10.00	20.00

2014 Vinylmation Star Wars Series 4

NNO	4-LOM	6.00	12.00
NNO	Bespin Princess Leia	6.00	12.00
NNO	Boba Fett Concept	20.00	40.00
	(combo topper)		
NNO	Boba Fett	15.00	30.00
	(combo topper)		
NNO	Bossk	6.00	12.00
NNO	Dagobah Luke Skywalker 9-Inch	30.00	60.00
	(LE 2000)		
NNO	Dengar	6.00	12.00
NNO	Han Solo Carbonite	50.00	100.00
	(LE 2000)		
NNO	Han Solo Hoth	6.00	12.00
NNO	Holographic Emperor	12.00	25.00
	(LE 2000)		
NNO	Jabba the Hutt and Salacious Crumb 9-Inch	30.00	60.00
	(LE 2000)		
NNO	Luke Skywalker Hoth	6.00	12.00

NNO	R2-D2 Dagobah	12.00	25.00
NNO	R2-D2	15.00	30.00
	(variant)		
NNO	R2-MK	8.00	15.00
NNO	Rancor and Malakili 9-and-3-Inch Combo	40.00	80.00
NNO	Snowtrooper	10.00	20.00
NNO	Tauntaun	6.00	12.00
NNO	Ugnaught	6.00	12.00
NNO	Wampa Attacked Luke		
	(variant)		
NNO	Wampa	15.00	30.00
	(chaser)		
NNO	Yoda 9-Inch		
	(LE 2000)		
NNO	Zuckuss	6.00	12.00

2015 Vinylmation Star Wars Series 5

NNO	Chopper	12.00	25.00
	(LE 2500)		
NNO	Death Star and Trooper 9-and-3-Inch Combo	40.00	80.00
	(LE 1000)		
NNO	Death Star Droid	8.00	15.00
NNO	Dr. Evazan	6.00	12.00
NNO	Duros		
NNO	Figrin D'an	15.00	30.00
	(instrument 1)		
NNO	Figrin D'an	20.00	40.00
	(instrument 2)		
NNO	Figrin D'an	20.00	40.00
	(instrument 3)		
NNO	Figrin D'an	15.00	30.00
	(instrument 4)		
NNO	Figrin D'an	20.00	40.00
	(instrument 5)		
NNO	Han Solo Stormtrooper	12.00	25.00
NNO	Heroes of Yavin Han		
	(LE 2500)		
NNO	Heroes of Yavin Luke	12.00	25.00
	(LE 2500)		
NNO	Inquisitor	20.00	40.00
NNO	Jabba the Hutt	6.00	12.00
NNO	Jawa	20.00	40.00
	(LE 2500)		
NNO	Labria	6.00	12.00
NNO	Luke Skywalker Stormtrooper	50.00	100.00
	(variant)		
NNO	Luke Skywalker X-Wing Pilot	10.00	20.00
	(combo topper)		
NNO	Momaw Nadon	6.00	12.00
NNO	Power Droid	10.00	25.00
	(LE 2500)		
NNO	Princess Leia	6.00	12.00
NNO	Sandtrooper	8.00	15.00
NNO	Snaggletooth	10.00	20.00
	(chaser)		
NNO	Tie Fighter Pilot	10.00	20.00
NNO	Zeb		
	(LE 2500)		

STAR WARS FILMS

1977 Star Wars

Han Solo and Chewbacca

COMPLETE SET W/STICKERS (330)	125.00	250.00
COMP.SER.1 SET W/STICKERS (66)	30.00	80.00
COMP.SER.2 SET W/STICKERS (66)	20.00	50.00
COMP.SER.3 SET W/STICKERS (66)	20.00	50.00
COMP.SER.4 SET W/STICKERS (66)	20.00	50.00
COMP.SER.5 SET W/STICKERS (66)	25.00	60.00
UNOPENED SER.1 BOX (36 PACKS)	1600.00	2000.00
UNOPENED SER.1 PACK (7 CARDS+1 STICKER)		
UNOPENED SER.2 BOX (36 PACKS)	500.00	600.00
UNOPENED SER.2 PACK (7 CARDS+1 STICKER)		
UNOPENED SER.3 BOX (36 PACKS)	400.00	500.00
UNOPENED SER.3 PACK (7 CARDS+1 STICKER)		
UNOPENED SER.4 BOX (36 PACKS)	450.00	600.00
UNOPENED SER.4 PACK (7 CARDS+1 STICKER)		
UNOPENED SER.5 BOX (36 PACKS)	350.00	500.00
UNOPENED SER.5 PACK (7 CARDS+1 STICKER)		
COMMON BLUE (1-66)	.30	.75
COMMON RED (67-132)	.25	.60
COMMON YELLOW (133-198)	.25	.60
COMMON GREEN (199-264)	.25	.60
COMMON ORANGE (265-330)	.25	.60
207A C-3PO Anthony Daniels ERR Obscene	30.00	80.00
207B C-3PO Anthony Daniels COR Airbrushed	.25	.60

1977 Star Wars Stickers

COMPLETE SET (55)	40.00	80.00
COMPLETE SERIES 1 (11)	6.00	15.00
COMPLETE SERIES 2 (11)	6.00	15.00
COMPLETE SERIES 3 (11)	6.00	15.00
COMPLETE SERIES 4 (11)	6.00	15.00
COMPLETE SERIES 5 (11)	6.00	15.00
COMMON STICKER (1-11)	.75	2.00
COMMON STICKER (12-22)	.60	1.50
COMMON STICKER (23-33)	.60	1.50
COMMON STICKER (34-44)	.60	1.50
COMMON STICKER (45-55)	.60	1.50
1 Luke Skywalker	1.25	3.00
7 Lord Darth Vader	1.25	3.00
36 Star Pilot Luke Skywalker	1.25	3.00
43 Stormtrooper Tool of the Empire	1.25	3.00

1978 Star Wars General Mills

COMPLETE SET (18)	12.00	30.00
COMMON CARD (1-18)	1.00	2.50

1977 Star Wars Tip Top Ice Cream

COMPLETE SET (15)	80.00	150.00
COMMON CARD	5.00	12.00
UNNUMBERED SET LISTED ALPHABETICALLY		
ALSO KNOWN AS R2-D2 SPACE ICE		

1977 Star Wars Wonder Bread

COMPLETE SET (16)	6.00	15.00
COMMON CARD (1-16)	.50	1.25

1995 Star Wars Widevision

Produced by Topps, the original Star Wars film is brought back to trading cards with photo images from the film along with behind-the-scenes photos and production art. Each full bleed front has a blue stripe on the bottom and holo-foil stamp; the backs have tons of trivia and behind-the-scenes information. Each card measures 4 5/8 by 2 1/2 inches (11.9 by 6.3 cm). The set does not have a checklist. Artwork by John Barry, Ivor Beddoes, John Berkey, Ron Cobb, Steve Gawley, Paul Huston, Joe Johnston, Tommy Jung, Ralph McQuarrie, Gary Meyers, John Mollo, Papuzza, Ronnie Shepherd, and Alex Tavoularis.

COMPLETE SET (120)	15.00	40.00
UNOPENED BOX (36 PACKS)	80.00	100.00
UNOPENED PACK (10 CARDS)	2.50	3.00
COMMON CARD (1-120)	.20	.50

1995 Star Wars Widevision Finest

COMPLETE SET (10)	40.00	100.00
COMMON CARD (1-10)	5.00	12.00
STATED ODDS 1:11		

2007 Star Wars 30th Anniversary

COMPLETE SET (120)	5.00	12.00
UNOPENED HOBBY BOX (24 PACKS)	200.00	225.00
UNOPENED HOBBY PACK (7 CARDS)	10.00	12.00
UNOPENED RETAIL BOX (24 PACKS)		
UNOPENED RETAIL PACK (7 CARDS)		
COMMON CARD (1-120)	.15	.40

*BLUE: 4X TO 10X BASIC CARDS
*RED: 8X TO 20X BASIC CARDS
*GOLD/30: 80X TO 150X BASIC CARDS

2007 Star Wars 30th Anniversary Animation Cels

COMPLETE SET (9)	6.00	15.00
COMMON CARD (1-9)	1.50	4.00
STATED ODDS 1:6 RETAIL		

2007 Star Wars 30th Anniversary Autographs

COMMON CARD (UNNUMBERED)	10.00	20.00
STATED ODDS 1:43 HOBBY		
NNO Anthony Daniels	700.00	1200.00
NNO Carrie Fisher	600.00	1000.00
NNO David Prowse	300.00	600.00
NNO George Roubichek	15.00	30.00
NNO Harrison Ford		
NNO Joe Viskocil	20.00	40.00
NNO John Dykstra	25.00	50.00
NNO John Williams	250.00	500.00
NNO Ken Ralston	20.00	40.00
NNO Kenny Baker	120.00	250.00
NNO Lorne Peterson	15.00	30.00
NNO Maria De Aragon	20.00	40.00
NNO Norman Reynolds	25.00	60.00
NNO Peter Mayhew	150.00	300.00
NNO Phil Tippet	25.00	50.00
NNO Richard Edlund	20.00	40.00
NNO Richard LeParmentier	10.00	20.00
NNO Rusty Goffe	25.00	50.00

2007 Star Wars 30th Anniversary Blister Bonus

COMPLETE SET (3)	3.00	8.00
COMMON CARD (1-3)	1.25	3.00
STATED ODDS 1:BLISTER PACK		

2007 Star Wars 30th Anniversary Magnets

COMPLETE SET (9)	12.00	30.00
COMMON CARD (UNNUMBERED)	1.50	4.00
STATED ODDS 1:8 RETAIL		

2007 Star Wars 30th Anniversary Original Series Box-Toppers

SERIES 1 (1-66) BLUE	12.00	30.00
SERIES 2 (67-132) RED	12.00	30.00
SERIES 3 (133-198) YELLOW	12.00	30.00
SERIES 4 (199-264) GREEN	12.00	30.00
SERIES 5 (265-330) ORANGE SP	30.00	80.00
STATED ODDS 1:BOX		

2007 Star Wars 30th Anniversary Sketches

COMPLETE ARTIST LIST (47)
STATED ODDS 1:50 HOBBY
UNPRICED DUE TO SCARCITY

1 Adam Hughes
2 Alexander Buechel
3 Allison Sohn
4 Amy Pronovost
5 Brandon McKinney
6 Brian Ashmore
7 Brian Denham
8 Brian Rood
9 Cat Staggs
10 Chris Eliopoulous
11 Christian Dalla Vecchia
12 Craig Rousseau
13 Cynthis Cummens
14 Dave Dorman
15 David Rabbitte
16 Davide Fabbri
17 Doug Cowan
18 Gabe Hernandez
19 Grant Gould
20 Ingrid Hardy
21 Jan Duursema
22 Jeff Chandler
23 Jessica Hickman
24 Joe Corroney
25 John Watkins-Chow
26 Joseph Booth
27 Josh Fargher
28 Josh Howard
29 Juan Carlos Ramos
30 Justin Chung
31 Katie Cook
32 Kevin Graham
33 Leah Mangue
34 Len Bellinger
35 Mark Brooks
36 Matt Busch
37 Otis Frampton
38 Paul Gutierrez
39 Phil Noto
40 Rafael Kayanen
41 Robert Teranishi
42 Russell Walks
43 Ryan Waterhouse
44 Sarah Wilkinson

45 Sean Pence
46 Stephane Roux
47 Tom Hodges

2007 Star Wars 30th Anniversary Triptych Puzzle

COMPLETE SET (27)	12.00	25.00
COMMON CARD (1-27)	.75	2.00
STATED ODDS 1:3		

2013 Star Wars Illustrated A New Hope

COMPLETE SET (100)	8.00	20.00
COMMON CARD (1-100)	.20	.50

*PURPLE: 2.5X TO 6X BASIC CARDS
*BRONZE: 5X TO 12X BASIC CARDS
*GOLD/10: 50X TO 120X BASIC CARDS
*P.P.BLACK/1: UNPRICED DUE TO SCARCITY
*P.P.CYAN/1: UNPRICED DUE TO SCARCITY
*P.P.MAGENTA/1: UNPRICED DUE TO SCARCITY
*P.P.YELLOW/1: UNPRICED DUE TO SCARCITY

2013 Star Wars Illustrated A New Hope Sketcha-graphs

1 Anthony Daniels
Aston Roy Cover/20
2 Anthony Daniels
Chad "CWM" McCown
3 Anthony Daniels
Chris Meeks
4 Anthony Daniels
Darrin Pepe
5 Anthony Daniels
Denae Frazier
6 Anthony Daniels
Grant Gould/48
7 Anthony Daniels
Jason Chalker
8 Anthony Daniels
Kris Penix
9 Anthony Daniels
Kyle Babbitt
10 Anthony Daniels
Robert Jimenez/45
11 Anthony Daniels
Robert Teranishi
12 Anthony Daniels
Scott Rorie
13 Anthony Daniels
Val Hochberg
14 Anthony Daniels
Paul "Gutz" Gutierrez
15 David Ackroyd
Aston Roy Cover
16 David Ackroyd

Darrin Pepe
17 David Ackroyd
Denae Frazier
18 David Ackroyd
Grant Gould
19 David Ackroyd
Jason Chalker
20 David Ackroyd
Kris Penix
21 David Ackroyd
Kyle Babbitt
22 David Ackroyd
Paul "Gutz" Gutierrez
23 David Ackroyd
Scott Rorie
24 David Ackroyd
Val Hochberg
25 David Paymer
Chad "CWM" McCown
26 David Paymer
Darrin Pepe
27 David Paymer
Denae Frazier
28 David Paymer
Grant Gould
29 David Paymer
Kris Penix
30 David Paymer
Kyle Babbitt
31 David Paymer
Mikey Babinski
32 David Paymer
Paul "Gutz" Gutierrez
33 David Paymer
Robert Teranishi
34 David Paymer
Scott Rorie
35 David Paymer
Val Hochberg
36 David Paymer
Wilson Ramos Jr.
37 Garrick Hagon
Aston Roy Cover
38 Garrick Hagon
Chad "CWM" McCown
39 Garrick Hagon
Chris Meeks
40 Garrick Hagon
Darrin Pepe
41 Garrick Hagon
Denae Frazier
42 Garrick Hagon
Grant Gould
43 Garrick Hagon
Jason Chalker
44 Garrick Hagon
Kris Penix
45 Garrick Hagon
Kyle Babbitt
46 Garrick Hagon
Mikey Babinski
47 Garrick Hagon
Paul "Gutz" Gutierrez
48 Garrick Hagon
Robert Jimenez
49 Garrick Hagon
Robert Teranishi
50 Garrick Hagon
Scott Rorie
51 Garrick Hagon
Val Hochberg
52 Kale Browne
Aston Roy Cover
53 Kale Browne
Chad "CWM" McCown
54 Kale Browne
Denae Frazier
55 Kale Browne
Grant Gould
56 Kale Browne
Jason Crosby
57 Kale Browne
Mikey Babinski
58 Kale Browne
Paul "Gutz" Gutierrez

59 Kale Browne
Robert Jimenez
60 Kale Browne
Robert Teranishi
61 Kale Browne
Scott Rorie
62 Kale Browne
Val Hochberg
63 Kale Browne
Wilson Ramos Jr.
64 Mark Hamill
Aston Roy Cover
65 Mark Hamill
Chad "CWM" McCown
66 Mark Hamill
Chris Meeks
67 Mark Hamill
Darrin Pepe
68 Mark Hamill
Denae Frazier
69 Mark Hamill
Grant Gould
70 Mark Hamill
Jason Chalker
71 Mark Hamill
Kyle Babbitt
72 Mark Hamill
Mikey Babinski
73 Mark Hamill
Robert Teranishi
74 Mark Hamill
Scott Rorie
75 Mark Hamill
Val Hochberg
76 Pam Rose
Aston Roy Cover
77 Pam Rose
Chad "CWM" McCown
78 Pam Rose
Chris Meeks
79 Pam Rose
Darrin Pepe
80 Pam Rose
Denae Frazier
81 Pam Rose
Grant Gould
82 Pam Rose
Jason Chalker
83 Pam Rose
Kris Penix
84 Pam Rose
Mikey Babinski
85 Pam Rose
Robert Jimenez
86 Pam Rose
Robert Teranishi
87 Pam Rose
Scott Rorie
88 Pam Rose
Val Hochberg
89 Peter Mayhew
Aston Roy Cover
90 Peter Mayhew
Chad "CWM" McCown
91 Peter Mayhew
Chris Meeks
92 Peter Mayhew
Darrin Pepe
93 Peter Mayhew
Denae Frazier
94 Peter Mayhew
Grant Gould
95 Peter Mayhew
Jason Chalker
96 Peter Mayhew
Kris Penix
97 Peter Mayhew
Kyle Babbitt

98 Peter Mayhew
Mikey Babinski
99 Peter Mayhew
Paul "Gutz" Gutierrez
100 Peter Mayhew
Robert Jimenez
101 Peter Mayhew
Robert Teranishi
102 Peter Mayhew
Scott Rorie
103 Peter Mayhew
Val Hochberg

2013 Star Wars Illustrated A New Hope Film Cels

COMPLETE SET (20)	250.00	500.00
COMMON CARD (FR1-FR20)	12.00	30.00
FR8 Greedo's Bounty	15.00	40.00
FR14 The Final Encounter	60.00	120.00

2013 Star Wars Illustrated A New Hope Movie Poster Reinterpretations

COMPLETE SET (9)	5.00	12.00
COMMON CARD (MP1-MP9)	1.25	3.00
*P.P.BLACK/1: UNPRICED DUE TO SCARCITY		
*P.P.CYAN/1: UNPRICED DUE TO SCARCITY		
*P.P.MAGENTA/1: UNPRICED DUE TO SCARCITY		
*P.P.YELLOW/1: UNPRICED DUE TO SCARCITY		
STATED ODDS 1:3		

2013 Star Wars Illustrated A New Hope One Year Earlier

COMPLETE SET (18)	5.00	12.00
COMMON CARD (OY1-OY18)	.60	1.50
*P.P.BLACK/1: UNPRICED DUE TO SCARCITY		
*P.P.CYAN/1: UNPRICED DUE TO SCARCITY		
*P.P.MAGENTA/1: UNPRICED DUE TO SCARCITY		
*P.P.YELLOW/1: UNPRICED DUE TO SCARCITY		
STATED ODDS 1:2		

2013 Star Wars Illustrated A New Hope Panorama Sketches

1 Adrianna Vanderstelt
2 Brandon Gallo
3 Brian Deguire
4 Choot McCan
5 Chris Hamer
6 Chris West
7 Christian Slade
8 Darrin Pepe
9 Dave Strong
10 David Green
11 David Rabbitte
12 GeckoArt/50*
13 Ingrid Hardy/15*
14 Irma Ahmed
15 Jake Myler/50*
16 Jason Chalker
17 Jason Crosby/50*
18 Jason Flowers
19 Jerry Vanderstelt
20 Joanne Ellen Patak
21 Joe Hogan
22 John Haun/50*
23 John Soukup/50*
24 Josh Howard
25 Justice41/25*
26 Kevin Graham
27 Kimberly Dunaway
28 Kris Penix
29 Lawrence Reynolds
30 Linzy Zorn
31 Marck Labas
32 Matt Busch
33 Matt Hebb/50*
34 Matte Chero/50*
35 McHero
36 Michael Locoduck Duron
37 Mikey Babinski
38 Pablo Diaz/50*
39 Patrick Richardson/50*
40 Rachel Kaiser/50*
41 Robert Hendrickson
42 Roberto Jimenez/50*
43 Scott Zambelli/50*
44 Shea Standefer
45 Stephanie Swanger

46 Steve Oatney
47 Tim Proctor
48 Todd Smith
49 Val Hochberg
50 Vanessa Banky
51 William O'Neill
52 Wilson Ramos Jr.

2013 Star Wars Illustrated A New Hope Radio Drama Puzzle

COMPLETE SET (6)	5.00	12.00
COMMON CARD (1-6)	1.50	4.00
*P.P.BLACK/1: UNPRICED DUE TO SCARCITY		
*P.P.CYAN/1: UNPRICED DUE TO SCARCITY		
*P.P.MAGENTA/1: UNPRICED DUE TO SCARCITY		
*P.P.YELLOW/1: UNPRICED DUE TO SCARCITY		
STATED ODDS 1:8		

2013 Star Wars Illustrated A New Hope The Mission Destroy the Death Star

COMPLETE SET (12)	30.00	60.00
COMMON CARD (1-12)	3.00	8.00
*P.P.BLACK/1: UNPRICED DUE TO SCARCITY		
*P.P.CYAN/1: UNPRICED DUE TO SCARCITY		
*P.P.MAGENTA/1: UNPRICED DUE TO SCARCITY		
*P.P.YELLOW/1: UNPRICED DUE TO SCARCITY		
STATED ODDS 1:12		

2013 Star Wars Illustrated A New Hope Promos

COMPLETE SET (4)	5.00	12.00
P1 Searching Mos Eisley	2.00	5.00
P2 The Rebellion's Imminent Victory	2.00	5.00
P3 Creating the Radio Play	2.00	5.00
P4 The Cast in Action	2.00	5.00

2017 Star Wars 40th Anniversary

COMPLETE SET (200)	15.00	40.00
UNOPENED BOX (24 PACKS)	100.00	120.00
UNOPENED PACK (8 CARDS)	4.25	5.00
COMMON CARD (1-200)	.20	.50
*GREEN: .5X TO 1.2X BASIC CARDS	.40	1.00
*BLUE: .6X TO 1.5X BASIC CARDS	.50	1.25
*PURPLE/100: 3X TO 8X BASIC CARDS	2.50	6.00
*GOLD/40: 6X TO 15X BASIC CARDS	5.00	12.00
*RED/1: UNPRICED DUE TO SCARCITY		
*P.P.BLACK/1: UNPRICED DUE TO SCARCITY		
*P.P.CYAN/1: UNPRICED DUE TO SCARCITY		
*P.P.MAGENTA/1: UNPRICED DUE TO SCARCITY		
*P.P.YELLOW/1: UNPRICED DUE TO SCARCITY		

2017 Star Wars 40th Anniversary Autographed Medallions

STATED PRINT RUN 10 SER.#'d SETS
UNPRICED DUE TO SCARCITY

AD Anthony Daniels
CF Carrie Fisher
HF Harrison Ford
KB Kenny Baker
MH Mark Hamill

2017 Star Wars 40th Anniversary Autographs

COMMON CARD	6.00	15.00
*RED/1: UNPRICED DUE TO SCARCITY		
*P.P.BLACK/1: UNPRICED DUE TO SCARCITY		
*P.P.CYAN/1: UNPRICED DUE TO SCARCITY		
*P.P.MAGENTA/1: UNPRICED DUE TO SCARCITY		
*P.P.YELLOW/1: UNPRICED DUE TO SCARCITY		
RANDOMLY INSERTED INTO PACKS		
AAAD Anthony Daniels		
AAAH Alan Harris	12.00	30.00
AAAL Al Lampert	12.00	30.00
AABF Barbara Frankland	10.00	25.00
AABL Bai Ling	8.00	20.00
AACB Caroline Blakiston		
AACF Carrie Fisher		
AACR Clive Revill	10.00	25.00
AADL Denis Lawson	10.00	25.00
AADR Deep Roy	8.00	20.00
AAEB Erik Bauersfeld		
AAFF Femi Taylor	8.00	20.00
AAGH Garrick Hagon	10.00	25.00
AAGR George Roubicek	10.00	25.00
AAHF Harrison Ford		
AAIM Ian McDiarmid		
AAJB Jeremy Bulloch	15.00	40.00
AAJG Julian Glover		
AAJK Jack Klaff	10.00	25.00
AAKB Kenny Baker		
AAMC Michael Carter		
AAMH Mark Hamill		
AAMW Matthew Wood	8.00	20.00
AAPS Paul Springer	8.00	20.00
AARP Ray Park		
AASC Stephen Costantino	10.00	25.00
AATR Tim Rose	8.00	20.00
AABDW Billy Dee Williams		
AACDW Corey Dee Williams	8.00	20.00
AAPBL Paul Blake	10.00	25.00

2017 Star Wars 40th Anniversary Celebration Orlando Promos

Luke Skywalker

COMPLETE SET (4)	225.00	450.00
COMMON CARD (C1-C4)		
*VOLUNTEER ED.: X TO X BASIC CARDS		
C1 Luke Skywalker	80.00	150.00
C2 Princess Leia	80.00	150.00
C3 Han Solo	60.00	120.00
C4 Darth Vader	50.00	100.00

2017 Star Wars 40th Anniversary Classic Stickers

COMMON CARD	12.00	30.00
STATED PRINT RUN 100 SER.#'d SETS		

2017 Star Wars 40th Anniversary Dual Autographs

STATED PRINT RUN 3 SER.#'d SETS

UNPRICED DUE TO SCARCITY

NNO Daniels/Baker

NNO Daniels/Mayhew

NNO Fisher/Davis

NNO Barclay/Carter

NNO Hamill/Baker

2017 Star Wars 40th Anniversary Medallions

COMMON CARD	8.00	20.00
MILLENNIUM FALCON (1-12)		
DEATH STAR (13-23)		
*BLUE/40: .5X TO 1.2X BASIC CARDS	10.00	25.00
*PURPLE/25: .6X TO 1.5X BASIC CARDS	12.00	30.00
*GOLD/10: 1.2X TO 3X BASIC CARDS	25.00	60.00
*RED/1: UNPRICED DUE TO SCARCITY		

2017 Star Wars 40th Anniversary Patches

COMMON CARD (1-20)	5.00	12.00
*BLUE/40: 6X TO 1.5X BASIC CARDS	8.00	20.00
*PURPLE/25: 1X TO 2.5X BASIC CARDS	12.00	30.00
*GOLD/10: 1.5X TO 4X BASIC CARDS	20.00	50.00
RANDOMLY INSERTED INTO PACKS		
TARGET EXCLUSIVE		

2017 Star Wars 40th Anniversary Quad Autographed Booklet

STATED PRINT RUN 2 SER.#'d SETS

UNPRICED DUE TO SCARCITY

NNO Hamill/Fisher/Daniels/Baker

2017 Star Wars 40th Anniversary Six-Person Autographed Booklet

STATED PRINT RUN 2 SER.#'d SETS

UNPRICED DUE TO SCARCITY

NNO Ford/Hamill/Fisher
Daniels/Baker/Mayhew

2017 Star Wars 40th Anniversary Sketches

COMPLETE ARTIST LIST (95)
STATED ODDS
UNPRICED DUE TO SCARCITY

NNO Adam Worton
NNO Alex Iniguez
NNO Andrew Lopez
NNO Angelina Benedetti
NNO Anil Sharma
NNO Anthony Skubis
NNO Ashleigh Popplewell
NNO Ben Abu Saada
NNO Bob Hepner
NNO Brad Hudson
NNO Brad Utterstrom
NNO Brandon Pyle
NNO Brendan Purchase
NNO Brent Ragland
NNO Can Baran
NNO Carlos Cabaleiro
NNO Cathy Razim
NNO Chad LaForce
NNO Chad Scheres
NNO Charlie Cody
NNO Chris West
NNO Clinton Yeager
NNO Corey Galal
NNO Dan Bergren
NNO Dan Burn Webster
NNO Dan Curto
NNO Daniel Cooney
NNO Danny Kidwell
NNO Darrin Pepe
NNO Dave Dabila
NNO David Rabbitte
NNO Dylan Riley
NNO Elfie Lebouleux
NNO Eric Lehtonen
NNO Eric Muller
NNO Frank Kadar
NNO Freddy Lopez
NNO George Joseph
NNO Ingrid Hardy
NNO Jamie Cosley
NNO Jamie Richards
NNO Jamie Thomas
NNO Jason Brower
NNO Jason Durden
NNO Jason Sobol
NNO Jay Machand
NNO Jeff Mallinson
NNO Jessica Hickman
NNO Jim Mehsling
NNO JM Smith
NNO John Sloboda

NNO Jon Gregory
NNO Kaela Croft
NNO Kallan Archer
NNO Kate Carleton
NNO Kelly Greider
NNO Kevin Graham
NNO Kevin P. West
NNO Kris Penix
NNO Kyle Babbitt
NNO Kyle Hickman
NNO Luke Preece
NNO Marcia Dye
NNO Mark Mangum
NNO Mark Stroud
NNO Marsha Parkins
NNO Matt Langford
NNO Matt Maldonado
NNO Matt Soffe
NNO Matt Steffens
NNO Matt Stewart
NNO Michael Mastermaker
NNO Michelle Rayner
NNO Mike Barnard
NNO Mike James
NNO Mohammad Jilani
NNO Neil Camera
NNO Norvierto P. Basio
NNO Phil Hassewer
NNO Rey Paez
NNO Rich Molinelli
NNO Robert Hendrickson
NNO Roy Cover
NNO Sarah Wilkinson
NNO Shane McCormack
NNO Solly Mohamed
NNO Stephanie Swanger
NNO Ted Dastick Jr.
NNO Tiffany Groves
NNO Tim Dowler
NNO Tim Proctor
NNO Tina Berardi
NNO Todd Aaron Smith
NNO Tom Carlton
NNO Ward Silverman

2017 Star Wars 40th Anniversary Triple Autographs

STATED PRINT RUN 3 SER.#'d SETS

UNPRICED DUE TO SCARCITY

TABDM Baker/Daniels/Mayhew
TAHBB Hamill/Barclay/Bauersfeld
TAHHK Hamill/Hagon/Klaff
TAPMW Park/McDiarmid/Wood

2017 Star Wars 1978 Sugar Free Wrappers Set

COMPLETE SET (49)	10.00	25.00
COMPLETE FACTORY SET (51)		
COMMON CARD (1-49)	.30	.75
*BLUE/75: 2X TO 5X BASIC CARDS	1.50	4.00
*GREEN/40: 4X TO 10X BASIC CARDS	3.00	8.00
*GOLD/10: 6X TO 15X BASIC CARDS	5.00	12.00
*RED/1: UNPRICED DUE TO SCARCITY		

1980 Star Wars Empire Strikes Back

"WELCOME, YOUNG LUKE!"

COMPLETE SET (352)	60.00	120.00
COMPLETE SET W/STICKERS (440)	75.00	150.00
COMPLETE SERIES 1 SET (132)	20.00	50.00
COMPLETE SERIES 1 SET W/STICKERS (165)	25.00	60.00
COMPLETE SERIES 2 SET (132)	15.00	40.00
COMPLETE SERIES 2 SET W/STICKERS (165)	20.00	50.00
COMPLETE SERIES 3 SET (88)	12.00	30.00
COMPLETE SERIES 3 SET W/STICKERS (110)	15.00	40.00
UNOPENED SERIES 1 BOX (36 PACKS)	150.00	200.00
UNOPENED SERIES 1 PACK (12 CARDS+1 STICKER)	5.00	6.00
UNOPENED SERIES 2 BOX (36 PACKS)	65.00	80.00
UNOPENED SERIES 2 PACK (12 CARDS+1 STICKER)	2.50	3.00
UNOPENED SERIES 3 BOX (36 PACKS)	65.00	80.00
UNOPENED SERIES 3 PACK (12 CARDS+1 STICKER)	2.50	3.00
COMMON SERIES 1 CARD (1-132)	.10	.25
COMMON SERIES 2 CARD (133-264)	.06	.15
COMMON SERIES 3 CARD (265-352)	.06	.15

1980 Star Wars Empire Strikes Back Stickers

COMPLETE SET (88)	15.00	40.00
COMPLETE SERIES 1 SET (33)	8.00	20.00
COMPLETE SERIES 2 SET (33)	6.00	15.00
COMPLETE SERIES 3 SET (22)	3.00	8.00
COMMON CARD (1-33)	.60	1.50
COMMON CARD (34-66)	.40	1.00
COMMON CARD (67-88)	.20	.50

1980 Star Wars Empire Strikes Back Twinkies New Zealand

COMPLETE SET (6)	15.00	40.00
COMMON CARD (UNNUMBERED)	4.00	10.00

1980 Star Wars Empire Strikes Back York Peanut Butter Discs

COMPLETE SET (6)	12.00	30.00
COMMON CARD (1-6)	3.00	8.00

1995 Star Wars Empire Strikes Back Widevision

Produced by Topps. The second movie in the original Star Wars trilogy is the topic for this set. The card fronts show a photo image from the film, with a purple stripe on the top and bottom, plus a holographic foil stamp in the bottom-right corner. The card backs feature story boards, production art, and production photos, accompanied by story text and behind-the-scenes narrative. This is another set where the cards measure 4 5/8 by 2 1/2 inches (11.9 by 6.3 cm). A checklist card was not produced for this set. Artwork on card backs by Ivor Beddoes, Joe Johnston, Ralph McQuarrie, John Mollo, Norman Reynolds, and Nilo Rodis-Janero.

COMPLETE SET (144)	12.00	30.00
UNOPENED BOX (36 PACKS)	30.00	40.00
UNOPENED PACK (9 CARDS)	1.00	1.25
COMMON CARD (1-144)	.25	.60

1995 Star Wars Empire Strikes Back Widevision Finest

COMPLETE SET (10)	40.00	100.00
COMMON CARD (C1-C10)	4.00	10.00
STATED ODDS 1:12		

1995 Star Wars Empire Strikes Back Widevision Mini Posters

These oversized poster cards measure 4" x 6" and were issued one per box.

COMPLETE SET (6)	40.00	80.00
COMMON CARD (1-6)	6.00	15.00
STATED ODDS 1:BOX		

1995 Star Wars Empire Strikes Back Widevision Promos

0 Darth Vader
P1 Han Solo Tortured
P2 AT-Ats
P3 Luke & Yoda
P4 Luke Hanging
P5 Boba Fett w/Han in Carbonite
P6 Leia, Luke, and Robots
NNO 3-Card Sheet
P1-P3

2010 Star Wars Empire Strikes Back 3-D Widevision

COMPLETE SET (48)	10.00	25.00
COMMON CARD (1-48)	.40	1.00
P1 Luke Skywalker PROMO	8.00	20.00

2010 Star Wars Empire Strikes Back 3-D Widevision Autographs

COMMON CARD	150.00	300.00
STATED ODDS 1:1,055		
1 Irvin Kershner	250.00	400.00
2 Ralph McQuarrie	500.00	800.00
4 David Prowse	500.00	800.00
6 Carrie Fisher	500.00	800.00
8 Mark Hamill	400.00	600.00

2010 Star Wars Empire Strikes Back 3-D Widevision Sketches

COMPLETE ARTIST LIST (109)
STATED ODDS 1:24 H, 1:72 R
UNPRICED DUE TO SCARCITY

1 Adrian Rivera
2 Alex Alderete
3 Alex Buechel
4 Beck Kramer
5 Ben Curtis Jones
6 Bill Pulkovski
7 Braden Lamb
8 Brandon Kenney
9 Brent Engstrom
10 Brian Ashmore
11 Brian Rood
12 Bruce Gerlach
13 Bryan Morton
14 Cal Slayton
15 Carolyn Edwards
16 Cassandra Siemon
17 Cat Staggs
18 Chris Eliopoulos
19 Chris Henderson
20 Chris Houghton
21 Chris Uminga
22 Clay McCormack
23 Cynthia Cummens Narcisi
24 Dan Bergren
25 Dan Curto
26 Dan Masso
27 Darrin Radimaker
28 David Day
29 David Rabbitte
30 Denise Vasquez
31 Dennis Budd
32 Erik Maell
33 Gabe Farber
34 Geoff Munn
35 Hayden Davis
36 Howard Shum
37 Ingrid Hardy
38 Irma Ahmed
39 Jake Minor
40 James Bukauskas
41 Jamie Snell
42 Jan Duursema
43 Jason Davies
44 Jason Hughes
45 Jason Keith Phillips
46 Jason Sobol
47 Jeff Confer
48 Jen Mercer
49 Jeremy Treece
50 Jerry Vanderstelt
51 Jessica Hickman
52 Jim Kyle
53 Joe Corroney
54 John Beatty
55 John Haun
56 John McCrea
57 John P. Wales
58 John Soukup
58 Rich Molinelli
59 Jon Morris
60 Juan Carlos Ramos
61 Karen Krajenbrink
62 Katie Cook
63 Katie McDee
64 Kevin Doyle

65 Kevin Graham
66 Kevin Liell
67 Lance Sawyer
68 Lauren Perry
69 Lawrence Snelly
70 Leah Mangue
71 Lee Kohse
72 Lin Workman
73 Lord Mesa
74 Mark Dos Santos
75 Mark McHaley
76 Mark Raats
77 Martheus Wade
78 Matt Minor
79 Matt Olson
80 Michael Duron
81 Monte Moore
82 Nolan Woodard
83 Randy Martinez
84 Rhiannon Owens
86 Rich Woodall
87 Robert Hendrickson
88 Robert Teranishi
89 Ryan Hungerford
90 Sarah Wilkinson
91 Scott Daly
92 Scott DM Simmons
93 Scott Rorie
94 Scott Zirkel
95 Sean Pence
96 Shea Standefer
97 Shelli Paroline
98 Soni Alcorn-Hender
99 Spencer Brinkerhoff III
100 Stephanie Yue
101 Steve Oatney
102 Steve Stanley
103 Steven Miller
104 Ted Dastick
105 Tim Proctor
106 Tod Allen Smith
107 Tom Hodges
108 Tomoko Taniguchi
109 Zack Giallongo

1996 Star Wars The Empire Strikes Back 3-Di

P1 AT-ATs

2015 Star Wars Illustrated Empire Strikes Back

COMPLETE SET (100)	10.00	25.00
COMMON CARD (1-100)	.20	.50
*PURPLE: 5X TO 12X BASIC CARDS	2.50	6.00
*BRONZE: 8X TO 20X BASIC CARDS	4.00	10.00
*GOLD/10: 20X TO 50X BASIC CARDS	10.00	25.00
*P.P.BLACK/1: UNPRICED DUE TO SCARCITY		
*P.P.CYAN/1: UNPRICED DUE TO SCARCITY		
*P.P.MAGENTA/1: UNPRICED DUE TO SCARCITY		
*P.P.YELLOW/1: UNPRICED DUE TO SCARCITY		

2015 Star Wars Illustrated Empire Strikes Back Celebration VII Promos

COMPLETE SET (10)	10.00	25.00
COMMON CARD (1-10)	1.50	4.00

2015 Star Wars Illustrated Empire Strikes Back Artist Autographs

COMPLETE ARTIST LIST (100)
UNPRICED DUE TO SCARCITY

1 Renegade Flight
Randy Martinez
2 Attacking the Convoy
Matt Busch
3 Reporting to Needa
Randy Martinez
4 Status Update
Matt Busch
5 Luke and Leia Confer
Randy Martinez
6 Presenting Commander Skywalker
Matt Busch
7 Echo 3 to Echo 7
Randy Martinez
8 Luke Attacked!
Matt Busch
9 Droids Identify
Randy Martinez
10 The Wampa Cave
Matt Busch
11 Luke Fights the Wampa
Randy Martinez
12 Solo Returns
Matt Busch
13 Working on the Falcon
Randy Martinez
14 Ben's Guidance
Matt Busch
15 Breaking the News
Randy Martinez
16 A Tender-ish Moment
Matt Busch
17 Stuck in the Snow
Randy Martinez
18 Shutting the Professor Up
Matt Busch
19 Han Rides Out
Randy Martinez
20 Discovering Luke
Matt Busch
21 Keeping Warm
Randy Martinez
22 Inside the Shelter
Matt Busch
23 Closing the Shield Doors
Randy Martinez

24 The Search Begins
Matt Busch
25 Rescue on Hoth
Randy Martinez
26 Luke's Visitors
Matt Busch
27 Zone 12 Moving East
Randy Martinez
28 Destroying the Probe
Matt Busch
29 Ordering the Evacuation
Randy Martinez
30 Ozzel's Bad News
Matt Busch
31 Captain Piett's Plan
Randy Martinez
32 Ozzel's Final Punishment
Matt Busch
33 Luke and Leia's Farewell
Randy Martinez
34 Walkers on the North Ridge
Matt Busch
35 Rogue Flight's Attack
Randy Martinez
36 Rogue Leader
Matt Busch
37 The Great Harpoon Plan
Randy Martinez
38 Walker Down!
Matt Busch
39 Rogue Leader Down!
Randy Martinez
40 Man vs. Walker
Matt Busch
41 Echo Base Invasion
Randy Martinez
42 Snowtrooper Invasion
Matt Busch
43 The Millennium Falcon Departs
Randy Martinez
44 Rogue Flight Reunion
Matt Busch
45 Against the Empire
Randy Martinez
46 Set Course for Dagobah
Matt Busch
47 Entering the Asteroid Field
Randy Martinez
48 Darth Vader's Interruption
Matt Busch
49 The Kiss
Randy Martinez
50 Mynocks in the Cave
Matt Busch
51 Out in the Cave
Randy Martinez
52 Monster in Space
Matt Busch
53 Contacting the Emperor
Randy Martinez
54 Crash Landing
Matt Busch
55 Meeting Yoda
Randy Martinez
56 Little Green Nuisance
Matt Busch
57 Dinner at the Hut
Randy Martinez
58 Yoda's Warning
Matt Busch
59 Jedi Training Begins
Randy Martinez
60 Harsh Lessons
Matt Busch
61 Spirits in the Cave
Randy Martinez
62 Bounty Hunters Assembled
Matt Busch

63 Boba Fett on the Spot
Randy Martinez
64 The Falcon's Escape
Matt Busch
65 Balancing Stones
Randy Martinez
66 Size Defeats Luke
Matt Busch
67 Master Yoda's Great Power
Randy Martinez
68 With the Garbage
Matt Busch
69 Luke's Vision
Randy Martinez
70 Bespin Arrival
Matt Busch
71 Introducing Lando
Randy Martinez
72 Threepio's Intrusion
Matt Busch
73 Ignoring the Master's Advice
Randy Martinez
74 Bringing Back Threepio
Matt Busch
75 Vader's Surprise
Randy Martinez
76 Standing Idly By
Matt Busch
77 Han's Torture
Randy Martinez
78 Han's Cell
Matt Busch
79 Chewbacca's Rage
Randy Martinez
80 I Know
Matt Busch
81 The Freezing of Han Solo
Randy Martinez
82 He's Alive!
Matt Busch
83 In Pursuit of Fett
Randy Martinez
84 Leia's Frantic Warning
Matt Busch
85 Meeting Vader
Randy Martinez
86 The Duel Begins
Matt Busch
87 A Quick Defeat?
Randy Martinez
88 Lando Tricks Back
Matt Busch
89 The East Platform
Randy Martinez
90 To the Falcon
Matt Busch
91 The Millennium Falcon Departs
Randy Martinez
92 Luke Overpowered
Matt Busch
93 The Duel Continues
Randy Martinez
94 Luke's Bitter Defeat
Matt Busch
95 Vader's Dark Truth
Randy Martinez
96 Through the Force
Matt Busch
97 Escape From Bespin
Randy Martinez
98 Watching the Escape
Matt Busch
99 Hyperdrive: Operational
Randy Martinez
100 New Hand, New Mission
Matt Busch

2015 Star Wars Illustrated Empire Strikes Back Film Cel Relics

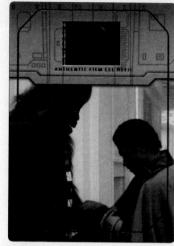

COMPLETE SET (25)	100.00	200.00
COMMON CARD (SKIP #'d)	6.00	15.00
FR2 Back at Echo Base	8.00	20.00
FR3 Monster in the Snow	8.00	20.00
FR6 The Imperial Walkers	10.00	25.00
FR7 Luke Vs. the AT-AT	8.00	20.00
FR8 Imperial Pursuit	10.00	25.00
FR9 Asteroid Field	8.00	20.00
FR10 Dagobah Landing	8.00	20.00
FR13 Message From the Emperor	12.00	30.00
FR15 Bounty Hunters Assemble	8.00	20.00
FR16 Failure at the Cave	10.00	25.00
FR20 A Most Gracious Host	10.00	25.00
FR25 You Are not a Jedi Yet	10.00	25.00
FR26 Lando's Redemption	8.00	20.00
FR27 Battle in the Gantry	10.00	25.00
FR28 The Truth Revealed	8.00	20.00
FR29 Rescuing Luke	15.00	40.00
FR30 Saying Farewell	8.00	20.00

2015 Star Wars Illustrated Empire Strikes Back Movie Poster Reinterpretations

COMPLETE SET (10)	8.00	20.00
COMMON CARD (MP1-MP10)	1.50	4.00

*P.P.BLACK/1: UNPRICED DUE TO SCARCITY
*P.P.CYAN/1: UNPRICED DUE TO SCARCITY
*P.P.MAGENTA/1: UNPRICED DUE TO SCARCITY
*P.P.YELLOW/1: UNPRICED DUE TO SCARCITY
STATED ODDS 1:3

2015 Star Wars Illustrated Empire Strikes Back
One Year Earlier

COMPLETE SET (18)	15.00	40.00
COMMON CARD (OY1-OY18)	1.50	4.00

*P.P.BLACK/1: UNPRICED DUE TO SCARCITY
*P.P.CYAN/1: UNPRICED DUE TO SCARCITY
*P.P.MAGENTA/1: UNPRICED DUE TO SCARCITY
*P.P.YELLOW/1: UNPRICED DUE TO SCARCITY
STATED ODDS 1:2

2015 Star Wars Illustrated Empire Strikes Back
Panorama Sketches

COMPLETE ARTIST LIST (97)
UNPRICED DUE TO SCARCITY

1 Adrianna Vanderstelt
2 Adrian Rivera
3 Andrew "Drone" Cosson
4 Andrew Jones
5 Angelina Benedetti
6 Art O'Callaghan
7 Barush Merling
8 Ben Dunn
9 Bill Pulkovski
10 Brandon Gallo
11 Brent Raglund
12 Brian K. O'Connell
13 Bruce Gerlach
14 Carla Rodriguez
15 Carlos Cabaleiro
16 Charles Hall
17 Chris Eliopoulos
18 Chris Henderson
19 Chris West
20 Dan Bergren
21 Dan Curto
22 Dan Gorman
23 Dan Nokes
24 Dan Smith
25 Daniel Benitez, Arturo "JAR" Ramìrez
26 Danny Haas
27 Darrin Pepe
28 David J. Williams
29 David Rabbitte
30 Denae Frazier
31 Elfie Lebouleux
32 Eric Bell
33 Eric Lehtonen
34 Eric McConnell
35 Erik Hodson
36 Erik Maell
37 FLOSI
38 Francois Chartier
39 Ingrid Hardy
40 Jared Hickman
41 Jason Adams

42 Jason Chalker
43 Jason Crosby
44 Jason Sobol
45 Jeff Zapata
46 Jeffrey "JSB" Benitez
47 Jenn DePaola
48 Jessica Hickman
49 Joanne Ellen Patak
50 Joe Corroney
51 Joe Hogan
52 Joel Carroll
53 John Soukup
54 Josh Bodwell
55 Kaela Croft
56 Kate Carleton
57 Kevin Doyle
58 Kimberly Dunaway
59 Kris Penix
60 Lak Lim
61 Lee Kohse
62 Lee Lightfoot
63 Marck Labas
64 Matt Busch
65 Matt Hebb
66 Michael "Locoduck" Duron
67 Michael Leavitt
68 Mick and Matt Glebe
69 Mikey Babinsky
70 Norvien Basio
71 Pablo Diaz
72 Pat Barrett
73 Patrick Richardson
74 Paul "Gutz" Gutierrez
75 Peejay Catacutan
76 Rhiannon Owens
77 Rich Kunz
78 Rich Molinelli
79 Robert Jimenez
80 Robert Teranishi
81 Ron Conley
82 Roy Cover
83 Russ Maheras
84 Sarah Wilkinson
85 Scott Zambelli
86 Sean Pence
87 Sol Mohamed
88 Stephanie Swanger
89 Steve Black
90 Steven Burch
91 Tanner Padlo
92 Thom "TG" Glinski
93 Thom Zahler
94 Tim Proctor
95 Tom Kelly
96 Tony Miello
97 Veronica O'Connell

2015 Star Wars Illustrated Empire Strikes Back
Sketchagraphs

1 Anthony Daniels
Adam Talley
2 Anthony Daniels
Carlos Cabaleiro
3 Anthony Daniels
Kevin Graham
4 Anthony Daniels
Kris Penix
5 Anthony Daniels
Mikey Babinski
6 Billy Dee Williams
Andrew "Drone" Cosson
7 Billy Dee Williams
Bill Pulkovski
8 Billy Dee Williams
Carlos Cabaleiro
9 Billy Dee Williams
Darrin Pepe
10 Billy Dee Williams

Jason Crosby
11 Billy Dee Williams
Jason Sobol
12 Billy Dee Williams
Kevin Graham
13 Billy Dee Williams
Kimberly Dunaway
14 Billy Dee Williams
Kyle Babbitt
15 Billy Dee Williams
Mikey Babinski
16 Billy Dee Williams
Rich Molinelli
17 Billy Dee Williams
Roy Cover
18 David Ackroyd
Erik Maell
19 David Ackroyd
Jason Crosby
20 David Ackroyd
Wilson Ramos Jr.
21 David Paymer
Erik Maell
22 Jay O. Sanders
Bruce Gerlach
23 Jay O. Sanders
Cal Sparrow
24 Jay O. Sanders
Carlos Cabaleiro
25 Jay O. Sanders
Dan Curto
26 Jay O. Sanders
Eric Lehtonen
27 Jay O. Sanders
Jason Crosby
28 Jay O. Sanders
Jason Sobol
29 Jay O. Sanders
Joe Hogan
30 Jay O. Sanders
John Soukup
31 Jay O. Sanders
Josh Bodwell
32 Jay O. Sanders
Kevin Graham
33 Jay O. Sanders
Kyle Babbitt
34 Jay O. Sanders
Mikey Babinski
35 Jay O. Sanders
Pat Barrett
36 Jay O. Sanders
Roy Cover
37 Jeremy Bulloch
Ben Dunn
38 Jeremy Bulloch
Bill Pulkovski
39 Jeremy Bulloch
Brandon Gallo
40 Jeremy Bulloch
Carlos Cabaleiro
41 Jeremy Bulloch
Dan Curto
42 Jeremy Bulloch
Danny Haas
43 Jeremy Bulloch
Eric Lehtonen
44 Jeremy Bulloch
Jason Crosby
45 Jeremy Bulloch
Jason Sobol
46 Jeremy Bulloch
Joe Hogan
47 Jeremy Bulloch
John Soukup
48 Jeremy Bulloch
Kyle Babbitt
49 Jeremy Bulloch

Mikey Babinski
50 Jeremy Bulloch
Rich Molinelli
51 Jeremy Bulloch
Roy Cover
52 Paul Hecht
Andrew "Drone" Cosson
53 Paul Hecht
Ashleigh Popplewell
54 Paul Hecht
Brandon Gallo
55 Paul Hecht
Bruce Gerlach
56 Paul Hecht
Carlos Cabaleiro
57 Paul Hecht
Dan Curto
58 Paul Hecht
Danny Haas
59 Paul Hecht
Eric Lehtonen
60 Paul Hecht
Jason Crosby
61 Paul Hecht
John Soukup
62 Paul Hecht
Josh Bodwell
63 Paul Hecht
Kate Carleton
64 Paul Hecht
Kevin Graham
65 Paul Hecht
Kimberly Dunaway
66 Paul Hecht
Kyle Babbitt
67 Paul Hecht
Mikey Babinski
68 Paul Hecht
Rich Molinelli
69 Paul Hecht
Roy Cover
70 Peter Friedman
Andrew "Drone" Cosson
71 Peter Friedman
Ben Dunn
72 Peter Friedman
Brandon Gallo
73 Peter Friedman
Bruce Gerlach
74 Peter Friedman
Cal Sparrow
75 Peter Friedman
Carlos Cabaleiro
76 Peter Friedman
Dan Curto
77 Peter Friedman
Eric Lehtonen
78 Peter Friedman
Jason Sobol
79 Peter Friedman
Joe Hogan
80 Peter Friedman
Kevin Graham
81 Peter Friedman
Kimberly Dunaway
82 Peter Friedman
Kyle Babbitt
83 Peter Friedman
Mikey Babinski
84 Peter Friedman
Pat Barrett
85 Peter Friedman
Roy Cover
86 Peter Michael Goetz
Andrew "Drone" Cosson
87 Peter Michael Goetz
Ashleigh Popplewell
88 Peter Michael Goetz

Ben Dunn
89 Peter Michael Goetz
Bruce Gerlach
90 Peter Michael Goetz
Cal Sparrow
91 Peter Michael Goetz
Carlos Cabaleiro
92 Peter Michael Goetz
Dan Curto
93 Peter Michael Goetz
Darrin Pepe
94 Peter Michael Goetz
Eric Lehtonen
95 Peter Michael Goetz
Jason Sobol
96 Peter Michael Goetz
Joe Hogan
97 Peter Michael Goetz
John Soukup
98 Peter Michael Goetz
Kate Carleton
99 Peter Michael Goetz
Kevin Graham
100 Peter Michael Goetz
Kimberly Dunaway
101 Peter Michael Goetz
Mikey Babinski
102 Peter Michael Goetz
Pat Barrett
103 Peter Michael Goetz
Rich Molinelli
104 Peter Michael Goetz
Roy Cover
105 Peter Mayhew
Adam Talley
106 Peter Mayhew
Andrew "Drone" Cosson
107 Peter Mayhew
Ben Dunn
108 Peter Mayhew
Bill Pulkovski
109 Peter Mayhew
Bruce Gerlach
110 Peter Mayhew
Carlos Cabaleiro
111 Peter Mayhew
Dan Gorman
112 Peter Mayhew
Eric Lehtonen
113 Peter Mayhew
Jason Crosby
114 Peter Mayhew
Jason Sobol
115 Peter Mayhew
John Soukup
116 Peter Mayhew
Josh Bodwell
117 Peter Mayhew
Kimberly Dunaway
118 Peter Mayhew
Mikey Babinski
NNO Sketchagraph Redemption Card

2015 Star Wars Illustrated Empire Strikes Back Sketches

COMPLETE ARTIST LIST (107)
UNPRICED DUE TO SCARCITY

1 Adam Talley
2 Adrianna Vanderstelt
3 Adrian Rivera
4 Andrew "Drone" Cosson
5 Andrew Jones
6 Angelina Benedetti
7 Art O'Callaghan
8 Ashleigh Popplewell
9 Barush Merling
10 Ben Dunn

11 Bill Pulkovski
12 Brandon Baselice
13 Brandon Gallo
14 Brent Raglund
15 Brian DeGuire
16 Brian K. O'Connell
17 Bruce Gerlach
18 Carla Rodriguez
19 Carlos Cabaleiro
20 Charles Hall
21 Chris Eliopoulos
22 Chris Henderson
23 Chris West
24 Dan Bergren
25 Dan Curto
26 Dan Gorman
27 Dan Nokes
28 Dan Smith
29 Daniel Benitez, Arturo "JAR" Ramìrez
30 Danny Haas
31 Darrin Pepe
32 David J. Williams
33 David Rabbitte
34 Denae Frazier
35 Elfie Lebouleux
36 Eric Bell
37 Eric Lehtonen
38 Eric McConnell
39 Frik Hodson
40 Erik Maell
41 FLOSI
42 Francois Chartier
43 Ingrid Hardy
44 Jared Hickman
45 Jason Adams
46 Jason Chalker
47 Jason Crosby
48 Jason Flowers
49 Jason Sobol
50 Jeff Zapata
51 Jeffrey "JSB" Benitez
52 Jenn DePaola
53 Jessica Hickman
54 Joanne Ellen Patak
55 Joe Corroney
56 Joe Hogan
57 Joel Biske
58 Joel Carroll
59 John Soukup
60 Josh Bodwell
61 Kaela Croft
62 Karen Hinson
63 Kate Carleton
64 Kevin Doyle
65 Kevin Graham
66 Kimberly Dunaway
67 Kris Penix
68 Lak Lim
69 Lee Kohse
70 Lee Lightfoot
71 Marck Labas
72 Matt Busch
73 Matt Hebb
74 Michael "Locoduck" Duron
75 Michael Leavitt
76 Mick and Matt Glebe
77 Mikey Babinsky
78 Norvien Basio
79 Pablo Diaz
80 Pat Barrett
81 Patrick Giles
82 Patrick Richardson
83 Paul "Gutz" Gutierrez
84 Peejay Catacutan
85 Rhiannon Owens
86 Rich Kunz
87 Rich Molinelli
88 Robert Jimenez

89 Robert Teranishi
90 Ron Conley
91 Roy Cover
92 Russ Maheras
93 Sarah Wilkinson
94 Scott Zambelli
95 Sean Pence
96 Sol Mohamed
97 Stephanie Swanger
98 Steve Black
99 Steven Burch
100 Tanner Padlo
101 Thom "TG" Glinski
102 Thom Zahler
103 Tim Proctor
104 Tod Allen Smith
105 Tom Kelly
106 Tony Miello
107 Veronica O'Connell

2015 Star Wars Illustrated Empire Strikes Back The Force Awakens Inserts

COMPLETE SET (4)	20.00	50.00
COMMON CARD (SKIP #'d)	8.00	20.00

2015 Star Wars Illustrated Empire Strikes Back The Mission Capture Skywalker

COMPLETE SET (10)	12.00	30.00
COMMON CARD (1-10)	2.50	6.00
*P.P.BLACK/1: UNPRICED DUE TO SCARCITY		
*P.P.CYAN/1: UNPRICED DUE TO SCARCITY		
*P.P.MAGENTA/1: UNPRICED DUE TO SCARCITY		
*P.P.YELLOW/1: UNPRICED DUE TO SCARCITY		
STATED ODDS 1:8		
3 Han Solo	3.00	8.00
9 Boba Fett	4.00	10.00

1983 Star Wars Return of the Jedi

COMPLETE SET (220)	15.00	40.00
COMMON CARD (1-220)	.15	.40

1983 Star Wars Return of the Jedi Stickers

COMPLETE SET W/O VARIANTS (55)	6.00	15.00
COMMON CARD (1-55)	.20	.50
STATED ODDS 1:1		

1996 Star Wars Return of the Jedi Widevision

COMPLETE SET (144)	10.00	25.00
UNOPENED BOX (24 PACKS)	50.00	60.00
UNOPENED PACK (9 CARDS)	1.50	2.00
COMMON CARD (1-144)	.20	.50

DIII Admiral Akbar

1996 Star Wars Return of the Jedi Widevision Finest

COMPLETE SET (10)	40.00	80.00
COMMON CARD (C1-C10)	4.00	10.00
STATED ODDS 1:12		

1996 Star Wars Return of the Jedi Widevision Mini Posters

These oversized poster cards measure 4" x 6" and were issued one per box.

COMPLETE SET (6)	40.00	80.00
COMMON CARD (1-6)	6.00	15.00
STATED ODDS 1:BOX		

1996 Star Wars Return of the Jedi Widevision Promos

0 Ghosts
P1 Han & Luke with Jabba
P2 Luke in Tree Chase
P3 Han, Leia, & Stormtroopers
P4 Emperor Palpatine
P5 Jabba the Hutt
P6 Luke, Han, & Chewbacca in Jabba's Palace
NNO 1-Card Sheet
Complete the Trilogy

2014 Star Wars Return of the Jedi 3-D Widevision

COMPLETE SET (44)	12.00	30.00
COMMON CARD (1-44)	.50	1.25
TOPPS WEBSITE EXCLUSIVE SET		

2014 Star Wars Return of the Jedi 3-D Widevision Autographs

COMMON CARD (UNNUMBERED)	12.00	30.00
STATED ODDS 1:SET		
NNO Alan Harris	30.00	60.00
NNO Barrie Holland	12.00	30.00
NNO Carrie Fisher		
NNO Femi Taylor	12.00	30.00
NNO Jeremy Bulloch	25.00	60.00
NNO Kenneth Colley	15.00	40.00
NNO Mark Hamill		
NNO Mike Quinn	25.00	50.00
NNO Peter Mayhew	50.00	100.00
NNO Tim Rose	25.00	60.00

2014 Star Wars Return of the Jedi 3-D Widevision Manufactured Patches

COMPLETE SET (4)	50.00	100.00
COMMON CARD	10.00	25.00
STATED ODDS ONE PATCH/SKETCH PER SET		

2014 Star Wars Return of the Jedi 3-D Widevision Sketch Card Relics

COMPLETE SET (5)
UNPRICED DUE TO SCARCITY

1 Ewok
2 Jabba's Sail Barge
3 Logray
4 Teebo
5 Wicket W. Warrick

1997 Star Wars Return of the Jedi Special Edition

NNO Crescent City Con XII

1999 Star Wars Episode One Widevision Series One

This Widevision formatted set covers the first film in the prequel trilogy. Produced by Topps, each card front displays an image from the film and each back has additional imagery plus narrative text. Cards measure 4 5/8 by 2 1/2 inches (11.9 by 6.3 cm). This product was available in both hobby (H) and retail (R) packs.

COMPLETE SET (80)	8.00	20.00
UNOPENED HOBBY BOX (36 PACKS)	45.00	60.00
UNOPENED HOBBY PACK (8 CARDS)	1.50	2.00
UNOPENED RETAIL BOX (11 PACKS)	30.00	45.00
UNOPENED RETAIL PACK (8 CARDS)	2.75	4.00
COMMON CARD (1-80)	.25	.50

1999 Star Wars Episode One Widevision Series
One Chrome

COMPLETE SET (8)	30.00	60.00
COMMON CARD (C1-C8)	4.00	10.00
STATED ODDS 1:12		

1999 Star Wars Episode One Widevision Series
One Expansion

COMPLETE SET (40)	30.00	60.00
COMMON CARD (X1-X40)	1.00	2.50
STATED ODDS 1:2		

1999 Star Wars Episode One Widevision Series
One Foil

COMPLETE SET (10)	30.00	60.00
COMMON CARD (F1-F10)	3.00	8.00

1999 Star Wars Episode One Widevision Series
One Stickers

COMPLETE SET (16)	8.00	20.00
COMMON CARD (S1-S16)	.60	1.50

1999 Star Wars Episode One Widevision Series
One Tin Inserts

COMPLETE SET (5)	12.00	30.00
COMMON CARD (1-5)	4.00	10.00
STATED ODDS ONE PER RETAIL TIN		
2 Darth Maul	5.00	12.00

1999 Star Wars Episode One Widevision Series
Two

More images from the film Star Wars Episode I: The Phantom Menace make up this second series. As with series one, each card front contains an image from the film while the backs have a narrative text, plus behind-the-scenes information along with a behind-the-scenes image or production drawing. The base set includes subsets, such as: Fantastic Characters (2-18), Environments of Wonder (19-24), Heroes in Flight (25-36), Podracing Thrills (37-54), The Land Battle (55-60), A Planet Beseiged (61-66), Galactic Warfare (67-72), The Force Is with Them (73-78). The set is rounded out by a checklist (80). Artwork by Doug Chiang, Iain McCaig, Drew Struzan, and Terryl Whitlach. It was available in both hobby (H) and retail (R).

COMPLETE SET (80)	8.00	20.00
UNOPENED HOBBY BOX (36 PACKS)	40.00	50.00
UNOPENED HOBBY PACK (8 CARDS)	1.25	1.50
UNOPENED RETAIL BOX (24 PACKS)	35.00	45.00
UNOPENED RETAIL PACK (8 CARDS)	1.50	1.75
COMMON CARD (1-80)	.25	.60

1999 Star Wars Episode One Widevision Series
Two Box-Toppers

COMPLETE SET (3)	10.00	20.00
COMMON CARD (1-3)	4.00	10.00
STATED ODDS 1:HOBBY BOX		

1999 Star Wars Episode One Widevision Series
Two Chrome Hobby

COMPLETE SET (4)	12.00	25.00
COMMON CARD (HC1-HC4)	4.00	10.00
STATED ODDS 1:18 HOBBY		

1999 Star Wars Episode One Widevision Series
Two Chrome Retail

COMPLETE SET (4)	20.00	40.00
COMMON CARD (C1-C4)	6.00	15.00
STATED ODDS 1:18 RETAIL		

1999 Star Wars Episode One Widevision Series
Two Embossed Hobby

COMPLETE SET (6)	8.00	20.00
COMMON CARD (HE1-HE6)	2.50	6.00
STATED ODDS 1:12 HOBBY		

1999 Star Wars Episode One Widevision Series
Two Embossed Retail

COMPLETE SET (6)	20.00	40.00
COMMON CARD (E1-E6)	4.00	10.00
STATED ODDS 1:12 RETAIL		

1999 Star Wars Episode One Widevision Series
Two Promos

P1 Racing with Conviction
P2 Sebulba's Deception

2000 Star Wars Episode One 3-D

Another Widevision effort from Topps covering the events of the Phantom Menace, this time in lenticular 3-D format. Each card measures 4 5/8 by 2 1/2 inches (11.9 by 6.3 cm).

COMPLETE SET (46)	20.00	40.00
UNOPENED BOX (36 PACKS)	45.00	60.00
UNOPENED PACK (2 CARDS)	1.50	2.00
COMMON CARD (1-46)	.50	1.25

2000 Star Wars Episode One 3-D Multi-Motion

COMPLETE SET (2)	10.00	25.00
COMMON CARD (1-2)	6.00	15.00

1999 Star Wars Episode I Bluebird Potato Chips New Zealand

12. QUI-GON AND WATTO

COMPLETE SET (30)	10.00	25.00
COMMON CARD (1-30)	.60	1.50

1999 Star Wars Episode I Family Toy

1 Obi-Wan	4.00	10.00
2 Darth Maul	4.00	10.00
3 (pod race)	4.00	10.00

1999 Star Wars Episode I Flip Images

COMPLETE SET (6)	5.00	12.00
COMMON CARD	1.25	3.00
UNNUMBERED SET		

1999 Star Wars Episode I Hallmark

H1 Anakin Skywalker and Obi-Wan Kenobi	2.00	5.00
H2 Obi-Wan Kenobi and Yoda	2.00	5.00
H3 Qui-Gon Jinn and Obi-Wan Kenobi	2.00	5.00

1999 Star Wars Episode I iKon

01. Padmé

This offering was produced by the Australian company, iKon Collectibles. The card fronts feature a bordered image from the film and the backs have either a glow-in-the-dark image (1-24) or puzzle image. The following card blocks form a 9-card puzzle: 25-33, 34-42, 43-51, and 52-60. There are two parallel versions (gold and silver) which are randomly inserted into packs. Limited to 5,000 boxes.

COMPLETE SET (60)	6.00	15.00
UNOPENED BOX (36 PACKS)		
UNOPENED PACK (6 CARDS)		
COMMON CARD (1-60)	.20	.50

*SILVER: 1.5X TO 4X BASIC CARDS
*GOLD: 2.5X TO 6X BASIC CARDS

1999 Star Wars Episode I KFC Australia

5/10   WE'VE GOT SOMETHING GOOD TO SHARE

COMPLETE SET (10)	3.00	8.00
COMMON CARD (1-10)	.50	1.25

1999 Star Wars Episode I KFC UK

1 Qui-Gon Jinn
2 R2-D2
3 Jar Jar Binks
4 Queen Amidala
5 Shmi Skywalker
6 Obi-Wan Kenobi
7 Senator Palpatine
8 Mace Windu
9 Destroyer Droid
10 Jabba the Hutt
11 Sebulba
12 Yoda
13 Darth Maul
14 C-3PO
15 Watto
16 Padme
17 Battle Droid
18 Nute Gunray
19 Darth Sidious
20 Anakin Skywalker

1999 Star Wars Episode I Pepsi Collector Can Contest Cards

1 Anakin Skywalker
2 Sebulba
3 Qui-Gon Jinn
4 Watto
5 Jabba the Hutt
6 Senator Palpatine
7 R2-D2
8 Darth Sidious
9 Darth Maul
10 Jar Jar Binks
11 Mace Windu
12 Obi-Wan Kenobi
13 Captain Panaka
14 Rune Haako
15 Ric Olie
16 Destroyer Droid
17 Queen Amidala
18 Padme
19 Shmi Skywalker
20 Battle Droid
21 Chancellor Valorum
22 C-3PO
23 Nute Gunray
24 Boss Nass

1999 Star Wars Episode I The Phantom Menace Harmony Foods

1 Heroes	2.00	5.00
2 Anakin	2.00	5.00
3 Jedi vs. Sith	2.00	5.00
4 Amidala	2.00	5.00
5 Jedi vs. Sith	2.00	5.00
6 Jedi	2.00	5.00
7 C-3PO	2.00	5.00
8 Sith Lord	2.00	5.00
9 Qui-Gon Jinn	2.00	5.00
10 Obi-Wan Kenobi	2.00	5.00
11 Podracing	2.00	5.00
12 Naboo Fighter	2.00	5.00
13 Battle Droids	2.00	5.00
14 Jar Jar Binks	2.00	5.00
15 Trade Federation Starfighter	2.00	5.00
16 Qui-Gon	2.00	5.00
17 Darth Maul	2.00	5.00

18 Podrace	2.00	5.00
19 R2-D2	2.00	5.00
20 Federation Fighter	2.00	5.00
21 Jedi Knight	2.00	5.00
22 Maul	2.00	5.00
23 Maul Hood	2.00	5.00
24 Qui-Gon	2.00	5.00

1999 Star Wars Episode I The Phantom Menace Kentucky Fried Chicken Employee Stickers

NNO Darth Maul	2.00	5.00
NNO Jar Jar Banks	2.00	5.00
NNO Obi-Wan Kenobi	2.00	5.00
NNO Queen Amidala	2.00	5.00
NNO Qui-Gon Jinn	2.00	5.00

1999 Star Wars Episode I The Phantom Menace Pepsi UK

1 Anakin Skywalker
2 Queen Amidala
3 Darth Maul
4 Jar Jar Binks
5 Obi-Wan Kenobi
6 Qui-Gon Jinn
7 Yoda

1999 Star Wars Episode I The Phantom Menace Show Promo

NNO DLP Exclusive Presentation

2001 Star Wars Episode I The Phantom Menace Walmart DVD Promos

1 Complete Podrace Grid Sequence
2 Extended Podrace Lap Two
3 The Waterfall Sequence
4 The Air Taxi Sequence

1999 Star Wars Episode I Star Mart

NNO Anakin Skywalker	2.00	5.00
NNO C-3PO	2.00	5.00
NNO Darth Maul	2.00	5.00
NNO R2-D2	2.00	5.00

2002 Star Wars Attack of the Clones

ANAKIN SKYWALKER

Based on the second installment in the sequel trilogy, this set displays an image from the film on the front and an additional image on the back, complete with narrative text and behind-the-scenes information. The base set includes the following subsets: The Characters (2-21), The Storyline (22-90), and Behind-the-Scenes (91-99). The set is rounded out with a checklist (100).

COMPLETE SET (100)	5.00	12.00
UNOPENED BOX (36 PACKS)	45.00	60.00
UNOPENED PACK (7 CARDS)	1.50	2.00
COMMON CARD (1-100)	.15	.40

2002 Star Wars Attack of the Clones Foil

COMPLETE SET (10)	6.00	15.00
COMMON CARD (1-10)	.75	2.00

2002 Star Wars Attack of the Clones Panoramic Fold-Outs

COMPLETE SET (5)	12.00	30.00
COMMON CARD (1-5)	3.00	8.00
STATED ODDS 1:12		

2002 Star Wars Attack of the Clones Prisms

COMPLETE SET (8)	8.00	20.00
COMMON CARD (1-8)	1.25	3.00

2002 Star Wars Attack of the Clones Promos

B1 UK Distribution		
(Album Exclusive)		
P1 The Saga Continues (Light Side)	1.25	3.00
(Non-Sport Update/Previews Exclusive)		
P2 The Saga Continues (Dark Side)	1.25	3.00
P3 The Saga Continues (Anakin & Clone Troopers)	1.25	3.00
P4 Star Wars Insider/Star Wars Gamer Exclusive	3.00	8.00
P5 The Saga Continues (Count Dooku)	1.25	3.00
(Wizard Exclusive)		
P6 Star Wars Celebration II Exclusive	3.00	8.00
NNO Best Buy Soundtrack Exclusive		

2002 Star Wars Attack of the Clones Widevision

This Topps produced set covers Episode II of the Star Wars saga. The card fronts contain photo images from the film and summarized narrative information on the backs along with a production photo or drawing. The cards measure roughly 4 5/8 by 2 1/2 inches (11.9 by 6.3 cm). Artwork produced by Robert Barnes, Doug Chiang, Ryan Church, Kurt Kaufman, Iain McCaig, Edwin Natividad, Durmont Power, Jay Shuster, Erik Tiemen, and Terryl Whitlach.

COMPLETE SET (80)	5.00	12.00
COMMON CARD (1-80)	.15	.40

2002 Star Wars Attack of the Clones Widevision Autographs

Notable names include: Ahmed Best, Frank Oz (1st autograph), Kenny Baker, and Silas Carson.

COMPLETE SET (24)	600.00	1200.00
COMMON CARD (1-24)	20.00	40.00
STATED ODDS 1:24		
2 Alethea McGrath	25.00	60.00
3 Amy Allen	30.00	60.00
7 Bonnie Piesse	40.00	80.00
8 Daniel Logan	75.00	125.00
10 Frank Oz	250.00	400.00
13 Joel Edgerton	20.00	50.00
14 Kenny Baker	100.00	200.00
22 Silas Carson/Ki-Adi-Mundi	25.00	50.00
23 Silas Carson/Nute Gunray	25.00	50.00

2002 Star Wars Attack of the Clones Widevision Promos

P1 Spider Droid	.60	1.50
(Non-Sport Update Exclusive)		
S1 Spider Droid		
(UK Exclusive)		

2002 Star Wars Attack of the Clones Widevision DVD Promos

W1 In Love And War	1.00	2.50
W2 R2D2 To The Rescue	1.00	2.50
W3 Jedi vs. Battle Droid	1.00	2.50
W4 Saved By Clone Troopers	1.00	2.50
W5 Yoda Prepares For Battle	1.00	2.50

2016 Star Wars Attack of the Clones 3-D Widevision

MEETING WITH THE CHANCELLOR

COMPLETE SET (44)	12.00	30.00
COMMON CARD (1-44)	.50	1.25

2016 Star Wars Attack of the Clones 3-D Widevision Autographs

*RED/1: UNPRICED DUE TO SCARCITY		
STATED ODDS 1:SET		
NNO Alan Ruscoe	15.00	40.00
NNO Amy Allen	60.00	120.00
NNO Anthony Daniels	80.00	150.00
NNO Daniel Logan	15.00	40.00
NNO Hassani Shapi	100.00	200.00
NNO Ian McDiarmid	150.00	300.00
(Chancellor Palpatine)		
NNO Ian McDiarmid	200.00	400.00
(Darth Sidious)		
NNO Jesse Jensen	30.00	80.00
NNO Jett Lucas	15.00	40.00
NNO Kenny Baker	80.00	150.00
NNO Matthew Wood	25.00	60.00
Magaloof		
NNO Oliver Ford	15.00	40.00
NNO Silas Carson	50.00	100.00
Ki-Adi-Mundi		
NNO Silas Carson	20.00	50.00
Nute Gunray		

2016 Star Wars Attack of the Clones 3-D Widevision Dual Autographs

COMPLETE SET (3)	
UNPRICED DUE TO SCARCITY	
1 Allen/Krishan	
2 Jensen/Shapi	
3 Carson/Jensen	

2016 Star Wars Attack of the Clones 3-D Widevision Medallions

COMPLETE SET (10)	175.00	350.00
COMMON CARD (MC1-MC10)	15.00	40.00
*SILVER/25: X TO X BASIC CARDS		
*GOLD/10: X TO X BASIC CARDS		
*RED/1: UNPRICED DUE TO SCARCITY		
STATED ODDS PATCH OR MEDALLION 1:1		

2016 Star Wars Attack of the Clones 3-D Widevision Patches

COMPLETE SET (12)	200.00	350.00
COMMON CARD (MP1-MP12)	15.00	40.00
*SILVER/25: X TO X BASIC CARDS		
*GOLD/10: X TO X BASIC CARDS		
*RED/1: UNPRICED DUE TO SCARCITY		
STATED ODDS PATCH OR MEDALLION 1:1		

2002 Star Wars Episode II Instant Win

NNO Anakin Skywalker
NNO C-3PO & R2-D2
NNO Jango Fett
NNO Obi-Wan Kenobi
NNO Padme Amidala

2002 Star Wars Episode II Jedi Fruit Rolls

COMPLETE SET (6)	5.00	12.00
UNNUMBERED SET		
1 Luke vs. Darth Vader	3.00	8.00
2 Luke vs. Darth Vader	3.00	8.00
3 Obi-Wan vs. Count Dooku	.75	2.00
4 Obi-Wan vs. Darth Vader	2.00	5.00
5 Obi-Wan vs. Jango Fett	.75	2.00
6 Qui-Gon Jinn vs. Darth Maul	1.25	3.00

2005 Star Wars Revenge of the Sith

MACE VS. PALPATINE

A Topps produced set devoted to the big conclusion in the prequel trilogy, Star Wars Episode III: Revenge of the Sith. The story is summarized with images on the front and text on the back. The base set includes the following subsets: Characters, Alliances, Storyline, Planets, Hardware, Production Art, and Behind-the-Scenes. This release came in many forms: hobby (H), retail (R), retail mini-boxes, retail tins, and retail bubble packs.

COMPLETE SET (90)	5.00	12.00
UNOPENED HOBBY BOX (36 PACKS)	65.00	80.00
UNOPENED HOBBY PACK (7 CARDS)	2.00	2.50
UNOPENED RETAIL BOX (24 PACKS)	30.00	40.00
UNOPENED RETAIL PACK (7 CARDS)	1.50	1.75
COMMON CARD (1-90)	.15	.40

2005 Star Wars Revenge of the Sith Blister Bonus

COMPLETE SET (3)	6.00	15.00
COMMON CARD (B1-B3)	2.50	6.00
STATED ODDS ONE PER BLISTER PACK		

2005 Star Wars Revenge of the Sith Embossed Foil

COMPLETE SET (10)	20.00	50.00
COMMON CARD (1-10)	2.50	6.00
STATED ODDS 1:6 RETAIL		

2005 Star Wars Revenge of the Sith Etched Foil Puzzle

COMPLETE SET (6)	12.00	30.00
COMMON CARD (1-6)	2.50	6.00
STATED ODDS 1:6		

2005 Star Wars Revenge of the Sith Flix-Pix

Produced by Topps UK. This was a separate product sold overseas. The basic design is similar to the Revenge of the Sith Flix-Pix inserts in the Widevision set. The card fronts feature a 3-D Lenticular image of various Star Wars scenes and characters while the backs feature a black-and-white image of another character.

COMPLETE SET (68)	50.00	100.00
UNOPENED BOX (36 PACKS)	100.00	150.00
UNOPENED PACK	3.00	5.00
COMMON CARD (1-68)	1.00	2.50
CL (TRI-FOLD INSERT)	.40	1.00

2005 Star Wars Revenge of the Sith Holograms

COMPLETE SET (3)	5.00	12.00
COMMON CARD (1-3)	2.00	5.00
STATED ODDS 1:14 RETAIL		

2005 Star Wars Revenge of the Sith Lenticular Morph Hobby

COMPLETE SET (2)	5.00	12.00
COMMON CARD (1-2)	3.00	8.00
STATED ODDS 1:24 HOBBY		

2005 Star Wars Revenge of the Sith Lenticular Morph Retail

COMPLETE SET (2)	5.00	12.00
COMMON CARD (1-2)	3.00	8.00
STATED ODDS 1:24 RETAIL		

2005 Star Wars Revenge of the Sith Sketches

ARTIST SKETCH CARD

COMPLETE ARTIST LIST (41)	
STATED ODDS 1:36	
GROUP A ODDS 1:777	
GROUP B ODDS 1:357	
GROUP C ODDS 1:493	
GROUP D ODDS 1:863	
GROUP E ODDS 1:194	
GROUP F ODDS 1:1,131	
GROUP G ODDS 1:134	
GROUP H ODDS 1:333	
GROUP I ODDS 1:221	
UNNUMBERED SET LISTED ALPHABETICALLY	
UNPRICED DUE TO SCARCITY	

1 Amy Pronovost B
2 Brandon McKinney B
3 Brent Woodside B
4 Brian Rood C
5 Cat Staggs A
6 Chris Eliopoulos A
7 Chris Trevas B
8 Christian Dalla Vecchia G
9 Cynthia Cummens B
10 Dan Norton E
11 Dan Parsons E
12 Dave Dorman B
13 Dave Fox A
14 David Rabbitte B
15 Davide Fabbri G
16 Grant Gould G
17 Howard Shum G
18 James Hodgkins F
19 Jeff Carlisle A
20 Jeff Chandler A
21 Joe Corroney C
22 John McCrea G
23 Joseph Booth C
24 Juan Carlos Ramos A
25 Justin Chung A
26 Kieron Dwyer B
27 Kilian Plunkett A
28 Matt Busch E
29 Matt Haley C
30 Mike Lilly C
31 Monte Moore A
32 Otis Frampton D
33 Paul Gutierrez E
34 Randy Martinez I
35 Robert Teranishi E
36 Russ Walks B
37 Ryan Benjamin E
38 Sarah Wilkinson E
39 Scott Erwert B
40 Thomas Hodges H
41 William O'Neill D

2005 Star Wars Revenge of the Sith Stickers

COMPLETE SET (10)	2.50	6.00
COMMON CARD (1-10)	.40	1.00
STATED ODDS 1:3 RETAIL		

2005 Star Wars Revenge of the Sith Tattoos

COMPLETE SET (10)	4.00	10.00
COMMON CARD (1-10)	1.00	2.50
STATED ODDS 1:3 RETAIL		

2005 Star Wars Revenge of the Sith Tin Gold

COMPLETE SET (6)	5.00	12.00
COMMON CARD (A-F)	1.00	2.50
STATED ODDS ONE PER TIN		

2005 Star Wars Revenge of the Sith Tin Story

COMPLETE SET (6)	5.00	12.00
COMMON CARD (1-6)	1.00	2.50
STATED ODDS ONE PER TIN		

2005 Star Wars Revenge of the Sith Promos

P1 The Circle is Complete GEN	1.00	2.50
P2 The Circle is Complete NSU	1.00	2.50
P3 The Circle is Complete	15.00	40.00
(Star Wars Shop)		
P4 The Circle is Complete	1.00	2.50
(Celebration III)		

P5 The Circle is Complete	1.00	2.50
(Wizard)		

2005 Star Wars Revenge of the Sith Medalionz

COMPLETE SET (24)	15.00	40.00
COMMON CARD (1-24)	1.00	2.50
*GOLD: .8X TO 2X BASIC MED.		
CL Checklist	.20	.50

2005 Star Wars Revenge of the Sith Widevision

Produced by Topps, this is the second set devoted to Revenge of the Sith, but it is in the Widevision format. Each card measures 4 5/8 by 2 1/2 inches (11.9 by 6.3 cm). An image from the film is illustrated on the card front, and narrative text plus an additional image is contained on the card back. It was available in both hobby (H) and retail (R). Autographs were randomly inserted with the most notable name being Samuel L. Jackson.

COMPLETE SET (80)	5.00	12.00
UNOPENED HOBBY BOX (24 PACKS)	25.00	40.00
UNOPENED HOBBY PACK (6 CARDS)	1.50	2.00
UNOPENED RETAIL BOX (24 PACKS)	25.00	40.00
UNOPENED RETAIL PACK (6 CARDS)	1.50	2.00
COMMON CARD (1-80)	.15	.40

2005 Star Wars Revenge of the Sith Widevision Autographs

COMMON CARD (UNNUMBERED)	25.00	50.00
STATED ODDS 1:48 HOBBY		
NNO Matthew Wood	50.00	100.00
NNO Peter Mayhew	50.00	100.00
NNO Samuel L. Jackson	600.00	1000.00

2005 Star Wars Revenge of the Sith Widevision Chrome Hobby

COMPLETE SET (10)	12.50	30.00
COMMON CARD (H1-H10)	1.50	4.00
STATED ODDS 1:6 HOBBY		

2005 Star Wars Revenge of the Sith Widevision Chrome Retail

COMPLETE SET (10)	15.00	40.00
COMMON CARD (R1-R10)	2.00	5.00
STATED ODDS 1:60 RETAIL		

2005 Star Wars Revenge of the Sith Widevision Flix-Pix

COMPLETE SET (10)	15.00	40.00
COMMON CARD (1-10)	2.00	5.00
STATED ODDS 1:6		

2015 Star Wars Revenge of the Sith 3-D Widevision

COMPLETE SET (44)	10.00	25.00
COMPLETE FACTORY SET (46)	60.00	120.00
COMMON CARD (1-44)	.40	1.00

2015 Star Wars Revenge of the Sith 3-D Widevision Autographs

COMMON CARD	15.00	40.00
*SILVER/15: UNPRICED DUE TO SCARCITY		
*GOLD/1: UNPRICED DUE TO SCARCITY		
1 Ian McDiarmid	250.00	500.00
2 Anthony Daniels		
3 Kenny Baker		
4 Peter Mayhew	60.00	120.00
5 Jeremy Bulloch	25.00	60.00
6 Bai Ling	30.00	80.00

2015 Star Wars Revenge of the Sith 3-D Widevision Medallions

COMPLETE SET (8)	100.00	200.00
COMMON CARD (1-8)	15.00	40.00

*SILVER/30: .6X TO 1.5X BASIC MEDALLIONS
*GOLD/1: UNPRICED DUE TO SCARCITY

2015 Star Wars Revenge of the Sith 3-D Widevision Patches

COMPLETE SET (4)	50.00	100.00
COMMON CARD	15.00	40.00

*SILVER/30: .6X TO 1.5X BASIC PATCHES
*GOLD/1: UNPRICED DUE TO SCARCITY

2015 Star Wars Revenge of the Sith 3-D Widevision Sketch Medallions

COMMON CARD	50.00	100.00
1 Anakin Skywalker	60.00	120.00
2 Darth Vader	50.00	100.00
3 Chewbacca	100.00	200.00
4 Clone Trooper	50.00	100.00
5 General Grievous	50.00	100.00
6 R2-D2	50.00	100.00
7 C-3PO	80.00	150.00
8 Yoda		

2017 Star Wars The Force Awakens 3-D Widevision

COMPLETE SET (44)	12.00	30.00
COMPLETE BOXED SET (46)		
COMMON CARD (1-44)	.40	1.00

2017 Star Wars The Force Awakens 3-D Widevision Dual Autographs

COMPLETE SET (5)
PARALLEL/1: UNPRICED DUE TO SCARCITY
UNPRICED DUE TO SCARCITY

NNO Fisher/Grunberg
NNO Ridley/Boyega
NNO Ridley/Hamill
NNO Boyega/Mayhew
NNO Hamill/Serkis

2016 Star Wars The Force Awakens Chrome

COMPLETE SET (100)	8.00	20.00
UNOPENED BOX (24 PACKS)	50.00	70.00
UNOPENED PACK (6 CARDS)	3.00	3.50
COMMON CARD (1-100)	.25	.60
*REFRACTOR: 1.2X TO 3X BASIC CARDS	.60	1.50
*PRISM REF./99: 5X TO 12X BASIC CARDS	3.00	8.00
*SHIMMER REF./50: 10X TO 25X BASIC CARDS	6.00	15.00
*PULSAR REF./10: 15X TO 40X BASIC CARDS	10.00	25.00

*SUPERFRACTOR/1: UNPRICED DUE TO SCARCITY
*P.P.BLACK/1: UNPRICED DUE TO SCARCITY
*P.P.CYAN/1: UNPRICED DUE TO SCARCITY
*P.P.MAGENTA/1: UNPRICED DUE TO SCARCITY
*P.P.YELLOW/1: UNPRICED DUE TO SCARCITY

2016 Star Wars The Force Awakens Chrome Autographs

COMMON CARD	5.00	12.00

*ATOMIC/99: .5X TO 1.2X BASIC CARDS
*PRISM/50: .6X TO 1.5X BASIC CARDS
*X-FRACTOR/25: .75X TO 2X BASIC CARDS
*SHIMMER/10: UNPRICED DUE TO SCARCITY
*PULSAR/5: UNPRICED DUE TO SCARCITY
*SUPERFRACTOR/1: UNPRICED DUE TO SCARCITY
*P.P.BLACK/1: UNPRICED DUE TO SCARCITY
*P.P.CYAN/1: UNPRICED DUE TO SCARCITY
*P.P.MAGENTA/1: UNPRICED DUE TO SCARCITY
*P.P.YELLOW/1: UNPRICED DUE TO SCARCITY
OVERALL AUTO ODDS 1:24

CAAB Anna Brewster	8.00	20.00
CABV Brian Vernel	10.00	25.00
CAGG Greg Grunberg	10.00	25.00
CAJS Joonas Suotamo	10.00	25.00
CAKS Kipsang Rotich	8.00	20.00
CAMD Mark Dodson	10.00	25.00
CAMQ Mike Quinn	8.00	20.00
CAPM Peter Mayhew	20.00	50.00
CASA Sebastian Armesto	8.00	20.00
CAYR Yayan Ruhian	10.00	25.00
CAMWG Matthew Wood	8.00	20.00

2016 Star Wars The Force Awakens Chrome Autographs Atomic Refractors

*ATOMIC/99: .5X TO 1.2X BASIC CARDS

CAJB John Boyega	120.00	200.00
CAWD Warwick Davis	12.00	30.00

2016 Star Wars The Force Awakens Chrome Autographs Prism Refractors

*PRISM/50: .6X TO 1.5X BASIC CARDS

CAAD Anthony Daniels		
CAAS Andy Serkis	120.00	200.00

2016 Star Wars The Force Awakens Chrome Autographs X-fractors

*X-FRACTORS: .75X TO 2X BASIC CARDS

CACF Carrie Fisher	120.00	250.00
CADR Daisy Ridley	1800.00	2200.00
CAEB Erik Bauersfeld		
CAHF Harrison Ford		
CAKB Kenny Baker	150.00	300.00
CAMH Mark Hamill		
CAMWU Matthew Wood		

2016 Star Wars The Force Awakens Chrome Behind-the-Scenes

COMPLETE SET (12)	10.00	25.00
COMMON CARD (1-12)	1.25	3.00
*SHIMMER REF./50: 1X TO 2.5X BASIC CARDS	3.00	8.00
*PULSAR REF./10: UNPRICED DUE TO SCARCITY		
*SUPERFRACTOR/1: UNPRICED DUE TO SCARCITY		
*P.P.BLACK/1: UNPRICED DUE TO SCARCITY		
*P.P.CYAN/1: UNPRICED DUE TO SCARCITY		
*P.P.MAGENTA/1: UNPRICED DUE TO SCARCITY		
*P.P.YELLOW/1: UNPRICED DUE TO SCARCITY		
STATED ODDS 1:4		

2016 Star Wars The Force Awakens Chrome Dual Autographs

COMPLETE SET (5)
STATED PRINT RUN 3 SER.#'d SETS
UNPRICED DUE TO SCARCITY

CDABF Fisher/Boyega
CDAHF Hamill/Fisher
CDAMA Marshall/Armesto
CDAMS Suotamo/Mayhew
CDAWB Mayhew/Walker

2016 Star Wars The Force Awakens Chrome Heroes of the Resistance

COMPLETE SET (18)	10.00	25.00
COMMON CARD (1-18)	.75	2.00
*SHIMMER REF./50: 1 X TO 2.5X BASIC CARDS	2.00	5.00
*PULSAR REF./10: UNPRICED DUE TO SCARCITY		
*SUPERFRACTOR/1: UNPRICED DUE TO SCARCITY		
*P.P.BLACK/1: UNPRICED DUE TO SCARCITY		
*P.P.CYAN/1: UNPRICED DUE TO SCARCITY		
*P.P.MAGENTA/1: UNPRICED DUE TO SCARCITY		
*P.P.YELLOW/1: UNPRICED DUE TO SCARCITY		
STATED ODDS 1:2		
1 Finn	1.25	3.00
2 Rey	1.25	3.00
3 Poe Dameron	1.00	2.50

9 BB-8	1.50	4.00
10 C-3PO	1.00	2.50
11 R2-D2	1.00	2.50
13 Han Solo	1.50	4.00
14 Chewbacca	1.00	2.50
18 General Leia Organa	1.00	2.50

2016 Star Wars The Force Awakens Chrome Medallions

COMPLETE SET (25)	200.00	400.00
COMMON CARD	3.00	8.00
*SILVER/25: .5X TO 1.2X BASIC CARDS		
*GOLD/10: UNPRICED DUE TO SCARCITY		
*PLATINUM/1: UNPRICED DUE TO SCARCITY		
M1 Han Solo	12.00	30.00
M2 General Leia Organa	12.00	30.00
M3 Admiral Ackbar	5.00	12.00
M4 Chewbacca	6.00	15.00
M5 Admiral Statura	5.00	12.00
M6 Snap Wexley	8.00	20.00
M7 Jess Testor Pava	8.00	20.00
M10 Poe Dameron	8.00	20.00
M11 Rey	20.00	50.00
M12 Finn	10.00	25.00
M13 BB-8	10.00	25.00
M14 Riot Control Stormtrooper	8.00	20.00
M16 Colonel Datoo	6.00	15.00
M17 Supreme Leader Snoke	6.00	15.00
M18 Flametrooper	5.00	12.00
M19 Kylo Ren	8.00	20.00
M20 Kylo Ren	8.00	20.00
M21 General Hux	5.00	12.00
M22 Captain Phasma	8.00	20.00
M23 FN-2187	10.00	25.00

2016 Star Wars The Force Awakens Chrome Patches

COMPLETE SET (27)	175.00	350.00
COMMON CARD (P1-P27)	5.00	12.00
*SHIMMER/199: .5X TO 1.2X BASIC CARDS		
*PULSAR/99: .6X TO 1.5X BASIC CARDS		
*SUPERFRACTOR/5: UNPRICED DUE TO SCARCITY		
P1 Rey/686	15.00	40.00
P2 Han Solo/299	8.00	20.00
P4 Finn/686	8.00	20.00
P7 Kylo Ren/401	6.00	15.00
P11 General Leia Organa/755	8.00	20.00
P15 BB-8/686	6.00	15.00
P16 Poe Dameron & BB-8/686	6.00	15.00
P17 Rey & BB-8/686	12.00	30.00
P18 R2-D2/686	6.00	15.00
P19 Rey/299	10.00	25.00
P20 Rey/686	10.00	25.00
P23 Han Solo & Chewbacca/737	10.00	25.00

2016 Star Wars The Force Awakens Chrome Power of the First Order

COMPLETE SET (9)	6.00	15.00
COMMON CARD (1-9)	.75	2.00
*SHIMMER REF./50: 1X TO 2.5X BASIC CARDS		
*PULSAR REF./10: UNPRICED DUE TO SCARCITY		
*SUPERFRACTOR/1: UNPRICED DUE TO SCARCITY		
*P.P.BLACK/1: UNPRICED DUE TO SCARCITY		
*P.P.CYAN/1: UNPRICED DUE TO SCARCITY		
*P.P.MAGENTA/1: UNPRICED DUE TO SCARCITY		
*P.P.YELLOW/1: UNPRICED DUE TO SCARCITY		
STATED ODDS 1:12		
1 Supreme Leader Snoke	1.50	4.00
2 Kylo Ren	1.50	4.00
3 General Hux	1.25	3.00
4 Captain Phasma	1.25	3.00

2016 Star Wars The Force Awakens Chrome Ships and Vehicles

COMPLETE SET (11)	6.00	15.00
COMMON CARD (1-11)	1.00	2.50
*SHIMMER REF./50: 1X TO 2.5X BASIC CARDS	2.50	6.00
*PULSAR REF./10: UNPRICED DUE TO SCARCITY		
*SUPERFRACTOR/1: UNPRICED DUE TO SCARCITY		
*P.P.BLACK/1: UNPRICED DUE TO SCARCITY		
*P.P.CYAN/1: UNPRICED DUE TO SCARCITY		
*P.P.MAGENTA/1: UNPRICED DUE TO SCARCITY		
*P.P.YELLOW/1: UNPRICED DUE TO SCARCITY		
STATED ODDS 1:8		

2016 Star Wars The Force Awakens Chrome Sketches

COMPLETE ARTIST LIST (24)
UNPRICED DUE TO SCARCITY

1 Alex Iniguez
2 Angelina Benedetti

3 Bob Stevlic
4 Brad Hudson
5 Brent Ragland
6 Carlos Cabaleiro
7 Daniel Parsons
8 Darrin Pepe
9 Eric Lehtonen
10 Jason Sobol
11 Jonathan Caustrita
12 Kevin Graham
13 Kevin P. West
14 Kris Penix
15 Marcia Dye
16 Matt Stewart
17 Rich Molinelli
18 Rob Teranishi
19 Robert Hendrickson
20 Sarah Wilkinson
21 Solly Mohamed
22 Stephanie Swanger
23 Tim Proctor
24 Tina Berardi

2016 Star Wars The Force Awakens Chrome Triple Autographs

COMPLETE SET (4)		
STATED PRINT RUN 3 SER.#'d SETS		
UNPRICED DUE TO SCARCITY		
CTAFBR Boyega/Fisher/Rose		
CTAFGQ Fisher/Grunberg/Quinn		
CTAHFB Hamill/Fisher/Boyega		
CTASMA Serkis/Marshall/Armesto		

2015 Star Wars The Force Awakens Dog Tags

COMPLETE SET (16)	15.00	40.00
COMMON CARD (1-16)	1.25	3.00
*GOLD: 1X TO 2.5X BASIC TAGS		
1 Kylo Ren	2.00	5.00
2 Rey	2.00	5.00
3 Finn	1.50	4.00
5 Captain Phasma	1.50	4.00
10 BB-8	2.50	6.00
11 Rey	2.00	5.00
12 Finn	1.50	4.00
13 Kylo Ren	2.00	5.00

2015 Star Wars The Force Awakens Dog Tags Target Exclusives

COMPLETE SET (2)	10.00	25.00
COMMON CARD (T1-T2)	5.00	12.00
*GOLD: .75X TO 2X BASIC TAGS		
EXCLUSIVE TO TARGET		
T2 BB-8	8.00	20.00

2015 Star Wars The Force Awakens Dog Tags Toys 'R' Us Exclusives

COMPLETE SET (2)	10.00	25.00
COMMON CARD (TR1-TR2)	6.00	15.00
*GOLD: 1X TO 2.5X BASIC TAGS		
EXCLUSIVE TO TOYS 'R' US		

2015 Star Wars The Force Awakens Dog Tags Walmart Exclusives

COMPLETE SET (2)	6.00	15.00
COMMON CARD (W1-W2)	4.00	10.00
*GOLD: 1X TO 2.5X BASIC TAGS		
EXCLUSIVE TO WALMART		

2016 Star Wars The Force Awakens Factory Set

Produced by Topps. This online exclusive brings three Star Wars base sets together for one stellar factory set. It is the first Star Wars factory set that Topps has produced. There are 310 total cards that have been taken from these three sets: Journey to the Force Awakens, The Force Awakens Series One, and The Force Awakens Series Two. Each card has a special "Topps Complete Set" foil stamp on it to signify its exclusivity.

COMPLETE FACTORY SET (310)	40.00	80.00
COMMON CARD	.15	.40
JOURNEY TO TFA (1-110)		
TFA SERIES ONE (1-100)		
TFA SERIES TWO (1-100)		
*LIM.ED./100: 6X TO 15X BASIC CARDS	2.50	6.00

2015 Star Wars The Force Awakens Glow-in-the-Dark Decals

Produced in conjunction with General Mills, this decal set was inserted in popular brands of breakfast cereal, such as Cheerios, Cinnamon Toast Crunch, etc. It features characters from the seventh film in the Star Wars saga, The Force Awakens. The Millennium Falcon decal was only offered as an exclusive decal within Reese's Puffs cereal at participating Kroger, thus making it a short-printed premium.

COMPLETE SET (7)	10.00	25.00
COMMON CARD	1.25	3.00
STATED ODDS 1:CEREAL BOX		
INSERTED IN BOXES OF GENERAL MILLS CEREAL		
MILLENNIUM FALCON IS KROGER EXCLUSIVE		
1 BB-8	2.50	6.00
2 C-3PO and R2-D2	1.50	4.00
3 Captain Phasma	2.00	5.00
5 Kylo Ren	2.00	5.00
6 Millennium Falcon SP	5.00	12.00
Kroger Exclusive		

2015 Star Wars The Force Awakens Series One

COMPLETE SET w/o SP (100)	10.00	25.00
COMMON CARD (1-100)	.20	.50
*LTSBR GREEN: .5X TO 1.2X BASIC CARDS		
*LTSBR BLUE: .6X TO 1.5X BASIC CARDS		
*LTSBR PURPLE: .75X TO 2X BASIC CARDS		
*FOIL/250: 4X TO 10X BASIC CARDS		
*GOLD/100: 6X TO 15X BASIC CARDS		
*PLATINUM/1: UNPRICED DUE TO SCARCITY		
*P.P.BLACK/1: UNPRICED DUE TO SCARCITY		
*P.P.CYAN/1: UNPRICED DUE TO SCARCITY		
*P.P.MAGENTA/1: UNPRICED DUE TO SCARCITY		
*P.P.YELLOW/1: UNPRICED DUE TO SCARCITY		
TARGET EXCLUSIVES SP 101-103		
100 Han Solo & Chewbacca return home	.75	2.00
101 Maz Kanata SP	3.00	8.00
102 Wollivan SP	3.00	8.00
103 Grummgar SP	3.00	8.00

2015 Star Wars The Force Awakens Series One Autographs

COMMON CARD	15.00	40.00
*LTSBR PURPLE/25: .75X TO 2X BASIC AUTOS		
*GOLD/10: UNPRICED DUE TO SCARCITY		
*IMP. RED/1: UNPRICED DUE TO SCARCITY		
*P.P.BLACK/1: UNPRICED DUE TO SCARCITY		
*P.P.CYAN/1: UNPRICED DUE TO SCARCITY		
*P.P.MAGENTA/1: UNPRICED DUE TO SCARCITY		
*P.P.YELLOW/1: UNPRICED DUE TO SCARCITY		
STATED ODDS 1:106 H; 1:12,334 R		
1 Anthony Daniels	120.00	250.00
2 Carrie Fisher	120.00	250.00
3 Daisy Ridley	800.00	1100.00
Mystery Redemption		
4 Harrison Ford		
5 John Boyega		
6 Kenny Baker	50.00	100.00
7 Peter Mayhew	30.00	80.00
8 Tim Rose	20.00	50.00

2015 Star Wars The Force Awakens Series One Behind-the-Scenes

COMPLETE SET (7)	5.00	12.00
COMMON CARD (1-7)	1.00	2.50
*LTSBR GREEN: .5X TO 1.2X BASIC CARDS		
*LTSBR BLUE: .6X TO 1.5X BASIC CARDS		
*LTSBR PURPLE: .75X TO 2X BASIC CARDS		
*FOIL/250: 4X TO 10X BASIC CARDS		
*GOLD/100: 6X TO 15X BASIC CARDS		
*PLATINUM/1: UNPRICED DUE TO SCARCITY		
*P.P.BLACK/1: UNPRICED DUE TO SCARCITY		
*P.P.CYAN/1: UNPRICED DUE TO SCARCITY		
*P.P.MAGENTA/1: UNPRICED DUE TO SCARCITY		
*P.P.YELLOW/1: UNPRICED DUE TO SCARCITY		
STATED ODDS 1:8 H; 1:5 R		

2015 Star Wars The Force Awakens Series One Character Montages

COMPLETE SET (8)	4.00	10.00
COMMON CARD (1-8)	.75	2.00

*LTSBR GREEN: .5X TO 1.2X BASIC CARDS
*LTSBR BLUE: .6X TO 1.5X BASIC CARDS
*LTSBR PURPLE: .75X TO 2X BASIC CARDS
*FOIL/250: 4X TO 10X BASIC CARDS
*GOLD/100: 6X TO 15X BASIC CARDS
*PLATINUM/1: UNPRICED DUE TO SCARCITY
*P.P.BLACK/1: UNPRICED DUE TO SCARCITY
*P.P.CYAN/1: UNPRICED DUE TO SCARCITY
*P.P.MAGENTA/1: UNPRICED DUE TO SCARCITY
*P.P.YELLOW/1: UNPRICED DUE TO SCARCITY
STATED ODDS 1:7 H; 1:4 R

1 Rey	1.50	4.00
5 Captain Phasma	1.25	3.00
7 BB-8	1.50	4.00

2015 Star Wars The Force Awakens Series One
Character Stickers

COMPLETE SET (18)	6.00	15.00
COMMON CARD (1-18)	.60	1.50

*LTSBR GREEN: .5X TO 1.2X BASIC CARDS
*LTSBR BLUE: .6X TO 1.5X BASIC CARDS
*LTSBR PURPLE: .75X TO 2X BASIC CARDS
*FOIL/250: 4X TO 10X BASIC CARDS
*GOLD/100: 6X TO 15X BASIC CARDS
*PLATINUM/1: UNPRICED DUE TO SCARCITY
*P.P.BLACK/1: UNPRICED DUE TO SCARCITY
*P.P.CYAN/1: UNPRICED DUE TO SCARCITY
*P.P.MAGENTA/1: UNPRICED DUE TO SCARCITY
*P.P.YELLOW/1: UNPRICED DUE TO SCARCITY
STATED ODDS 1:3 H; 1:2 R

1 Rey	1.25	3.00
5 Captain Phasma	1.00	2.50
8 BB-8	1.25	3.00
12 Rey	1.25	3.00

2015 Star Wars The Force Awakens Series One
Concept Art

COMPLETE SET (20)	8.00	20.00
COMMON CARD (1-20)	.75	2.00

*LTSBR GREEN: .5X TO 1.2X BASIC CARDS
*LTSBR BLUE: .6X TO 1.5X BASIC CARDS
*LTSBR PURPLE: .75X TO 2X BASIC CARDS
*FOIL/250: 4X TO 10X BASIC CARDS
*GOLD/100: 6X TO 15X BASIC CARDS
*PLATINUM/1: UNPRICED DUE TO SCARCITY
*P.P.BLACK/1: UNPRICED DUE TO SCARCITY
*P.P.CYAN/1: UNPRICED DUE TO SCARCITY
*P.P.MAGENTA/1: UNPRICED DUE TO SCARCITY
*P.P.YELLOW/1: UNPRICED DUE TO SCARCITY
STATED ODDS 1:3 H; 1:2 R

2015 Star Wars The Force Awakens Series One
Dual Autographs

UNPRICED DUE TO SCARCITY

1 Anthony Daniels and Kenny Baker
2 Anthony Daniels and Peter Mayhew
3 Carrie Fisher and Anthony Daniels
4 Mike Quinn and Tim Rose

2015 Star Wars The Force Awakens Series One
First Order Rises

COMPLETE SET (9)	6.00	15.00
COMMON CARD (1-9)	1.25	3.00

*LTSBR GREEN: .5X TO 1.2X BASIC CARDS
*LTSBR BLUE: .6X TO 1.5X BASIC CARDS
*LTSBR PURPLE: .75X TO 2X BASIC CARDS
*FOIL/250: 4X TO 10X BASIC CARDS
*GOLD/100: 6X TO 15X BASIC CARDS
*PLATINUM/1: UNPRICED DUE TO SCARCITY
*P.P.BLACK/1: UNPRICED DUE TO SCARCITY
*P.P.CYAN/1: UNPRICED DUE TO SCARCITY
*P.P.MAGENTA/1: UNPRICED DUE TO SCARCITY
*P.P.YELLOW/1: UNPRICED DUE TO SCARCITY
STATED ODDS 1:6 H; 1:4 R

2 Captain Phasma	1.50	4.00

2015 Star Wars The Force Awakens Series One
First Order Stormtrooper Costume Relics

COMMON CARD	12.00	30.00

*BRONZE/99: .75X TO 2X BASIC CARDS
*SILVER/50: 1.2X TO 3X BASIC CARDS
*GOLD/10: 2X TO 5X BASIC CARDS
*PLATINUM/1: UNPRICED DUE TO SCARCITY

2015 Star Wars The Force Awakens Series One
Locations

COMPLETE SET (9)	3.00	8.00
COMMON CARD (1-9)	.60	1.50

*LTSBR GREEN: .5X TO 1.2X BASIC CARDS
*LTSBR BLUE: .6X TO 1.5X BASIC CARDS
*LTSBR PURPLE: .75X TO 2X BASIC CARDS

*FOIL/250: 4X TO 10X BASIC CARDS
*GOLD/100: 6X TO 15X BASIC CARDS
*PLATINUM/1: UNPRICED DUE TO SCARCITY
*P.P.BLACK/1: UNPRICED DUE TO SCARCITY
*P.P.CYAN/1: UNPRICED DUE TO SCARCITY
*P.P.MAGENTA/1: UNPRICED DUE TO SCARCITY
*P.P.YELLOW/1: UNPRICED DUE TO SCARCITY
STATED ODDS 1:6 H; 1:4 R

2015 Star Wars The Force Awakens Series One
Medallions

COMMON CARD (M1-M66)	8.00	20.00
STATED ODDS 1:BOX		

2015 Star Wars The Force Awakens Series One
Movie Scenes

COMPLETE SET (20)	5.00	12.00
COMMON CARD (1-20)	.50	1.25

*LTSBR GREEN: .5X TO 1.2X BASIC CARDS
*LTSBR BLUE: .60X TO 1.5X BASIC CARDS
*LTSBR PURPLE: .75X TO 2X BASIC CARDS
*FOIL/250: 4X TO 10X BASIC CARDS
*GOLD/100: 6X TO 15X BASIC CARDS
*PLATINUM/1: UNPRICED DUE TO SCARCITY
*P.P.BLACK/1: UNPRICED DUE TO SCARCITY
*P.P.CYAN/1: UNPRICED DUE TO SCARCITY
*P.P.MAGENTA/1: UNPRICED DUE TO SCARCITY
*P.P.YELLOW/1: UNPRICED DUE TO SCARCITY
STATED ODDS 1:3 H; 1:2 R

2015 Star Wars The Force Awakens Series One
Sketches

1 Alejandro Iniguez
2 Bob Stevlic
3 Brent Ragland
4 Carlos Cabaleiro
6 Dan Parsons
5 Dan Bergren
7 Doug Cowan
8 Francois Chartier
9 Gabe Farber

10 Ingrid Hardy
11 Jeff Mallinson
12 Justin Mauk
13 Kris Penix
14 Kyle Babbitt
16 Rob Teranishi
17 Robert Hendrickson
18 Sarah Wilkinson
19 Sean Pence
20 Stephanie Swanger
15 Lord Mesa

2015 Star Wars The Force Awakens Series One
Triple Autographs

UNPRICED DUE TO SCARCITY

1 Carrie Fisher
Peter Mayhew
  Anthony Daniels

2015 Star Wars The Force Awakens Series One
Weapons

COMPLETE SET (10)	4.00	10.00
COMMON CARD (1-10)	.60	1.50
*LTSBR GREEN: .5X TO 1.2X BASIC CARDS		
*LTSBR BLUE: .6X TO 1.5X BASIC CARDS		
*LTSBR PURPLE: .75X TO 2X BASIC CARDS		
*FOIL/250: 4X TO 10X BASIC CARDS		
*GOLD/100: 6X TO 15X BASIC CARDS		
*PLATINUM/1: UNPRICED DUE TO SCARCITY		
*P.P.BLACK/1: UNPRICED DUE TO SCARCITY		
*P.P.CYAN/1: UNPRICED DUE TO SCARCITY		
*P.P.MAGENTA/1: UNPRICED DUE TO SCARCITY		
*P.P.YELLOW/1: UNPRICED DUE TO SCARCITY		
STATED ODDS 1:6 H; 1:3 R		
1 Kylo Ren's lightsaber	1.25	3.00
9 Han Solo's Blaster	.75	2.00

2016 Star Wars The Force Awakens Series Two

COMPLETE SET W/O SP (100)	10.00	25.00
COMPLETE SET W/SP (102)	20.00	50.00
UNOPENED HOBBY BOX (24 PACKS)	60.00	100.00
UNOPENED HOBBY PACK (8 CARDS)	2.50	4.00
COMMON CARD (1-100)	.20	.50
*LTSBR GREEN: .5X TO 1.2X BASIC CARDS		
*LTSBR BLUE: .6X TO 1.5X BASIC CARDS		
*LTSBR PURPLE: .75X TO 2X BASIC CARDS		
*FOIL: 4X TO 10X BASIC CARDS		
*GOLD/100: 6X TO 15X BASIC CARDS		
*PLATINUM/1: UNPRICED DUE TO SCARCITY		
*P.P.BLACK/1: UNPRICED DUE TO SCARCITY		
*P.P.CYAN/1: UNPRICED DUE TO SCARCITY		
*P.P.MAGENTA/1: UNPRICED DUE TO SCARCITY		
*P.P.YELLOW/1: UNPRICED DUE TO SCARCITY		
101 Finding Luke Skywalker SP	6.00	15.00
102 The Lightsaber Returned SP	10.00	25.00

2016 Star Wars The Force Awakens Series Two
Autographs

COMMON CARD	8.00	20.00
*LTSBR PURPLE/50: .5X TO 1.2X BASIC AUTOS		
*FOIL/25: .75X TO 2X BASIC AUTOS		
*GOLD/10: UNPRICED DUE TO SCARCITY		
*IMP. RED/1: UNPRICED DUE TO SCARCITY		
*P.P.BLACK/1: UNPRICED DUE TO SCARCITY		
*P.P.CYAN/1: UNPRICED DUE TO SCARCITY		
*P.P.MAGENTA/1: UNPRICED DUE TO SCARCITY		
*P.P.YELLOW/1: UNPRICED DUE TO SCARCITY		
1 David Acord	20.00	50.00
FN-2199		
2 David Acord	15.00	40.00
Teedo		
4 Kenny Baker	50.00	100.00
5 Erik Bauersfeld		
6 John Boyega	150.00	300.00
7 Anna Brewster	12.00	30.00
8 Dante Briggins	12.00	30.00
9 Thomas Brodie-Sangster	10.00	25.00
10 Aidan Cook	12.00	30.00
11 Anthony Daniels	50.00	100.00
12 Warrick Davis	10.00	25.00

13 Harrison Ford		
14 Greg Grunberg	15.00	40.00
15 Carrie Fisher	120.00	250.00
17 Jessica Henwick	15.00	40.00
18 Brian Herring	60.00	120.00
19 Andrew Jack	10.00	25.00
20 Billie Lourd	15.00	40.00
21 Rocky Marshall	10.00	25.00
22 Peter Mayhew	25.00	60.00
25 Arti Shah	12.00	30.00
26 Kiran Shah	10.00	25.00
27 Joonas Suotamo	15.00	40.00
28 Brian Vernel	10.00	25.00
29 Dame Harriet Walter	12.00	30.00
30 Paul Warren	10.00	25.00

2016 Star Wars The Force Awakens Series Two
Card Trader Characters

COMPLETE SET (9)		
COMMON CARD (1-9)	50.00	100.00
STATED PRINT RUN 100 SER.#'d SETS		
1 BB-8	60.00	120.00
3 Finn	60.00	120.00
5 Kylo Ren	80.00	150.00
6 Captain Phasma	80.00	150.00
7 Poe Dameron	60.00	120.00
8 Rey	120.00	200.00

2016 Star Wars The Force Awakens Series Two
Character Poster Inserts

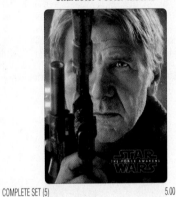

COMPLETE SET (5)	5.00	12.00
COMMON CARD (1-5)	1.50	4.00
*P.P.BLACK/1: UNPRICED DUE TO SCARCITY		
*P.P.CYAN/1: UNPRICED DUE TO SCARCITY		
*P.P.MAGENTA/1: UNPRICED DUE TO SCARCITY		
*P.P.YELLOW/1: UNPRICED DUE TO SCARCITY		
STATED ODDS 1:24		
1 Rey	2.50	6.00
2 Finn	2.50	6.00
5 Han Solo	2.00	5.00

2016 Star Wars The Force Awakens Series Two
Character Stickers

COMPLETE SET (18)	6.00	15.00
COMMON CARD (1-18)	.50	1.25
*P.P.BLACK/1: UNPRICED DUE TO SCARCITY		
*P.P.CYAN/1: UNPRICED DUE TO SCARCITY		

*P.P.MAGENTA/1: UNPRICED DUE TO SCARCITY		
*P.P.YELLOW/1: UNPRICED DUE TO SCARCITY		
1 Finn	.75	2.00
2 Rey	1.00	2.50
5 Han Solo	1.00	2.50
6 Leia Organa	.75	2.00
8 Poe Dameron	1.25	3.00
11 BB-8	1.25	3.00
12 Unkar Plutt	.60	1.50
13 General Hux	.75	2.00
15 Admiral Ackbar	.60	1.50
16 Stormtrooper	.75	2.00
18 Maz Kanata	.60	1.50

2016 Star Wars The Force Awakens Series Two
Concept Art

COMPLETE SET (9)	5.00	12.00
COMMON CARD (1-9)	1.00	2.50
*P.P.BLACK/1: UNPRICED DUE TO SCARCITY		
*P.P.CYAN/1: UNPRICED DUE TO SCARCITY		
*P.P.MAGENTA/1: UNPRICED DUE TO SCARCITY		
*P.P.YELLOW/1: UNPRICED DUE TO SCARCITY		

2016 Star Wars The Force Awakens Series Two
Dual Autographs

STATED PRINT RUN 3 SER.#'d SETS
UNPRICED DUE TO SCARCITY

1 John Boyega as Finn, Carrie Fisher as Leia Organa
2 Carrie Fisher as Leia Organa, Tim Rose as Admiral Ackbar
3 Anthony Daniels as C-3PO, Peter Mayhew as Chewbacca

2016 Star Wars The Force Awakens Series Two
Dual Medallion Autographs

STATED PRINT RUN 5 SER.#'d SETS
UNPRICED DUE TO SCARCITY

1 John Boyega as Finn, Carrie Fisher as Leia Organa
2 Carrie Fisher as Leia Organa, Mike Quinn as Nien Nunb
3 Mike Quinn as Nien Nunb, Tim Rose as Admiral Ackbar
4 Carrie Fisher as Leia Organa, Anthony Daniels as C-3PO
5 Anthony Daniels as C-3PO, Peter Mayhew as Chewbacca

2016 Star Wars The Force Awakens Series Two
Dual Medallions

STATED PRINT RUN 5 SER.#'d SETS
UNPRICED DUE TO SCARCITY

1 Kylo Ren, Captain Phasma
2 Rey, Finn
3 Stormtrooper, TIE Fighter Pilot
4 Finn, Poe Dameron
5 Han Solo, Rey

2016 Star Wars The Force Awakens Series Two
Galactic Connexions

COMPLETE SET (5)	120.00	250.00
COMMON CARD (1-5)	30.00	80.00
STATED PRINT RUN 100 ANNCD SETS		
WAL-MART EXCLUSIVE		
3 BB-8	50.00	100.00

2016 Star Wars The Force Awakens Series Two
Heroes of the Resistance

COMPLETE SET (16)	8.00	20.00
COMMON CARD (1-16)	.75	2.00
*P.P.BLACK/1: UNPRICED DUE TO SCARCITY		
*P.P.CYAN/1: UNPRICED DUE TO SCARCITY		
*P.P.MAGENTA/1: UNPRICED DUE TO SCARCITY		
*P.P.YELLOW/1: UNPRICED DUE TO SCARCITY		
2 Poe Dameron	1.00	2.50
3 Finn	1.00	2.50
4 Rey	1.25	3.00
5 Han Solo	1.50	4.00
16 BB-8	1.50	4.00

2016 Star Wars The Force Awakens Series Two
Maz's Castle

COMPLETE SET (9)	5.00	12.00
COMMON CARD (1-9)	.75	2.00
*P.P.BLACK/1: UNPRICED DUE TO SCARCITY		
*P.P.CYAN/1: UNPRICED DUE TO SCARCITY		
*P.P.MAGENTA/1: UNPRICED DUE TO SCARCITY		
*P.P.YELLOW/1: UNPRICED DUE TO SCARCITY		

2016 Star Wars The Force Awakens Series Two
Medallions

POE DAMERON

COMMON CARD	4.00	10.00
*SILVER p/r 244-399: .5X TO 1.2X BASIC CARDS		
*SILVER p/r 120-199: .6X TO 1.5X BASIC CARDS		

---

*SILVER p/r 50-99: 1X TO 2.5X BASIC CARDS		
*GOLD p/r 120-199: .6X TO 1.5X BASIC CARDS		
*GOLD p/r 74-100: .75X TO 2X BASIC CARDS		
*GOLD p/r 25-50: 1.2X TO 3X BASIC CARDS		
*PLATINUM p/r 16-25: X TO X BASIC CARDS		
*PLATINUM p/r 5-15: UNPRICED DUE TO SCARCITY		
*PLATINUM/1: UNPRICED DUE TO SCARCITY		
1 Kylo Ren	6.00	15.00
2 General Hux	5.00	12.00
3 Captain Phasma	5.00	12.00
4 FN-2187	5.00	12.00
6 Kylo Ren	6.00	15.00
12 Kylo Ren	6.00	15.00
13 Maz Kanata	5.00	12.00
14 Rey	6.00	15.00
15 BB-8	5.00	12.00
16 Han Solo	8.00	20.00
17 Chewbacca	5.00	12.00
18 Finn	6.00	15.00
19 Rey	6.00	15.00
22 Colonel Datoo	6.00	15.00
23 Captain Phasma	5.00	12.00
24 Finn	5.00	12.00
27 BB-8	5.00	12.00
28 Resistance X-Wing Fighter	5.00	12.00
29 Nien Nunb	6.00	15.00
30 C-3PO	6.00	15.00
31 R2-D2	8.00	20.00
32 Jess Testor Pava	10.00	25.00
33 Snap Wexley	6.00	15.00
34 Admiral Statura	6.00	15.00
35 Admiral Ackbar	6.00	15.00
36 Major Brance	5.00	12.00

2016 Star Wars The Force Awakens Series Two
Power of the First Order

POWER OF THE FIRST ORDER

COMPLETE SET (11)	5.00	12.00
COMMON CARD (1-11)	.40	1.00
*P.P.BLACK/1: UNPRICED DUE TO SCARCITY		
*P.P.CYAN/1: UNPRICED DUE TO SCARCITY		
*P.P.MAGENTA/1: UNPRICED DUE TO SCARCITY		
*P.P.YELLOW/1: UNPRICED DUE TO SCARCITY		
1 Kylo Ren	1.25	3.00
2 General Hux	1.00	2.50
3 Captain Phasma	1.25	3.00
11 Supreme Leader Snoke	1.00	2.50

2016 Star Wars The Force Awakens Series Two
Quad Autographed Booklet

STATED PRINT RUN 1 SER.#'d SET
UNPRICED DUE TO SCARCITY

1 John Boyega as Finn, Carrie Fisher as Leia Organa, Tim Rose as Admiral Ackbar, Mike Quin as Nien Nunb

---

2016 Star Wars The Force Awakens Series Two
Sketches

1 Bob Stevlic
2 Brent Ragland
3 Brian Kong
4 Carlos Cabaleiro
5 Dan Parsons
6 Dan Bergren
7 Doug Cowan
8 Eric Lehtonen
9 Francois Chartier
10 Gabe Farber
11 Ingrid Hardy
12 Jeff Mallinson
13 Kris Penix
14 Kyle Babbit
15 Rob Teranishi
16 Robert Hendrickson
17 Stephanie Swanger

2016 Star Wars The Force Awakens Series Two
Triple Autographs

STATED PRINT RUN 3 SER.#'d SETS
UNPRICED DUE TO SCARCITY

1 John Boyega as Finn, Carrie Fisher as Leia Organa, Peter Mayhew as Chewbacca
2 Carrie Fisher as Leia Organa, Tim Rose as Admiral Ackbar, Mike Quinn as Nien Nunb

2016 Star Wars Rogue One Series One

COMPLETE SET (90)	8.00	20.00
UNOPENED BOX (24 PACKS)	80.00	100.00
UNOPENED PACK (8 CARDS)	3.00	4.00
COMMON CARD (1-90)	.25	.60
*DEATH STAR BL.: .6X TO 1.5X BASIC CARDS		
*GREEN SQ.: .75X TO 2X BASIC CARDS		
*BLUE SQ.: 1X TO 2.5X BASIC CARDS		
*GRAY SQ./100: 4X TO 10X BASIC CARDS		
*GOLD SQ./50: 6X TO 15X BASIC CARDS		
*ORANGE SQ./1: UNPRICED DUE TO SCARCITY		
*P.P.BLACK/1: UNPRICED DUE TO SCARCITY		
*P.P.CYAN/1: UNPRICED DUE TO SCARCITY		
*P.P.MAGENTA/1: UNPRICED DUE TO SCARCITY		
*P.P.YELLOW/1: UNPRICED DUE TO SCARCITY		

2016 Star Wars Rogue One Series One Autographs

COMMON CARD	10.00	25.00
*BLACK/50: .6X TO 1.5X BASIC CARDS		
*GOLD/10: UNPRICED DUE TO SCARCITY		

*P.P.BLACK/1: UNPRICED DUE TO SCARCITY
*P.P.CYAN/1: UNPRICED DUE TO SCARCITY
*P.P.MAGENTA/1: UNPRICED DUE TO SCARCITY
*P.P.YELLOW/1: UNPRICED DUE TO SCARCITY
RANDOMLY INSERTED INTO PACKS

1	Donnie Yen as Chirrut Imwe	100.00	200.00
2	Felicity Jones as Jyn Erso	300.00	600.00
3	Forest Whitaker as Saw Gerrera	100.00	200.00
4	Genevieve O'Reilly as Mon Mothma	15.00	40.00

2016 Star Wars Rogue One Series One Blueprints of Ships and Vehicles

COMPLETE SET (8)	5.00	12.00
COMMON CARD (BP1-BP8)	1.00	2.50

*P.P.BLACK/1: UNPRICED DUE TO SCARCITY
*P.P.CYAN/1: UNPRICED DUE TO SCARCITY
*P.P.MAGENTA/1: UNPRICED DUE TO SCARCITY
*P.P.YELLOW/1: UNPRICED DUE TO SCARCITY
RANDOMLY INSERTED INTO PACKS

2016 Star Wars Rogue One Series One Character Icons

COMPLETE SET (11)	8.00	20.00
COMMON CARD (CI1-CI11)	1.25	3.00

*P.P.BLACK/1: UNPRICED DUE TO SCARCITY
*P.P.CYAN/1: UNPRICED DUE TO SCARCITY
*P.P.MAGENTA/1: UNPRICED DUE TO SCARCITY
*P.P.YELLOW/1: UNPRICED DUE TO SCARCITY
RANDOMLY INSERTED INTO PACKS

2016 Star Wars Rogue One Series One Character Stickers

COMPLETE SET (18)	10.00	25.00
COMMON CARD (CS1-CS18)	.75	2.00

*P.P.BLACK/1: UNPRICED DUE TO SCARCITY
*P.P.CYAN/1: UNPRICED DUE TO SCARCITY
*P.P.MAGENTA/1: UNPRICED DUE TO SCARCITY
*P.P.YELLOW/1: UNPRICED DUE TO SCARCITY
RANDOMLY INSERTED INTO PACKS

2016 Star Wars Rogue One Series One Dual Autographs

COMPLETE SET (3)
UNPRICED DUE TO SCARCITY

1 Forest Whitaker
Donnie Yen
2 Genevieve O'Reilly

Forest Whitaker
3 Paul Kasey
Nick Kellington

2016 Star Wars Rogue One Series One Gallery

COMPLETE SET (10)	4.00	10.00
COMMON CARD (G1-G10)	.50	1.25

*P.P.BLACK/1: UNPRICED DUE TO SCARCITY
*P.P.CYAN/1: UNPRICED DUE TO SCARCITY
*P.P.MAGENTA/1: UNPRICED DUE TO SCARCITY
*P.P.YELLOW/1: UNPRICED DUE TO SCARCITY
RANDOMLY INSERTED INTO PACKS

G1	Jyn Erso	.75	2.00
G2	Jyn Erso	.75	2.00
G3	Jyn Erso	.75	2.00
G4	Jyn Erso	.75	2.00
G5	Jyn Erso	.75	2.00
G6	Jyn Erso	.75	2.00
G7	Jyn Erso	.75	2.00

2016 Star Wars Rogue One Series One Heroes of the Rebel Alliance

COMPLETE SET (14)	8.00	20.00
COMMON CARD (HR1-HR14)	1.00	2.50

*P.P.BLACK/1: UNPRICED DUE TO SCARCITY
*P.P.CYAN/1: UNPRICED DUE TO SCARCITY
*P.P.MAGENTA/1: UNPRICED DUE TO SCARCITY
*P.P.YELLOW/1: UNPRICED DUE TO SCARCITY
RANDOMLY INSERTED INTO PACKS

HR1	Jyn Erso	1.50	4.00
HR4	Chirrut IMWE	1.25	3.00

2016 Star Wars Rogue One Series One Medallions

COMMON CARD	4.00	10.00

*BRONZE: SAME VALUE AS BASIC
*SILVER/99: .5X TO 1.2X BASIC CARDS

---

*GOLD/50: .6X TO 1.5X BASIC CARDS
*PLATINUM/1: UNPRICED DUE TO SCARCITY
RANDOMLY INSERTED INTO PACKS

5	Captain Cassian Andor with X-Wing	6.00	15.00
6	Captain Cassian Andor with U-Wing	6.00	15.00
7	Chirrut Imwe with Y-Wing	6.00	15.00
8	Darth Vader with Death Star	6.00	15.00
9	Darth Vader with Imperial Star Destroyer	6.00	15.00
10	Death Trooper with Imperial Star Destroyer	6.00	15.00
14	Edrio Two Tubes with U-Wing	6.00	15.00
15	Jyn Erso with X-Wing	8.00	20.00
16	Jyn Erso with U-Wing	8.00	20.00
17	Jyn Erso with Death Star	8.00	20.00
18	K-2SO with X-Wing	5.00	12.00
20	Moroff with U-Wing	5.00	12.00
24	Shoretrooper with AT-ACT	5.00	12.00
25	Stormtrooper with AT-ST	5.00	12.00
27	TIE Fighter Pilot with TIE Striker	5.00	12.00

2016 Star Wars Rogue One Series One Montages

COMPLETE SET (9)	5.00	12.00
COMMON CARD (M1-M9)	1.00	2.50

*P.P.BLACK/1: UNPRICED DUE TO SCARCITY
*P.P.CYAN/1: UNPRICED DUE TO SCARCITY
*P.P.MAGENTA/1: UNPRICED DUE TO SCARCITY
*P.P.YELLOW/1: UNPRICED DUE TO SCARCITY
STATED ODDS 1:

2016 Star Wars Rogue One Series One Sketches

COMPLETE ARTIST LIST (78)
UNPRICED DUE TO SCARCITY

1 Achilleas Kokkinakis
2 Alex Iniguez
3 Anil Sharma
4 Anthony Skubis
5 Ben AbuSaada
6 Bill Pulkovski
7 Bob Hepner
8 Bob Stevlic
9 Brad Hudson
10 Brad Tabar
11 Brad Utterstrom
12 Brendan Purchase
13 Brent Ragland
14 Brett Farr
15 Brian Kong
16 Carlos Cabaleiro

2016 Star Wars Rogue One Series One Triple Autograph

COMPLETE SET (1)
UNPRICED DUE TO SCARCITY

1 Donnie Yen
Nick Kellington
Paul Kasey

2016 Star Wars Rogue One Series One Villains of the Galactic Empire

DEATH TROOPER

COMPLETE SET (8)	6.00	15.00
COMMON CARD (VE1-VE8)	1.00	2.50
*P.P.BLACK/1: UNPRICED DUE TO SCARCITY		
*P.P.CYAN/1: UNPRICED DUE TO SCARCITY		
*P.P.MAGENTA/1: UNPRICED DUE TO SCARCITY		
*P.P.YELLOW/1: UNPRICED DUE TO SCARCITY		

2017 Star Wars Rogue One Series Two

KRENNIC AND TARKIN CONFER

COMPLETE SET (100)	10.00	25.00
UNOPENED BOX (24 PACKS)	120.00	160.00
UNOPENED PACK (8 CARDS)	6.00	8.00
COMMON CARD (1-100)	.20	.50
*DTHSTR BLACK: .6X TO 1.5X BASIC CARDS		
*GREEN SQ: .75X TO 2X BASIC CARDS		
*BLUE SQ: 1X TO 2.5X BASIC CARDS		
*GRAY SQ/100: 5X TO 12X BASIC CARDS		
*GOLD SQ/50: 10X TO 25X BASIC CARDS		
*RED/1: UNPRICED DUE TO SCARCITY		
*P.P.BLACK/1: UNPRICED DUE TO SCARCITY		
*P.P.CYAN/1: UNPRICED DUE TO SCARCITY		
*P.P.MAGENTA/1: UNPRICED DUE TO SCARCITY		
*P.P.YELLOW/1: UNPRICED DUE TO SCARCITY		

2017 Star Wars Rogue One Series Two Autographs

FELICITY JONES AS JYN ERSO

COMMON CARD	10.00	25.00
*BLACK/50: .6X TO 1.5X BASIC CARDS		
*GOLD/10: 1.2X TO 3X BASIC CARDS		
*ORANGE/1: UNPRICED DUE TO SCARCITY		
*P.P.BLACK/1: UNPRICED DUE TO SCARCITY		
*P.P.CYAN/1: UNPRICED DUE TO SCARCITY		
*P.P.MAGENTA/1: UNPRICED DUE TO SCARCITY		
*P.P.YELLOW/1: UNPRICED DUE TO SCARCITY		
STATED ODDS 1:36		
JONES, WHITAKER, AND KELLINGTON		
DO NOT HAVE BASE AUTOGRAPHS		

DY Donnie Yen	80.00	150.00
RA Riz Ahmed	120.00	200.00
WD Warwick Davis	12.00	30.00

2017 Star Wars Rogue One Series Two Autographs Black

*BLACK/50: .6X TO 1.5X BASIC CARDS
STATED ODDS 1:163
STATED PRINT RUN 50 SER.#'d SETS

FJ Felicity Jones	300.00	600.00
FW Forest Whitaker	100.00	200.00
NK Nick Kellington	20.00	50.00

2017 Star Wars Rogue One Series Two Character Stickers

BISTAN

COMPLETE SET (18)	30.00	80.00
COMMON CARD (CS1-CS18)	2.50	6.00
STATED ODDS 1:12		
CS1 Jyn Erso	5.00	12.00
CS8 Director Krennic	3.00	8.00
CS9 Darth Vader	4.00	10.00
CS10 K-2SO	3.00	8.00
CS14 Chirrut Imwe	4.00	10.00
CS18 Admiral Raddus	3.00	8.00

2017 Star Wars Rogue One Series Two Dual Autographs

GENEVIEVE O'REILLY AS MON MOTHMA

FELICITY JONES AS JYN ERSO

UNPRICED DUE TO SCARCITY

FJFW Jones/Whitaker
FJGO Jones/O'Reilly
GOAP O'Reilly/Petrie

2017 Star Wars Rogue One Series Two Heroes of the Rebel Alliance

BODHI ROOK

COMPLETE SET (10)	6.00	15.00
COMMON CARD (HR1-HR10)	1.00	2.50
*P.P.BLACK/1: UNPRICED DUE TO SCARCITY		
*P.P.CYAN/1: UNPRICED DUE TO SCARCITY		
*P.P.MAGENTA/1: UNPRICED DUE TO SCARCITY		
*P.P.YELLOW/1: UNPRICED DUE TO SCARCITY		
STATED ODDS 1:7		

2017 Star Wars Rogue One Series Two Movie Posters

COMPLETE SET (10)	30.00	80.00
COMMON CARD (1-10)	3.00	8.00
*P.P.BLACK/1: UNPRICED DUE TO SCARCITY		
*P.P.CYAN/1: UNPRICED DUE TO SCARCITY		
*P.P.MAGENTA/1: UNPRICED DUE TO SCARCITY		
*P.P.YELLOW/1: UNPRICED DUE TO SCARCITY		
STATED ODDS 1:24		
1 United States Theatrical Poster	6.00	15.00
5 Cassian Andor Character Poster	4.00	10.00
6 Bodhi Rook Character Poster	5.00	12.00
7 Chirrut Imwe Character Poster	6.00	15.00
9 K-2SO Character Poster	6.00	15.00

2017 Star Wars Rogue One Series Two Patches

COMMON CARD	5.00	12.00
*SILVER/100: .5X TO 1.2X BASIC CARDS		
*GOLD/50: .6X TO 1.5X BASIC CARDS		
*RED/10: 1.2X TO 3X BASIC CARDS		
*ORANGE/1: UNPRICED DUE TO SCARCITY		

2017 Star Wars Rogue One Series Two Prime Forces

COMPLETE SET (10)	8.00	20.00
COMMON CARD (PF1-PF10)	1.50	4.00
*P.P.BLACK/1: UNPRICED DUE TO SCARCITY		
*P.P.CYAN/1: UNPRICED DUE TO SCARCITY		
*P.P.MAGENTA/1: UNPRICED DUE TO SCARCITY		
*P.P.YELLOW/1: UNPRICED DUE TO SCARCITY		
STATED ODDS 1:2		

2017 Star Wars Rogue One Series Two Sketches

COMPLETE ARTIST LIST (75)
STATED ODDS 1:32

UNPRICED DUE TO SCARCITY

1 Achilleas Kokkinakis
2 Andrew Lopez
3 Angelina Benedetti
4 Anil Sharma
5 Anthony Skubis
6 Ben AbuSaada
7 Bill Pulkovski
8 Bob Hepner
9 Brad Hudson
10 Brendan Purchase
11 Brent Engstrom
12 Brent Ragland
13 Brett Farr
14 Bruce Gerlach
15 Can Baran
16 Carlos Cabaleiro
17 Cathy Razim
18 Chad LaForce
19 Charlie Cody
20 Cliff Thomas
21 Clinton Yeager
22 Corey Galal
23 Dan Curto
24 Daniel Cooney
25 Danny Kidwell
26 Darrin Pepe
27 Dennis Gortakowski
28 Elfie Lebouleux
29 Eric Lehtonen
30 Erik Maell
31 Freddy Lopez
32 George Joseph
33 Ingrid Hardy
34 Jamie Cosley
35 Jason Davies
36 Jason Durden
37 Jason Sobol
38 Jay Manchand
39 Jim Mehsling
40 JM Smith
41 Jonathan Caustrita
42 Jordan Maison
43 Joshua Bommer
44 Kallan Archer
45 Kate Carleton
46 Kevin Graham
47 Kevin Liell
48 Kevin P. West
49 Kris Penix
50 Kyle Hickman
51 Lee Lightfoot
52 Luke Preece
53 Marcia Dye
54 Mark Mangum
55 Marsha Parkins
56 Matt Langford
57 Matt Soffe
58 Matt Steffens
59 Matt Stewart
60 Melike Acar
61 Mick and Matt Glebe
62 Mike Barnard
63 Mohammad Jilani
64 Neil Camera
65 Patrick Giles
66 Phil Hassewer
67 Randy Siplon
68 Rich Molinelli
69 Robert Hendrickson
70 Roy Cover
71 Ryan Moffett
72 Shaow Siong
73 Solly Mohamed
74 Steve Potter
75 Ted Dastick Jr.
76 Tim Proctor
77 Tina Berardi
78 Todd Aaron Smith

2017 Star Wars Rogue One Series Two Triple Autographs

STATED ODDS 1:11,771
UNPRICED DUE TO SCARCITY

FJDYFW Jones/Yen/Whitaker
FJGOAP Jones/O'Reilly/Petrie
FWPKAC Whitaker/Kasey/Cook

2017 Star Wars Rogue One Series Two Troopers

COMPLETE SET (10)	8.00	20.00
COMMON CARD (TR1-TR10)	1.50	4.00
*P.P.BLACK/1: UNPRICED DUE TO SCARCITY		
*P.P.CYAN/1: UNPRICED DUE TO SCARCITY		
*P.P.MAGENTA/1: UNPRICED DUE TO SCARCITY		
*P.P.YELLOW/1: UNPRICED DUE TO SCARCITY		
STATED ODDS 1:2		

2017 Star Wars Rogue One Series Two Villains of the Galactic Empire

COMPLETE SET (10)	12.00	30.00
COMMON CARD (VG1-VG10)	2.50	6.00
*P.P.BLACK/1: UNPRICED DUE TO SCARCITY		
*P.P.CYAN/1: UNPRICED DUE TO SCARCITY		
*P.P.MAGENTA/1: UNPRICED DUE TO SCARCITY		
*P.P.YELLOW/1: UNPRICED DUE TO SCARCITY		
STATED ODDS 1:7		

2009 Art of Star Wars Comics Postcards

COMPLETE SET (100)	12.00	30.00
COMMON CARD (1-100)	.25	.60

2014 Disney Store Star Wars North America

COMPLETE SET (9)	10.00	25.00
COMMON CARD (1-10)	.75	2.00
US/CANADA EXCLUSIVE		
1 Luke Skywalker	2.00	5.00
4 Darth Vader	2.00	5.00
7 Princess Leia	2.00	5.00
9 Han Solo	2.00	5.00

2014 Disney Store Star Wars United Kingdom

COMPLETE SET (12)	15.00	40.00
COMMON CARD (1-12)	1.00	2.50
UK EXCLUSIVE		
1 Chewbacca	1.25	3.00
2 Darth Vader	4.00	10.00
4 Han Solo	4.00	10.00
6 Luke Skywalker	3.00	8.00
8 Obi-Wan Kenobi	1.25	3.00
9 Princess Leia Organa	3.00	8.00
10 R2-D2 and C-3PO	1.25	3.00
11 Stormtrooper	1.25	3.00

2008 Family Guy Episode IV A New Hope

COMPLETE SET (50)	5.00	12.00
COMMON CARD (1-50)	.15	.40
CL1 ISSUED AS CASE EXCLUSIVE		
CL1 Evil Empire CI	12.00	25.00

2008 Family Guy Episode IV A New Hope Droid Chat

COMPLETE SET (3)	5.00	12.00
COMMON CARD (DC1-DC3)	2.00	5.00
STATED ODDS 1:23		

2008 Family Guy Episode IV A New Hope Promos

P1 Left half w/Han	1.00	2.50
Pi Right half w/Leia	1.00	2.50

2008 Family Guy Episode IV A New Hope Puzzle

COMPLETE SET (9)	4.00	10.00
COMMON CARD (NH1-NH9)	.75	2.00
STATED ODDS 1:7		

2008 Family Guy Episode IV A New Hope Scenes from Space

COMPLETE SET (6)	4.00	10.00
COMMON CARD (S1-S6)	1.25	3.00
STATED ODDS 1:11		

2008 Family Guy Episode IV A New Hope Spaceships and Transports

COMPLETE SET (9)	4.00	10.00
COMMON CARD (ST1-ST9)	1.00	2.50
STATED ODDS 1:9		

2008 Family Guy Episode IV A New Hope What Happens Next?

COMPLETE SET (6)	4.00	10.00
COMMON CARD (WN1-WN6)	1.25	3.00
STATED ODDS 1:11		

2015 Star Wars Original Trilogy Series Bikkuriman Stickers

COMPLETE SET (24)	30.00	80.00
COMMON CARD	2.00	5.00

2015 Star Wars Prequel Trilogy Series Bikkuriman Stickers

COMPLETE SET (24)	25.00	60.00
COMMON CARD	1.25	3.00

1996 Star Wars 3-Di Widevision

COMPLETE SET (63)	30.00	60.00
COMMON CARD (1-63)	.60	1.50
1M STATED ODDS 1:24		
1M Death Star Explosion	6.00	15.00

1996 Star Wars 3-Di Widevision Promos

3Di1 Darth Vader	2.50	6.00
3Di2 Luke Skywalker	12.00	30.00

1997 Star Wars Adventure Journal

NNO One of a Kind by Doug Shuler
NNO To Fight Another Day by Mike Vilardi
NNO Mist Encounter by Doug Shuler

1984 Star Wars C-3PO's Cereal Masks

Produced by Kellogg's. A long time ago in a cereal box at the local grocery store, Kellogg's produced these unique cardboard masks. Each mask was printed on the backside of C-3PO's cereal boxes and they featured some of the most popular Star Wars characters of the film franchise. The masks came with holes for the eyes, nose and string to use for binding around a person's head.

COMPLETE SET (6)	150.00	300.00
COMMON CARD	12.00	30.00
STATED ODDS 1:CEREAL BOX		
1 C-3PO	60.00	120.00
2 Chewbacca	25.00	60.00
5 Stormtrooper	15.00	40.00
6 Yoda	15.00	40.00

2016 Star Wars Card Trader

SAVAGE OPRESS
STAR WARS: THE CLONE WARS.

COMPLETE SET (100)	6.00	15.00
UNOPENED BOX (24 PACKS)	35.00	50.00
UNOPENED PACK (6 CARDS)	2.00	3.00
COMMON CARD (1-100)	.12	.30
*BLUE: .6X TO 1.5X BASIC CARDS	.20	.50
*RED: 1.2X TO 3X BASIC CARDS	.40	1.00
*GREEN/99: 6X TO 15X BASIC CARDS	2.00	5.00
*ORANGE/50: 12X TO 30X BASIC CARDS	4.00	10.00
*BAT.DAM./10: 30X TO 80X BASIC CARDS	10.00	25.00
*SLAVE I/5: UNPRICED DUE TO SCARCITY		

2016 Star Wars Card Trader Actor Digital Autographs

COMPLETE SET (20)
COMMON CARD (DA1-DA20)
*RED/10: UNPRICED DUE TO SCARCITY
*GOLD/5: UNPRICED DUE TO SCARCITY
STATED ODDS 1:788
STATED PRINT RUN 25 SER.#'d SETS
UNPRICED DUE TO LACK OF MARKET INFO

DA1 Billy Dee Williams
DA2 Steve Blum
DA3 Vanessa Marshall
DA4 Tiya Sircar
DA5 Taylor Gray
DA6 Daniel Logan
DA7 Daniel Logan
DA8 Ray Park
DA9 Nika Futterman
DA10 Warwick Davis
DA11 Phil Eason
DA12 Michonne Bourriague

DA13 Mike Quinn
DA14 David Bowers
DA15 Ashley Eckstein
DA16 John Ratzenberger
DA17 Hassani Shapi
DA18 Andy Secombe
DA19 Zachariah Jensen
DA20 Caroline Blakiston

2016 Star Wars Card Trader Bounty

COMPLETE SET (20)	15.00	40.00
COMMON CARD (B1-B20)	1.25	3.00
STATED ODDS 1:5		

2016 Star Wars Card Trader Classic Artwork

CHEWBACCA

COMPLETE SET (20)	15.00	40.00
COMMON CARD (CA1-CA20))	1.25	3.00
STATED ODDS 1:5		

2016 Star Wars Card Trader Film Quotes

COMPLETE SET (20)	10.00	25.00
COMMON CARD (FQ1-FQ20)	1.00	2.50
STATED ODDS 1:4		

2016 Star Wars Card Trader Galactic Moments

GALACTIC MOMENTS
Lucas Begins
Filming Star Wars: A New Hope

COMPLETE SET (20)	15.00	40.00
COMMON CARD (GM1-GM20)	1.25	3.00
STATED ODDS 1:5		

2016 Star Wars Card Trader Reflections

REFLECTIONS
Darth Vader & Obi-Wan Kenobi

COMPLETE SET (7)	12.00	30.00
COMMON CARD (R1-R7)	2.50	6.00
STATED ODDS 1:8		

2016 Star Wars Card Trader Topps Choice

COMPLETE SET (13)	15.00	40.00
COMMON CARD (TC1-TC13)	2.00	5.00
STATED ODDS 1:16		
TC4 Kabe	8.00	20.00
TC7 Lak Sivrak	3.00	8.00
TC10 Bo-Katan Kryze	3.00	8.00
TC13 Todo 360	2.50	6.00

2017 Star Wars Celebration Orlando Cartamundi Playing Card Promos

1 Princess Leia	3.00	8.00
2 Luke	4.00	10.00
3 Darth Vader	5.00	12.00
4 Boba Fett	4.00	10.00

1999 Star Wars Chrome Archives

BOBA FETT ATTACKS!

Produced by Topps, this set revisits various cards from the '70's and '80's and updates them with chromium technology. Both the card fronts and backs replicate a card from the original vintage sets. The base set is divided into three 30-card subsets. They are as follows: A New Hope (1-30), Empire Strikes Back (31-60), and Return of the Jedi (61-90). Artwork by Greg and Tim Hildebrandt.

COMPLETE SET (90)	10.00	25.00
UNOPENED BOX (36 PACKS)	65.00	80.00
UNOPENED PACK (5 CARDS)	2.00	2.50
COMMON CARD (1-90)	.20	.50

1999 Star Wars Chrome Archives Clearzone

COMPLETE SET (4)	7.50	20.00
COMMON CARD (C1-C4)	2.50	6.00

1999 Star Wars Chrome Archives Double Sided

COMPLETE SET (9)	40.00	100.00
COMMON CARD (C1-C9)	6.00	15.00

1999 Star Wars Chrome Archives Promos

P1 Hate me, Luke! Destroy me!	1.00	2.50
P2 Welcome, young Luke	1.00	2.50

2014 Star Wars Chrome Perspectives

COMPLETE SET (100)	30.00	60.00
UNOPENED BOX (24 PACKS)	175.00	200.00
UNOPENED PACK (6 CARDS)	8.00	10.00
COMMON CARD (1E-50E)	.40	1.00
COMMON CARD (1R-50R)	.40	1.00
*REFRACTOR: 1.2X TO 3X BASIC CARDS		
*PRISM: 1.5X TO 4X BASIC CARDS		
*X-FRACTOR/99: 3X TO 8X BASIC CARDS		
*GOLD REF./50: 6X TO 15X BASIC CARDS		
*SUPERFRACTOR/1: UNPRICED DUE TO SCARCITY		
*P.P.BLACK/1: UNPRICED DUE TO SCARCITY		
*P.P.CYAN/1: UNPRICED DUE TO SCARCITY		
*P.P.MAGENTA/1: UNPRICED DUE TO SCARCITY		
*P.P.YELLOW/1: UNPRICED DUE TO SCARCITY		

2014 Star Wars Chrome Perspectives Autograph Sketches

1 Anthony Wheeler
2 Ashleigh Popplewell
3 Bob Stevlic
4 Brandon Gallo
5 Brian DeGuire
6 Charles Hall
7 Chris Ring
8 Chris West
9 Dan Curto
10 Dan Gorman
11 Darrin Pepe
12 Eric Lehtonen
13 Flosi
14 Hayden Davis
15 Irma Ahmed
17 Jason Chalker
18 Jason Crosby
19 JD
20 Jeff Chandler
21 Jeff Zapata
22 Jimenez
23 Joe Hogan
24 John Soukup
25 Jon Rademacher
26 Jorge Baeza
27 Justin Schillerberg
28 Kevin Doyle
29 Kris Penix
30 Lin Workman
31 Melike Acar
32 Michael Duron
33 Mikey Babinski
34 Otto
35 Patricia Ross
36 Patrick Hamill
37 Richard Molinelli
38 Robert Hendrickson
39 Robert Teranishi
40 Roy Cover
41 Tina Berardi
42 Tom Kelly
43 Val Hochberg

2014 Star Wars Chrome Perspectives Autographs

COMMON CARD	8.00	20.00
*GOLD REF./10: UNPRICED DUE TO SCARCITY		
*SUPERFRACTOR/1: UNPRICED DUE TO SCARCITY		
*P.P.BLACK/1: UNPRICED DUE TO SCARCITY		
*P.P.CYAN/1: UNPRICED DUE TO SCARCITY		
*P.P.MAGENTA/1: UNPRICED DUE TO SCARCITY		
*P.P.YELLOW/1: UNPRICED DUE TO SCARCITY		
STATED ODDS 1 PER BOX W/SKETCHES		

1 Angus MacInnes	15.00	40.00
2 Anthony Daniels		
3 Billy Dee Williams	50.00	100.00
4 Carrie Fisher	200.00	500.00
5 Harrison Ford EXCH	1000.00	4000.00
8 James Earl Jones	150.00	300.00
9 Jeremy Bulloch	30.00	60.00
11 Julian Glover	15.00	40.00
12 Kenneth Colley	12.00	25.00
13 Mark Capri	12.00	25.00
14 Mark Hamill		

2014 Star Wars Chrome Perspectives Empire Priority Targets

COMPLETE SET (10)	8.00	20.00
COMMON CARD (1-10)	1.25	3.00
*P.P.BLACK/1: UNPRICED DUE TO SCARCITY		
*P.P.CYAN/1: UNPRICED DUE TO SCARCITY		
*P.P.MAGENTA/1: UNPRICED DUE TO SCARCITY		
*P.P.YELLOW/1: UNPRICED DUE TO SCARCITY		
STATED ODDS 1:4		

2014 Star Wars Chrome Perspectives Empire Propaganda

COMPLETE SET (10)	15.00	40.00
COMMON CARD (1-10)	3.00	8.00
*P.P.BLACK/1: UNPRICED DUE TO SCARCITY		
*P.P.CYAN/1: UNPRICED DUE TO SCARCITY		
*P.P.MAGENTA/1: UNPRICED DUE TO SCARCITY		
*P.P.YELLOW/1: UNPRICED DUE TO SCARCITY		
STATED ODDS 1:24		

2014 Star Wars Chrome Perspectives Helmet Medallions

COMPLETE SET (30)	75.00	200.00
COMMON CARD (1-30)	5.00	12.00
*GOLD/50: 1.2X TO 3X BASIC MEDALLIONS		
STATED ODDS 1:24		

2014 Star Wars Chrome Perspectives Rebel Propaganda

COMPLETE SET (10)	12.00	30.00
COMMON CARD (1-10)	2.00	5.00
*P.P.BLACK/1: UNPRICED DUE TO SCARCITY		
*P.P.CYAN/1: UNPRICED DUE TO SCARCITY		
*P.P.MAGENTA/1: UNPRICED DUE TO SCARCITY		
*P.P.YELLOW/1: UNPRICED DUE TO SCARCITY		
STATED ODDS 1:12		

2014 Star Wars Chrome Perspectives Rebel Training

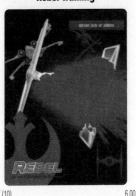

COMPLETE SET (10)	6.00	15.00
COMMON CARD (1-10)	1.25	3.00

*P.P.BLACK/1: UNPRICED DUE TO SCARCITY
*P.P.CYAN/1: UNPRICED DUE TO SCARCITY
*P.P.MAGENTA/1: UNPRICED DUE TO SCARCITY
*P.P.YELLOW/1: UNPRICED DUE TO SCARCITY
STATED ODDS 1:8

2014 Star Wars Chrome Perspectives Sketches

1 Angelina Benedetti
2 Anthony Wheeler
3 Ashleigh Popplewell
4 Bill Pulkovski
5 Bob Stevlic
6 Brandon Gallo
7 Brian DeGuire
8 Charles Hall
9 Chris "Urbnpop" Hamer
10 Chris Ring
11 Chris West
12 Christian N. (CNS) St. Pierre
13 Dan Curto
14 Dan Gorman
15 Darrin Pepe
16 Denae Frazier
17 Dennis Budd
18 Eric Lehtonen
19 Erik Maell
20 FLOSI
21 Hayden Davis
22 Irma "Aimo" Ahmed
23 j(ay)
24 Jan Duursema
25 Jason Adams
26 Jason Chalker
27 Jason Crosby
28 Jason Flowers
29 Jeff Chandler
30 Jeff Zapata
31 Joann Ellen Patak
32 Joe Corroney
33 Joe Hogan
34 John Sloboda
35 John Soukup
36 Jon Rademacher
37 Jorge Baeza
38 Josh R.
39 Justin Chung
40 Justin Schillerberg
41 Karen Hinson
42 Ken Branch
43 Kevin Doyle
44 Kevin Graham
45 Kimberly Dunaway
46 Kris Penix
47 Krist West
48 Kyle Babbitt
49 Louis (LDM) De Martinis
50 Lin Workman
51 Lord Mesa
52 Lynne Anderson
53 Mark Labas
54 Melike Acar
55 Michael "Locoduck" Duron
56 Mikey Babinski
57 Otto Dieffenbach
58 Patricia Ross
59 Patrick (PG) Giles
60 Patrick Hamill
61 Randy Martinez
62 Rich "RAM" Molinelli
63 Robert Hendrickson
64 Robert Jimenez
65 Robert Teranishi
66 Roy Cover
67 Scott Zambelli
68 Sean Pence
69 Sian Mandrake
70 Solly Mohamed
71 Stephanie Swanger
72 Tim Proctor
73 Tina Berardi
74 Tod Allen Smith
75 Tom Kelly
76 Tom Krohne
77 Val Hochberg
78 Veronica O'Connell
79 William O'Neill

2014 Star Wars Chrome Perspectives Triple Autograph

UNPRICED DUE TO SCARCITY

1 H. Ford/M. Hamill/C. Fisher EXCH

2014 Star Wars Chrome Perspectives Wanted Posters Rebellion

COMPLETE SET (10)	5.00	12.00
COMMON CARD (1-10)	.75	2.00

.*P.P.BLACK/1: UNPRICED DUE TO SCARCITY
*P.P.CYAN/1: UNPRICED DUE TO SCARCITY
*P.P.MAGENTA/1: UNPRICED DUE TO SCARCITY
*P.P.YELLOW/1: UNPRICED DUE TO SCARCITY
STATED ODDS 1:2

2015 Star Wars Chrome Perspectives Jedi vs. Sith

COMPLETE SET (100)	25.00	60.00
UNOPENED BOX (24 PACKS)	60.00	70.00
UNOPENED PACK (6 CARDS)	3.00	4.00
COMMON CARD	.40	1.00

*REFRACTOR: 1.2X TO 3X BASIC CARDS
*PRISM REF/199: 1.5X TO 4X BASIC CARDS
*X-FRACTOR/99: 3X TO 8X BASIC CARDS
*GOLD REF/50: 6X TO 15X BASIC CARDS
*P.P.BLACK/1: UNPRICED DUE TO SCARCITY
*P.P.CYAN/1: UNPRICED DUE TO SCARCITY
*P.P.MAGENTA/1: UNPRICED DUE TO SCARCITY
*P.P.YELLOW/1: UNPRICED DUE TO SCARCITY

2015 Star Wars Chrome Perspectives Jedi vs. Sith Autographs

COMMON CARD	6.00	15.00

*PRISM REF./50: .75X TO 2X BASIC AUTOS
* X-FRACTORS/25: 1.2X TO 3X BASIC AUTOS
*GOLD REF./10: UNPRICED DUE TO SCARCITY
*SUPERFRACTOR/1: UNPRICED DUE TO SCARCITY
*P.P.BLACK/1: UNPRICED DUE TO SCARCITY
*P.P.CYAN/1: UNPRICED DUE TO SCARCITY
*P.P.MAGENTA/1: UNPRICED DUE TO SCARCITY
*P.P.YELLOW/1: UNPRICED DUE TO SCARCITY
MARK HAMILL HAS NO BASE AUTO

1	Carrie Fisher	400.00	600.00
2	David Prowse	30.00	80.00
3	Peter Mayhew	25.00	60.00
4	Ray Park	20.00	50.00
5	Matthew Wood	10.00	25.00
8	Michaela Cottrell	10.00	25.00
9	Nalini Krishan	12.00	30.00
11	Jerome Blake	10.00	25.00
16	Sam Witwer	10.00	25.00
17	Barbara Goodson	10.00	25.00
18	Olivia D'Abo	10.00	25.00
21	Ashley Eckstein	10.00	25.00

2015 Star Wars Chrome Perspectives Jedi vs. Sith
Jedi Hunt

COMPLETE SET (10)	10.00	25.00
COMMON CARD (1-10)	2.00	5.00

*P.P.BLACK/1: UNPRICED DUE TO SCARCITY
*P.P.CYAN/1: UNPRICED DUE TO SCARCITY
*P.P.MAGENTA/1: UNPRICED DUE TO SCARCITY
*P.P.YELLOW/1: UNPRICED DUE TO SCARCITY
STATED ODDS 1:4

2015 Star Wars Chrome Perspectives Jedi vs. Sith
Jedi Information Guide

COMPLETE SET (10)	20.00	50.00
COMMON CARD (1-10)	4.00	10.00

*P.P.BLACK/1: UNPRICED DUE TO SCARCITY
*P.P.CYAN/1: UNPRICED DUE TO SCARCITY
*P.P.MAGENTA/1: UNPRICED DUE TO SCARCITY
*P.P.YELLOW/1: UNPRICED DUE TO SCARCITY
STATED ODDS 1:12

2015 Star Wars Chrome Perspectives Jedi vs. Sith
Jedi Training

COMPLETE SET (10)	12.00	30.00
COMMON CARD (1-10)	2.50	6.00

*P.P.BLACK/1: UNPRICED DUE TO SCARCITY
*P.P.CYAN/1: UNPRICED DUE TO SCARCITY

*P.P.MAGENTA/1: UNPRICED DUE TO SCARCITY
*P.P.YELLOW/1: UNPRICED DUE TO SCARCITY
STATED ODDS 1:24

2015 Star Wars Chrome Perspectives Jedi vs. Sith
Medallions

COMPLETE SET (36)	120.00	250.00
COMMON CARD (1-36)	5.00	12.00

*SILVER/150: .6X TO 1.5X BASIC CARDS
*GOLD/50: .75X TO 2X BASIC CARDS
OVERALL MEDALLION ODDS 1:BOX

2015 Star Wars Chrome Perspectives Jedi vs. Sith
Rare Dual Autographs

COMMON CARD	25.00	60.00

*P.P.BLACK/1: UNPRICED DUE TO SCARCITY
*P.P.CYAN/1: UNPRICED DUE TO SCARCITY
*P.P.MAGENTA/1: UNPRICED DUE TO SCARCITY
*P.P.YELLOW/1: UNPRICED DUE TO SCARCITY

NNO	A.Allen/O.Shoshan	50.00	100.00
NNO	A.Eckstein/N.Futterman		
NNO	A.Eckstein/O.D'Abo	50.00	100.00
NNO	M.Cottrell/Z.Jensen	50.00	100.00
NNO	N.Futterman/B.Goodson	25.00	60.00

2015 Star Wars Chrome Perspectives Jedi vs. Sith
Sith Fugitives

COMPLETE SET (10)	8.00	20.00
COMMON CARD (1-10)	1.50	4.00

*P.P.BLACK/1: UNPRICED DUE TO SCARCITY
*P.P.CYAN/1: UNPRICED DUE TO SCARCITY
*P.P.MAGENTA/1: UNPRICED DUE TO SCARCITY
*P.P.YELLOW/1: UNPRICED DUE TO SCARCITY
STATED ODDS 1:2

2015 Star Wars Chrome Perspectives Jedi vs. Sith
Sith Propaganda

COMPLETE SET (10)	12.00	30.00
COMMON CARD (1-10)	2.50	6.00

*P.P.BLACK/1: UNPRICED DUE TO SCARCITY
*P.P.CYAN/1: UNPRICED DUE TO SCARCITY
*P.P.MAGENTA/1: UNPRICED DUE TO SCARCITY
*P.P.YELLOW/1: UNPRICED DUE TO SCARCITY
STATED ODDS 1:8

2015 Star Wars Chrome Perspectives Jedi vs. Sith
Sketches

1 Aaron Lambert
2 Achilleas Kokkinakis
3 Adam Talley
4 Adrian Rivera
5 Alex Ironhed Sanchez
6 Andrew Drone Cosson
7 Bill Pulkovski
8 Brad Hudson
9 Brad Utterstrom
10 Brent Ragland
11 Carla Rodriguez
12 Carlos Cabaleiro
13 Chad McCown
14 Charles Dowd
15 Charles Hall
16 Chris Ehnot
17 Chris Henderson
18 Chris West
19 Crystal Bamboota Fontan
20 Dan Bergren
21 Dan Nokes
22 Dan Parsons
23 Dan Smif Smith
24 Danny Haas
25 Darrin Pepe
26 David Valentine
27 Denae Frazier
28 Eric Kowalick
29 Eric Lehtonen
30 Erik Maell
31 Francois Chartier
32 Gavin Hunt
33 Howard Russell
34 Ingrid Hardy
35 Irma Aimo Ahmed
36 Jamie Cosley
37 Jared Hickman
38 Jason Adams
39 Jason Brower
40 Jason Chalker
41 Jason Flowers
42 Jeffrey Benitez
43 Jessica Hickman
44 Joe Hogan
45 John Soukup
46 Jordan Maison
47 Josh Bodwell
48 Josh Lyman
49 Kaela Croft
50 Karen Hinson
51 Kate Carleton
52 Kevin Graham
53 Kevin West
54 Kimberly Dunaway

55 Kris Penix
56 Kyle Babbitt
57 Lak Lim
58 Laura Guzzo
59 Lee Lightfoot
60 Lord Mesa
61 Marcia Dye
62 Marck Labas
63 Mark Hammermeister
64 Mark Picirilli
65 Matt Stewart
66 Matthew Sutton
67 Melike Acar
68 Michael Leavitt
69 Michael Locoduck Duron
70 Mick/Matt Glebe
71 Norvien Basio
72 Omar Maya Velazquez
73 Pablo Diaz
74 Patricia Ross
75 Patrick Giles
76 Paul Gutz Guttierez
77 Peter Zuno Chan
78 Rich Kunz
79 Rich Molinelli
80 Robert Hendrickson
81 Robert Teranishi
82 Roy Cover
83 Ryan van der Draaij
84 Sarah Wilkinson
85 Scott Houseman
86 Scott Zambelli
87 Sean Pence
88 Sol Mohamed
89 Stephanie Swanger
90 Steven Burch
91 Sue Thomas
92 Tanner Padlo
93 Ted Dastick Jr.
94 Tim Dowler
95 Tim Shay
96 Tina Berardi
97 Tom Carlton
98 Tomoko Taniguchi
99 Tressina Bowling
100 Ward Silverman
101 Wilson Ramos Jr.

2015 Star Wars Chrome Perspectives Jedi vs. Sith The Force Awakens

Poe Dameron in his X-Wing
® & TM Lucasfilm Ltd.

COMPLETE SET (8)	20.00	50.00
COMMON CARD	4.00	10.00

*MATTE BACK: .6X TO1.5X BASIC CARDS
STATED ODDS 1:24

2015 Star Wars Chrome Perspectives Jedi vs. Sith Ultra Rare Dual Autographs

*P.P.BLACK/1: UNPRICED DUE TO SCARCITY
*P.P.CYAN/1: UNPRICED DUE TO SCARCITY
*P.P.MAGENTA/1: UNPRICED DUE TO SCARCITY
*P.P.YELLOW/1: UNPRICED DUE TO SCARCITY
STATED PRINT RUN 3 SER.#'d SETS
UNPRICED DUE TO SCARCITY

1 I.McDiarmid/D.Prowse
2 I.McDiarmid/R.Park
3 M.Hamill/C.Fisher

2015 Star Wars Chrome Perspectives Jedi vs. Sith Ultra Rare Triple Autographs

*P.P.BLACK/1: UNPRICED DUE TO SCARCITY
*P.P.CYAN/1: UNPRICED DUE TO SCARCITY
*P.P.MAGENTA/1: UNPRICED DUE TO SCARCITY
*P.P.YELLOW/1: UNPRICED DUE TO SCARCITY
UNPRICED DUE TO SCARCITY

1 M.Hamill/D.Prowse/I.McDiarmid
2 M.Hamill/D.Prowse/R.Park

2004 Star Wars Clone Wars Cartoon

ASAJJ VENTRESS

This Topps-produced set is based on the Cartoon Network series of the same name. Each card front contains an animated image from the show and the backs have an additional image plus narrative text and behind-the-scenes facts. The base set is made up of the following subsets: The Characters (1-8), The Episodes (10-73), and Dark Horse Gallery (74-89, which contain images from the comic book series). The set is rounded out with a checklist (90). This product was released as both hobby (pre-printed with H) and retail packs (pre-printed with $1.99). Both versions contain the same inserts with the same ratios; however, sketch cards are hobby exclusive. Artwork by Patrick Blaine, Ben Caldwell, Brian Chung, Mozart Couto, Jan Duursema, Tomas Giorello, and Kev Walker.

COMPLETE SET (90)	5.00	12.00
UNOPENED HOBBY BOX (36 PACKS)	50.00	60.00
UNOPENED HOBBY PACK (7 CARDS)	1.50	2.00
UNOPENED RETAIL BOX (36 PACKS)	55.00	65.00
UNOPENED RETAIL PACK (7 CARDS)	1.75	2.25
COMMON CARD (1-90)	.15	.40

2004 Star Wars Clone Wars Cartoon Autographs

COMMON CARD	12.00	30.00

2004 Star Wars Clone Wars Cartoon Battle Motion

COMPLETE SET (10)	15.00	40.00
COMMON CARD (B1-B10)	2.00	5.00

2004 Star Wars Clone Wars Cartoon Sketches

COMPLETE ARTIST LIST (13)
RANDOMLY INSERTED INTO PACKS
UNPRICED DUE TO SCARCITY

1 Joe Corroney
2 Dave Dorman
3 Davide Fabbri
4 Tomas Giorello
5 Rafael Kayanan
6 John McCrea
7 Pop Mhan
8 Rodolfo Migliari
9 Kilian Plunkett
10 Paul Ruddish
11 Genndy Tartakovsky
12 Robert Teranishi
13 Doug Wheatley

2004 Star Wars Clone Wars Cartoon Stickers

COUNT DOOKU

COMPLETE SET (10)	3.00	8.00
COMMON CARD (1-10)	.40	1.00

2008 Star Wars Clone Wars

ROTTA THE HUTTLET

COMPLETE SET (90)	5.00	12.00
UNOPENED BOX (36 PACKS)	40.00	50.00
UNOPENED PACK (7 CARDS)	1.50	2.00
COMMON CARD (1-90)	.15	.40

*GOLD: 8X TO 20X BASIC CARD

2008 Star Wars Clone Wars Foil

COMPLETE SET (10)	12.00	25.00
COMMON CARD (1-10)	2.00	5.00

STATED ODDS 1:3 RETAIL

2008 Star Wars Clone Wars Animation Cels

COMPLETE SET (10)	7.50	15.00
COMMON CARD (1-10)	1.25	3.00

STATED ODDS 1:6
ALSO KNOWN AS THE WHITE CELS

2008 Star Wars Clone Wars Blue Animation Cels

COMPLETE SET (5)	15.00	40.00
COMMON CARD	4.00	10.00

STATED ODDS 1:6 WALMART PACKS

2008 Star Wars Clone Wars Red Animation Cels

COMPLETE SET (5)	20.00	50.00
COMMON CARD	5.00	12.00

STATED ODDS 1:6 TARGET PACKS

2008 Star Wars Clone Wars Coins Purple

COMPLETE SET (12)	15.00	40.00
COMMON CARD (1-12)	2.50	6.00

*RED: SAME VALUE
*YELLOW: SAME VALUE
PURPLE ODDS 2:WALMART/MEIER BONUS BOX
RED ODDS 2:TARGET BONUS BOX
YELLOW ODDS 2:TRU BONUS BOX

2008 Star Wars Clone Wars Motion

COMPLETE SET (5)	4.00	8.00
COMMON CARD (1-5)	1.25	3.00

STATED ODDS 1:8 RETAIL

2008 Star Wars Clone Wars Sketches

COMPLETE ARTIST LIST (110)
STATED ODDS 1:24 HOBBY
UNPRICED DUE TO SCARCITY

1 Amy Pronovost
2 Anthony Ermio
3 Ben Curtis Jones
4 Bosco Ng
5 Brent Engstrom
6 Brian Ashmore
7 Brian Denham
8 Brian Kalin O'Connell
9 Brian Kong
10 Brian Miller
11 Bryan Morton
12 Cat Staggs
13 Chelsea Brown
14 Chris Henderson
15 Chris Trevas
16 Christian Dalla Vecchia
17 Clay McCormack
18 Cynthia Cummens
19 Dan Parsons
20 Daniel Cooney
21 Danny Keller
22 Dave Filoni
23 Dave Fox
24 David Le Merrer
25 David Rabbitte
26 Davide Fabbri
27 Dennis Budd
28 Don Pedicini Jr.
29 Doug Cowan
30 Dwayne Clare
31 Edward Pun
32 Erik Maell
33 Francis Hsu
34 Gabe Hernandez
35 Giancarlo Volpe
36 Grant Gould
37 Hamilton Cline
38 Howard Shum
39 Ingrid Hardy
40 Irma Ahmed (Aimo)
41 Jackson Sze
42 Jake Minor
43 Jake Myler
44 James Bukauskas (Bukshot)
45 James Hodgkins
46 Jamie Snell
47 Jan Duursema
48 Jason Hughes
49 Jason Potratz
50 Jason Potratz
Jack Hai
51 Jason Sobol
52 Jeff Carlisle
53 Jeff Chandler
54 Jessica Hickman
55 Jim Kyle
56 Joanne Ellen Mutch
57 Joe Corroney
58 Joel Carroll
59 John McCrea
60 John Watkins-Chow
61 Jon Morris
62 Josh Fargher
63 Josh Howard
64 Juan Carlos Ramos
65 Justin Chung
66 Karen Krajenbrink
67 Kate Bradley
68 Kate Glasheen
69 Katie Cook-Wilcox
70 Keith Phillips
71 Kelsey Mann
72 Kevin Doyle
73 Kevin Graham
74 Kilian Plunkett
75 Kyle Babbitt
76 Lance Sawyer
77 Le Tang
78 Leah Mangue
79 Lee Kohse
80 Len Bellinger
81 Lord Mesa
82 Mark McHaley
83 Mark Walters
84 Matt Gaser
85 Matt Olsen
86 Matthew Goodmanson
87 Michael Duron
88 Nicole Falk
89 Noah Albrecht
90 Pat Presley
91 Patrick Hamill
92 Paul Alan Ballard
93 Paul Gutierrez
94 Randy Bantog
95 Rich Molinelli
96 Rich Woodall
97 Rob Teranishi
98 Russel G. Chong
99 Sergio Paez
100 Shelli Paroline
101 Spencer Brinkerhoff
102 Stephanie Yue
103 Steven Oatney
104 Steward Lee
105 Thang Le
106 Tod Smith
107 Tom Hodges
108 Wayne Lo
109 William O'Neill
110 Zack Giallongo

2008 Star Wars Clone Wars Promos

P1 Group of four	1.50	4.00
White back GEN		
P2 Group of four	1.50	4.00
Color back SDCC		

2008 Star Wars Clone Wars Stickers

COMPLETE SET (90)	15.00	40.00
COMMON CARD (1-90)	.40	1.00

2008 Star Wars Clone Wars Stickers Die-Cut Magnets

COMPLETE SET (9)	10.00	25.00
COMMON CARD (1-9)	2.00	5.00

STATED ODDS 1:12

2008 Star Wars Clone Wars Stickers Die-Cut Pop-Ups

YODA

COMPLETE SET (10)	3.00	8.00
COMMON CARD (1-10)	.60	1.50
STATED ODDS 1:3		

2008 Star Wars Clone Wars Stickers Foil

COMPLETE SET (10)	5.00	12.00
COMMON CARD (1-10)	.75	2.00
STATED ODDS 1:3		

2008 Star Wars Clone Wars Stickers Temporary Tattoos

COMPLETE SET (10)	6.00	15.00
COMMON CARD (1-10)	1.00	2.50
STATED ODDS 1:4		

2008 Star Wars Clone Wars Stickers Tin Lid Stickers

COMPLETE SET (6)	12.00	30.00
STATED ODDS 1 PER TIN		
1 Anakin	3.00	8.00
2 Obi-Wan	3.00	8.00
3 Anakin and Obi-Wan	3.00	8.00
4 Clone Troopers	3.00	8.00
5 Yoda	3.00	8.00
6 Anakin and Ahsoka	3.00	8.00

2010 Star Wars Clone Wars Rise of the Bounty Hunters

COMPLETE SET (90)	4.00	10.00
UNOPENED BOX (24 PACKS)	15.00	20.00
UNOPENED PACK (7 CARDS)	.75	1.00
COMMON CARD (1-90)	.10	.30
*SILVER/100: 20X TO 50X BASIC CARDS		
*GOLD/1: UNPRICED DUE TO SCARCITY		

2010 Star Wars Clone Wars Rise of the Bounty Hunters Animator Sketches

COMPLETE ARTIST LIST (6)
STATED ODDS 1:335
UNPRICED DUE TO SCARCITY

1 Animator Sketch Redemption
2 A. Kirk
3 Brian Kalin O'Connell
4 Carlo Sansonetti
5 Chris Glenn
6 Juan Hernandez
7 Ken Min
8 Killian Plunkett
9 Polina Hristova

10 Vince Lee
11 Will Nichols

2010 Star Wars Clone Wars Rise of the Bounty Hunters Cels Red

| COMPLETE SET (5) | 8.00 | 20.00 |
| COMMON CARD (1-5) | 3.00 | 8.00 |

2010 Star Wars Clone Wars Rise of the Bounty Hunters Cels Yellow

| COMPLETE SET (5) | 6.00 | 15.00 |
| COMMON CARD (1-5) | 2.50 | 6.00 |

2010 Star Wars Clone Wars Rise of the Bounty Hunters Foil

COMPLETE SET (20)	8.00	20.00
COMMON CARD (1-20)	.60	1.50
STATED ODDS 1:3		

2010 Star Wars Clone Wars Rise of the Bounty Hunters Motion

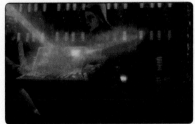

COMPLETE SET (5)	6.00	15.00
COMMON CARD (1-5)	1.50	4.00
STATED ODDS 1:6		

2010 Star Wars Clone Wars Rise of the Bounty Hunters Sketches

1 Adrien Rivera
2 Alex Buechel
3 Amy Pronovost
4 Beck Kramer
5 Bill Pulkovski
6 Bob Stevlic
7 Braden Lamb
8 Brent Engstrom
9 Brian Miller
10 Brian Rood
11 Bruce Gerlach
12 Cal Slayton
13 Cat Staggs
14 Dan Bergren
15 Dan Masso
16 David Day
17 David Rabbitte
18 Denise Vasquez
19 Don Pedicini Jr

20 Doug Cowan
21 Gabe Farber
22 Gary Kezele
23 Geoff Munn
24 George Davis
25 Grant Gould
26 Hayden Davis
27 Howard Shum
28 Ingrid Hardy
29 Irma Ahmed
30 Jamie Snell
31 Jason Hughes
32 Jason Keith Philips
33 Jason Sobol
34 Jeff Confer
35 Jeremy Treece
36 Jerry Gaylord
37 Jessica Hickman
38 Jim Kyle
39 John Beatty
40 John P. Wales
41 John Soukup
42 Jon Morris
43 Juan Carlos Ramos
44 Katie Cook
45 Kevin Doyle
46 Kevin Graham
47 Kevin Liell
48 Lance Sawyer
49 Lawrence Snelly
50 Lee Kohse
51 M. Jason Reed
52 Mark Slater
53 Martheus Wade
54 Matt Minor
55 Michael Duron
56 Nolan Woodard
57 Otis Frampton
58 Patrick Richardson
59 Randy Martinez
60 Rhiannon Owens
61 Rich Molinelli
62 Robert Teranishi
63 Ryan Hungerford
64 Sarah Wilkinson
65 Scott Zambelli
66 Shea Standefer
67 Shelli Paroline
68 Spencer Brinkerhoff
69 Stephanie Yue
70 Steve Oatney
71 Tim Proctor
72 Tod Allen Smith
73 Tom Hodges
74 Zack Giallongo

2010 Star Wars Clone Wars Rise of the Bounty Hunters Promos

| P1 Cad Bane and Others | 1.25 | 3.00 |
| P3 Pre Vizsla and Mandalorian Death Watch | 1.25 | 3.00 |

2009 Star Wars Clone Wars Widevision

COMPLETE SET (80)	5.00	12.00
UNOPENED BOX (24 PACKS)	60.00	70.00
UNOPENED PACK (7 CARDS)	2.50	3.00
COMMON CARD (1-80)	.15	.40
*SILVER: 5X TO 12X BASIC CARDS		

2009 Star Wars Clone Wars Widevision Animation Cels

THREEPIO AND JAR JAR

COMPLETE SET (10)	6.00	15.00
COMMON CARD (1-10)	.75	2.00
STATED ODDS 1:4		

2009 Star Wars Clone Wars Widevision Animator Sketches

COMPLETE ARTIST LIST (23)
STATED ODDS 1:223
OVERALL ODDS WITH ARTIST SKETCHES 1:24
UNPRICED DUE TO SCARCITY

20 Thang Le
23 Wayne Lo
2 Bosco Ng
8 Don Ta
12 Ken Min
10 Jackson Sze
4 Chris Voy
16 Randy Bantog
21 Tim Brock
17 Russell Chong
1 Anthony Ermio
6 Dave Filoni
7 Davide Le Merrer
5 Darren Marshall
3 Brian Kalin O'Connell
18 Sergio Paez
13 Kilian Plunkett
15 Pat Presley
19 Stew Lee
11 Jacob Stephens
14 Le Tang
22 Vince Lee
9 Giancarlo Volpe

2009 Star Wars Clone Wars Widevision Artist Sketches

COMPLETE ARTIST LIST (105)
STATED ODDS 1:27 HOBBY PACKS
STATED ODDS 1:48 RETAIL PACKS
OVERALL ODDS WITH ANIMATOR SKETCHES 1:24
UNPRICED DUE TO SCARCITY

DAY David Day
97 Stephanie Yue
AHME Irma Ahmed
94 Soni Alcorn-Hender
10 Brian Ashmore
67 Kyle Babbitt
23 Dan Bergren
12 Brian Miller
95 Spencer Brinkerhoff III
32 Dennis Budd
3 Alex Buechel
45 James Bukauskas
6 Bernard Chang
19 Chris Henderson
76 Matte Chero
60 Justin Chung
39 Hamilton Cline
63 Katie Cook
54 Joe Corroney
51 Jerome Dabos
100 Ted Dastick Jr.
40 Hayden Davis
11 Brian Denham
20 Colleen Doran

64 Kevin Doyle
77 Michael Duron (Locoduck)
26 Darla Ecklund
81 Nina Edlund
17 Carolyn Edwards
9 Brent Engstrom
80 Nicole Falk
37 Gabe Farber
58 Josh Fargher
2 Agnieszka Garbowska
14 Bruce Gerlach
105 Zack Giallongo
62 Kate Glasheen
38 Grant Gould
65 Kevin Graham
42 Ingrid Hardy
52 Jess Hickman
103 Tom Hodges
47 Jason Hughes
44 Jake Minor
5 Ben Curtis Jones
46 Jamie Snell
24 Danny Kelly
72 Lee Kohse
61 Karen Krajenbrink
53 Jim Kyle
8 Braden Lamb
66 Kevin Liell
69 Laura Martin
70 Lawrence Snelly
34 Erik Maell
71 Leah Mangue
74 Mark McHaley
73 Lord Mesa
75 Matt Minor
85 Rich Molinelli
78 Monte Moore
9 Jon Morris
15 Bryan Morton
22 Cynthia (Cummens) Narcisi
82 Nolan Woodward
98 Steve Oatney
84 Rhiannon Owens
93 Shelli Paroline
33 Don Pedicini Jr.
92 Sean Pence
48 Jason Keith Phillips
101 Tim Proctor
4 Amy Pronovost
7 Bill Pulkovski
30 David Rabbitte
25 Darin Radimaker
59 Juan Carlos Ramos
88 Robert Hendrickson
79 Adrian Rivera
83 Randy Martinez
13 Brian Rood
21 Craig Rousseau
96 Stephane Roux
86 Rich Woodall
68 Lance Sawyer
79 Neil Segura
41 Howard Shum
91 Scott D. M. Simmons
99 Steven Miller
49 Jason Sobol
16 Carlo Sinfuego Soriano
56 John Soukup
18 Cat Staggs
27 Dave Pops Tata
87 Rob Teranishi
50 Jeremy Treece
35 Francis Tsai
102 Tod Allen Smith
104 Uko Smith
31 Denise Vasquez
36 Frank Villarreal
55 John P. Wales
89 Russ Walks
90 Sarah Wilkinson
29 David Green

2009 Star Wars Clone Wars Widevision Autographs

MATT LANTER
ANAKIN SKYWALKER

COMMON CARD	8.00	20.00
STATED ODDS 1:67		
AD Anthony Daniels		
CT Catherine Taber	12.00	30.00
IA Ian Abercrombie	12.00	30.00
NF Nika Futterman	12.00	30.00
TK Tom Kane	12.00	30.00
DBB Dee Bradley Baker	12.00	30.00
MW1 Matthew Wood/Droids	10.00	25.00
MW2 Matthew Wood/Grievous	10.00	25.00

2009 Star Wars Clone Wars Widevision Foil Characters

GENERAL GRIEVOUS

COMPLETE SET (20)	15.00	40.00
COMMON CARD (1-20)	1.00	2.50
STATED ODDS 1:3		

2009 Star Wars Clone Wars Widevision Motion

COMPLETE SET (5)	6.00	15.00
COMMON CARD (1-5)	1.50	4.00
STATED ODDS 1:8		

2009 Star Wars Clone Wars Widevision Season Two Previews

SEASON 2 PREVIEW

COMPLETE SET (8)	3.00	8.00
COMMON CARD (PV1-PV8)	.50	1.25
STATED ODDS 1:2		

1995 Star Wars Day

NNO Millennium Falcon w/X-Wings and TIE Fighters

2015 Star Wars Disney Pixar Cars Promos

COMPLETE SET (5)	30.00	80.00
COMMON CARD	10.00	25.00

2015 Star Wars Disney Store
The Force Awakens Promos

Finn on the run!

COMPLETE SET (8)	20.00	50.00
COMMON CARD (SKIP #'d)	4.00	10.00
11 BB-8 on the move!	6.00	15.00
67 Kylo Ren ignites his Lightsaber!	5.00	12.00
96 The Millennium Falcon	5.00	12.00

2011 Star Wars Dog Tags

COMPLETE SET (24)	25.00	60.00
UNOPENED BOX (PACKS)		
UNOPENED PACK (1 TAG+1 CARD)		
COMMON TAG (1-24)	2.00	5.00
*SILVER: .5X TO 1.2X BASIC TAGS	2.50	6.00
*RAINBOW: 1.2X TO 3X BASIC TAGS	6.00	15.00

2001 Star Wars Evolution

This all-foil set from Topps covers the various characters in the first four of six Star Wars films, showing two images of a particular character on the card fronts and featuring a front image and character information on the backs.

COMPLETE SET (93)	5.00	12.00
UNOPENED BOX (36 PACKS)	45.00	60.00
UNOPENED PACK (8 CARDS)	1.50	2.00
COMMON CARD (1-93)	.15	.40

2001 Star Wars Evolution Autographs

COMMON CARD	15.00	40.00
GROUP A/1000* STATED ODDS 1:37		
GROUP B/400* STATED ODDS 1:919		
GROUP C/300* STATED ODDS 1:2450		
GROUP D/100* STATED ODDS 1:3677		
NNO Andrew Secombe/1000*	20.00	50.00
NNO Anthony Daniels/100*	1000.00	1500.00
NNO Billy Dee Williams/300*	200.00	400.00
NNO Carrie Fisher/100*	1000.00	1500.00
NNO Ian McDiarmid/400*	250.00	500.00
NNO James Earl Jones/1000*	125.00	200.00
NNO Jeremy Bulloch/1000*	50.00	100.00
NNO Kenneth Colley/1000*	20.00	50.00
NNO Kenny Baker/1000*	125.00	200.00
NNO Lewis MacLeod	35.00	70.00
NNO Mercedes Ngoh/1000*	20.00	50.00
NNO Michonne Bourriague/1000*	20.00	50.00
NNO Peter Mayhew/400*	100.00	200.00
NNO Phil Brown/1000*	25.00	60.00
NNO Warwick Davis/1000*	20.00	50.00

2001 Star Wars Evolution Insert A

COMPLETE SET (12)	15.00	30.00
COMMON CARD (1A-12A)	1.50	4.00
STATED ODDS 1:6		

2001 Star Wars Evolution Insert B

COMPLETE SET (8)	20.00	40.00
COMMON CARD (1B-8B)	2.50	6.00
STATED ODDS 1:12		

2001 Star Wars Evolution Promos

Anakin Skywalker

COMMON CARD	1.00	2.50
P3 Nien Nunb ALPHA CON	3.00	8.00
P4 Anakin Skywalker SDCC	2.00	5.00

2006 Star Wars Evolution Update

Using the same format as the first set, this one encompasses characters from all six films. The card fronts illustrate an all-foil finish and the backs contain character information. It was released in both hobby (H) and retail (R) packs. Artwork by Jan Duursema and Dan Parsons.

COMPLETE SET (90)	5.00	12.00
UNOPENED BOX (24 PACKS)	40.00	50.00
UNOPENED PACK (6 CARDS)	2.00	2.25
COMMON CARD (1-90)	.15	.40
1D ISSUED AS DAMAGED AUTO REPLACEMENT		
CL1 Luke Connections CL	.40	1.00
CL2 Leia Connections CL	.40	1.00
1D Luke Skywalker SP	2.00	5.00
P1 Obi-Wan Kenobi PROMO	1.00	2.50
P2 Darth Vader PROMO	1.00	2.50

2006 Star Wars Evolution Update Autographs

SLY MOORE

COMMON CARD (UNNUMBERED)	10.00	25.00
STATED ODDS 1:24 HOBBY		
GROUP A ODDS 1:2,005		
GROUP B ODDS 1:231		
GROUP C ODDS 1:81		
GROUP D ODDS 1:259		
GROUP E ODDS 1:48		
NNO Alec Guinness		
NNO Bob Keen B	25.00	50.00
NNO David Barclay B	25.00	50.00
NNO George Lucas		
NNO Hayden Christensen A	600.00	1000.00
NNO James Earl Jones A	200.00	400.00
NNO John Coppinger B	25.00	50.00
NNO Mike Edmonds B	25.00	50.00

NNO	Mike Quinn B	25.00	50.00
NNO	Peter Cushing		
NNO	Toby Philpott B	25.00	50.00
NNO	Wayne Pygram B	50.00	100.00

2006 Star Wars Evolution Update Etched Foil Puzzle

COMPLETE SET (6)	6.00	15.00
COMMON CARD (1-6)	1.25	3.00
STATED ODDS 1:6		

2006 Star Wars Evolution Update Galaxy Crystals

COMPLETE SET (10)	12.50	30.00
COMMON CARD (G1-G10)	1.50	4.00
STATED ODDS 1:4 RETAIL		

2006 Star Wars Evolution Update Insert A

COMPLETE SET (20)	20.00	40.00
COMMON CARD (1A-20A)	1.50	4.00
STATED ODDS 1:6		

2006 Star Wars Evolution Update Insert B

COMPLETE SET (15)	20.00	40.00
COMMON CARD (1B-15B)	2.00	5.00
STATED ODDS 1:12		

2006 Star Wars Evolution Update Luke and Leia

COMPLETE SET (2)	1000.00	2000.00
COMMON CARD (1-2)	600.00	1200.00
STATED ODDS 1:1975 HOBBY		
STATED PRINT RUN 100 SER. #'d SETS		

2016 Star Wars Evolution

COMPLETE SET (100)	8.00	20.00
UNOPENED BOX (24 PACKS)	60.00	75.00
UNOPENED PACK (8 CARDS)	2.50	3.00
COMMON CARD (1-100)	.15	.40
*LTSBR BLUE: 4X TO 10X BASIC CARDS		
*LTSBR PURPLE: 8X TO 20X BASIC CARDS		
*GOLD/50: 15X TO 40X BASIC CARDS		
*IMP.RED/1: UNPRICED DUE TO SCARCITY		
*P.P.BLACK/1: UNPRICED DUE TO SCARCITY		
*P.P.CYAN/1: UNPRICED DUE TO SCARCITY		
*P.P.MAGENTA/1: UNPRICED DUE TO SCARCITY		
*P.P.YELLOW/1: UNPRICED DUE TO SCARCITY		

2016 Star Wars Evolution Autographs

COMMON CARD	6.00	15.00
*PURPLE/25: .6X TO 1.5X BASIC CARDS		
*GOLD/10: UNPRICED DUE TO SCARCITY		
*IMP.RED/1: UNPRICED DUE TO SCARCITY		
*P.P.BLACK/1: UNPRICED DUE TO SCARCITY		
*P.P.CYAN/1: UNPRICED DUE TO SCARCITY		
*P.P.MAGENTA/1: UNPRICED DUE TO SCARCITY		
*P.P.YELLOW/1: UNPRICED DUE TO SCARCITY		
RANDOMLY INSERTED INTO PACKS		
NNO	Alan Harris	8.00	20.00
NNO	Amy Allen	10.00	25.00
NNO	Andy Serkis	150.00	300.00
NNO	Angus MacInnes	20.00	50.00
NNO	Ashley Eckstein	20.00	50.00
NNO	Catherine Taber	8.00	20.00
NNO	Clive Revill	25.00	60.00
NNO	Dee Bradley Baker	8.00	20.00
NNO	Deep Roy	10.00	25.00
NNO	Denis Lawson	30.00	80.00
NNO	Dickey Beer	15.00	40.00
NNO	Freddie Prinze Jr.	60.00	120.00
NNO	George Takei	15.00	40.00
NNO	Greg Grunberg	15.00	40.00
NNO	Harriet Walter	12.00	30.00
NNO	Hugh Quarshie	20.00	50.00
NNO	Jeremy Bulloch	20.00	50.00
NNO	Jerome Blake	10.00	25.00
NNO	John Boyega	100.00	200.00
NNO	John Ratzenberger	8.00	20.00
NNO	Keisha Castle-Hughes	10.00	25.00
NNO	Kenneth Colley	12.00	30.00

NNO	Matthew Wood	12.00	30.00
NNO	Mercedes Ngoh	20.00	50.00
NNO	Michael Carter	20.00	50.00
NNO	Mike Quinn	8.00	20.00
NNO	Orli Shoshan	8.00	20.00
NNO	Paul Blake	8.00	20.00
NNO	Peter Mayhew	80.00	150.00
NNO	Phil Lamarr	15.00	40.00
NNO	Ray Park	25.00	60.00
NNO	Sam Witwer	8.00	20.00
NNO	Stephen Stanton	10.00	25.00
NNO	Taylor Gray	10.00	25.00
NNO	Tim Dry	12.00	30.00
NNO	Tiya Sircar	8.00	20.00
NNO	Tom Kane	10.00	25.00
NNO	Vanessa Marshall	8.00	20.00
NNO	Warwick Davis	12.00	30.00

2016 Star Wars Evolution Dual Autographs

COMPLETE SET (7)		
STATED PRINT RUN 3 SER.#'d SETS		
UNPRICED DUE TO SCARCITY		

NNO Eckstein
Baker
NNO McDiarmid
Revill
NNO McDiarmid
Wood
NNO Bulloch
Logan
NNO Hamill
Roy
NNO Carter
Wood
NNO Park
Witwer

2016 Star Wars Evolution Dual Patch Banner Books

COMPLETE SET (8)		
STATED PRINT RUN 5 SER.#'d SETS		
UNPRICED DUE TO SCARCITY		

NNO Bail Organa
Padme Amidala
NNO Count Dooku
General Grievous
NNO Emperor Palpatine
Darth Vader
NNO Finn
Rey
NNO Kanan Jarrus
Ezra Bridger
NNO Kylo Ren
Captain Phasma
NNO Luke Skywalker
Princess Leia
NNO Yoda
Mace Windu

2016 Star Wars Evolution Evolution of the Lightsaber

COMPLETE SET (9)	12.00	30.00
COMMON CARD (EL1-EL9)	2.00	5.00
*P.P.BLACK/1: UNPRICED DUE TO SCARCITY		
*P.P.CYAN/1: UNPRICED DUE TO SCARCITY		
*P.P.MAGENTA/1: UNPRICED DUE TO SCARCITY		
*P.P.YELLOW/1: UNPRICED DUE TO SCARCITY		
STATED ODDS 1:8		

2016 Star Wars Evolution Evolution of Vehicles and Ships

COMPLETE SET (18)	8.00	20.00
COMMON CARD (EV1-EV18)	.75	2.00
*P.P.BLACK/1: UNPRICED DUE TO SCARCITY		
*P.P.CYAN/1: UNPRICED DUE TO SCARCITY		
*P.P.MAGENTA/1: UNPRICED DUE TO SCARCITY		
*P.P.YELLOW/1: UNPRICED DUE TO SCARCITY		
STATED ODDS 1:2		

2016 Star Wars Evolution Lenticular Morph

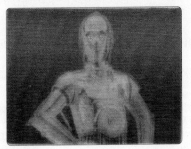

COMPLETE SET (9)	60.00	120.00
COMMON CARD (1-9)	6.00	15.00
STATED ODDS 1:72		
1 Darth Vader	10.00	25.00
2 Luke Skywalker	10.00	25.00
3 Leia Organa	8.00	20.00
4 Han Solo	10.00	25.00
9 Chewbacca	8.00	20.00

2016 Star Wars Evolution Marvel Star Wars Comics

COMPLETE SET (17)	12.00	30.00
COMMON CARD (EC1-EC17)	1.50	4.00
*P.P.BLACK/1: UNPRICED DUE TO SCARCITY		
*P.P.CYAN/1: UNPRICED DUE TO SCARCITY		
*P.P.MAGENTA/1: UNPRICED DUE TO SCARCITY		
*P.P.YELLOW/1: UNPRICED DUE TO SCARCITY		
STATED ODDS 1:4		

2016 Star Wars Evolution Patches

COMMON CARD	5.00	12.00
*SILVER/50: 5X TO 1.2X BASIC CARDS		
*GOLD/25: .6X TO 1.5X BASIC CARDS		
*IMP.RED/1: UNPRICED DUE TO SCARCITY		
*PLATINUM/10: UNPRICED DUE TO SCARCITY		
NNO Admiral Ackbar	6.00	15.00
NNO Ahsoka Tano	6.00	15.00
NNO BB-8	8.00	20.00
NNO Chancellor Palpatine	6.00	15.00
NNO Clone Trooper	6.00	15.00
NNO Darth Vader	6.00	15.00
NNO Ezra Bridger	6.00	15.00
NNO General Hux	6.00	15.00
NNO Grand Moff Tarkin	8.00	20.00
NNO Han Solo	8.00	20.00
NNO Kylo Ren	8.00	20.00
NNO Luke Skywalker	6.00	15.00
NNO Mon Mothma	6.00	15.00
NNO Poe Dameron	6.00	15.00
NNO Princess Leia Organa	6.00	15.00
NNO Qui-Gon Jinn	6.00	15.00
NNO Rey	10.00	25.00
NNO Senator Amidala	6.00	15.00
NNO Supreme Leader Snoke	6.00	15.00

2016 Star Wars Evolution Quad Autograph

STATED PRINT RUN 1 SER.#'d SET
UNPRICED DUE TO SCARCITY

1 Bulloch
Morton
  Beers
  Logan

2016 Star Wars Evolution Sketches

1 Alex Buechel
2 Angelina Benedetti
3 Brad Hudson
4 Brent Ragland
5 Brian Kong
6 Carlos Cabaleiro
7 Christopther West
8 Dan Bergren
9 Dan Parsons
10 Darrin Pepe

11 David Rabbitte
12 Elfie Lebouleux
13 Eli Rutten
14 Eric Lehtonen
15 Francois Chartier
16 Jason Brower
17 Jason Crosby
18 Jason Flowers
19 Jason Sobol
20 Jeff West
21 Jeffrey Benitez
22 Jennifer Allyn
23 Jonathan Caustrita
24 Keith Carter
25 Kevin West
26 Kris Penix
27 Kyle Babbit
28 Lin Workman
29 Marcia Dye
30 Matthew Fletcher
31 Patrick Richardson
32 Rich Molinelli
33 Roy Cover
34 Scott Jones
35 Scott Rorie
36 Seth Ismart
37 Solly Mohamed
38 Stephanie Swanger
39 Strephon Taylor
40 Tim Proctor
41 Tim Shay
42 Tina Berardi

2016 Star Wars Evolution SP Inserts

COMPLETE SET (9)	250.00	500.00
COMMON CARD (1-9)	25.00	60.00
STATED PRINT RUN 100 SER.#'d SETS		
1 Luke	30.00	80.00
Stormtrooper Disguise		
2 Leia	30.00	80.00
Boussh Disguise		
5 Vader	50.00	100.00
Birth of the Dark Lord		
6 Boba Fett	30.00	80.00
Skiff Battle		

2016 Star Wars Evolution Stained Glass Pairings

COMPLETE SET (9)	20.00	50.00
COMMON CARD (1-9)	2.50	6.00
STATED ODDS 1:24		
1 Luke Skywalker	5.00	12.00
Princess Leia		
2 Han Solo	4.00	10.00
Lando Calrissian		
4 Darth Sidious	4.00	10.00
Darth Maul		
5 Darth Vader	3.00	8.00
Grand Moff Tarkin		
6 Kylo Ren	3.00	8.00
Captain Phasma		
7 Chewbacca	3.00	8.00
C-3PO		
9 Rey	6.00	15.00
Finn		

2016 Star Wars Evolution Triple Autographs

COMPLETE SET (4)
STATED PRINT RUN 3 SER.#'d SETS
UNPRICED DUE TO SCARCITY

1 Blakinston
Crowley
Rose
2 McDiarmid
Wood
Blake
3 Bulloch
Morton
Beer
4 Gray
Eckstein
Baker

2007 Star Wars Family Guy Blue Harvest DVD Promos

This little gem was included with Family Guy Blue Harvest DVD Boxed Set. The card fronts contain and image of the animation depicted in the Blue Harvest episode. The basic design pays homage to the vintage 1977 Star Wars set that was produced by Topps. The card backs feature a puzzle piece which, along with all the others, produces an image. Besides the English version, there are 3 other known language versions: German, Italian, and Spanish.

COMPLETE SET (12)	5.00	12.00
COMMON CARD (UNNUMBERED)	.75	2.00

*GERMAN: SAME VALUE AS ENGLISH
*ITALIAN: SAME VALUE AS ENGLISH
*SPANISH: SAME VALUE AS ENGLISH

1996 Star Wars Finest

Topps produced this set that combines artist-inspired imagery and chromium card stock. Each card back features character information plus a drawing in metallic ink. The base set contains the following subsets: Rebel Alliance (2-10, Rebels and Affiliates (11-18), Imperial Command (19-27, Imperials and Affiliates (28-36), Force Users (37-45), Spies Smugglers and Rogues (46-54), Indigenous Life Forms (55-63), Mos Eisley Can-

tina (64-72), Jabba's Palace (73-81), and Droids (82-90). Artwork by Den Beauvais, Dan Brereton, Mike Butkus, Joe Chiodo, Hugh Fleming, Tony Harris, Lou Harrison, Mark Harrison, Rick Hoberg, Ray Lago, Mike Manley, Brandon McKinney, Chris Moeller, Joe Phillips, Marc Sasso, Juda Tverski, Jon Van Fleet, and Russell Walks

COMPLETE SET (90)	10.00	25.00
UNOPENED BOX (36 PACKS)	45.00	60.00
UNOPENED PACK (5 CARDS)	1.50	2.00
COMMON CARD (1-90)	.20	.50

*REF.: 5X TO 12X BASIC CARDS

1996 Star Wars Finest Embossed

COMPLETE SET (6)	10.00	25.00
COMMON CARD (F1-F6)	2.00	5.00

1996 Star Wars Finest Matrix

COMPLETE SET (4)	6.00	15.00
COMMON CARD (M1-M4)	2.00	5.00

NNO Exchange Card

1996 Star Wars Finest Promos

COMPLETE SET (3)	2.50	6.00
COMMON CARD (SWF1-SWF3)	1.00	2.50
B1 Han Solo & Chewbacca	3.00	8.00
(Album Exclusive)		
SWF1 Boba Fett	1.00	2.50
SWF2 Republic City	1.00	2.50
SWF3 Jedi Council Chamber	1.00	2.50
NNO 1-Card Sheet		
NNO 1-Card Sheet Refractor		
NNO Star Wars Goes Split Level	200.00	400.00

2015 Star Wars Galactic Connexions

COMPLETE SET (75)	8.00	20.00
COMMON DISC	.20	.50

*FOIL: .6X TO 1.5X BASIC DISCS
*BLK: .75X TO 2X BASIC DISCS
*HOLOFOIL: .75X TO 2X BASIC DISCS
*BLK FOIL: 1.5X TO 4X BASIC DISCS
*CLR: 1.5X TO 4X BASIC DISCS
*PATTERN FOIL: 2X TO 5X BASIC DISCS
*BLK PATTERN FOIL: 2.5X TO 6X BASIC DISCS
*JABBA SLIME GREEN: 3X TO 8X BASIC DISCS
*CLR FOIL: 4X TO 10X BASIC DISCS
*LTSABER RED: 4X TO 10X BASIC DISCS
*CLR PATTERN FOIL: 8X TO 20X BASIC DISCS
*C-3PO GOLD: 10X TO 25X BASIC DISCS
*DEATH STAR SILVER: 12X TO 30X BASIC DISCS
*SOLID GOLD: 20X TO 50X BASIC DISCS

2015 Star Wars Galactic Connexions Battle Damaged Border

1 Darth Vader	250.00	500.00
Red		
2 Han Solo	150.00	300.00
Red		
3 Luke Skywalker	120.00	250.00
Red		
4 Obi-Wan Kenobi		
Red		
5 Princess Leia Organa		
Red		

2015 Star Wars Galactic Connexions Blue Starfield Exclusives

COMPLETE SET (10)	10.00	25.00
COMMON DISC	1.50	4.00

2015 Star Wars Galactic Connexions SDCC Promos

COMPLETE SET (6)	100.00	200.00
COMMON DISC	12.00	30.00
4 Stormtrooper	30.00	80.00
Red		
5 Stormtrooper	20.00	50.00
Gold		

2015 Star Wars Galactic Connexions Series 2

COMPLETE SET (75)	8.00	20.00
COMMON DISC	.20	.50

*GRAY FOIL: .6X TO 1.5X BASIC DISCS
*BLK: .75X TO 2X BASIC DISCS
*GRAY: .75X TO 2X BASIC DISCS
*BLK FOIL: 1.5X TO 4X BASIC DISCS
*CLR: 1.5X TO 4X BASIC DISCS
*GRAY PATTERN FOIL: 2X TO 5X BASIC DISCS
*BLK PATTERN FOIL: 2.5X TO 6X BASIC DISCS
*JABBA SLIME GREEN: 3X TO 8X BASIC DISCS
*CLR FOIL: 4X TO 10X BASIC DISCS
*LTSABER PURPLE: 4X TO 10X BASIC DISCS
*LTSABER RED: 4X TO 10X BASIC DISCS
*CLR PATTERN FOIL: 8X TO 20X BASIC DISCS
*C-3PO GOLD: 10X TO 25X BASIC DISCS
*DEATH STAR SILVER: 12X TO 30X BASIC DISCS
*SOLID GOLD: 20X TO 50X BASIC DISCS

2012 Star Wars Galactic Files

COMPLETE SET (350)	25.00	50.00
UNOPENED BOX (24 PACKS)	80.00	100.00
UNOPENED PACK (12 CARDS)	4.00	5.00
COMMON CARD (1-350)	.15	.40
*BLUE: 8X TO 20X BASIC CARDS	3.00	8.00
*RED: 20X TO 50X BASIC CARDS	8.00	20.00
*GOLD/1: UNPRICED DUE TO SCARCITY		
*P.P.BLACK/1: UNPRICED DUE TO SCARCITY		
*P.P.CYAN/1: UNPRICED DUE TO SCARCITY		
*P.P.MAGENTA/1: UNPRICED DUE TO SCARCITY		
*P.P.YELLOW/1: UNPRICED DUE TO SCARCITY		
76 Darth Vader (Jedi Purge) SP	12.00	30.00
96 Luke Skywalker (Stormtrooper) SP	12.00	30.00
125B Princess Leia (Despair) SP	12.00	30.00

2012 Star Wars Galactic Files Autographs

COMMON CARD	12.00	30.00
STATED ODDS ONE AUTO OR PATCH PER HOBBY BOX		
1 Amy Allen	15.00	40.00
4 Carrie Fisher	250.00	400.00
5 Daniel Logan	15.00	40.00
6 Felix Silla	15.00	40.00
7 Harrison Ford	2500.00	4000.00
8 Irvin Kershner	600.00	1000.00
9 Jake Lloyd	15.00	40.00
10 James Earl Jones	200.00	400.00
11 Jeremy Bulloch	30.00	60.00
12 Mark Hamill	300.00	500.00
13 Matthew Wood	25.00	50.00
15 Peter Mayhew	25.00	50.00
16 Ray Park	25.00	50.00

2012 Star Wars Galactic Files Classic Lines

COMPLETE SET (10)	3.00	8.00
COMMON CARD (CL1-CL10)	.75	2.00
STATED ODDS 1:4		

2012 Star Wars Galactic Files Duels of Fate

COMPLETE SET (10)	4.00	10.00
COMMON CARD (DF1-DF10)	1.00	2.50
STATED ODDS 1:6		

2012 Star Wars Galactic Files Galactic Moments

COMPLETE SET (20)	20.00	40.00
COMMON CARD (GM1-GM20)	1.50	4.00
STATED ODDS 1:6		

2012 Star Wars Galactic Files Heroes on Both Sides

COMPLETE SET (10)	4.00	10.00
COMMON CARD (HB1-HB10)	1.00	2.50
STATED ODDS 1:6		

2012 Star Wars Galactic Files I Have a Bad Feeling About This

COMPLETE SET (8)	3.00	8.00
COMMON CARD (BF1-BF8)	.75	2.00
STATED ODDS 1:4		

2012 Star Wars Galactic Files Patches

COMMON CARD	8.00	20.00
STATED ODDS ONE AUTO OR PATCH PER HOBBY BOX		
PR1 X-Wing Fighter Pilots: Red Leader	50.00	100.00
Garven Dreis		
PR2 X-Wing Fighter Pilots: Red Two	50.00	100.00
Wedge Antilles		
PR3 X-Wing Fighter Pilots: Red Three	50.00	100.00
Biggs Darklighter		
PR4 X-Wing Fighter Pilots: Red Four	50.00	100.00
John D. Branon		
PR5 X-Wing Fighter Pilots: Red Five	100.00	200.00
Luke Skywalker		
PR6 X-Wing Fighter Pilots: Red Six	50.00	100.00
Jek Porkins		
PR12 Jedi Starfighter Pilots	12.00	30.00

Obi-Wan Kenobi		
PR13 Jedi Starfighter Pilots	15.00	40.00
Anakin Skywalker		
PR14 Jedi Starfighter Pilots	12.00	30.00
Plo Koon		
PR17 Snowspeeder Pilots: Rogue Leader	75.00	150.00
Luke Skywalker		
PR18 Snowspeeder Pilots: Rogue Two	40.00	80.00
Zev Senesca		
PR19 Snowspeeder Pilots: Rogue Three	40.00	80.00
Wedge Antilles		
PR20 Snowspeeder Pilots: Rogue Four	30.00	60.00
Derek Hobbie Kuvian		
PR21 Snowspeeder Pilots: Rogue Leader	30.00	60.00
(Gunner) Dak Ralter		
PR23 Death Star Command	15.00	40.00
Grand Moff Tarkin		
PR24 Death Star Command	15.00	40.00
Darth Vader		
PR25 Millennium Falcon Pilots	35.00	70.00
Han Solo		
PR26 Millennium Falcon Pilots	15.00	40.00
Chewbacca		
PR27 Millennium Falcon Pilots: Gold Leader	25.00	50.00
Lando Calrissian		
PR28 Millennium Falcon Pilots: Gold Leader	15.00	40.00
Nien Numb		

2012 Star Wars Galactic Files Sketches

1 Adam Talley/200*
2 Alex Buechel/50*
3 Amy Pronovost/50*
4 Angelina Benedetti/100*
5 Ashleigh Popplewell/100*
6 Bill Pulkovski
7 Bob Stevlic/100*
8 Brent Engstrom
9 Brian DeGuire/100*
10 Chris Raimo/100*
11 Clay Rodery/100*
12 Dan Bergren/50*
13 Darla Ecklund
14 Dave Strong/100*
15 David Green
16 David Rabbitte/130*
17 Denae Frazier/50*
18 Denise Vasquez/100*
19 Diego Jourdan
20 Eli Rutten/50*
21 Gary Kezele/50*
22 Howard Shum
23 Ian Roberts/101*
24 Ingrid Hardy/50*
25 Irma Ahmed/100*
26 Jamie Snell/100*
27 Jason Durden
28 Jason Goad
29 Jason Sobol
30 Jay Shimko
31 Jennifer Mercer
32 Jeremy Scott
33 Joe Hogan
34 John Ottinger
35 Justin Chung
36 Kate Glasheen
37 Katie Cook
38 Kevin Bloomfield
39 Kevin Reinke
40 Kimberly Dunaway
41 Lak Lim
42 Lance Sawyer
43 Lark Sudol
44 Leah Mangue
45 Lee Kohse
46 Lee Lightfoot
47 Lin Workman
48 Lord Mesa
49 M. Jason Reed
50 Mario Rojas
51 Matte Chero
52 Mike Hampton
53 Mike Vasquez
54 Mikey Babinski

55 Nina Edlund
56 Pablo Diaz
57 Puis Calzada
58 Rachel Kaiser
59 Randy Martinez
60 Rhiannon Owens
61 Rich Molinelli
62 Robert Teranishi
63 Russ Maheras
64 Scott Rorie
65 Scott Zambelli
66 Stephanie Swanger
67 Ted Dastick
68 Tim Proctor
69 Trev Murphy
70 Tyler Scarlet
71 Val Hochberg
72 Van Davis
73 Vanessa Banky Farano
74 Wilson Ramos Jr.
75 Adrian Rivera
76 Tony Miello

2013 Star Wars Galactic Files 2

COMPLETE SET (353)	20.00	50.00
COMP.SET W/O SP (350)	12.00	30.00
UNOPENED BOX (24 PACKS)	70.00	80.00
UNOPENED PACK (12 CARDS)	3.00	4.00
COMMON CARD (351-699)	.15	.40
COMMON SP	4.00	10.00
*BLUE/350: 2X TO 5X BASIC CARDS		
*RED/35: 15X TO 40X BASIC CARDS		
*GOLD/10: 50X TO 120X BASIC CARDS		
*P.P.BLACK/1: UNPRICED DUE TO SCARCITY		
*P.P.CYAN/1: UNPRICED DUE TO SCARCITY		
*P.P.MAGENTA/1: UNPRICED DUE TO SCARCITY		
*P.P.YELLOW/1: UNPRICED DUE TO SCARCITY		
463b Han Solo Stormtrooper SP	4.00	10.00
481b Luke Skywalker Bacta Tank SP	4.00	10.00
510b Princess Leia Slave Girl SP	4.00	10.00

2013 Star Wars Galactic Files 2 Autographs

COMMON CARD	12.00	30.00
STATED ODDS 1:55		
UNNUMBERED SET		
NNO Alan Harris	15.00	40.00
NNO Ashley Eckstein	15.00	40.00
NNO Billy Dee Williams	60.00	120.00
NNO Carrie Fisher	200.00	350.00
NNO Chris Parsons	15.00	40.00

NNO Ian McDiarmid	400.00	600.00
NNO James Earl Jones	200.00	350.00
NNO Jeremy Bulloch	20.00	50.00
NNO John Ratzenberger	20.00	50.00
NNO Mark Hamill	350.00	500.00
NNO Peter Mayhew	20.00	50.00
NNO Tom Kane	15.00	40.00

2013 Star Wars Galactic Files 2 Dual Autographs

ANNOUNCED COMBINED PRINT RUN 200

NNO A.Eckstein/T.Kane	100.00	200.00
NNO J.Bulloch/A.Harris	100.00	200.00
NNO J.Jones/I.McDiarmid		
NNO C.Fisher/M.Hamill		
NNO H.Ford/P.Mayhew		

2013 Star Wars Galactic Files 2 Classic Lines

COMPLETE SET (10)	3.00	8.00
COMMON CARD (CL1-CL10)	.60	1.50
*P.P.BLACK/1: UNPRICED DUE TO SCARCITY		
*P.P.CYAN/1: UNPRICED DUE TO SCARCITY		
*P.P.MAGENTA/1: UNPRICED DUE TO SCARCITY		
*P.P.YELLOW/1: UNPRICED DUE TO SCARCITY		
STATED ODDS 1:4		

2013 Star Wars Galactic Files 2 Galactic Moments

COMPLETE SET (20)	30.00	60.00
COMMON CARD (GM1-GM20)	2.00	5.00
*P.P.BLACK/1: UNPRICED DUE TO SCARCITY		
*P.P.CYAN/1: UNPRICED DUE TO SCARCITY		
*P.P.MAGENTA/1: UNPRICED DUE TO SCARCITY		
*P.P.YELLOW/1: UNPRICED DUE TO SCARCITY		
STATED ODDS 1:12		

2013 Star Wars Galactic Files 2 Honor the Fallen

COMPLETE SET (10)	4.00	10.00

COMMON CARD (HF1-HF10)	.75	2.00
*P.P.BLACK/1: UNPRICED DUE TO SCARCITY		
*P.P.CYAN/1: UNPRICED DUE TO SCARCITY		
*P.P.MAGENTA/1: UNPRICED DUE TO SCARCITY		
*P.P.YELLOW/1: UNPRICED DUE TO SCARCITY		
STATED ODDS 1:6		

2013 Star Wars Galactic Files 2 Medallions

COMMON CARD (MD1-MD30)	10.00	25.00
STATED ODDS 1:55		
MD1 Luke Skywalker	20.00	50.00
MD3 Han Solo	20.00	50.00
MD4 Chewbacca	15.00	40.00
MD5 Lando Calrissian	12.00	30.00
MD6 Han Solo	150.00	250.00
MD7 Boba Fett	35.00	70.00
MD9 Princess Leia Organa	20.00	50.00
MD12 General Veers	20.00	50.00
MD13 Jawa	20.00	50.00
MD14 C-3PO	35.00	70.00
MD15 R2-D2	20.00	50.00
MD16 R5-D4	12.00	30.00
MD18 Darth Sidious	12.00	30.00
MD19 Luke Skywalker	35.00	70.00
MD20 Obi-Wan Kenobi	12.00	30.00
MD21 C-3PO & R2-D2	40.00	80.00
MD23 Darth Vader	15.00	40.00
MD24 Stormtrooper	12.00	30.00
MD25 Obi-Wan Kenobi	12.00	30.00
MD26 Plo Koon	12.00	30.00
MD27 Captain Panaka	12.00	30.00
MD28 Qui-Gon Jinn	12.00	30.00
MD29 Obi-Wan Kenobi	15.00	40.00
MD30 Queen Amidala	50.00	100.00

2013 Star Wars Galactic Files 2 Ripples in the Galaxy

COMPLETE SET (10)	4.00	10.00
COMMON CARD (RG1-RG10)	.75	2.00
*P.P.BLACK/1: UNPRICED DUE TO SCARCITY		
*P.P.CYAN/1: UNPRICED DUE TO SCARCITY		
*P.P.MAGENTA/1: UNPRICED DUE TO SCARCITY		
*P.P.YELLOW/1: UNPRICED DUE TO SCARCITY		
STATED ODDS 1:6		

2013 Star Wars Galactic Files 2 Sketches

1 Adam Talley/200*
2 Adrian Rivera
3 Angelina Benedetti
4 Beck Seashols
5 Bill Gallo
6 Bill Pulkovski
7 Bob Stevlic
8 Brett Farr
9 Brian DeGuire/50*
10 Bruce Gerlach
11 Chad McCown

12 Chris Dee/100*
13 Chris Henderson/100*
14 Chris Ramiro
15 Chris West
16 Christian Slade
17 Christopher West/200*
18 Coleen Doran
19 Dan Curto
20 Dan Gorman
21 Dave Strong
22 David Day
23 David Green
24 David Strong/106*
25 Denae Frazier
26 Denise Vasquez
27 Dennis Budd
28 Dennis Salvatier
29 Doran Leia
30 Elfie Lebouleux
31 Eric Kanalish
32 Eric Lehtonen
33 Erik Hodson
34 Erik Maell
35 Gary Kezele/100*
36 Gavin Hunt
37 George Deep
38 Hayden Davis
39 Ian Yoshio Roberts
40 Ingrid Hardy/25*
41 Irma Ahmed (Aimo)/100*
42 Jason Adams
43 Jason Davies
44 Jason Durden/100*
45 Jason Hughes
46 Jason Sobol
47 Jeff Carlisle
48 Jenn DePaola
49 Jennifer Mercer
50 Jeremy Scott
51 Jerry Fleming
52 Jessica Hickman
53 Joe Corroney
54 Joe Hogan/200*
55 John Ottinger
56 John Soukup/100*
57 JP Wales
58 Kate Glasheen/100*
59 Kevin Bloomfield/100*
60 Kevin Doyle/100*
61 Kimberly Dunaway
62 Kris Penix
63 Lak Lim
64 Lance Sawyer
65 Lark Sudol
66 Lee Bradley/100*
67 Lee Lightfoot/100*
68 Lord Mesa/100*
69 Mark Evans
70 Mary Zorilita Bellamy/100*
71 Matt Hebb
72 Matte Chero/100*
73 Michael Banks
74 Michael Duron
75 Mike Babinski
76 Mike Hampton
77 Mike Vasquez
78 Monte Moore
79 Pablo Diaz
80 Patricia Ross/100*
81 Peter Chan
82 Robert Hendrickson/50*
83 Robert Teranishi
84 Roy Aston Cover/100*
85 Russ Maheras
86 Sarah Wilkinson
87 Scott Houseman/100*
88 Scott Zambelli/100*
89 Sean Pence/25*
90 Sian Mandrake
91 Stephanie Swanger/100*
92 Strephon Taylor
93 Steve Lydic
94 Steve Oatney

95 Tim Proctor
96 Tod Allen Smith/200*
97 Tomoko Taniguchi
98 Val Hochberg
99 Vanessa Banky Farano
100 Wayne Barnes
101 Wilson Ramos
102 Zach Giallongo

2013 Star Wars Galactic Files 2 The Weak Minded

COMPLETE SET (7)	2.50	6.00
COMMON CARD (WM1-WM7)	.60	1.50

*P.P.BLACK/1: UNPRICED DUE TO SCARCITY
*P.P.CYAN/1: UNPRICED DUE TO SCARCITY
*P.P.MAGENTA/1: UNPRICED DUE TO SCARCITY
*P.P.YELLOW/1: UNPRICED DUE TO SCARCITY
STATED ODDS 1:3

2017 Star Wars Galactic Files Reborn

COMPLETE SET (200)	10.00	25.00
UNOPENED BOX (24 PACKS)	80.00	100.00
UNOPENED PACK (6 CARDS)	4.00	5.00
COMMON CARD	.15	.40

*ORANGE: .75X TO 2X BASIC CARDS
*BLUE: 1.2X TO 3X BASIC CARDS
*GREEN/199: 4X TO 10X BASIC CARDS
*PURPLE/99: 8X TO 20X BASIC CARDS
*GOLD/10: 20X TO 50X BASIC CARDS
*RED/1: UNPRICED DUE TO SCARCITY
*P.P.BLACK/1: UNPRICED DUE TO SCARCITY
*P.P.CYAN/1: UNPRICED DUE TO SCARCITY
*P.P.MAGENTA/1: UNPRICED DUE TO SCARCITY
*P.P.YELLOW/1: UNPRICED DUE TO SCARCITY

2017 Star Wars Galactic Files Reborn Autographs

COMMON CARD
*PURPLE/99: X TO X BASIC CARDS
*GOLD/10: UNPRICED DUE TO SCARCITY

*RED/1: UNPRICED DUE TO SCARCITY
*P.P.BLACK/1: UNPRICED DUE TO SCARCITY
*P.P.CYAN/1: UNPRICED DUE TO SCARCITY
*P.P.MAGENTA/1: UNPRICED DUE TO SCARCITY
*P.P.YELLOW/1: UNPRICED DUE TO SCARCITY

NNO Adam Driver		
NNO Adrienne Wilkinson	6.00	15.00
NNO Alan Tudyk	120.00	250.00
NNO Andy Serkis		
NNO Anna Graves	8.00	20.00
NNO Anthony Daniels		
NNO Ashley Eckstein		
NNO Brian Blessed	8.00	20.00
NNO Bruce Spence		
NNO Carrie Fisher		
NNO Catherine Taber	15.00	40.00
NNO Clive Revill		
NNO Daisy Ridley		
NNO Dave Barclay	10.00	25.00
NNO David Bowers	6.00	15.00
NNO Dee Bradley	12.00	30.00
NNO Denis Lawson		
NNO Donnie Yen	60.00	120.00
NNO Erik Bauersfeld	25.00	60.00
NNO Felicity Jones		
NNO Forest Whitaker	75.00	150.00
NNO Freddie Prinze		
NNO George Takei	12.00	30.00
NNO Harrison Ford		
NNO Hassani Shapi	8.00	20.00
NNO Jeremy Bulloch	20.00	50.00
NNO Jerome Blake	6.00	15.00
NNO Jesse Jensen	6.00	15.00
NNO Jim Cummings	6.00	15.00
NNO John Boyega		
NNO Julian Glover		
NNO Kath Soucie	8.00	20.00
NNO Kenny Baker		
NNO Keone Young	20.00	50.00
NNO Lewis MacLeod		
NNO Mark Hamill		
NNO Mary Oyaya	12.00	30.00
NNO Megan Udall	6.00	15.00
NNO Michael Carter	8.00	20.00
NNO Michonne Bourriague	6.00	15.00
NNO Nika Futterman	12.00	30.00
NNO Oliver Ford	8.00	20.00
NNO Oliver Walpole	10.00	25.00
NNO Olivia D'Abo	8.00	20.00
NNO Phil Eason	6.00	15.00
NNO Phil LaMarr	10.00	25.00
NNO Rajia Baroudi	8.00	20.00
NNO Ray Park	30.00	75.00
NNO Rena Owen	6.00	15.00
NNO Riz Ahmed	60.00	120.00
NNO Rohan Nichol	10.00	25.00
NNO Sam Witwer	15.00	40.00
NNO Stephen Stanton	25.00	60.00
NNO Tom Kane		
NNO Tom Kenny	6.00	15.00
NNO Wayne Pygram	8.00	20.00
NNO Zac Jensen	8.00	20.00

2017 Star Wars Galactic Files Reborn Dual Autographs

COMPLETE SET (9)	
STATED PRINT RUN SER.#'d SETS	
UNPRICED DUE TO SCARCITY	
NNO Blakiston/Rose	

NNO Fisher/Blakiston
NNO Taber/LaMarr
NNO McDiarmid/Carson
NNO Glover/Colley
NNO Nichol/Brown
NNO Carson/Allen
NNO Stanton/Kenny
NNO Gray/Soucie

2017 Star Wars Galactic Files Reborn Famous Quotes

COMPLETE SET (15)	8.00	20.00
COMMON CARD (MQ1-MQ15)	1.00	2.50

*PURPLE/99: X TO X BASIC CARDS
*GOLD/10: UNPRICED DUE TO SCARCITY
*RED/1: UNPRICED DUE TO SCARCITY
*P.P.BLACK/1: UNPRICED DUE TO SCARCITY
*P.P.CYAN/1: UNPRICED DUE TO SCARCITY
*P.P.MAGENTA/1: UNPRICED DUE TO SCARCITY
*P.P.YELLOW/1: UNPRICED DUE TO SCARCITY

2017 Star Wars Galactic Files Reborn Galactic Moments

COMPLETE SET (9)	8.00	20.00
COMMON CARD (GM1-GM9)	1.25	3.00

*PURPLE/99: X TO X BASIC CARDS
*GOLD/10: UNPRICED DUE TO SCARCITY
*RED/1: UNPRICED DUE TO SCARCITY
*P.P.BLACK/1: UNPRICED DUE TO SCARCITY
*P.P.CYAN/1: UNPRICED DUE TO SCARCITY
*P.P.MAGENTA/1: UNPRICED DUE TO SCARCITY
*P.P.YELLOW/1: UNPRICED DUE TO SCARCITY

2017 Star Wars Galactic Files Reborn Locations

COMPLETE SET (10)	6.00	15.00
COMMON CARD (L1-L10)	1.00	2.50

*PURPLE/99: X TO X BASIC CARDS
*GOLD/10: UNPRICED DUE TO SCARCITY
*RED/1: UNPRICED DUE TO SCARCITY
*P.P.BLACK/1: UNPRICED DUE TO SCARCITY
*P.P.CYAN/1: UNPRICED DUE TO SCARCITY
*P.P.MAGENTA/1: UNPRICED DUE TO SCARCITY
*P.P.YELLOW/1: UNPRICED DUE TO SCARCITY

2017 Star Wars Galactic Files Reborn Six Signature Autograph

COMPLETE SET (1)
STATED PRINT RUN SER.#'d SETS
UNPRICED DUE TO SCARCITY

NNO McDiarmid/Wood/Carson/Pygram/Colley/Glover

2017 Star Wars Galactic Files Reborn Sketches

COMPLETE ARTIST LIST (80)
STATED ODDS
UNPRICED DUE TO SCARCITY

NNO Adam Schickling
NNO Alex Iniguez
NNO Andrew Fry
NNO Andrew Lopez
NNO Anil Sharma
NNO Anthony Skubis
NNO Ben AbuSaada
NNO Brad Hudson
NNO Brandon Blevins
NNO Brendan Purchase
NNO Brendan Shaw
NNO Brett Farr
NNO Brian Jackson
NNO Brian Kong
NNO Bruce Gerlach
NNO Carlos Cabaleiro
NNO Cathy Razim
NNO Chris Clark
NNO Chris Henderson
NNO Chris Meeks
NNO Clinton Yeager
NNO Dan Bergren
NNO Daniel Cooney
NNO Darrin Pepe
NNO Dean Drummond
NNO Don Pedicini Jr.
NNO Eddie Price
NNO Eric Lehtonen
NNO Eric White
NNO Humberto Fuentes
NNO Ibrahim Ozkan
NNO J. P. Perez
NNO Jamie Thomas
NNO Jason Sobol
NNO Jay Manchand
NNO Jeff Meuth
NNO Jennifer Allyn
NNO Jessica Hickman
NNO Jim Mehsling
NNO Jonathan Caustrita
NNO Jordan Maison
NNO Joshua Bommer
NNO Juan Rosales
NNO Kaela Croft
NNO Kallan Archer
NNO Kate Carleton
NNO Kelly Greider
NNO Kevin Liell
NNO Kris Penix
NNO Kyle Babbitt
NNO Kyle Hickman
NNO Lak Lim
NNO Louise Draper
NNO Marcia Dye
NNO Mark Mangum

NNO Marsha Parkins
NNO Matthew Pruno
NNO Matthew Sutton
NNO Matt Maldonado
NNO Matt Steffens
NNO Matt Stewart
NNO Michael Duron
NNO Michelle Rayner
NNO Mike Barnard
NNO Mike James
NNO Norvierto P. Basio
NNO Pablo Diaz
NNO Patrick Giles
NNO Paul Andrews
NNO Phil Hassewer
NNO Roy Cover
NNO Scott Houseman
NNO Shane McCormack
NNO Shaow Siong
NNO Solly Mohamed
NNO Stephanie Rosales
NNO Tiffany Groves
NNO Tim Smith
NNO Tod Smith
NNO Veronica O'Connell

2017 Star Wars Galactic Files Reborn Triple Autographs

COMPLETE SET (8)
STATED PRINT RUN SER.#'d SETS
UNPRICED DUE TO SCARCITY

NNO Fisher/Barclay/Carter
NNO Revill/Colley/Glover
NNO Prinze Jr./Gray/Eckstein
NNO Grunberg/Rotich/Rose
NNO McDiarmid/Park/Blake
NNO Hamill/Baker/Daniels
NNO Wood/Carson/Blake
NNO Witwer/Goodson/Futterman

2017 Star Wars Galactic Files Reborn Vehicle Medallions

COMMON CARD	5.00	12.00

*SILVER/99: .6X TO 1.5X BASIC CARDS
*GOLD/50: 1.2X TO 3X BASIC CARDS
*RED/1: UNPRICED DUE TO SCARCITY

2017 Star Wars Galactic Files Reborn Vehicles

COMPLETE SET (20)	10.00	25.00
COMMON CARD (V1-V20)	.75	2.00

*PURPLE/99: 1.5X TO 4X BASIC CARDS
*GOLD/10: UNPRICED DUE TO SCARCITY
*RED/1: UNPRICED DUE TO SCARCITY
*P.P.BLACK/1: UNPRICED DUE TO SCARCITY
*P.P.CYAN/1: UNPRICED DUE TO SCARCITY
*P.P.MAGENTA/1: UNPRICED DUE TO SCARCITY
*P.P.YELLOW/1: UNPRICED DUE TO SCARCITY

2017 Star Wars Galactic Files Reborn Weapons

CHEWBACCA'S BOWCASTER

COMPLETE SET (10)	6.00	15.00
COMMON CARD (W1-W10)	1.00	2.50

*PURPLE/99: 1.2X TO 3X BASIC CARDS
*GOLD/10: UNPRICED DUE TO SCARCITY
*RED/1: UNPRICED DUE TO SCARCITY
*P.P.BLACK/1: UNPRICED DUE TO SCARCITY
*P.P.CYAN/1: UNPRICED DUE TO SCARCITY
*P.P.MAGENTA/1: UNPRICED DUE TO SCARCITY
*P.P.YELLOW/1: UNPRICED DUE TO SCARCITY

1993-95 Star Wars Galaxy

This was the first Star Wars trading card series that Topps had released since the Return of the Jedi sets, a 10-year hiatus! However, everyone's favorite chewing gum company did not disappoint with this offering. The card fronts feature artwork by various artists, while the card backs feature production art, poster art, production photos, and informative text concerning the images on each card. There are a grand total of 365 base cards in between the three series, each containing various subsets and artwork by a considerable number of different artists. Some notable artist names include: Alec Guiness, Tim and Greg Hildebrandt, Jeffrey Jones, Joe Jusko, Jack Kirby, Ralph McQuarrie, Frank Miller, Jim Steranko, Boris Vallejo, and Mike Zeck.

COMPLETE SET (365)	15.00	40.00
COMP.SER 1 SET (140)	6.00	15.00
COMP.SER 2 SET (135)	6.00	15.00
COMP.SER 3 SET (90)	6.00	15.00
UNOPENED SER.1 BOX (36 PACKS)	30.00	40.00
UNOPENED SER.1 PACK (8 CARDS)	1.00	1.25
UNOPENED SER.2 BOX (36 PACKS)	20.00	30.00
UNOPENED SER.2 PACK (8 CARDS)	.75	1.00
UNOPENED SER.3 BOX (36 PACKS)	20.00	30.00
UNOPENED SER.3 PACK (7 CARDS)	.75	1.00
COMMON CARD (1-365)	.15	.40

*MIL.FALCON FOIL: .8X TO 2X BASIC CARDS
*FIRST DAY: 1X TO 2.5X BASIC CARDS
DARTH VADER FOIL UNNUMBERED 4.00 10.00

1993-95 Star Wars Galaxy Clearzone

COMPLETE SET (6)	15.00	40.00
COMMON CARD (E1-E6)	3.00	8.00

1993-95 Star Wars Galaxy Etched Foil

COMPLETE SET (18)	60.00	120.00
COMMON CARD (1-18)	3.00	8.00

1993-95 Star Wars Galaxy LucasArts

COMPLETE SET (12)	6.00	15.00
COMMON CARD (L1-L12)	.60	1.50
L1 Dark Forces Display Art	.60	1.50
L2 Dark Forces Ad Art	.60	1.50
L3 Dark Trooper	.60	1.50
L4 Keith Carter	.60	1.50
L5 TIE Fighter	.60	1.50
L6 Defender of the Empire	.60	1.50
L7 Keith Carter	.60	1.50
L8 X-Wing	.60	1.50
L9 The Farlander Papers	.60	1.50
L10 Keith Carter	.60	1.50
L11 Rebel Assault	.60	1.50

1993-95 Star Wars Galaxy Promos

0 Ralph McQuarrie (Darth Vader)	2.50	6.00
0 Drew Sturzan artwork (SW Galaxy Magazine)	1.25	3.00
0 Ken Steacy Art		
P1 Jae Lee/Rancor Monster(dealer cello pack)	1.25	4.00
P1 Jae Lee/Rancor Monster/AT-AT		
P1 Rancor Card		
AT-AT/Yoda 5X7		
P2 Chris Sprouse/Luke building lightsaber (NSU)	2.00	5.00
P2 Snowtrooper (Convention exclusive)	1.50	4.00
P3 Yoda Shrine SP	150.00	300.00
P3 Darth Vader on Hoth (NSU)	1.25	3.00
P4 Dave Gibbons/C-3PO and Jawas (SW Galaxy 1 Tin Set)		
P4 Luke on Dagobah/Art Suydam	.60	1.50
P5 Joe Phillips/Han and Chewbacca (Cards Illustrated)	2.00	5.00

P5 AT-AT	.75	2.00
P6 Tom Taggart/Boba Fett (Hero)	2.50	6.00
P6 Luke with lightsaber (SW Galaxy Magazine)		
P7 Leia with Jacen and Jania (Wizard Magazine)	2.00	5.00
P8 Boba Fett and Darth Vader (Cards Illustrated)	4.00	10.00
140 Look for Series Two (Bend Ems Toys)		
DH2 Cam Kennedy artwork/BobaFett	2.50	6.00
DH3 Cam Kennedy artwork/Millennium Falcon		
NNO Jim Starlin/Stormtrooper and Ewoks (Triton #3)	1.50	4.00
NNO Tim Truman/Tuskan Raiders	3.00	8.00
NNO Boba Fett	3.00	8.00
NNO AT-AT 5 x 7 (Previews)		
NNO Boba Fett/Dengar (Classic Star Wars)	2.00	5.00
NNO Jabba the Hutt (NSU/Starlog/Wizard)	1.25	3.00
NNO Princess Leia (NSU)	1.50	4.00
NNO Sandtrooper (Wizard Magazine)	1.50	4.00
NNO Truce at Bakura (Bantam exclusive)	4.00	10.00
NNO Princess Leia/Sandtrooper 2-Card Panel (Advance exclusive)		
NNO Jabba the Hutt, Obi-Wan/Darth Vader 5X7 (Previews exclusive)		
DH1A Cam Kennedy artwork/Battling Robots (Dark Lords of the Sith comic) Series at line 8		
DH1B Cam Kennedy artwork/Battling Robots (Dark Lords of the Sith comic) Series at line 9		
SWB1 Grand Moff Tarkin (album exclusive)	2.00	5.00

1999 Star Wars Galaxy Collector

SW0 Episode I
(Non-Sport Update Gummie Award Exclusive)
SW1 R2-D2
SW2 Old Republic City
SW3 Jedi Council Chamber
SW4 Ric Olie
SW5 Naboo Fighters
SW6 Captain Panaka & R2-D2
SW7 Battle Droids
SW8 Obi-Wan Kenobi
SW9 Nuna Bird

1996 Star Wars Galaxy Magazine Cover Gallery

C1 Dark Emperor
C2 Luke with Grenade
C3 Han vs. Weasel
C4 Darth Vader

1995 Star Wars Galaxy Magazine Finest Promos

SWGM1 (art by Ralph McQuarrie; SW Galaxy Mag Issue 1, 1995)
SWGM2 (art by Joe Johnston; SW Galaxy Mag Issue 2, 1995)
SWGM3 AT-AT (art by Ralph McQuarrie; SW Galaxy Mag Issue 3, 1995)
SWGM4 Luke on X-Wing (art by Ralph McQuarrie; SW Galaxy Mag Issue 4, 1995)

2009 Star Wars Galaxy Series 4

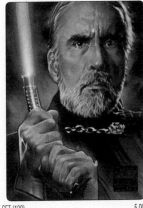

COMPLETE SET (120)	5.00	12.00
UNOPENED BOX (24 PACKS)	70.00	80.00
UNOPENED PACK (7 CARDS)	3.00	4.00
UNOPENED BOX (24 PACKS)	100.00	120.00
UNOPENED PACK (7 CARDS)	5.00	6.00
COMMON CARD (1-120)	.15	.40

*P.P.BLACK/1: UNPRICED DUE TO SCARCITY
*P.P.CYAN/1: UNPRICED DUE TO SCARCITY
*P.P.MAGENTA/1: UNPRICED DUE TO SCARCITY
*P.P.YELLOW/1: UNPRICED DUE TO SCARCITY

2009 Star Wars Galaxy Series 4 Silver Foil

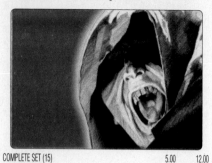

COMPLETE SET (15)	5.00	12.00
COMMON CARD (1-15)	.60	1.50

*BRONZE: 2X TO 5X BASIC CARDS
*GOLD: .8X TO 2X BASIC CARDS
*SILVER REF./1: UNPRICED DUE TO SCARCITY
STATED ODDS 1:3

2009 Star Wars Galaxy Series 4 Die-Cut Sketches

COMPLETE ARTIST LIST (51)
STATED ODDS 1:191 HOBBY
UNPRICED DUE TO SCARCITY

1 Amy Vutiya
2 Andy Heng
3 Art Denka
4 Artbot 138
5 Ayleen Gaspar
6 Brian Kong
7 Brian Slivka
8 Bryce Ward
9 Chanmen
10 Daniel Cantrell
11 Datadub
12 Fetts
13 Gargamel Katope
14 George Gaspar
15 Ghanmenu
16 Gio Chiappetta
17 Goccodo
18 Hans Yim
19 iguodo
20 Jaguar Nono
21 Jason Atomic
22 Jeff McMillan
23 Jeremy Madl
24 Jesse Moore
25 JK5
26 Justin Rudy
27 Kemilyn
28 Kerry Lee
29 L'amour Supreme
30 Luc Hudson
31 Mad Barbarian
32 Matt Doughty
33 MCA
34 McEavill
35 Michael Leavitt
36 Mishka NYC
37 Neil Winn
38 Natalie To
39 Nick the Ring
40 Nix Toxic
41 Patrick Francisco
42 Phetus
43 Rob Ames
44 Russell Walks
45 RYCA
46 Sara! Antoinette Martin
47 Simeon Lipman
48 Sket One
49 $uckadelic
50 Tulip
51 Urban Medium

2009 Star Wars Galaxy Series 4 Etched Foil

COMPLETE SET (6)	6.00	12.00
COMMON CARD (1-6)	1.50	4.00

STATED ODDS 1:6

2009 Star Wars Galaxy Series 4 Galaxy Evolutions

COMPLETE SET (6)	30.00	80.00
COMMON CARD (1-6)	8.00	20.00

STATED ODDS 1:24 RETAIL

2009 Star Wars Galaxy Series 4 Lost Galaxy

COMPLETE SET (5)	12.00	25.00
COMMON CARD (1-5)	3.00	8.00

STATED ODDS 1:24
YODA'S WORLD/999 STATED ODDS 1:277
JOHN RHEAUME AUTO STATED ODDS 1:2,789

NNO Yoda's World/999	15.00	30.00
NNOAU Yoda's World		
Rheaume AU		

2009 Star Wars Galaxy Series 4 Sketches

COMPLETE ARTIST LIST (98)
STATED ODDS 1:24 HOBBY
UNPRICED DUE TO SCARCITY

1 Allison Sohn
2 Amy Pronovost
3 Art Grafunkel
4 Brent Engstrom
5 Brent Schoonover
6 Brian Kong
7 Brian Miller
8 Brian Rood
9 Bruce Gerlach
10 Bryan Morton
11 Carolyn Edwards
12 Cat Staggs
13 Chris Henderson
14 Cynthia Cummens
15 Dan Cooney
16 Daniel Bergren
17 David Rabbitte
18 Denise Vasquez
19 Dennis Budd
20 Don Pedicini Jr.
21 Doug Cowan
22 Edward Pun
23 Erik Maell
24 Gabe Hernandez
25 Grant Gould
26 Howard Shum
27 Ingrid Hardy
28 Irma Aimo Ahmed
29 Jake Minor
30 Jamie Snell
31 Jason Davies
32 Jason Hughes
33 Jason Keith Phillips
34 Jason Sobol
35 Javier Guzman
36 Jeff Carlisle
37 Jerry Vanderstelt
38 Jessica Hickman
39 Jim Kyle
40 Joanne Ellen Mutch
41 Joe Corroney
42 Joel Carroll
43 John McCrea
44 John Soukup
45 John Watkins-Chow
46 Jon Morris
47 Jon Ocampo
48 Joseph Booth
49 Josh Fargher
50 Josh Howard
51 Justin Chung
52 Justin Jusscope Orr
53 Karen Krajenbrink
54 Kate Glasheen
55 Kate Red Bradley
56 Katie Cook
57 Katie McDee
58 Ken Branch
59 Kevin Caron
60 Kevin Doyle
61 Kevin Graham
62 Kyle Babbitt
63 Lance Sawyer
64 Leah Mangue
65 Lee Kohse
66 Len Bellinger
67 Lord Mesa
68 Mark McHaley
69 Mark Walters
70 Matt Minor
71 Micheal Locoduck Duron
72 Monte Moore
73 Nate Lovett
74 Nathan E. Hamill
75 Nicole Falk
76 Nik Neocleous
77 Nina Edlund
78 Noah Albrecht
79 Otto Dieffenbach
80 Patrick Hamill
81 Patrick Richardson
82 Paul Allan Ballard
83 Paul Gutierrez
84 Pete Pachoumis
85 Randy Martinez
86 Randy Siplon
87 Rich Molinelli
88 Rich Woodall
89 Russell Walks
90 Sarah Wilkinson
91 Scott Zirkel
92 Sean Pence

93 Spencer Brinkerhoff
94 Stephanie Yue
95 Ted Dastick Jr.
96 Tod Allen Smith
97 Tom Hodges
98 Zack Giallongo

2009 Star Wars Galaxy Series 4 Sketches Retail Red

COMPLETE ARTIST LIST (43)

1 Brent Engstrom
2 Brent Schoonover
3 Brian Kong
4 Brian Miller
5 Brian Rood
6 Bryan Morton
7 Cat Staggs
8 Chris Henderson
9 Dan Cooney
10 David Rabbitte
11 Don Pedicini Jr.
12 Gabe Hernandez
13 Grant Gould
14 Howard Shum
15 Ingrid Hardy
16 Jamie Snell
17 Jason Davies
18 Jason Keith Phillips
19 Jason Sobol
20 Javier Guzman
21 Jessica Hickman
22 Jim Kyle
23 John McCrea
24 Jon Morris
25 Karen Krajenbrink
26 Kate Glasheen
27 Katie McDee
28 Kevin Doyle
29 Kevin Graham
30 Leah Mangue
31 Lee Kohse
32 Matt Minor
33 Nicole Falk
34 Paul Allan Ballard
35 Paul Gutierrez
36 Randy Martinez
37 Rich Molinelli
38 Rich Woodall
39 Russell Walks
40 Sarah Wilkinson
41 Sean Pence
42 Ted Dastick Jr.
43 Tom Hodges

2009 Star Wars Galaxy Series 4 Promos

P1A Ventress	1.50	4.00
Dooku GEN		
P1B Starcruiser crash/ (Fan Club Excl.)	6.00	15.00
P2 Vader	.50	1.00
Padme NSU		
P3 Group shot WW	2.00	5.00

2010 Star Wars Galaxy Series 5

COMPLETE SET (120)	8.00	20.00
COMMON CARD (1-120)	.15	.40

*P.P.BLACK/1: UNPRICED DUE TO SCARCITY
*P.P.CYAN/1: UNPRICED DUE TO SCARCITY
*P.P.MAGENTA/1: UNPRICED DUE TO SCARCITY
*P.P.YELLOW/1: UNPRICED DUE TO SCARCITY

2010 Star Wars Galaxy Series 5 Etched Foil

COMPLETE SET (6)	4.00	10.00
COMMON CARD (1-6)	1.25	3.00
STATED ODDS 1:6 H/R		

2010 Star Wars Galaxy Series 5 Silver Foil

COMPLETE SET (15)	6.00	15.00
COMMON CARD (1-15)	.60	1.50

*BRONZE FOIL: 1.2X TO 3X BASIC CARDS
*GOLD FOIL/770: 6X TO 15X BASIC CARDS
*SILVER REFR./1: UNPRICED DUE TO SCARCITY
STATED ODDS 1:3 H/R

2010 Star Wars Galaxy Series 5 Artist Sketches

COMPLETE ARTIST LIST (113)
STATED ODDS 1:24 HOBBY, 1:72 RETAIL
UNPRICED DUE TO SCARCITY

1 Adrien Rivera
2 Alex Buechel
3 Amy Pronovost
4 Art Grafunkel
5 Ben Curtis Jones
6 Bill Pulkovski
7 Braden D. Lamb
8 Brandon Kenney
9 Brent Engstrom
10 Brian Kong
11 Brian Miller
12 Brian Rood
13 Bruce Gerlach
14 Bryan Morton
15 Cat Staggs
16 Chris Henderson
17 Chris Uminga
18 Chrissie Zullo
19 Craig Rousseau
20 Cynthia Narcisi
21 Dan Bergren
22 Dan Masso
23 Darla Ecklund
24 Darrin Radimaker
25 Dave Tata
26 David Day
27 David Rabbitte
28 Denise Vasquez
29 Dennis Budd
30 Dustin Foust
31 Erik Maell
32 Frank Villarreal
33 Gabe Farber
34 Grant Gould
35 Hayden Davis
36 Howard Shum
37 Ingrid Hardy
38 Irma Ahmed
39 Jake Minor
40 James Bukauskas
41 Jamie Snell
42 Jason Davies
43 Jason Keith Phillips
44 Jason Sobol
45 Jay Fosgitt
46 Jennifer Mercer
47 Jeremy Treece
48 Jerry Vanderstelt
49 Jessica Hickman
50 Jim Kyle
51 Joe Corroney
52 John Beatty
53 John Haun
54 John P. Wales
55 John Soukup
56 John Watkins-Chow
57 Jon Morris
58 Justin Chung
59 Karen Krajenbrink
60 Kate Bradley
61 Kate Glasheen
62 Katie Cook
63 Kevin Doyle
64 Kevin Graham
65 Kevin Liell
66 Kyle Babbitt
67 Lance Sawyer
68 Lawrence Snelly
69 Leah Mangue
70 Lee Kohse
71 Len Bellinger
72 Lord Mesa
73 Mark McHaley
74 Mark Walters
75 Martheus Wade
76 Matt Busch
77 Matt Minor
78 Matte Chero
79 Michael Duron
80 Monte Moore

81 Nicole Falk
82 Nina Edlund
83 Nolan Woodard
84 Otto Dieffenbach
85 Patrick Schoenmaker
86 Paul Allan Ballard
87 Randy Martinez
88 Randy Siplon
89 Rhiannon Owens
90 Rich Molinelli
91 Rich Woodall
92 Robert Hendrickson
93 Robert Teranishi
94 Russ Walks
95 Ryan Hungerford
96 Sarah Wilkinson
97 Scott DM Simmons
98 Scott Rorie
99 Sean Pence
100 Shea Standefer
101 Shelli Paroline
102 Soni Alcorn-Hender
103 Spencer Brinkerhoff III
104 Stephanie Yue
105 Steve Oatney
106 Steve Stanley
107 Steven Miller
108 Ted Dastick Jr.
109 Tim Proctor
110 Tod Allen Smith
111 Tom Hodges
112 Wilson Ramos Jr.
113 Zack Giallongo

2010 Star Wars Galaxy Series 5 Autographs

COMMON CARD	30.00	80.00
STATED ODDS 1:274 HOBBY		
JB Jeremy Bulloch	50.00	100.00
JJ James Earl Jones	75.00	150.00
MH Mark Hamill	300.00	450.00

2010 Star Wars Galaxy Series 5 Die-Cut Sketches

COMPLETE ARTIST LIST (38)
STATED ODDS 1:192 HOBBY
UNPRICED DUE TO SCARCITY

1 Adriean Koleric
2 Angie Dutchess
3 Anthony Ausgang
4 Appro Nation
5 Auxpeer
6 Bill McMullen
7 Billy Roids
8 Brian Flynn
9 Buff Monster
10 Burt Banger
11 Colin Walton
12 Collin David
13 Dangeruss
14 Devil Robots
15 Gothic Hangman
16 Hariken
17 Hiroshi Namiki
18 Ilanena
19 Jared Deal
20 Jason Adams
21 Jason Atomic
22 Jesse Hernandez
23 Kano
24 King
25 Kosbe
26 Len Bellinger
27 Michael Leavitt
28 Mike Kelly
29 Mio Murakami
30 Mr. Den
31 Plasticgod
32 Rolo Ledesma
33 Russell Walks
34 Skull Toys
35 $uckadelic
36 Touma
37 Tulip
38 Uamou

2010 Star Wars Galaxy Series 5 Lost Galaxy

COMPLETE SET (5)	10.00	25.00
COMMON CARD (1-5)	3.00	8.00
STATED ODDS 1:24 HOBBY		

2010 Star Wars Galaxy Series 5 Manga Sketches

COMPLETE ARTIST LIST (8)
COMMON CARD
STATED ODDS 1:274 HOBBY

1 Axer
2 Dax Gordine
3 Eric Vedder
4 J.Rosero (2NGAW)
5 Tim Smith
6 Tomoko Taniguchi
7 Vanessa Duran
8 Wilson Ramos Jr.

2011 Star Wars Galaxy Series 6

COMPLETE SET (120)	8.00	20.00
COMMON CARD (1-120)	.15	.40

*P.P.BLACK/1: UNPRICED DUE TO SCARCITY
*P.P.CYAN/1: UNPRICED DUE TO SCARCITY
*P.P.MAGENTA/1: UNPRICED DUE TO SCARCITY
*P.P.YELLOW/1: UNPRICED DUE TO SCARCITY

2011 Star Wars Galaxy Series 6 Silver Foil

COMPLETE SET (10)	6.00	15.00
COMMON CARD (1-10)	1.00	2.50

*BRONZE: 1.2X TO 3X BASIC CARDS
*GOLD/600: 4X TO 10X BASIC CARDS
UNPRICED REFR. PRINT RUN 1
STATED ODDS 1:3

2011 Star Wars Galaxy Series 6 Animation Cels

COMPLETE SET (9)	20.00	40.00
COMMON CARD (1-9)	3.00	8.00
STATED ODDS 1:4 RETAIL		

2011 Star Wars Galaxy Series 6 Etched Foil

COMPLETE SET (6)	5.00	12.00
COMMON CARD (1-6)	1.25	3.00
STATED ODDS 1:6		

2011 Star Wars Galaxy Series 6 Sketchagraphs

1 Amy Allen
Adam Hughes
2 Amy Allen
Alex Buechel
3 Amy Allen
Allison Sohn
4 Amy Allen
Brian Rood
5 Amy Allen
Cat Staggs
6 Amy Allen
Doug Cowan
7 Amy Allen
Grant Gould
8 Amy Allen
Jamie Snell
9 Amy Allen
Jim Kyle
10 Amy Allen
John Haun
11 Amy Allen
Kevin Doyle
12 Amy Allen
Kevin Graham
13 Amy Allen
Lin Workman
14 Amy Allen
Kyle Babbitt
15 Amy Allen
Otis Frampton
16 Amy Allen
Randy Martinez
17 Amy Allen
Rich Molinelli
18 Amy Allen
Sarah Wilkinson
19 Amy Allen
Sean Pence
20 Amy Allen
Steve Stanley
21 Amy Allen
Tim Proctor
22 Amy Allen
Tom Hodges
23 Carrie Fisher
Adam Hughes
24 Carrie Fisher
Alex Buechel
25 Carrie Fisher
Allison Sohn
26 Carrie Fisher
Brian Rood
27 Carrie Fisher
Cat Staggs
28 Carrie Fisher
Doug Cowan
29 Carrie Fisher
Grant Gould
30 Carrie Fisher
Jamie Snell
31 Carrie Fisher
Jim Kyle
32 Carrie Fisher
John Haun
33 Carrie Fisher
Kevin Doyle
34 Carrie Fisher
Kevin Graham
35 Carrie Fisher
Lin Workman
36 Carrie Fisher
Kyle Babbitt
37 Carrie Fisher
Otis Frampton
38 Carrie Fisher
Randy Martinez
39 Carrie Fisher
Rich Molinelli

40 Carrie Fisher
Sarah Wilkinson
41 Carrie Fisher
Sean Pence
42 Carrie Fisher
Steve Stanley
43 Carrie Fisher
Tim Proctor
44 Carrie Fisher
Tom Hodges
45 Jake Lloyd
Adam Hughes
46 Jake Lloyd
Alex Buechel
47 Jake Lloyd
Allison Sohn
48 Jake Lloyd
Brian Rood
49 Jake Lloyd
Cat Staggs
50 Jake Lloyd
Doug Cowan
51 Jake Lloyd
Grant Gould
52 Jake Lloyd
Jamie Snell
53 Jake Lloyd
Jim Kyle
54 Jake Lloyd
John Haun
55 Jake Lloyd
Kevin Doyle
56 Jake Lloyd
Kevin Graham
57 Jake Lloyd
Lin Workman
58 Jake Lloyd
Kyle Babbitt
59 Jake Lloyd
Otis Frampton
60 Jake Lloyd
Randy Martinez
61 Jake Lloyd
Rich Molinelli
62 Jake Lloyd
Sarah Wilkinson
63 Jake Lloyd
Sean Pence
64 Jake Lloyd
Steve Stanley
65 Jake Lloyd
Tim Proctor
66 Jake Lloyd
Tom Hodges
67 John Morton
Adam Hughes
68 John Morton
Alex Buechel
69 John Morton
Allison Sohn
70 John Morton
Brian Rood
71 John Morton
Cat Staggs
72 John Morton
Doug Cowan
73 John Morton
Grant Gould
74 John Morton
Jamie Snell
75 John Morton
Jim Kyle
76 John Morton
John Haun
77 John Morton
Kevin Doyle
78 John Morton
Kevin Graham
79 John Morton
Lin Workman
80 John Morton
Kyle Babbitt
81 John Morton

Otis Frampton
82 John Morton
Randy Martinez
83 John Morton
Rich Molinelli
84 John Morton
Sarah Wilkinson
85 John Morton
Sean Pence
86 John Morton
Steve Stanley
87 John Morton
Tim Proctor
88 John Morton
Tom Hodges
89 Jon Berg
Adam Hughes
90 Jon Berg
Alex Buechel
91 Jon Berg
Allison Sohn
92 Jon Berg
Brian Rood
93 Jon Berg
Cat Staggs
94 Jon Berg
Doug Cowan
95 Jon Berg
Grant Gould
96 Jon Berg
Jamie Snell
97 Jon Berg
Jim Kyle
98 Jon Berg
John Haun
99 Jon Berg
Kevin Doyle
100 Jon Berg
Kevin Graham
101 Jon Berg
Lin Workman
102 Jon Berg
Kyle Babbitt
103 Jon Berg
Otis Frampton
104 Jon Berg
Randy Martinez
105 Jon Berg
Rich Molinelli
106 Jon Berg
Sarah Wilkinson
107 Jon Berg
Sean Pence
108 Jon Berg
Steve Stanley
109 Jon Berg
Tim Proctor
110 Jon Berg
Tom Hodges
111 Mark Hamill
Adam Hughes
112 Mark Hamill
Alex Buechel
113 Mark Hamill
Allison Sohn
114 Mark Hamill
Brian Rood
115 Mark Hamill
Cat Staggs
116 Mark Hamill
Doug Cowan
117 Mark Hamill
Grant Gould
118 Mark Hamill
Jamie Snell
119 Mark Hamill
Jim Kyle
120 Mark Hamill
John Haun
121 Mark Hamill
Kevin Doyle
122 Mark Hamill
Kevin Graham

123 Mark Hamill
Lin Workman
124 Mark Hamill
Kyle Babbitt
125 Mark Hamill
Otis Frampton
126 Mark Hamill
Randy Martinez
127 Mark Hamill
Rich Molinelli
128 Mark Hamill
Sarah Wilkinson
129 Mark Hamill
Sean Pence
130 Mark Hamill
Steve Stanley
131 Mark Hamill
Tim Proctor
132 Mark Hamill
Tom Hodges
133 Mike Quinn
Adam Hughes
134 Mike Quinn
Alex Buechel
135 Mike Quinn
Allison Sohn
136 Mike Quinn
Brian Rood
137 Mike Quinn
Cat Staggs
138 Mike Quinn
Doug Cowan
139 Mike Quinn
Grant Gould
140 Mike Quinn
Jamie Snell
141 Mike Quinn
Jim Kyle
142 Mike Quinn
John Haun
143 Mike Quinn
Kevin Doyle
144 Mike Quinn
Kevin Graham
145 Mike Quinn
Lin Workman
146 Mike Quinn
Kyle Babbitt
147 Mike Quinn
Otis Frampton
148 Mike Quinn
Randy Martinez
149 Mike Quinn
Rich Molinelli
150 Mike Quinn
Sarah Wilkinson
151 Mike Quinn
Sean Pence
152 Mike Quinn
Steve Stanley
153 Mike Quinn
Tim Proctor
154 Mike Quinn
Tom Hodges
155 Orli Shoshan
Adam Hughes
156 Orli Shoshan
Alex Buechel
157 Orli Shoshan
Allison Sohn
158 Orli Shoshan
Brian Rood
159 Orli Shoshan
Cat Staggs
160 Orli Shoshan
Doug Cowan
161 Orli Shoshan
Grant Gould
162 Orli Shoshan
Jamie Snell
163 Orli Shoshan
Jim Kyle
164 Orli Shoshan

John Haun
165 Orli Shoshan
Kevin Doyle
166 Orli Shoshan
Kevin Graham
167 Orli Shoshan
Lin Workman
168 Orli Shoshan
Kyle Babbitt
169 Orli Shoshan
Otis Frampton
170 Orli Shoshan
Randy Martinez
171 Orli Shoshan
Rich Molinelli
172 Orli Shoshan
Sarah Wilkinson
173 Orli Shoshan
Sean Pence
174 Orli Shoshan
Steve Stanley
175 Orli Shoshan
Tim Proctor
176 Orli Shoshan
Tom Hodges
177 Ray Park
Adam Hughes
178 Ray Park
Alex Buechel
179 Ray Park
Allison Sohn
180 Ray Park
Brian Rood
181 Ray Park
Cat Staggs
182 Ray Park
Doug Cowan
183 Ray Park
Grant Gould
184 Ray Park
Jamie Snell
185 Ray Park
Jim Kyle
186 Ray Park
John Haun
187 Ray Park
Kevin Doyle
188 Ray Park
Kevin Graham
189 Ray Park
Lin Workman
190 Ray Park
Kyle Babbitt
191 Ray Park
Otis Frampton
192 Ray Park
Randy Martinez
193 Ray Park
Rich Molinelli
194 Ray Park
Sarah Wilkinson
195 Ray Park
Sean Pence
196 Ray Park
Steve Stanley
197 Ray Park
Tim Proctor
198 Ray Park
Tom Hodges

2011 Star Wars Galaxy Series 6 Sketches

1 Adrian Rivera
2 Agnes Garbowska
3 Alex Buechel
4 Amy Pronovost
5 Art O'Callaghan
6 Beck Seashols
7 Bill Pulkovski
8 Bob Stevlic
9 Braden D. Lamb
10 Brent Engstrom
11 Brian Kong
12 Bruce Gerlach

13 Bryan Morton
14 Cat Staggs
15 Charles Hall
16 Chris Henderson
17 Cynthia Narcisi
18 D Douglas
19 Dan Bergren
20 David Day
21 David Green
22 David Rabbitte
23 Denae Frazier
24 Dennis Budd
25 Dennis Hart
26 Don Pedicini Jr.
27 Doug Cowan
28 Eli Rutten
29 Erik Maell
30 Gabe Farber
31 Gary Kezele
32 Geoff Munn
33 Hayden Davis
34 Ingrid Hardy
35 Irma Ahmed
36 Jamie Snell
37 Jason Adams
38 Jason Durden
39 Jason Keith Phillips
40 Jason Sobol
41 Jason Williams
42 Jay Shimko
43 Jerry The Franchize Gaylord
44 Jessica Hickman
45 Jim Kyle
46 Joe Corroney
47 Joe Hogan
48 John Haun
49 Jonathan D. Gordon
50 Juan Carlos Ramos
51 Kate Bradley
52 Katie Cook
53 Kevin Doyle
54 Kevin Graham
55 Kevin Liell
56 Kyle Babbitt
57 Lawrence Reynolds
58 Leah Mangue
59 Lee Kohse
60 Len Bellinger
61 Lin Workman
62 Linzy Zorn
63 Lord Mesa
64 M. Jason Reed
65 Manny Mederos
66 Martheus Wade
67 Matt Busch
68 Matthew Minor
69 Michael Locoduck Duron
70 Mick and Matt Glebe
71 Monte Moore
72 Nina Edlund
73 Nolan Woodard
74 Otis Frampton
75 Rachel Kaiser
76 Randy Martinez
77 Rhiannon Owens
78 Rich Woodall
79 Robert Hendrickson
80 Robert Teranishi
81 Russell Walks
82 Ryan Hungerford
83 Sanna U
84 Sarah Wilkinson
85 Scott Rorie
86 Scott Zambelli
87 Sean Pence
88 Shea Standefer
89 Shelli Paroline
90 Soni Alcorn-Hender
91 Stephanie Swanger
92 Steve Miller
93 Steve Oatney
94 Steve Stanley
95 Ted Dastick Jr.

96 Tim Proctor
97 Tim Smith
98 Tod Smith
99 Tom Hodges
100 Tomoko Taniguchi
101 Vanessa Banky Farano
102 Wilson Ramos Jr.
103 Zack Giallongo

2011 Star Wars Galaxy Series 6 Sketches Die-Cuts

1 Abe Lincoln Jr.
2 Arbito
3 Aya Kakeda
4 Billy Roids
5 Brian Mead
6 Burt Banger
7 Chris Ryniak
8 Dan Bina
9 Dan Goodsell
10 Dave Savage
11 Doktor A
12 Free Humanity
13 Gothic Hangman
14 JRYU
15 Jason Atomic
16 Jermaine Rogers
17 John Spanky Stokes
18 Jon-Paul Kaiser
19 Jordana Lake
20 Julie West
21 Larz
22 Len Bellinger
23 Lorne Colon
24 Lou Pimentel
25 Luke Gibbons-Reich
26 Martin Hsu
27 Martina Secondo Russo
Frank Russo
28 Marty Hansen THEGODBEAST
29 Mike Egan
30 Mike Mendez NEMO
31 Mio Murakami
32 Nathan Hamill
33 olive47
34 Omen
35 Ritzy Periwinkle
36 Sarah Jo Marks
37 Scott Tolleson
38 Sergey Safonov
39 SHAWNIMALS
40 Stella Bouzakis
41 Steve Talkowski
42 Steven Daily
43 The Sucklord
44 Tyson Bodnarchuk
45 VISE ONE
46 Wade Lageose

2011 Star Wars Galaxy Series 6 Sketches Retail Red

1 Alex Buechel
2 Bill Pulkovski
3 Chris Henderson
4 David Day
5 David Rabbitte
6 Erik Maell
7 Howard Shum
8 Jerry The Franchize Gaylord
9 John P. Wales
10 Justin Chung
11 Mark Slater
12 Michael Locoduck Duron
13 Mick and Matt Glebe
14 Rhiannon Owens
15 Scott Zambelli
16 Shea Standefer
17 Shelli Paroline
18 Stephanie Swanger
19 Wilson Ramos Jr.
20 Zack Giallongo
21 Stephanie Yue
22 Lee Bradley
23 Don Pedicini Jr.

24 Ted Dastick Jr.
25 Tim Proctor
26 Tim Smith 3
27 Tod Smith
28 Beck Seashols
29 Juan Carlos Ramos

2012 Star Wars Galaxy Series 7

COMPLETE SET (110)	8.00	20.00
UNOPENED BOX (24 PACKS)	60.00	70.00
UNOPENED PACK (7 CARDS)	2.50	3.00
COMMON CARD (1-110)	.15	.40

*P.P.BLACK/1: UNPRICED DUE TO SCARCITY
*P.P.CYAN/1: UNPRICED DUE TO SCARCITY
*P.P.MAGENTA/1: UNPRICED DUE TO SCARCITY
*P.P.YELLOW/1: UNPRICED DUE TO SCARCITY

2012 Star Wars Galaxy Series 7 Silver Foil

COMPLETE SET (15)	6.00	15.00
COMMON CARD (1-15)	.75	2.00

*BRONZE: 1.5X TO 4X SILVER
*GOLD: 3X TO 8X SILVER
*SILVER REF./1: UNPRICED DUE TO SCARCITY
STATED ODDS 1:3

2012 Star Wars Galaxy Series 7 Cels

COMPLETE SET (9)	35.00	70.00
COMMON CARD (1-9)	4.00	10.00

2012 Star Wars Galaxy Series 7 Etched Foil

COMPLETE SET (6)	5.00	12.00
COMMON CARD (1-6)	1.50	4.00

*ORIG.ART/1: UNPRICED DUE TO SCARCITY
STATED ODDS 1:6

2012 Star Wars Galaxy Series 7 Sketchagraphs

1 Alan Flyng
Kevin Doyle
2 Alan Flyng
Brian Rood
3 Alan Flyng
Steve Oatney
4 Alan Flyng
Dan Bergren
5 Alan Flyng
Bruce Gerlach
6 Alan Flyng
Gabe Farber
7 Alan Flyng
Kyle Babbitt
8 Alan Flyng
Hayden Davis
9 Alan Flyng
David Day
10 Alan Flyng
Jamie Snell
11 Alan Flyng
Sarah Wilkinson
12 Alan Flyng
John Haun
13 Alan Flyng
Gary Kezele
14 Alan Flyng
Kevin Graham
15 Alan Flyng
Matthew Minor
16 Alan Flyng
Leah Mangue
17 Alan Flyng
Jake Minor
18 Alan Flyng
Rich Molinelli
19 Alan Flyng
Tom Hodges
20 Alan Flyng
Robert Teranishi
21 Alan Flyng
Jim Kyle
22 Alan Flyng
Sean Pence
23 Alan Flyng
Robert Hendrickson
24 Alan Flyng
Tim Proctor
25 Alan Flyng
Allison Sohn
26 Ashley Eckstein/Allison Sohn
27 Ashley Eckstein/Brian Rood
28 Ashley Eckstein/Bruce Gerlach
29 Ashley Eckstein/Dan Bergren
30 Ashley Eckstein/David Day
31 Ashley Eckstein/Gabe Farber
32 Ashley Eckstein/Gary Kezele
33 Ashley Eckstein/Hayden Davis
34 Ashley Eckstein/Jake Minor

35 Ashley Eckstein/Jamie Snell
36 Ashley Eckstein/Jim Kyle
37 Ashley Eckstein/John Haun
38 Ashley Eckstein/Kevin Doyle
39 Ashley Eckstein/Kevin Graham
40 Ashley Eckstein/Kyle Babbitt
41 Ashley Eckstein/Leah Mangue
42 Ashley Eckstein/Matthew Minor
43 Ashley Eckstein/Rich Molinelli
44 Ashley Eckstein/Robert Hendrickson
45 Ashley Eckstein/Robert Teranishi
46 Ashley Eckstein/Sarah Wilkinson
47 Ashley Eckstein/Sean Pence
48 Ashley Eckstein/Steve Oatney
49 Ashley Eckstein/Tim Proctor
50 Ashley Eckstein/Tom Hodges
51 Ben Burtt/Allison Sohn
52 Ben Burtt/Brian Rood
53 Ben Burtt/Bruce Gerlach
54 Ben Burtt/Dan Bergren
55 Ben Burtt/David Day
56 Ben Burtt/Gabe Farber
57 Ben Burtt/Gary Kezele
58 Ben Burtt/Hayden Davis
59 Ben Burtt/Jake Minor
60 Ben Burtt/Jamie Snell
61 Ben Burtt/Jim Kyle
62 Ben Burtt/John Haun
63 Ben Burtt/Kevin Doyle
64 Ben Burtt/Kevin Graham
65 Ben Burtt/Kyle Babbitt
66 Ben Burtt/Leah Mangue
67 Ben Burtt/Matthew Minor
68 Ben Burtt/Rich Molinelli
69 Ben Burtt/Robert Hendrickson
70 Ben Burtt/Robert Teranishi
71 Ben Burtt/Sarah Wilkinson
72 Ben Burtt/Sean Pence
73 Ben Burtt/Steve Oatney
74 Ben Burtt/Tim Proctor
75 Ben Burtt/Tom Hodges
76 Carrie Fisher/Allison Sohn
77 Carrie Fisher/Brian Rood
78 Carrie Fisher/Bruce Gerlach
79 Carrie Fisher/Dan Bergren
80 Carrie Fisher/David Day
81 Carrie Fisher/Gabe Farber
82 Carrie Fisher/Gary Kezele
83 Carrie Fisher/Hayden Davis
84 Carrie Fisher/Jake Minor
85 Carrie Fisher/Jamie Snell
86 Carrie Fisher/Jim Kyle
87 Carrie Fisher/John Haun
88 Carrie Fisher/Kevin Doyle
89 Carrie Fisher/Kevin Graham
90 Carrie Fisher/Kyle Babbitt
91 Carrie Fisher/Leah Mangue
92 Carrie Fisher/Matthew Minor
93 Carrie Fisher/Rich Molinelli
94 Carrie Fisher/Robert Hendrickson
95 Carrie Fisher/Robert Teranishi
96 Carrie Fisher/Sarah Wilkinson
97 Carrie Fisher/Sean Pence
98 Carrie Fisher/Steve Oatney
99 Carrie Fisher/Tim Proctor
100 Carrie Fisher/Tom Hodges
101 Catherine Taber/Allison Sohn
102 Catherine Taber/Brian Rood
103 Catherine Taber/Bruce Gerlach
104 Catherine Taber/Dan Bergren
105 Catherine Taber/David Day
106 Catherine Taber/Gabe Farber
107 Catherine Taber/Gary Kezele
108 Catherine Taber/Hayden Davis
109 Catherine Taber/Jake Minor
110 Catherine Taber/Jamie Snell
111 Catherine Taber/Jim Kyle
112 Catherine Taber/John Haun
113 Catherine Taber/Kevin Doyle
114 Catherine Taber/Kevin Graham
115 Catherine Taber/Kyle Babbitt
116 Catherine Taber/Leah Mangue
117 Catherine Taber/Matthew Minor

118 Catherine Taber/Rich Molinelli
119 Catherine Taber/Robert Hendrickson
120 Catherine Taber/Robert Teranishi
121 Catherine Taber/Sarah Wilkinson
122 Catherine Taber/Sean Pence
123 Catherine Taber/Steve Oatney
124 Catherine Taber/Tim Proctor
125 Catherine Taber/Tom Hodges
126 Dickey Beer/Allison Sohn
127 Dickey Beer/Brian Rood
128 Dickey Beer/Bruce Gerlach
129 Dickey Beer/Dan Bergren
130 Dickey Beer/David Day
131 Dickey Beer/Gabe Farber
132 Dickey Beer/Gary Kezele
133 Dickey Beer/Hayden Davis
134 Dickey Beer/Jake Minor
135 Dickey Beer/Jamie Snell
136 Dickey Beer/Jim Kyle
137 Dickey Beer/John Haun
138 Dickey Beer/Kevin Doyle
139 Dickey Beer/Kevin Graham
140 Dickey Beer/Kyle Babbitt
141 Dickey Beer/Leah Mangue
142 Dickey Beer/Matthew Minor
143 Dickey Beer/Rich Molinelli
144 Dickey Beer/Robert Hendrickson
145 Dickey Beer/Robert Teranishi
146 Dickey Beer/Sarah Wilkinson
147 Dickey Beer/Sean Pence
148 Dickey Beer/Steve Oatney
149 Dickey Beer/Tim Proctor
150 Dickey Beer/Tom Hodges
151 James Arnold Taylor/Allison Sohn
152 James Arnold Taylor/Brian Rood
153 James Arnold Taylor/Bruce Gerlach
154 James Arnold Taylor/Dan Bergren
155 James Arnold Taylor/David Day
156 James Arnold Taylor/Gabe Farber
157 James Arnold Taylor/Gary Kezele
158 James Arnold Taylor/Hayden Davis
159 James Arnold Taylor/Jake Minor
160 James Arnold Taylor/Jamie Snell
161 James Arnold Taylor/Jim Kyle
162 James Arnold Taylor/John Haun
163 James Arnold Taylor/Kevin Doyle
164 James Arnold Taylor/Kevin Graham
165 James Arnold Taylor/Kyle Babbitt
166 James Arnold Taylor/Leah Mangue
167 James Arnold Taylor/Matthew Minor
168 James Arnold Taylor/Rich Molinelli
169 James Arnold Taylor/Robert Hendrickson
170 James Arnold Taylor/Robert Teranishi
171 James Arnold Taylor/Sarah Wilkinson
172 James Arnold Taylor/Sean Pence
173 James Arnold Taylor/Steve Oatney
174 James Arnold Taylor/Tim Proctor
175 James Arnold Taylor/Tom Hodges
176 Mark Hamill/Allison Sohn
177 Mark Hamill/Brian Rood
178 Mark Hamill/Bruce Gerlach
179 Mark Hamill/Dan Bergren
180 Mark Hamill/David Day
181 Mark Hamill/Gabe Farber
182 Mark Hamill/Gary Kezele
183 Mark Hamill/Hayden Davis
184 Mark Hamill/Jake Minor
185 Mark Hamill/Jamie Snell
186 Mark Hamill/Jim Kyle
187 Mark Hamill/John Haun
188 Mark Hamill/Kevin Doyle
189 Mark Hamill/Kevin Graham
190 Mark Hamill/Kyle Babbitt
191 Mark Hamill/Leah Mangue
192 Mark Hamill/Matthew Minor
193 Mark Hamill/Rich Molinelli
194 Mark Hamill/Robert Hendrickson
195 Mark Hamill/Robert Teranishi
196 Mark Hamill/Sarah Wilkinson
197 Mark Hamill/Sean Pence
198 Mark Hamill/Steve Oatney
199 Mark Hamill/Tim Proctor
200 Mark Hamill/Tom Hodges

201 Matt Wood/Allison Sohn
202 Matt Wood/Brian Rood
203 Matt Wood/Bruce Gerlach
204 Matt Wood/Dan Bergren
205 Matt Wood/David Day
206 Matt Wood/Gabe Farber
207 Matt Wood/Gary Kezele
208 Matt Wood/Hayden Davis
209 Matt Wood/Jake Minor
210 Matt Wood/Jamie Snell
211 Matt Wood/Jim Kyle
212 Matt Wood/John Haun
213 Matt Wood/Kevin Doyle
214 Matt Wood/Kevin Graham
215 Matt Wood/Kyle Babbitt
216 Matt Wood/Leah Mangue
217 Matt Wood/Matthew Minor
218 Matt Wood/Rich Molinelli
219 Matt Wood/Robert Hendrickson
220 Matt Wood/Robert Teranishi
221 Matt Wood/Sarah Wilkinson
222 Matt Wood/Sean Pence
223 Matt Wood/Steve Oatney
224 Matt Wood/Tim Proctor
225 Matt Wood/Tom Hodges
226 Peter Mayhew/Allison Sohn
227 Peter Mayhew/Brian Rood
228 Peter Mayhew/Bruce Gerlach
229 Peter Mayhew/Dan Bergren
230 Peter Mayhew/David Day
231 Peter Mayhew/Gabe Farber
232 Peter Mayhew/Gary Kezele
233 Peter Mayhew/Hayden Davis
234 Peter Mayhew/Jake Minor
235 Peter Mayhew/Jamie Snell
236 Peter Mayhew/Jim Kyle
237 Peter Mayhew/John Haun
238 Peter Mayhew/Kevin Doyle
239 Peter Mayhew/Kevin Graham
240 Peter Mayhew/Kyle Babbitt
241 Peter Mayhew/Leah Mangue
242 Peter Mayhew/Matthew Minor
243 Peter Mayhew/Rich Molinelli
244 Peter Mayhew/Robert Hendrickson
245 Peter Mayhew/Robert Teranishi
246 Peter Mayhew/Sarah Wilkinson
247 Peter Mayhew/Sean Pence
248 Peter Mayhew/Steve Oatney
249 Peter Mayhew/Tim Proctor
250 Peter Mayhew/Tom Hodges
251 Timothy Zahn/Allison Sohn
252 Timothy Zahn/Brian Rood
253 Timothy Zahn/Bruce Gerlach
254 Timothy Zahn/Dan Bergren
255 Timothy Zahn/David Day
256 Timothy Zahn/Gabe Farber
257 Timothy Zahn/Gary Kezele
258 Timothy Zahn/Hayden Davis
259 Timothy Zahn/Jake Minor
260 Timothy Zahn/Jamie Snell
261 Timothy Zahn/Jim Kyle
262 Timothy Zahn/John Haun
263 Timothy Zahn/Kevin Doyle
264 Timothy Zahn/Kevin Graham
265 Timothy Zahn/Kyle Babbitt
266 Timothy Zahn/Leah Mangue
267 Timothy Zahn/Matthew Minor
268 Timothy Zahn/Rich Molinelli
269 Timothy Zahn/Robert Hendrickson
270 Timothy Zahn/Robert Teranishi
271 Timothy Zahn/Sarah Wilkinson
272 Timothy Zahn/Sean Pence
273 Timothy Zahn/Steve Oatney
274 Timothy Zahn/Tim Proctor
275 Timothy Zahn/Tom Hodges
276 Tom Kane/Allison Sohn
277 Tom Kane/Brian Rood
278 Tom Kane/Bruce Gerlach
279 Tom Kane/Dan Bergren
280 Tom Kane/David Day
281 Tom Kane/Gabe Farber
282 Tom Kane/Gary Kezele
283 Tom Kane/Hayden Davis

284 Tom Kane/Jake Minor
285 Tom Kane/Jamie Snell
286 Tom Kane/Jim Kyle
287 Tom Kane/John Haun
288 Tom Kane/Kevin Doyle
289 Tom Kane/Kevin Graham
290 Tom Kane/Kyle Babbitt
291 Tom Kane/Leah Mangue
292 Tom Kane/Matthew Minor
293 Tom Kane/Rich Molinelli
294 Tom Kane/Robert Hendrickson
295 Tom Kane/Robert Teranishi
296 Tom Kane/Sarah Wilkinson
297 Tom Kane/Sean Pence
298 Tom Kane/Steve Oatney
299 Tom Kane/Tim Proctor
300 Tom Kane/Tom Hodges

2012 Star Wars Galaxy Series 7 Sketches

1 Adrian Rivera
2 Agnes Garbowska
3 Alex Buechel
4 Amy Beth Christenson
5 Ashleigh Popplewell
6 Beck Seashols
7 Ben Dale
8 Bill Pulkovski
9 Bob Stevlic
10 Brandon Kenney
11 Brent Engstrom
12 Brian DeGuire
13 Brian Miller
14 Brian Rood
15 Bruce Gerlach
16 Cal Slayton
17 Charles Hall
18 Chris Henderson
19 Colin Walton
20 Cory Hamscher
21 Cynthia Narcisi
22 D Douglas
23 Dan Bergren
24 Dan Curto
25 Darla Ecklund
26 David Day
27 David Rabbitte
28 Denae Frazier
29 Denis Medri
30 Dennis Budd
31 Don Pedicini Jr.
32 Eli Rutten
33 Erik Maell
34 Gabe Farber
35 Gary Kezele
36 Hayden Davis
37 Ingrid Hardy
38 Irma Ahmed
39 Jamie Snell
40 Jason Atomic
41 Jason Davies
42 Jason Durden
43 Jason Hughes
44 Jason Sobol
45 Jason Keith Phillips
46 Jay Shimko
47 Jerry Ma
48 Jim Kyle

49 Joe Corroney
50 Joe Hogan
51 John Beatty
52 John Soukup
53 John P Wales
54 Jonathan D. Gordon
55 Kate Glasheen
56 Katie Cook
57 Keven Reinke
58 Kevin Doyle
59 Kevin Graham
60 Kevin Liell
61 Killian Plunkett
62 Kyle Babbitt
63 Lak Lim
64 Lance Sawyer
65 Lawrence Reynolds
66 Lee Bradley
67 Lee Kohse
68 Lin Workman
69 Lord Mesa
70 Mark McHaley
71 Mark Slater
72 Mike Duron
73 Nathan Hamill
74 Nathen Reinke
75 Nicole Falk
76 Nigel Sade
77 Nina Edlund
78 Pat Presley
79 Patrick Richardson
80 Patrick Schoenmaker
81 Randy Martinez
82 Randy Siplon
83 Rhiannon Owens
84 Rich Molinelli
85 Rob Liefeld
86 Robert Hendrickson
87 Russell Walks
88 Scott Rorie
89 Scott Zambelli
90 Shea Standefer
91 Shelli Paroline
92 Sian Mandrake
93 Steph Swanger
94 Ted Dastick Jr.
95 Tim Proctor
96 Tod Allen Smith
97 Tom Hodges
98 Trev Murphy
99 Vanessa Banky Farano
100 Veronica O'Connell
101 Zack Giallongo
102 Brian Kong
103 Cat Staggs
104 Chris Glenn
105 Cole Higgins
106 David Green
107 Eric Komalieh
108 Jenn DePaola
109 Jessica Hickman
110 Linzy Zorn
111 Marat Mychaels
112 Matt Busch
113 Mikey Babinski
114 Nicole Goff
115 Sarah Wilkinson
116 Sean Pence
117 Vince Lee
118 Will Nichols
119 Lizzie Carr

2012 Star Wars Galaxy Series 7 Sketches Retail Red

1 Adrian Rivera
2 Agnes Garbowska
3 Beck Seashols
4 Bruce Gerlach
5 David Rabbitte
6 Denae Frazier
7 Denis Medri
8 Erik Maell
9 Howard Shum

10 Jason Davies
11 Jason Durden
12 Jay Shimko
13 Jessica Hickman
14 Joe Hogan
15 John P Wales
16 Jonathan D. Gordon
17 Kate Glasheen
18 Kevin Doyle
19 Lee Bradley
20 Lee Kohse
21 Lord Mesa
22 Mark Slater
23 Rich Molinelli
24 Scott Zambelli
25 Shelli Paroline
26 Sian Mandrake
27 Steph Swanger
28 Tod Allen Smith
29 Trev Murphy
30 Veronica O'Connell
31 Wilson Ramos Jr.

2004 Star Wars Heritage

BLESSINGS FROM BEYOND

In this retro-style set, Topps uses the same format as the original Star Wars cards from the '70's and '80's, in both design and card stock. All six movies are covered (with some images of the 1997 re-releases included). The fronts have an image encased in a border while the backs have story text. As an added piece of nostalgia, a stick of gum is inserted in every pack; however, the gum is no wrapped so collectors don't have to worry about that pesky gum stain. Each film in the series contains its own subset. Artwork by Jan Duursema and Dan Parsons. The set comes in both hobby (H) and retail (R) packs.

COMPLETE SET (120)	8.00	20.00
UNOPENED BOX (36 PACKS)	65.00	70.00
UNOPENED PACK (5 CARDS)	2.00	2.50
COMMON CARD (1-120)	.15	.40

2004 Star Wars Heritage Alphabet Stickers

COMPLETE SET (30)	12.00	30.00
STATED ODDS 1:3 RETAIL		

2004 Star Wars Heritage Autographs

DARTH VADER

STATED ODDS 1:578

NNO	Carrie Fisher	200.00	400.00
NNO	James Earl Jones	100.00	200.00
NNO	Mark Hamill	600.00	1000.00

2004 Star Wars Heritage Etched Wave One

COMPLETE SET (6)	6.00	15.00
COMMON CARD (1-6)	1.25	3.00
STATED ODDS 1:9		

2004 Star Wars Heritage Etched Wave Two

COMPLETE SET (6)	6.00	15.00
COMMON CARD (1-6)	1.25	3.00
STATED ODDS 1:9		

2004 Star Wars Heritage Sketches

COMPLETE ARTIST LIST (32)
RANDOMLY INSERTED INTO PACKS
UNPRICED DUE TO SCARCITY

1 Ray Lago
2 Ryan Benjamin
3 Matt Busch
4 Jeff Carlisle
5 Brian Ching
6 Cynthia Cummens
7 Dave Dorman
8 Jan Duursema
9 Tommy Edwards
10 Chris Eliopoulos
11 Davide Fabbri
12 Tom Hodges
13 James Hodgkins
14 Jeff Johnson
15 Rafael Kayanan
16 Mike Lemos
17 Mike Lilly
18 Randy Martinez
19 John McCrea
20 Brandon McKinney
21 Mary Mitchell
22 Jake Myler
23 William O'Neil
24 Dan Parsons
25 Dimitri Patelis
26 Sean Phillips
27 Kilian Plunkett
28 David Rabitte
29 Ron Randall
30 Robert Teranishi
31 Chris Trevas
32 Russell Walks

2004 Star Wars Heritage Promos

Return of the Jedi

P1	The Phantom Menace	2.00	5.00
P2	Attack of the Clones	6.00	15.00
P3	Episode III SDCC	.75	2.00
P4	A New Hope NSU	.75	2.00
P5	Empire Strikes Back NSU	.75	2.00
P6	Return of the Jedi	2.00	5.00
S1	Empire Strikes Back CT UK	2.50	6.00

2015 Star Wars High Tek

COMPLETE SET w/o SP (112)	60.00	120.00
COMPLETE SET w/SP (127)	250.00	500.00
UNOPENED BOX (8 CARDS)	100.00	120.00
COMMON CARD (1-112)	.40	1.00

*DS CORE: .5X TO 1.2X BASIC CARDS
*HOTH TAC.: .5X TO 1.2X BASIC CARDS
*TIE FRONT: .6X TO 1.5X BASIC CARDS
*VADER TIE: .6X TO 1.5X BASIC CARDS
*MIL.FALCON: .75X TO 2X BASIC CARDS
*STAR DEST.: .75X TO 2X BASIC CARDS
*CARBON: 1X TO 2.5X BASIC CARDS
*EMP.THRONE: 1X TO 2.5X BASIC CARDS
*DS EXT.: 2X TO 5X BASIC CARDS
*TIE WING: 2X TO 5X BASIC CARDS
TIDAL/99: 1.2X TO 3X BASIC CARDS
GOLD RAINBOW/50: 1.5X TO 4X BASIC CARDS
CLOUDS/25: 2X TO 5X BASIC CARDS
RED ORBIT/5: UNPRICED DUE TO SCARCITY
BLACK GALACTIC/1: UNPRICED DUE TO SCARCITY
*P.P.BLACK/1: UNPRICED DUE TO SCARCITY
*P.P.CYAN/1: UNPRICED DUE TO SCARCITY
*P.P.MAGENTA/1: UNPRICED DUE TO SCARCITY
*P.P.YELLOW/1: UNPRICED DUE TO SCARCITY

1A	Luke	3.00	8.00
	lightsaber		
1B	Luke	10.00	25.00
	blaster SP		
1C	Luke	12.00	30.00
	Jedi Knight SP		
2A	Leia	3.00	8.00
	A New Hope		
2B	Leia	15.00	40.00
	Bespin uniform SP		
2C	Leia	120.00	200.00

	Slave SP		
3A	Han Solo	4.00	10.00
	blaster		
3B	Han Solo	20.00	50.00
	Bespin SP		
3C	Han Solo	12.00	30.00
	Endor SP		
4	Darth Vader	5.00	12.00
5A	The Emperor	2.00	5.00
5B	Sheev Palpatine SP	4.00	10.00
5C	Darth Sidious SP	12.00	30.00
6	Yoda	1.25	3.00
7A	C-3PO	4.00	10.00
	shiny chrome		
7B	C-3PO	8.00	20.00
	dirty chrome SP		
8	R2-D2	1.25	3.00
9	Chewbacca	1.25	3.00
10A	Lando	2.00	5.00
	cape		
10B	Lando	8.00	20.00
	blaster SP		
11	Boba Fett	2.00	5.00
36A	Anakin Skywalker	1.25	3.00
36B	Anakin	6.00	15.00
	two lightsabers SP		
37A	Obi-Wan Kenobi	1.25	3.00
37B	Obi-Wan	12.00	30.00
	young SP		
37C	Obi-Wan	8.00	20.00
	old SP		
40A	Padme	1.25	3.00
	dark dress		
40B	Padme Amidala	10.00	25.00
	white outfit SP		
42	Darth Maul	1.25	3.00
44B	Boba Fett	25.00	60.00
	armor SP		
88	Anakin Skywalker	1.25	3.00
94	The Inquisitor	.75	2.00
106	Finn	3.00	8.00
107	Kylo Ren	3.00	8.00
108	Rey	5.00	12.00
109	Poe Dameron	3.00	8.00
110	BB-8	4.00	10.00
111	Captain Phasma	3.00	8.00
112	Flametrooper	2.00	5.00

2015 Star Wars High Tek Armor Tek

JANGO FETT ARMOR TEK

COMPLETE SET (10)	120.00	250.00
COMMON CARD (AT1-AT10)	8.00	20.00
STATED PRINT RUN 50 SER.#'d SETS		

AT1	Boba Fett	15.00	40.00
AT3	Commander Cody	15.00	40.00
AT4	Darth Vader	20.00	50.00
AT5	Jango Fett	12.00	30.00
AT7	Luke Skywalker	12.00	30.00
AT8	Sabine Wren	10.00	25.00
AT9	Poe Dameron	15.00	40.00
AT10	Kylo Ren	15.00	40.00

2015 Star Wars High Tek Autographs

COMMON CARD	6.00	15.00

*TIDAL/75: .5X TO 1.2X BASIC AUTOS
*GOLD RAINBOW/50: .6X TO 1.5X BASIC AUTOS
*CLOUDS/25: .75X TO 2X BASIC AUTOS
*RED ORBIT/5: UNPRICED DUE TO SCARCITY
*P.P.BLACK/1: UNPRICED DUE TO SCARCITY
*P.P.CYAN/1: UNPRICED DUE TO SCARCITY
*P.P.MAGENTA/1: UNPRICED DUE TO SCARCITY
*P.P.YELLOW/1: UNPRICED DUE TO SCARCITY

14	Alan Harris	8.00	20.00
57	Amy Allen	10.00	25.00
90	Andy Secombe	8.00	20.00
7	Anthony Daniels	80.00	150.00
102	Ashley Eckstein	10.00	25.00
49	Bai Ling	8.00	20.00
10	Billy Dee Williams	25.00	60.00
78	Bruce Spence	8.00	20.00
2	Carrie Fisher	200.00	400.00
4	David Prowse	120.00	250.00
105	Dee Bradley Baker	12.00	30.00
6	Deep Roy	20.00	50.00
23	Dickey Beer	10.00	25.00
29	Dickey Beer	15.00	40.00
104	George Takei	30.00	80.00
3	Harrison Ford		
11	Jeremy Bulloch	20.00	50.00
106	John Boyega	400.00	600.00
27	John Ratzenberger	10.00	25.00
56	Keisha Castle-Hughes	20.00	50.00
1	Mark Hamill		
84	Matthew Wood	25.00	60.00
25	Michael Carter	25.00	60.00
68	Nalini Krishan	8.00	20.00
54	Oliver Ford Davies	8.00	20.00
28	Pam Rose	30.00	80.00
12	Paul Blake	10.00	25.00
30	Paul Brooke	15.00	40.00
9	Peter Mayhew	25.00	60.00
42	Ray Park	20.00	50.00
61	Silas Carson	10.00	25.00
80	Silas Carson	10.00	25.00
96	Taylor Gray	10.00	25.00
16	Tim Rose	10.00	25.00
100	Tiya Sircar	12.00	30.00
97	Vanessa Marshall	8.00	20.00
20	Warwick Davis	12.00	30.00
79	Wayne Pygram	10.00	25.00

2015 Star Wars High Tek Moments of Power

COMPLETE SET (15)	175.00	350.00
COMMON CARD (MP1-MP15)	8.00	20.00
STATED PRINT RUN 50 SER.#'d SETS		

MP1	Anakin Skywalker	10.00	25.00
MP2	Darth Maul	12.00	30.00
MP3	Obi-Wan Kenobi	15.00	40.00
MP4	Padme Amidala	12.00	30.00
MP6	Yoda	12.00	30.00
MP7	The Emperor	10.00	25.00
MP8	Han Solo	20.00	50.00
MP9	Luke Skywalker	15.00	40.00
MP10	Boba Fett	15.00	40.00
MP11	Chewbacca	10.00	25.00
MP13	Princess Leia Organa	15.00	40.00
MP15	Darth Vader	20.00	50.00

2015 Star Wars High Tek Sketches

1	Achilleas Kokkinakis
2	Adam Talley
3	Adrian Rivera
4	Alejandro Iniquez
5	Andrew Cosson
6	Bob Stevlic
7	Brad Hudson
8	Brent Ragland
9	Brian Reedy
10	Brian Kong
11	Bruce Gerlach
12	Carlos Cabaleiro
13	Christopther West
14	Crystal Bam Fontan
15	Dan Curto
16	Dan Bergren
17	Darrin Pepe
18	Dave Strong
19	Eli Ruttan
20	Eric Lehtonen
21	Francois Chartier
22	Irma Ahmed
23	Jeffrey Benitez
24	Jessica Hickman
25	Joe Hogan
26	John Haun
27	Jonathan Caustrita
28	Kate Carleton
29	Kevin West
30	Kevin Graham
31	Kevin Doyle
32	Kevin Liell
33	Kyle Babbitt
34	Kyle Hickman
35	Lawrence Reynolds
36	Lee Lightfoot
37	Marcia Dye
38	Matt Hebb
39	Matthew Stewart
40	Matthew Sutton
41	Michael Cohen
42	Mike Hampton
43	Norvien Basio
44	Patrick Giles
45	Rich Molinelli
46	Ron Conley
47	Russ Maheras
48	Solly Mohamed
49	Stephanie Swanger
50	Ted Dastick
51	Tim Dowler
52	Tim Proctor
53	Tom Carlton
54	Tom Zahler
55	Jeremy M. Jack
56	Veronica O'Connell

2015 Star Wars High Tek Tek Heads

COMPLETE SET (15)	150.00	275.00
COMMON CARD (TH1-TH15)	6.00	15.00
STATED PRINT RUN 50 SER.#'d SETS		

TH1	Darth Vader	20.00	50.00
TH2	C-3PO	10.00	25.00
TH3	Luke Skywalker	10.00	25.00
TH4	R2-D2	8.00	20.00
TH5	IG-88	8.00	20.00
TH7	BB-8	12.00	30.00
TH8	FX-7	8.00	20.00
TH10	2-1B	10.00	25.00
TH12	R7-A7	10.00	25.00
TH13	General Grievous	8.00	20.00
TH14	Chopper	10.00	25.00

2016 Star Wars High Tek

COMPLETE SET W/O SP (112)	100.00	200.00
COMPLETE SET W/SP (127)	300.00	600.00
UNOPENED BOX (1 PACK/8 CARDS)	50.00	60.00
COMMON CARD (SW1-SW112)	1.25	3.00

*F1P1: SAME VALUE AS BASIC
*F1P2: SAME VALUE AS BASIC
*F1P3: .75X TO 2X BASIC CARDS
*F1P4: .75X TO 2X BASIC CARDS
*F1P5: 1.5X TO 4X BASIC CARDS
*F2P1: SAME VALUE AS BASIC
*F2P2: SAME VALUE AS BASIC
*F2P3: .75X TO 2X BASIC CARDS
*F2P4: 1X TO 2.5X BASIC CARDS
*F2P5: 1.50X TO 4X BASIC CARDS
*BLUE RAIN/99: .75X TO 2X BASIC CARDS
*GOLD RAIN/50: 1.5X TO 4X BASIC CARDS
*ORANGE MAGMA/25: 3X TO 6X BASIC CARDS
*GREEN CUBE/10: 4X TO 10X BASIC CARDS
*RED ORBIT/5: 6X TO 15X BASIC CARDS
*BLACK GALACTIC/1: UNPRICED DUE TO SCARCITY
*P.P.BLACK/1: UNPRICED DUE TO SCARCITY
*P.P.CYAN/1: UNPRICED DUE TO SCARCITY
*P.P.MAGENTA/1: UNPRICED DUE TO SCARCITY
*P.P.YELLOW/1: UNPRICED DUE TO SCARCITY

SW60A Kylo Ren	15.00	40.00
Dark Side Disciple SP		
SW72A General Leia Organa	25.00	60.00
Resistance Leader SP		
SW75A Rey	15.00	40.00
Jakku Scavenger SP		
SW75B Rey	80.00	150.00
Force Sensitive SP		
SW75C Rey	60.00	120.00
Starkiller Base Duel SP		
SW76A FN-2187	30.00	80.00
First Order Stormtrooper SP		
SW76B Flametrooper	12.00	30.00
First Order Infantry SP		
SW76C Snowtrooper	12.00	30.00
First Order Infantry SP		
SW76D TIE Pilot	12.00	30.00
First Order Pilot SP		
SW84A Han Solo	50.00	100.00
Smuggler SP		
SW87A Finn	30.00	80.00
Resistance Warrior SP		
SW87B Finn	20.00	50.00
Resistance Fighter SP		
SW88A Chewbacca	30.00	80.00
Millennium Falcon Co-Pilot SP		
SW100A Poe Dameron	25.00	60.00
Resistance Messenger SP		
SW100B Poe Dameron	15.00	40.00
Resistance Pilot SP		

2016 Star Wars High Tek Armor Tek

COMPLETE SET (11)		
COMMON CARD (AT1-AT11)	8.00	20.00
STATED PRINT RUN 50 SER.#'d SETS		
AT1 Kylo Ren	15.00	40.00
AT2 Captain Phasma	12.00	30.00
AT3 Poe Dameron	10.00	25.00
AT6 First Order Tie Fighter Pilot	12.00	30.00
AT7 First Order Stormtrooper	12.00	30.00
AT8 Rey	20.00	50.00
AT9 Stormtrooper (Heavy Gunner)	10.00	25.00
AT11 Sidon Ithano	12.00	30.00

2016 Star Wars High Tek Autographs

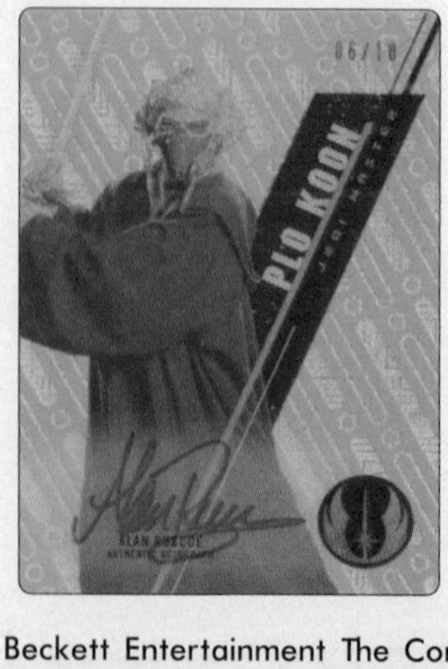

COMMON CARD	5.00	12.00
*BLUE RAIN/75: .5X TO 1.2X BASIC CARDS		
*GOLD RAIN/50: .6X TO 1.5X BASIC CARDS		
*ORANGE MAGMA/25: .75X TO 2X BASIC CARDS		
*GREEN CUBE/10: UNPRICED DUE TO SCARCITY		
*RED ORBIT/5: UNPRICED DUE TO SCARCITY		
*BLACK GALACTIC: UNPRICED DUE TO SCARCITY		
*P.P.BLACK/1: UNPRICED DUE TO SCARCITY		
*P.P.CYAN/1: UNPRICED DUE TO SCARCITY		
*P.P.MAGENTA/1: UNPRICED DUE TO SCARCITY		
*P.P.YELLOW/1: UNPRICED DUE TO SCARCITY		
STATED ODDS 1:		
1 Adam Driver		
3 Aidan Cook/Cookie Tuggs	8.00	20.00
4 Alan Ruscoe/Bib Fortuna	6.00	15.00
6 Amy Allen	8.00	20.00
7 Andy Serkis	50.00	100.00
8 Anna Brewster	8.00	20.00
9 Anthony Daniels		
10 Ashley Eckstein	10.00	25.00
11 Billy Dee Williams		
12 Brian Herring		
13 Brian Vernel	6.00	15.00
14 Carrie Fisher		
15 Catherine Taber	6.00	15.00
17 Cristina da Silva	8.00	20.00
19 Daisy Ridley		
20 Dave Barclay	8.00	20.00
21 David Acord/Med.Droid	6.00	15.00
22 David Acord/Voiceover	6.00	15.00
23 David Bowers	6.00	15.00
24 Dee Bradley Baker	6.00	15.00
25 Denis Lawson		
26 Dickey Beer		
28 Freddie Prinze Jr.		
29 Greg Grunberg		
30 Harriet Walter	6.00	15.00
31 Harrison Ford		
32 Hugh Quarshie		
33 Jeremy Bulloch	12.00	30.00
35 Jessica Henwick		
37 John Boyega		
38 Julie Dolan	8.00	20.00
39 Kiran Shah	6.00	15.00
40 Marc Silk	6.00	15.00
42 Mark Dodson/S.Crumb	6.00	15.00
43 Mark Hamill		
45 Michael Kingma	6.00	15.00
47 Mike Edmonds	6.00	15.00
48 Mike Quinn	8.00	20.00
50 Paul Blake	6.00	15.00
51 Paul Springer	6.00	15.00
54 Ray Park		
57 Sam Witwer	8.00	20.00
59 Sebastian Armesto	6.00	15.00
60 Silas Carson	8.00	20.00
62 Taylor Gray	6.00	15.00
63 Tim Rose	6.00	15.00
64 Tiya Sircar	6.00	15.00
66 Tosin Cole	10.00	25.00
67 Warwick Davis		

2016 Star Wars High Tek Autographs Gold Rainbow

*GOLD RAINBOW/50: .6X TO 1.5X BASIC CARDS		
STATED ODDS 1:		
12 Brian Herring	25.00	60.00
25 Denis Lawson	15.00	40.00
67 Warwick Davis	12.00	30.00

2016 Star Wars High Tek Autographs Orange Magma Diffractor

*ORANGE MAGMA/25: .75X TO 2X BASIC CARDS		
14 Carrie Fisher	250.00	500.00
28 Freddie Prinze Jr.	30.00	80.00
37 John Boyega	120.00	250.00

2016 Star Wars High Tek Living Tek

COMPLETE SET (13)		
COMMON CARD (LT1-LT13)	6.00	15.00
STATED PRINT RUN 50 SER.#'d SETS		
LT1 Crusher Roodown	10.00	25.00
LT2 Luke Skywalker	15.00	40.00
LT3 C-3PO	8.00	20.00
LT4 BB-8	12.00	30.00
LT5 GA-97	8.00	20.00
LT6 Luggabeast	8.00	20.00
LT7 PZ-4CO	8.00	20.00
LT9 B-U4D	12.00	30.00
LT11 Sidon Ithano	12.00	30.00
LT12 HURID-327	8.00	20.00
LT13 R2-D2	8.00	20.00

2015 Star Wars Honey Maid

These cards were imprinted on the backs of special Honey Maid graham crackers. They feature many of the popular characters from the classic trilogy, including Darth Vader, Yoda, Boba Fett, Luke Skywalker, and Han Solo. In their original condition, cards came in 6-card panels.

COMPLETE SET (12)	3.00	8.00
COMMON CARD	.40	1.00
PAN1 Obi-Wan Kenobi	2.00	5.00
Darth Vader		
Han Solo		
Chewbacca		
Storm Trooper		
C-3PO		
PAN2 R2-D2	2.00	5.00
The Emperor		
Yoda		
Luke Skywalker		
Boba Fett		
Princess Leia Organa		

2013 Star Wars Jedi Legacy

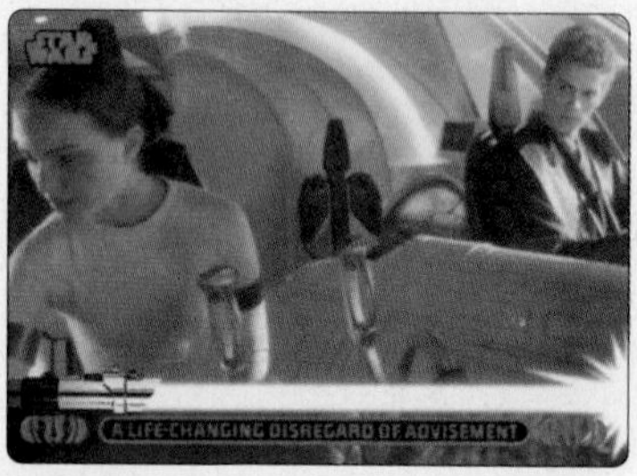

COMPLETE SET (90)	6.00	15.00
UNOPENED BOX (24 PACKS)	60.00	70.00
UNOPENED PACK (8 CARDS)	2.50	3.00
COMMON CARD (1A-45L)	.20	.50
*BLUE: 1.2X TO 3X BASIC CARDS		
*MAGENTA: 4X TO 10X BASIC CARDS		
*GREEN: X TO X BASIC CARDS		
*GOLD/10: 50X TO 120X BASIC CARDS		
*P.P.BLACK/1: UNPRICED DUE TO SCARCITY		
*P.P.CYAN/1: UNPRICED DUE TO SCARCITY		
*P.P.MAGENTA/1: UNPRICED DUE TO SCARCITY		
*P.P.YELLOW/1: UNPRICED DUE TO SCARCITY		

2013 Star Wars Jedi Legacy Autographs

COMMON CARD (UNNUMBERED)	10.00	25.00
STATED ODDS 1:72		
NNO Alan Harris	20.00	50.00
NNO Anthony Daniels	200.00	400.00
NNO Billy Dee Williams	125.00	250.00
NNO Carrie Fisher	300.00	500.00
NNO Harrison Ford	1750.00	2500.00
NNO Ian McDiarmid	300.00	500.00
NNO James Earl Jones	150.00	300.00
NNO Jeremy Bulloch	30.00	60.00
NNO John Morton	15.00	40.00
NNO Kenneth Colley	15.00	40.00
NNO Kenny Baker	30.00	60.00
NNO Mark Hamill	400.00	600.00
NNO Tim Rose	15.00	40.00

2013 Star Wars Jedi Legacy Chewbacca Fur Relics

COMMON CARD (CR1-CR4)	75.00	150.00
STATED ODDS 1:720		

2013 Star Wars Jedi Legacy Connections

COMPLETE SET (15)	5.00	12.00
COMMON CARD (C1-C15)	.60	1.50
*P.P.BLACK/1: UNPRICED DUE TO SCARCITY		
*P.P.CYAN/1: UNPRICED DUE TO SCARCITY		
*P.P.MAGENTA/1: UNPRICED DUE TO SCARCITY		
*P.P.YELLOW/1: UNPRICED DUE TO SCARCITY		
STATED ODDS 1:2		

2013 Star Wars Jedi Legacy Ewok Fur Relics

COMMON CARD (ER1-ER4)	20.00	50.00
STATED ODDS 1:120		
ER1 Wicket W. Warrick	35.00	70.00
ER4 Widdle Warrick	50.00	100.00

2013 Star Wars Jedi Legacy Film Cels

COMMON CARD (FR1-FR30)	10.00	25.00
STATED ODDS 1:BOX		
FR6 Darth Vader	20.00	50.00

2013 Star Wars Jedi Legacy Dual Film Cels

COMPLETE SET (6)	120.00	250.00
COMMON CARD (DFR1-DFR6)	20.00	50.00
STATED ODDS 1:144		
DFR1 Darth Vader/Luke Skywalker	30.00	60.00

2013 Star Wars Jedi Legacy Triple Film Cels

COMPLETE SET (10)	250.00	500.00
COMMON CARD (TFR1-TFR10)	30.00	60.00
STATED ODDS 1:144		

2013 Star Wars Jedi Legacy Influencers

COMPLETE SET (18)	5.00	12.00
COMMON CARD (I1-I18)	.50	1.25
*P.P.BLACK/1: UNPRICED DUE TO SCARCITY		
*P.P.CYAN/1: UNPRICED DUE TO SCARCITY		
*P.P.MAGENTA/1: UNPRICED DUE TO SCARCITY		
*P.P.YELLOW/1: UNPRICED DUE TO SCARCITY		
STATED ODDS 1:2		

2013 Star Wars Jedi Legacy Jabba's Sail Barge Relics

COMPLETE SET (5)	300.00	600.00
COMMON CARD (JR1-JR5)	50.00	100.00
STATED ODDS 1:336		
JR1 Luke Skywalker	125.00	200.00
JR2 Leia Organa	100.00	175.00
JR3 Boba Fett	75.00	150.00

2013 Star Wars Jedi Legacy The Circle is Now Complete

COMPLETE SET (12)	35.00	70.00
COMMON CARD (CC1-CC12)	4.00	10.00
*P.P.BLACK/1: UNPRICED DUE TO SCARCITY		
*P.P.CYAN/1: UNPRICED DUE TO SCARCITY		
*P.P.MAGENTA/1: UNPRICED DUE TO SCARCITY		
*P.P.YELLOW/1: UNPRICED DUE TO SCARCITY		
STATED ODDS 1:12		
NNO1 Luke Skywalker PROMO		

2015 Star Wars Journey to The Force Awakens

Star Wars: The Force Awakens™

COMPLETE SET (110)	10.00	25.00
COMMON CARD (1-110)	.20	.50

*JABBA SLIME GREEN: .5X TO 1.2X BASIC CARDS
*BLACK: .6X TO 1.5X BASIC CARDS
*DEATH STAR SILVER: .75X TO 2X BASIC CARDS
*LTSBR. NEON PINK: 1.5X TO 4X BASIC CARDS
*PURPLE: 4X TO 10X BASIC CARDS
*HOTH ICE/150: 6X TO 15X BASIC CARDS
*GOLD/50: 10X TO 25X BASIC CARDS
*HOLOGRAM/25: 15X TO 40X BASIC CARDS
*RED IMPERIAL/1: UNPRICED DUE TO SCARCITY
*P.P. BLACK/1: UNPRICED DUE TO SCARCITY
*P.P. CYAN/1: UNPRICED DUE TO SCARCITY
*P.P. MAGENTA/1: UNPRICED DUE TO SCARCITY
*P.P. YELLOW/1: UNPRICED DUE TO SCARCITY

2015 Star Wars Journey to The Force Awakens
Autographs

ALAN HARRIS
AUTHENTIC AUTOGRAPH

COMMON CARD	8.00	20.00

*SILVER/50: .75X TO 2X BASIC AUTOS
*GOLD/10: UNPRICED DUE TO SCARCITY
*RED/1: UNPRICED DUE TO SCARCITY
*P.P.BLACK/1: UNPRICED DUE TO SCARCITY
*P.P.CYAN/1: UNPRICED DUE TO SCARCITY
*P.P.MAGENTA/1: UNPRICED DUE TO SCARCITY
*P.P.YELLOW/1: UNPRICED DUE TO SCARCITY

NNO Alan Harris	12.00	30.00
NNO Amy Allen	25.00	60.00
NNO Angus MacInnes	10.00	25.00
NNO Anthony Daniels	200.00	400.00
NNO Ashley Eckstein	15.00	40.00
NNO Bai Ling	15.00	40.00
NNO Billy Dee Williams	50.00	100.00
NNO Caroline Blakiston	10.00	25.00
NNO Carrie Fisher	120.00	250.00
NNO David Prowse	80.00	150.00
NNO Dickey Beer	10.00	25.00
NNO Femi Taylor	12.00	30.00
NNO Hassani Shapi	12.00	30.00
NNO Ian McDiarmid	150.00	300.00
NNO Jeremy Bulloch	50.00	100.00
NNO Jerome Blake	10.00	25.00
NNO John Ratzenberger	12.00	30.00
NNO Kenji Oates	10.00	25.00
NNO Kenneth Colley	10.00	25.00
NNO Kenny Baker	60.00	120.00
NNO Mark Hamill	225.00	350.00
NNO Michonne Bourriague	12.00	30.00
NNO Mike Quinn	25.00	60.00
NNO Nika Futterman	10.00	25.00
NNO Olivia d'Abo	80.00	150.00
NNO Orli Shoshan	10.00	25.00
NNO Pam Rose	10.00	25.00

NNO Peter Mayhew	30.00	80.00
NNO Ray Park	25.00	60.00
NNO Rohan Nichol	12.00	30.00
NNO Steven Blum	10.00	25.00
NNO Taylor Gray	12.00	30.00
NNO Tiya Sircar	25.00	60.00
NNO Vanessa Marshall	15.00	40.00
NNO Wayne Pygram	12.00	30.00

2015 Star Wars Journey to The Force Awakens
Behind-the-Scenes

The Birth of 2-1B

COMPLETE SET (9)	5.00	12.00
COMMON CARD (BTS1-BTS9)	1.00	2.50

*P.P.BLACK/1: UNPRICED DUE TO SCARCITY
*P.P.CYAN/1: UNPRICED DUE TO SCARCITY
*P.P.MAGENTA/1: UNPRICED DUE TO SCARCITY
*P.P.YELLOW/1: UNPRICED DUE TO SCARCITY

2015 Star Wars Journey to The Force Awakens
Blueprints

MILLENNIUM FALCON

COMPLETE SET (8)	15.00	40.00
COMMON CARD (BP1-BP8)	3.00	8.00
BP1 BB-8	6.00	15.00
BP3 Millennium Falcon	5.00	12.00
BP4 X-Wing Fighter	4.00	10.00

2015 Star Wars Journey to The Force Awakens
Character Stickers

BB-8

COMPLETE SET (18)	15.00	40.00
COMMON CARD (S1-S18)	1.25	3.00

*P.P.BLACK/1: UNPRICED DUE TO SCARCITY
*P.P.CYAN/1: UNPRICED DUE TO SCARCITY
*P.P.MAGENTA/1: UNPRICED DUE TO SCARCITY
*P.P.YELLOW/1: UNPRICED DUE TO SCARCITY

S1 Luke Skywalker	1.50	4.00
S2 Han Solo	2.00	5.00
S9 BB-8	2.50	6.00

S10 Captain Phasma	1.50	4.00
S11 Kylo Ren	2.00	5.00
S14 Darth Vader	2.00	5.00
S15 Boba Fett	1.50	4.00
S17 Kylo Ren	2.00	5.00
S18 Yoda	1.50	4.00

2015 Star Wars Journey to The Force Awakens
Choose Your Destiny

CHEWBACCA

COMPLETE SET (9)	12.00	30.00
COMMON CARD (CD1-CD9)	2.50	6.00

2015 Star Wars Journey to The Force Awakens
Classic Captions

Stormtroopers attack!

COMPLETE SET (8)	15.00	40.00
COMMON CARD (CC1-CC8)	4.00	10.00

2015 Star Wars Journey to The Force Awakens
Cloth Stickers

STAR WARS

COMPLETE SET (9)	8.00	20.00
COMMON CARD (CS1-CS9)	1.50	4.00
CS6 Kylo Ren	2.00	5.00
CS9 Kylo Ren (w/TIE Fighters)	2.00	5.00

2015 Star Wars Journey to The Force Awakens
Concept Art

CONCEPT ART
THE IMPERIAL AT-AT

COMPLETE SET (9)	5.00	12.00
COMMON CARD (CA1-CA9)	1.00	2.50

*P.P.BLACK/1: UNPRICED DUE TO SCARCITY
*P.P.CYAN/1: UNPRICED DUE TO SCARCITY
*P.P.MAGENTA/1: UNPRICED DUE TO SCARCITY
*P.P.YELLOW/1: UNPRICED DUE TO SCARCITY

2015 Star Wars Journey to The Force Awakens Dual Autographs

STATED PRINT RUN 3 SER.#'d SETS
UNPRICED DUE TO SCARCITY

1 Mark Hamill/Kenny Baker
2 Ian McDiarmid/Wayne Pygram
3 Peter Mayhew/Anthony Daniels
4 Mark Hamill/David Prowse

2015 Star Wars Journey to The Force Awakens Family Legacy Matte Backs

COMPLETE SET (8)	10.00	25.00
COMMON CARD (FL1-FL8)	1.50	4.00
*GLOSSY: .5X TO 1.2X BASIC CARDS		
*P.P.BLACK/1: UNPRICED DUE TO SCARCITY		
*P.P.CYAN/1: UNPRICED DUE TO SCARCITY		
*P.P.MAGENTA/1: UNPRICED DUE TO SCARCITY		
*P.P.YELLOW/1: UNPRICED DUE TO SCARCITY		
FL1 Boba Fett and Jango Fett	2.00	5.00
FL2 Anakin Skywalker and Luke Skywalker	2.00	5.00
FL3 Padme Amidala and Leia Organa	2.00	5.00

2015 Star Wars Journey to The Force Awakens Heroes of the Resistance

COMPLETE SET (9)	6.00	15.00
COMMON CARD (R1-R9)	1.25	3.00
*P.P.BLACK/1: UNPRICED DUE TO SCARCITY		
*P.P.CYAN/1: UNPRICED DUE TO SCARCITY		
*P.P.MAGENTA/1: UNPRICED DUE TO SCARCITY		
*P.P.YELLOW/1: UNPRICED DUE TO SCARCITY		
R4 BB-8	2.00	5.00
R8 The Millennium Falcon	1.50	4.00

2015 Star Wars Journey to The Force Awakens Patches

COMPLETE SET (20)	150.00	300.00
COMMON CARD (P1-P20)	8.00	20.00
P1 First Order Kylo Ren	12.00	30.00
P3 First Order Captain Phasma	12.00	30.00
P9 X-Wing Fighter BB-8	12.00	30.00
P18 BB-8 BB-8	12.00	30.00

2015 Star Wars Journey to The Force Awakens Power of the First Order

COMPLETE SET (8)	6.00	15.00
COMMON CARD (FD1-FD8)	1.25	3.00
*P.P.BLACK/1: UNPRICED DUE TO SCARCITY		
*P.P.CYAN/1: UNPRICED DUE TO SCARCITY		
*P.P.MAGENTA/1: UNPRICED DUE TO SCARCITY		
*P.P.YELLOW/1: UNPRICED DUE TO SCARCITY		
FD1 Kylo Ren	2.00	5.00
FD2 Captain Phasma	1.50	4.00

2015 Star Wars Journey to The Force Awakens Silhouette Foil

COMPLETE SET (8)	4.00	10.00
COMMON CARD (1-8)	.75	2.00
*P.P.BLACK/1: UNPRICED DUE TO SCARCITY		
*P.P.CYAN/1: UNPRICED DUE TO SCARCITY		
*P.P.MAGENTA/1: UNPRICED DUE TO SCARCITY		
*P.P.YELLOW/1: UNPRICED DUE TO SCARCITY		
ERRONEOUSLY LISTED AS A 9-CARD SET		
ON THE CARD BACKS		
5 Kylo Ren	1.50	4.00
7 Captain Phasma	1.25	3.00

2015 Star Wars Journey to The Force Awakens Sketches

1 Achilleas Kokkinakis
2 Adam Talley
3 Adrian Rivera
4 Alex Iniguez
5 Andrew "Drone" Cosson
6 Bien Flores
7 Brian Reedy
8 Bruce Gerlach
9 Chris Henderson
10 Chris Raimo
11 Dan Gorman
12 Dan Parsons
13 Daniel Contois
14 Danny Haas
15 Darrin Pepe
16 David Rabbitte
17 Don Pedicini Jr.
18 Eric Lehtonen
19 Fer Galicia
20 FLOSI
21 Francois Chartier
22 Greg Pedersen
23 Ingrid Hardy
24 Irma "Aimo" Ahmed
25 J. Peltz
26 Jan Duursema
27 Jason Adams
28 Jason Brower
29 Jason Chalker
30 Jason Crosby
31 Jason Flowers
32 Jason Martin
33 Jeff Mallinson
34 Jessica Hickman
35 Joel Biske
36 John Sloboda
37 Josh Lyman
38 Justin ...
39 Karen Hallion
40 Kimberly Dunaway
41 Kiley Beecher
42 Kris Penix
43 Lord Mesa
44 Marcia "MDYE" Dye
45 Marco D. Carrillo
46 Matt Hebb
47 Matt Stewart
48 Michael "Locoduck" Duron
49 Michael Cohen
50 Nicole Falk
51 Omar Maya Velazquez
52 Otis Frampton
53 Pablo Diaz
54 Rich Molinelli
55 Robert Hendrickson
56 Robert Jimenez
57 Robert Teranishi
58 Sarah Wilkinson
59 Scott Blair
60 Shane McCormack
61 Solly Mohamed
62 Stephanie Swanger
63 Strephon Taylor
64 Sue Thomas
65 Tim Proctor
66 Tina Berardi
67 Todd Aaron Smith
67 Ward Silverman
69 Wilson Ramos Jr.

2015 Star Wars Journey to The Force Awakens
Triple Autographs

STATED PRINT RUN 5 SER.#'d SETS

UNPRICED DUE TO SCARCITY

1 McDiarmid/Park/Pygram

2 Prowse/Park/Pygram

2015 Star Wars Journey to The Force Awakens
Promos

P1 Luke Skywalker	6.00	15.00
(SDCC Marvel Star Wars Lando exclusive)		
P2 Luke Skywalker	2.00	5.00
(Star Wars Insider)		
P3 Darth Vader	2.00	5.00
(Star Wars Insider)		
P4 Princess Leia	2.00	5.00
(Star Wars Insider)		
P5 Han Solo	2.00	5.00
(Star Wars Insider)		
P6 Kanan Jarrus	5.00	12.00
(NYCC exclusive)		

2015 Star Wars Journey to The Force Awakens UK

OMPLETE SET (208)	30.00	80.00
COMMON CARD	.30	.75

LEY Yoda

LEBF Boba Fett

LECH Chewbacca

LEHS Han Solo

LELC Lando Calrissian

LELS Luke Skywalker

LEPL Princess Leia

LER2 R2-D2

LEST Stormtrooper

LETE The Emperor

2017 Star Wars Journey to The Last Jedi

Heroes United

COMPLETE SET (110)	12.00	30.00
UNOPENED BOX (24 PACKS)	85.00	100.00
UNOPENED PACK (8 CARDS)	3.00	4.00
COMMON CARD (1-110)	.20	.50
*GREEN STAR.: .5X TO 1.2X BASIC CARDS	.25	.60
*PINK STAR.: .6X TO 1.5X BASIC CARDS	.30	.75
*BLACK STAR.: .75X TO 2X BASIC CARDS	.40	1.00
*SILVER STAR.: 1.2X TO 3X BASIC CARDS	.60	1.50
*PURPLE STAR.: 2X TO 5X BASIC CARDS	1.00	2.50
*WHITE STAR./199: 12X TO 30X BASIC CARDS	6.00	15.00
*ORANGE STAR./50: 15X TO 40X BASIC CARDS	8.00	20.00
*GOLD STAR./25: 25X TO 60X BASIC CARDS	12.00	30.00
*IMP. RED/1: UNPRICED DUE TO SCARCITY		
*P.P.BLACK/1: UNPRICED DUE TO SCARCITY		
*P.P.CYAN/1: UNPRICED DUE TO SCARCITY		
*P.P.MAGENTA/1: UNPRICED DUE TO SCARCITY		
*P.P.YELLOW/1: UNPRICED DUE TO SCARCITY		

2017 Star Wars Journey to The Last Jedi Allies

HAN SOLO   CHEWBACCA

COMPLETE SET (5)	50.00	100.00
COMMON CARD (1-5)	10.00	25.00
*P.P.BLACK/1: UNPRICED DUE TO SCARCITY		
*P.P.CYAN/1: UNPRICED DUE TO SCARCITY		
*P.P.MAGENTA/1: UNPRICED DUE TO SCARCITY		
*P.P.YELLOW/1: UNPRICED DUE TO SCARCITY		
STATED ODDS 1:		
GAMESTOP EXCLUSIVE		

2017 Star Wars Journey to The Last Jedi Autographs

LANDO CALRISSIAN

COMMON CARD (UNNUMBERED)

*PURPLE/99: X TO X BASIC CARDS

*ORANGE/25: X TO X BASIC CARDS

*GOLD/10: X TO X BASIC CARDS

*IMP. RED/1: UNPRICED DUE TO SCARCITY

*P.P.BLACK/1: UNPRICED DUE TO SCARCITY

*P.P.CYAN/1: UNPRICED DUE TO SCARCITY

*P.P.MAGENTA/1: UNPRICED DUE TO SCARCITY

*P.P.YELLOW/1: UNPRICED DUE TO SCARCITY

STATED ODDS 1:

AAD	Adam Driver		
AAE	Ashley Eckstein		
AAP	Alistair Petrie		
AAS	Andy Serkis		
AAT	Alan Tudyk		
ABD	Ben Daniels	20.00	50.00
ABH	Brian Herring		
ABL	Billie Lourd		
ABW	Billy Dee Williams		
ACD	Cristina da Silva	12.00	30.00
ACF	Carrie Fisher		
ACR	Clive Revill		
ACT	Catherine Taber		
ADB	Dee Bradley Baker	12.00	30.00
ADC	Dave Champman	20.00	50.00
ADL	Daniel Logan	12.00	30.00
ADP	Duncan Pow		
ADR	Daisy Ridley		
ADY	Donnie Yen		
AFJ	Felicity Jones		
AFP	Freddie Prinze Jr.		
AFW	Forest Whitaker		
AGC	Gwendoline Christie		
AGT	George Takei		
AHC	Hayden Christensen		
AHF	Harrison Ford		
AIU	Iko Uwais		
AIW	Ian Whyte	10.00	25.00
AJB	John Boyega		
AJC	Jim Cummings	10.00	25.00
AJD	Julie Dolan	10.00	25.00
AJI	Jason Isaacs		
AKB	Kenny Baker		
AKF	Kate Fleetwood		
AKY	Keone Young	15.00	40.00
AMH	Mark Hamill		
APB	Paul Blake	15.00	40.00
APM	Peter Mayhew		
APW	Paul Warren	10.00	25.00
ARA	Riz Ahmed		
ARC	Richard Cunningham	12.00	30.00
ARP	Ray Park		
ASG	Stefan Grube	12.00	30.00
ASR	Scott Richardson	15.00	40.00
ASW	Sam Witwer		
ATB	Thomas Brodie-Sangster		
ATC	Tosin Cole		
ATK	Tom Kane		
ATW	Tom Wilton	12.00	30.00
AWP	Wayne Pygram	10.00	25.00
AYR	Yayan Ruhian		
AZD	Zarene Dallas	12.00	30.00
AADA	Anthony Daniels		
AADX	Adam Driver Unmasked		
ACAR	Cecp Arif Rahman	15.00	40.00
ADAR	Derek Arnold		
ADBA	Dave Barclay	10.00	25.00
ADRX	Daisy Ridley Scavenger		
AGGA	Gloria Garcia	12.00	30.00
AGGA	Greg Grunberg		
AIMD	Ian McDiarmid		
AIME	Ian McElhinney	12.00	30.00
AJBL	Jerome Blake	10.00	25.00
AJBU	Jeremy Bulloch		
ASDB	Sharon Duncan-Brewster	15.00	40.00

2017 Star Wars Journey to The Last Jedi Blueprints

COMPLETE SET (7)	8.00	20.00
COMMON CARD (1-7)	2.00	5.00

*P.P.BLACK/1: UNPRICED DUE TO SCARCITY
*P.P.CYAN/1: UNPRICED DUE TO SCARCITY
*P.P.MAGENTA/1: UNPRICED DUE TO SCARCITY
*P.P.YELLOW/1: UNPRICED DUE TO SCARCITY
STATED ODDS 1:

2017 Star Wars Journey to The Last Jedi Character Retro Stickers

COMPLETE SET (18)	100.00	200.00
COMMON CARD (1-18)	6.00	15.00

*P.P.BLACK/1: UNPRICED DUE TO SCARCITY
*P.P.CYAN/1: UNPRICED DUE TO SCARCITY
*P.P.MAGENTA/1: UNPRICED DUE TO SCARCITY
*P.P.YELLOW/1: UNPRICED DUE TO SCARCITY
STATED ODDS 1:

2017 Star Wars Journey to The Last Jedi Characters

COMPLETE SET (16)	12.00	30.00
COMMON CARD (1-16)	1.25	3.00

*P.P.BLACK/1: UNPRICED DUE TO SCARCITY
*P.P.CYAN/1: UNPRICED DUE TO SCARCITY
*P.P.MAGENTA/1: UNPRICED DUE TO SCARCITY
*P.P.YELLOW/1: UNPRICED DUE TO SCARCITY
STATED ODDS 1:

2017 Star Wars Journey to The Last Jedi Choose Your Destiny

GENERAL LEIA ORGANA

COMPLETE SET (10)	8.00	20.00
COMMON CARD (1-10)	1.25	3.00

*P.P.BLACK/1: UNPRICED DUE TO SCARCITY
*P.P.CYAN/1: UNPRICED DUE TO SCARCITY
*P.P.MAGENTA/1: UNPRICED DUE TO SCARCITY
*P.P.YELLOW/1: UNPRICED DUE TO SCARCITY
STATED ODDS 1:

2017 Star Wars Journey to The Last Jedi Darkness Rises

COMPLETE SET (6)	6.00	15.00
COMMON CARD (1-6)	1.50	4.00

2017 Star Wars Journey to The Last Jedi Dual Autographs

COMPLETE SET (4)
STATED PRINT RUN SER.#'d SETS
UNPRICED DUE TO SCARCITY

NNO Serkis/Driver
NNO Ridley/Driver
NNO Ridley/Herring
NNO Grunberg/Lourd

2017 Star Wars Journey to The Last Jedi Family Legacy

GENERAL LEIA ORGANA   KYLO REN

COMPLETE SET (6)	5.00	12.00
COMMON CARD (1-6)	1.25	3.00

*P.P.BLACK/1: UNPRICED DUE TO SCARCITY
*P.P.CYAN/1: UNPRICED DUE TO SCARCITY
*P.P.MAGENTA/1: UNPRICED DUE TO SCARCITY
*P.P.YELLOW/1: UNPRICED DUE TO SCARCITY
STATED ODDS 1:

2017 Star Wars Journey to The Last Jedi Illustrated Characters

PORGS

COMPLETE SET (14)	10.00	25.00
COMMON CARD (1-14)	1.00	2.50

*P.P.BLACK/1: UNPRICED DUE TO SCARCITY
*P.P.CYAN/1: UNPRICED DUE TO SCARCITY
*P.P.MAGENTA/1: UNPRICED DUE TO SCARCITY

*P.P.YELLOW/1: UNPRICED DUE TO SCARCITY
STATED ODDS 1:

2017 Star Wars Journey to The Last Jedi Patches

COMMON CARD (UNNUMBERED)	5.00	12.00
*ORANGE/99: .75X TO 2X BASIC CARDS	10.00	25.00
*GOLD/25: 1.2X TO 3X BASIC CARDS	15.00	40.00

*IMP. RED/1: UNPRICED DUE TO SCARCITY
STATED ODDS 1:

2017 Star Wars Journey to The Last Jedi Rey Continuity

COMPLETE SET (5)	4.00	10.00
COMMON CARD (1-5)	1.00	2.50

*P.P.BLACK/1: UNPRICED DUE TO SCARCITY
*P.P.CYAN/1: UNPRICED DUE TO SCARCITY
*P.P.MAGENTA/1: UNPRICED DUE TO SCARCITY
*P.P.YELLOW/1: UNPRICED DUE TO SCARCITY
STATED ODDS 1:

2017 Star Wars Journey to The Last Jedi Six-Person Autographed Booklet

COMPLETE SET (1)
STATED PRINT RUN SER.#'d SETS
UNPRICED DUE TO SCARCITY

NNO Ford/Hamill/Fisher/Ridley/Boyega/Herring

2017 Star Wars Journey to The Last Jedi Sketches

COMPLETE ARTIST LIST (134)
STATED ODDS
UNPRICED DUE TO SCARCITY

NNO Achilleas Kokkinakis
NNO Adam Worton
NNO Alex Iniguez
NNO Alex Mines
NNO Andrew Fry
NNO Andrew Lopez
NNO Andy Duggan
NNO Angelina Benedetti
NNO Anil Sharma

NNO Anthony Skubis
NNO Ashleigh Popplewell
NNO Ben AbuSaada
NNO Ben Goddard
NNO Bobby Blakely
NNO Brad Hudson
NNO Brandon Pyle
NNO Brendan Purchase
NNO Brendan Shaw
NNO Brent Ragland
NNO Brent Scotchmer
NNO Brett Farr
NNO Bruce Gerlach
NNO Bryan Silverbax
NNO Bryan Snuffer
NNO Bryce King II
NNO Carlos Cabaleiro
NNO Cathy Razim
NNO Chad LaForce
NNO Chad Scheres
NNO Charlie Cody
NNO Chris Clark
NNO Chris Willdig
NNO Clinton Yeager
NNO Corey Galal
NNO D.J. Coffman
NNO Dan Curto
NNO Dan Gorman
NNO Daniel Cooney
NNO Danny Kidwell
NNO Darrin Pepe
NNO Dave Dabila
NNO Dave Fowler
NNO Dean Drummond
NNO Dennis Gortakowski
NNO Dylan Riley
NNO Eddie Price
NNO Eric Lehtonen
NNO Eric White
NNO Freddy Lopez
NNO Garrett Dix
NNO Gavin Williams
NNO George Joseph
NNO GERALD GARCIA
NNO Ibrahim Ozkan
NNO Ingrid Hardy
NNO J Hammond
NNO J. P. Perez
NNO Jamie Cosley
NNO Jamie Richards
NNO Jason Brower
NNO Jason Heil
NNO Jason Sobol
NNO Jay Manchand
NNO Jay Salce
NNO Jeff Mallinson
NNO Jerry Bennett
NNO Jessica Hickman
NNO Jim Mehsling
NNO Jim O'Riley
NNO JM Smith
NNO John Soukup
NNO Jonathan Caustrita
NNO Jordan Maison
NNO Joshua Bommer
NNO Kaela Croft
NNO Kallan Archer
NNO Kevin Liell
NNO Kris Penix
NNO Kyle Babbitt
NNO Kyle Newman
NNO Lawrence Reynolds
NNO Lee Lightfoot
NNO Louise Draper
NNO Marcia Dye
NNO Mark Mangum
NNO Marsha Parkins
NNO Matt Applegate
NNO Matt Langford
NNO Matt Maldonado
NNO Matt Steffens
NNO Matt Stewart
NNO Matthew Buttich
NNO Matthew Sutton
NNO Melike Acar
NNO Michael Brady
NNO Michael Duron
NNO Michael Mastermaker
NNO Michelle Rayner
NNO Mick and Matt Glebe
NNO Mike Barnard
NNO Mohamed Jilani
NNO Neil Camera

NNO Nicholas Baltra
NNO Nick Justus
NNO Nolan Dykstra
NNO Norvierto P. Basio
NNO Pablo Diaz
NNO Patrick Giles
NNO Phil Hassewer
NNO Phillip Trujillo
NNO Preston Asevedo
NNO Ray Richardson
NNO Rey Paez
NNO Rich Molinelli
NNO Richard Serrao
NNO Rob Teranishi
NNO Robert Hendrickson
NNO Rory McQueen
NNO Roy Cover
NNO Ryan Edwards
NNO Scott Jones
NNO Shane Molina
NNO Shaow Siong
NNO Solly Mohamed
NNO Stephanie Swanger
NNO Ted Dastick Jr.
NNO Tim Dowler
NNO Tim Proctor
NNO Tina Berardi
NNO Tod Smith
NNO Todd Rayner
NNO Trent Westbrook
NNO Vincenzo D'Ippolito
NNO Ward Silverman

2017 Star Wars Journey to The Last Jedi Triple Autographs

COMPLETE SET (2)
STATED PRINT RUN SER.#'d SETS
UNPRICED DUE TO SCARCITY

NNO Serkis/Driver/Christie
NNO Ridley/Driver/Boyega

1996 Star Wars Laser

O Star Wars 20th Anniversary Commemorative Magazine

2016 Star Wars LEGO Droid Tales

COMPLETE SET (9)   15.00   40.00
UNOPENED PACK (3 CARDS)   6.00   8.00
COMMON CARD (DT1-DT9)
ONE PACK INSERTED INTO
STAR WARS LEGO DROID TALES DVD

1995 Star Wars Mastervisions

Various paintings from the Star Wars Galaxy are presented in this set produced by Topps. Each card is 24-point stock and measures 6 1/2 by 10 inches (16.5 by 25.4 cm). Artwork by John Alvin, Ken Barr, Frank Brunner, J. Scott Campbell, Tom Cantrell, Dave Dorman, Hugh Fleming, Mark Harrison, Greg and Tim Hildebrandt, Miran Kim, Ray Lago, Gene Lemery, Ralph McQuarrie, Chris Moeller, Don Punchatz, Kazuhiko Sano, Bill Schmidt, Bill Sienkiewicz, Ken Steacy, Brian Stelfreeze, Drew Struzan, Boris Vallejo,

John Van Fleet, and Michael Whelan.
COMPLETE BOXED SET (36)   10.00   25.00
COMMON CARD (1-36)   .30   .75

1995 Star Wars Mastervisions Promos

COMMON CARD   .75   2.00
P2 Luke on Hoth   1.25   3.00
(Star Wars Galaxy Magazine Exclusive)

2015 Star Wars Masterwork

COMPLETE SET w/o SP (50)   60.00   120.00
UNOPENED BOX (4 MINIBOXES)   300.00   350.00
UNOPENED MINIBOX (5 CARDS)   80.00   95.00
COMMON CARD (1-50)   2.00   5.00
COMMON CARD (51-75)   5.00   12.00
*BLUE/299: .5X TO 1.2X BASIC CARDS
*BLUE SP/299: .2X TO .50X BASIC CARDS
*SILVER/99: .75X TO 2X BASIC CARDS
*SILVER SP/99: .3X TO .80X BASIC CARDS
*GREEN/50: 1.2X TO 3X BASIC CARDS
*GREEN SP/50: .5X TO 1.2X BASIC CARDS
*P.P.BLACK/1: UNPRICED DUE TO SCARCITY
*P.P.CYAN/1: UNPRICED DUE TO SCARCITY
*P.P.MAGENTA/1: UNPRICED DUE TO SCARCITY
*P.P.YELLOW/1: UNPRICED DUE TO SCARCITY

2015 Star Wars Masterwork Autographs

COMMON CARD   10.00   25.00
*FRAMED/28: X TO X BASIC CARDS
*FOIL/25: X TO X BASIC CARDS
*CANVAS/10: UNPRICED DUE TO SCARCITY
*WOOD/1: UNPRICED DUE TO SCARCITY
STATED ODDS 1:4

NNO Alan Harris   12.00   30.00
NNO Amy Allen   12.00   30.00
NNO Angus MacInnes   12.00   30.00
NNO Anthony Daniels   120.00   250.00
NNO Ashley Eckstein   20.00   50.00
NNO Billy Dee Williams   120.00   250.00
NNO Carrie Fisher   500.00   800.00
NNO Dickey Beer   12.00   30.00
NNO Gerald Home   15.00   40.00
NNO Harrison Ford   1800.00 3000.00
NNO James Earl Jones   150.00   300.00
NNO Jeremy Bulloch   25.00   60.00
NNO Jerome Blake   12.00   30.00
NNO John Morton   20.00   50.00
NNO John Ratzenberger   15.00   40.00
NNO Kenneth Colley   12.00   30.00

NNO	Kenny Baker	60.00	120.00
NNO	Mark Hamill	350.00	600.00
NNO	Mike Quinn	12.00	30.00
NNO	Oliver Ford Davies	15.00	40.00
NNO	Pam Rose	12.00	30.00
NNO	Paul Brooke	25.00	60.00
NNO	Peter Mayhew	50.00	100.00
NNO	Phil Eason	15.00	40.00
NNO	Rusty Goffe	15.00	40.00
NNO	Tim Rose	25.00	60.00
NNO	Wayne Pygram	15.00	40.00
NNO	Zachariah Jensen	15.00	40.00

2015 Star Wars Masterwork Companions

COMPLETE SET (10)		25.00	60.00
COMMON CARD (C1-C10)		10.00	10.00

*RAINBOW/299: .6X TO 1.5X BASIC CARDS
*CANVAS/99: 1X TO 2.5X BASIC CARDS
*WOOD/50: 1.2X TO 3X BASIC CARDS
*CLEAR ACE./25: 1.5X TO 4X BASIC CARDS
*METAL/10: UNPRICED DUE TO SCARCITY
*GOLDEN METAL/1: UNPRICED DUE TO SCARCITY
*P.P.BLACK/1: UNPRICED DUE TO SCARCITY
*P.P.CYAN/1: UNPRICED DUE TO SCARCITY
*P.P.MAGENTA/1: UNPRICED DUE TO SCARCITY
*P.P.YELLOW/1: UNPRICED DUE TO SCARCITY

C1	Han Solo and Chewbacca	6.00	15.00
C2	Luke and Leia	6.00	15.00
C3	Vader and Palpatine	5.00	12.00
C5	C-3PO and R2-D2	5.00	12.00
C8	R2-D2 and Luke Skywalker	5.00	12.00
C10	Boba Fett and Jango Fett	5.00	12.00

2015 Star Wars Masterwork Defining Moments

COMPLETE SET (10)		25.00	60.00
COMMON CARD (DM1-DM10)		4.00	10.00

*RAINBOW/299: .6X TO 1.5X BASIC CARDS
*CANVAS/99: 1X TO 2.5X BASIC CARDS
*WOOD/50: 1.2X TO 3X BASIC CARDS
*CLEAR ACE./25: 1.5X TO 4X BASIC CARDS
*METAL/10: UNPRICED DUE TO SCARCITY
*GOLDEN METAL/1: UNPRICED DUE TO SCARCITY
*P.P.BLACK/1: UNPRICED DUE TO SCARCITY
*P.P.CYAN/1: UNPRICED DUE TO SCARCITY
*P.P.MAGENTA/1: UNPRICED DUE TO SCARCITY
*P.P.YELLOW/1: UNPRICED DUE TO SCARCITY

DM1	Darth Vader	5.00	12.00
DM2	Luke Skywalker	5.00	12.00
DM3	Han Solo	8.00	20.00
DM4	Princess Leia Organa	5.00	12.00
DM7	Anakin Skywalker	5.00	12.00
DM8	Obi-Wan Kenobi	5.00	12.00
DM10	Chewbacca	5.00	12.00

2015 Star Wars Masterwork Dual Autograph Booklets

STATED PRINT RUN 5 SER. #'d SETS
UNPRICED DUE TO SCARCITY

1 Anthony Daniels/Kenny Baker
2 Billy Dee Williams/Mike Quinn
3 Jeremy Bulloch/Chris Parsons
4 Mark Hamill/James Earl Jones

2015 Star Wars Masterwork Gold-Stamped Sketches

1 Adam Talley
2 Adrian Rivera
3 Bill Pulkovski
4 Brandon Gallo
5 Brent Ragland
6 Brian DeGuire
7 Brian Kong
8 Chad "CWM" McCown
9 Chris Henderson
10 Christian N. St. Pierre
11 Clay McCormack
12 Dan Bergren
13 Dan Cooney
14 Dan Parsons
15 Daniel Contois
16 Darrin Pepe
17 David J. Williams
18 Davide Fabbri
19 Denae Frazier
20 Don Pedicini Jr
21 Eric Kowalick
22 Erik Hodson
23 Francois Chartier
24 Gavin Hunt
25 Gyula Nemeth
26 Irma "Aimo" Ahmed
27 James Henry Smith
28 Jamie Snell
29 Jason Crosby
30 Jason Davies
31 Jason Durden
32 Jeff Carlisle
33 Jeff "GeckoArt" Chandler
34 Jeff Confer
35 Jeff Zapata
36 Jeffrey Benitez
37 John Haun
38 Jon Morris
39 Jorge Baeza
40 Karen Hallion
41 Karen Hinson
42 Ken Branch
43 Ken Knudtsen
44 Kevin Doyle
45 Kevin Graham
46 Kimberly Dunaway
47 Kris Penix
48 Lawrence Reynolds
49 Lee Kohse
50 Lin Workman
51 Lord Mesa
52 Marck Labas
53 Mark Hammermeister
54 Mary Bellamy
55 Michael "Locoduck" Duron
56 Mick & Matt Glebe
57 Mikey Babinsky
58 Nick "NIK" Neocleus
59 Omar Maya Velasquez
60 Pablo Diaz

61 Patrick Giles
62 Rhiannon Owens
63 Rich Molinelli
64 Robert Hendrickson
65 Robert Jimenez
66 Robert Teranishi
67 Russ Maheras
68 Scott Houseman
69 Scott Zambelli
70 Stephanie Swanger
71 Steven Black
72 Steven Burch
73 Strephon Taylor
74 Ted Dastick Jr
75 Terry Pavlet
76 Tim Proctor
77 Tod Allen Smith
78 Tom Hodges
79 Wilson Ramos, Jr.
80 Zuno

2015 Star Wars Masterwork Puzzle Sketches

1 Brian DeGuire
2 Chris Raimo
3 Jason Crosby
4 Joe Hogan
5 Lawrence Reynolds
6 Lord Mesa
7 Nik Neocleous
8 Pablo Diaz
9 Steve Burch
10 Tomoko Taniguchi

2015 Star Wars Masterwork Return of the Jedi Bunker Relics Bronze

COMMON CARD		12.00	30.00

*SILVER/77: .75X TO 2X BASIC CARDS
CARDS 1, 2, 3, 4, 10, 12 SER.#'d TO 155
CARDS 5, 6, 7, 8, 9, 11 SER.#'d TO 255

1	Han Solo/155	20.00	50.00
2	Princess Leia Organa/155	20.00	50.00
3	Chewbacca/155	15.00	40.00
4	Luke Skywalker/155	25.00	60.00
10	Ewok (frame)/155	15.00	40.00
12	Han, Leia & Luke/155	20.00	50.00

2015 Star Wars Masterwork Scum and Villainy

COMPLETE SET (10)		25.00	60.00
COMMON CARD (SV1-SV10)		4.00	10.00

*RAINBOW/299: 1.5X TO 6X BASIC CARDS

*CANVAS/99: 1X TO 2.5X BASIC CARDS
*WOOD/50: 1.2X TO 3X BASIC CARDS
*CLEAR ACE./25: 1.5X TO 4X BASIC CARDS
*METAL/10: UNPRICED DUE TO SCARCITY
*GOLDEN METAL/1: UNPRICED DUE TO SCARCITY
*P.P.BLACK/1: UNPRICED DUE TO SCARCITY
*P.P.CYAN/1: UNPRICED DUE TO SCARCITY
*P.P.MAGENTA/1: UNPRICED DUE TO SCARCITY
*P.P.YELLOW/1: UNPRICED DUE TO SCARCITY

SV1	Boba Fett	6.00	15.00
SV2	Jabba the Hutt	5.00	12.00
SV4	General Grievous	6.00	15.00
SV5	Jango Fett	5.00	12.00
SV8	Ponda Baba	6.00	15.00
SV9	Bossk	5.00	12.00
SV10	Tusken Raider	6.00	15.00

2015 Star Wars Masterwork Sketch Booklets

UNPRICED DUE TO SCARCITY

1 Chris Raimo
2 Darrin Pepe
3 Jeff Zapata
4 Patrick Giles
5 Steven Black

2015 Star Wars Masterwork Sketches

1 Aaron Smith
2 Adam Talley
3 Adrian Rivera
4 Adrianna Vanderstelt
5 Alex Buechel
6 Andrew "Drone" Cosson
7 Anthony Pugh
8 Bill Maus
9 Bill Pulkovski
10 Bob Stevlic
11 Brandon Bracamonte
12 Brandon Gallo
13 Brent Ragland
14 Brian DeGuire
15 Brian Kong
16 Chris Hamer
17 Chris Henderson
18 Chris Raimo
19 Chris Ring
20 Chris West
21 Christian N. St. Pierre
22 Clay McCormack
23 Dan Bergren
24 Dan Cooney
25 Dan Gorman
26 Dan Parsons
27 Dan Smith
28 Dana Black
29 Daniel Contois
30 Darin Radimaker
31 Darrin Pepe
32 David J. Williams

33 David Rabbitte
34 Davide Fabbri
35 Denae Frazier
36 Don Pedicini Jr.
37 Doug Cowan
38 Elfie Lebouleux
39 Eric Kowalick
40 Eric Lehtonen
41 Erik Hodson
42 Francois Chartier
43 Gary Kezele
44 Gavin Hunt
45 GeckoArt
46 Grant Gould
47 Gyula Nemeth
48 Ingrid Hardy
49 Irma "Aimo" Ahmed
50 James "Bukshot" Bukauskas
51 James Henry Smith
52 Jamie Snell
53 Jason Adams
54 Jason Chalker
55 Jason Crosby
56 Jason Davies
57 Jason Durden
58 Jason Flowers
59 Jason Goad
60 Jason M. Kincaid
61 Jason Sobol
62 Jason Walker
63 Jay Kretzer
64 Jeff "GeckoArt" Chandler
65 Jeff Carlisle
66 Jeff Confer
67 Jeff Mallinson
68 Jeff Parsons
69 Jeff Zapata
70 Jeffrey Benitez
71 Jenn DePaola
72 Joe Allard
73 Joe Corroney
74 Joe Hogan
75 Joel Biske
76 John Haun
77 John Sloboda
78 John Soukup
79 Jon Morris
80 Jorge Baeza
81 Justin Chung
82 Kaela Croft
83 Karen Hallion
84 Karen Hinson
85 Ken Branch
86 Ken Knudtsen
87 Kent Archer
88 Kevin Doyle
89 Kevin Graham
90 Kimberly Dunaway
91 Kris Penix
92 Kyle Babbitt
93 Lak Lim
94 Lark Sudol
95 Lawrence Reynolds
96 Lee Kohse
97 Lee Lightfoot
98 Lin Workman
99 LinZy Zom
100 Lizzy "ELC" Carr
101 Lord Mesa
102 Marcia Dye
103 Marck Labas
104 Mark Hammermeister
105 Mark Pingitore
106 Martheus Wade
107 Mary Bellamy
108 Mat Nastos
109 Matt Minor
110 Matthew Kirscht
111 Melike Acar
112 Michael "Locoduck" Duron
113 Michael Leavitt
114 Mick & Matt Glebe
115 Mike Hampton
116 Mike Mayhew
117 Mike Vasquez
118 Mikey Babinsky
119 Monte Moore
120 Nathan Hamill
121 Nick Neocleus
122 Nicole Falk
123 Omar Maya Velazquez
124 Pablo Diaz
125 Patrick Giles

126 Paul "Gutz" Gutierrez
127 Puiz Calzada
128 Rhiannon Owens
129 Rich Molinelli
130 Robert Hendrickson
131 Robert Jimenez
132 Robert Teranishi
133 Ron Conley
134 Roy Cover
135 Russ Maheras
136 Russell Walks
137 Sarah Wilkinson
138 Scott Houseman
139 Scott Rorie
140 Scott Zambelli
141 Sean Pence
142 Sol Mohamed
143 Stephanie Swanger
144 Steve Oatney
145 Steven Black
146 Steven Burch
147 Strephon Taylor
148 Ted Dastick Jr
149 Terry Pavlet
150 Tim Dowler
151 Tim Proctor
152 Tim Shay
153 Tina Berardi
154 Tod Allen Smith
155 Tom Hodges
156 Tomoko Taniguchi
157 Tony Miello
158 Tyler Scarlett
159 Val Hochberg
160 Wilson Ramos, Jr.
161 Zuno

2015 Star Wars Masterwork Stamp Relics

COMMON CARD		20.00	50.00
STATED ODDS 1:CASE			
NNO	Anakin vs. Obi-Wan	50.00	100.00
NNO	Ben (Obi-Wan) Kenobi	30.00	80.00
NNO	Boba Fett	60.00	120.00
NNO	C-3PO	25.00	60.00
NNO	Darth Maul	50.00	100.00
NNO	Darth Vader	30.00	80.00
NNO	Emperor Palpatine	30.00	80.00
NNO	Han Solo and Chewbacca	50.00	100.00
NNO	Luke Skywalker	30.00	80.00
NNO	The Millennium Falcon	50.00	100.00
NNO	X-Wing Fighter	30.00	80.00

2015 Star Wars Masterwork Triple Autograph

STATED PRINT RUN 2 SER. #'d SETS
UNPRICED DUE TO SCARCITY

1 Mark Hamill
Harrison Ford
Carrie Fisher

2015 Star Wars Masterwork Weapons Lineage Medallions

COMPLETE SET (30)	250.00	500.00
COMMON CARD	8.00	20.00

*SILVER/50: 1.2X TO 3X BASIC CARDS
*GOLD/10: UNPRICED DUE TO SCARCITY
STATED ODDS 1:6

NNO Anakin Skywalker	10.00	25.00
Mace Windu's Lightsaber		
NNO Anakin Skywalker	12.00	30.00
Anakin Skywalker's Lightsaber		
NNO B. Fett's Blaster	10.00	25.00
NNO B. Fett's Blaster	12.00	30.00
NNO Darth Maul's Lightsaber	10.00	25.00
NNO Vader	10.00	25.00
Vader's Lightsaber		
NNO Vader	10.00	25.00
Vader's Lightsaber		
NNO Vader	10.00	25.00
Vader's Lightsaber		
NNO Vader Solo's Blaster	12.00	30.00
NNO Darth Vader	15.00	40.00
Luke Skywalker's Lightsaber		
NNO Han Solo	12.00	30.00
Han Solo's Blaster		
NNO Han Solo	12.00	30.00
Han Solo's Blaster		
NNO Han Solo	15.00	40.00
Luke Skywalker's Lightsaber		
NNO Luke Skywalker	10.00	25.00
Luke Skywalker's Lightsaber		
NNO Luke Skywalker	10.00	25.00
Luke Skywalker's Lightsaber		
NNO Mace Windu	10.00	25.00
Mace Windu's Lightsaber		
NNO Princess Leia Organa	10.00	25.00
Stormtrooper Blaster Rifle		
NNO Leia	12.00	30.00
Leia's Blaster		
NNO R2-D2	10.00	25.00
Luke's Lightsaber		
NNO Stormtrooper	12.00	30.00
Stormtrooper Blaster Rifle		
NNO Yoda	15.00	40.00
Yoda's Lightsaber		

2015 Star Wars Masterwork Wood Sketches

UNPRICED DUE TO SCARCITY

1 Adam Talley
2 Alex Buechel
3 Bill Pulkovski
4 Brent Raglund
5 Chris West
6 Christian N. St. Pierre
7 Dan Cooney
8 Dan Parsons
9 Darrin Pepe
10 David J. Williams
11 Davide Fabbri
12 Denae Frazier
13 Don Pedicini Jr.
14 Elfie Lebouleux
15 Eric Lehtonen
16 Erik Hodson
17 Francois Chartier
18 Gavin Hunt
19 Gyula Nemeth
20 Jason Crosby
21 Jason Davies
22 Jason Flowers
23 Jason Goad
24 Jay Kretzer
25 Jeff Carlisle
26 Jeff Mallinson
27 Jeff Zapata
28 Jeffrey Benitez
29 John Soukup
30 Jon Morris
31 Ken Branch
32 Kent Archer
33 Kevin Doyle
34 Kevin Graham
35 Kimberly Dunaway
36 Lee Kohse
37 Lee Lightfoot
38 Lord Mesa
39 Marck Labas
40 Mary Bellamy
41 Mat Nastos
42 Matt Smith
43 Melike Acar
44 Mick & Matt Glebe
45 Monte Moore
46 Nick "NIK" Neocleus
47 Pablo Diaz
48 Rich Molinelli
49 Robert Hendrickson
50 Robert Jimenez
51 Robert Teranishi
52 Roy Cover
53 Russ Maheras
54 Scott Rorie
55 Sol Mohamed
56 Stephanie Swanger
57 Steven Burch
58 Strephon Taylor
59 Ted Dastick Jr.
60 Tim Dowler
61 Tim Proctor
62 Todd Aaron Smith
63 Val Hochberg
64 Zuno

2016 Star Wars Masterwork

COMPLETE SET W/SP (75)	200.00	400.00
COMPLETE SET W/O SP (50)	30.00	80.00
UNOPENED BOX (4 PACKS)	150.00	200.00
UNOPENED PACK (5 CARDS)	50.00	60.00
COMMON CARD (1-75)	2.00	5.00
COMMON SP (51-75)	4.00	10.00

*BLUE MET.: SAME VALUE | 2.00 | 5.00
*BLUE MET.SP: SAME VALUE | 4.00 | 10.00
*SILVER MET./99: .75X TO 1.5X BASIC CARDS | 3.00 | 8.00
*SILVER MET.SP/99: 30X TO .75X BASIC CARDS | 3.00 | 8.00
*GREEN MET./50: 1.2X TO 3X BASIC CARDS | 6.00 | 15.00
*GREEN MET.SP/50: .6X TO 1.5X BASIC CARDS | 6.00 | 15.00
*LTSBR PURP./50: 1.5X TO 4X BASIC CARDS | 8.00 | 20.00
*LTSBR PURP.SP/25: .75X TO 2X BASIC CARDS | 8.00 | 20.00
*GOLD/1: UNPRICED DUE TO SCARCITY
*P.P.BLACK/1: UNPRICED DUE TO SCARCITY
*P.P.CYAN/1: UNPRICED DUE TO SCARCITY
*P.P.MAGENTA/1: UNPRICED DUE TO SCARCITY
*P.P.YELLOW/1: UNPRICED DUE TO SCARCITY

66 Han Solo SP	6.00	15.00
71 Rey SP	8.00	20.00

2016 Star Wars Masterwork Alien Identification Guide

COMPLETE SET (10)	20.00	50.00
COMMON CARD (AI1-AI10)	2.50	6.00

*FOIL/299: .6X TO 1.5X BASIC CARDS | 3.00 | 8.00
*CANVAS/99: .75X TO 2X BASIC CARDS | 5.00 | 12.00
*WOOD/50: 1X TO 2.5X BASIC CARDS | 6.00 | 15.00
*SILVER/10: UNPRICED DUE TO SCARCITY
*GOLD/1: UNPRICED DUE TO SCARCITY
*P.P.BLACK/1: UNPRICED DUE TO SCARCITY
*P.P.CYAN/1: UNPRICED DUE TO SCARCITY
*P.P.MAGENTA/1: UNPRICED DUE TO SCARCITY
*P.P.YELLOW/1: UNPRICED DUE TO SCARCITY
STATED ODDS 1:4

2016 Star Wars Masterwork Autographs

COMMON CARD	6.00	15.00

*FOIL/50: .6X TO 1.5X BASIC CARDS
*CANVAS/25: .75X TO 2X BASIC CARDS
*WOOD/10: UNPRICED DUE TO SCARCITY
*SILVER/10: UNPRICED DUE TO SCARCITY
*GOLD/1: UNPRICED DUE TO SCARCITY
*P.P.BLACK/1: UNPRICED DUE TO SCARCITY
*P.P.CYAN/1: UNPRICED DUE TO SCARCITY
*P.P.MAGENTA/1: UNPRICED DUE TO SCARCITY
*P.P.YELLOW/1: UNPRICED DUE TO SCARCITY

5 Andy Serkis	80.00	150.00
8 Ashley Eckstein	12.00	30.00
11 Caroline Blakiston	8.00	20.00
14 Clive Revill	12.00	30.00
15 Corey Dee Williams	8.00	20.00
19 David Ankrum	8.00	20.00
20 David Barclay	8.00	20.00
24 Dickey Beer	10.00	25.00
34 Jeremy Bulloch	15.00	40.00
39 John Coppinger	8.00	20.00
47 Mark Dodson	10.00	25.00
50 Matthew Wood	8.00	20.00
55 Mike Edmonds	8.00	20.00
56 Mike Quinn	8.00	20.00
65 Sam Witwer	8.00	20.00
73 Tim Dry	8.00	20.00
74 Tim Rose	8.00	20.00
75 Tiya Sircar	8.00	20.00

2016 Star Wars Masterwork Autographs Canvas

*CANVAS/25: .75X TO 2X BASIC CARDS
STATED ODDS 1:25
STATED PRINT RUN 25 SER.#'d SETS

1 Adam Driver	800.00	1200.00

5 Andy Serkis	150.00	300.00
7 Anthony Daniels	80.00	150.00
10 Billy Dee Williams		
12 Carrie Fisher	200.00	400.00
16 Daisy Ridley	1200.00	2000.00
23 Denis Lawson	25.00	60.00
26 Freddie Prinze Jr.	30.00	80.00
29 Greg Grunberg	12.00	30.00
31 Harrison Ford/1		
32 Hugh Quarshie		
38 John Boyega		
42 Julian Glover		
43 Keisha Castle-Hughes		
48 Mark Hamill	250.00	500.00
52 Michael Carter	12.00	30.00
60 Peter Mayhew		
61 Ray Park		
79 Warwick Davis	15.00	40.00

2016 Star Wars Masterwork Autographs Foil

*FOIL/50: .6X TO 1.5X BASIC CARDS
STATED ODDS 1:30
STATED PRINT RUN 50 SER.#'d SETS

3 Alan Harris		
7 Anthony Daniels	50.00	100.00
12 Carrie Fisher		
14 Clive Revill		
15 Corey Dee Williams		
19 David Ankrum		
20 David Barclay		
23 Denis Lawson		
25 Femi Taylor		
26 Freddie Prinze Jr.		
27 Garrick Hagon		
28 George Takei	15.00	40.00
29 Greg Grunberg	10.00	25.00
31 Harrison Ford/1		
32 Hugh Quarshie	10.00	25.00
33 Jack Klaff		
38 John Boyega	120.00	250.00
40 John Morton		
41 John Ratzenberger		
43 Keisha Castle-Hughes		
44 Kenneth Colley		
47 Mark Dodson		
51 Mercedes Ngoh		
52 Michael Carter		
59 Paul Blake		
60 Peter Mayhew	30.00	80.00
61 Ray Park		
67 Sean Crawford		
76 Toby Philpott		
79 Warwick Davis		

2016 Star Wars Masterwork Dual Autographs

STATED ODDS 1:4,658

NNO Fisher/Baker		
NNO Barclay/Philpott	25.00	60.00
NNO McDiarmid/Revill		
NNO Blake/Bowers	20.00	50.00
NNO Hamill/Ridley		
NNO Hamill/Baker		
NNO Pygram/Stanton	15.00	40.00

2016 Star Wars Masterwork Gold-Stamped Sketches

COMPLETE ARTIST LIST (26)
STATED ODDS 1:110
UNPRICED DUE TO SCARCITY

1 Alex Iniguez/18*
2 Brad Hudson/16*

3 Brent Ragland/10*	
4 Brian Kong/24*	
5 Carlos Cabaleiro/27*	
6 Chris Meeks/15*	
7 Dan Bergren/9*	
8 Darrin Pepe/7*	
9 Eric Lehtonen/9*	
10 Gus Mauk/9*	
11 Ingrid Hardy/3*	
12 Jason Brower/5*	
13 Jason Sobol/11*	
14 Jessica Hickman/20*	
15 Kevin Liell/16*	
16 Kris Penix/10*	
17 Lee Lightfoot/8*	
18 Marcia Dye/9*	
19 Matthew Stewart/14*	
20 Melike Acar/8*	
21 Rob Teranishi/37*	
22 Roy Cover/9*	
23 Solly Mohamed/23*	
24 Stephanie Swanger/9*	
25 Tim Proctor/5*	
26 Tina Berardi/4*	

2016 Star Wars Masterwork Great Rivalries

COMPLETE SET (10)	15.00	40.00
COMMON CARD (GR1-GR10)	2.50	6.00

*FOIL/299: .6X TO 1.5X BASIC CARDS
*CANVAS/99: .75X TO 2X BASIC CARDS
*WOOD/50: 1X TO 2.5X BASIC CARDS
*SILVER/10: UNPRICED DUE TO SCARCITY
*GOLD/1: UNPRICED DUE TO SCARCITY
*P.P.BLACK/1: UNPRICED DUE TO SCARCITY
*P.P.CYAN/1: UNPRICED DUE TO SCARCITY
*P.P.MAGENTA/1: UNPRICED DUE TO SCARCITY
*P.P.YELLOW/1: UNPRICED DUE TO SCARCITY
STATED ODDS 1:2

2016 Star Wars Masterwork Medallion Relics

COMMON CARD	5.00	12.00
*SILVER/99: .6X TO 1.5X BASIC CARDS	8.00	20.00
*GOLD/10: 1.5X TO 4X BASIC CARDS	20.00	50.00

*PLATINUM/1: UNPRICED DUE TO SCARCITY
STATED ODDS 1:7

NNO Han Solo Hoth	6.00	15.00
NNO Han Solo Starkiller Base	6.00	15.00
NNO Han Solo Yavin	6.00	15.00
NNO Kylo Ren Starkiller Base		
NNO Rey Starkiller Base	6.00	15.00

2016 Star Wars Masterwork Quad Autographed Booklet

STATED ODDS 1:20,960
UNPRICED DUE TO SCARCITY

1 McDiarmid/Jones/Glover/Colley

2016 Star Wars Masterwork Show of Force

COMPLETE SET (10)	25.00	60.00
COMMON CARD (SF1-SF10)	3.00	8.00
*FOIL/299: .6X TO 1.5X BASIC CARDS	5.00	12.00
*CANVAS/99: .75X TO 2X BASIC CARDS	6.00	15.00
*WOOD/50: 1X TO 2.5X BASIC CARDS	8.00	20.00

*SILVER/10: UNPRICED DUE TO SCARCITY
*GOLD/1: UNPRICED DUE TO SCARCITY
*P.P.BLACK/1: UNPRICED DUE TO SCARCITY
*P.P.CYAN/1: UNPRICED DUE TO SCARCITY
*P.P.MAGENTA/1: UNPRICED DUE TO SCARCITY
*P.P.YELLOW/1: UNPRICED DUE TO SCARCITY
STATED ODDS 1:4

SF10 Rey	4.00	10.00

2016 Star Wars Masterwork Sketch Booklets

COMPLETE ARTIST LIST (18)
STATED ODDS 1:4,195
UNPRICED DUE TO SCARCITY

1 Brad Hudson/2*
2 Brent Ragland/1*
3 Brian Kong/1*
4 Carlos Cabaleiro/1*
5 Chris Meeks/1*
6 Dan Bergren/2*
7 Darrin Pepe/1*
8 Eric Lehtonen/2*
9 Gus Mauk/1*
10 Jason Brower/1*
11 Kris Penix/2*
12 Lee Lightfoot/1*
13 Marcia Dye/2*
14 Melike Acar/1*
15 Rob Teranishi/2*
16 Solly Mohamed/1*
17 Stephanie Swanger/2*
18 Tim Proctor/2*

2016 Star Wars Masterwork Sketches

COMPLETE ARTIST LIST (31)
STATED ODDS 1:30
UNPRICED DUE TO SCARCITY

1 Alex Iniguez/53*
2 Brad Hudson/54*
3 Brent Ragland/27*
4 Brian Kong/62*
5 Carlos Cabaleiro/78*
6 Dan Bergren/33*
7 Dan Cooney/105*

8 Darrin Pepe/32*
9 Eric Lehtonen/27*
10 Gus Mauk/36*
11 Ingrid Hardy/12*
12 Jamie Cosley/52*
13 Jason Brower/25*
14 Jason Sobol/47*
15 Jessica Hickman/48*
16 Jordan Maison/39*
17 Joshua Bommer/6*
18 Kevin Liell/45*
19 Kris Penix/26*
20 Kyle Babbit/5*
21 Lee Lightfoot/50*
22 Marcia Dye/22*
23 Matthew Stewart/43*
24 Melike Acar/20*
25 Rob Teranishi/193*
26 Roy Cover/25*
27 Scott Houseman/25*
28 Solly Mohamed/52*
29 Stephanie Swanger/28*
30 Tim Proctor/13*
31 Tina Berardi/20*

2016 Star Wars Masterwork Stamp Relics

COMPLETE SET (12)	100.00	200.00
COMMON CARD	8.00	20.00
*BRONZE/99: .6X TO 1.5X BASIC CARDS	12.00	30.00
*SILVER/50: .75X TO 2X BASIC CARDS	15.00	40.00
*GOLD/10: UNPRICED DUE TO SCARCITY		
*PLATINUM/1: UNPRICED DUE TO SCARCITY		
STATED ODDS 1:13		
STATED PRINT RUN 249 SER.#'d SETS		
NNO Han Solo	10.00	25.00
NNO Rey	12.00	30.00

2016 Star Wars Masterwork Triple Autographs

STATED ODDS 1:4,658
UNPRICED DUE TO SCARCITY

1 McDiarmid/Colley/Glover
2 Hamill/Boyega/Ridley
3 Hamill/Fisher/Baker

2016 Star Wars Masterwork Wood Sketches

COMPLETE ARTIST LIST (24)
STATED ODDS 1:442
UNPRICED DUE TO SCARCITY

1 Alex Iniguez/10*
2 Brad Hudson/15*
3 Brent Ragland/1*
4 Carlos Cabaleiro/15*
5 Chris Meeks/5*
6 Dan Bergren/4*

---

7 Darrin Pepe/3*
8 Eric Lehtonen/10*
9 Gus Mauk/10*
10 Ingrid Hardy/2*
11 Jason Brower/10*
12 Jessica Hickman/11*
13 Joshua Bommer/3*
14 Kris Penix/4*
15 Kyle Babbit/5*
16 Lee Lightfoot/10*
17 Marcia Dye/5*
18 Melike Acar/7*
19 Rob Teranishi/2*
20 Roy Cover/14*
21 Solly Mohamed/8*
22 Stephanie Swanger/2*
23 Tim Proctor/5*
24 Tina Berardi/9*

2017 Star Wars May the 4th Be with You

COMPLETE SET (20)	12.00	30.00
COMPLETE FACTORY SET (21)		
COMMON CARD (1-20)	1.00	2.50
*SILVER/10: 6X TO 15X BASIC CARDS	15.00	40.00
*GOLD/1: UNPRICED DUE TO SCARCITY		

2017 Star Wars May the 4th Be with You Autographs

COMMON CARD	10.00	25.00
*SILVER/10: .6X TO 1.5X BASIC AUTOS		
*GOLD/1: UNPRICED DUE TO SCARCITY		
STATED ODDS 1:SET		
1A Harrison Ford		
2A Mark Hamill	400.00	600.00
3A Carrie Fisher		
4A Kenny Baker		
5A Anthony Daniels	175.00	300.00
7A Jeremy Bulloch	25.00	60.00
8A Ian McDiarmid	250.00	400.00
10A Billy Dee Williams		
14A Kenneth Colley	12.00	30.00
16A Erik Bauersfeld	25.00	60.00
16A Tim Rose	15.00	40.00
19A Paul Blake		

1994-96 Star Wars Metal Promos

P1 Star Wars Episode IV	6.00	15.00
P2 The Empire Strikes Back	6.00	15.00
P3 Return of the Jedi	6.00	15.00

1996 Star Wars Metal Art of Ralph McQuarrie

COMPLETE SET (20)	10.00	25.00
COMMON CARD (1-20)	1.00	2.50
COA Certificate of Authenticity		

1998 Star Wars Metal Bounty Hunters

COMPLETE SET (5)	2.50	6.00
COMMON CARD (1-5)	1.00	2.50
HSJH Han Solo and Jabba the Hutt SE		

1995 Star Wars Metal Dark Empire I

COMPLETE SET (6)	3.00	8.00
COMMON CARD (1-6)	1.00	2.50

1996 Star Wars Metal Dark Empire II

COMPLETE SET (6)	3.00	8.00
COMMON CARD (1-6)	1.00	2.50

1998 Star Wars Metal Jedi Knights

COMPLETE SET (5)	3.00	8.00
COMMON CARD (1-5)	1.00	2.50
MES Mos Eisley Spaceport SE	1.50	4.00

1998 Star Wars Metal Jedi Knights Avon

COMPLETE SET (4)	3.00	8.00
COMMON CARD (1-4)	1.00	2.50
WIC Wampa Ice Creature SE	1.50	4.00

1997 Star Wars Metal Shadows of the Empire

COMPLETE SET (6)	4.00	10.00
COMMON CARD (1-6)	1.00	2.50

2015 Star Wars Micro Collector Packs

COMPLETE SET (36)	60.00	120.00
COMMON CARD (1-36)	1.50	4.00
NNO 3-D Glasses	.40	1.00

2015 Star Wars Micro Collector Packs 3-D Posters

COMPLETE SET (6)	3.00	8.00
COMMON CARD	.60	1.50
STATED ODDS 1:1		

2015 Star Wars Micro Collector Packs Micro-Comics

COMPLETE SET (6)	4.00	10.00
COMMON CARD	.75	2.00
STATED ODDS 1:1		

1996 Star Wars Multimotion

2M Star Wars 20th Anniversary Commemorative Magazine

1999 Star Wars The New Jedi Order

NNO SDCC Exclusive

2015 Star Wars NYCC Oversized Exclusives

COMPLETE SET (70)	75.00	150.00
COMMON CARD (1-70)	2.00	5.00

1995 Star Wars The Power of the Force

NNO Luke Skywalker

2011 Star Wars Power Plates

COMPLETE SET W/SP (30)	75.00	150.00
COMP.SET W/O SP (24)	50.00	100.00
UNOPENED BOX (48 PACKS)	120.00	150.00
UNOPENED PACK (1 PLATE)	2.50	8.00
COMMON PLATE	3.00	8.00
COMMON PLATE SP	5.00	12.00
SP STATED ODDS 1:8		

1999 Star Wars Preview Guide

NNO Pod Racers 5.00
(Orange County Register Exclusive)

1997 Star Wars Quality Bakers

COMPLETE SET (10)	12.00	30.00
COMMON CARD (1-10)	2.00	5.00

2016 Star Wars Rancho Obi-Wan Little Debbie

COMPLETE SET (12)	20.00	50.00
COMMON CARD (1-12)	2.50	6.00
STATED ODDS 1:1 BOXES OF STAR CRUNCH		

2015 Star Wars Rebels

COMPLETE SET (100)	6.00	15.00
UNOPENED BOX (24 PACKS)	40.00	50.00
UNOPENED PACK (6 CARDS)	2.00	2.50
COMMON CARD (1-100)	.12	.30
*FOIL: 2X TO 5X BASIC CARDS		

2015 Star Wars Rebels Stickers

COMPLETE SET (20)	5.00	12.00
COMMON CARD (1-20)	.40	1.00

2015 Star Wars Rebels Tattoos

COMPLETE SET (10)	6.00	15.00
COMMON CARD (1-10)	1.00	2.50
STATED ODDS 1:8		

2017 Star Wars Rebels Season 4 Preview Set

COMPLETE SET (25)
UNOPENED BOXED SET (27 CARDS)
COMMON CARD
*GREEN/50: X TO X BASIC CARDS
*PURPLE/25: X TO X BASIC CARDS
*SILVER/10: X TO X BASIC CARDS
*GOLD/5: UNPRICED DUE TO SCARCITY
*RED/1: UNPRICED DUE TO SCARCITY

1 Kanan Jarrus
2 Ezra Bridger
3 Hera Syndulla
4 Sabine Wren
5 Zeb Orrelios
6 Chopper
7 Rex
8 Ahsoka Tano
9 Darth Maul
10 The Grand Inquisitor
11 The Fifth Brother
12 The Seventh Sister
13 Tarkin
14 Lando Calrissian
15 Saw Gerrera
16 Obi-Wan Kenobi
17 Mon Mothma
18 Governor Pryce
19 Princess Leia Organa
20 Bail Organa
21 Bendu
22 Hondo Ohnaka
23 Agent Kallus
24 Grand Admiral Thrawn
25 Darth Vader

2017 Star Wars Rebels Season 4 Preview Set Autographs

COMMON CARD
*GREEN/50: X TO X BASIC CARDS
*PURPLE/25: X TO X BASIC CARDS
*SILVER/10: X TO X BASIC CARDS
*GOLD/5: UNPRICED DUE TO SCARCITY
*RED/1: UNPRICED DUE TO SCARCITY
STATED ODDS 1:1 PER BOX SET

NNO Freddie Prinze Jr.
NNO Taylor Gray
NNO Vanessa Marshall
NNO Tiya Sircar
NNO Steve Blum
NNO Ashley Eckstein
NNO Sam Witwer
NNO Jason Isaacs
NNO Philip Anthony Rodriguez
NNO Sarah Michelle Gellar
NNO Stephen Stanton
NNO Billy Dee Williams
NNO Forest Whitaker
NNO Stephen Stanton

NNO Genevieve OiReilly
NNO Mary Elizabeth McGlynn
NNO Phil Lamarr
NNO Tom Baker
NNO Jim Cummings

2014 Star Wars Rebels Subway Promos

COMPLETE SET (6)	6.00	15.00
COMMON CARD	1.50	4.00

2016 Star Wars Rogue One Mission Briefing

JYN ERSO

Produced by Topps. This trading card set is dedicated to the first stand alone Star Wars film, Rogue One. The card fronts are a retro homage to the 1983 Return of the Jedi set. They contain a red-bordered photo image from various Star Wars films while the backs also contain a retro design for ROTJ that includes narrative text and an illustration of the Death Star. The backs of cards 101-109 form a 9-card puzzle image while the back of card 110 contains a depiction of the entire puzzle image.

COMPLETE SET (110)	8.00	20.00
UNOPENED BOX (24 PACKS)	85.00	100.00
UNOPENED PACK (8 CARDS)	4.00	5.00
COMMON CARD (1-110)	.20	.50
*BLACK: .75X TO 2X BASIC CARDS	.40	1.00
*GREEN: 1.2X TO 3X BASIC CARDS	.60	1.50
*BLUE: 1.5X TO 4X BASIC CARDS	.75	2.00
*GRAY/100: 8X TO 20X BASIC CARDS	4.00	10.00
*GOLD/50: 12X TO 30X BASIC CARDS	6.00	15.00
*ORANGE/1: UNPRICED DUE TO SCARCITY		
*P.P.BLACK/1: UNPRICED DUE TO SCARCITY		
*P.P.CYAN/1: UNPRICED DUE TO SCARCITY		
*P.P.MAGENTA/1: UNPRICED DUE TO SCARCITY		
*P.P.YELLOW/1: UNPRICED DUE TO SCARCITY		

2016 Star Wars Rogue One Mission Briefing Autographs

JASON ISAACS

AS THE GRAND INQUISITOR

COMMON CARD	6.00	15.00
*BLACK/50: .6X TO 1.5X BASIC AUTOS		
*BLUE/25: 1.2X TO 3X BASIC AUTOS		
*GOLD/10: UNPRICED DUE TO SCARCITY		

NNO	Adrienne Wilkinson	12.00	30.00
NNO	Al Lampert	10.00	25.00
NNO	Anna Graves	15.00	40.00
NNO	Anthony Daniels		
NNO	Ashley Eckstein		
NNO	Barbara Frankland	10.00	25.00
NNO	Billy Dee Williams		
NNO	Brian Blessed	8.00	20.00
NNO	Candice Orwell	12.00	30.00
NNO	Caroline Blakiston		
NNO	Carrie Fisher		
NNO	Catherine Taber		
NNO	Clive Revill	12.00	30.00
NNO	Corey Dee Williams	10.00	25.00
NNO	Dave Barclay		
NNO	David Ankrum	10.00	25.00
NNO	Deep Roy		
NNO	Denis Lawson	15.00	40.00
NNO	Dermot Crowley		
NNO	Eric Lopez	10.00	25.00
NNO	Femi Taylor	8.00	20.00
NNO	Freddie Prinze Jr.		
NNO	Garrick Hagon	10.00	25.00
NNO	George Roubicek	10.00	25.00
NNO	George Takei		
NNO	Glyn Baker	10.00	25.00
NNO	Harrison Ford		
NNO	Hugh Quarshie		
NNO	Ian Liston	10.00	25.00
NNO	Ian McDiarmid		
NNO	Jack Klaff	8.00	20.00
NNO	Jason Isaacs		
NNO	Jeremy Bulloch		
NNO	Jett Lucas		
NNO	Jim Cummings	12.00	30.00
NNO	John Coppinger	15.00	40.00
NNO	John Ratzenberger	10.00	25.00
NNO	Julian Glover		
NNO	Kath Soucie	15.00	40.00
NNO	Kenneth Colley	8.00	20.00
NNO	Kenny Baker		
NNO	Lloyd Sherr	10.00	25.00
NNO	Mark Dodson		
NNO	Mark Hamill		
NNO	Mary Oyaya		
NNO	Matthew Wood	12.00	30.00
NNO	Megan Udall	10.00	25.00
NNO	Mercedes Ngoh	8.00	20.00
NNO	Meredith Salenger	15.00	40.00
NNO	Michael Carter		
NNO	Michaela Cottrell	8.00	20.00
NNO	Mike Edmonds	12.00	30.00
NNO	Oliver Walpole	10.00	25.00
NNO	Paul Blake		
NNO	Paul Springer	12.00	30.00
NNO	Phil Lamarr		
NNO	Rajia Baroudi	12.00	30.00
NNO	Ray Park	15.00	40.00
NNO	Rich Oldfield	15.00	40.00
NNO	Rusty Goffe	10.00	25.00
NNO	Sam Witwer	15.00	40.00
NNO	Scott Capurro	12.00	30.00
NNO	Sean Crawford	10.00	25.00
NNO	Stephen Stanton	8.00	20.00
NNO	Taylor Gray		
NNO	Tim Rose		
NNO	Tom Kane	8.00	20.00
NNO	Tom Kenny	15.00	40.00
NNO	Warwick Davis		
NNO	Wayne Pygram	10.00	25.00

2016 Star Wars Rogue One Mission Briefing Character Foil

COMPLETE SET (9)	12.00	20.00
COMMON CARD (1-9)	2.00	5.00

*P.P.BLACK/1: UNPRICED DUE TO SCARCITY
*P.P.CYAN/1: UNPRICED DUE TO SCARCITY
*P.P.MAGENTA/1: UNPRICED DUE TO SCARCITY
*P.P.YELLOW/1: UNPRICED DUE TO SCARCITY
STATED ODDS 1:8

2016 Star Wars Rogue One Mission Briefing Comic Strips Inserts

COMPLETE SET (12)	8.00	20.00
COMMON CARD (1-12)	1.25	3.00

*P.P.BLACK/1: UNPRICED DUE TO SCARCITY
*P.P.CYAN/1: UNPRICED DUE TO SCARCITY
*P.P.MAGENTA/1: UNPRICED DUE TO SCARCITY
*P.P.YELLOW/1: UNPRICED DUE TO SCARCITY

2016-17 Star Wars Rogue One Mission Briefing Darth Vader Continuity

COMMON CARD (1-15)	3.00	8.00
MISSION BRIEFING (1-5)		
SERIES ONE (6-10)		
SERIES TWO (11-15)		

*P.P.BLACK/1: UNPRICED DUE TO SCARCITY
*P.P.CYAN/1: UNPRICED DUE TO SCARCITY
*P.P.MAGENTA/1: UNPRICED DUE TO SCARCITY
*P.P.YELLOW/1: UNPRICED DUE TO SCARCITY
STATED ODDS 1:12

2016 Star Wars Rogue One Mission Briefing The Death Star

COMPLETE SET (9)	6.00	15.00
COMMON CARD (1-9)	.75	2.00

*P.P.BLACK/1: UNPRICED DUE TO SCARCITY
*P.P.CYAN/1: UNPRICED DUE TO SCARCITY
*P.P.MAGENTA/1: UNPRICED DUE TO SCARCITY
*P.P.YELLOW/1: UNPRICED DUE TO SCARCITY
STATED ODDS 1:4

2016 Star Wars Rogue One Mission Briefing Dual Autographs

STATED PRINT RUN 3 SER.#'d SETS
UNPRICED DUE TO SCARCITY

1 C.Fisher
C.Blakiston
2 M.Hamill
D.Lawson

2016 Star Wars Rogue One Mission Briefing Heroes of the Rebel Alliance

COMPLETE SET (9)	10.00	25.00
COMMON CARD (1-9)	1.50	3.00

*P.P.BLACK/1: UNPRICED DUE TO SCARCITY
*P.P.CYAN/1: UNPRICED DUE TO SCARCITY
*P.P.MAGENTA/1: UNPRICED DUE TO SCARCITY
*P.P.YELLOW/1: UNPRICED DUE TO SCARCITY
STATED ODDS 1:8

1	Luke Skywalker	2.00	5.00
2	Princess Leia	2.00	5.00
3	Han Solo	2.00	5.00
4	Chewbacca	1.50	4.00
6	Obi-Wan Kenobi	1.50	4.00
7	R2-D2	1.50	4.00

2016 Star Wars Rogue One Mission Briefing Mission Briefing Monday

COMPLETE SET (36)	150.00	300.00
COMMON CARD	6.00	15.00
NOV.7, 2016 (MBME1-MBME6)/206*		
NOV.14, 2016 (MBM1-MBM5)/226*		
NOV.21, 2016 (MBM6-MBM10)/218*		
NOV.28, 2016 (MBM11-MBM15)/212*		
DEC.5, 2016 (MBM16-MBM20)/224*		
DEC.12, 2016 (MBM21-MBM25)/234*		
DEC.19, 2016 (MBM26-MBM30)/252*		

2016 Star Wars Rogue One Mission Briefing Montages

COMPLETE SET (9)	15.00	40.00
COMMON CARD (1-9)	3.00	8.00

*P.P.BLACK/1: UNPRICED DUE TO SCARCITY
*P.P.CYAN/1: UNPRICED DUE TO SCARCITY
*P.P.MAGENTA/1: UNPRICED DUE TO SCARCITY
*P.P.YELLOW/1: UNPRICED DUE TO SCARCITY
STATED ODDS 1:24

1	Storming the Beach	3.00	8.00
2	Imperial Assault	3.00	8.00
3	Jyn Erso	5.00	12.00
4	Within Rebel Base	3.00	8.00
5	Patrol of the Empire	3.00	8.00
6	Fearsome Death Trooper	3.00	8.00
7	Director Krennic	3.00	8.00
8	In Flames	3.00	8.00
9	Rebel Ensemble	3.00	8.00

2016 Star Wars Rogue One Mission Briefing NYCC Exclusives

_K-2SO_

COMPLETE SET (10)	12.00	30.00
COMMON CARD (E1-E10)	2.00	5.00
2016 NYCC EXCLUSIVE		

2016 Star Wars Rogue One Mission Briefing Patches

COMPLETE SET (12)	50.00	100.00
COMMON CARD (M1-M12)	3.00	8.00
*GRAY/100: .75X TO 2X BASIC CARDS		
*GOLD/50: 1.5X TO 4X BASIC CARDS		
*RED/10: 3X TO 8X BASIC CARDS		
STATED ODDS 1:26		
MP1 Jyn Erso	6.00	15.00
MP3 L-1 Droid	5.00	12.00
MP4 Admiral Raddus	4.00	10.00
MP6 TIE Fighter Pilot	4.00	10.00
MP7 Shoretrooper	4.00	10.00
MP10 Captain Cassian Andor	5.00	12.00
MP11 Bistan	4.00	10.00

2016 Star Wars Rogue One Mission Briefing Quad Autograph

STATED PRINT RUN 2 SER.#'d SETS
UNPRICED DUE TO SCARCITY

1 Hamill
Lawson
  Klaff
  Hagon

2016 Star Wars Rogue One Mission Briefing Sketches

COMPLETE ARTIST LIST (33)
UNPRICED DUE TO SCARCITY

1 Alex Iniguez
2 Angelina Benedetti
3 Bill Pulkovski
4 Brad Hudson
5 Brent Ragland
6 Brian Kong
7 Carlos Cabaleiro
8 Chris Meeks
9 Dan Parsons
10 Danny Haas
11 Darrin Pepe
12 Eric Lehtonen
13 Francois Chartier
14 Hayden Davis
15 Ingrid Hardy
16 James Henry Smith
17 Jamie Cosley
18 Jason Bommer
19 Jason Sobol
20 Jeff Mallinson
21 Jessica Hickman
22 Jonathan Caustrita
23 Kevin Liell
24 Kevin P. West
25 Kyle Babbitt
26 Marcia Dye
27 Matt Stewart
28 Rob Teranishi
29 Robert Hendrickson
30 Roy Cover
31 Solly Mohamed
32 Stephanie Swanger
33 Tina Berardi

2016 Star Wars Rogue One Mission Briefing Stickers

DEATH TROOPER

COMPLETE SET (18)	10.00	25.00
COMMON CARD (1-18)	1.00	2.50
*P.P.BLACK/1: UNPRICED DUE TO SCARCITY		
*P.P.CYAN/1: UNPRICED DUE TO SCARCITY		
*P.P.MAGENTA/1: UNPRICED DUE TO SCARCITY		
*P.P.YELLOW/1: UNPRICED DUE TO SCARCITY		
STATED ODDS 1:12		
1 Jyn Erso	1.50	4.00
13 Darth Vader	2.00	5.00

2016 Star Wars Rogue One Mission Briefing Triple Autographs

STATED PRINT RUN 3 SER.#'d SETS
UNPRICED DUE TO SCARCITY

1 Fisher
Blakiston
  Crowley
2 Hamill
Lawson
  Hagon

2016 Star Wars Rogue One Mission Briefing Villains of the Galactic Empire

GENERAL VEERS
VILLAINS OF THE GALACTIC EMPIRE

COMPLETE SET (8)	8.00	20.00
COMMON CARD (1-8)	1.25	3.00
*P.P.BLACK/1: UNPRICED DUE TO SCARCITY		
*P.P.CYAN/1: UNPRICED DUE TO SCARCITY		
*P.P.MAGENTA/1: UNPRICED DUE TO SCARCITY		
*P.P.YELLOW/1: UNPRICED DUE TO SCARCITY		
STATED ODDS 1:8		
1 Darth Vader	1.25	5.00

1999 Star Wars Sci-Fi Expo Celebrity Promos

P1 Garrick Hagon	8.00	20.00
(Biggs Darklighter)		
P2 Peter Mayhew	8.00	20.00
(Chewbacca)		

2003 Star Wars SDCC Exhibitor Promos

1 Boba Fett
2 Yoda
3 bald woman
4 character shootout

1997 Star Wars SE Trilogy 3-D Doritos Discs

COMPLETE SET (20)	5.00	12.00
COMMON CARD	.40	1.00

1997 Star Wars SE Trilogy 3-D Doritos-Cheetos

COMPLETE SET (6)	3.00	8.00
COMMON CARD (1-6)	.75	2.00

1996 Star Wars Shadows of the Empire

The artwork of the Brothers Hildebrandt highlight this painted set featuring characters from the novel of the same name (which is set between The Empire Strikes Back and Return of the Jedi).The insert cards for this set are interestingly numbered as part of the base set.

COMPLETE SET (100)	15.00	40.00
COMMON CARD (1-72, 83-100)	.15	.40
COMMON ETCHED (73-78)	2.00	5.00
COMMON EMBOSSED (79-82)	3.00	8.00
73-78 STATED ODDS 1:9		
79-82 STATED ODDS 1:18		

1996 Star Wars Shadows of the Empire Promos

SOTE1 Xizor	2.00	5.00
SOTE2 Darth Vader	2.00	5.00
SOTE3 Luke Skywalker	2.00	5.00

SOTE4 Dash Rendar & Leebo	2.00	5.00
SOTE5 Boba Fett	8.00	15.00
(Convention Exclusive)		
SOTE6 Guri	2.00	5.00
SOTE7 C-3PO & R2-D2	2.00	5.00
NNO Reservation Coupon		
(Shop Exclusive)		
NNO SOTE3-SOTE1 (Luke Skywalker/Darth Vader)		

1996 Star Wars Shadows of the Empire Xizor Promos

SOTE Foil Background w/Line Pattern Embossing		
SOTE Foil Background w/Ripple Pattern Embossing		
SOTE Foil w/Line Pattern Embossing		
SOTE Non-Foil Background w/Line Pattern Embossing		
SOTE Non-Foil Background w/Ripple Pattern Embossing		

1997 Star Wars Stickers US

COMPLETE SET (66)	7.50	20.00
COMMON CARD (1-66)	.20	.50
PRODUCED BY PANINI		

1997 Star Wars Trilogy The Complete Story

The Emperor's Lightning

COMPLETE SET (72)	6.00	15.00
COMMON CARD (1-72)	.25	.60
0 Promo	1.00	2.00

1997 Star Wars Trilogy The Complete Story Laser

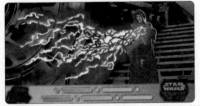

COMPLETE SET (6)	6.00	15.00
COMMON CARD (LC1-LC6)	1.25	3.00
STATED ODDS 1:9		

1997 Star Wars Trilogy Merlin

Produced and issued in England by Merlin Productions, this set features full-bleed photo images from the films with narrative text and an additional image on the back of each card. The cards cover all three films with each one having its own subset: A New Hope (1-35), Empire Strikes Back (36-70), and Return of the Jedi (71-105). Additional subsets include: Character Profiles (106-115) and Vehicle Profiles (116-124). The checklist (125) rounds out the set. No inserts were produced for this release.

COMPLETE SET (125)	10.00	25.00
UNOPENED BOX (48 PACKS)	25.00	40.00
UNOPENED PACK (5 CARDS)	1.00	1.25
COMMON CARD (1-125)	.15	.40

1997 Star Wars Trilogy Merlin Case-Toppers

COMPLETE SET (3)	20.00	50.00
COMMON CARD (P1-P3)	8.00	20.00
STATED ODDS 1:CASE		

1997 Star Wars Trilogy Special Edition

Produced by Topps, this was the second version of the Trilogy set and it was only available as a hobby issue. All three of the original Star Wars re-releases are featured. The card fronts feature mostly photo images with some production art. The card backs feature production notes and film facts with an additional image that differs from that on the fronts. A holographic foil stamp is included on the fronts and the images are bordered from top to bottom with gold ink. The cards measure 4 5/8 by 2 1/2 inches (11.9 by 6.3 cm). Artwork by Tyruben Ellingson, George Hull, Claudia Mullaly, Derek Thompson, and Terryl Whitlatch.

| COMPLETE SET (72) | 6.00 | 15.00 |
| UNOPENED BOX (36 PACKS) | 80.00 | 100.00 |

UNOPENED PACK (9 CARDS)	2.50	3.00
COMMON CARD (1-72)	.15	.40
13D ISSUED AS BOX TOPPER		
13D X-Wings Departing	6.00	15.00

1997 Star Wars Trilogy Special Edition Holograms

COMPLETE SET (2)	10.00	25.00
COMMON CARD (1-2)	6.00	15.00
STATED ODDS 1:18		

1997 Star Wars Trilogy Special Edition Laser

COMPLETE SET (6)	6.00	15.00
COMMON CARD (LC1-LC6)	1.25	3.00
STATED ODDS 1:9		

1997 Star Wars Trilogy Special Edition Promos

P1 Three Stormtroopers	4.00	10.00
P2 Jabba at the Falcon	1.25	3.00
P3 X-Wings	1.25	3.00
P4 Sandcrawler	3.00	8.00
P5 Jawa and Landspeeder	3.00	8.00
P6 Millennium Falcon	3.00	8.00
P7 Landspeeder	1.25	3.00
P8 3 Aliens Singing	1.25	3.00

1997 Star Wars Trilogy Special Edition Holland Promos

NNO Millennium Falcon		
NNO Mos Eisley		
NNO X-Wings		

1997 Star Wars Trilogy Special Edition Kenner Promos

H1 Millennium Falcon	4.00	10.00
H2 Rebel Pyramid	4.00	10.00
H3 Han and Jabba	4.00	10.00
H4 Robot Mechanics	4.00	10.00

1997 Star Wars Trilogy Special Edition Micro Machine Promos

G1 X-Wing w/R2-D2	4.00	10.00
G2 X-Wing and TIE Fighter	4.00	10.00
G3 Landspeeder	4.00	10.00
G4 Town	4.00	10.00
G5 Jawa on Creature	4.00	10.00

1997 Star Wars Trilogy Special Edition Frito Lay

1 Han and Chewbacca make…
2 Luke again faces his father…
3 An X-Wing, the most…
4 The starships and fighters…
5 Darth Vader's shuttle…
6 Han takes aim…

1997 Star Wars Trilogy Special Edition TV Week Magazine Australian

1 Darth Vader…
2 Luke Rescues Leia…
3 C-3PO & R2-D2…
4 Friends and Fighters…

1997 Star Wars Trilogy Theater Promos Thai

| NNO Star Wars | | |
| NNO The Empire Strikes Back | | |

| NNO Return of the Jedi | | |
| NNO The Star Wars Trilogy | | |

1997 Star Wars Vehicles

Produced by Topps/Top Cow Productions. The various modes of transportation seen in the original three Star Wars films are depicted here, drawn by various comic book artists. The backs have information about the vehicles depicted. The base set has a metallic finish, as well as a small foil stamp. Artwork by Joe Benitez, Nathan Cabrera, Anthony Chun, David Detrick, Jeff Do Los Santos, D-Tron, David Finch, Trent Kaniuga, Victor Llamas, Chris Moeller, Brandon Peterson, Bobby Rubio, Marc Silvestri, Aaron Sowd, Billy Tan, and Michael Turner.

COMPLETE SET (72)	5.00	12.00
UNOPENED BOX (36 PACKS)	40.00	50.00
UNOPENED PACK (5 CARDS)	1.25	1.50
COMMON CARD (1-72)	.15	.40

1997 Star Wars Vehicles 3-D

COMPLETE SET (3)	25.00	60.00
COMMON CARD	8.00	20.00
STATED ODDS 1:36		
3 Princess Leia	15.00	40.00
Luke Skywalker		

1997 Star Wars Vehicles Cut-Away

X-WING

COMPLETE SET (4)	7.50	20.00
COMMON CARD (C1-C4)	2.50	6.00
STATED ODDS 1:18		

1997 Star Wars Vehicles Promos

P1A Darth Vader & Stormtroopers on Speeder Bikes chromium)/3200*	12.00	30.00
P1B Darth Vader & Stormtroopers on Speeder Bikes (refractor)/320*	30.00	75.00
P2A Stormtroopers on Speeder Bikes (chromium)/1600*	20.00	50.00
P2B Stormtroopers on Speeder Bikes (refractor)/160*	50.00	100.00
NNO 2-Card Sheet		

TCG

1995 Star Wars Premiere

COMPLETE SET (324) 75.00 150.00
BOOSTER BOX (36 PACKS) 75.00 150.00
BOOSTER PACK (15 CARDS) 3.00 6.00
RELEASED IN DECEMBER 1995

1 5D6-RA-7 (Fivedesix) R1 1.25 3.00
2 Admiral Motti R2 .75 2.00
3 Chief Bast U1 .30 .75
4 Colonel Wullf Yularen U1 .30 .75
5 Commander Praji U2 .30 .75
6 Darth Vader R1 .30 .75
7 Dathcha U1 3.00 8.00
8 Death Star Trooper C2 10.00 25.00
9 Djas Puhr R2 .30 .75
10 Dr. Evazan R2 .12 .30
11 DS-61-2 U1 .75 2.00
12 DS-61-3 R1 .75 2.00
13 EG-6 (Eegee-Six) U2 .30 .75
14 Feltipern Trevagg U1 .75 2.00
15 Garindan R2 .75 2.00
16 General Tagge R2 .75 2.00
17 Grand Moff Tarkin R1 3.00 8.00
18 Imperial Pilot C2 .12 .30
19 Imperial Trooper Guard C2 .12 .30
20 Jawa DARK C2 .12 .30
21 Kitik Keed'kak R1 1.25 3.00
22 Labria R2 .12 .30
23 Lieutenant Tanbris U2 .75 2.00
24 LIN-V8M (Elleyein-Veeateemm) C1 .30 .75
25 Miiiyoom Onith U2 .30 .75
26 MSE-6 ëMousei Droid U1 .30 .75
27 Myo R2 .75 2.00
28 Ponda Baba U1 .30 .75
29 Prophetess U1 .30 .75
30 R1-G4 (Arone-Geefour) C2 .12 .30
31 R4-M9 (Arfour-Emmnine) C2 .12 .30
32 Stormtrooper C3 .12 .30
33 Tonnika Sisters R1 1.25 3.00
34 Tusken Raider C2 .12 .30
35 WED-9-M1 ëBanthai Droid R2 .75 2.00
36 Wuher U2 .30 .75
37 Blaster Scope C2 .30 .75
38 Caller DARK U2 .30 .75
39 Comlink C1 .12 .30
40 Droid Detector C2 .12 .30
41 Fusion Generator Supply Tanks DARK C2 .12 .30
42 Observation Holocam U2 .30 .75
43 Restraining Bolt DARK C2 .30 .75
44 Stormtrooper Backpack C2 .30 .75
45 Stormtrooper Utility Belt C2 .30 .75
46 A Disturbance In The Force U1 .30 .75
47 Baniss Keeg C2 .30 .75
48 Blast Door Controls U2 .30 .75

49 Blaster Rack U1 .30 .75
50 Dark Hours U2 .30 .75
51 Death Star Sentry U1 .30 .75
52 Disarmed DARK R1 1.25 3.00
53 Expand The Empire R1 1.25 3.00
54 Fear Will Keep Them In Line R2 .75 2.00
55 I Find Your Lack Of Faith Disturbing R1 1.25 3.00
56 I'ive Lost Artoo! U1 .30 .75
57 Jawa Pack U1 .30 .75
58 Juri Juice R2 .75 2.00
59 Ket Maliss C2 .12 .30
60 Lateral Damage R2 .75 2.00
61 Luke? Luuuuke! U1 .30 .75
62 Macroscan C2 .12 .30
63 Molator R1 1.25 3.00
64 Organa's Ceremonial Necklace R1 1.25 3.00
65 Presence Of The Force R1 1.25 3.00
66 Reactor Terminal U2 .30 .75
67 Send A Detachment Down R1 1.25 3.00
68 Sunsdown U1 .30 .75
69 Tactical Re-Call R2 .75 2.00
70 Wrong Turn U1 .30 .75
71 Your Eyes Can Deceive You U1 1.25 3.00
72 Alter DARK U1 .30 .75
73 Boring Conversation Anyway R1 1.25 3.00
74 Charming To The Last R2 .75 2.00
75 Collateral Damage C2 .12 .30
76 Counter Assault C1 .12 .30
77 Dark Collaboration R1 1.25 3.00
78 Dark Jedi Presence R1 4.00 10.00
79 Dark Maneuvers C2 .12 .30
80 Dead Jawa C2 .12 .30
81 Elis Helrot U2 .30 .75
82 Emergency Deployment U1 .30 .75
83 Evacuate? U2 .30 .75
84 Full Scale Alert U2 .30 .75
85 Gravel Storm U2 .30 .75
86 I Have You Now R2 .75 2.00
87 Imperial Barrier DARK C2 .12 .30
88 Imperial Code Cylinder C2 .12 .30
89 Imperial Reinforcements C1 .12 .30
90 It's Worse C2 .12 .30
91 I've Got A Problem Here C2 .12 .30
92 Kintan Strider C1 .12 .30
93 Limited Resources U2 .30 .75
94 Local Trouble R1 1.25 3.00
95 Lone Pilot R2 .75 2.00
96 Lone Warrior R2 .75 2.00
97 Look Sir, Droids R1 1.25 3.00
98 Moment Of Triumph R2 .75 2.00
99 Nevar Yalnal R2 .75 2.00
100 Ommni Box C2 .12 .30
101 Overload C2 .12 .30
102 Physical Choke R1 1.25 3.00
103 Precise Attack C2 .12 .30
104 Scanning Crew C2 .12 .30
105 Sense DARK U1 .30 .75
106 Set For Stun C2 .12 .30
107 Takeel C2 .12 .30
108 Tallon Roll C2 .12 .30
109 The Circle Is Now Complete R1 1.25 3.00
110 The Empire's Back U1 .30 .75
111 Trinto Duaba U1 .30 .75
112 Trooper Charge U2 .30 .75
113 Tusken Scavengers C2 .12 .30
114 Utinni! DARK R1 1.25 3.00
115 Vader's Eye R1 1.25 3.00
116 We're All Gonna Be A Lot Thinner! R11.25 3.00
117 You Overestimate Their Chances C1 .30 .75
118 Your Powers Are Weak, Old Man R1 .12 .30

119 Alderaan DARK R1 1.25 3.00
120 Dantooine DARK U1 .30 .75
121 Death Star: Central Core U2 .30 .75
122 Death Star: Detention Block Corridor C1 .12 .30
123 Death Star: Docking Bay 327 DARK C2 .12 .30
124 Death Star: Level 4 Military Corridor U1 .30 .75
125 Death Star: War Room U2 .30 .75
126 Kessel U2 .75 2.00
127 Tatooine DARK C2 .12 .30
128 Tatooine: Cantina DARK R2 .75 2.00
129 Tatooine: Docking Bay 94 DARK C2 .12 .30
130 Tatooine: Jawa Camp DARK C1 .12 .30
131 Tatooine: Jundland Wastes C1 .12 .30
132 Tatooine: Larsí Moisture Farm DARK C1 .12 .30
133 Tatooine: Mos Eisley DARK C1 .12 .30
134 Yavin 4 DARK C2 .12 .30
135 Yavin 4: Docking Bay DARK C2 .12 .30
136 Yavin 4: Jungle DARK U1 .30 .75
137 Black 2 R1 2.50 6.00
138 Black 3 U1 .30 .75
139 Devastator R1 2.50 6.00
140 Imperial-Class Star Destroyer U1 .75 2.00
141 TIE Advanced x1 U2 .30 .75
142 TIE Fighter C2 .12 .30
143 TIE Scout C2 .12 .30
144 Vader's Custom TIE R1 4.00 10.00
145 Bantha U2 .30 .75
146 Lift Tube DARK C2 .12 .30
147 Sandcrawler DARK R2 .75 2.00
148 Ubrikkian 9000 Z001 C2 .12 .30
149 Assault Rifle R2 .75 2.00
150 Blaster Rifle DARK C1 .12 .30
151 Boosted TIE Cannon U1 .30 .75
152 Dark Jedi Lightsaber U1 .40 1.00
153 Gaderffii Stick C2 .12 .30
154 Han Seeker R2 .75 2.00
155 Imperial Blaster DARK C2 .12 .30
156 Ion Cannon U1 .30 .75
157 Laser Projector U2 .30 .75
158 Light Repeating Blaster Rifle R1 1.25 3.00
159 Luke Seeker R2 .75 2.00
160 Timer Mine DARK C2 .12 .30
161 Turbolaser Battery R2 .75 2.00
162 Vader's Lightsaber R1 3.00 8.00
163 2X-3KPR (Tooex) U1 .30 .75
164 Beru Lars U2 .30 .75
165 Biggs Darklighter R2 .75 2.00
166 BoShek U1 .30 .75
167 C-3PO (See-Threepio) R1 3.00 8.00
168 CZ-3 (Seezee-Three) C1 .12 .30
169 Dice Ibegon R2 .75 2.00
170 Dutch R1 2.50 6.00
171 Figrin D'an U2 .30 .75
172 General Dodonna U1 .30 .75
173 Han Solo R1 5.00 12.00
174 Jawa LIGHT C2 .12 .30
175 Jek Porkins U1 .30 .75
176 Kabe U1 .30 .75
177 KaliFalnl Cindros R1 1.25 3.00
178 Leesub Sirln R2 .12 .30
179 Leia Organa R1 .30 .75
180 LIN-V8K (Elleyein-Veeatekay) C1 4.00 10.00
181 Luke Skywalker R1 6.00 15.00
182 Momaw Nadon C2 .30 .75
183 Obi-Wan Kenobi R1 4.00 10.00
184 Owen Lars U1 .30 .75
185 Pops U1 .30 .75

186 R2-X2 (Artoo-Extoo) C2 .12 .30
187 R4-E1 (Arfour-Eeone) C2 .12 .30
188 Rebel Guard C2 .12 .30
189 Rebel Pilot C2 .12 .30
190 Rebel Trooper C3 .12 .30
191 Red Leader R1 2.50 6.00
192 Shistavanen Wolfman C2 .12 .30
193 Talz C2 .12 .30
194 WED-9-M1 'Bantha' Droid R2 .75 2.00
195 Wioslea U1 .30 .75
196 Caller LIGHT U2 .30 .75
197 Electrobinoculars C2 .12 .30
198 Fusion Generator Supply Tanks LIGHT C2 .12 .30
199 Hydroponics Station U2 .30 .75
200 Restraining Bolt LIGHT C2 .12 .30
201 Targeting Computer U1 .30 .75
202 Tatooine Utility Belt C2 .12 .30
203 Vaporator C2 .12 .30
204 A Tremor In The Force U1 .30 .75
205 Affect Mind R1 1.25 3.00
206 Beggar R1 1.25 3.00
207 Crash Site Memorial U1 .30 .75
208 Death Star Plans R1 1.25 3.00
209 Demotion R2 .75 2.00
210 Disarmed Light R1 1.25 3.00
211 Ellorrs Madak C2 .12 .30
212 Eyes In The Dark U1 .30 .75
213 Jawa Siesta U1 .30 .75
214 Kessel LIGHT U2 1.25 3.00
215 K'lor'slug R1 .30 .75
216 Lightsaber Proficiency R1 1.25 3.00
217 Mantellian Savrip R2 .75 2.00
218 Nightfall U1 .30 .75
219 Obi-Wan's Cape R1 .30 .75
220 Our Most Desperate Hour R1 1.25 3.00
221 Plastoid Armor U2 .30 .75
222 Rebel Planners R2 .75 2.00
223 Restricted Deployment U1 .30 .75
224 Revolution R1 1.25 3.00
225 Rycar Ryjerd U1 .30 .75
226 Sai'torr Kal Fas C2 .12 .30
227 Special Modifications U1 .30 .75
228 Traffic Control U2 .30 .75
229 Tusken Breath Mask U1 .30 .75
230 Yavin Sentry U2 .30 .75
231 Yerka Mig U1 .12 .30
232 A Few Maneuvers C2 .12 .30
233 Alter LIGHT U1 .30 .75
234 Beru Stew U2 .30 .75
235 Cantina Brawl R1 1.25 3.00
236 Collision! C2 .12 .30
237 Combined Attack C2 .12 .30
238 Don't Get Cocky R1 1.25 3.00
239 Don't Underestimate Our Chances C1 .12 .30
240 Droid Shutdown C2 .12 .30
241 Escape Pod U2 .30 .75
242 Friendly Fire C2 .12 .30
243 Full Throttle R2 .75 2.00
244 Gift Of The Mentor R1 1.25 3.00
245 Hanís Back U2 .30 .75
246 Hanís Dice C2 .12 .30
247 Hear Me Baby, Hold Together C2 .12 .30
248 Help Me Obi-Wan Kenobi R1 1.25 3.00
249 How Did We Get Into This Mess? U2 .30 .75
250 Hyper Escape C2 .12 .30
251 Into The Garbage Chute, Flyboy R2 .12 .30
252 It Could Be Worse C2 .75 2.00
253 I've Got A Bad Feeling About This C2 .12 .30
254 Jedi Presence R1 1.25 3.00
255 Krayt Dragon Howl R1 1.25 3.00

256 Leia's Back U2 .30 .75
257 Luke's Back U2 .30 .75
258 Move Along... R1 1.25 3.00
259 Nabrun Leids U2 .30 .75
260 Narrow Escape C2 .12 .30
261 Noble Sacrifice R2 .75 2.00
262 Old Ben C2 .12 .30
263 On The Edge R2 .75 2.00
264 Out Of Nowhere U2 .30 .75
265 Panic U1 .30 .75
266 Radar Scanner C2 .12 .30
267 Rebel Barrier C2 .12 .30
268 Rebel Reinforcements C1 .12 .30
269 Return Of A Jedi U2 .30 .75
270 Scomp Link Access C2 .12 .30
271 Sense LIGHT U1 .30 .75
272 Skywalkers R1 1.25 3.00
273 Solo Han R2 .75 2.00
274 Spaceport Speeders U2 .30 .75
275 Surprise Assault C1 .12 .30
276 Thank The Maker R2 .75 2.00
277 The Bith Shuffle C2 .12 .30
278 The Force Is Strong With This One R2 .75 2.00
279 This Is All Your Fault U1 .30 .75
280 Utinni! LIGHT R1 1.25 3.00
281 Warriorís Courage R2 .75 2.00
282 Weíre Doomed C2 .12 .30
283 Alderaan LIGHT U2 .75 2.00
284 Dantooine LIGHT U1 .30 .75
285 Death Star: Detention Block Control Room U2 .30 .75
286 Death Star: Docking Bay 327 LIGHT C2 .12 .30
287 Death Star: Trash Compactor U1 .30 .75
288 Kessel LIGHT U2 .30 .75
289 Tatooine LIGHT C2 .12 .30
290 Tatooine: Cantina LIGHT R2 .75 2.00
291 Tatooine: Docking Bay 94 LIGHT C2 .12 .30
292 Tatooine: Dune Sea C1 .12 .30
293 Tatooine: Jawa Camp LIGHTC1 .12 .30
294 Tatooine: Larsí Moisture Farm LIGHT U2 .30 .75
295 Tatooine: Mos Eisley LIGHT U2 .30 .75
296 Tatooine: Obi-Wanís Hut R1 1.25 3.00
297 Yavin 4 C2 .12 .30
298 Yavin 4: Docking Bay LIGHT C1 .12 .30
299 Yavin 4: Jungle LIGHT C2 1.25 3.00
300 Yavin 4: Massassi Throne Room R1 .30 .75
301 Yavin 4: Massassi War Room U2 .30 .75
302 Corellian Corvette U2 .40 1.00
303 Gold 1 R2 .75 2.00
304 Gold 5 R2 .75 2.00
305 Millenium Falcon R1 3.00 8.00
306 Red 1 U1 .30 .75
307 Red 3 R2 .75 2.00
308 X-wing C2 .12 .30
309 Y-wing C2 .12 .30
310 Lift Tube LIGHT C2 .12 .30
311 Luke's X-34 Landspeeder U2 .30 .75
312 Sandcrawler LIGHT R2 .75 2.00
313 SoroSuub V-35 Landspeeder C2 .12 .30
314 Blaster C2 .12 .30
315 Blaster Rifle LIGHT C2 .12 .30
316 Hanís Heavy Blaster Pistol R2 .75 2.00
317 Jedi Lightsaber U1 .30 .75
318 Leiaís Sporting Blaster U1 .30 .75
319 Obi-Wanís Lightsaber R1 2.50 6.00
320 Proton Torpedoes C2 .12 .30
321 Quad Laser Cannon U1 .30 .75
322 Tagge Seeker R2 .75 2.00
323 Tarkin Seeker R2 .75 2.00
324 Timer Mine LIGHT C2 .12 .30

1996 Star Wars Hoth

COMPLETE SET (163)	50.00	100.00
BOOSTER BOX (36 PACKS)	50.00	100.00
BOOSTER PACK (15 CARDS)	2.00	4.00
RELEASED IN NOVEMBER 1996		
1 AT-AT Driver C2	.12	.30
2 Admiral Ozzel R1	1.25	3.00
3 Captain Lennox U1	.40	1.00
4 Captain Piett R2	1.25	3.00
5 FX-10 (Effex-ten) C2	.12	.30
6 General Veers R1	3.00	8.00
7 Imperial Gunner C2	.12	.30
8 Lieutenant Cabbel U2	.40	1.00
9 Probe Droid C2	.12	.30
10 Snowtrooper C3	.12	.30
11 Snowtrooper Officer C1	.12	.30
12 Wampa R2	1.25	3.00
13 Deflector Shield Generators U2	.40	1.00
14 Evacuation Control U1	.40	1.00
15 Portable Fusion Generator C2	.12	.30
16 Probe Antennae U2	.40	1.00
17 Breached Defenses U2	.40	1.00
18 Death Mark R1	1.25	3.00
19 Death Squadron U1	.40	1.00
20 Frostbite LIGHT C2	.12	.30
21 Frozen Dinner R1	1.25	3.00
22 High Anxiety R1	1.25	3.00
23 Ice Storm LIGHT U1	.40	1.00
24 Image Of The Dark Lord R2	1.25	3.00
25 Imperial Domination U1	.40	1.00
26 Meteor Impact? R1	1.25	3.00
27 Mournful Roar R1	1.25	3.00
28 Responsibility Of Command R1	1.25	3.00
29 Silence Is Golden U2	.40	1.00
30 The Shield Doors Must Be Closed U1	.40	1.00
31 This Is Just Wrong R1	1.25	3.00
32 Too Cold For Speeders U1	.40	1.00
33 Weapon Malfunction R1	1.25	3.00
34 Target The Main Generator R2	1.25	3.00
35 A Dark Time For The Rebellion C1	.12	.30
36 Cold Feet C2	.12	.30
37 Collapsing Corridor R2	1.25	3.00
38 ComScan Detection C2	.12	.30
39 Crash Landing U1	.40	1.00
40 Debris Zone R2	1.25	3.00
41 Direct Hit U1	.40	1.00
42 Exhaustion U2	.40	1.00
43 Exposure U1	.40	1.00
44 Furry Fury R2	1.25	3.00
45 He Hasnít Come Back Yet C2	.12	.30
46 Iíd Just As Soon Kiss A Wookiee C2	.12	.30
47 Imperial Supply C1	.12	.30
48 Lightsaber Deficiency U1	.40	1.00
49 Oh, Switch Off C2	.12	.30
50 Our First Catch Of The Day C2	.12	.30
51 Probe Telemetry C2	.12	.30
52 Scruffy-Looking Nerf Herder R2	1.25	3.00
53 Self-Destruct Mechanism U1	.40	1.00
54 Stop Motion C2	.12	.30
55 Tactical Support R2	1.25	3.00
56 Thatís It, The Rebels Are There! U2	.40	1.00
57 Trample R1	1.25	3.00
58 Turn It Off! Turn It Off! C1	.12	.30
59 Walker Barrage U1	.40	1.00
60 Wall Of Fire U1	.40	1.00
61 Yaggle Gakkle R2	1.25	3.00
62 Hoth DARK U2	.40	1.00
63 Hoth: Defensive Perimeter LIGHT C2	.12	.30
64 Hoth: Echo Command Center (War Room) LIGHT U2	.40	1.00
65 Hoth: Echo Corridor DARK U2	.40	1.00
66 Hoth: Echo Docking Bay LIGHT C2	.12	.30
67 Hoth: Ice Plains C2	.12	.30
68 Hoth: North Ridge LIGHT C2	.12	.30
69 Hoth: Wampa Cave R2	1.25	3.00
70 Ord Mantell LIGHT U2	.40	1.00
71 Stalker R1	4.00	10.00
72 Tyrant R1	3.00	8.00
73 Blizzard 1 R1	2.50	6.00
74 Blizzard 2 R2	1.25	3.00
75 Blizzard Scout 1 R1	2.50	6.00
76 Blizzard Walker U2	.40	1.00
77 AT-AT Cannon U1	.40	1.00
78 Echo Base Operations R2	1.25	3.00
79 Infantry Mine LIGHT C2	.12	.30
80 Probe Droid Laser U2	.40	1.00
81 Vehicle Mine LIGHT C2	.12	.30
82 2-1B (Too-Onebee) R1	1.25	3.00
83 Cal Alder U2	.40	1.00
84 Commander Luke Skywalker R1	6.00	15.00
85 Dack Ralter R2	1.25	3.00
86 Derek ëHobbieí Klivian U1	.40	1.00
87 Electro-Rangefinder U1	.40	1.00
88 Echo Base Trooper Officer C1	.12	.30
89 Echo Trooper Backpack C2	.12	.30
90 FX-7 (Effex-Seven) C2	.12	.30
91 General Carlist Rieekan R2	1.25	3.00
92 Jeroen Webb U1	.40	1.00
93 K-3PO (Kay-Threepio) R1	1.25	3.00
94 Major Bren Derlin R2	1.25	3.00
95 R2 Sensor Array C2	.12	.30
96 R5-M2 (Arfive-Emmtoo) C2	.12	.30
97 Rebel Scout C1	.12	.30
98 Rogue Gunner C2	.12	.30
99 Romas Lock Navander U2	.40	1.00
100 Shawn Valdez U1	.40	1.00
101 Tamizander Rey U2	.40	1.00
102 Tauntaun Handler C2	.12	.30
103 Tigran Jamiro U1	.40	1.00
104 Toryn Farr U1	.40	1.00
105 WED-1016 ëTechieí Droid C1	.12	.30
106 Wes Janson R2	1.25	3.00
107 Wyron Serper U2	.40	1.00
108 Zev Senesca R2	1.25	3.00
109 Artillery Remote R2	1.25	3.00
110 EG-4 (Eegee-Four) C1	.12	.30
111 Hoth LIGHT U2	.40	1.00
112 R-3PO (Ar-Threepio) DARK R2	1.25	3.00
112 R-3PO (Ar-Threepio) LIGHT R2	1.25	3.00
113 Bacta Tank R2	2.00	5.00
114 Disarming Creature R1	1.25	3.00
115 Echo Base Trooper C3	.12	.30
116 E-web Blaster C1	.12	.30
117 Frostbite DARK C2	.12	.30
118 Ice Storm DARK U1	.40	1.00
119 Tauntaun Bones U1	.40	1.00
120 The First Transport Is Away! R1	1.25	3.00
121 Attack Pattern Delta U1	.40	1.00
122 Dark Dissension R1	1.25	3.00
123 Fall Back! C2	.12	.30
124 I Thought They Smelled Bad On The Outside R1	1.25	3.00
125 It Can Wait C2	.12	.30
126 Lucky Shot U1	.40	1.00
127 Nice Of You Guys To Drop By C2	.12	.30
128 One More Pass U1	.40	1.00
129 Perimeter Scan C2	.12	.30
130 Rug Hug R1	1.25	3.00
131 Under Attack U1	.40	1.00
132 Walker Sighting U2	.40	1.00
133 Whoís Scruffy-Looking? R1	1.25	3.00
134 You Have Failed Me For The Last Time R1	1.25	3.00
135 You Will Go To The Dagobah System R1	1.25	3.00
136 Hoth Survival Gear C2	.12	.30
137 Hoth: Defensive Perimeter DARK C2	.12	.30
138 Hoth: Echo Command Center (War Room) DARK U2	.40	1.00
139 Hoth: Echo Corridor LIGHT C2	.12	.30
140 Hoth: Echo Docking Bay DARK C2	.12	.30
141 Hoth: Echo Med Lab C2	.12	.30
142 Hoth: Main Power Generators U2	.40	1.00
143 Hoth: North Ridge DARK C2	.12	.30
144 Hoth: Snow Trench C2	.12	.30
145 Ord Mantell DARK C2	.12	.30
146 Medium Transport U2	.40	1.00
147 Rogue 1 R1	2.50	6.00
148 Rogue 2 R2	1.25	3.00
149 Rogue 3 R1	2.50	6.00
150 Snowspeeder U2	.40	1.00
151 Tauntaun C2	.12	.30
152 Anakinís Lightsaber R1	6.00	15.00
153 Atgar Laser Cannon U2	.40	1.00
154 Concussion Grenade R1	1.25	3.00
155 Dual Laser Cannon U1	.40	1.00
156 Golan Laser Battery U1	.40	1.00
157 Infantry Mine DARK C2	.12	.30
158 Medium Repeating Blaster Cannon C1	.12	.30
159 Planet Defender Ion Cannon R2	1.25	3.00
160 Power Harpoon U1	.40	1.00
161 Surface Defense Cannon R2	1.25	3.00
162 Vehicle Mine DARK C2	.12	.30

1996 Star Wars Jedi Pack

COMPLETE SET (11)	3.00	8.00
RELEASED IN 1996		
1 Hyperoute Navigation Chart PM	.40	1.00
2 Dark Forces PM	.40	1.00
3 Eriadu PM	.40	1.00
4 For Luck PM	.40	1.00
5 Gravity Shadow PM	.40	1.00
6 Han PM	.40	1.00
7 Leia PM	.40	1.00
8 Lukeís T-16 Skyhopper PM	.40	1.00
9 Motti PM	.40	1.00
10 Tarkin PM	.40	1.00
11 Tedn Dahai PM	.40	1.00

1996 Star Wars A New Hope

COMPLETE SET (162)	50.00	100.00
BOOSTER BOX (36 PACKS)	50.00	100.00
BOOSTER PACK (15 CARDS)	2.00	4.00
RELEASED IN JULY 1996		
1 Advosze C2	.12	.30
2 Captain Khurgee U1	.40	1.00
3 DS-61-4 R2	1.25	3.00
4 Dannik Jerriko R1	1.25	3.00
5 Danz Borin U2	.40	1.00
6 Death Star R2	4.00	10.00
7 Defel C2	.12	.30
8 Greedo R1	3.00	8.00
9 Hem Dazon R1	1.25	3.00
10 IT-O (Eyetee-Oh) R1	1.25	3.00
11 Imperial Commander C2	.12	.30
12 Imperial Squad Leader C3	.12	.30
13 Lirin Carín U2	.40	1.00
14 Lt. Pol Treidum C1	.12	.30
15 Lt. Shann Childsen U1	.40	1.00
16 Mosep U2	.40	1.00
17 Officer Evax C1	.12	.30
18 R2-Q2 (Artoo-Kyootoo) C2	.12	.30
19 R3-T6 (Arthree-Teesix) R1	1.25	3.00
20 R5-A2 (Arfive-Aytoo) C2	.12	.30
21 Reegesk U2	.40	1.00
22 Reserve Pilot U1	.40	1.00
23 Rodian C2	.12	.30
24 Tech Moír U2	.40	1.00
25 Trooper Davin Felth R2	1.25	3.00
26 U-3PO (Yoo-Threepio) R1	1.25	3.00
27 URoRRuRiRiR U2	.40	1.00
28 WED15-I7 ëSeptoidí Droid U2	.40	1.00
29 Dianoga R2	1.25	3.00
30 Death Star Tractor Beam R2	1.25	3.00
31 Hypo R1	1.25	3.00
32 Laser Gate U2	.40	1.00
33 Maneuver Check R2	1.25	3.00
34 Tractor Beam U1	.40	1.00
35 Astromech Shortage U2	.40	1.00
36 Besieged R2	1.25	3.00
37 Come With Me C2	.12	.30
38 Dark Waters R2	1.25	3.00
39 Hyperwave Scan U1	.40	1.00
40 Imperial Justice C2	.12	.30
41 Krayt Dragon Bones U1	.40	1.00
42 Merc Sunlet C2	.12	.30
43 Program Trap U1	.40	1.00
44 Spice Mines Of Kessel R1	1.25	3.00
45 Swilla Corey C2	.12	.30
46 Tentacle C2	.12	.30
47 Thereíll Be Hell To Pay U2	.40	1.00
48 Undercover LIGHT U2	.40	1.00
49 Commence Primary Ignition R2	1.25	3.00
50 Evader U1	.40	1.00
51 Ghhhk C2	.12	.30
52 Iím On The Leader R1	1.25	3.00
53 Informant U1	.40	1.00
54 Monnok C2	.12	.30
55 Ngíok C2	.12	.30
56 Oo-ta Goo-ta, Solo? C2	.12	.30
57 Retract the Bridge R1	1.25	3.00
58 Sniper U1	.40	1.00
59 Stunning Leader C2	.12	.30
60 This Is Some Rescue! U1	.40	1.00
61 We Have A Prisoner C2	.12	.30
62 Death Star Gunner C1	.12	.30
63 Death Star: Conference Room U1	.40	1.00
64 Imperial Holotable R1	1.25	3.00
65 Kashyyyk LIGHTC1	.12	.30
66 Kiffex R1	1.25	3.00
67 Ralltiir LIGHT C1	.12	.30
68 Sandcrawler: Droid Junkheap R1	1.25	3.00
69 Tatooine: Bluffs R1	1.25	3.00
70 Black 4 U2	.40	1.00
71 Conquest R1	4.00	10.00
72 TIE Assault Squadron U1	.40	1.00
73 TIE Vanguard C2	.12	.30
74 Victory-Class Star Destroyer U1	.40	1.00
75 Bespin Motors Void Spider THX 1138 C2	.12	.30
76 Mobquet A-1 Deluxe Floater C2	.12	.30
77 Enhanced TIE Laser Cannon C2	.12	.30
78 Jawa Blaster C2	.12	.30
79 Leia Seeker R2	1.25	3.00
80 Superlaser R2	2.00	5.00
81 URoRRuRiRiRís Hunting Rifle U1	.40	1.00
82 Arcona C2	.12	.30
83 Brainiac R1	2.50	6.00
84 Chewbacca R2	6.00	15.00
85 Commander Evram Lajaie C1	.12	.30
86 Commander Vanden Willard U2	.40	1.00
87 Corellian C2	.12	.30
88 Doikk Naits U2	.40	1.00
89 Garouf Lafoe U2	.40	1.00
90 Het Nkik U2	.40	1.00
91 Hunchback R1	1.25	3.00
92 Ickabel Gíont U2	.40	1.00
93 Magnetic Suction Tube DARK R2	1.25	3.00
94 Nalan Cheel U2	.40	1.00
95 R2-D2 (Artoo-Detoo) R2	6.00	15.00
96 R5-D4 (Arfive-Defour) C2	.12	.30
97 RA-7 (Aray-Seven) C2	.12	.30
98 Rebel Commander C2	.12	.30
99 Rebel Squad Leader C3	.12	.30
100 Rebel Tech C1	.12	.30
101 Saurin C2	.12	.30
102 Tiree U2	.40	1.00
103 Tzizvvt R2	1.25	3.00
104 Wedge Antilles R1	6.00	15.00
105 Zutton C1	.12	.30
106 Fire Extinguisher U2	.40	1.00
107 Magnetic Suction Tube LIGHT R2	1.25	3.00
108 Rectenna C2	.12	.30
109 Remote C2	.12	.30
110 Sensor Panel U1	.40	1.00
111 Cell 2187 R1	1.25	3.00
112 Commence Recharging R2	1.25	3.00
113 Eject! Eject! C2	.12	.30
114 Grappling Hook C2	.12	.30
115 Logistical Delay U2	.40	1.00
116 Lukeís Cape R1	1.25	3.00
117 M-HYD ëBinaryí Droid U1	.40	1.00
118 Scanner Techs U1	.40	1.00
119 Solomahal C2	.12	.30
120 Theyíre On Dantooine R1	1.25	3.00
121 Undercover DARK U2	.40	1.00
122 Whatíre You Tryiní To Push On Us? U2	.40	1.00
123 Attack Run R2	1.25	3.00
124 Advance Preparation U1	.40	1.00
125 Alternatives To Fighting U1	.40	1.00
126 Blast The Door, Kid! C2	.12	.30
127 Blue Milk C2	.12	.30
128 Corellian Slip C2	.12	.30
129 Double Agent R2	1.25	3.00
130 Grimtaash C2	.12	.30
131 Houjix C2	.12	.30
132 I Have A Very Bad Feeling About This C2	.12	.30
133 Iím Here To Rescue You U1	.40	1.00
134 Let The Wookiee Win R1	5.00	12.00
135 Out Of Commission U2	.40	1.00
136 Quite A Mercenary C2	.12	.30
137 Sabotage U1	.40	1.00
138 Sorry About The Mess U1	.40	1.00
139 Wookiee Roar R1	1.25	3.00
140 Y-wing Assault Squadron U1	.40	1.00
141 Clakidor VII R2	1.25	3.00
142 Corellia R1	1.25	3.00
143 Death Star: Trench R2	1.25	3.00
144 Dejarik Hologameboard R1	1.25	3.00
145 Kashyyyk DARK C1	.12	.30
146 Ralltiir DARK C1	.12	.30
147 Sandcrawler: Loading Bay R1	1.25	3.00
148 Yavin 4: Massassi Ruins U1	.40	1.00
149 Youíre All Clear Kid! R1	1.25	3.00
150 Gold 2 U1	.40	1.00
151 Red 2 R1	1.25	3.00
152 Red 5 R1	3.00	8.00
153 Red 6 U1	.40	1.00
154 Tantive IV R1	4.00	10.00
155 Yavin 4: Briefing Room U1	.40	1.00
156 Incom T-16 Skyhopper C2	.12	.30
157 Rogue Bantha U1	.40	1.00
158 Bowcaster R2	1.25	3.00
159 Jawa Ion Gun C2	.12	.30
160 Lukeís Hunting Rifle U1	.40	1.00
161 Motti Seeker R2	1.25	3.00
162 SW-4 Ion Cannon R2	1.25	3.00

1997 Star Wars Cloud City

COMPLETE SET (180)	50.00	100.00
BOOSTER BOX (60 PACKS)	50.00	100.00
BOOSTER PACK (9 CARDS)	2.00	4.00
RELEASED IN NOVEMBER 1997		
1 Ability, Ability, Ability C	.12	.30
2 Abyss U	.40	1.00
3 Access Denied C	.12	.30
4 Advantage R	1.25	3.00
5 Aiiii! Aaa! Agggggggggg! R	1.25	3.00
6 All My Urchins R	1.25	3.00
7 All Too Easy R	1.25	3.00
8 Ambush R	1.25	3.00
9 Armed And Dangerous U	.40	1.00
10 Artoo, Come Back At Once! R	1.25	3.00
11 As Good As Gone C	.12	.30
12 Atmospheric Assault R	1.25	3.00
13 Beldonís Eye R	1.25	3.00
14 Bespin DARK U	.40	1.00
15 Bespin LIGHT U	.40	1.00
16 Bespin: Cloud City DARK U	.40	1.00
17 Bespin: Cloud City LIGHT U	.40	1.00
18 Binders C	.12	.30
19 Bionic Hand R	1.25	3.00
20 Blasted Droid C	.12	.30
21 Blaster Proficiency C	.12	.30

22 Boba Fett R 8.00 20.00
23 Boba Fettís Blaster Rifle R 3.00 8.00
24 Bounty C .12 .30
25 Brief Loss Of Control R 1.25 3.00
26 Bright Hope R 1.25 3.00
27 Captain Bewil R 1.25 3.00
28 Captain Han Solo R 8.00 20.00
29 Captive Fury U .40 1.00
30 Captive Pursuit C .12 .30
31 Carbon-Freezing U .40 1.00
32 Carbonite Chamber Console U .40 1.00
33 Chasm U .40 1.00
34 Chief Retwin R 1.25 3.00
35 Civil Disorder C .12 .30
36 Clash Of Sabers U .40 1.00
37 Cloud Car DARK C .12 .30
38 Cloud Car LIGHT C .12 .30
39 Cloud City Blaster DARK C .12 .30
40 Cloud City Blaster LIGHT C .12 .30
41 Cloud City Engineer C .12 .30
42 Cloud City Sabacc DARK U .40 1.00
43 Cloud City Sabacc LIGHT U .40 1.00
44 Cloud City Technician C .12 .30
45 Cloud City Trooper DARK C .12 .30
46 Cloud City Trooper LIGHT C .12 .30
47 Cloud City: Carbonite Chamber DARK U .40 1.00
48 Cloud City: Carbonite Chamber LIGHT U .40 1.00
49 Cloud City: Chasm Walkway DARK C .12 .30
50 Cloud City: Chasm Walkway LIGHT C .12 .30
51 Cloud City: Dining Room R 1.25 3.00
52 Cloud City: East Platform (Docking Bay) C .12 .30
53 Cloud City: Guest Quarters R 1.25 3.00
54 Cloud City: Incinerator DARK C .12 .30
55 Cloud City: Incinerator LIGHT C .12 .30
56 Cloud City: Lower Corridor DARK U .40 1.00
57 Cloud City: Lower Corridor LIGHT U .40 1.00
58 Cloud City: Platform 327 (Docking Bay) C .12 .30
59 Cloud City: Security Tower C .12 .30
60 Cloud City: Upper Plaza Corridor DARK C .12 .30
61 Cloud City: Upper Plaza Corridor LIGHT U .40 1.00
62 Clouds DARK C .12 .30
63 Clouds LIGHT C .12 .30
64 Commander Desanne U .40 1.00
65 Computer Interface C .12 .30
66 Courage Of A Skywalker R 1.25 3.00
67 Crack Shot U .40 1.00
68 Cyborg Construct U .40 1.00
69 Dark Approach R 1.25 3.00
70 Dark Deal R 1.25 3.00
71 Dark Strike C .12 .30
72 Dash C .12 .30
73 Despair R 1.25 3.00
74 Desperate Reach U .40 1.00
75 Dismantle On Sight R 1.25 3.00
76 Dodge C .12 .30
77 Double Back U .40 1.00
78 Double-Crossing, No-Good Swindler C .12 .30
79 E Chu Ta C .12 .30
80 E-3P0 R 1.25 3.00
81 End This Destructive Conflict R 1.25 3.00
82 Epic Duel R 2.00 5.00
83 Fall Of The Empire U .40 1.00
84 Fall Of The Legend U .40 1.00
85 Flight Escort R 1.25 3.00
86 Focused Attack R 1.25 3.00
87 Force Field R 1.25 3.00
88 Forced Landing R 1.25 3.00
89 Frozen Assets R 1.25 3.00
90 Gamblerís Luck R 1.25 3.00
91 Glancing Blow R 1.25 3.00
92 Haven R 1.25 3.00
93 Heís All Yours, Bounty Hunter R 1.25 3.00
94 Heart Of The Chasm U .40 1.00
95 Hero Of A Thousand Devices U .40 1.00
96 Higher Ground R 1.25 3.00
97 Hindsight R 1.25 3.00
98 Hopping Mad R 1.25 3.00
99 Human Shield C .12 .30
100 I Am Your Father R 1.25 3.00
101 I Donít Need Their Scum, Either R 1.25 3.00
102 I Had No Choice R 1.25 3.00
103 Imperial Decree U .40 1.00
104 Imperial Trooper Guard Dainsom U .40 1.00
105 Impressive, Most Impressive R 1.25 3.00
106 Innocent Scoundrel U .40 1.00
107 Interrogation Array R 1.25 3.00
108 Into The Ventilation Shaft, Lefty R 1.25 3.00
109 Itís A Trap! U .40 1.00
110 Kebyc U .40 1.00
111 Keep Your Eyes Open C .12 .30
112 Lando Calrissian DARK R 5.00 12.00
113 Lando Calrissian LIGHT R 5.00 12.00
114 Landoís Wrist Comlink U .40 1.00
115 Leia Of Alderaan R 2.00 5.00
116 Levitation Attack U .40 1.00
117 Lieutenant Cecius U .40 1.00
118 Lieutenant Sheckil R 1.25 3.00
119 Lift Tube Escape C .12 .30
120 Lobot R 2.50 6.00
121 Lukeís Blaster Pistol R 1.25 3.00
122 Mandalorian Armor R 2.00 5.00
123 Mostly Armless R 1.25 3.00
124 NOOOOOOOOOOOO! R 1.25 3.00
125 Obsidian 7 R 2.00 5.00
126 Obsidian 8 R 2.00 5.00
127 Off The Edge R 1.25 3.00
128 Old Pirates R 1.25 3.00
129 Out Of Somewhere U .40 1.00
130 Path Of Least Resistance C .12 .30
131 Point Man R 1.25 3.00
132 Prepare The Chamber U .40 1.00
133 Princess Leia R 4.00 10.00
134 Projective Telepathy U .40 1.00
135 Protector R 1.25 3.00
136 Punch It! R 1.25 3.00
137 Put That Down C .12 .30
138 Redemption R 2.50 6.00
139 Release Your Anger R 1.25 3.00
140 Rendezvous Point On Tatooine R 1.25 3.00
141 Rescue In The Clouds C .12 .30
142 Restricted Access C .12 .30
143 Rite Of Passage C .12 .30
144 Shattered Hope U .40 1.00
145 Shocking Information C .12 .30
146 Shocking Revelation C .12 .30
147 Slave I R 4.00 10.00
148 Slip Sliding Away R 1.25 3.00
149 Smoke Screen R 1.25 3.00
150 Somersault C .12 .30
151 Sonic Bombardment U .40 1.00
152 Special Delivery C .12 .30
153 Surprise R 1.25 3.00
154 Surreptitious Glance R 1.25 3.00
155 Swing-And-A-Miss U .40 1.00
156 The Emperorís Prize R 1.25 3.00
157 This Is Even Better R 1.25 3.00
158 This Is Still Wrong R 1.25 3.00
159 Tibanna Gas Miner DARK C .12 .30
160 Tibanna Gas Miner LIGHT C .12 .30
161 TIE Sentry Ships C .12 .30
162 Treva Horme U .40 1.00
163 Trooper Assault C .12 .30
164 Trooper Jerrol Blendin U .40 1.00
165 Trooper Utris Mitoc U .40 1.00
166 Ugloste R 1.25 3.00
167 Ugnaught C .12 .30
168 Uncontrollable Fury R 1.25 3.00
169 Vaderís Bounty R 1.25 3.00
170 Vaderís Cape R 1.25 3.00
171 Weíll Find Han R 1.25 3.00
172 Weíre The Bait R 1.25 3.00
173 Weapon Levitation U .40 1.00
174 Weapon Of An Ungrateful Son U .40 1.00
175 Weather Vane DARK U .40 1.00
176 Weather Vane LIGHT U .40 1.00
177 Why Didnít You Tell Me? R 1.25 3.00
178 Wiorkettle U .40 1.00
179 Wookiee Strangle R 1.25 3.00
180 You Are Beaten U .40 1.00

1997 Star Wars Dagobah

COMPLETE SET (181) 50.00 100.00
BOOSTER BOX (60 PACKS) 50.00 100.00
BOOSTER PACK (9 CARDS) 1.50 3.00
RELEASED ON APRIL 23, 1997

1 3,720 To 1 C .12 .30
2 4-LOM R 2.50 6.00
3 4-LOMís Concussion Rifle R 2.00 5.00
4 A Dangerous Time C .12 .30
5 A Jediís Strength U .40 1.00
6 Anger, Fear, Aggression C .12 .30
7 Anoat DARK U .40 1.00
8 Anoat LIGHT U .40 1.00
9 Apology Accepted C .12 .30
10 Asteroid Field DARK C .12 .30
11 Asteroid Field LIGHT C .12 .30
12 Asteroid Sanctuary C .12 .30
13 Asteroids Do Not Concern Me R 1.25 3.00
14 Astroid Sanctuary C .12 .30
15 Astromech Translator C .12 .30
16 At Peace R 1.25 3.00
17 Avenger R 4.00 10.00
18 Away Put Your Weapon U .40 1.00
19 Awwww, Cannot Get Your Ship Out C .12 .30
20 Bad Feeling Have I R 1.25 3.00
21 Big One DARK U .40 1.00
22 Big One LIGHT U .40 1.00
23 Big One: Asteroid Cave or Space Slug Belly DARK U .40 1.00
24 Big One: Asteroid Cave or Space Slug Belly LIGHT U .40 1.00
25 Blasted Varmints C .12 .30
26 Bog-wing DARK C .12 .30
27 Bog-wing LIGHT C .12 .30
28 Bombing Run R 1.25 3.00
29 Bossk R 3.00 8.00
30 Bosskís Mortar Gun R 2.00 5.00
31 Broken Concentration R 1.25 3.00
32 Captain Needa R 2.00 5.00
33 Close Call C .12 .30
34 Closer?! U .40 1.00
35 Comm Chief C .12 .30
36 Commander Brandei U .40 1.00
37 Commander Gherant U .40 1.00
38 Commander Nemet U .40 1.00
39 Control DARK U .40 1.00
40 Control LIGHT U .40 1.00
41 Corporal Derdram U .40 1.00
42 Corporal Vandolay U .40 1.00
43 Corrosive Damage R 1.25 3.00
44 Dagobah U .40 1.00
45 Dagobah: Bog Clearing R 1.25 3.00
46 Dagobah: Cave R 1.25 3.00
47 Dagobah: Jungle U .40 1.00
48 Dagobah: Swamp U .40 1.00
49 Dagobah: Training Area C .12 .30
50 Dagobah: Yodaís Hut R 2.00 5.00
51 Defensive Fire C .12 .30
52 Dengar R 1.25 3.00
53 Dengarís Blaster Carbine R 1.25 3.00
54 Descent Into The Dark R 1.25 3.00
55 Do, Or Do Not C .12 .30
56 Domain Of Evil U .40 1.00
57 Dragonsnake R 1.25 3.00
58 Droid Sensorscope C .12 .30
59 Effective Repairs R 1.25 3.00
60 Egregious Pilot Error R 1.25 3.00
61 Encampment C .12 .30
62 Executor R 8.00 20.00
63 Executor: Comm Station U .40 1.00
64 Executor: Control Station U .40 1.00
65 Executor: Holotheatre R 1.25 3.00
66 Executor: Main Corridor C .12 .30
67 Executor: Meditation Chamber R 1.25 3.00
68 Failure At The Cave R 1.25 3.00
69 Fear C .12 .30
70 Field Promotion R 1.25 3.00
71 Flagship R 1.25 3.00
72 Flash Of Insight U .40 1.00
73 Found Someone You Have U .40 1.00
74 Frustration R 1.25 3.00
75 Great Warrior C .12 .30
76 Grounded Starfighter U .40 1.00
77 Hanís Toolkit R 1.25 3.00
78 He Is Not Ready C .12 .30
79 Hiding In The Garbage R 1.25 3.00
80 HoloNet Transmission U .40 1.00
81 Houndís Tooth R 2.50 6.00
82 I Have A Bad Feeling About This R 1.25 3.00
83 I Want That Ship R 1.25 3.00
84 IG-2000 R 2.00 5.00
85 IG-88 R 4.00 10.00
86 IG-88ís Neural Inhibitor R 2.00 5.00
87 IG-88ís Pulse Cannon R 2.00 5.00
88 Imbalance U .40 1.00
89 Imperial Helmsman C .12 .30
90 Ineffective Maneuver U .40 1.00
91 It Is The Future You See R 1.25 3.00
92 Jedi Levitation R 1.25 3.00
93 Knowledge And Defense C .12 .30
94 Landing Claw R 1.25 3.00
95 Lando System? R 1.25 3.00
96 Levitation U .40 1.00
97 Lieutenant Commander Ardan U .40 1.00
98 Lieutenant Suba R 1.25 3.00
99 Lieutenant Venka U .40 1.00
100 Light Maneuvers R 1.25 3.00
101 Location, Location, Location R 1.25 3.00
102 Lost In Space R 1.25 3.00
103 Lost Relay C .12 .30
104 Lukeís Backpack R 1.25 3.00
105 Mist Hunter R 2.00 5.00
106 Moving To Attack Position C .12 .30
107 Much Anger In Him R 1.25 3.00
108 Mynock DARK C .12 .30
109 Mynock LIGHT C .12 .30
110 Never Tell Me The Odds C .12 .30
111 No Disintegrations! R 1.25 3.00
112 Nudj C .12 .30
113 Obi-Wanís Apparition R 1.25 3.00
114 Order To Engage R 1.25 3.00
115 Polarized Negative Power Coupling R 1.25 3.00
116 Portable Fusion Generator C .12 .30
117 Precision Targeting U .40 1.00
118 Proton Bombs U .40 1.00
119 Punishing One R 2.00 5.00
120 Quick Draw C .12 .30
121 Raithal DARK R 1.25 3.00
122 Raithal LIGHT U .40 1.00
123 Rebel Flight Suit C .12 .30
124 Recoil In Fear C .12 .30
125 Reflection R 1.25 3.00
126 Report To Lord Vader R 1.25 3.00
127 Res Luk Raíauf R 1.25 3.00
128 Retractable Arm C .12 .30
129 Rogue Asteroid DARK C .12 .30
130 Rogue Asteroid LIGHT C .12 .30
131 Rycarís Run R 1.25 3.00
132 Scramble U .40 1.00
133 Shoo! Shoo! U .40 1.00
134 Shot In The Dark U .40 1.00
135 Shut Him Up Or Shut Him Down U .40 1.00
136 Size Matters Not R 1.25 3.00
137 Sleen C .12 .30
138 Smugglerís Blues R 1.25 3.00
139 Something Hit Us! U .40 1.00
140 Son of Skywalker R 8.00 20.00
141 Space Slug DARK R 1.25 3.00
142 Space Slug LIGHT U .40 1.00
143 Star Destroyer: Launch Bay C .12 .30
144 Starship Levitation U .40 1.00
145 Stone Pile R 1.25 3.00
146 Sudden Impact U .40 1.00
147 Take Evasive Action C .12 .30
148 The Dark Path R 1.25 3.00
149 The Professor R 1.25 3.00
150 There Is No Try C .12 .30
151 Theyíd Be Crazy To Follow Us C .12 .30
152 This Is More Like It R 1.25 3.00
153 This Is No Cave R 1.25 3.00
154 Those Rebels Wonít Escape Us C .12 .30
155 Through The Force Things You Will See R 1.25 3.00
156 TIE Avenger C .12 .30
157 TIE Bomber U .40 1.00
158 Tight Squeeze R 1.25 3.00
159 Transmission Terminated U .40 1.00
160 Tunnel Vision U .40 1.00
161 Uncertain Is The Future C .12 .30
162 Unexpected Interruption R 1.25 3.00
163 Vine Snake DARK C .12 .30
164 Vine Snake LIGHT C .12 .30
165 Visage Of The Emperor R 1.25 3.00
166 Visored Vision C .12 .30
167 Voyeur C .12 .30
168 Warrant Officer MíKae U .40 1.00
169 Wars Not Make One Great U .40 1.00
170 We Can Still Outmaneuver Them R 1.25 3.00
171 We Donít Need Their Scum R 1.25 3.00
172 WHAAAAAAAAAOOOOW! R 1.25 3.00
173 What Is Thy Bidding, My Master? R 1.25 3.00
174 Yoda R 8.00 20.00
175 Yoda Stew U .40 1.00
176 Yoda, You Seek Yoda R 1.25 3.00
177 Yodaís Gimer Stick R 1.25 3.00
178 Yodaís Hope U .40 1.00
179 You Do Have Your Moments U .40 1.00
180 Zuckuss R 2.00 5.00
181 Zuckussí Snare Rifle R 1.25 3.00

1997 Star Wars First Anthology

COMPLETE SET (6) 3.00 8.00
RELEASED IN 1997

1 Boba Fett PV .75 2.00
2 Commander Wedge Antilles PV .75 2.00
3 Death Star Assault Squadron PV .75 2.00
4 Hit And Run PV .75 2.00
5 Jabbaís Influence PV .75 2.00
6 X-wing Assault Squadron PV .75 2.00

1997 Star Wars Rebel Leaders

COMPLETE SET (2) 1.25 3.00
RELEASED IN 1997

1 Gold Leader In Gold 1 PM 1.00 2.50
2 Red Leader In Red 1 PM 1.00 2.50

1998 Star Wars Enhanced Premiere

COMPLETE SET (6) 3.00 8.00
RELEASED IN 1998

1 Boba Fett With Blaster Rifle PM .75 2.00
2 Darth Vader With Lightsaber PM .75 2.00
3 Han With Heavy Blaster Pistol PM .75 2.00
4 Leia With Blaster Rifle PM .75 2.00
5 Luke With Lightsaber PM .75 2.00
6 Obi-Wan With Lightsaber PM .75 2.00

1998 Star Wars Jabba's Palace

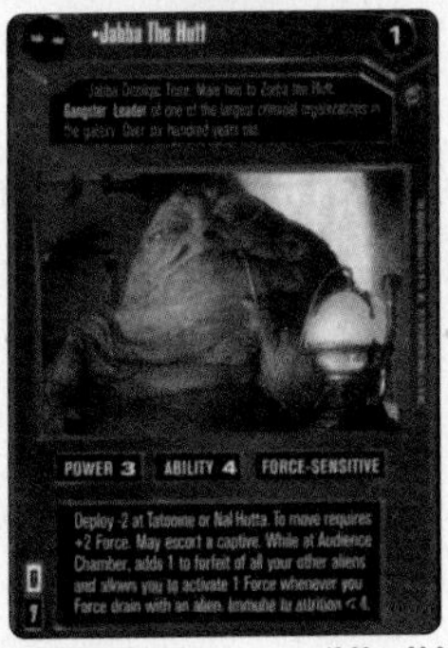

COMPLETE SET (180) 40.00 80.00
BOOSTER BOX (60 PACKS) 40.00 80.00
BOOSTER PACK (9 CARDS) 1.00 2.00
RELEASED IN MAY 1998

1 8D8 R 1.25 3.00
2 A Gift U .40 1.00
3 Abyssin C .12 .30
4 Abyssin Ornament U .40 1.00
5 All Wrapped Up U .40 1.00
6 Amanaman R 1.25 3.00
7 Amanin C .12 .30
8 Antipersonnel Laser Cannon U .40 1.00
9 Aqualish C .12 .30
10 Arc Welder U .40 1.00
11 Ardon Vapor Crell R 1.25 3.00
12 Artoo R 3.00 8.00
13 Artoo, I Have A Bad Feeling About This U .40 1.00
14 Attark R 1.25 3.00
15 Aved Luun R 1.25 3.00
16 Bíomarr Monk C .12 .30
17 Bane Malar R 1.25 3.00
18 Bantha Fodder C .12 .30
19 Barada R 1.25 3.00
20 Baragwin C .12 .30
21 Bargaining Table U .40 1.00
22 Beedo R 1.25 3.00
23 BG-J38 R 1.25 3.00
24 Bib Fortuna R 1.25 3.00
25 Blaster Deflection R 1.25 3.00
26 Bo Shuda U .40 1.00
27 Bubo U .40 1.00
28 Cane Adiss U .40 1.00
29 Chadra-Fan C .12 .30
30 Chevin C .12 .30
31 Choke C .12 .30
32 Corellian Retort U .40 1.00
33 CZ-4 C .12 .30
34 Den Of Thieves U .40 1.00
35 Dengarís Modified Riot Gun R 1.25 3.00
36 Devaronian C .12 .30
37 Donít Forget The Droids C .12 .30
38 Double Laser Cannon R 1.25 3.00
39 Droopy McCool R 1.25 3.00
40 Dune Sea Sabacc DARK U .40 1.00
41 Dune Sea Sabacc LIGHT U .40 1.00
42 Elom C .12 .30
43 Ephant Mon R 1.25 3.00
44 EV-9D9 R 1.25 3.00
45 Fallen Portal U .40 1.00
46 Florn Lamproid C .12 .30
47 Fozec R 1.25 3.00
48 Gailid R 1.25 3.00
49 Gamorrean Ax C .12 .30
50 Gamorrean Guard C .12 .30
51 Garon Nas Tal R 1.25 3.00
52 Geezum R 1.25 3.00
53 Ghoel R 1.25 3.00
54 Giran R 1.25 3.00
55 Gran C .12 .30
56 Hinemthe C .12 .30
57 Herat R 1.25 3.00
58 Hermi Odle R 1.25 3.00
59 Hidden Compartment U .40 1.00
60 Hidden Weapons U .40 1.00
61 Holoprojector U .40 1.00
62 Hutt Bounty R 1.25 3.00
63 Hutt Smooch U .40 1.00
64 I Must Be Allowed To Speak R 1.25 3.00
65 Information Exchange U .40 1.00
66 Ishi Tib C .12 .30
67 Ithorian C .12 .30
68 JiQuille R 1.25 3.00
69 Jabba the Hutt R 4.00 10.00
70 Jabbaís Palace Sabacc DARK U .40 1.00
71 Jabbaís Palace Sabacc LIGHT U .40 1.00
72 Jabbaís Palace: Audience Chamber DARK U .40 1.00
73 Jabbaís Palace: Audience Chamber LIGHT U .40 1.00
74 Jabbaís Palace: Droid Workshop U .40 1.00
75 Jabbaís Palace: Dungeon U .40 1.00
76 Jabbaís Palace: Entrance Cavern DARK U .40 1.00
77 Jabbaís Palace: Fntrance Cavern LIGHT U .40 1.00
78 Jabbaís Palace: Rancor Pit U .40 1.00
79 Jabbaís Sail Barge R 2.50 6.00
80 Jabbaís Sail Barge: Passenger Deck R1.25 3.00
81 Jedi Mind Trick R 1.25 3.00
82 Jess R 1.25 3.00
83 Jet Pack U .40 1.00
84 Kalit R 1.25 3.00
85 Ke Chu Ke Kakuta? C .12 .30
86 Kiffex R 1.25 3.00
87 Kirdo III R 1.25 3.00
88 Kithaba R 1.25 3.00
89 Kitonak C .12 .30
90 Klaatu R 1.25 3.00
91 Klatooinian Revolutionary C .12 .30
92 Laudica R 1.25 3.00
93 Leslomy Tacema R 1.25 3.00
94 Life Debt R 1.25 3.00
95 Loje Nella R 1.25 3.00
96 Malakili R 1.25 3.00
97 Mandalorian Mishap U .40 1.00
98 Max Rebo R 1.25 3.00
99 Mos Eisley Blaster DARK C .12 .30
100 Mos Eisley Blaster LIGHT C .12 .30
101 Murttoc Yine R 1.25 3.00
102 Nal Hutta R 1.25 3.00
103 Nar Shaddaa Wind Chimes U .40 1.00
104 Nikto C .12 .30
105 Nizuc Bek R 1.25 3.00
106 None Shall Pass C .12 .30
107 Nysad R 1.25 3.00
108 Oola R 1.25 3.00
109 Ortolan C .12 .30
110 Ortugg R 1.25 3.00
111 Palejo Reshad R 1.25 3.00
112 Pote Snitkin R 1.25 3.00
113 Princess Leia Organa R 3.00 8.00
114 Projection Of A Skywalker U .40 1.00
115 Pucumir Thryss R 1.25 3.00
116 Quarren C .12 .30
117 Quick Reflexes C .12 .30
118 Rikik Dínec, Hero Of The Dune Sea R1.25 3.00
119 Rancor R 2.50 6.00
120 Rayc Ryjerd R 1.25 3.00
121 Ree-Yees R 1.25 3.00
122 Rennek R 1.25 3.00
123 Resistance U .40 1.00
124 Revealed U .40 1.00
125 Saelt-Marae R 1.25 3.00
126 Salacious Crumb R 1.25 3.00
127 Sandwhirl DARK U .40 1.00
128 Sandwhirl LIGHT U .40 1.00
129 Scum And Villainy R 1.25 3.00
130 Sergeant Doallyn R 1.25 3.00
131 Shasa Tiel R 1.25 3.00
132 Sic-Six C .12 .30
133 Skiff DARK C .12 .30
134 Skiff LIGHT C .12 .30
135 Skrilling C .12 .30
136 Skull U .40 1.00
137 Snivvian C .12 .30
138 Someone Who Loves You U .40 1.00
139 Strangle R 1.25 3.00
140 Tamtel Skreej R 2.50 6.00
141 Tanus Spijek R 1.25 3.00
142 Tatooine: Desert DARK C .12 .30
143 Tatooine: Desert LIGHT C .12 .30
144 Tatooine: Great Pit Of Carkoon U .40 1.00
145 Tatooine: Hutt Canyon U .40 1.00
146 Tatooine: Jabbaís Palace U .40 1.00
147 Taym Dren-garen R 1.25 3.00
148 Tessek R 1.25 3.00
149 The Signal C .12 .30
150 Thermal Detonator R 2.00 5.00
151 Thul Fain R 1.25 3.00
152 Tibrin R 1.25 3.00
153 Torture C .12 .30
154 Trandoshan C .12 .30
155 Trap Door U .40 1.00
156 Twilek Advisor C .12 .30
157 Ultimatum U .40 1.00
158 Unfriendly Fire R 1.25 3.00
159 Vedain R 1.25 3.00
160 Velken Tezeri R 1.25 3.00
161 Vibro-Ax DARK C .12 .30
162 Vibro-Ax LIGHT C .12 .30
163 Vizam R 1.25 3.00
164 Vul Tazaene R 1.25 3.00
165 Weapon Levitation U .40 1.00
166 Weequay Guard C .12 .30
167 Weequay Hunter C .12 .30
168 Weequay Marksman U .40 1.00
169 Weequay Skiff Master C .12 .30
170 Well Guarded U .40 1.00
171 Whiphid C .12 .30
172 Wittin R 1.25 3.00
173 Woof R 1.25 3.00
174 Worrt U .40 1.00
175 Wounded Wookiee U .40 1.00
176 Yarkora C .12 .30
177 Yarna dialí Gargan U .40 1.00
178 You Will Take Me To Jabba Now C .12 .30
179 Yoxgit R 1.25 3.00
180 Yuzzum C .12 .30

1998 Star Wars Official Tournament Sealed Deck

COMPLETE SET (18) 4.00 10.00
RELEASED IN 1998

1 Arleil Schous PM .40 1.00
2 Black Squadron TIE PM .40 1.00
3 Chall Bekan PM .40 1.00
4 Corulag DARK PM .40 1.00
5 Corulag LIGHT PM .40 1.00
6 Dreadnaught-Class Heavy Cruiser PM.40 1.00
7 Faithful Service PM .40 1.00
8 Forced Servitude PM .40 1.00
9 Gold Squadron Y-wing PM .40 1.00
10 Itís a Hit! PM .40 1.00
11 Obsidian Squadron TIE PM .40 1.00
12 Rebel Trooper Recruit PM .40 1.00
13 Red Squadron X-wing PM .40 1.00
14 Stormtrooper Cadet PM .40 1.00
15 Tarkinís Orders PM .40 1.00
16 Tatooine: Jundland Wastes PM .40 1.00
17 Tatooine: Tusken Canyon PM .40 1.00
18 Z-95 Headhunter PM .40 1.00

1998 Star Wars Second Anthology

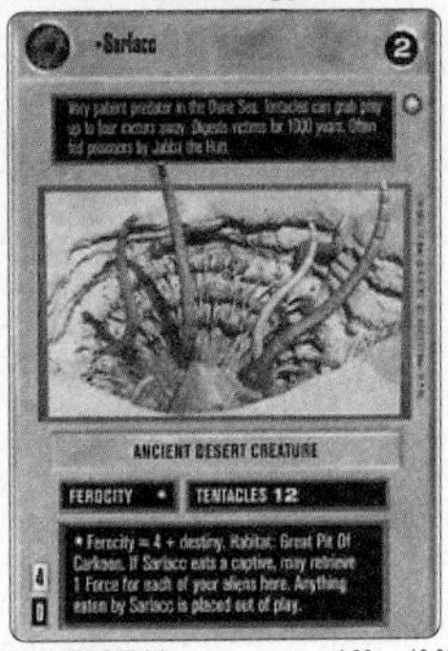

COMPLETE SET (6) 4.00 10.00
RELEASED IN 1998

1 Flagship Operations PV 1.00 2.50
2 Mon Calamari Star Cruiser PV 1.00 2.50
3 Mon Mothma PV 1.00 2.50
4 Rapid Deployment PV 1.00 2.50
5 Sarlacc PV 1.00 2.50
6 Thunderflare PV 1.00 2.50

1998 Star Wars Special Edition

COMPLETE SET (324) 75.00 150.00
BOOSTER BOX (30 PACKS) 60.00 120.00
BOOSTER PACK (9 CARDS) 3.00 6.00
RELEASED IN NOVEMBER 1998

1 ISB Operations Empireís Sinister Agents R 1.00 2.50
2 2X-7KPR (Tooex) C .12 .30
3 A Bright Center To The Universe U .40 1.00
4 A Day Long Remembered U .40 1.00
5 A Real Hero R 1.00 2.50
6 Air-2 Racing Swoop C .12 .30
7 Ak-rev U .40 1.00
8 Alderaan Operative C .12 .30
9 Alert My Star Destroyer! C .12 .30
10 All Power To Weapons C .12 .30
11 All Wings Report In R 1.00 2.50
12 Anoat Operative DARK C .12 .30
13 Anoat Operative LIGHT C .12 .30
14 Antilles Maneuver C .12 .30
15 ASP-707 (Ayesspee) F .60 1.50
16 Balanced Attack U .40 1.00
17 Bantha Herd R .75 2.00
18 Barquin Dían U .40 1.00
19 Ben Kenobi R 2.00 5.00
20 Blast Points C .12 .30
21 Blown Clear U .40 1.00
22 Boba Fett R 1.50 4.00
23 Boelo R 1.00 2.50
24 Bossk In Houndís Tooth R 1.00 2.50
25 Bothan Spy C .12 .30
26 Bothawui F .60 1.50
27 Bothawui Operative C .12 .30
28 Brangus Glee R .75 2.00
29 Bren Quersey U .40 1.00
30 Bron Burs R .75 2.00
31 B-wing Attack Fighter F .60 1.50
32 Camie R 1.00 2.50
33 Carbon Chamber Testing My Favorite Decoration R 1.00 2.50
34 Chyler U .40 1.00
35 Clakídor VII Operative U .40 1.00
36 Cloud City Celebration R 1.00 2.50
37 Cloud City Occupation R 1.25 3.00
38 Cloud City: Casino DARK U .40 1.00
39 Cloud City: Casino LIGHT U .40 1.00
40 Cloud City: Core Tunnel U .40 1.00
41 Cloud City: Downtown Plaza DARK R1.00 2.50
42 Cloud City: Downtown Plaza LIGHT R1.00 2.50
43 Cloud City: Interrogation Room C .12 .30
44 Cloud City: North Corridor C .12 .30
45 Cloud City: Port Town District U .40 1.00
46 Cloud City: Upper Walkway C .12 .30
47 Cloud City: West Gallery DARK C .12 .30
48 Cloud City: West Gallery LIGHT C .12 .30
49 Colonel Feyn Gospic R 1.00 2.50
50 Combat Cloud Car F .60 1.50
51 Come Here You Big Coward! C .12 .30
52 Commander Wedge Antilles R 1.00 2.50
53 Coordinated Attack C .12 .30
54 Corellia Operative U .40 1.00
55 Corellian Engineering Corporation R1.00 2.50
56 Corporal Grenwick R .75 2.00
57 Corporal Prescott U .40 1.00
58 Corulag Operative C .12 .30
59 Coruscant Celebration R .75 2.00
60 Coruscant DARK R 2.50 6.00
61 Coruscant LIGHT R 1.00 2.50
62 Coruscant: Docking Bay C .12 .30
63 Coruscant: Imperial City U .40 1.00
64 Coruscant: Imperial Square R 1.25 3.00
65 Counter Surprise Assault R 1.00 2.50
66 Dagobah U .40 1.00
67 Dantooine Base Operations More Dangerous Than You Realize R .75 2.00
68 Dantooine Operative C .12 .30
69 Darklighter Spin C .12 .30
70 Darth Vader, Dark Lord Of The Sith R6.00 15.00
71 Death Squadron Star Destroyer R 1.00 2.50
72 Death Star Assault Squadron R 1.00 2.50
73 Death Star R 1.25 3.00
74 Death Star: Detention Block Control Room C .12 .30
75 Death Star: Detention Block Corridor C.12 .30
76 Debnoli R 1.00 2.50
77 Desert DARK F .60 1.50
78 Desert LIGHT F .60 1.50
79 Desilijic Tattoo U .40 1.00
80 Desperate Tactics C .12 .30
81 Destroyed Homestead R 1.00 2.50
82 Dewback C .12 .30
83 Direct Assault C .12 .30
84 Disruptor Pistol DARK F .60 1.50
85 Disruptor Pistol LIGHT F .60 1.50
86 Docking And Repair Facilities R 1.00 2.50
87 Dodo Bodonawieedo U .40 1.00
88 Donít Tread On Me R 1.00 2.50
89 Down With The Emperor! U .40 1.00
90 Dr. Evazanís Sawed-off Blaster U .40 1.00
91 Draw Their Fire U .40 1.00
92 Dreaded Imperial Starfleet R 1.25 3.00
93 Droid Merchant C .12 .30
94 Dune Walker R 1.25 3.00
95 Echo Base Trooper Rifle C .12 .30
96 Elyhek Rue U .40 1.00
97 Entrenchment R .75 2.00
98 Eriadu Operative C .12 .30
99 Executor: Docking Bay U .40 1.00
100 Farm F .60 1.50
101 Feltipern Trevaggís Stun Rifle U .40 1.00
102 Firepower C .12 .30
103 Firin Morett U .40 1.00
104 First Aid F .60 1.50
105 First Strike U .40 1.00
106 Flare-S Racing Swoop C .12 .30
107 Flawless Marksmanship C .12 .30
108 Floating Refinery C .12 .30
109 Fondor U .40 1.00
110 Forest DARK F .60 1.50
111 Forest LIGHT F .60 1.50
112 Gela Yeens U .40 1.00
113 General McQuarrie R .75 2.00
114 Gold 3 U .40 1.00
115 Gold 4 U .40 1.00
116 Gold 6 U .40 1.00
117 Goo Nee Tay R 1.00 2.50
118 Greeata U .40 1.00
119 Grondorn Muse R .75 2.00
120 Harc Seff U .40 1.00
121 Harvest R 1.25 3.00
122 Heavy Fire Zone C .12 .30
123 Heroes Of Yavin R .75 2.00
124 Heroic Sacrifice U .40 1.00
125 Hidden Base Systems Will Slip Through Your Fingers R 1.50 4.00
126 Hit And Run R .75 2.00

127 Hol Okand U .40 1.00
128 Homing Beacon R 1.00 2.50
129 Hoth Sentry U .40 1.00
130 Hunt Down And Destroy The Jedi 1.50 4.00
Their Fire Has Gone Out Of The Universe R
131 Hunting Party R 1.00 2.50
132 I Canít Shake Him! C .12 .30
133 Iasa, The Traitor Of Jawa Canyon R.75 2.00
134 IM4-099 F .60 1.50
135 Imperial Atrocity R 3.00 8.00
136 Imperial Occupation 1.00 2.50
Imperial Control R
137 Imperial Propaganda R 3.00 8.00
138 In Range C .12 .30
139 Incom Corporation R .75 2.00
140 InCom Engineer C .12 .30
141 Intruder Missile DARK F .60 1.50
142 Intruder Missile LIGHT F .60 1.50
143 Itís Not My Fault! F .60 1.50
144 Jabba R 1.00 2.50
145 Jabbaís Influence R .75 2.00
146 Jabbaís Space Cruiser R 1.25 3.00
147 Jabbaís Through With You U .40 1.00
148 Jabbaís Twerps U .40 1.00
149 Joh Yowza R .75 2.00
150 Jungle DARK F .60 1.50
151 Jungle LIGHT F .60 1.50
152 Kalitís Sandcrawler R 1.00 2.50
153 Kashyyyk Operative DARK U .40 1.00
154 Kashyyyk Operative LIGHT U .40 1.00
155 Kessel Operative U .40 1.00
156 Ketwol R .75 2.00
157 Kiffex Operative DARK U .40 1.00
158 Kiffex Operative LIGHT U .40 1.00
159 Kirdo III Operative C .12 .30
160 Koensayr Manufacturing R 1.00 2.50
161 Krayt Dragon R 1.00 2.50
162 Kuat Drive Yards R 1.25 3.00
163 Kuat U .40 1.00
164 Landoís Blaster Rifle R 1.00 2.50
165 Legendary Starfighter C .12 .30
166 Leiaís Blaster Rifle R 1.00 2.50
167 Lieutenant Lepira U .40 1.00
168 Lieutenant Naytaan U .40 1.00
169 Lieutenant Tarn Mison R 1.00 2.50
170 Lobel C .12 .30
171 Lobot R 1.00 2.50
172 Local Defense U .40 1.00
173 Local Uprising / Liberation R 1.00 2.50
174 Lyn Me U .40 1.00
175 Major Palo Torshan R 1.00 2.50
176 Makurth F .60 1.50
177 Maneuvering Flaps C .12 .30
178 Masterful Move C .12 .30
179 Mechanical Failure R .75 2.00
180 Meditation R 1.25 3.00
181 Medium Bulk Freighter U .40 1.00
182 Melas R 1.00 2.50
183 Mind What You Have Learned 1.25 3.00
Save You It Can R
184 Moisture Farmer C .12 .30
185 Nal Hutta Operative C .12 .30
186 Neb Dulo U .40 1.00
187 Nebit R 1.00 2.50
188 Niado Duegad U .40 1.00
189 Nick Of Time U .40 1.00
190 No Bargain U .40 1.00
191 Old Times R .75 2.00
192 On Target C .12 .30
193 One-Arm R 1.00 2.50
194 Oppressive Enforcement U .40 1.00
195 Ord Mantell Operative C .12 .30
196 Organized Attack C .12 .30
197 OS-72-1 In Obsidian 1 R 1.00 2.50
198 OS-72-10 R 1.00 2.50
199 OS-72-2 In Obsidian 2 R 1.00 2.50
200 Outer Rim Scout R 1.50 4.00
201 Overwhelmed C .12 .30
202 Patrol Craft DARK C .12 .30
203 Patrol Craft LIGHT C .12 .30
204 Planetary Subjugation U .40 1.00
205 Ponda Babaís Hold-out Blaster U .40 1.00
206 Portable Scanner C .12 .30
207 Power Pivot C .12 .30
208 Precise Hit C .12 .30
209 Pride Of The Empire C .12 .30
210 Princess Organa R 1.25 3.00
211 Put All Sections On Alert C .12 .30
212 R2-A5 (Artoo-Ayfive) U .40 1.00
213 R3-A2 (Arthree-Aytoo) U .40 1.00
214 R3-T2 (Arthree-Teetoo) R 1.00 2.50

215 Raithal Operative C .12 .30
216 Ralltiir Freighter Captain F .60 1.50
217 Ralltiir Operations 1.50 4.00
In The Hands Of The Empire R
218 Ralltiir Operative C .12 .30
219 Rapid Fire C .12 .30
220 Rappertunie U .40 1.00
221 Rebel Ambush C .12 .30
222 Rebel Base Occupation R .75 2.00
223 Rebel Fleet R 1.00 2.50
224 Red 10 U .40 1.00
225 Red 7 U .40 1.00
226 Red 8 U .40 1.00
227 Red 9 U .40 1.00
228 Relentless Pursuit C .12 .30
229 Rendezvous Point R 1.00 2.50
230 Rendili F .60 1.50
231 Rendili StarDrive R .75 2.00
232 Rescue The Princess 1.00 2.50
Sometimes I Amaze Even Myself R
233 Return To Base R 1.00 2.50
234 Roche U .40 1.00
235 Rock Wart F .60 1.50
236 Rogue 4 R 1.50 4.00
237 Ronto DARK C .12 .30
238 Ronto LIGHT C .12 .30
239 RRíururrr R 1.00 2.50
240 Ryle Torsyn U .40 1.00
241 Rystall R 1.50 4.00
242 Sacrifice F .60 1.50
243 Sandspeeder F .60 1.50
244 Sandtrooper F .60 1.50
245 Sarlacc R 1.00 2.50
246 Scrambled Transmission U .40 1.00
247 Scurrier F .60 1.50
248 Secret Plans U .40 1.00
249 Sentinel-Class Landing Craft F .60 1.50
250 Sergeant Edian U .40 1.00
251 Sergeant Hollis R 1.00 2.50
252 Sergeant Major Bursk U .40 1.00
253 Sergeant Major Enfield R .75 2.00
254 Sergeant Merril U .40 1.00
255 Sergeant Narthax R 1.00 2.50
256 Sergeant Torent R 1.00 2.50
257 S-Foils C .12 .30
258 SFS L-s9.3 Laser Cannons C .12 .30
259 Short-Range Fighters R 1.00 2.50
260 Sienar Fleet Systems R 1.00 2.50
261 Slayn and Korpil Facilities R .75 2.00
262 Slight Weapons Malfunction C .12 .30
263 Soth Petikkin R .75 2.00
264 Spaceport City DARK F .60 1.50
265 Spaceport City LIGHT F .60 1.50
266 Spaceport Docking Bay DARK F .60 1.50
267 Spaceport Docking Bay LIGHT F .60 1.50
268 Spaceport Prefectís Office F .60 1.50
269 Spaceport Street DARK F .60 1.50
270 Spaceport Street LIGHT F .60 1.50
271 Spiral R 1.25 3.00
272 Star Destroyer! R 1.00 2.50
273 Stay Sharp! U .40 1.00
274 Steady Aim C .12 .30
275 Strategic Reserves R 1.00 2.50
276 Suppressive Fire C .12 .30
277 Surface Defense R 1.00 2.50
278 Swamp DARK F .60 1.50
279 Swamp LIGHT F .60 1.50
280 Swoop Mercenary F .60 1.50
281 Sy Snootles R 1.00 2.50
282 T-47 Battle Formation R 1.00 2.50
283 Tarkinís Bounty U .40 1.00
284 Tatooine Celebration R 1.25 3.00
285 Tatooine Occupation R 1.50 4.00
286 Tatooine: Anchorhead F .60 1.50
287 Tatooine: Beggarís Canyon R .75 2.00
288 Tatooine: Jabbaís Palace C .12 .30
289 Tatooine: Jawa Canyon DARK U .40 1.00
290 Tatooine: Jawa Canyon LIGHT U .40 1.00
291 Tatooine: Krayt Dragon Pass F .60 1.50
292 Tatooine: Tosche Station C .12 .30
293 Tauntaun Skull C .12 .30
294 Tawss Khaa R .75 2.00
295 The Planet That Itís Farthest From U.40 1.00
296 Thedit R 1.00 2.50
297 Theron Nett U .40 1.00
298 Theyíre Coming In Too Fast! C .12 .30
299 Theyíre Tracking Us C .12 .30
300 Theyíve Shut Down .12 .30
The Main Reactor C
301 Tibrin Operative C .12 .30
302 TIE Defender Mark I F .60 1.50

303 TK-422 R 1.00 2.50
304 Trooper Sabacc DARK F .60 1.50
305 Trooper Sabacc LIGHT F .60 1.50
306 Uh-oh! U .40 1.00
307 Umpass-stay R .75 2.00
308 UríRuír R 1.00 2.50
309 URoRRuRíRíRís Bantha R 1.00 2.50
310 Uutkik R 1.00 2.50
311 Vaderís Personal Shuttle R 1.00 2.50
312 Vengeance R 1.00 2.50
313 Wakeelmui U .40 1.00
314 Watch Your Back! C .12 .30
315 Weapons Display C .12 .30
316 Wise Advice U .40 1.00
317 Wittinís Sandcrawler R 1.00 2.50
318 Womp Rat C .12 .30
319 Wookiee F .60 1.50
320 Wrist Comlink C .12 .30
321 X-wing Assault Squadron R 1.00 2.50
322 X-wing Laser Cannon C .12 .30
323 Yavin 4 Trooper F .60 1.50
324 Yavin 4: Massassi Headquarters R1.00 2.50

1999 Star Wars Endor

COMPLETE SET (180) 75.00 150.00
BOOSTER BOX (30 PACKS) 75.00 150.00
BOOSTER PACK (9 CARDS) 3.50 7.00
RELEASED IN JUNE 1999

1 AT-ST Pilot C .12 .30
2 Biker Scout Trooper C .12 .30
3 Colonel Dyer R 1.25 3.00
4 Commander Igar R 1.25 3.00
5 Corporal Avarik U .40 1.00
6 Corporal Drazin U .40 1.00
7 Corporal Drelosyn R 1.25 3.00
8 Corporal Misik R 1.00 2.50
9 Corporal Oberk R 1.25 3.00
10 Elite Squadron Stormtrooper C .12 .30
11 Lieutenant Arnet U .40 1.00
12 Lieutenant Grond U .40 1.00
13 Lieutenant Renz R .75 2.00
14 Lieutenant Watts R 1.25 3.00
15 Major Hewex R .75 2.00
16 Major Marquand R 1.50 4.00
17 Navy Trooper C .12 .30
18 Navy Trooper Fenson R 1.00 2.50
19 Navy Trooper Shield Technician C .12 .30
20 Navy Trooper Vesden U .40 1.00
21 Sergeant Barich R 2.00 5.00
22 Sergeant Elsek U .40 1.00
23 Sergeant Irol R 1.50 4.00
24 Sergeant Tarl U .40 1.00
25 Sergeant Wallen R 1.50 4.00
26 An Entire Legion Of My Best Troops U.40 1.00
27 Aratech Corporation R 1.00 2.50
28 Battle Order U .40 1.00
29 Biker Scout Gear U .40 1.00
30 Closed Door R .75 2.00
31 Crossfire R 3.00 8.00
32 Early Warning Network R .75 2.00
33 Empireís New Order R .75 2.00
34 Establish Secret Base R 1.50 4.00
35 Imperial Academy Training C .12 .30
36 Imperial Arrest Order U .40 1.00
37 Ominous Rumors R .75 2.00
38 Perimeter Patrol R 1.00 2.50
39 Pinned Down U .40 1.00
40 Relentless Tracking R .75 2.00
41 Search And Destroy U .40 1.00
42 Security Precautions R 2.50 6.00
43 Well-earned Command R .75 2.00
44 Accelerate C .12 .30
45 Always Thinking With Your Stomach R2.50 6.00
46 Combat Readiness C .12 .30

47 Compact Firepower C .12 .30
48 Counterattack R .75 2.00
49 Dead Ewok C .12 .30
50 Donít Move! C .12 .30
51 Eee Chu Wawa! C .12 .30
52 Endor Scout Trooper C .12 .30
53 Freeze! U .40 1.00
54 Go For Help! C .12 .30
55 High-speed Tactics U .40 1.00
56 Hot Pursuit C .12 .30
57 Imperial Tyranny C .12 .30
58 Itís An Older Code R .75 2.00
59 Main Course U .40 1.00
60 Outflank C .12 .30
61 Pitiful Little Band C .12 .30
62 Scout Recon C .12 .30
63 Sneak Attack C .12 .30
64 Wounded Warrior R 1.50 4.00
65 You Rebel Scum R 1.00 2.50
66 Carida U .40 1.00
67 Endor Occupation R .75 2.00
68 Endor: Ancient Forest U .40 1.00
69 Endor: Back Door LIGHT U .40 1.00
70 Endor: Bunker LIGHT U .40 1.00
71 Endor: Dark Forest R 2.50 6.00
72 Endor: Dense Forest LIGHT C .12 .30
73 Endor: Ewok Village LIGHT U .40 1.00
74 Endor: Forest Clearing U .40 1.00
75 Endor: Great Forest LIGHT C .12 .30
76 Endor: Landing Platform .12 .30
(Docking Bay) LIGHT C
77 Endor DARK U .40 1.00
78 Lambda-class Shuttle C .12 .30
79 Speeder Bike LIGHT C .12 .30
80 Tempest 1 R .75 2.00
81 Tempest Scout 1 R 1.00 2.50
82 Tempest Scout 2 R 2.00 5.00
83 Tempest Scout 3 R .75 2.00
84 Tempest Scout 4 R 2.50 6.00
85 Tempest Scout 5 R 2.00 5.00
86 Tempest Scout 6 R 2.50 6.00
87 Tempest Scout U .40 1.00
88 AT-ST Dual Cannon R 6.00 15.00
89 Scout Blaster C .12 .30
90 Speeder Bike Cannon U .40 1.00
91 Captain Yutani U .40 1.00
92 Chewbacca of Kashyyyk R .75 2.00
93 Chief Chirpa R 1.00 2.50
94 Corporal Beezer U .40 1.00
95 Corporal Delevar U .40 1.00
96 Corporal Janse U .40 1.00
97 Corporal Kensaric R 1.25 3.00
98 Daughter of Skywalker R 10.00 20.00
99 Dresselian Commando C .12 .30
100 Endor LIGHT U .40 1.00
101 Ewok Sentry C .12 .30
102 Ewok Spearman C .12 .30
103 Ewok Tribesman C .12 .30
104 General Crix Madine R 1.00 2.50
105 General Solo R .75 2.00
106 Graak R .75 2.00
107 Kazak R 1.00 2.50
108 Lieutenant Greeve R .75 2.00
109 Lieutenant Page R 1.50 4.00
110 Logray R .75 2.00
111 Lumat U .40 1.00
112 Mon Mothma R 1.25 3.00
113 Orrimaarko R .75 2.00
114 Paploo U .40 1.00
115 Rabin U .40 1.00
116 Romba R .75 2.00
117 Sergeant Brooks Carlson R .75 2.00
118 Sergeant Bruckman R .75 2.00
119 Sergeant Junkin U .40 1.00
120 Teebo R .75 2.00
121 Threepio R 1.25 3.00
122 Wicket R .75 2.00
123 Wuta U .40 1.00
124 Aim High R 1.00 2.50
125 Battle Plan U .40 1.00
126 Commando Training C .12 .30
127 Count Me In R .75 2.00
128 I Hope Sheís All Right U .40 1.00
129 I Wonder Who They Found U .40 1.00
130 Insurrection U .40 1.00
131 Thatís One R .75 2.00
132 Wokling R 6.00 15.00
133 Deactivate The Shield Generator R1.25 3.00
134 Careful Planning C .12 .30
135 Covert Landing U .40 1.00

136 Endor Operations 2.50 6.00
Imperial Outpost R
137 Ewok And Roll C .12 .30
138 Ewok Log Jam C .12 .30
139 Ewok Rescue C .12 .30
140 Firefight C .12 .30
141 Fly Casual R .75 2.00
142 Free Ride U .40 1.00
143 Get Alongside That One U .40 1.00
144 Here We Go Again R .75 2.00
145 I Have A Really Bad .12 .30
Feeling About This C
146 I Know R 1.25 3.00
147 Lost In The Wilderness R .75 2.00
148 Rapid Deployment R .75 2.00
149 Sound The Attack C .12 .30
150 Surprise Counter Assault R .75 2.00
151 Take The Initiative C .12 .30
152 This Is Absolutely Right R .75 2.00
153 Throw Me Another Charge U .40 1.00
154 Were You Looking For Me? R 4.00 10.00
155 Wookiee Guide C .12 .30
156 Yub Yub! C .12 .30
157 Chandrila U .40 1.00
158 Endor Celebration R .75 2.00
159 Endor: Back Door DARK U .40 1.00
160 Endor: Bunker DARK U .40 1.00
161 Endor: Chief Chirpaís Hut R 3.00 8.00
162 Endor: Dense Forest DARK C .12 .30
163 Endor: Ewok Village DARK U .40 1.00
164 Endor: Great Forest DARK C .12 .30
165 Endor: Hidden Forest Trail U .40 1.00
166 Endor: Landing Platform .12 .30
(Docking Bay) DARK C
167 Endor: Rebel Landing Site (Forest) R2.50 6.00
168 Rebel Strike Team 1.25 3.00
Garrison Destroyed R
169 Tydirium R 1.25 3.00
170 YT-1300 Transport C .12 .30
171 Chewieís AT-ST R 3.00 8.00
172 Ewok Glider C .12 .30
173 Speeder Bike DARK C .12 .30
174 A280 Sharpshooter Rifle R 2.50 6.00
175 BlasTech E-11B Blaster Rifle C .12 .30
176 Chewbaccaís Bowcaster R 2.50 6.00
177 Ewok Bow C .12 .30
178 Ewok Catapult U .40 1.00
179 Ewok Spear C .12 .30
180 Explosive Charge U .40 1.00

1999 Star Wars Enhanced Cloud City

COMPLETE SET (12) 12.00 25.00
RELEASED IN 1999

1 4-LOM With Concussion Rifle PM 1.50 4.00
2 Any Methods Necessary PM 2.00 5.00
3 Boba Fett in Slave I PM 1.00 2.50
4 Chewie With Blaster Rifle PM 1.00 2.50
5 Crush The Rebellion PM 1.25 3.00
6 Dengar In Punishing One PM 1.00 2.50
7 IG-88 With Riot Gun PM 3.00 8.00
8 Lando In Millennium Falcon PM 1.00 2.50
9 Lando With Blaster Pistol PM 1.00 2.50
10 Quiet Mining Colony 1.00 2.50
Independent Operation PM
11 This Deal Is Getting Worse 1.00 2.50
All The Time
Pray I Donít Alter It Any Further
12 Z-95 Bespin Defense Fighter PM 1.00 2.50

1999 Star Wars Enhanced Jabba's Palace

COMPLETE SET (12) 20.00 40.00
RELEASE IN 1999

1 Bossk With Mortar Gun PM 1.00 2.50
2 Boushh PM 1.25 3.00
3 Court Of The Vile Gangster 1.00 2.50
I Shall Enjoy Watching You Die PM
4 Dengar With Blaster Carbine PM 1.00 2.50
5 IG-88 In IG-2000 PM 1.00 2.50
6 Jodo Kast PM 1.50 4.00
7 Mara Jade, The Emperorís Hand PM10.00 20.00
8 Mara Jadeís Lightsaber PM 1.50 4.00
9 Master Luke PM 2.50 6.00
10 See-Threepio PM 1.00 2.50
11 You Can Either Profit By This... 1.00 2.50
Or Be Destroyed PM
12 Zuckuss In Mist Hunter PM 1.25 3.00

2000 Star Wars Death Star II

COMPLETE SET (182)	200.00	300.00
BOOSTER BOX (30 PACKS)	150.00	250.00
BOOSTER PACK (11 CARDS)	5.00	9.00
RELEASED IN JULY 2000		
1 Accuser R	1.25	3.00
2 Admiral Ackbar XR	1.25	3.00
3 Admiral Chiraneau R	1.50	4.00
4 Admiral Piett XR	1.00	2.50
5 Anakin Skywalker R	1.00	2.50
6 Aquaris C	.12	.30
7 A-wing C	.12	.30
8 A-wing Cannon C	.12	.30
9 Baron Soontir Fel R	1.50	4.00
10 Battle Deployment R	1.25	3.00
11 Black 11 R	1.00	2.50
12 Blue Squadron 5 U	.40	1.00
13 Blue Squadron B-wing R	1.50	4.00
14 Bring Him Before Me Take Your Fatherís Place R	1.00	2.50
15 B-wing Attack Squadron R	1.00	2.50
16 B-wing Bomber C	.12	.30
17 Capital Support R	1.00	2.50
18 Captain Godherdt U	.40	1.00
19 Captain Jonus U	.40	1.00
20 Captain Sarkli R	1.00	2.50
21 Captain Verrack U	.40	1.00
22 Captain Yorr U	.40	1.00
23 Chimaera R	2.50	6.00
24 Close Air Support C	.12	.30
25 Colonel Cracken R	1.00	2.50
26 Colonel Davod Jon U	.40	1.00
27 Colonel Jendon R	1.00	2.50
28 Colonel Salm U	.40	1.00
29 Combat Response C	.12	.30
30 Combined Fleet Action R	1.00	2.50
31 Commander Merrejk R	1.25	3.00
32 Concentrate All Fire R	1.00	2.50
33 Concussion Missiles DARK C	.12	.30
34 Concussion Missiles LIGHT C	.12	.30
35 Corporal Marmor U	.40	1.00
36 Corporal Midge U	.40	1.00
37 Critical Error Revealed C	.12	.30
38 Darth Vaderís Lightsaber R	1.00	2.50
39 Death Star II R	1.25	3.00
40 Death Star II: Capacitors C	.12	.30
41 Death Star II: Coolant Shaft C	.12	.30
42 Death Star II: Docking Bay C	.12	.30
43 Death Star II: Reactor Core C	.12	.30
44 Death Star II: Throne Room R	1.00	2.50
45 Defiance R	1.25	3.00
46 Desperate Counter C	.12	.30
47 Dominator R	1.00	2.50
48 DS-181-3 U	.40	1.00
49 DS-181-4 U	.40	1.00
50 Emperor Palpatine UR	30.00	60.00
51 Emperorís Personal Shuttle R	1.00	2.50
52 Emperorís Power U	.40	1.00
53 Endor Shield U	.40	1.00
54 Enhanced Proton Torpedoes C	.12	.30
55 Fighter Cover R	2.00	5.00
56 Fighters Coming In R	1.00	2.50
57 First Officer Thaneespi R	1.00	2.50
58 Flagship Executor R	1.25	3.00
59 Flagship Operations R	1.00	2.50
60 Force Lightning R	2.00	5.00
61 Force Pike C	.12	.30
62 Gall C	.12	.30
63 General Calrissian R	1.00	2.50
64 General Walex Blissex U	.40	1.00
65 Gold Squadron 1 R	1.00	2.50
66 Gray Squadron 1 U	.40	1.00
67 Gray Squadron 2 U	.40	1.00
68 Gray Squadron Y-wing Pilot C	.12	.30
69 Green Leader R	1.00	2.50
70 Green Squadron 1 R	1.00	2.50
71 Green Squadron 3 R	1.00	2.50
72 Green Squadron A-wing R	1.25	3.00
73 Green Squadron Pilot C	.12	.30
74 Head Back To The Surface C	.12	.30
75 Heading For The Medical Frigate C	.12	.30
76 Heavy Turbolaser Battery DARK C	.12	.30
77 Heavy Turbolaser Battery LIGHT C	.12	.30
78 Home One R	4.00	10.00
79 Home One: Docking Bay C	.12	.30
80 Home One: War Room R	1.25	3.00
81 Honor Of The Jedi U	.40	1.00
82 I Feel The Conflict U	.40	1.00
83 Iíll Take The Leader R	2.50	6.00
84 Iím With You Too R	1.50	4.00
85 Imperial Command R	4.00	10.00
86 Inconsequential Losses C	.12	.30
87 Independence R	1.25	3.00
88 Insertion Planning C	.12	.30
89 Insignificant Rebellion U	.40	1.00
90 Intensify The Forward Batteries R	1.00	2.50
91 Janus Greejatus R	1.00	2.50
92 Judicator R	1.50	4.00
93 Karie Neth U	.40	1.00
94 Keir Santage U	.40	1.00
95 Kin Kian U	.40	1.00
96 Launching The Assault R	1.00	2.50
97 Leave Them To Me C	.12	.30
98 Letís Keep A Little Optimism Here C	.12	.30
99 Liberty R	1.25	3.00
100 Lieutenant Blount R	1.00	2.50
101 Lieutenant Endicott U	.40	1.00
102 Lieutenant Hebsly U	.40	1.00
103 Lieutenant síToo Vees U	.40	1.00
104 Lieutenant Telsij U	.40	1.00
105 Lord Vader R	10.00	20.00
106 Luke Skywalker, Jedi Knight UR	30.00	60.00
107 Lukeís Lightsaber R	1.50	4.00
108 Luminous U	.40	1.00
109 Major Haashín U	.40	1.00
110 Major Mianda U	.40	1.00
111 Major Olander Brit U	.40	1.00
112 Major Panno U	.40	1.00
113 Major Rhymer U	.40	1.00
114 Major Turr Phennir U	.40	1.00
115 Masanya R	1.50	4.00
116 Menace Fades C	.12	.30
117 Mobilization Points C	.12	.30
118 Moff Jerjerrod R	1.00	2.50
119 Mon Calamari DARK C	.12	.30
120 Mon Calamari LIGHT C	.12	.30
121 Mon Calamari Star Cruiser R	1.25	3.00
122 Myn Kyneugh R	1.00	2.50
123 Nebulon-B Frigate U	.40	1.00
124 Nien Nunb R	1.25	3.00
125 Obsidian 10 U	.40	1.00
126 Onyx 1 R	1.25	3.00
127 Onyx 2 U	.40	1.00
128 Operational As Planned C	.12	.30
129 Orbital Mine C	.12	.30
130 Our Only Hope U	.40	1.00
131 Overseeing It Personally R	1.00	2.50
132 Prepared Defenses C	.12	.30
133 Rebel Leadership R	3.00	8.00
134 Red Squadron 1 R	1.00	2.50
135 Red Squadron 4 U	.40	1.00
136 Red Squadron 7 U	.40	1.00
137 Rise, My Friend R	1.00	2.50
138 Royal Escort C	.12	.30
139 Royal Guard C	.12	.30
140 Saber 1 R	6.00	15.00
141 Saber 2 U	.40	1.00
142 Saber 3 U	.40	1.00
143 Saber 4 U	.40	1.00
144 Scimitar 1 U	.40	1.00
145 Scimitar 2 U	.40	1.00
146 Scimitar Squadron TIE C	.12	.30
147 Scythe 1 U	.40	1.00
148 Scythe 3 U	.40	1.00
149 Scythe Squadron TIE C	.12	.30
150 SFS L-s7.2 TIE Cannon C	.12	.30
151 Sim Aloo R	1.00	2.50
152 Something Special Planned For Them C	.12	.30
153 Squadron Assignments C	.12	.30
154 Staging Areas C	.12	.30
155 Strike Planning R	1.00	2.50
156 Strikeforce C	.12	.30
157 Sullust DARK C	.12	.30
158 Sullust LIGHT C	.12	.30
159 Superficial Damage C	.12	.30
160 Superlaser Mark II U	.40	1.00
161 Taking Them With Us R	1.25	3.00
162 Tala 1 R	1.00	2.50
163 Tala 2 R	1.00	2.50
164 Ten Numb R	1.00	2.50
165 That Thingís Operational R	1.00	2.50
166 The Emperorís Shield R	1.00	2.50
167 The Emperorís Sword R	1.00	2.50
168 The Time For Our Attack Has Come C	.12	.30
169 The Way Of Things U	.40	1.00
170 There Is Good In Him I Can Save Him R	1.00	2.50
171 Thunderflare R	1.00	2.50
172 TIE Interceptor C	.12	.30
173 Twilight Is Upon Me R	1.00	2.50
174 Tycho Celchu R	1.25	3.00
175 Visage R	1.00	2.50
176 Weíre In Attack Position Now R	2.50	6.00
177 Wedge Antilles, Red Squadron Leader R	1.50	4.00
178 You Cannot Hide Forever U	.40	1.00
179 You Must Confront Vader R	1.50	4.00
180 Young Fool R	1.00	2.50
181 Your Destiny C	.12	.30
182 Your Insight Serves You Well U	.40	1.00

2000 Star Wars Jabba's Palace Sealed Deck

COMPLETE SET (20)	5.00	12.00
RELEASE DATE FALL, 2000		
1 Agents In The Court No Love For The Empire PM	.40	1.00
2 Hutt Influence PM	.40	1.00
3 Jabbaís Palace: Antechamber PM	.40	1.00
4 Jabbaís Palace: Lower Passages PM	.40	1.00
5 Lando With Vibro-Ax PM	.40	1.00
6 Let Them Make The First Move My Kind Of Scum Fearless And Inventive PM	.40	1.00
7 Mercenary Pilot PM	.40	1.00
8 Mighty Jabba PM	.40	1.00
9 No Escape PM	.40	1.00
10 Ounee Ta PM	.40	1.00
11 Palace Raider PM	.40	1.00
12 Power Of The Hutt PM	.40	1.00
13 Racing Skiff DARK PM	.40	1.00
14 Racing Skiff LIGHT PM	.40	1.00
15 Seeking An Audience PM	.40	1.00
16 Stun Blaster DARK PM	.40	1.00
17 Stun Blaster LIGHT PM	.40	1.00
18 Tatooine: Desert Heart PM	.40	1.00
19 Tatooine: Hutt Trade Route (Desert) PM	.40	1.00
20 Underworld Contacts PM	.40	1.00

2000 Star Wars Reflections II

COMPLETE SET (54)	20.00	50.00
BOOSTER BOX (30 PACKS)	150.00	250.00
BOOSTER PACK (11 CARDS)	5.00	10.00
RELEASED IN DECEMBER 2000		
1 There Is No Try and Oppressive Enforcement PM	.60	1.50
2 Abyssin Ornament and Wounded Wookiee PM	.40	1.00
3 Agents Of Black Sun Vengence Of The Dark Prince PM	.40	1.00
4 Alter and Collateral Damage PM	.60	1.50
5 Alter and Friendly Fire PM	.60	1.50
6 Arica PM	2.00	5.00
7 Artoo and Threepio PM	.60	1.50
8 Black Sun Fleet PM	.40	1.00
9 Captain Gilad Pellaeon PM	.60	1.50
10 Chewbacca, Protector PM	.60	1.50
11 Control and Set For Stun PM	.60	1.50
12 Control and Tunnel Vision PM	1.00	2.50
13 Corran Horn PM	1.50	4.00
14 Dark Maneuvers and Tallon Roll PM	1.00	2.50
15 Dash Rendar PM	1.25	3.00
16 Defensive Fire and Hutt Smooch PM	.40	1.00
17 Do, Or Do Not and Wise Advice PM	.40	1.00
18 Dr Evazan and Ponda Baba PM	.40	1.00
19 Evader and Monnok PM	.60	1.50
20 Ghhhk and Those Rebels Wonít Escape Us PM	.40	1.00
21 Grand Admiral Thrawn PM	2.50	6.00
22 Guri PM	1.25	3.00
23 Houjix and Out Of Nowhere PM	.60	1.50
24 Jabbaís Prize PM	.40	1.00
25 Kir Kanos PM	.40	1.00
26 LE-BO2D9 [Leebo] PM	.40	1.00
27 Luke Skywalker, Rebel Scout PM	1.00	2.50
28 Mercenary Armor PM	.40	1.00
29 Mirax Terrik PM	.60	1.50
30 Nar Shaddaa Wind Chimes and Out Of Somewhere PM	.40	1.00
31 No Questions Asked PM	.40	1.00
32 Obi-Waníís Journal PM	.40	1.00
33 Ommni Box and Itís Worse PM	.40	1.00
34 Out of Commission and Transmission Terminated PM	1.00	2.50
35 Outrider PM	.60	1.50
36 Owen Lars and Beru Lars PM	.40	1.00
37 Path Of Least Resistance and Revealed PM	.40	1.00
38 Prince Xizor PM	1.50	4.00
39 Pulsar Skate PM	.40	1.00
40 Sense and Recoil In Fear PM	.60	1.50
41 Sense and Uncertain Is The Future PM	.60	1.50
42 Shocking Information and Grimtaash PM	.40	1.00
43 Sniper and Dark Strike PM	.40	1.00
44 Snoova PM	1.00	2.50
45 Sorry About The Mess and Blaster Proficiency PM	.60	1.50
46 Stinger PM	.40	1.00
47 Sunsdown and Too Cold For Speeders PM	.40	1.00
48 Talon Karrde PM	.60	1.50
49 The Bith Shuffle and Desperate Reach PM	.40	1.00
50 The Emperor PM	1.50	4.00
51 Vigo PM	1.50	4.00
52 Virago PM	.40	1.00
53 Watch Your Step This Place Can Be A Little Rough PM	.40	1.00
54 Yoda Stew and You Do Have Your Moments PM	.40	1.00

2000 Star Wars Third Anthology

COMPLETE SET (6)	4.00	10.00
RELEASED IN 2000		
1 A New Secret Base PM	1.00	2.50
2 Artoo-Detoo In Red 5 PM	1.00	2.50
3 Echo Base Garrison PM	1.00	2.50
4 Massassi Base Operations One In A Million PM	1.00	2.50
5 Prisoner 2187 PM	1.00	2.50
6 Set Your Course For Alderaan The Ultimate Power In The Universe PM	1.00	2.50

2001 Star Wars Coruscant

COMPLETE SET (188)	120.00	250.00
BOOSTER BOX (30 PACKS)	300.00	400.00
BOOSTER PACK (11 CARDS)	12.00	15.00
RELEASED IN AUGUST 2001		
1 A Tragedy Has Occurred U	.40	1.00
2 A Vergence In The Force U	.40	1.00
3 Accepting Trade Federation Control U	.40	1.00
4 Aks Moe R	1.25	3.00
5 All Wings Report In and Darklighter Spin R	6.00	15.00
6 Allegations Of Corruption U	.40	1.00
7 Alter DARK U	.40	1.00
8 Alter LIGHT U	.40	1.00
9 Another Pathetic Lifeform U	.40	1.00
10 Are You Brain Dead?! R	1.50	4.00
11 Ascertaining The Truth U	.40	1.00
12 Baseless Accusations C	.12	.30
13 Baskol Yeesrim U	.40	1.00
14 Battle Droid Blaster Rifle C	.12	.30
15 Battle Order and First Strike R	1.00	2.50
16 Battle Plan and Draw Their Fire R	1.50	4.00
17 Begin Landing Your Troops U	.40	1.00
18 Blockade Flagship: Bridge R	3.00	8.00
19 Captain Madakor R	1.00	2.50
20 Captain Panaka R	1.00	2.50
21 Chokk U	.40	1.00
22 Control DARK U	.40	1.00
23 Control LIGHT U	.40	1.00
24 Coruscant DARK C	.12	.30
25 Coruscant LIGHT C	.12	.30
26 Coruscant Guard DARK C	.12	.30
27 Coruscant Guard LIGHT C	.12	.30
28 Coruscant: Docking Bay DARK C	.12	.30
29 Coruscant: Docking Bay LIGHT C	.12	.30
30 Coruscant: Galactic Senate DARK C	.12	.30
31 Coruscant: Galactic Senate LIGHT C	.12	.30
32 Coruscant: Jedi Council Chamber R	3.00	8.00
33 Credits Will Do Fine C	.12	.30
34 Darth Maul, Young Apprentice R	15.00	30.00
35 Daultay Dofine R	1.25	3.00
36 Depa Billaba R	1.25	3.00
37 Destroyer Droid R	12.00	25.00
38 Dioxis R	1.00	2.50
39 Do They Have A Code Clearance? R	1.00	2.50
40 Droid Starfighter C	.12	.30
41 Drop! U	.40	1.00
42 Edcel Bar Gane C	.12	.30
43 Enter The Bureaucrat U	.40	1.00
44 Establish Control U	.40	1.00
45 Free Ride and Endor Celebration R	1.50	4.00
46 Freon Drevan U	.40	1.00
47 Gardulla The Hutt U	.40	1.00
48 Graxol Kelvyyn U	.40	1.00
49 Grotto Werribee R	1.25	3.00
50 Gungan Warrior C	.12	.30
51 Horox Ryyder C	.12	.30
52 I Will Not Defer U	.40	1.00
53 Iíve Decided To Go Back C	.12	.30
54 Imperial Arrest Order and Secret Plans R	3.00	8.00
55 Imperial Artillery R	3.00	8.00
56 Inconsequential Barriers C	.12	.30
57 Insurrection and Aim High R	2.50	6.00
58 Jawa DARK C	.12	.30
59 Jawa LIGHT C	.12	.30
60 Keder The Black R	1.00	2.50
61 Ki-Adi-Mundi U	.40	1.00
62 Kill Them Immediately C	.12	.30
63 Lana Dobreed U	.40	1.00
64 Laser Cannon Battery U	.40	1.00
65 Liana Merian U	.40	1.00
66 Lieutenant Williams U	.40	1.00
67 Little Real Power C	.12	.30
68 Lott Dod R	1.25	3.00
69 Mace Windu R	10.00	20.00
70 Malastare DARK U	.40	1.00
71 Malastare LIGHT U	.40	1.00
72 Mas Amedda U	.40	1.00
73 Master Qui-Gon R	3.00	8.00
74 Masterful Move and Endor Occupation R	2.00	5.00
75 Maul Strikes R	2.00	5.00
76 Maulís Sith Infiltrator R	3.00	8.00
77 Might Of The Republic R	2.50	6.00
78 Mind Tricks Donít Work On Me U	.40	1.00
79 Mindful Of The Future C	.12	.30
80 Motion Supported U	.40	1.00
81 Murr Danod R	1.00	2.50
82 My Lord, Is That Legal? I Will Make It Legal U	.40	1.00
83 My Loyal Bodyguard U	.40	1.00
84 Naboo Blaster C	.12	.30
85 Naboo Blaster Rifle DARK C	.12	.30
86 Naboo Blaster Rifle LIGHT C	.12	.30
87 Naboo Defense Fighter C	.12	.30

88 Naboo Fighter Pilot C .12 .30
89 Naboo Security Officer Blaster C .12 .30
90 Naboo DARK U .40 1.00
91 Naboo LIGHT U .40 1.00
92 Naboo: Battle Plains DARK C .12 .30
93 Naboo: Battle Plains LIGHT C .12 .30
94 Naboo: Swamp DARK C .12 .30
95 Naboo: Swamp LIGHT C .12 .30
96 Naboo: Theed Palace Courtyard DARK C .12 .30
97 Naboo: Theed Palace Courtyard LIGHT C .12 .30
98 Naboo: Theed Palace Docking Bay DARK C .12 .30
99 Naboo: Theed Palace Docking Bay LIGHT C .12 .30
100 Naboo: Theed Palace Throne Room DARK C .12 .30
101 Naboo: Theed Palace Throne Room LIGHT C .12 .30
102 Neimoidian Advisor U .40 1.00
103 Neimoidian Pilot C .12 .30
104 New Leadership Is Needed C .12 .30
105 No Civility, Only Politics C .12 .30
106 No Money, No Parts, No Deal! Youíre A Slave? U .40 1.00
107 Nute Gunray R 1.00 2.50
108 Odin Nesloor U .40 1.00
109 On The Payroll Of The Trade Federation C .12 .30
110 Orn Free Taa C .12 .30
111 Our Blockade Is Perfectly Legal U .40 1.00
112 P-59 R 3.00 8.00
113 P-60 R 1.50 4.00
114 Panakaís Blaster R 1.25 3.00
115 Passel Argente C .12 .30
116 Phylo Gandish R 1.50 4.00
117 Plea To The Court U .40 1.00
118 Plead My Case To The Senate Sanity And Compassion U .40 1.00
119 Plo Koon R 3.00 8.00
120 Queen Amidala, Ruler Of Naboo R 5.00 10.00
121 Queenís Royal Starship R 1.25 3.00
122 Radiant VII R 1.50 4.00
123 Rebel Artillery R 3.00 8.00
124 Republic Cruiser C .12 .30
125 Reveal Ourselves To The Jedi C .12 .30
126 Ric Olie R 1.00 2.50
127 Rune Haako R 1.00 2.50
128 Sabe R 1.25 3.00
129 Sache U .40 1.00
130 Secure Route U .40 1.00
131 Security Battle Droid C .12 .30
132 Security Control U .40 1.00
133 Sei Taria U .40 1.00
134 Senator Palpatine (head and shoulders) R 3.00 8.00
135 Senator Palpatine (head shot) R 15.00 30.00
136 Sense DARK U .40 1.00
137 Sense LIGHT U .40 1.00
138 Short Range Fighters and Watch Your Back! R 2.50 6.00
139 Speak With The Jedi Council R 3.00 8.00
140 Squabbling Delegates R 1.25 3.00
141 Stay Here, Where Itís Safe C .12 .30
142 Supreme Chancellor Valorum R 1.00 2.50
143 Tatooine DARK U .40 1.00
144 Tatooine LIGHT U .40 1.00
145 Tatooine: Marketplace DARK C .12 .30
146 Tatooine: Marketplace LIGHT C .12 .30
147 Tatooine: Mos Espa Docking Bay DARK C .12 .30
148 Tatooine: Mos Espa Docking Bay LIGHT C .12 .30
149 Tatooine: Wattoís Junkyard DARK C .12 .30
150 Tatooine: Wattoís Junkyard LIGHT C .12 .30
151 TC-14 R 1.00 2.50
152 Televan Koreyy R 1.00 2.50
153 Tendau Bendon U .40 1.00
154 Tey How U .40 1.00
155 The Gravest Of Circumstances U .40 1.00
156 The Hyperdrive Generatorís Gone Weíll Need A New One U .40 1.00
157 The Phantom Menace R 5.00 10.00
158 The Point Is Conceded C .12 .30
159 They Will Be No Match For You R 1.00 2.50
160 Theyíre Still Coming Through! U .40 1.00
161 This Is Outrageous! U .40 1.00
162 Thrown Back C .12 .30
163 Tikkes C .12 .30
164 Toonbuck Toora U .40 1.00
165 Trade Federation Battleship U .40 1.00
166 Trade Federation Droid Control Ship R 1.25 3.00
167 Tusken Raider C .12 .30
168 Vote Now! DARK R 1.00 2.50
169 Vote Now! LIGHT R 1.25 3.00
170 We Must Accelerate Our Plans R 10.00 20.00
171 We Wish To Board At Once R 2.00 5.00
172 Weíre Leaving C .12 .30
173 Wipe Them Out, All Of Them U .40 1.00
174 Yade M'rak U .40 1.00
175 YanÈ U .40 1.00
176 Yarua U .40 1.00
177 Yeb Yeb Ademíthorn C .12 .30
178 Yoda, Senior Council Member R 2.50 6.00
179 You Cannot Hide Forever and Mobilization Points R 2.50 6.00
180 You've Got A Lot Of Guts Coming Here R 1.25 3.00
181 Your Insight Serves You Well and Staging Areas R 1.00 2.50
182 Coruscant Dark Side List 1 .12 .30
183 Coruscant Dark Side List 2 .12 .30
184 Coruscant Light Side List 1 .12 .30
185 Coruscant Light Side List 2 .12 .30
186 Coruscant Rule Card 1 .12 .30
187 Coruscant Rule Card 2 .12 .30
188 Coruscant Rule Card 3 .12 .30

2001 Star Wars Reflections III

COMPLETE SET (96) 80.00 150.00
BOOSTER BOX (30 PACKS) 250.00 350.00
BOOSTER PACK (11 CARDS) 7.50 15.00
RELEASED IN 2001

1 A Close Race PM 1.00 2.50
2 A Remote Planet PM 1.00 2.50
3 A Tragedy Has Occured PM 1.25 3.00
4 A Useless Gesture PM 1.00 2.50
5 Aim High PM 1.25 3.00
6 Allegations of Coruption PM 1.00 2.50
7 An Unusual Amount Of Fear PM 1.00 2.50
8 Another Pathetic Lifeform PM 1.00 2.50
9 Armament Dismantled PM 1.00 2.50
10 Battle Order PM 1.00 2.50
11 Battle Plan PM 1.25 3.00
12 Bib Fortuna PM 1.00 2.50
13 Blizzard 4 PM 2.00 5.00
14 Blockade Flagship: Hallway PM 1.00 2.50
15 Blow Parried PM 1.00 2.50
16 Boba Fett, Bounty Hunter PM 6.00 12.00
17 Chewie, Enraged PM 1.50 4.00
18 Clinging To The Edge PM 1.00 2.50
19 Colo Claw Fish DARK PM 1.00 2.50
20 Colo Claw Fish LIGHT PM 1.00 2.50
21 Come Here You Big Coward PM 1.25 3.00
22 Conduct Your Search PM 1.25 3.00
23 Crossfire PM 1.00 2.50
24 Dark Rage PM 1.00 2.50
25 Darth Maulís Demise PM 1.00 2.50
26 Deep Hatred PM 1.00 2.50
27 Desperate Times PM 1.00 2.50
28 Diversionary Tactics PM 1.00 2.50
29 Do They Have A Code Clearance? PM 1.25 3.00
30 Do, Or Do Not PM 1.00 2.50
31 Donít Do That Again PM 1.00 2.50
32 Echo Base Sensors PM 1.25 3.00
33 Energy Walls DARK PM 1.00 2.50
34 Energy Walls LIGHT PM 1.00 2.50
35 Ewok Celebration PM 1.00 2.50
36 Fall Of A Jedi PM 1.00 2.50
37 Fanfare PM 1.00 2.50
38 Fear Is My Ally PM 1.00 2.50
39 Force Push PM 1.25 3.00
40 Han, Chewie, and The Falcon PM 6.00 12.00
41 He Can Go About His Business PM 1.00 2.50
42 Horace Vancil PM 1.00 2.50
43 Inner Strength PM 1.00 2.50
44 Jabba Desilijic Tiure PM 1.00 2.50
45 Jar Jarís Electropole PM 1.00 2.50
46 Jedi Leap PM 1.00 2.50
47 Lando Calrissian, Scoundrel PM 2.00 5.00
48 Landoís Not A System, Heís A Man PM 1.00 2.50
49 Leave them to Me PM 1.00 2.50
50 Leia, Rebel Princess PM 2.50 6.00
51 Letís Keep A Little Optimism Here PM 1.00 2.50
52 Lord Maul PM 7.50 15.00
53 Maulís Double-Bladed Lightsaber PM 2.00 5.00
54 Naboo: Theed Palace Generator Core DARK PM 1.00 2.50
55 Naboo: Theed Palace Generator Core LIGHT PM 1.00 2.50
56 Naboo: Theed Palace Generator DARK PM 1.00 2.50
57 Naboo: Theed Palace Generator LIGHT PM 1.00 2.50
58 No Escape PM 1.00 2.50
59 No Match For A Sith PM 1.00 2.50
60 Obi-Wan Kenobi, Jedi Knight PM 1.50 4.00
61 Obi-Wanís Lightsaber PM 1.00 2.50
62 Only Jedi Carry That Weapon PM 1.00 2.50
63 Opee Sea Killer DARK PM 1.00 2.50
64 Opee Sea Killer LIGHT PM 1.00 2.50
65 Oppressive Enforcement PM 1.00 2.50
66 Ounee Ta PM 1.00 2.50
67 Planetary Defenses PM 1.00 2.50
68 Prepare For A Surface Attack PM 1.00 2.50
69 Qui-Gon Jinn, Jedi Master PM 2.50 6.00
70 Qui-Gonís End PM 1.25 3.00
71 Reistance PM 1.00 2.50
72 Sando Aqua Monster DARK PM 1.00 2.50
73 Sando Aqua Monster LIGHT PM 1.00 2.50
74 Secret Plans PM 1.00 2.50
75 Sio Bibble PM 1.00 2.50
76 Stormtrooper Garrison PM 5.00 10.00
77 Strike Blockaded PM 1.00 2.50
78 The Ebb Of Battle PM 1.00 2.50
79 The Hutts Are Gangsters PM 1.00 2.50
80 There Is No Try PM 1.25 3.00
81 They Must Never Again Leave This City PM 1.00 2.50
82 Thok and Thug PM 1.00 2.50
83 Through The Corridor PM 1.00 2.50
84 Ultimatum PM 1.00 2.50
85 Unsalvageable PM 1.00 2.50
86 Weíll Let Fate-a Decide, Huh? PM 1.00 2.50
87 Weapon Of A Fallen Mentor PM 1.00 2.50
88 Weapon Of A Sith PM 1.00 2.50
89 Where Are Those Droidekas?! PM 1.00 2.50
90 Wipe Them Out, All Of Them PM 1.00 2.50
91 Wise Advice PM 1.00 2.50
92 Yoda, Master Of The Force PM 5.00 10.00
93 You Cannot Hide Forever PM 1.00 2.50
94 Youíve Never Won A Race? PM 1.00 2.50
95 Your Insight Serves You Well PM 1.00 2.50
96 Your Ship? PM 1.25 3.00

2001 Star Wars Tatooine

COMPLETE SET (95) 25.00 60.00
BOOSTER BOX (30 PACKS) 50.00 100.00
BOOSTER PACK (11 CARDS) 2.50 5.00
RELEASED IN MAY 2001

1 A Jediís Concentration C .12 .30
2 A Jediís Focus C .12 .30
3 A Jediís Patience C .12 .30
4 A Jediís Resilience U .40 1.00
5 A Million Voices Crying Out R .75 2.00
6 A Step Backward U .40 1.00
7 Anakinís Podracer R .75 2.00
8 Aurra Sing R 1.50 4.00
9 Ben Quadinarosí Podracer C .12 .30
10 Boonta Eve Podrace DARK R .75 2.50
11 Boonta Eve Podrace LIGHT R .75 2.00
12 Brisky Morning Munchen R .75 2.00
13 Caldera Righim C .12 .30
14 Changing The Odds C .12 .30
15 Daroe R .75 2.00
16 Darth Maul R 1.50 4.00
17 Deneb Both U .40 1.00
18 Donít Do That Again C .12 .30
19 Dud Boltís Podracer C .12 .30
20 Either Way, You Win U .40 1.00
21 End Of A Reign R .75 2.00
22 Entering The Arena U .40 1.00
23 Eopie C .12 .30
24 Eventually Youíll Lose U .40 1.00
25 Fanfare C .12 .30
26 Gamall Wironicc U .40 1.00
27 Ghana Gleemort U .40 1.00
28 Gragra U .40 1.00
29 Great Shot, Kid! R .75 2.00
30 Grugnak U .40 1.00
31 His Name Is Anakin C .12 .30
32 Hit Racer U .40 1.00
33 I Canít Believe Heís Gone C .12 .30
34 I Did It! R .75 2.00
35 I Will Find Them Quickly, Master R .75 2.00
36 Iím Sorry R .75 2.00
37 If The Trace Was Correct U .40 1.00
38 Jar Jar Binks R .75 2.00
39 Jedi Escape C .12 .30
40 Join Me! U .40 1.00
41 Keeping The Empire Out Forever R .75 2.00
42 Lathe U .40 1.00
43 Lightsaber Parry C .12 .30
44 Loci Rosen U .40 1.00
45 Losing Track C .12 .30
46 Maulís Electrobinoculars C .12 .30
47 Maulís Lightsaber R .75 2.00
48 Neck And Neck U .40 1.00
49 Ni Chuba Na?? C .12 .30
50 Obi-wan Kenobi, Padawan Learner R 1.00 2.50
51 Padme Naberrie R 2.00 5.00
52 Pit Crews U .40 1.00
53 Pit Droid C .12 .30
54 Podrace Prep U .40 1.00
55 Podracer Collision U .40 1.00
56 Quietly Observing U .40 1.00
57 Qui-Gon Jinn R 1.50 4.00
58 Qui-Gon Jinnís Lightsaber R 1.00 2.50
59 Rachalt Hyst U .40 1.00
60 Sebulba R .75 2.00
61 Sebulbaís Podracer R .75 2.00
62 Shmi Skywalker R .75 2.00
63 Sith Fury C .12 .30
64 Sith Probe Droid R 1.00 2.50
65 Start Your Engines! U .40 1.00
66 Tatooine: City Outskirts U .40 1.00
67 Tatooine: Desert Landing Site R .75 2.00
68 Tatooine: Mos Espa DARK C .12 .30
69 Tatooine: Mos Espa LIGHT C .12 .30
70 Tatooine: Podrace Arena DARK C .12 .30
71 Tatooine: Podrace Arena LIGHT C .12 .30
72 Tatooine: Podracer Bay C .12 .30
73 Tatooine: Slave Quarters U .40 1.00
74 Teemto Pagaliesí Podracer C .12 .30
75 The Camp C .12 .30
76 The Shield Is Down! R .75 2.00
77 There Is No Conflict C .12 .30
78 Threepio With His Parts Showing R 1.25 3.00
79 Too Close For Comfort U .40 1.00
80 Vaderís Anger C .12 .30
81 Watto R 1.25 3.00
82 Wattoís Box C .12 .30
83 Wattoís Chance Cube U .40 1.00
84 We Shall Double Our Efforts! R .75 2.00
85 What Was It U .40 1.00
86 Yotts Orren U .40 1.00
87 You May Start Your Landing R .75 2.00
88 You Swindled Me! U .40 1.00
89 You Want This, Donít You? C .12 .30
90 Youíll Find Iím Full Of Surprises U .40 1.00
91 Tatooine Dark Side List .12 .30
92 Tatooine Light Side List .12 .30
93 Tatooine Rule Card 1 .12 .30
94 Tatooine Rule Card 2 .12 .30
95 Tatooine Rule Card 3 .12 .30

2001 Star Wars Theed Palace

COMPLETE SET (121) 80.00 150.00
BOOSTER BOX (30 PACKS) 400.00 500.00
BOOSTER PACK (11 CARDS) 15.00 20.00
RELEASED IN DECEMBER 2001
FINAL EXPANSION PRODUCT BY DECIPHER

1 3B3-10 U .30 .75
2 3B3-1204 U .30 .75
3 3B3-21 U .30 .75
4 3B3-888 U .30 .75
5 AAT Assault Leader R 1.00 2.50
6 AAT Laser Cannon U .30 .75
7 Activate The Droids C .12 .30
8 After Her! R .75 2.00
9 Amidalaís Blaster R .75 2.00
10 Armored Attack Tank U .30 .75
11 Artoo, Brave Little Droid R 1.50 4.00
12 Ascension Guns U .30 .75
13 At Last We Are Getting Results C .12 .30
14 Battle Droid Officer C .12 .30
15 Battle Droid Pilot C .12 .30
16 Big Boomers! C .12 .30
17 Blockade Flagship R 1.50 4.00
18 Blockade Flagship: Docking Bay DARK U .30 .75
19 Blockade Flagship: Docking Bay LIGHT U .30 .75
20 Bok Askol U .30 .75
21 Booma C .12 .30
22 Boss Nass R 1.25 3.00
23 Bravo 1 R .75 2.00
24 Bravo 2 U .30 .75
25 Bravo 3 U .30 .75
26 Bravo 4 U .30 .75
27 Bravo 5 U .30 .75
28 Bravo Fighter R .75 2.00
29 Captain Tarpals R .75 2.00
30 Captain Tarpalsí Electropole C .12 .30
31 Captian Daultay Dofine R .75 2.00
32 Cease Fire! C .12 .30
33 Corporal Rushing U .30 .75
34 Dams Denna U .30 .75
35 Darth Maul With Lightsaber R 12.00 25.00
36 Darth Sidious R 25.00 50.00
37 DFS Squadron Starfighter C .12 .30
38 DFS-1015 U .30 .75
39 DFS-1308 R .75 2.00
40 DFS-327 C .12 .30
41 Droid Racks R 1.25 3.00
42 Droid Starfighter Laser Cannons C .12 .30
43 Drop Your Weapons C .12 .30
44 Electropole C .12 .30
45 Energy Shell Launchers C .12 .30
46 Fambaa C .12 .30
47 Fighters Straight Ahead U .30 .75
48 General Jar Jar R 1.25 3.00
49 Get To Your Ships! C .12 .30
50 Gian Speeder C .12 .30
51 Gimme A Lift! R .75 2.00
52 Gungan Energy Shield C .12 .30
53 Gungan General C .12 .30
54 Gungan Guard C .12 .30
55 Halt! C .12 .30
56 Iíll Try Spinning R .75 2.00
57 Infantry Battle Droid C .12 .30
58 Invasion / In Complete Control U .30 .75
59 Itís On Automatic Pilot C .12 .30
60 Jerus Jannick U .30 .75
61 Kaadu C .12 .30
62 Letís Go Left R .75 2.00
63 Lieutenant Arven Wendik U .30 .75
64 Lieutenant Chamberlyn U .30 .75
65 Lieutenant Rya Kirsch U .30 .75
66 Mace Windu, Jedi Master R 7.50 15.00

67 Master, Destroyers! R 1.00 2.50
68 Multi Troop Transport U .30 .75
69 Naboo Celebration R .75 2.00
70 Naboo Occupation R 1.00 2.50
71 Naboo: Boss Nassís Chambers U .30 .75
72 Naboo: Otoh Gunga Entrance U .30 .75
73 Naboo: Theed Palace Hall U .30 .75
74 Naboo: Theed Palace Hallway U .30 .75
75 No Giben Up, General Jar Jar! R .75 2.00
76 Nothing Can Get Through Are Shield R1.00 2.50
77 Nute Gunray, Neimoidian Viceroy R2.00 5.00
78 Officer Dolphe U .30 .75
79 Officer Ellberger U .30 .75
80 Officer Perosei U .30 .75
81 OOM-9 U .30 .75
82 Open Fire! C .12 .30
83 OWO-1 With Backup R 1.25 3.00
84 Panaka, Protector Of The Queen R 2.50 6.00
85 Proton Torpedoes C .12 .30
86 Queen Amidala R 10.00 20.00
87 Qui-Gon Jinn With Lightsaber R 7.50 15.00
88 Rayno Vaca U .30 .75
89 Rep Been U .30 .75
90 Ric Olie, Bravo Leader R .75 2.00
91 Rolling, Rolling, Rolling R 1.00 2.50
92 Royal Naboo Security Officer C .12 .30
93 Rune Haako, Legal Counsel R 1.25 3.00
94 Senate Hovercam DARK R 1.00 2.50
95 Senate Hovercam LIGHT R 1.00 2.50
96 Sil Unch U .30 .75
97 Single Trooper Aerial Platform C .12 .30
98 SSA-1015 U .30 .75
99 SSA-306 U .30 .75
100 SSA-719 R 1.25 3.00
101 STAP Blaster Cannons C .12 .30
102 Steady, Steady C .12 .30
103 Take Them Away C .12 .30
104 Take This! C .12 .30
105 Tank Commander C .12 .30
106 The Deflector Shield Is Too Strong R.75 2.00
107 There They Are! U .30 .75
108 They Win This Round R .75 2.00
109 This Is Not Good C .12 .30
110 Trade Federation Landing Craft C .12 .30
111 TT-6 R 1.00 2.50
112 TT-9 R .75 2.00
113 We Didnít Hit It C .12 .30
114 We Donít Have Time For This R 1.00 2.50
115 We Have A Plan .12 .30
They Will Be Lost And Confused C
116 Weíre Hit Artoo C .12 .30
117 Wesa Gotta Grand Army C .12 .30
118 Wesa Ready To Do Our-sa Part C .12 .30
119 Whoooo! C .12 .30
120 Theed Palace Dark Side List .12 .30
121 Theed Palace Light Side List .12 .30

2002 Star Wars Attack of the Clones

Darth Tyranus
CHARACTER · DARK JEDI MASTER
Pay 1 Force → Tyranus gets +2 power for this attack.
Pay 3 Force → Evade 3 (Prevent up to 3 damage to Tyranus.)
Pay 2 Force → Deflect 1 (Prevent 1 damage to Tyranus, and Tyranus may do that much damage to a unit of your choice in the Character arena.)
"The battle is far from over."

COMPLETE SET (180) 30.00 80.00
BOOSTER BOX (36 PACKS) 20.00 40.00
BOOSTER PACK (11 CARDS) 1.00 1.50
*FOIL: .75X TO 2X BASIC CARDS
RELEASED IN APRIL 2002

1 Anakin Skywalker (A) R .60 1.50
2 Anakin Skywalker (B) R .60 1.50
3 Assassin Droid ASN-121 (A) R .60 1.50
4 Bail Organa (A) R .60 1.50
5 Battle Fatigue R .60 1.50
6 Boba Fett (A) R .60 1.50
7 Captain Typho (A) R .60 1.50
8 Clear the Skies R .60 1.50
9 Clone Officer R .60 1.50
10 Dark Rendezvous R .60 1.50
11 Dark Side's Command R .60 1.50
12 Dark Side's Compulsion R .60 1.50
13 Darth Sidious (A) R .60 1.50
14 Darth Tyranus (A) R .60 1.50
15 Destruction of Hope R .60 1.50
16 Dexter Jettster (A) R .60 1.50
17 Geonosian Sentry R .60 1.50
18 Hero's Duty R .60 1.50
19 Hero's Flaw R .60 1.50
20 Interference in the Senate R .60 1.50
21 Jango Fett (A) R .60 1.50
22 Jango Fett (B) R .60 1.50
23 Jar Jar Binks (A) R .60 1.50
24 Jedi Call for Help R .60 1.50
25 Jedi Council Summons R .60 1.50
26 Jedi Knight's Deflection R .60 1.50
27 Lama Su (A) R .60 1.50
28 Luxury Airspeeder U .20 .50
29 A Moment's Rest R .60 1.50
30 Naboo Defense Station R .60 1.50
31 Obi-Wan Kenobi (A) R .60 1.50
32 Obi-Wan's Starfighter (A) R .60 1.50
33 Order Here R .60 1.50
34 PadmÈ Amidala (A) R .60 1.50
35 PadmÈ Amidala (B) R .60 1.50
36 PadmÈ's Yacht (A) R .60 1.50
37 Plo Koon (A) R .60 1.50
38 Plot the Secession R .60 1.50
39 Power Dive R .60 1.50
40 Queen Jamillia (A) R .60 1.50
41 R2-D2 (A) R .60 1.50
42 San Hill (A) U .20 .50
43 Second Effort R .60 1.50
44 Seek the Council's Wisdom R .60 1.50
45 Shu Mai (A) U .20 .50
46 Slave I (A) R .60 1.50
47 Spirit of the Fallen R .60 1.50
48 Target the Senator R .60 1.50
49 Taun We (A) R .60 1.50
50 Trade Federation Battleship Core R .60 1.50
51 Tyranus's Edict R .60 1.50
52 Tyranus's Geonosian Speeder (A) R .60 1.50
53 Tyranus's Solar Sailer (A) R .60 1.50
54 Tyranus's Wrath R .60 1.50
55 War Will Follow R .60 1.50
56 Ward of the Jedi R .60 1.50
57 Windu's Solution R .60 1.50
58 Yoda (A) R .60 1.50
59 Yoda's Intervention R .60 1.50
60 Zam Wesell (A) R .60 1.50
61 Acklay U .20 .50
62 Anakin Skywalker (C) U .20 .50
63 Anakin's Inspiration U .20 .50
64 AT-TE Walker 23X U .20 .50
65 AT-TE Walker 71E R .60 1.50
66 Attract Enemy Fire U .20 .50
67 C-3PO (A) U .20 .50
68 Capture Obi-Wan U .20 .50
69 Chancellor Palpatine (A) R .60 1.50
70 Chase the Villain U .20 .50
71 Cheat the Game U .20 .50
72 Cliegg Lars (A) U .20 .50
73 Clone Warrior 4/163 U .20 .50
74 Clone Warrior 5/373 U .20 .50
75 Commerce Guild Droid Platoon U .20 .50
76 CordÈ (A) U .20 .50
77 Coruscant Freighter AA-9 (A) U .20 .50
78 Dark Speed U .20 .50
79 Darth Tyranus (B) U .20 .50
80 Departure Time U .20 .50
81 Destroyer Droid, P Series U .20 .50
82 Down in Flames U .20 .50
83 Droid Control Ship U .20 .50
84 Elan Sleazebaggano (A) R .60 1.50
85 Geonosian Guard U .20 .50
86 Geonosian Warrior U .20 .50
87 Go to the Temple U .20 .50
88 Infantry Battle Droid, B1 Series U .20 .50
89 Jango Fett (C) U .20 .50
90 Jawa Sandcrawler U .20 .50
91 Jedi Patrol U .20 .50
92 Kaminoan Guard U .20 .50
93 Kit Fisto (A) U .20 .50
94 Master and Apprentice U .20 .50
95 Naboo Security Guard U .20 .50
96 Naboo Spaceport U .20 .50
97 Nexu U .20 .50
98 Nute Gunray (A) U .20 .50
99 Obi-Wan Kenobi (B) U .20 .50
100 PadmÈ Amidala (C) U .20 .50
101 Poggle the Lesser (A) U .20 .50
102 Reek U .20 .50
103 Republic Assault Ship U .20 .50
104 Republic Cruiser C .10 .25
105 Shaak Ti (A) U .20 .50
106 Ship Arrival U .20 .50
107 Splinter the Republic U .20 .50
108 Strength of Hate U .20 .50
109 Subtle Assassination U .20 .50
110 Super Battle Droid 8EX U .20 .50
111 Trade Federation Battleship U .20 .50
112 Trade Federation C-9979 U .20 .50
113 Tyranus's Gift U .20 .50
114 Underworld Connections U .20 .50
115 Wat Tambor (A) U .20 .50
116 Watto (A) U .20 .50
117 Weapon Response U .20 .50
118 Wedding of Destiny U .20 .50
119 Yoda (B) U .20 .50
120 Zam's Airspeeder (A) U .20 .50
121 Anakin Skywalker (D) C .10 .25
122 Battle Droid Squad C .10 .25
123 Bravo N-1 Starfighter C .10 .25
124 Chancellor's Guard Squad C .10 .25
125 Clone Platoon C .10 .25
126 Clone Squad C .10 .25
127 Commerce Guild Droid 81 C .10 .25
128 Commerce Guild Starship C .10 .25
129 Corellian Star Shuttle C .10 .25
130 Darth Tyranus (C) C .10 .25
131 Destroyer Droid Squad C .10 .25
132 Droid Starfighter DFS-4CT C .10 .25
133 Droid Starfighter Squadron C .10 .25
134 Droid Starfighter Wing C .10 .25
135 Elite Jedi Squad C .10 .25
136 Flying Geonosian Squad C .10 .25
137 Geonosian Defense Platform C .10 .25
138 Geonosian Fighter C .10 .25
139 Geonosian Squad C .10 .25
140 Gozanti Cruiser C .10 .25
141 Hatch a Clone C .10 .25
142 Hero's Dodge C .10 .25
143 High-Force Dodge C .10 .25
144 Hyperdrive Ring C .10 .25
145 InterGalactic Banking Clan Starship C.10 .25
146 Jango Fett (D) C .10 .25
147 Jedi Starfighter 3R3 C .10 .25
148 Knockdown C .10 .25
149 Lost in the Asteroids C .10 .25
150 Lull in the Fighting C .10 .25
151 Mending C .10 .25
152 N-1 Starfighter C .10 .25
153 Naboo Cruiser C .10 .25
154 Naboo Royal Starship C .10 .25
155 Naboo Senatorial Escort C .10 .25
156 Naboo Starfighter Squadron C .10 .25
157 Obi-Wan Kenobi (C) C .10 .25
158 Padawan's Deflection C .10 .25
159 PadmÈ Amidala (D) C .10 .25
160 Patrol Speeder C .10 .25
161 Peace on Naboo C .10 .25
162 Pilot's Dodge C .10 .25
163 Recon Speeder U .10 .25
164 Republic Attack Gunship UH-478 C.10 .25
165 Repulsorlift Malfunction C .10 .25
166 Return to Spaceport C .10 .25
167 Rickshaw C .10 .25
168 Slumming on Coruscant C .10 .25
169 Sonic Shockwave C .10 .25
170 Speeder Bike Squadron C .10 .25
171 Starship Refit C .10 .25
172 Surge of Power C .10 .25
173 Swoop Bike C .10 .25
174 Take the Initiative C .10 .25
175 Target Locked C .10 .25
176 Taylander Shuttle C .10 .25
177 Techno Union Starship C .10 .25
178 Trade Federation War Freighter C .10 .25
179 Walking Droid Fighter C .10 .25
180 Zam Wesell (B) C .10 .25

2002 Star Wars A New Hope

Darth Vader
CHARACTER · DARK JEDI KNIGHT · SITH LORD
Pay 2 Force → Vader gets +2 power for this attack.
Pay 3 Force → Evade 3 (Prevent up to 3 damage to Vader.)
"I find your lack of faith disturbing."

COMPLETE SET (180) 30.00 80.00
BOOSTER BOX (36 PACKS) 25.00 50.00
BOOSTER PACK (11 CARDS) 1.50 3.00
*FOIL: .8X TO 2X BASIC CARDS
RELEASED IN OCTOBER 2002

1 Admiral Motti (A) R .60 1.50
2 Beru Lars (A) R .60 1.50
3 Blaster Barrage R .60 1.50
4 Capture the Falcon R .60 1.50
5 Contingency Plan R .60 1.50
6 Dannik Jerriko (A) R .60 1.50
7 Darth Vader (A) R 1.25 3.00
8 Desperate Confrontation R .75 2.00
9 Destroy Alderaan R .60 1.50
10 Dianoga (A) R .60 1.50
11 Disturbance in the Force R .60 1.50
12 It's Not Over Yet R .60 1.50
13 EG-6 Power Droid R .60 1.50
14 Elite Stormtrooper Squad R .60 1.50
15 Figrin D'an (A) R .75 2.00
16 Greedo (A) R .60 1.50
17 Hold 'Em Off R .60 1.50
18 Imperial Blockade R .60 1.50
19 Imperial Navy Helmsman R .60 1.50
20 Imperial Sentry Droid R .60 1.50
21 IT-0 Interrogator Droid R .75 2.00
22 Jawa Leader R .60 1.50
23 Krayt Dragon R .60 1.50
24 Leia's Kiss R .60 1.50
25 Luke Skywalker (B) R .60 1.50
26 Luke Skywalker (A) R .60 1.50
27 Luke's Speeder (A) R .60 1.50
28 Luke's X-Wing (A) R .60 1.50
29 Momaw Nadon (A) R 1.00 2.50
30 Most Desperate Hour R .60 1.50
31 No Escape R .60 1.50
32 Obi-Wan Kenobi (E) R .60 1.50
33 Obi-Wan's Prowess R .60 1.50
34 Obi-Wan's Task R .60 1.50
35 Our Only Hope R .60 1.50
36 Owen Lars (A) R .60 1.50
37 Plan of Attack R .60 1.50
38 Princess Leia (A) R .60 1.50
39 Protection of the Master R .60 1.50
40 R5-D4 (A) R .60 1.50
41 Rebel Crew Chief R .60 1.50
42 Rebel Lieutenant R .60 1.50
43 Regroup on Yavin R .60 1.50
44 Sandtrooper R .60 1.50
45 Starfighter's End R .60 1.50
46 Stormtrooper TK-421 R .60 1.50
47 Strategy Session R .60 1.50
48 Strike Me Down R .60 1.50
49 Surprise Attack R .60 1.50
50 Tantive IV (A) R .60 1.50
51 Tarkin's Stench R .60 1.50
52 TIE Fighter Elite Pilot U .20 .50
53 Tiree (A) R .60 1.50
54 Tractor Beam R .60 1.50
55 URoRRuR'R'R (A) R .60 1.50
56 Imperial Manipulation R .60 1.50
57 Vader's Leadership R .60 1.50
58 Vader's TIE Fighter (A) R .60 1.50
59 Wedge Antilles (A) R .60 1.50
60 Yavin 4 Hangar Base R .60 1.50
61 Astromech Assistance U .20 .50
62 Benefits of Training U .20 .50
63 Biggs Darklighter (A) U .20 .50
64 C-3PO (C) U .20 .50
65 Commander Praji (A) U .20 .50
66 Tatooine Sandcrawler U .20 .50
67 Darth Vader (B) U .20 .50
68 Death Star Hangar Bay U .20 .50
69 Death Star Plans U .20 .50
70 Death Star Scanning Technician U .20 .50
71 Death Star Superlaser Gunner U .20 .50
72 Death Star Turbolaser Gunner U .20 .50
73 Demonstration of Power U .20 .50
74 Devastator (A) U .20 .50
75 Dissolve the Senate U .20 .50
76 Error in Judgment U .20 .50
77 Fate of the Dragon U .20 .50
78 General Dodonna (A) U .20 .50
79 General Tagge (A) U .20 .50
80 Han's Courage U .20 .50
81 Imperial Control Station U .20 .50
82 Imperial Navy Lieutenant U .20 .50
83 Insignificant Power U .20 .50
84 Into the Garbage Chute C .10 .25
85 Jawa U .20 .50
86 Jawa Collection Team U .20 .50
87 Jedi Extinction U .20 .50
88 Jon Dutch Vander (A) U .20 .50
89 Learning the Force U .20 .50
90 Lieutenant Tanbris (A) U .20 .50
91 LIN Demolitionmech U .20 .50
92 Luke Skywalker (C) U .20 .50
93 Luke's Warning U .20 .50
94 Mounted Stormtrooper U .20 .50
95 Mouse Droid U .20 .50
96 Obi-Wan Kenobi (F) U .20 .50
97 Oil Bath U .20 .50
98 Princess Leia (B) U .20 .50
99 R2-D2 (C) U .20 .50
100 Rebel Blockade Runner U .20 .50
101 Rebel Control Officer U .20 .50
102 Rebel Control Post U .20 .50
103 Rebel Marine U .20 .50
104 Rebel Surrender U .20 .50
105 Rebel Trooper U .20 .50
106 Remote Seeker Droid U .20 .50
107 Press the Advantage U .20 .50
108 Stabilize Deflectors U .20 .50
109 Star Destroyer Commander U .20 .50
110 Stormtrooper Charge U .20 .50
111 Stormtrooper DV-692 U .20 .50
112 Stormtrooper Squad Leader U .20 .50
113 Stormtrooper TK-119 U .20 .50
114 Support in the Senate U .20 .50
115 Disrupt the Power System U .20 .50
116 Tatooine Speeder U .20 .50
117 Tusken Sharpshooter U .20 .50
118 Vader's Interference U .20 .50
119 Vader's TIE Fighter (B) U .60 1.50
120 Wuher (A) U .20 .50
121 Air Cover C .10 .25
122 Precise Blast C .10 .25
123 Stay Sharp C .10 .25
124 Carrack Cruiser C .10 .25
125 Darth Vader (C) C .10 .25
126 Death Star Cannon Tower C .10 .25
127 Death Star Guard Squad C .10 .25
128 Domesticated Bantha C .10 .25
129 Flare-S Swoop C .10 .25
130 Ground Support C .10 .25
131 Imperial Detention Block C .10 .25
132 Imperial Star Destroyer C .10 .25
133 Incom T-16 Skyhopper C .10 .25
134 Into Hiding C .10 .25
135 Jawa Squad C .10 .25
136 Jawa Supply Trip C .10 .25
137 Jump to Lightspeed C .10 .25
138 Luke Skywalker (D) C .10 .25
139 Luke's Repairs C .10 .25
140 Moisture Farm C .10 .25
141 Planetary Defense Turret C .10 .25
142 Nowhere to Run C .10 .25
143 Obi-Wan Kenobi (G) C .10 .25
144 Jedi Intervention C .10 .25
145 Obi-Wan's Plan C .10 .25
146 Penetrate the Shields C .10 .25
147 Preemptive Shot C .10 .25
148 Princess Leia (C) C .10 .25
149 Rebel Fighter Wing C .10 .25
150 Rebel Honor Company C .10 .25
151 Rebel Marine Squad C .10 .25
152 Rebel Pilot C .10 .25
153 Rebel Squad C .10 .25
154 Rescue C .10 .25
155 Slipping Through C .10 .25
156 SoruSuub V-35 Courier C .10 .25
157 Synchronized Assault C .10 .25
158 Stormtrooper Assault Team C .10 .25
159 Stormtrooper DV-523 C .10 .25

160 Stormtrooper Patrol C	.10	.25
161 Stormtrooper Squad C	.10	.25
162 TIE Fighter DS-3-12 C	.10	.25
163 TIE Fighter DS-73-3 C	.10	.25
164 TIE Fighter DS-55-6 C	.10	.25
165 TIE Fighter DS-61-9 C	.10	.25
166 TIE Fighter Pilot C	.10	.25
167 TIE Fighter Squad C	.10	.25
168 Tusken Squad C	.10	.25
169 Vader's Grip U	.10	.25
170 Victory-Class Star Destroyer C	.10	.25
171 Well-Aimed Shot C	.10	.25
172 X-wing Red One C	.10	.25
173 X-wing Red Three C	.10	.25
174 X-wing Red Two C	.10	.25
175 X-wing Attack Formation C	.10	.25
176 Y-wing Gold One C	.10	.25
177 Y-wing Gold Squadron C	.10	.25
178 YT-1300 Transport C	.10	.25
179 YV-664 Light Freighter C	.10	.25
180 Z-95 Headhunter C	.10	.25

2002 Star Wars Sith Rising

COMPLETE SET (90)	15.00	40.00
BOOSTER BOX (36 PACKS)	25.00	50.00
BOOSTER PACK (11 CARDS)	1.00	2.00

*FOIL: .75X TO 2X BASIC CARDS
RELEASED IN JULY 2002

1 Aayla Secura (A) R	.60	1.50
2 Anakin Skywalker (E) R	.60	1.50
3 Aurra Sing (A) R	.60	1.50
4 Chancellor Palpatine (B) R	.60	1.50
5 Clone Captain R	.60	1.50
6 Clone Facility R	.60	1.50
7 Darth Maul (A) R	.60	1.50
8 Darth Maul (C) R	.60	1.50
9 Darth Sidious (B) R	.60	1.50
10 Darth Tyranus (D) R	.60	1.50
11 Geonosian Picadors R	.60	1.50
12 Impossible Victory R	.60	1.50
13 Jango Fett (E) R	.60	1.50
14 Jedi Bravery R	.60	1.50
15 Jedi Starfighter Wing R	.60	1.50
16 Jocasta Nu (A) R	.60	1.50
17 Mace Windu (A) R	.60	1.50
18 Mace Windu (C) R	.60	1.50
19 Massiff R	.60	1.50
20 Nute Gunray (B) R	.60	1.50
21 Republic Drop Ship R	.60	1.50
22 Sio Bibble (A) R	.60	1.50
23 Sith Infiltrator (A) R	.60	1.50
24 Slave I (B) R	.60	1.50
25 Super Battle Droid 5TE R	.60	1.50
26 Trade Federation Control Core R	.60	1.50
27 Tusken Camp R	.60	1.50
28 Twilight of the Republic R	.60	1.50
29 Unfriendly Fire R	.60	1.50
30 Yoda (C) R	.60	1.50
31 Aiwha Rider U	.20	.50
32 C-3PO (B) U	.20	.50
33 Careful Targeting U	.20	.50
34 Clever Escape U	.20	.50
35 Clone Trooper 6/298 U	.20	.50
36 Darth Maul (B) U	.20	.50
37 Darth Tyranus (E) U	.20	.50
38 Destroyer Droid, W Series U	.20	.50
39 Female Tusken Raider U	.20	.50
40 Fog of War U	.20	.50
41 Geonosian Scout U	.20	.50
42 Halifire Droid U	.20	.50
43 Homing Spider Droid U	.20	.50
44 Infantry Battle Droid U	.20	.50
45 Jedi Heroes U	.20	.50
46 Jedi Starfighter Scout U	.20	.50
47 Mace Windu (B) U	.20	.50
48 Moment of Truth U	.20	.50
49 Obi_Wan Kenobi (D) U	.20	.50
50 Out of His Misery U	.20	.50
51 PadmÈ Amidala (E) U	.20	.50
52 Passel Argente (A) U	.20	.50
53 Price of Failure U	.20	.50
54 R2-D2 (B) U	.20	.50
55 Recognition of Valor U	.20	.50
56 Sun Fac (A) U	.20	.50
57 Techno Union Warship U	.20	.50
58 Trade Federation Offensive U	.20	.50
59 Tusken Raider U	.20	.50
60 Visit the Lake Retreat U	.20	.50
61 Acclamator-Class Assault Ship C	.10	.25
62 Aggressive Negotiations C	.10	.25
63 Anakin Skywalker (F) C	.10	.25
64 AT-TE Troop Transport C	.10	.25
65 Battle Droid Assault Squad C	.10	.25
66 Brutal Assault C	.10	.25
67 Clone Trooper Legion C	.10	.25
68 Commerce Guild Cruiser C	.10	.25
69 Commerce Guild Spider Droid C	.10	.25
70 Concentrated Fire C	.10	.25
71 Corsucant Speeder C	.10	.25
72 Darth Maul (D) C	.10	.25
73 Diplomatic Cruiser C	.10	.25
74 Droid Starfighter DFS-1VR C	.10	.25
75 Geonosian Artillery Battery C	.10	.25
76 Geonosian Defense Fighter C	.10	.25
77 Maul's Strategy C	.10	.25
78 Mobile Assault Cannon C	.10	.25
79 Naboo Starfighter Wing C	.10	.25
80 Nubian Yacht C	.10	.25
81 Padawan and Senator C	.10	.25
82 Reassemble C-3PO C	.10	.25
83 Republic LAAT/i Gunship C	.10	.25
84 Retreat Underground R	.10	.25
85 Run the Gauntlet C	.10	.25
86 Senatorial Cruiser C	.10	.25
87 Shoot Her or Something C	.10	.25
88 Super Battle Droid Squad C	.10	.25
89 Suppressing Fire C	.10	.25
90 Trade Federation Warship C	.10	.25

2003 Star Wars Battle of Yavin

COMPLETE SET (105)	60.00	120.00
BOOSTER BOX (36 PACKS)	30.00	50.00
BOOSTER PACK (11 CARDS)	2.50	5.00

*FOIL: .75X TO 2X BASIC CARDS
RELEASED IN MARCH 2003

1 Artoo's Repairs R	2.00	5.00
2 Blow This Thing R	1.50	4.00
3 Celebrate the Victory R	.75	2.00
4 Chariot Light Assault Vehicle R	.75	2.00
5 Chewbacca (B) R	4.00	10.00
6 Chewbacca (A) R	4.00	10.00
7 Chief Bast (A) R	2.00	5.00
8 Colonel Wulff Yularen (A) R	2.00	5.00
9 Darth Vader (D) R	4.00	10.00
10 Death Star (A) R	3.00	8.00
11 Death Star (C) R	3.00	8.00
12 Garven Dreis (A) R	1.25	3.00
13 Grand Moff Tarkin (A) R	3.00	8.00
14 Han Solo (B) R	5.00	12.00
15 Han Solo (A) R	4.00	10.00
16 Hero's Potential R	.20	.50
17 Jek Porkins (A) R	.60	1.50
18 Lieutenant Shann Childsen (A) R	1.25	3.00
19 Luke Skywalker (E) R	4.00	10.00
20 Luke's Skyhopper (A) R	.20	.50
21 Luke's X-wing (B) R	2.00	5.00
22 Millennium Falcon (A) R	2.00	5.00
23 Millennium Falcon (B) R	2.00	5.00
24 Millennium Falcon (C) R	2.00	5.00
25 Obi-Wan Kenobi (H) R	4.00	10.00
26 Obi-Wan's Guidance R	.75	2.00
27 Princess Leia (D) R	1.25	3.00
28 R2-X2 (A) R	1.25	3.00
29 R2-Q5 (A) R	1.25	3.00
30 Rebel Ground Crew Chief R	.75	2.00
31 Second Wave R	1.25	3.00
32 Stormtrooper Commander R	4.00	10.00
33 Vader's Fury R	2.00	5.00
34 X-wing Squadron R	2.00	5.00
35 Your Powers Are Weak R	1.25	3.00
36 Alien Rage U	.40	1.00
37 C-3PO (D) U	.40	1.00
38 Chewbacca (C) U	.40	1.00
39 Commander Willard (A) U	.40	1.00
40 Countermeasures U	.40	1.00
41 Darth Vader (E) U	.40	1.00
42 Death Star (B) U	.40	1.00
43 Death Star Trooper U	.40	1.00
44 Deflectors Activated U	.40	1.00
45 Grand Moff Tarkin (B) U	.40	1.00
46 Grand Moff Tarkin (C) U	.40	1.00
47 Han Solo (C) U	.40	1.00
48 Heavy Fire Zone U	.40	1.00
49 Imperial Dewback U	.40	1.00
50 Interrogation Droid U	.40	1.00
51 Jawa Crawler U	.40	1.00
52 Jawa Scavenger U	.40	1.00
53 Labria (A) U	.40	1.00
54 Let the Wookiee Win U	.40	1.00
55 Luke Skywalker (F) U	.40	1.00
56 Luke's Speeder (B) U	.40	1.00
57 Mobile Command Base U	.40	1.00
58 Obi-Wan's Handiwork U	.40	1.00
59 Princess Leia (E) U	.40	1.00
60 R2-D2 (D) U	.40	1.00
61 Rebel Armored Freerunner U	.40	1.00
62 Refit on Yavin U	.40	1.00
63 Sabers Locked U	.40	1.00
64 Stormtrooper KE-829 U	.40	1.00
65 Tatooine Hangar U	.40	1.00
66 Tusken Raider Squad U	.40	1.00
67 Tusken War Party U	.40	1.00
68 Untamed Ronto U	.40	1.00
69 WED Treadwell U	.40	1.00
70 Womp Rat U	.40	1.00
71 Accelerate C	.20	.50
72 Blast It! C	.20	.50
73 Chewbacca (D) C	.20	.50
74 Corellian Corvette C	.20	.50
75 Creature Attack C	.20	.50
76 Luke Skywalker (G) C	.20	.50
77 Darth Vader (F) C	.20	.50
78 Death Star Turbolaser Tower C	.20	.50
79 Dewback Patrol C	.20	.50
80 Escape Pod C	.20	.50
81 Greedo's Marksmanship C	.20	.50
82 Han Solo (D) C	.20	.50
83 Han's Evasion C	.20	.50
84 Imperial Landing Craft C	.20	.50
85 Jawa Salvage Team C	.20	.50
86 Juggernaut U	.20	.50
87 Star Destroyer C	.20	.50
88 Malfunction C	.20	.50
89 Outrun C	.20	.50
90 Pilot's Speed C	.20	.50
91 Rebel Defense Team C	.20	.50
92 Sandtrooper Squad C	.20	.50
93 Stormtrooper Assault C	.20	.50
94 Stormtrooper TK-875 C	.20	.50
95 Stormtrooper Platoon C	.20	.50
96 Stormtrooper Regiment C	.20	.50
97 TIE Defense Squadron C	.20	.50
98 TIE Fighter DS-73-5 C	.20	.50
99 TIE Fighter DS-29-4 C	.20	.50
100 TIE Fighter DS-55-2 C	.20	.50
101 Trust Your Feelings C	.20	.50
102 Visit to Mos Eisley C	.20	.50
103 X-wing Red Squadron C	.20	.50
104 X-wing Red Ten C	.20	.50
105 Y-wing Gold Two C	.20	.50

2003 Star Wars The Empire Strikes Back

COMPLETE SET (210)	100.00	200.00
BOOSTER BOX (36 PACKS)	400.00	550.00
BOOSTER PACK (11 CARDS)	1.25	2.50

*FOIL: .75X TO 2X BASIC CARDS
RELEASED IN NOVEMBER 2003

1 2-1B Medical Droid (A) R	1.25	3.00
2 Admiral Firmus Piett (B) R	1.25	3.00
3 AT-AT Assault Group R	1.25	3.00
4 Avenger (A) R	4.00	10.00
5 Blizzard Force Snowtrooper R	1.25	3.00
6 Blizzard One (A) R	1.25	3.00
7 C-3PO (E) R	1.25	3.00
8 Captain Lorth Needa (A) R	1.25	3.00
9 Carbon Freezing Chamber R	5.00	12.00
10 Chewbacca (E) U	1.25	3.00
11 Chewbacca (G) R	1.25	3.00
12 Dack Ralter (A) R	1.25	3.00
13 Dangerous Gamble R	1.25	3.00
14 Dark Cave R	1.25	3.00
15 Darth Vader (H) R	2.00	5.00
16 Darth Vader (I) R	3.00	8.00
17 Decoy Tactics R	1.25	3.00
18 Desperate Times R	1.25	3.00
19 Echo Base R	3.00	8.00
20 Emperor's Bidding R	1.25	3.00
21 Emperor's Prize R	1.25	3.00
22 Executor (A) R	1.25	3.00
23 Failed for the Last Time R	1.25	3.00
24 Future Sight R	1.25	3.00
25 FX-7 Medical Droid (A) R	1.25	3.00
26 General Carlist Rieekan (A) R	1.25	3.00
27 General Maximilian Veers (B) R	1.25	3.00
28 Go for the Legs R	1.25	3.00
29 Han Solo (G) R	2.00	5.00
30 Jedi Test R	1.25	3.00
31 Jedi's Failure R	1.25	3.00
32 K-3PO (A) R	1.25	3.00
33 Kiss From Your Sister R	1.25	3.00
34 Lando Calrissian (A) R	2.50	6.00
35 Lando Calrissian (D) R	2.50	6.00
36 Lieutenant Wes Janson (A) R	2.00	5.00
37 Lobot (A) R	1.25	3.00
38 Luke Skywalker (J) R	6.00	15.00
39 Luke Skywalker (K) R	5.00	12.00
40 Luke's Snowspeeder (A) R	4.00	10.00
41 Luke's Wrath R	1.25	3.00
42 Luke's X-wing (c) R	2.00	5.00
43 Major Bren Derlin (A) R	1.25	3.00
44 Mara Jade (A) R	1.25	3.00
45 Millennium Falcon (E) R	2.00	5.00
46 Millennium Falcon (F) R	2.00	5.00
47 Millennium Falcon (G) R	2.00	5.00
48 Obi-Wan's Spirit (A) R	1.25	3.00
49 Occupation R	1.25	3.00
50 Parting of Heroes R	1.25	3.00
51 Planetary Ion Cannon R	1.25	3.00
52 Princess Leia (G) R	2.00	5.00
53 Quest for Truth R	1.25	3.00
54 R2-D2 (G) R	1.25	3.00
55 R2-D2's Heroism R	1.25	3.00
56 Rally the Defenders R	1.25	3.00
57 Sacrifice R	1.25	3.00
58 Search for the Rebels R	1.25	3.00
59 Stormtrooper Swarm R	1.25	3.00
60 Streets of Cloud City R	1.25	3.00
61 Toryn Farr (A) R	1.25	3.00
62 Vader's Imperial Shuttle (A) R	2.00	5.00
63 Wampa Cave R	1.25	3.00
64 Wedge Antilles (B) R	4.00	10.00
65 Wedge's Snowspeeder (A) R	4.00	10.00
66 Yoda (F) R	1.25	3.00
67 Yoda (G) R	1.25	3.00
68 Yoda (H) R	1.25	3.00
69 Yoda's Training R	1.25	3.00
70 Zev Senesca (A) R	1.25	3.00
71 3,720 to 1 U	.40	1.00
72 Admiral Firmus Piett (A) U	.40	1.00
73 Admiral Kendal Ozzel (A) U	.40	1.00
74 Outmaneuver Them U	.40	1.00
75 All Terrain Troop Transport U	.40	1.00
76 Anti-Infantry Laser Battery U	.40	1.00
77 Asteroid Field U	.40	1.00
78 AT-AT Driver U	.40	1.00
79 Blizzard Force AT-ST U	.40	1.00
80 Battle the Wampa U	.40	1.00
81 Cloud City Penthouse U	.40	1.00
82 Cloud City Prison U	.40	1.00
83 Bespin Twin-Pod Cloud Car U	.40	1.00
84 Blockade U	.40	1.00
85 Bright Hope (A) U	.40	1.00
86 C-3PO (F) U	.40	1.00
87 Change in Destiny U	.40	1.00
88 Chewbacca (F) R	.40	1.00
89 Darth Vader (G) R	.40	1.00
90 Darth Vader (K) U	.40	1.00
91 Death Mark U	.40	1.00
92 Derek Hobbie Klivian (A) U	.40	1.00
93 Don't Get All Mushy U	.40	1.00
94 Dragonsnake U	.40	1.00
95 Emergency Repairs U	.40	1.00
96 Carbon Freeze U	.40	1.00
97 Executor Bridge U	.40	1.00
98 Executor Hangar U	.40	1.00
99 Quicker Easier More Seductive U	.40	1.00
100 General Maximilian Veers (A) U	.40	1.00
101 Han Enchained U	.40	1.00
102 Han Solo (F) U	.40	1.00
103 Hoth Icefields U	.40	1.00
104 Imperial Fleet U	.40	1.00
105 Imperial Misdirection U	.40	1.00
106 Jungles of Dagobah U	.40	1.00
107 Lambda-Class Shuttle U	.40	1.00
108 Lando Calrissian (C) U	.40	1.00
109 Leia's Warning U	.40	1.00
110 Luke Skywalker (I) U	.40	1.00
111 Medical Center U	.40	1.00
112 Millennium Falcon (D) U	.40	1.00
113 Mynock U	.40	1.00
114 Painful Reckoning U	.40	1.00
115 Princess Leia (H) U	.40	1.00
116 Probe Droid U	.40	1.00
117 Probot U	.40	1.00
118 R2-D2 (F) U	.40	1.00
119 Rebel Fleet U	.40	1.00
120 Rebel Hoth Army U	.40	1.00
121 Rebel Trenches U	.40	1.00
122 Rebel Troop Cart U	.40	1.00
123 Redemption (A) U	.40	1.00
124 See You In Hell U	.40	1.00
125 Self Destruct U	.40	1.00
126 Shield Generator U	.40	1.00
127 Snowspeeder Rogue Ten U	.40	1.00
128 Snowspeeder Squad U	.40	1.00
129 Snowtrooper Elite Squad U	.40	1.00
130 Stormtrooper Sentry U	.40	1.00
131 Surprise Reinforcements U	.40	1.00
132 TIE Bomber Pilot U	.40	1.00
133 TIE Bomber Squad U	.40	1.00
134 TIE Pursuit Pilot U	.40	1.00
135 Torture Room U	.40	1.00
136 Vader's Call U	.40	1.00
137 Vicious Attack U	.40	1.00
138 Wampa U	.40	1.00
139 Yoda's Hut U	.40	1.00
140 725 to 1 C	.20	.50
141 All Terrain Armored Transport C	.20	.50
142 All Terrain Scout Transport C	.20	.50
143 Alter the Deal C	.20	.50
144 Antivehicle Laser Cannon C	.20	.50
145 Armor Plating C	.20	.50
146 Space Slug C	.20	.50
147 Blizzard Force AT-AT C	.20	.50
148 Precise Attack C	.20	.50
149 Belly of the Beast C	.20	.50
150 Cloud City Battleground C	.20	.50
151 Cloud City Dining Hall C	.20	.50
152 Cloud City Landing Platform C	.20	.50
153 Bespin System C	.20	.50
154 Blizzard C	.20	.50
155 Bogwing C	.20	.50
156 Close the Shield Doors C	.20	.50
157 Darth Vader (J) C	.20	.50
158 Vader's Vengeance C	.20	.50

159 Dagobah System C	.20	.50
160 Explore the Swamps C	.20	.50
161 Float Away C	.20	.50
162 Force Throw C	.20	.50
163 Gallofree Medium Transport C	.20	.50
164 Ground Assault C	.20	.50
165 Han Solo (E) C	.20	.50
166 Han's Attack U	.20	.50
167 Han's Promise C	.20	.50
168 Hanging Around C	.20	.50
169 Hope of Another C	.20	.50
170 Hoth Battle Plains C	.20	.50
171 Hoth System C	.20	.50
172 Imperial II-Class Star Destroyer C	.20	.50
173 Jedi Master's Meditation C	.20	.50
174 Jedi Trap C	.20	.50
175 Kuat Lancer-Class Frigate C	.20	.50
176 Kuat Nebulon-B Frigate C	.20	.50
177 Lando Calrissian (B) C	.20	.50
178 Lando's Repairs C	.20	.50
179 Leap into the Chasm C	.20	.50
180 Luke Skywalker (H) C	.20	.50
181 Meditation Chamber C	.20	.50
182 Navy Trooper C	.20	.50
183 Princess Leia (F) C	.20	.50
184 Probe the Galaxy C	.20	.50
185 Rebel Command Center C	.20	.50
186 Rebel Escape Squad C	.20	.50
187 Rebel Hangar C	.20	.50
188 Rebel Trench Defenders C	.20	.50
189 Rebel Assault Frigate C	.20	.50
190 Dreadnaught Heavy Cruiser C	.20	.50
191 Snowspeeder Rogue Two C	.20	.50
192 Snowstorm C	.20	.50
193 Snowtrooper Heavy Weapons Team C	.20	.50
194 Snowtrooper Squad C	.20	.50
195 Snowtrooper Guard C	.20	.50
196 Imperial II Star Destroyer C	.20	.50
197 Strange Lodgings C	.20	.50
198 Swamps of Dagobah C	.20	.50
199 Tauntaun C	.20	.50
200 Tauntaun Mount C	.20	.50
201 TIE Bomber EX-1-2 C	.20	.50
202 TIE Bomber EX-1-8 C	.20	.50
203 TIE Fighter EX-4-9 C	.20	.50
204 TIE Fighter OS-72-8 C	.20	.50
205 TIE Pursuit Squad C	.20	.50
206 Trust Her Instincts C	.20	.50
207 Visions of the Future C	.20	.50
208 Well-Earned Meal C	.20	.50
209 X-wing Rogue Seven C	.20	.50
210 Y-wing Gold Six C	.20	.50

2003 Star Wars Jedi Guardians

COMPLETE SET (105)	60.00	120.00
BOOSTER BOX (36 PACKS)	120.00	250.00
BOOSTER PACK (11 CARDS)	5.00	7.00
*FOIL: .75X TO 2X BASIC CARDS		
RELEASED IN JULY 2003		

1 Adi Gallia (A) R	1.25	3.00
2 Anakin Skywalker (H) R	1.25	3.00
3 Aurra Sing (B) R	1.25	3.00
4 Boba Fett (B) R	1.25	3.00
5 Coup de Grace U	1.25	3.00
6 Dark Dreams R	1.25	3.00
7 Darth Maul (E) R	3.00	8.00
8 Darth Sidious (C) R	1.25	3.00
9 Darth Tyranus (F) R	2.00	5.00
10 Eeth Koth (A) R	1.25	3.00
11 Even Piell (A) R	1.25	3.00
12 Furious Charge C	1.25	3.00
13 Gather the Council R	1.25	3.00
14 Guidance of the Chancellor C	1.25	3.00

15 Homing Missile R	1.25	3.00
16 Jango Fett (G) R	1.25	3.00
17 Jedi Council Quorum R	1.25	3.00
18 Jedi Youngling R	1.25	3.00
19 Ki-Adi-Mundi (A) R	1.25	3.00
20 Kouhun R	1.25	3.00
21 Mace Windu (D) R	2.50	6.00
22 Trade Federation Battle Freighter C	1.25	3.00
23 Obi-Wan Kenobi (I) R	1.25	3.00
24 Obi-Wan's Starfighter (B) R	2.00	5.00
25 Oppo Rancisis (A) R	1.25	3.00
26 Padme Amidala (F) R	1.25	3.00
27 Plo Koon (B) R	1.25	3.00
28 R2-D2 (E) R	1.25	3.00
29 Remember the Prophecy R	1.25	3.00
30 Saesee Tiin (A) R	1.25	3.00
31 Senator Tikkes (A) R	1.25	3.00
32 Shaak Ti (B) R	2.00	5.00
33 Shmi Skywalker (A) R	2.00	5.00
34 Slave I (C) R	1.25	3.00
35 Trade Federation Blockade Ship C	1.25	3.00
36 Rapid Recovery R	1.25	3.00
37 Tipoca Training Ground R	1.25	3.00
38 Trade Federation Core Ship C	1.25	3.00
39 Tyranus's Geonosis Speeder (B) C	1.25	3.00
40 Unified Attack U	1.25	3.00
41 Yoda (D) R	5.00	12.00
42 Zam Wesell (D) R	1.25	3.00
43 Zam's Airspeeder (B) R	1.25	3.00
44 Battle Droid Division U	.40	1.00
45 Battle Protocol Droid (A) U	.40	1.00
46 Call for Reinforcements U	.40	1.00
47 Tyranus's Power C	.40	1.00
48 Clone Cadet U	.40	1.00
49 Coleman Trebor (A) U	.40	1.00
50 Corporate Alliance Tank Droid U	.40	1.00
51 Coruscant Air Bus U	.40	1.00
52 Depa Billaba (A) U	.40	1.00
53 Executioner Cart U	.40	1.00
54 FA-4 (A) U	.40	1.00
55 Jango Fett (F) U	.40	1.00
56 Jedi Arrogance U	.40	1.00
57 Jedi Training Exercise U	.40	1.00
58 Jedi Knight's Survival U	.40	1.00
59 Jedi Superiority U	.40	1.00
60 Lightsaber Gift U	.40	1.00
61 Lightsaber Loss U	.40	1.00
62 Neimoidian Shuttle (A) U	.40	1.00
63 Obi-Wan Kenobi (J) U	.40	1.00
64 Orray U	.40	1.00
65 Padme's Yacht (B) U	.40	1.00
66 Underworld Investigations C	.40	1.00
67 Protocol Battle Droid (A) U	.40	1.00
68 Qui-Gon Jinn (B) U	.40	1.00
69 Republic Communications Tower U	.40	1.00
70 RIC-920 U	.40	1.00
71 Sun-Fac (B) U	.40	1.00
72 Tactical leadership U	.40	1.00
73 Tame the Beast U	.40	1.00
74 Train For War U	.40	1.00
75 Tyranus's Return U	.40	1.00
76 Tyranus's Solar Sailer (B) U	.40	1.00
77 Yoda (E) U	.40	1.00
78 Zam Wesell (C) U	.40	1.00
79 Anakin Skywalker (I) C	.20	.50
80 Mobile Artillery Division C	.20	.50
81 Captured Reek C	.20	.50
82 Clone Fire Team C	.20	.50
83 Close Pursuit C	.20	.50
84 Darth Tyranus (G) C	.20	.50
85 Destroyer Droid Team U	.20	.50
86 Diplomatic Barge C	.20	.50
87 Droid Deactivation C	.20	.50
88 Droid Starfighter Assault Wing C	.20	.50
89 Trade Federation Droid Bomber C	.20	.50
90 Forward Command Center C	.20	.50
91 Geonosian Fighter Escort C	.20	.50
92 Gondola Speeder C	.20	.50
93 Gunship Offensive C	.20	.50
94 Jedi Starfighter Squadron C	.20	.50
95 Obi-Wan's Maneuver C	.20	.50
96 Plan for the Future C	.20	.50
97 Republic Assault Transport C	.20	.50
98 Republic Attack Gunship C	.20	.50
99 Republic Light Assault Cruiser C	.20	.50
100 Republic Hyperdrive Ring C	.20	.50
101 Sabaoth Starfighter C	.20	.50
102 Scurrier C	.20	.50
103 Separatist Battle Droid C	.20	.50
104 Shaak C	.20	.50
105 Synchronized Systems C	.20	.50

2004 Star Wars The Phantom Menace

COMPLETE SET (90)	50.00	100.00
BOOSTER BOX (36 PACKS)	200.00	250.00
BOOSTER PACK (11 CARDS)	1.50	3.00
*FOIL: .75X TO 2X BASIC CARDS		
RELEASED IN JULY 2004		

1 Ann and Tann Gella (A) R	2.00	5.00
2 Aurra Sing (C) R	1.25	3.00
3 Bongo Sub R	1.25	3.00
4 Boss Nass (A) R	1.25	3.00
5 C-9979 R	1.25	3.00
6 Corridors of Power R	1.25	3.00
7 Dark Woman (A) R	1.25	3.00
8 Darth Maul (F) R	2.00	5.00
9 Duel of the Fates R	1.25	3.00
10 Fambaa Shield Beast R	1.25	3.00
11 Fight on All Fronts R	1.25	3.00
12 Gardulla the Hutt (A) R	1.25	3.00
13 Gas Attack R	1.25	3.00
14 Gungan Grand Army R	1.50	4.00
15 Guardian Mantis (A) R	1.25	3.00
16 In Disguise R	1.25	3.00
17 Jar Jar Binks (B) R	1.25	3.00
18 Jedi Temple R	1.25	3.00
19 Ki-Adi-Mundi (B) R	2.00	5.00
20 Marauder-Class Corvette R	1.25	3.00
21 Negotiate the Peace R	1.25	3.00
22 Nute Gunray (C) R	1.25	3.00
23 Orn Free Taa (A) R	1.25	3.00
24 Otoh Gunga R	1.25	3.00
25 Podracing Course R	1.25	3.00
26 Quinlan Vos (A) R	1.25	3.00
27 Sando Aqua Monster R	1.25	3.00
28 Sith Infiltrator (B) R	1.25	3.00
29 Walking Droid Starfighter R	1.25	3.00
30 Watto's Shop R	1.25	3.00
31 A'Sharad Hett (A) U	1.25	3.00
32 Anakin Skywalker (J) U	3.00	8.00
33 Anakin's Podracer (A) U	2.00	5.00
34 Bravo Starfighter U	.40	1.00
35 Captain Panaka (A) U	.40	1.00
36 Captain Tarpals (A) U	.40	1.00
37 Citadel Cruiser U	.40	1.00
38 Colo Claw Fish U	.40	1.00
39 Discuss It in Committee U	.40	1.00
40 Durge (A) U	.40	1.00
41 Falumpaset U	.40	1.00
42 Gungan Battle Wagon U	.40	1.00
43 Gungan Catapult U	.40	1.00
44 Inferno (A) U	.40	1.00
45 Kaadu Scout U	.40	1.00
46 Let the Cube Decide U	.40	1.00
47 Modified YV-330 (A) U	.40	1.00
48 Naboo System U	.40	1.00
49 Qui-Gon Jinn (D) U	.40	1.00
50 Ric Olié (A) U	.40	1.00
51 Royal Cruiser U	.40	1.00
52 Rune Haako (A) U	.40	1.00
53 Sebulba (A) U	.40	1.00
54 Sebulba's Podracer (A) U	.40	1.00
55 Streets of Theed U	.40	1.00
56 Trade Federation Hangar U	.40	1.00
57 Trade Federation MTT U	.40	1.00
58 Vilmarh Grahrk (A) U	.40	1.00
59 Watto (B) U	.40	1.00
60 Yaddle (A) U	.40	1.00
61 A Bigger Fish C	.20	.50
62 Aayla Secura (B) C	.20	.50
63 Blockade (TPM) C	.20	.50
64 Blockade Battleship C	.20	.50
65 CloakShape Fighter C	.20	.50
66 Darth Sidious (D) C	.20	.50
67 Delta Six Jedi Starfighter C	.20	.50

68 Eopie C	.20	.50
69 Finis Valorum (B) C	.20	.50
70 Flash Speeder C	.20	.50
71 Gian Speeder C	.20	.50
72 Gungan Kaadu Squad C	.20	.50
73 Jedi Transport C	.20	.50
74 Melt Your Way In C	.20	.50
75 Mos Espa C	.20	.50
76 Naboo Pilot C	.20	.50
77 Obi-Wan Kenobi (K) C	.20	.50
78 Opee Sea Killer C	.20	.50
79 Podrace C	.20	.50
80 Qui-Gon Jinn (C) C	.20	.50
81 Sith Probe Droid C	.20	.50
82 Sneak Attack C	.20	.50
83 Swamps of Naboo C	.20	.50
84 TC-14 (A) C	.20	.50
85 Theed Power Generator C	.20	.50
86 Theed Royal Palace C	.20	.50
87 Trade Federation AAT C	.20	.50
88 Trade Federation STAP C	.20	.50
89 Unconventional Maneuvers C	.20	.50
90 Yinchorri Fighter C	.20	.50

2004 Star Wars Return of the Jedi

COMPLETE SET (109)	50.00	100.00
BOOSTER BOX (36 PACKS)	100.00	200.00
BOOSTER PACK (11 CARDS)	3.00	5.00
*FOIL: .75X TO 2X BASIC CARDS		
RELEASED IN OCTOBER 2004		

1 Admiral Ackbar (A) R	1.25	3.00
2 Anakin Skywalker (K) R	1.25	3.00
3 Anakin's Spirit (A) R	1.25	3.00
4 Bargain with Jabba R	1.25	3.00
5 Bib Fortuna (A) R	1.25	3.00
6 Chewbacca (J) R	1.25	3.00
7 Darth Vader (P) R	1.25	3.00
8 Death Star II (B) R	1.25	3.00
9 Emperor Palpatine (E) R	1.25	3.00
10 Endor Imperial Fleet R	1.25	3.00
11 Endor Rebel Fleet R	1.25	3.00
12 Endor Shield Generator R	1.25	3.00
13 Ephant Mon (A) R	1.25	3.00
14 Endor Regiment R	1.25	3.00
15 Free Tatooine R	1.25	3.00
16 Han Solo (K) R	1.25	3.00
17 Home One (A) R	1.25	3.00
18 Honor the Fallen R	1.25	3.00
19 Jabba the Hutt (A) R	1.25	3.00
20 Jabba's Dancers R	1.25	3.00
21 Jabba's Palace R	1.25	3.00
22 Jabba's Spies R	1.25	3.00
23 Lando Calrissian (H) R	1.25	3.00
24 Luke Skywalker (N) R	1.25	3.00
25 Malakili (A) R	1.25	3.00
26 Max Rebo Band (A) R	1.25	3.00
27 Mixed Battlegroup R	1.25	3.00
28 Mon Mothma (A) R	1.25	3.00
29 Nien Nunb (A) R	1.25	3.00
30 Occupied Tatooine R	1.25	3.00
31 Progress Report R	1.25	3.00
32 Rancor R	1.25	3.00
33 Reactor Core R	1.25	3.00
34 Salacious B. Crumb (A) R	1.25	3.00
35 Sarlacc (A) R	1.25	3.00
36 Scythe Squadron (A) R	1.25	3.00
37 Throne Room R	1.25	3.00
38 Trap Door! R	1.25	3.00
39 Vader's Guile R	1.25	3.00
40 Yoda's Spirit (A) R	1.25	3.00
41 Baited Trap U	.40	1.00
42 Boba Fett (H) U	.40	1.00
43 C-3PO (H) U	.40	1.00

44 Captain Lennox (A) U	.40	1.00
45 Chief Chirpa (A) U	.40	1.00
46 Darth Vader (N) U	.40	1.00
47 Desperate Bluff U	.40	1.00
48 Emperor Palpatine (D) U	.40	1.00
49 Ewok Village U	.40	1.00
50 Free Bespin U	.40	1.00
51 Free Endor U	.40	1.00
52 Han Solo (J) U	.40	1.00
53 Ionization Weapons U	.40	1.00
55 Jabba the Hutt (C) U	.40	1.00
56 Jabba's Sail Barge (A) U	.40	1.00
57 Lando Calrissian (I) U	.40	1.00
58 Luke Skywalker (O) U	.40	1.00
59 Millennium Falcon (J) U	.40	1.00
60 Occupied Bespin U	.40	1.00
61 Occupied Endor U	.40	1.00
62 Princess Leia (J) U	.40	1.00
63 R2-D2 (I) U	.40	1.00
64 Rancor Pit U	.40	1.00
65 Red Squadron X-wing U	.40	1.00
66 Skiff U	.40	1.00
67 Vader's Summons U	.40	1.00
68 Wicket W. Warrick (A) U	.40	1.00
69 Wookiee Hug U	.40	1.00
70 Worrt U	.40	1.00
71 A-wing C	.20	.50
72 B-wing C	.20	.50
73 Cantina Bar Mob C	.20	.50
74 Chewbacca (K) C	.20	.50
75 Close Quarters C	.20	.50
76 Elite Royal Guard C	.20	.50
77 Darth Vader (O) C	.20	.50
78 Death Star Battalion C	.20	.50
79 Death Star II (A) C	.20	.50
80 Decoy C	.20	.50
81 Dune Sea C	.20	.50
82 Elite Squad C	.20	.50
83 Emperor Palpatine (C) C	.20	.50
84 Ewok Artillery C	.20	.50
85 Ewok Glider C	.20	.50
86 Fly Casual C	.20	.50
87 Force Lightning C	.20	.50
88 Forest AT-AT C	.20	.50
89 Forest AT-ST C	.20	.50
90 Endor Attack Squad C	.20	.50
91 Forests of Endor C	.20	.50
92 Free Coruscant C	.20	.50
93 Gray Squadron Y-wing C	.20	.50
94 High-Speed Dodge C	.20	.50
95 Imperial Speeder Bike C	.20	.50
96 Imperial-Class Star Destroyer C	.20	.50
97 Jabba's Guards C	.20	.50
98 Lightsaber Throw C	.20	.50
99 Log Trap C	.20	.50
100 Luke Skywalker (M) C	.20	.50
101 Mon Calamari Cruiser C	.20	.50
102 Occupied Coruscant C	.20	.50
103 Oola (A) C	.20	.50
104 Princess Leia (K) C	.20	.50
105 Rebel Scouts C	.20	.50
106 Royal Guards C	.20	.50
107 Scout Trooper C	.20	.50
108 Surprising Strength C	.20	.50
109 TIE Interceptor C	.20	.50
110 Savage Attack C	.20	.50

2004 Star Wars Rogues and Scoundrels

COMPLETE SET (105)	50.00	100.00
BOOSTER BOX (36 PACKS)	40.00	80.00
BOOSTER PACK (11 CARDS)	1.50	3.00
*FOIL: .75X TO 2X BASIC CARDS		
RELEASED IN APRIL 2004		

1 Admiral Firmus Piett (C) R	1.25	3.00
2 Boba Fett (G) R	1.25	3.00
3 Bossk (A) R	1.25	3.00
4 Call For Hunters R	1.25	3.00
5 Chewbacca (I) R	1.25	3.00
6 Commander Nemet (A) R	1.25	3.00
7 Dantooine System R	1.25	3.00
8 Dark Sacrifice R	1.25	3.00
9 Dengar (A) R	1.25	3.00
10 Doctor Evazan (A) R	1.25	3.00
11 Guri (A) R	1.25	3.00
12 Han Solo (I) R	1.25	3.00
13 Het Nkik (A) R	1.25	3.00
14 Hounds Tooth (A) R	1.25	3.00
15 IG-2000 (A) R	1.25	3.00
16 IG-88 (A) R	1.25	3.00
17 Dune Sea Krayt Dragon R	1.25	3.00
18 Lando Calrissian (F) R	1.25	3.00
19 Lando Calrissian (G) R	1.25	3.00
20 Lando's Influence R	1.25	3.00
21 Lobot (B) R	1.25	3.00
22 Mara Jade (B) R	1.25	3.00
23 Millennium Falcon (I) R	1.25	3.00
24 Mist Hunter (A) R	1.25	3.00
25 Modal Nodes (A) R	1.25	3.00
26 Prince Xizor (A) R	1.25	3.00
27 Princess Leia (I) R	1.25	3.00
28 Slave 1 (F) R	1.25	3.00
29 Stinger (A) R	1.25	3.00
30 Take A Prisoner R	1.25	3.00
31 Trash Compactor R	1.25	3.00
32 Virago (A) R	1.25	3.00
33 Yoda (I) R	1.25	3.00
34 Yoda's Lesson R	1.25	3.00
35 Zuckuss (A) R	1.25	3.00
36 4 Lom (A) U	.40	1.00
37 AT-AT U	.40	1.00
38 Bespin Cloud Car Squad U	.40	1.00
39 Big Asteroid U	.40	1.00
40 Boba Fett (F) U	.40	1.00
41 C 3PO (G) U	.40	1.00
42 Chewbacca (H) U	.40	1.00
43 Cloud City Wing Guard U	.40	1.00
44 Darth Vader (M) U	.40	1.00
45 Death Star Control Room U	.40	1.00
46 Garindan (A) U	.40	1.00
47 Greedo (B) U	.40	1.00
48 Han Solo (H) U	.40	1.00
49 Han's Sacrifice U	.40	1.00
50 Holoprojection Chamber U	.40	1.00
51 Human Shield U	.40	1.00
52 Kessel System U	.40	1.00
53 Lando Calrissian (E) U	.40	1.00
54 Lando's Trickery U	.40	1.00
55 Luke Skywalker (L) U	.40	1.00
56 Luke's X-wing (D) U	.40	1.00
57 Millennium Falcon (H) U	.40	1.00
58 Ponda Baba (A) U	.40	1.00
59 Punishing One (A) U	.40	1.00
60 R2-D2 (H) U	.40	1.00
61 Redoubled Effort U	.40	1.00
62 E-3PO (A) U	.40	1.00
63 Slave 1 (E) U	.40	1.00
64 Slave 1 (D) U	.40	1.00
65 Space Slug (RaS) U	.40	1.00
66 Outrider (A) U	.40	1.00
67 Ugnaught U	.40	1.00
68 Vendetta U	.40	1.00
69 Enraged Wampa U	.40	1.00
70 Lars Homestead U	.40	1.00
71 2-1B's Touch C	.20	.50
72 Bantha Herd C	.20	.50
73 Base Guards C	.20	.50
74 Bespin Patrol Cloud Car C	.20	.50
75 Boba Fett (C) C	.20	.50
76 Boba Fett (D) C	.20	.50
77 Boba Fett (E) C	.20	.50
78 Darth Vader (L) C	.20	.50
79 Dash Rendar (A) C	.20	.50
80 Disrupting Strike C	.20	.50
81 Falcon's Needs C	.20	.50
82 Jabba's Death Mark C	.20	.50
83 Kabe (A) C	.20	.50
84 Kyle Katarn (A) C	.20	.50
85 Lando System? C	.20	.50
86 Leebo (A) C	.20	.50
87 Luke's Garage C	.20	.50
88 Luke's Vow C	.20	.50
89 Medium Asteroid C	.20	.50
90 Mos Eisley C	.20	.50
91 Mos Eisley Cantina C	.20	.50
92 Muftak C	.20	.50
93 No Good To Me Dead C	.20	.50
94 Ord Mantell System C	.20	.50
95 Sleen C	.20	.50
96 Small Asteroid C	.20	.50
97 Zutton (A) C	.20	.50
98 Star Destroyer (RaS) C	.20	.50
99 Stormtrooper Detachment C	.20	.50
100 Streets Of Tatooine C	.20	.50
101 Tatooine Desert C	.20	.50
102 Tie Fighter C	.20	.50
103 Tusken Warrior C	.20	.50
104 Unmodified Snowspeeder C	.20	.50
105 X Wing Escort C	.20	.50

2005 Star Wars Revenge of the Sith

COMPLETE SET (110) 50.00 100.00
BOOSTER BOX (36 PACKS) 30.00 60.00
BOOSTER PACK (11 CARDS) 1.25 2.50
*FOIL: .75X TO 2X BASIC CARDS
RELEASED IN MAY 2005

1 Anakin Skywalker (M) R	1.25	3.00
2 Bail Organa (B) R	1.25	3.00
3 Chewbacca (M) R	1.25	3.00
4 Commerce Guild Droid 81-X R	1.25	3.00
5 Commerce Guild Starship (ROTS) R	1.25	3.00
6 Coruscant Shuttle R	1.25	3.00
7 Darth Sidious (G) R	1.25	3.00
8 Darth Tyranus (I) R	1.25	3.00
9 Darth Vader (R) R	1.25	3.00
10 Darth Vader (S) R	1.25	3.00
11 Dismiss R	1.25	3.00
12 Droid Security Escort R	1.25	3.00
13 Engine Upgrade R	1.25	3.00
14 Foil R	1.25	3.00
15 Palpatine's Sanctum R	1.25	3.00
16 Grand Moff Tarkin (D) R	1.25	3.00
17 It Just Might Work R	1.25	3.00
18 Jar Jar Binks (C) R	1.25	3.00
19 Lightsaber Quick Draw R	1.25	3.00
20 Mace Windu (F) R	1.25	3.00
21 Mas Amedda (A) R	1.25	3.00
22 Mustafar Battle Grounds R	1.25	3.00
23 Mustafar System R	1.25	3.00
24 Nos Monster R	1.25	3.00
25 Obi-Wan Kenobi (N) R	1.25	3.00
26 PadmE Amidala (G) R	1.25	3.00
27 R4-P17 (A) R	1.25	3.00
28 Rage of Victory R	1.25	3.00
29 Recusant-Class Light Destroyer R	1.25	3.00
30 Republic Fighter Wing R	1.25	3.00
31 Sacrifice the Expendable R	1.25	3.00
32 Separatist Fleet R	1.25	3.00
33 Spinning Slash R	1.25	3.00
34 Strike with Impunity R	1.25	3.00
35 Stubborn Personality R	1.25	3.00
36 Super Battle Droid 7EX R	1.25	3.00
37 Theta-Class Shuttle R	1.25	3.00
38 Unexpected Attack R	1.25	3.00
39 Venator-Class Destroyer R	1.25	3.00
40 Yoda (K) R	1.25	3.00
41 Acclamator II-Class Assault Ship U	.40	1.00
42 AT-AP U	.40	1.00
43 C-3PO (I) U	.40	1.00
44 Chancellor's Office U	.40	1.00
45 Combined Squadron Tactics U	.40	1.00
46 Confusion U	.40	1.00
47 Darth Sidious (F) U	.40	1.00
48 Darth Vader (Q) U	.40	1.00
49 Destroyer Droid, Q Series U	.40	1.00
50 Droid Missiles U	.40	1.00
51 Elite Guardian U	.40	1.00
52 Hardcell-Class Transport U	.40	1.00
53 Jedi Concentration U	.40	1.00
54 Jedi Master's Deflection U	.40	1.00
55 Kashyyyk System U	.40	1.00
56 Naboo Star Skiff U	.40	1.00
57 Nute Gunray (D) U	.40	1.00
58 Obi-Wan Kenobi (L) U	.40	1.00
59 PadmE Amidala (H) U	.40	1.00
60 Patrol Mode Vulture Droid U	.40	1.00
61 GH-7 Medical Droid U	.40	1.00
62 R2-D2 (J) U	.40	1.00
63 Thread The Needle U	.40	1.00
64 Thwart U	.40	1.00
65 Treachery U	.40	1.00
66 Techno Union Interceptor U	.40	1.00
67 Utapau System U	.40	1.00
68 Vehicle Shields Package U	.40	1.00
69 Vehicle Weapons Package U	.40	1.00
70 Yoda (J) U	.40	1.00
71 Anakin Skywalker (L) C	.20	.50
72 Anakin's Starfighter (A) C	.20	.50
73 ARC-170 Starfighter C	.20	.50
74 AT-RT C	.20	.50
75 BARC Speeder C	.20	.50
76 Blaster Pistol C	.20	.50
77 Blaster Rifle C	.20	.50
78 Buzz Droid C	.20	.50
79 Chewbacca (L) C	.20	.50
80 Coruscant Emergency Ship C	.20	.50
81 Darth Sidious (E) C	.20	.50
82 Darth Tyranus (H) C	.20	.50
83 DC0052 Intergalactic Airspeeder C	.20	.50
84 Diving Attack C	.20	.50
85 Droid Battlestaff C	.20	.50
86 Droid Tri-Fighter C	.20	.50
87 Force Dodge C	.20	.50
88 HAVw A6 Juggernaut C	.20	.50
89 Homing Missiles Salvo C	.20	.50
90 IBC Hailfire Droid C	.20	.50
91 Instill Doubt C	.20	.50
92 InterGalactic Banking Clan Cruiser C	.20	.50
93 Jedi Lightsaber C	.20	.50
94 Jedi Piloting C	.20	.50
95 Meditate C	.20	.50
96 Obi-Wan Kenobi (M) C	.20	.50
97 Plo Koon's Starfighter (A) C	.20	.50
98 Power Attack C	.20	.50
99 Republic Assault Gunboat C	.20	.50
100 Security Droid C	.20	.50
101 Sith Lightsaber C	.20	.50
102 STAP Squad C	.20	.50
103 Surge of Strength C	.20	.50
104 Tank Droid C	.20	.50
105 TF Battle Droid Army C	.20	.50
106 Trade Federation Cruiser C	.20	.50
107 Unity of the Jedi C	.20	.50
108 Utapau Sinkhole C	.20	.50
109 Vulture Droid Starfighter C	.20	.50
110 V-wing Clone Starfighter C	.20	.50

2013 Star Wars Force Attax Clone Wars Series 5

1 Anakin Skywalker	1.50	4.00
2 Obi-Wan Kenobi	1.50	4.00
3 Ahsoka Tano	1.50	4.00
4 Yoda	1.50	4.00
5 Mace Windu	1.50	4.00
6 Kit Fisto	1.50	4.00
7 Luminara Unduli	1.50	4.00
8 Barriss Offee	1.50	4.00
9 Eeth Koth	1.50	4.00
10 Adi Gallia	1.50	4.00
11 Ima-Gun Di	1.50	4.00
12 Quinlas Vos	1.50	4.00
13 Tera Sinube	1.50	4.00
14 Cin Drallig	1.50	4.00
15 Tiplee	1.50	4.00
16 Tiplar	1.50	4.00
17 Jedi Temple Guard	1.50	4.00
18 R2-D2	1.50	4.00
19 C-3PO	1.50	4.00
20 Huyang	1.50	4.00
21 WAC-47	1.50	4.00
22 AZI-3	1.50	4.00
23 Chancellor Palpatine	1.50	4.00
24 Senator Bail Organa	1.50	4.00
25 Captain Ackbar	1.50	4.00
26 Finis Valorum	1.50	4.00
27 Admiral Wullf Yularen	1.50	4.00
28 Admiral Kilian	1.50	4.00
29 Lieutenant Tan Divo	1.50	4.00
30 Steela Gerrera	1.50	4.00
31 Clone Commander Cody	1.50	4.00
32 Clone Captain Rex	1.50	4.00
33 Clone Commander Wolffe	1.50	4.00
34 Clone Trooper Fives	1.50	4.00
35 Clone Commander Colt	1.50	4.00
36 Clone ARF Trooper (white)	1.50	4.00
37 Clone ARF Trooper (camo)	1.50	4.00
38 Clone Trooper (standing)	1.50	4.00
39 Clone Trooper (aiming)	1.50	4.00
40 Yoda's Jedi Starfighter	1.50	4.00
41 Anakin's Jedi Starfighter (side)	1.50	4.00
42 Ahsoka's Jedi Starfighter (rear)	1.50	4.00
43 Y-Wing Starfighter	1.50	4.00
44 Republic Attack Cruiser	1.50	4.00
45 Republic Frigate	1.50	4.00
46 Twilight	1.50	4.00
47 Republic Attack Gunship	1.50	4.00
48 Republic Medical Base	1.50	4.00
49 Republic Escape Pod	1.50	4.00
50 Republic Assault Ship	1.50	4.00
51 Tantive IV	1.50	4.00
52 Naboo Cruiser	1.50	4.00
53 Coruscant Speeder	1.50	4.00
54 AT-TE Walker	1.50	4.00
55 Naboo Scout Carrier	1.50	4.00
56 Crucible	1.50	4.00
57 Kaminoan Flight Pod	1.50	4.00
58 Darth Sidious	1.50	4.00
59 Count Dooku	1.50	4.00
60 Darth Maul	1.50	4.00
61 Savage Opress	1.50	4.00
62 Asajj Ventress	1.50	4.00
63 General Grievous	1.50	4.00
64 Senator Rush Clovis	1.50	4.00
65 Riff Tamson	1.50	4.00
66 Osi Sobeck	1.50	4.00
67 Bec Lawise	1.50	4.00
68 Nix Card	1.50	4.00
69 Nossor Ri	1.50	4.00
70 Nala Se	1.50	4.00
71 Lama Su	1.50	4.00
72 Mother Talzin	1.50	4.00
73 Battle Droid	1.50	4.00
74 Commando Droid	1.50	4.00
75 Droid Starfighter	1.50	4.00
76 Droid Gunship	1.50	4.00
77 Count Dooku's Solar Sailer	1.50	4.00
78 General Grievous' Speeder	1.50	4.00
79 Trident Drill Ship	1.50	4.00
80 Commerce Guild Destroyer	1.50	4.00
81 Trade Federation Battleship	1.50	4.00
82 Umbaran Starfighter	1.50	4.00
83 STAP	1.50	4.00
84 Pre Vizsla	1.50	4.00
85 Bo-Katan	1.50	4.00
86 Death Watch Torch Trooper	1.50	4.00
87 Ziton Moj	1.50	4.00
88 Cad Bane	1.50	4.00
89 Embo	1.50	4.00
90 Bossk	1.50	4.00
91 Rako Hardeen	1.50	4.00
92 Twazzi	1.50	4.00
93 Derrown	1.50	4.00
94 Seripas	1.50	4.00
95 Lom Pyke	1.50	4.00
96 Garnac	1.50	4.00
97 Ratter	1.50	4.00
98 Jabba The Hutt	1.50	4.00
99 Ziro The Hutt	1.50	4.00
T1 Anakin Skywalker	1.50	4.00
Yoda (LE)		
100 Slave I	1.50	4.00
101 Trandoshan Speeder	1.50	4.00
102 Jedi Knight #1	1.50	4.00
103 Jedi Knight #2	1.50	4.00
104 Jedi Knight #3	1.50	4.00
105 Jedi Knight #4	1.50	4.00
106 Jedi Knight #5	1.50	4.00
107 Jedi Knight #6	1.50	4.00
108 Jedi Knight #7	1.50	4.00
109 Jedi Knight #8	1.50	4.00
110 Jedi Knight #9	1.50	4.00
111 Sith #1	1.50	4.00
112 Sith #2	1.50	4.00
113 Sith #3	1.50	4.00
114 Sith #4	1.50	4.00
115 Sith #5	1.50	4.00
116 Sith #6	1.50	4.00
117 Sith #7	1.50	4.00
118 Sith #8	1.50	4.00
119 Sith #9	1.50	4.00
120 Bounty Hunter #1	1.50	4.00
121 Bounty Hunter #2	1.50	4.00
122 Bounty Hunter #3	1.50	4.00
123 Bounty Hunter #4	1.50	4.00
124 Bounty Hunter #5	1.50	4.00
125 Bounty Hunter #6	1.50	4.00
126 Bounty Hunter #7	1.50	4.00
127 Bounty Hunter #8	1.50	4.00
128 Bounty Hunter #9	1.50	4.00
129 Anakin Skywalker	1.50	4.00
130 Obi-Wan Kenobi	1.50	4.00
131 Ahsoka Tano	1.50	4.00
132 Yoda	1.50	4.00
133 Mace Windu	1.50	4.00
134 Aalya Secura	1.50	4.00
135 Luminara Unduli	1.50	4.00
136 Barriss Offee	1.50	4.00
137 Adi Gallia	1.50	4.00
138 Shaak Ti	1.50	4.00
139 Ima-Gun Di	1.50	4.00
140 Pong Krell	1.50	4.00
141 Force Priestess	1.50	4.00
142 R2-D2	1.50	4.00
143 C-3PO	1.50	4.00
144 AZI-3	1.50	4.00
145 Clone Commander Cody	1.50	4.00
146 Clone Captain Rex	1.50	4.00
147 Darth Sidious	1.50	4.00
148 Count Dooku	1.50	4.00
149 Darth Maul	1.50	4.00
150 Savage Opress	1.50	4.00
151 General Grievous	1.50	4.00
152 Nala Se	1.50	4.00
153 Pre Vizsla	1.50	4.00
154 Bo-Katan	1.50	4.00
155 Cad Bane	1.50	4.00
156 Pyke	1.50	4.00
157 Black Sun Leader	1.50	4.00
158 Boba Fett	1.50	4.00
159 Bossk	1.50	4.00
160 Embo	1.50	4.00
161 Anakin Skywalker	1.50	4.00
162 Obi-Wan Kenobi	1.50	4.00
163 Ahsoka Tano	1.50	4.00
164 Yoda	1.50	4.00
165 Mace Windu	1.50	4.00
166 Ima-Gun Di	1.50	4.00
167 Shaak Ti	1.50	4.00
168 Luminara Unduli	1.50	4.00
169 Barriss Offee	1.50	4.00
170 Force Priestess	1.50	4.00
171 R2-D2	1.50	4.00
172 Darth Sidious	1.50	4.00
173 Count Dooku	1.50	4.00
174 Darth Maul	1.50	4.00
175 Asajj Ventress	1.50	4.00
176 Mother Talzin	1.50	4.00
LEAS Anakin Skywalker (LEG)	1.50	4.00
LEAT Ahsoka Tano (LEG)	1.50	4.00
LECR Klon-Captain Rex (LEG)	1.50	4.00
LEDM Darth Maul (LEG)	1.50	4.00
LEDS Darth Sidious (LEG)	1.50	4.00
LEFP Macht-Priesterin (LEG)	1.50	4.00
LEOK Obi-Wan Kenobi (LEG)	1.50	4.00
LEPV Pre Vizsla (LEG)	1.50	4.00
LEPV Pre Vizsla (LE)	1.50	4.00
LESO Savage Opress (LEG)	1.50	4.00

2014 Star Wars Force Attax Movie Series 3

1 Luke Skywalker 1.50 4.00
2 Han Solo 1.50 4.00
3 Leia Organa 1.50 4.00
4 Chewbacca 1.50 4.00
5 Obi-Wan Kenobi 1.50 4.00
6 Yoda 1.50 4.00
7 Lando Calrissian 1.50 4.00
8 Admiral Ackbar 1.50 4.00
9 Mon Calamari 1.50 4.00
10 Prune Face 1.50 4.00
11 Nien Nunb 1.50 4.00
12 Rebel Trooper 1.50 4.00
13 Rebel Commando 1.50 4.00
14 Owen Lars 1.50 4.00
15 Beru Lars 1.50 4.00
16 R2-D2 1.50 4.00
17 C-3PO 1.50 4.00
18 2-1B Medical Droid 1.50 4.00
19 Protocol Droid 1.50 4.00
20 R1-G4 1.50 4.00
21 Training Remote 1.50 4.00
22 Momaw Nadon 1.50 4.00
23 Dice Ibegon 1.50 4.00
24 Yoxgit 1.50 4.00
25 Wicket 1.50 4.00
26 Logray 1.50 4.00
27 Paploo 1.50 4.00
28 Teebo 1.50 4.00
29 Romba 1.50 4.00
30 Millennium Falcon 1.50 4.00
31 X-Wing Starfighter 1.50 4.00
32 Y-Wing Starfighter 1.50 4.00
33 B-Wing Starfighter 1.50 4.00
34 A-Wing Starfighter 1.50 4.00
35 Tantive 4 1.50 4.00
36 Medical Frigate 1.50 4.00
37 Headquarters Frigate 1.50 4.00
38 Rebel Transport 1.50 4.00
39 Snowspeeder 1.50 4.00
40 T-16 Skyhopper 1.50 4.00
41 Landspeeder 1.50 4.00
42 Emperor Palpatine 1.50 4.00
43 Darth Vader 1.50 4.00
44 Grand Moff Tarkin 1.50 4.00
45 Moff Jerjerrod 1.50 4.00
46 General Veers 1.50 4.00
47 Captain Lennox 1.50 4.00
48 Lieutenant Cabbel 1.50 4.00
49 Captain Khurgee 1.50 4.00
50 Stormtrooper 1.50 4.00
51 Snowtrooper 1.50 4.00
52 Sandtrooper 1.50 4.00
53 TIE Fighter Pilot 1.50 4.00
54 Janus Greejatus 1.50 4.00
55 Sim Aloo 1.50 4.00
56 Star Destroyer 1.50 4.00
57 Super Star Destroyer 1.50 4.00
58 TIE Fighter 1.50 4.00
59 TIE Interceptor 1.50 4.00
60 TIE Advanced 1.50 4.00
61 TIE Bomber 1.50 4.00
62 Imperial Shuttle 1.50 4.00
63 AT-ST Walker 1.50 4.00
64 AT-AT Walker 1.50 4.00
65 Speeder Bike 1.50 4.00
66 Probe Droid Capsule 1.50 4.00
67 Probot 1.50 4.00
68 R2-Q5 1.50 4.00
69 Demolition Droid 1.50 4.00
70 Death Star 1.50 4.00
71 Death Star 2 1.50 4.00
72 Jabba the Hutt 1.50 4.00
73 Bib Fortuna 1.50 4.00
74 Salacious Crumb 1.50 4.00
75 Amanaman 1.50 4.00
76 Boba Fett 1.50 4.00
77 Bossk 1.50 4.00
78 IG-88 1.50 4.00
79 Boushh 1.50 4.00
80 Gamorrean Guard 1.50 4.00
81 Umpass-Stay 1.50 4.00
82 Klaatu 1.50 4.00
83 Lathe 1.50 4.00
84 Harc Seff 1.50 4.00
85 Melas 1.50 4.00
86 Brock Starsher 1.50 4.00
87 Muftak 1.50 4.00
88 Tusken Raider 1.50 4.00
89 Jawa 1.50 4.00
90 EV-9D9 1.50 4.00
91 Slave I 1.50 4.00
92 Sandcrawler 1.50 4.00
93 Sailbarge 1.50 4.00
94 Desert Skiff 1.50 4.00
95 Anakin Skywalker 1.50 4.00
96 Obi-Wan Kenobi 1.50 4.00
97 Mace Windu 1.50 4.00
98 Qui-Gon Jinn 1.50 4.00
99 Kit Fisto 1.50 4.00
T1 R2-D2 (LE) 1.50 4.00
100 Ki-Adi-Mundi 1.50 4.00
101 Shaak Ti 1.50 4.00
102 Saesee Tiin 1.50 4.00
103 Plo Koon 1.50 4.00
104 Agen Kolar 1.50 4.00
105 Luminara Unduli 1.50 4.00
106 Stass Allie 1.50 4.00
107 Ma'Kis'Shaalas 1.50 4.00
108 J'oopi She 1.50 4.00
109 Cin Drallig 1.50 4.00
110 Youngling 1.50 4.00
111 Queen Amidala 1.50 4.00
112 Chancellor Palpatine 1.50 4.00
113 Chancellor Valorum 1.50 4.00
114 Bail Organa 1.50 4.00
115 Dorme 1.50 4.00
116 Captain Typho 1.50 4.00
117 Clone Trooper (blue) 1.50 4.00
118 Clone Trooper (orange) 1.50 4.00
119 Clone Trooper (yellow) 1.50 4.00
120 Clone Trooper (red) 1.50 4.00
121 Clone Trooper (white) 1.50 4.00
122 Jar Jar Binks 1.50 4.00
123 Gungan Soldier 1.50 4.00
124 Tion Meddon 1.50 4.00
125 Utapaun Warrior 1.50 4.00
126 Mustafarian 1.50 4.00
127 PK-4 Droid 1.50 4.00
128 Pit Droid 1.50 4.00
129 Otoga 222 Droid 1.50 4.00
130 Forklift Droid 1.50 4.00
131 Bettybot 1.50 4.00
132 Jedi Attack Cruiser 1.50 4.00
133 Jedi Starfighter (red) 1.50 4.00
134 Jedi Starfighter (yellow) 1.50 4.00
135 ARC-170 Starfighter 1.50 4.00
136 Darth Sidious 1.50 4.00
137 Count Dooku 1.50 4.00
138 Darth Maul 1.50 4.00
139 General Grievous 1.50 4.00
140 Destroyer Droid 1.50 4.00
141 Magnaguard 1.50 4.00
142 Crab Droid 1.50 4.00
143 Battle Droid 1.50 4.00
144 Battle Droid Pilot 1.50 4.00
145 TC-14 1.50 4.00
146 Droid Tri-Fighter 1.50 4.00
147 Wheel Bike 1.50 4.00
148 MTT 1.50 4.00
149 Droid Starfighter 1.50 4.00
150 The Invisible Hand 1.50 4.00
151 Droid Control Ship 1.50 4.00
152 Theta-Class Shuttle 1.50 4.00
153 Jango Fett 1.50 4.00
154 Aurra Sing 1.50 4.00
155 Zam Wesell 1.50 4.00
156 Watto 1.50 4.00
157 Alliance Strike Force 1 1.50 4.00
158 Alliance Strike Force 2 1.50 4.00
159 Alliance Strike Force 3 1.50 4.00
160 Alliance Strike Force 4 1.50 4.00
161 Strike Force 1.50 4.00
162 Alliance Strike Force 6 1.50 4.00
163 Alliance Strike Force 7 1.50 4.00
164 Alliance Strike Force 8 1.50 4.00
165 Alliance Strike Force 9 1.50 4.00
166 Empire Strike Force 1 1.50 4.00
167 Empire Strike Force 2 1.50 4.00
168 Empire Strike Force 3 1.50 4.00
169 Empire Strike Force 4 1.50 4.00
170 Strike Force 1.50 4.00
171 Empire Strike Force 6 1.50 4.00
172 Empire Strike Force 7 1.50 4.00
173 Empire Strike Force 8 1.50 4.00
174 Empire Strike Force 9 1.50 4.00
175 Republic Strike Force 1 1.50 4.00
176 Republic Strike Force 2 1.50 4.00
177 Republic Strike Force 3 1.50 4.00
178 Republic Strike Force 4 1.50 4.00
179 Strike Force 1.50 4.00
180 Republic Strike Force 6 1.50 4.00
181 Republic Strike Force 7 1.50 4.00
182 Republic Strike Force 8 1.50 4.00
183 Republic Strike Force 9 1.50 4.00
184 Separatist Strike Force 1 1.50 4.00
185 Separatist Strike Force 2 1.50 4.00
186 Separatist Strike Force 3 1.50 4.00
187 Separatist Strike Force 4 1.50 4.00
188 Strike Force 1.50 4.00
189 Separatist Strike Force 6 1.50 4.00
190 Separatist Strike Force 7 1.50 4.00
191 Separatist Strike Force 8 1.50 4.00
192 Separatist Strike Force 9 1.50 4.00
193 Luke Skywalker 1.50 4.00
Princess Leia
194 Han Solo 1.50 4.00
Chewbacca
195 R2-D2 1.50 4.00
C-3PO
196 Princess Leia 1.50 4.00
Wicket
197 Obi-Wan Kenobi 1.50 4.00
Luke Skywalker
198 Emperor Palpatine 1.50 4.00
Darth Vader
199 Qui-Gon Jinn 1.50 4.00
Obi-Wan Kenobi
200 Anakin Skywalker 1.50 4.00
Obi-Wan Kenobi
201 Mace Windu 1.50 4.00
Obi-Wan Kenobi
202 Luminara Unduli 1.50 4.00
Barriss Offee
203 Yoda 1.50 4.00
Chewbacca
204 Jango Fett 1.50 4.00
Boba Fett
205 Luke Skywalker 1.50 4.00
206 Han Solo 1.50 4.00
207 Princess Leia 1.50 4.00
208 Chewbacca 1.50 4.00
209 Lando Calrissian 1.50 4.00
210 R2-D2 1.50 4.00
211 C-3PO 1.50 4.00
212 Anakin Skywalker 1.50 4.00
213 Obi-Wan Kenobi 1.50 4.00
214 Yoda 1.50 4.00
215 Mace Windu 1.50 4.00
216 Queen Amidala 1.50 4.00
217 Clone Lieutenant Galle 1.50 4.00
218 Darth Maul 1.50 4.00
219 Count Dooku 1.50 4.00
220 General Grievous 1.50 4.00
221 Darth Vader 1.50 4.00
222 Jabba the Hutt 1.50 4.00
223 Jango Fett 1.50 4.00
224 Boba Fett 1.50 4.00
225 Luke Skywalker 1.50 4.00
226 Han Solo 1.50 4.00
227 Princess Leia 1.50 4.00
228 Chewbacca 1.50 4.00
229 Anakin Skywalker 1.50 4.00
230 Obi-Wan Kenobi 1.50 4.00
231 Yoda 1.50 4.00
232 Mace Windu 1.50 4.00
233 Qui-Gon Jinn 1.50 4.00
234 Queen Amidala 1.50 4.00
235 Boba Fett 1.50 4.00
236 Darth Maul 1.50 4.00
237 Count Dooku 1.50 4.00
238 General Grievous 1.50 4.00
239 Darth Vader 1.50 4.00
240 Emperor Palpatine 1.50 4.00
LE1 Luke Skywalker (LE) 1.50 4.00
LE2 Han Solo (LEG) 1.50 4.00
LE3 Prinzessin Leia (LEG) 1.50 4.00
LE4 Lando Calrissian (LEG) 1.50 4.00
LE5 Darth Vader (LEG) 1.50 4.00
LE6 Anakin Skywalker (LEG) 1.50 4.00
LE7 Yoda (LEG) 1.50 4.00
LE8 C-3PO (LEG) 1.50 4.00
LE9 R2-D2 (LEG) 1.50 4.00
LE10 Chewbacca (LEG) 1.50 4.00
LE11 Boba Fett (LEG) 1.50 4.00

2015 Star Wars Between the Shadows

12710633 A Heroís Trial .75 2.00
12720634 Luke Skywalker .75 2.00
12730635 Speeder Bike .75 2.00
12740636 Lukeís Lightsaber .75 2.00
12750637 I Am a Jedi .75 2.00
12760065 Heat of Battle .75 2.00
12810638 The Masterís Domain .75 2.00
12820639 Yoda .75 2.00
12830640 Bogwing .75 2.00
12840641 Yodaís Hut .75 2.00
12850089 Lightsaber Deflection .75 2.00
12860642 The Jediís Resolve .75 2.00
12910643 Following Fate .75 2.00
12920644 Obi-Wan Kenobi .75 2.00
12930106 R2-D2 .75 2.00
12940645 Obi-Wanís Lightsaber .75 2.00
12950646 Noble Sacrifice .75 2.00
12960133 Target of Opportunity .75 2.00
13010647 Journey Through the Swamp.75 2.00
13020648 Jubba Bird .75 2.00
13030648 Jubba Bird .75 2.00
13040649 Knobby White Spider .75 2.00
13050650 Life Creates It .75 2.00
13060651 Size Matters Not .75 2.00
13110652 Sacrifice at Endor .75 2.00
13120653 Ewok Hunter .75 2.00
13130653 Ewok Hunter .75 2.00
13140654 Funeral Pyre .75 2.00
13150655 Unexpected Assistance .75 2.00
13160656 Retreat to the Forest .75 2.00
13210657 Commando Raid .75 2.00
13220658 Lieutenant Judder Page .75 2.00
13230659 Pageís Commandos .75 2.00
13240659 Pageís Commandos .75 2.00
13250065 Heat of Battle .75 2.00
13260133 Target of Opportunity .75 2.00
13310660 Calling In Favors .75 2.00
13320661 Talon Karrde .75 2.00
13330662 Skipray Blastboat .75 2.00
13340662 Skipray Blastboat .75 2.00
13350663 Dirty Secrets .75 2.00
13360664 Clever Ruse .75 2.00
13410665 No Disintegrations .75 2.00
13420666 Boba Fett .75 2.00
13430667 Freelance Hunter .75 2.00
13440668 Flamethrower .75 2.00
13450378 Prized Possession .75 2.00
13460669 Entangled .75 2.00
13510670 Masterful Manipulation .75 2.00
13520671 Prince Xizor .75 2.00
13530672 Black Sun Headhunter .75 2.00
13540673 Debt Collector .75 2.00
13550674 Shadows of the Empire .75 2.00
13560675 The Princeís Scheme .75 2.00
13610676 All Out Brawl .75 2.00
13620677 Zekka Thyne .75 2.00
13630673 Debt Collector .75 2.00
13640678 Armed to the Teeth .75 2.00
13650669 Entangled .75 2.00
13660169 Heat of Battle .75 2.00
13710679 The Best That Credits Can Buy.75 2.00
13720680 Virago .75 2.00
13730672 Black Sun Headhunter .75 2.00
13740681 Rise of the Black Sun .75 2.00
13750682 Warning Shot .75 2.00
13760170 Target of Opportunity .75 2.00
13810683 The Hunters .75 2.00
13820684 Boushh .75 2.00
13830685 Snoova .75 2.00
13840686 A Better Offer .75 2.00
13850542 Pay Out .75 2.00
13860687 Show of Force .75 2.00
13910688 The Investigation .75 2.00
13920689 Ysanne Isard .75 2.00
13930690 Imperial Intelligence Officer .75 2.00
13940690 Imperial Intelligence Officer .75 2.00
13950691 Confiscation .75 2.00
13960692 Official Inquiry .75 2.00
14010693 Family Connections .75 2.00
14020694 General Tagge .75 2.00
14030695 Security Task Force .75 2.00
14040695 Security Task Force .75 2.00
14050696 Imperial Discipline .75 2.00
14060697 Precision Fire .75 2.00

2015 Star Wars Chain of Command

1611 A Heroís Beginning .75 2.00
1612 Lukeís X-34 Landspeeder .75 2.00
1613 Owen Lars .75 2.00
1614 Moisture Vaporator .75 2.00
1615 Unfinished Business .75 2.00
1616 Supporting Fire .75 2.00
1621 Breaking the Blockade .75 2.00
1622 Smuggling Freighter .75 2.00
1623 Smuggling Freighter .75 2.00
1624 Duros Smuggler .75 2.00
1625 Duros Smuggler .75 2.00
1626 Surprising Maneuver .75 2.00
1631 The Imperial Bureaucracy .75 2.00
1632 Sate Pestage .75 2.00
1633 Advisor to the Emperor .75 2.00
1634 Quarren Bureaucrat .75 2.00
1635 Endless Bureaucracy .75 2.00
1636 Supporting Fire .75 2.00
1641 The Last Grand Admiral .75 2.00
1642 Grand Admiral Thrawn .75 2.00
1643 Noghri Bodyguard .75 2.00
1644 Noghri Bodyguard .75 2.00
1645 Chain of Command 2.00 5.00
1646 Supporting Fire .75 2.00
1651 Nar Shaddaa Drift .75 2.00
1652 Race Circut Champion .75 2.00
1653 Racing Swoop .75 2.00
1654 Racing Swoop .75 2.00
1655 Black Market Exchange .75 2.00
1656 Cut Off .75 2.00

2015 Star Wars Draw Their Fire

14610722 The Survivors	.75	2.00
14620723 Qu Rahn	.75	2.00
14630724 Sulon Sympathizer	.75	2.00
14640725 Shien Training	.75	2.00
14650061 Force Rejuvenation	.75	2.00
14660256 Protection	.75	2.00
14710726 Called to Arms	.75	2.00
14720727 Gray Squadron Gunner	.75	2.00
14730728 Gray Squadron Y-Wing	.75	2.00
14740729 Advanced Proton Torpedoes	.75	2.00
14750730 Desperation	.75	2.00
14760133 Target of Opportunity	.75	2.00
14810731 The Daring Escape	.75	2.00
14820732 LE-BO2D9	.75	2.00
14830733 Outrider	.75	2.00
14840734 Spacer Cantina	.75	2.00
14850735 Punch It	.75	2.00
14860702 Stay on Target	.75	2.00
14910736 The Emperorís Sword	.75	2.00
14920737 Maarek Stele	.75	2.00
14930738 Delta One	.75	2.00
14940739 Advanced Concussion Missiles	.75	2.00
14950740 Hand of the Emperor	.75	2.00
14960169 Heat of Battle	.75	2.00
15010741 Guarding the Wing	.75	2.00
15020742 DS-61-3	.75	2.00
15030743 Black Squadron Fighter	.75	2.00
15040743 Black Squadron Fighter	.75	2.00
15050744 Elite Pilot Training	.75	2.00
15060170 Target of Opportunity	.75	2.00

2015 Star Wars Imperial Entanglement

17110838 House Edge	.75	2.00
17120839 Lando Calrissian	.75	2.00
17130840 Herglic Sabacc Addict	.75	2.00
17140022 Cloud City Casino	.75	2.00
17150841 Sabacc Shift	.75	2.00
17160842 The Gamblerís Trick	.75	2.00
17210843 Debt of Honor	.75	2.00
17220844 Chewbacca	.75	2.00
17230845 Wookiee Defender	.75	2.00
17240846 Kashyyyk Resistance Hideout	.75	2.00
17250847 Wookiee Rage	.75	2.00
17260256 Protection	.75	2.00
17310848 Fortune and Fate	.75	2.00
17320849 Lady Luck	.75	2.00
17330850 Cloud City Technician	.75	2.00
17340850 Cloud City Technician	.75	2.00
17350851 Central Computer	.75	2.00
17360133 Target of Opportunity	.75	2.00
17410852 Honor Among Thieves	.75	2.00
17420853 Mirax Terrik	.75	2.00
17430854 Fringer Captain	.75	2.00
17440854 Fringer Captain	.75	2.00
17450855 Special Discount	.75	2.00
17460856 One Last Trick	.75	2.00
17510857 Renegade Reinforcements	.75	2.00
17520858 Corporal Dansra Beezer	.75	2.00
17530210 Renegade Squadron Operative	.75	2.00
17540859 Hidden Backup	.75	2.00
17550860 Directed Fire	.75	2.00
17560861 Last Minute Reinforcements	.75	2.00
17610862 Mysteries of the Rim	.75	2.00
17620863 Outer Rim Mystic	.75	2.00
17630863 Outer Rim Mystic	.75	2.00
17640864 Niman Training	.75	2.00
17650864 Niman Training	.75	2.00
17660865 Force Illusion	.75	2.00
17710866 Planning the Rescue	.75	2.00
17720867 General Airen Cracken	.75	2.00
17730868 Alliance Infiltrator	.75	2.00
17740869 Superior Intelligence	.75	2.00
17750870 Undercover	.75	2.00
17760117 Rescue Mission	.75	2.00
17810871 The Tarkin Doctrine	.75	2.00
17820872 Grand Moff Tarkin	.75	2.00
17830873 Stormtrooper Assault Team	.75	2.00
17840874 Rule by Fear	.75	2.00
17850875 Moment of Triumph	.75	2.00
17860171 Twist of Fate	.75	2.00
17910876 Might of the Empire	.75	2.00
17920877 Chimaera	.75	2.00
17930878 DP20 Corellian Gunship	.75	2.00
17940879 Fleet Staging Area	.75	2.00
17950392 Tractor Beam	.75	2.00
17960880 The Empire Strikes Back	.75	2.00
18010881 Enforced Loyalty	.75	2.00
18020882 Colonel Yularen	.75	2.00
18030883 Lieutenant Mithel	.75	2.00
18040884 MSE-6 ìMouseî Droid	.75	2.00
18050024 Control Room	.75	2.00
18060885 The Imperial Fist	.75	2.00
18110886 Imperial Entanglements	.75	2.00
18120887 Imperial Raider	.75	2.00
18130888 VT-49 Decimator	.75	2.00
18140888 VT-49 Decimator	.75	2.00
18150889 Customs Blockade	.75	2.00
18160890 Ion Cannon	.75	2.00
18210891 Phantoms of Imdaar	.75	2.00
18220892 TIE Phantom	.75	2.00
18230892 TIE Phantom	.75	2.00
18240893 Enhanced Laser Cannon	.75	2.00
18250894 Fighters Coming In!	.75	2.00
18260169 Heat of Battle	.75	2.00
18310895 Brothers of the Sith	.75	2.00
18320896 Gorc	.75	2.00
18330897 Pic	.75	2.00
18340898 Telepathic Connection	.75	2.00
18350062 Force Stasis	.75	2.00
18360899 Force Invisibility	.75	2.00
18410900 The Huttís Menagerie	.75	2.00
18420901 Malakili	.75	2.00
18430902 Jabbaís Rancor	.75	2.00
18440903 Bubo	.75	2.00
18450904 Underground Entertainment	.75	2.00
18460905 Jabbaís Summons	.75	2.00

2015 Star Wars Jump to Lightspeed

1661 The Forgotten Masters	.75	2.00
1662 Tira Saa	.75	2.00
1663 Lost Master	.75	2.00
1664 Lost Master	.75	2.00
1665 A Gift from the Past	.75	2.00
1666 Echoes of the Force	.75	2.00
1671 Heroes of the Rebellion	.75	2.00
1672 Tycho Celchu	.75	2.00
1673 Wes Janson	.75	2.00
1674 Rogue Six	.75	2.00
1675 Rogue Nine	.75	2.00
1676 Ready for Takeoff	.75	2.00
1681 That Bucket of Bolts	.75	2.00
1682 Han Solo	.75	2.00
1683 Millennium Falcon	.75	2.00
1684 Well Paid	.75	2.00
1685 Well Paid	.75	2.00
1686 Heat of Battle	.75	2.00
1691 The Reawakening	.75	2.00
1692 Arden Lyn	.75	2.00
1693 Dark Side Apprentice	.75	2.00
1694 Return to Darkness	.75	2.00
1695 Give in to Your Anger	.75	2.00
1696 Give in to Your Anger	.75	2.00
1701 Behind the Black Sun	.75	2.00
1702 Guri	.75	2.00
1703 Freelance Assassin	.75	2.00
1704 Hidden Vibroknife	.75	2.00
1705 Threat Removal	.75	2.00
1706 Heat of Battle	.75	2.00

2015 Star Wars Ready for Takeoff

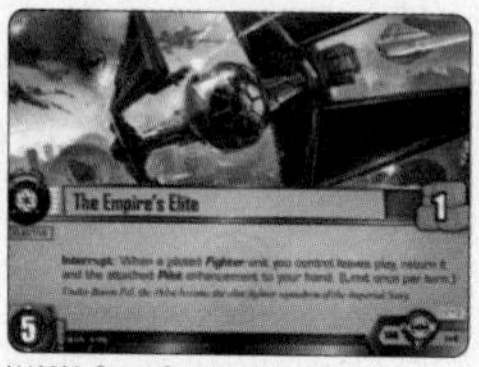

14110698 Rogue Squadron Assault	.75	2.00
14120699 Derek ìHobbieî Klivian	.75	2.00
14130700 Rogue Squadron X-Wing	.75	2.00
14140700 Rogue Squadron X-Wing	.75	2.00
14150701 Pilot Ready Room	.75	2.00
14160702 Stay on Target	.75	2.00
14210703 Memories of Taanab	.75	2.00
14220704 Lando Calrissian	.75	2.00
14230705 System Patrol Craft	.75	2.00
14240705 System Patrol Craft	.75	2.00
14250706 Conner Net	.75	2.00
14260707 A Little Maneuver	.75	2.00
14310708 Black Squadron Formation	.75	2.00
14320709 ìMauleri Mithel	.75	2.00
14330710 Black Two	.75	2.00
14340146 TIE Advanced	.75	2.00
14350711 Death Star Ready Room	.75	2.00
14360712 Stay on Target	.75	2.00
14410713 The Empireís Elite	.75	2.00
14420714 Baron Fel	.75	2.00
14430715 181st TIE Interceptor	.75	2.00
14440715 181st TIE Interceptor	.75	2.00
14450716 Flight Academy	.75	2.00
14460712 Stay on Target	.75	2.00
14510717 The Grand Heist	.75	2.00
14520718 Niles Ferrier	.75	2.00
14530719 Novice Starship Thief	.75	2.00
14540719 Novice Starship Thief	.75	2.00
14550720 Pirate Hideout	.75	2.00
14560721 Salvage Operation	.75	2.00

2016 Star Wars Destiny Awakening

COMPLETE SET (174 CARDS)	450.00	650.00
BOOSTER BOX (36 PACKS)	80.00	120.00
BOOSTER PACK (5 CARDS AND 1 DICE)	4.00	6.00
UNLISTED C	.10	.20
UNLISTED U	.25	.40
UNLISTED R	3.00	5.00

RELEASED IN NOVEMBER, 2016

1 Captain Phasma L	10.00	15.00
2 First Order Stormtrooper R	3.00	5.00
3 General Grievous R	3.00	5.00
4 General Veers R	3.00	5.00
5 AT ST L	8.00	12.00
6 First Order TIE Fighter R	3.00	5.00
7 Commanding Presence L	10.00	15.00
8 F 11D Rifle S	2.00	3.50
9 Count Dooku R	3.00	5.00
10 Darth Vader L	30.00	35.00
11 Kylo Ren S	1.50	2.50
12 Nightsister R	3.00	5.00
13 Force Choke L	15.00	20.00
14 Immobilize R	3.00	5.00
15 Kylo Rens Lightsaber L	15.00	20.00
16 Sith Holocron R	10.00	13.00
17 Infantry Grenades R	3.00	5.00
18 Speeder Bike Scout R	3.00	5.00
19 Bala Tik R	3.00	5.00
20 Jabba the Hutt L	20.00	25.00
21 Jango Fett R	3.00	5.00
22 Tusken Raider R	3.00	5.00
23 Crime Lord L	10.00	15.00
24 Flame Thrower R	3.00	5.00
25 Gaffi Stick R	3.00	5.00
26 On the Hunt R	3.00	5.00
27 Admiral Ackbar R	3.00	5.00
28 Leia Organa R	3.00	5.00
29 Poe Dameron L	20.00	25.00
30 Rebel Trooper R	3.00	5.00
31 Launch Bay L	7.00	10.00
32 Black One L	5.00	8.00
33 Scout R	3.00	5.00
34 Survival Gear R	3.00	5.00
35 Luke Skywalker L	20.00	25.00
36 Padawan R	3.00	5.00
37 Qui Gon Jinn R	3.00	5.00
38 Rey S	2.00	3.50
39 Force Protection R	3.00	5.00
40 Jedi Robes R	3.00	5.00
41 Luke Skywalkers Lightsaber L	10.00	15.00
42 One With the Force L	20.00	25.00
43 BB 8 R	3.00	5.00
44 Reys Staff R	3.00	5.00
45 Finn S	2.00	3.50
46 Han Solo L	15.00	20.00
47 Hired Gun R	3.00	5.00
48 Padme Amidala R	3.00	5.00
49 Millennium Falcon L	10.00	15.00
50 Diplomatic Immunity R	3.00	5.00
51 DL 44 Heavy Blaster Pistol R	3.00	5.00
52 Infiltrate R	3.00	5.00
53 Outpost R	3.00	5.00
54 DH 17 Blaster Pistol R	3.00	5.00
55 IQA 11 Blaster Rifle R	3.00	5.00
56 Promotion R	3.00	5.00
57 Force Throw S	7.00	10.00
58 Force Training R	3.00	5.00
59 Lightsaber S	2.00	3.50
60 Mind Probe S	5.00	8.00
61 Comlink R	3.00	5.00
62 Datapad R	3.00	5.00
63 Holdout Blaster R	15.00	20.00
64 Black Market R	3.00	5.00
65 Cunning R	3.00	5.00
66 Jetpack R	3.00	5.00
67 Thermal Detonator L	20.00	25.00
68 Cannon Fodder C	.10	.20
69 Closing the Net C	.10	.20
70 Endless Ranks U	1.50	2.00
71 Occupation C	.10	.20
72 Probe C	.10	.20
73 Sweep the Area C	.10	.20
74 Tactical Mastery U	2.00	3.00
75 The Best Defense U	.25	.40
76 Drudge Work C	.10	.20
77 Local Garrison U	.25	.40
78 Personal Escort C	.10	.20
79 Abandon All Hope U	.25	.40
80 Boundless Ambition C	.10	.20
81 Enrage C	.10	.20
82 Feel Your Anger C	.10	.20
83 Force Strike U	.75	1.25
84 Intimidate C	.10	.20
85 Isolation C	.10	.20
86 No Mercy U	2.00	3.00
87 Pulling the Strings C	.10	.20
88 Emperors Favor U	.25	.40
89 Power of the Dark Side S	.40	.60
90 Hidden in Shadow U	.25	.40
91 Nowhere to Run U	.25	.40
92 Ace in the Hole U	.75	1.25
93 Armed to the Teeth C	.10	.20
94 Confiscation U	.25	.40
95 Fight Dirty U	.25	.40
96 Go for the Kill C	.10	.20
97 He Doesnt Like You C	.10	.20
98 Lying in Wait C	.10	.20
99 Backup Muscle C	.10	.20
100 My Kind of Scum C	.10	.20
101 Underworld Connections U	1.00	1.50
102 Prized Possession U	.25	.40
103 Commando Raid U	.25	.40
104 Defensive Position C	.10	.20
105 Field Medic C	.10	.20
106 Hit and Run C	.10	.20
107 Its a Trap U	.75	1.25
108 Natural Talent C	.10	.20
109 Rearm U	.25	.40
110 Retreat U	.25	.40
111 Strategic Planning C	.10	.20
112 Surgical Strike C	.10	.20
113 Resistance HQ U	.25	.40
114 Anticipate U	.25	.40
115 Defensive Stance C	.10	.20
116 Force Misdirection C	.10	.20
117 Heroism C	.10	.20
118 Noble Sacrifice C	.10	.20
119 Patience C	.10	.20
120 Return of the Jedi U	.25	.40
121 Riposte C	.10	.20
122 Willpower U	.40	.60
123 Jedi Council U	.25	.40
124 Awakening S	.60	1.00
125 The Force is Strong C	.10	.20
126 Daring Escape U	.25	.40
127 Dont Get Cocky C	.10	.20
128 Draw Attention C	.10	.20
129 Hyperspace Jump U	.25	.40
130 Let the Wookiee Win U	.25	.40
131 Negotiate C	.10	.20
132 Scavenge C	.10	.20
133 Shoot First U	.25	.40
134 Smuggling C	.10	.20
135 Play the Odds U	.25	.40
136 Street Informants C	.10	.20
137 Second Chance U	1.50	2.50
138 Award Ceremony C	.10	.20
139 Dug In U	2.00	3.00
140 Firepower C	.10	.20
141 Leadership U	.40	.60
142 Logistics C	.10	.20
143 Squad Tactics C	.10	.20
144 Supporting Fire U	.25	.40
145 Deflect C	.10	.20
146 Disturbance in the Force C	.10	.20
147 Mind Trick U	.40	.60
148 The Power of the Force C	.10	.20
149 Use the Force S	.75	1.25
150 It Binds All Things U	1.25	2.00
151 Aim S	.50	.80
152 All In U	1.50	2.00
153 Block C	.10	.20
154 Close Quarters Assault S	1.00	1.50
155 Dodge C	.10	.20
156 Flank U	.25	.40
157 Take Cover C	.10	.20
158 Disarm C	.10	.20
159 Electroshock U	4.00	6.00
160 Reversal U	1.00	1.50
161 Scramble C	.10	.20
162 Unpredictable C	.10	.20
163 Infamous U	1.50	2.50
164 Hunker Down C	.10	.20
165 Command Center U	.25	.40
166 Echo Base U	.25	.40
167 Emperors Throne Room U	.25	.40
168 Frozen Wastes S	.60	1.00
169 Imperial Armory C	.10	.20
170 Jedi Temple C	.10	.20
171 Rebel War Room C	.10	.20
172 Mos Eisley Spaceport C	.10	.20
173 Separatist Base C	.10	.20
174 Starship Graveyard S	1.50	2.50

2016 Star Wars Force Attax The Force Awakens

COMPLETE SET (224 CARDS)
RELEASED IN 2016

1 Luke Skywalker .20 .35
2 Princess Leia .20 .35
3 Han Solo .20 .35
4 Chewbacca .20 .35
5 Obi Wan Kenobi .20 .35
6 Yoda .20 .35
7 Lando Calrissian .20 .35
8 Mon Mothma .20 .35
9 General Jan Dodonna .20 .35
10 General Rieekan .20 .35
11 Lobot .20 .35
12 Owen Lars .20 .35
13 Beru Lars .20 .35
14 Rebel Trooper .20 .35
15 Rebel Commando .20 .35
16 C 3PO .20 .35
17 R2 D2 .20 .35
18 2 1B Medical Droid .20 .35
19 K 3PO .20 .35
20 FX 7 Medical Droid .20 .35
21 Training Remote .20 .35
22 Admiral Ackbar .20 .35
23 Mon Calamari .20 .35
24 Crix Madine .20 .35
25 Orrimaarko .20 .35
26 Wicket .20 .35
27 Logray .20 .35
28 Paploo .20 .35
29 Teebo .20 .35
30 Tokkat .20 .35
31 Romba .20 .35
32 Ten Numb .20 .35
33 Tauntaun .20 .35
34 Darth Vader .20 .35
35 Emperor Palpatine .20 .35
36 Grand Moff Tarkin .20 .35
37 Moff Jerjerrod .20 .35
38 General Veers .20 .35
39 Captain Lennox .20 .35
40 Captain Khurgee .20 .35
41 Lieutenant Cabbel .20 .35
42 Lieutenant Sheckil .20 .35
43 Admiral Piett .20 .35
44 TIE Fighter Pilot .20 .35
45 Scout Trooper .20 .35
46 Stormtrooper .20 .35
47 Sandtrooper .20 .35
48 Snowtrooper .20 .35
49 Probot .20 .35
50 Interrogation Droid .20 .35
51 Death Star Droid .20 .35
52 Imperial Astromech Droid .20 .35
53 R2 Q5 .20 .35
54 Boba Fett .20 .35
55 Jabba The Hutt .20 .35
56 Bib Fortuna .20 .35
57 Salacious B Crumb .20 .35
58 Oola .20 .35
59 Yarna D Al Gargan .20 .35
60 Amanaman .20 .35
61 Bossk .20 .35
62 IG 88 .20 .35
63 Boushh .20 .35
64 Snaggletooth .20 .35
65 Gamorrean Guard .20 .35
66 Jawa .20 .35
67 Tusken Raider .20 .35
68 Muftak .20 .35
69 Umpass Stay .20 .35
70 Klaatu .20 .35
71 Harc Seff .20 .35
72 Brock Starsher .20 .35
73 EV 9D9 .20 .35
74 Millennium Falcon .20 .35
75 Tantive IV .20 .35
76 Y Wing Starfighter .20 .35
77 X Wing Starfighter .20 .35
78 A Wing Starfighter .20 .35
79 B Wing Starfighter .20 .35
80 Home One .20 .35
81 Nebulon B Frigate .20 .35
82 Rebel Transport .20 .35
83 Snowspeeder .20 .35
84 Landspeeder .20 .35
85 T 16 Skyhopper .20 .35
86 Death Star .20 .35
87 Death Star II .20 .35
88 Star Destroyer .20 .35
89 Super Star Destroyer .20 .35
90 TIE Fighter .20 .35
91 TIE Interceptor .20 .35
92 Darth Vader s TIE Advanced .20 .35
93 TIE Bomber .20 .35
94 Imperial Shuttle .20 .35
95 Speeder Bike .20 .35
96 AT ST Walker .20 .35
97 AT AT Walker .20 .35
98 Probe Droid Capsule .20 .35
99 Slave 1 .20 .35
100 Jabba s Sail Barge .20 .35
101 Desert Skiff .20 .35
102 Finn .20 .35
103 Rey .20 .35
104 Poe Dameron .20 .35
105 BB 8 .20 .35
106 Han Solo .20 .35
107 Chewbacca .20 .35
108 General Leia Organa .20 .35
109 C 3PO .20 .35
110 R2 D2 .20 .35
111 Lor San Tekka .20 .35
112 Kylo Ren .20 .35
113 General Hux .20 .35
114 Captain Phasma .20 .35
115 Stormtrooper .20 .35
116 Stormtrooper .20 .35
117 Snowtrooper .20 .35
118 TIE Fighter Pilot .20 .35
119 Rey s Speeder .20 .35
120 Millennium Falcon .20 .35
121 X Wing Starfighter .20 .35
122 Poe s X Wing Starfighter .20 .35
123 The Finalizer .20 .35
124 First Order Transporter .20 .35
125 Rebel Strikeforce 1 .20 .35
126 Rebel Strikeforce 2 .20 .35
127 Rebel Strikeforce 3 .20 .35
128 Rebel Strikeforce 4 .20 .35
129 Rebel Strikeforce 5 .20 .35
130 Rebel Strikeforce 6 .20 .35
131 Rebel Strikeforce 7 .20 .35
132 Rebel Strikeforce 8 .20 .35
133 Rebel Strikeforce 9 .20 .35
134 Empire Strikeforce 1 .20 .35
135 Empire Strikeforce 2 .20 .35
136 Empire Strikeforce 3 .20 .35
137 Empire Strikeforce 4 .20 .35
138 Empire Strikeforce 5 .20 .35
139 Empire Strikeforce 6 .20 .35
140 Empire Strikeforce 7 .20 .35
141 Empire Strikeforce 8 .20 .35
142 Empire Strikeforce 9 .20 .35
143 Rebel Strikeforce 1 .20 .35
144 Rebel Strikeforce 2 .20 .35
145 Rebel Strikeforce 3 .20 .35
146 Rebel Strikeforce 4 .20 .35
147 Rebel Strikeforce 5 .20 .35
148 Rebel Strikeforce 6 .20 .35
149 Rebel Strikeforce 7 .20 .35
150 Rebel Strikeforce 8 .20 .35
151 Rebel Strikeforce 9 .20 .35
152 First Order Strikeforce 1 .20 .35
153 First Order Strikeforce 2 .20 .35
154 First Order Strikeforce 3 .20 .35
155 First Order Strikeforce 4 .20 .35
156 First Order Strikeforce 5 .20 .35
157 First Order Strikeforce 6 .20 .35
158 First Order Strikeforce 7 .20 .35
159 First Order Strikeforce 8 .20 .35
160 First Order Strikeforce 9 .20 .35
161 Luke Skywalker .20 .35
162 Princess Leia .20 .35
163 Han Solo .20 .35
164 Chewbacca .20 .35
165 Obi Wan Kenobi .20 .35
166 Yoda .20 .35
167 Lando Calrissian .20 .35
168 C 3PO .20 .35
169 R2 D2 .20 .35
170 Admiral Ackbar .20 .35
171 Darth Vader .20 .35
172 Emperor Palpatine .20 .35
173 Stormtrooper .20 .35
174 AT AT Pilot .20 .35
175 AT ST Pilot .20 .35
176 Jabba The Hutt .20 .35
177 Boba Fett .20 .35
178 Dengar .20 .35
179 Millennium Falcon .20 .35
180 X Wing Starfighter .20 .35
181 TIE Interceptor .20 .35
182 Star Destroyer .20 .35
183 Finn .20 .35
184 Rey .20 .35
185 Poe Dameron .20 .35
186 BB 8 .20 .35
187 Chewbacca .20 .35
188 Kylo Ren .20 .35
189 Captain Phasma .20 .35
190 Stormtrooper .20 .35
191 TIE Fighter .20 .35
192 Millennium Falcon .20 .35
193 Luke Skywalker .20 .35
194 Princess Leia .20 .35
195 Han Solo .20 .35
196 Chewbacca .20 .35
197 Obi Wan Kenobi .20 .35
198 Yoda .20 .35
199 Lando Calrissian .20 .35
200 C 3PO .20 .35
201 R2 D2 .20 .35
202 Darth Vader .20 .35
203 Emperor Palpatine .20 .35
204 Boba Fett .20 .35
205 Finn .20 .35
206 Poe Dameron .20 .35
207 Kylo Ren .20 .35
208 Captain Phasma .20 .35
209 Finn .20 .35
210 Rey .20 .35
211 Poe Dameron .20 .35
212 BB 8 .20 .35
213 Han Solo .20 .35
214 Chewbacca .20 .35
215 C 3PO .20 .35
216 R2 D2 .20 .35
217 Kylo Ren .20 .35
218 General Hux .20 .35
219 Captain Phasma .20 .35
220 Stormtrooper .20 .35
221 Stormtrooper .20 .35
222 Snowtrooper .20 .35
223 Flametrooper .20 .35
224 Riot Control Stormtrooper .20 .35

2016 Star Wars Force Attax Extra The Force Awakens

COMPLETE SET (138 CARDS) 100.00 250.00
1 Finn .75 2.00
2 Rey .75 2.00
3 Poe Dameron .75 2.00
4 BB 8 .75 2.00
5 Han Solo .75 2.00
6 Chewbacca .75 2.00
7 General Organa .75 2.00
8 Admiral Ackbar .75 2.00
9 Admiral Statura .75 2.00
10 Major Ematt .75 2.00
11 Major Brance .75 2.00
12 Snap Wexley .75 2.00
13 Jess Testor Pava .75 2.00
14 Ello Asty .75 2.00
15 Nien Nunb .75 2.00
16 Korr Sella .75 2.00
17 Vober Dand .75 2.00
18 Pamich Nerro .75 2.00
19 Kaydel Ko .75 2.00
20 Goss Toowers .75 2.00
21 Bollie Prindel .75 2.00
22 Resistance Soldier .75 2.00
23 C 3PO .75 2.00
24 R2 D2 .75 2.00
25 4B EG 6 .75 2.00
26 PZ 4CO .75 2.00
27 M9 G8 .75 2.00
28 B U4D .75 2.00
29 GA 97 .75 2.00
30 Kylo Ren .75 2.00
31 General Hux .75 2.00
32 Captain Phasma .75 2.00
33 Lieutenant Mitaka .75 2.00
34 Colonel Datoo .75 2.00
35 Chief Petty Officer Unamo .75 2.00
36 Petty Officer Thanisson .75 2.00
37 Fleet Engineer .75 2.00
38 Lieutenant Rodinon .75 2.00
39 Technician Mandetat .75 2.00
40 Stormtrooper .75 2.00
41 Flametrooper .75 2.00
42 Snowtrooper .75 2.00
43 Riot Control Stormtrooper .75 2.00
44 TIE Fighter Pilot .75 2.00
45 Millennium Falcon .75 2.00
46 The Erevana .75 2.00
47 Resistance Transport .75 2.00
48 X Wing Starfighter .75 2.00
49 Poe Dameron s X Wing .75 2.00
50 Rey s Speeder .75 2.00
51 The Finalizer .75 2.00
52 Kylo Ren s Command Shuttle .75 2.00
53 TIE Fighter .75 2.00
54 Special Forces TIE Fighter .75 2.00
55 Unkar Plutt .75 2.00
56 Unkar s Thug .75 2.00
57 Unkar s Thug .75 2.00
58 Teedo .75 2.00
59 Athgar Heece .75 2.00
60 Bobbajo .75 2.00
61 Crusher Roodown .75 2.00
62 Sarco Plank .75 2.00
63 Constable Zuvio .75 2.00
64 Bala Tik .75 2.00
65 Guavian Security Soldier .75 2.00
66 Guavian Security Soldier .75 2.00
67 Tasu Leech .75 2.00
68 Volzang Li Thrull .75 2.00
69 Crokind Shand .75 2.00
70 Razoo Qin Fee .75 2.00
71 Maz Kanata .75 2.00
72 Captain Ithano .75 2.00
73 Grummgar .75 2.00
74 Bazine Netal .75 2.00
75 Strono Cookie Tuggs .75 2.00
76 Wollivan .75 2.00
77 Quiggold .75 2.00
78 Pru Sweevant .75 2.00
79 Prashee and Cratinus .75 2.00
80 Hassk Triplets .75 2.00
81 Jashco Phurus .75 2.00
82 Gwellis Bagnoro .75 2.00
83 Praster Ommlen .75 2.00
84 Happabore .75 2.00
85 Luggabeast .75 2.00
86 Rathtar .75 2.00
87 FN 2187 and Poe Dameron .75 2.00
88 Rey and Finn .75 2.00
89 Han and Chewbacca .75 2.00
90 Han and Leia .75 2.00
91 R2 D2 and C 3PO .75 2.00
92 BB 8 and R2 D2 .75 2.00
93 Rey Finn and BB 8 .75 2.00
94 Han Chewbacca Rey and Finn .75 2.00
95 Kylo Ren and Captain Phasma .75 2.00
96 Grummgar and Bazine .75 2.00
97 Finn .75 2.00
98 Rey .75 2.00
99 Poe Dameron .75 2.00
100 Han Solo .75 2.00
101 Chewbacca .75 2.00
102 BB 8 .75 2.00
103 C 3PO .75 2.00
104 Kylo Ren .75 2.00
105 General Hux .75 2.00
106 Captain Phasma .75 2.00
107 Riot Control Stormtrooper .75 2.00
108 Stormtrooper .75 2.00
109 Maz Kanata .75 2.00
110 Captain Ithano .75 2.00
111 Tasu Leech .75 2.00
112 Bala Tik .75 2.00
113 Starkiller Base .75 2.00
114 The Finalizer .75 2.00
115 Kylo Ren s Command Shuttle .75 2.00
116 TIE Fighter .75 2.00
117 Millennium Falcon .75 2.00
118 The Erevana .75 2.00
119 X Wing Starfighter .75 2.00
120 Poe Dameron s X Wing .75 2.00
121 Finn .75 2.00
122 Rey .75 2.00
123 Poe Dameron .75 2.00
124 Han Solo .75 2.00
125 Luke Skywalker .75 2.00
126 Kylo Ren .75 2.00
127 Captain Phasma .75 2.00
128 Stormtrooper .75 2.00
129 Finn .75 2.00
130 Rey .75 2.00
131 Poe Dameron .75 2.00
132 Han Solo .75 2.00
133 Chewbacca .75 2.00
134 BB 8 .75 2.00
135 Kylo Ren .75 2.00
136 Captain Phasma .75 2.00
137 Maz Kanata .75 2.00
138 Unkar Plutt .75 2.00

2017 Star Wars Destiny Spirit of Rebellion

COMPLETE SET (160 CARDS) 400.00 550.00
BOOSTER BOX (36 PACKS) 100.00 130.00
BOOSTER PACK (5 CARDS AND 1 DICE) 4.00 6.00
UNLISTED C .10 .20
UNLISTED U .25 .40
UNLISTED R 3.00 5.00
RELEASED ON APRIL 28TH, 2017

1 Death Trooper R 4.00 6.00
2 FN 2199 R 2.50 4.00
3 Director Krennic L 8.00 12.00
4 TIE Pilot R 2.50 4.00
5 E Web Emplacement R 7.00 10.00
6 Imperial Discipline R 2.50 4.00
7 DT 29 Heavy Blaster Pistol R 2.50 4.00
8 Z6 Riot Control Baton L 20.00 25.00
9 Asajj Ventress R 2.50 4.00
10 Darth Vader R 2.50 4.00
11 Palpatine L 20.00 25.00
12 Royal Guard R 2.50 4.00
13 Commando Shuttle R 2.50 4.00
14 Force Lightning L 15.00 20.00
15 Lightsaber Pike R 7.00 10.00
16 Lure of Power R 2.50 4.00
17 Interrogation Droid R 2.50 4.00
18 Aurra Sing R 2.50 4.00
19 Guavian Enforcer R 2.50 4.00
20 IG 88 L 8.00 12.00
21 Unkar Plutt R 2.50 4.00
22 Slave I L 8.00 12.00
23 Blackmail L 8.00 12.00
24 Personal Shield R 2.50 4.00
25 Vibroknucklers R 2.50 4.00
26 Baze Malbus L 8.00 12.00

27 Mon Mothma R 2.50 4.00
28 Rebel Commando R 2.50 4.00
29 Temmin "Snap" Wexley R 2.50 4.00
30 C 3PO R 2.50 4.00
31 U Wing L 8.00 12.00
32 A180 Blaster R 2.50 4.00
33 Overkill R 2.50 4.00
34 Jedi Acolyte R 2.50 4.00
35 Chirrut Œmwe R 2.50 4.00
36 Luminara Unduli R 2.50 4.00
37 Obi Wan Kenobi L 8.00 12.00
38 Delta 7 Interceptor R 2.50 4.00
39 Handcrafted Light Bow L 8.00 12.00
40 Force Heal R 2.50 4.00
41 Journals of Ben Kenobi R 2.50 4.00
42 R2 D2 R 2.50 4.00
43 Chewbacca L 8.00 12.00
44 Jyn Erso R 2.50 4.00
45 Maz Kanata R 2.50 4.00
46 Outer Rim Smuggler R 2.50 4.00
47 Smuggling Freighter R 2.50 4.00
48 Bowcaster L 8.00 12.00
49 Lone Operative R 2.50 4.00
50 Mazs Goggles L 8.00 12.00
51 Supply Line R 2.50 4.00
52 Astromech R 2.50 4.00
53 Rocket Launcher L 30.00 35.00
54 Force Push R 2.50 4.00
55 Force Speed L 50.00 65.00
56 Makashi Training R 2.50 4.00
57 Vibroknife R 15.00 20.00
58 Quadjumper L 8.00 12.00
59 Ascension Gun R 7.00 10.00
60 Con Artist R 2.50 4.00
61 Battle Formation C .10 .20
62 Imperial War Machine U .25 .40
63 Lockdown C .10 .20
64 Sustained Fire U .25 .40
65 Traitor U .25 .40
66 Trench Warfare C .10 .20
67 Undying Loyalty C .10 .20
68 We Have Them Now U .40 .60
69 Attrition C .10 .20
70 Imperial Inspection U .40 .60
71 Anger U .75 1.25
72 Lightsaber Throw U .60 1.00
73 Manipulate C .10 .20
74 No Disintegrations C .10 .20
75 Now You Will Die C .10 .20
76 Rise Again U 1.00 1.50
77 The Price of Failure C .10 .20
78 Dark Presence U 1.00 1.50
79 Now I Am The Master C .10 .20
80 Doubt C .10 .20
81 Arms Deal C .10 .20
82 Bait and Switch C .10 .20
83 Friends in High Places U .25 .40
84 Loose Ends U .25 .40
85 One Quarter Portion C .10 .20
86 Relentless Pursuit C .10 .20
87 Scrap Buy U .25 .40
88 Salvage Stand C .10 .20
89 Armor Plating U .60 1.00
90 Emergency Evacuation U .25 .40
91 Friendly Fire U .25 .40
92 Guerrilla Warfare C .10 .20
93 Our Only Hope U .25 .40
94 Rebel Assault C .10 .20
95 Sensor Placement U .25 .40
96 Spirit of Rebellion C .10 .20
97 Planetary Uprising U .60 1.00
98 Spy Net C .10 .20
99 Tactical Aptitude C .10 .20
100 Caution U .75 1.25
101 Destiny C .10 .20
102 Determination C .10 .20
103 Guard U .25 .40
104 Krayt Dragon Howl C .10 .20
105 My Ally Is The Force U .60 1.00
106 Synchronicity C .10 .20
107 Your Eyes Can Decive You U .25 .40
108 Protective Mentor C .10 .20
109 Confidence C .10 .20
110 Garbagell Do C .10 .20
111 Hold On C .10 .20
112 Rebel U .25 .40
113 Long Con C .10 .20
114 Loth Cat and Mouse C .10 .20
115 Never Tell Me the Odds U .25 .40
116 Planned Explosion U .25 .40
117 Double Dealing C .10 .20
118 Life Debt U .25 .40
119 Bombing Run U .25 .40
120 Collateral Damage C .10 .20
121 Salvo U .40 .60
122 Suppression C .10 .20
123 Aftermath C .10 .20
124 Air Superiority C .10 .20
125 Training U 2.00 2.50
126 Wingman C .10 .20
127 Decisive Blow C .10 .20
128 High Ground C .10 .20
129 Momentum Shift U .25 .40
130 Overconfidence C .10 .20
131 Premonitions U .25 .40
132 Rejuvenate C .10 .20
133 Trust Your Instincts U 1.25 2.00
134 Meditate C .10 .20
135 Force Illusion U 2.00 3.00
136 Evade C .10 .20
137 New Orders U .60 1.00
138 Parry C .10 .20
139 Swiftness C .10 .20
140 Resolve U .25 .40
141 Ammo Belt C .10 .20
142 Bolt Hole C .10 .20
143 Cheat U .75 1.25
144 Diversion C .10 .20
145 Fair Trade U .25 .40
146 Friends in Low Places C .10 .20
147 Sabotage U .25 .40
148 Improvisation C .10 .20
149 Outmaneuver C .10 .20
150 Fast Hands U 5.00 7.00
151 Carbon Freezing Chamber U .25 .40
152 Cargo Hold C .10 .20
153 Docking Bay C .10 .20
154 Ewok Village C .10 .20
155 Mazs Castle U .25 .40
156 Moisture Farm U .25 .40
157 Otoh Gunga C .10 .20
158 Secluded Beach C .10 .20
159 Secret Facility U .25 .40
160 War Torn Streets C .10 .20

2017 Star Wars Destiny Empire at War

COMPLETE SET (160 CARDS) 300.00 550.00
BOOSTER BOX (36 PACKS) 85.00 120.00
BOOSTER PACK (5 CARDS) 3.00 5.00
UNLISTED C .10 .20
UNLISTED U .40 .60
UNLISTED R 2.00 5.00
RELEASED IN FALL 2017

1 †Ciena Ree† Adept Pilot R 2.00 5.00
2 †General Hux† Aspiring Commander R2.00 5.00
3 †MagnaGuard R 2.00 5.00
4 †Thrawn†Master Strategist L 15.00 20.00
5 †AT DP R 2.00 5.00
6 †Probe Droid R 2.00 5.00
7 †T 7 Ion Disruptor Rifle L 8.00 15.00
8 †Quinlan Vos† Dark Disciple R 2.00 5.00
9 †Servant of the Dark Side R 2.00 5.00
10 †Seventh Sister† Agile Inquisitor L8.00 15.00
11 †Grand Inquisitor† Sith Loyalist L 8.00 15.00
12 †Darth Vaders TIE Advanced R 2.00 5.00
13 †ID9 Seeker Droid R 2.00 5.00
14 †Temptation R 2.00 5.00
15 †Grand Inquisitors Lightsaber L 8.00 15.00
16 †Bazine Netal† Master Manipulator R2.00 5.00
17 †Bossk† Wookiee Slayer R 2.00 5.00
18 †Cad Bane† Vicious Mercenary L15.00 20.00
19 †Gamorrean Guard R 2.00 5.00
20 †Hounds Tooth L 8.00 15.00
21 †Cable Launcher R 2.00 5.00
22 †LL 30 Blaster Pistol R 2.00 5.00
23 †Relby V10 Mortar Gun R 2.00 5.00
24 †General Rieekan† Defensive Mastermind R 2.00 5.00
25 †Hera Syndulla† Phoenix Leader R2.00 5.00
26 †K 2SO† Reprogrammed Droid L 8.00 15.00
27 †Rookie Pilot R 2.00 5.00
28 †Ghost L 8.00 15.00
29 †Y Wing R 2.00 5.00
30 †A280 Blaster Rifle R 2.00 5.00
31 †Ahsoka Tano† Force Operative L20.00 25.00
32 †Jedi Instructor R 2.00 5.00
33 †Kanan Jarrus† Rebel Jedi R 2.00 5.00
34 †Mace Windu† Jedi Champion L 8.00 15.00
35 †Training Remote R 2.00 5.00
36 †Master of the Council L 8.00 15.00
37 †Coordination R 2.00 5.00
38 †Ezra Bridger† Force sensitive Thief R2.00 5.00
39 †Lando Calrissian† Galactic Entrepreneur R 2.00 5.00
40 †Sabine Wren† Explosives Expert L8.00 15.00
41 †Wookiee Warrior R 2.00 5.00
42 †Chopper L 8.00 15.00
43 †Energy Slingshot R 2.00 5.00
44 †Tough Haggler R 2.00 5.00
45 †T 47 Airspeeder R 2.00 5.00
46 †LR1K Sonic Cannon L 8.00 15.00
47 †Electrostaff R 2.00 5.00
48 †Natural Pilot R 2.00 5.00
49 †Ancient Lightsaber L 35.00 45.00
50 †Psychometry R 2.00 5.00
51 †Shoto Lightsaber R 2.00 5.00
52 †Weapons Cache R 2.00 5.00
53 †BD 1 Cutter Vibro AX R 2.00 5.00
54 †Extortion R 2.00 5.00
55 †X 8 Night Sniper L 8.00 15.00
56 †Z 95 Headhunter R 2.00 5.00
57 †Chance Cube R 2.00 5.00
58 †EMP Grenades R 2.00 5.00
59 †Lead by Example R 2.00 5.00
60 †Scatterblaster R 2.00 5.00
61 †Commandeer U .40 .60
62 †Crossfire C .10 .20
63 †Drop Your Weapon! U .40 .60
64 †Imperial Backing U .40 .60
65 †Prepare for War C .10 .20
66 †Red Alert C .10 .20
67 †Ruthless Tactics C .10 .20
68 †Take Prisoner U .40 .60
69 †Imperial HQ C .10 .20
70 †As You Command C .10 .20
71 †Cornered Prey C .10 .20
72 †Indomitable C .10 .20
73 †It Will All Be Mine U .40 .60
74 †Kill Them All C .10 .20
75 †Unyielding U .40 .60
76 †Insidious C .10 .20
77 †Hate U .40 .60
78 †Anarchy U .40 .60
79 †Bounty Postings C .10 .20
80 †Buy Out U .40 .60
81 †Coercion U .40 .60
82 †Only Business Matters C .10 .20
83 †Pilfered Goods U .40 .60
84 †Twin Shadows U .40 .60
85 †Hutt Ties C .10 .20
86 †Deadly U .40 .60
87 †No Survivors C .10 .20
88 †Detention Center U .40 .60
89 †All Quiet On The Front U .40 .60
90 †Entrenched U .40 .60
91 †Fortuitous Strike C .10 .20
92 †Rearguard C .10 .20
93 †Reckless Reentry U .40 .60
94 †Strike Briefing C .10 .20
95 †Swift Strike C .10 .20
96 †Rally Aid U .40 .60
97 †Shield Generator C .10 .20
98 †At Peace C .10 .20
99 †Bestow C .10 .20
100 †Bring Balance U .40 .60
101 †Reaping The Crystal U .40 .60
102 †Secret Mission C .10 .20
103 †Trust The Force C .10 .20
104 †Funeral Pyre C .10 .20
105 †Yodas Quarters U .40 .60
106 †Fearless U .40 .60
107 †Against The Odds C .10 .20
108 †Appraise C .10 .20
109 †Bad Feeling C .10 .20
110 †Double Cross U .40 .60
111 †Impersonate U .40 .60
112 †Local Patrol C .10 .20
113 †Quick Escape U .40 .60
114 †Tenacity C .10 .20
115 †Running Interference U .40 .60
116 †Thermal Paint C .10 .20
117 †Defiance C .10 .20
118 †Covering Fire C .10 .20
119 †Deploy Squadron C .10 .20
120 †Fall Back U .40 .60
121 †Feint U .40 .60
122 †Flanking Maneuver U .40 .60
123 †Heat Of Battle C .10 .20
124 †Pinned Down C .10 .20
125 †The Day is Ours C .10 .20
126 †Drop Zone U .40 .60
127 †Tech Team C .10 .20
128 †Battle of Wills U .40 .60
129 †Force Vision C .10 .20
130 †Lightsaber Pull C .10 .20
131 †Lightsaber Training C .10 .20
132 †No Surrender C .10 .20
133 †Something familiar U .40 .60
134 †Voices Cry Out C .10 .20
135 †Keen Instincts U .40 .60
136 †Battle Rage C .10 .20
137 †Disable C .10 .20
138 †Persuade C .10 .20
139 †Pickpocket C .10 .20
140 †Threaten U .40 .60
141 †Trickery U .40 .60
142 †Truce C .10 .20
143 †Stolen Cache C .10 .20
144 †Hidden Agenda U .40 .60
145 †Mandalorian Armor C .10 .20
146 †Dangerous Mission C .10 .20
147 †Endurance U .40 .60
148 †Partnership C .10 .20
149 †Recycle C .10 .20
150 †Rend C .10 .20
151 †Roll On C .10 .20
152 †Plastoid Armor C .10 .20
153 †BOmarr Monastery† Teth C .10 .20
154 †Fort Anaxes† Anaxes U .40 .60
155 †Garel Spaceport† Garel U .40 .60
156 †Imperial Academy† Lothal U .40 .60
157 †Main Plaza† Vashka C .10 .20
158 †Medical Center† Kaliida Shoals U.40 .60
159 †Port District† Bespin U .40 .60
160 †Weapons Factory Alpha† Cymoon 1 U .40 .60

2017 Star Wars Force Attax Universe

COMPLETE SET (272 CARDS) 70.00 110.00
BOOSTER BOX (36 PACKS) 50.00 80.00
BOOSTER PACK (5 CARDS) 2.00 3.50
RELEASED IN FEBRUARY, 2017

1 Anakin Skywalker .25 .40
2 Boss Nass .25 .40
3 C 3PO .25 .40
4 Captain Panaka .25 .40
5 Jar Jar Binks .25 .40
6 Naboo Pilot .25 .40
7 Obi Wan Kenobi .25 .40
8 Padme Amidala .25 .40
9 Qui Gon Jinn .25 .40
10 R2 D2 .25 .40
11 Senator Palpatine .25 .40
12 Shmi Skywalker .25 .40
13 Sio Bibble .25 .40
14 Battle Droid .25 .40
15 Darth Maul .25 .40
16 Darth Sidious .25 .40
17 Destroyer Droid .25 .40
18 Nute Gunray .25 .40
19 Sebulba .25 .40
20 Watto .25 .40
21 Droid Control Ship .25 .40
22 N 1 Starfighter .25 .40
23 Naboo Royal Starship .25 .40
24 Sith Infiltrator .25 .40
25 Anakin Skywalker .25 .40
26 C 3PO .25 .40
27 Captain Typho .25 .40
28 Chancellor Palpatine .25 .40
29 Clone Trooper .25 .40
30 Dexter Jettster .25 .40
31 Ki Adi Mundi .25 .40
32 Lama Su .25 .40
33 Mace Windu .25 .40
34 Obi Wan Kenobi .25 .40
35 Padme Amidala .25 .40
36 R2 D2 .25 .40
37 Yoda .25 .40
38 Count Dooku .25 .40
39 Geonosian Warrior .25 .40
40 Jango Fett .25 .40
41 Poggle The Lesser .25 .40
42 Shu Mai .25 .40
43 Super Battle Droid .25 .40
44 Wat Tambor .25 .40
45 Zam Wesell .25 .40
46 Jedi Starfighter .25 .40
47 Republic Gunship .25 .40
48 Slave 1 .25 .40
49 Aayla Secura .25 .40
50 Anakin Skywalker .25 .40
51 Bail Organa .25 .40
52 C 3PO .25 .40
53 Clone Trooper .25 .40
54 Commander Cody .25 .40
55 Kit Fisto .25 .40
56 Mace Windu .25 .40
57 Obi Wan Kenobi .25 .40
58 Padme Amidala .25 .40
59 Plo Koon .25 .40
60 R2 D2 .25 .40
61 Yoda .25 .40
62 Count Dooku .25 .40
63 Darth Sidious .25 .40
64 General Grievous .25 .40
65 San Hill .25 .40
66 Magnaguard .25 .40
67 Muckraker Crab Droid .25 .40
68 ARC 170 Starfighter .25 .40
69 The Invisible Hand .25 .40
70 Jedi Attack Cruiser .25 .40
71 Jedi Starfighter .25 .40
72 Soulless One Belbullab 22 Starfighter .25 .40
73 Admiral Raddus .25 .40
74 Baze Malbus .25 .40
75 Bistan .25 .40
76 Bodhi Rook .25 .40
77 Cassian Andor .25 .40
78 Chirrut Imwe .25 .40
79 Edrio Two Tubes .25 .40
80 General Draven .25 .40
81 Jyn Erso .25 .40
82 K 2SO .25 .40
83 Mon Mothma .25 .40
84 Moroff .25 .40
85 Pao .25 .40
86 Saw Gerrera .25 .40
87 Darth Vader .25 .40
88 Death Trooper .25 .40
89 Director Krennic .25 .40
90 Galen Erso .25 .40
91 Shoretrooper .25 .40
92 Stormtrooper .25 .40
93 AT ACT .25 .40
94 Death Star .25 .40
95 Rebel U Wing Fighter .25 .40
96 TIE Striker .25 .40
97 Beru Lars .25 .40
98 C 3PO .25 .40
99 Chewbacca .25 .40
100 General Dodonna .25 .40
101 Han Solo .25 .40
102 Jawa .25 .40
103 Luke Skywalker .25 .40
104 Obi Wan Kenobi .25 .40
105 Owen Lars .25 .40
106 Princess Leia .25 .40
107 R2 D2 .25 .40
108 Darth Vader .25 .40
109 Grand Moff Tarkin .25 .40
110 Imperial Gunner .25 .40
111 Sandtrooper .25 .40

112 Stormtrooper .25 .40
113 TIE Fighter Pilot .25 .40
114 Tusken Raider .25 .40
115 Death Star .25 .40
116 Millennium Falcon .25 .40
117 Tantive IV .25 .40
118 TIE Fighter .25 .40
119 X Wing Starfighter .25 .40
120 Y Wing Starfighter .25 .40
121 C 3PO .25 .40
122 Chewbacca .25 .40
123 General Rieekan .25 .40
124 Lando Calrissian .25 .40
125 Leia Organa .25 .40
126 Lobot .25 .40
127 Luke Skywalker .25 .40
128 R2 D2 .25 .40
129 Rebel Trooper .25 .40
130 Yoda .25 .40
131 Admiral Ozzel .25 .40
132 Admiral Piett .25 .40
133 Boba Fett .25 .40
134 Bossk .25 .40
135 Darth Vader .25 .40
136 General Veers .25 .40
137 IG 88 .25 .40
138 Snowtrooper .25 .40
139 AT AT .25 .40
140 The Executor .25 .40
141 Medical Frigate .25 .40
142 Slave 1 .25 .40
143 Snowspeeder .25 .40
144 Star Destroyer .25 .40
145 Admiral Ackbar .25 .40
146 C 3PO .25 .40
147 Chewbacca .25 .40
148 Han Solo .25 .40
149 Lando Calrissian .25 .40
150 Leia Organa .25 .40
151 Luke Skywalker .25 .40
152 Mon Mothma .25 .40
153 Nien Nunb .25 .40
154 R2 D2 .25 .40
155 Wicket .25 .40
156 Bib Fortuna .25 .40
157 Boba Fett .25 .40
158 Darth Vader .25 .40
159 Emperor Palpatine .25 .40
160 Gamorrean Guard .25 .40
161 Jabba The Hutt .25 .40
162 Scout Trooper .25 .40
163 AT ST .25 .40
164 A Wing Starfighter .25 .40
165 Death Star II .25 .40
166 Millennium Falcon .25 .40
167 Speeder Bike .25 .40
168 TIE Interceptor .25 .40
169 Admiral Statura .25 .40
170 BB 8 .25 .40
171 C 3PO .25 .40
172 Chewbacca .25 .40
173 Finn .25 .40
174 General Leia Organa .25 .40
175 Han Solo .25 .40
176 Lor San Tekka .25 .40
177 Luke Skywalker .25 .40
178 Maz Kanata .25 .40
179 Poe Dameron .25 .40
180 R2 D2 .25 .40
181 Rey .25 .40
182 Captain Phasma .25 .40
183 Flametrooper .25 .40
184 General Hux .25 .40
185 Kylo Ren .25 .40
186 Stormtrooper .25 .40
187 Tasu Leech .25 .40
188 Unkar Plutt .25 .40
189 The Finalizer .25 .40
190 Millennium Falcon .25 .40
191 Poe Dameron s X Wiing .25 .40
192 Starkiller Base .25 .40
193 Star Wars The Phantom Menace .25 .40
194 Star Wars Attack of The Clones .25 .40
195 Star Wars Revenge of The Sith .25 .40
196 Star Wars Rogue One .25 .40
197 Star Wars A New Hope .25 .40
198 Star Wars The Empire Strikes Back.25 .40
199 Star Wars Return of The Jedi .25 .40
200 Star Wars The Force Awakens .25 .40
201 Star Wars The Phantom Menace .25 .40
202 Star Wars The Phantom Menace .25 .40
203 Star Wars The Phantom Menace .25 .40
204 Star Wars Attack of The Clones .25 .40
205 Star Wars Attack of The Clones .25 .40
206 Star Wars Attack of The Clones .25 .40
207 Star Wars Revenge of The Sith .25 .40
208 Star Wars Revenge of The Sith .25 .40
209 Star Wars Revenge of The Sith .25 .40
210 Star Wars Rogue One .25 .40
211 Star Wars Rogue One .25 .40
212 Star Wars Rogue One .25 .40
213 Star Wars A New Hope .25 .40
214 Star Wars A New Hope .25 .40
215 Star Wars A New Hope .25 .40
216 Star Wars The Empire Strikes Back.25 .40
217 Star Wars The Empire Strikes Back.25 .40
218 Star Wars The Empire Strikes Back.25 .40
219 Star Wars Return of The Jedi .25 .40
220 Star Wars Return of The Jedi .25 .40
221 Star Wars Return of The Jedi .25 .40
222 Star Wars The Force Awakens .25 .40
223 Star Wars The Force Awakens .25 .40
224 Star Wars The Force Awakens .25 .40
225 Aurra Sing .25 .40
226 Jar Jar Binks .25 .40
227 Yaddle .25 .40
228 Podracer .25 .40
229 Boba Fett .25 .40
230 Jocasta Nu .25 .40
231 Mas Amedda .25 .40
232 Geonosian Starfighter .25 .40
233 Commander Bly .25 .40
234 Darth Vader .25 .40
235 Tarful .25 .40
236 Droid Tri Fighter .25 .40
237 Death Trooper .25 .40
238 K 2SO .25 .40
239 Saw Gerrera .25 .40
240 Death Star .25 .40
241 Barquin D an .25 .40
242 Captain Khurgee .25 .40
243 R5 D4 .25 .40
244 TIE Advanced .25 .40
245 Dengar .25 .40
246 Ugnaught .25 .40
247 TIE Bomber .25 .40
248 X Wing .25 .40
249 General Madine .25 .40
250 Max Rebo .25 .40
251 Royal Guard .25 .40
252 Imperial Shuttle .25 .40
253 Bala Tik .25 .40
254 Riot Control Stormtrooper .25 .40
255 Sidon Ithano .25 .40
256 Kylo Ren s Command Shuttle .25 .40
257 Qui Gon Jinn .25 .40
258 Darth Maul .25 .40
259 Yoda .25 .40
260 Count Dooku .25 .40
261 Anakin Skywalker .25 .40
262 Obi Wan Kenobi .25 .40
263 Jyn Erso .25 .40
264 Director Krennic .25 .40
265 Princess Leia .25 .40
266 Han Solo .25 .40
267 Darth Vader .25 .40
268 Boba Fett .25 .40
269 Luke Skywalker .25 .40
270 Emperor Palpatine .25 .40
271 Rey .25 .40
272 Kylo Ren .25 .40

MINIATURES

2004 Star Wars Rebel Storm Miniatures

COMPLETE SET (60) 120.00 250.00
RELEASED ON SEPTEMBER 3, 2004

1 4-LOM R 5.00 10.00
2 Bespin Guard C .30 .75
3 Boba Fett VR 15.00 40.00
4 Bossk R 5.00 10.00
5 Bothan Spy U .60 1.50
6 C-3PO R 5.00 10.00
7 Chewbacca R 6.00 12.00
8 Commando on Speeder Bike VR 15.00 25.00
9 Darth Vader, Dark Jedi R 6.00 12.00
10 Darth Vader, Sith Lord VR 12.50 25.00
11 Dengar R 5.00 10.00
12 Duros Mercenary U .60 1.50
13 Elite Hoth Trooper U .60 1.50
14 Elite Rebel Trooper C .30 .75
15 Elite Snowtrooper U .60 1.50
16 Elite Stormtrooper U .60 1.50
17 Emperor Palpatine VR 15.00 30.00
18 Ewok C .30 .75
19 Gamorrean Guard U .60 1.50
20 General Veers R 5.00 10.00
21 Grand Moff Tarkin R 5.00 10.00
22 Greedo R 5.00 10.00
23 Han Solo R 5.00 10.00
24 Heavy Stormtrooper U .60 1.50
25 Hoth Trooper C .30 .75
26 IG-88 R 5.00 10.00
27 Imperial Officer U .60 1.50
28 Ithorian Scout U .60 1.50
29 Jabba the Hutt VR 12.50 25.00
30 Jawa C .30 .75
31 Lando Calrissian R 5.00 10.00
32 Luke Skywalker, Jedi Knight VR 18.00 30.00
33 Luke Skywalker, Rebel R 6.00 12.00
34 Mara Jade Emperor's Hand R 5.00 10.00
35 Mon Calamari Mercenary C .30 .75
36 Obi-Wan Kenobi VR 12.50 25.00
37 Princess Leia, Captive VR 12.50 25.00
38 Princess Leia, Senator R 6.00 12.00
39 Probe Droid VR 10.00 20.00
40 Quarren Assassin U .60 1.50
41 R2-D2 R 6.00 12.00
42 Rebel Commando U .60 1.50
43 Rebel Officer U .60 1.50
44 Rebel Pilot C .30 .75
45 Rebel Trooper C .30 .75
46 Rebel Trooper C .30 .75
47 Royal Guard U .60 1.50
48 Sandtrooper on Dewback VR 10.00 20.00
49 Scout Trooper on Bike VR 10.00 20.00
50 Scout Trooper U .60 1.50
51 Snowtrooper C .30 .75
52 Stormtrooper C .30 .75
53 Stormtrooper C .30 .75
54 Stormtrooper C .30 .75
55 Stormtrooper Officer U .60 1.50
56 Tusken Raider C .30 .75
57 Twi'lek Bodyguard U .60 1.50
58 Twi'lek Scoundrel C .30 .75
59 Wampa VR 10.00 20.00
60 Wookiee Soldier C .30 .75

2004 Star Wars Clone Strike Miniatures

COMPLETE SET (60) 150.00 300.00
RELEASED ON DECEMBER 13, 2004

1 48 Super Battle Droid U .60 1.50
2 Aayla Secura VR 12.00 20.00
3 Aerial Clone Trooper Captain R 6.00 12.00
4 Agen Kolar R 6.00 12.00
5 Anakin Skywalker VR 15.00 25.00
6 Aqualish Spy C .30 .75
7 ARC Trooper U .60 1.50
8 Asajj Ventress R 6.00 12.00
9 Aurra Sing VR 20.00 35.00
10 Battle Droid C .30 .75
11 Battle Droid C .30 .75
12 Battle Droid C .30 .75
13 Battle Droid Officer U .60 1.50
14 Battle Droid on STAP R 6.00 12.00
15 Captain Typho R 6.00 12.00
16 Clone Trooper C .30 .75
17 Clone Trooper C .30 .75
18 Clone Trooper Commander U .60 1.50
19 Clone Trooper Grenadier C .30 .75
20 Clone Trooper Sergeant C .30 .75
21 Count Dooku VR 15.00 25.00
22 Dark Side Acolyte U .60 1.50
23 Darth Maul VR 18.00 30.00
24 Darth Sidious VR 15.00 25.00
25 Destroyer Droid R 6.00 12.00
26 Devaronian Bounty Hunter C .30 .75
27 Durge R 6.00 12.00
28 Dwarf Spider Droid R 6.00 12.00
29 General Grievous VR 18.00 30.00
30 General Kenobi R 6.00 12.00
31 Geonosian Drone C .30 .75
32 Geonosian Overseer U .60 1.50
33 Geonosian Picador on Orray R 6.00 12.00
34 Geonosian Soldier U .60 1.50
35 Gran Raider C .30 .75
36 Gungan Cavalry on Kaadu R 6.00 12.00
37 Gungan Infantry C .30 .75
38 Ishi Tib Scout U .60 1.50
39 Jango Fett R 6.00 12.00
40 Jedi Guardian U .60 1.50
41 Ki-Adi-Mundi R 6.00 12.00
42 Kit Fisto R 6.00 12.00
43 Klatooinian Enforcer C .30 .75
44 Luminara Unduli R 6.00 12.00
45 Mace Windu VR 15.00 25.00
46 Naboo Soldier U .60 1.50
47 Nikto Soldier C .30 .75
48 Padme Amidala VR 12.00 20.00
49 Plo Koon R 6.00 12.00
50 Quarren Raider U .60 1.50
51 Qui-Gon Jinn VR 12.00 20.00
52 Quinlan Vos VR 12.00 20.00
53 Rodian Mercenary U .60 1.50
54 Saesee Tiin R 6.00 12.00
55 Security Battle Droid C .30 .75
56 Super Battle Droid U .60 1.50
57 Weequay Mercenary C .30 .75
58 Wookiee Commando U .60 1.50
59 Yoda VR 18.00 30.00
60 Zam Wesell R 6.00 12.00

2005 Star Wars Revenge of the Sith Miniatures

COMPLETE SET (61) 120.00 250.00
RELEASED ON APRIL 2, 2005

1 49 Nautolan Soldier C .30 .75
2 Agen Kolar, Jedi Master R 6.00 12.00
3 Alderaan Trooper U .75 1.50
4 Anakin Skywalker, Jedi Knight R 6.00 12.00
5 Anakin Skywalker Sith Apprentice VR15.00 25.00
6 AT-RT VR 15.00 25.00
7 Bail Organa VR 10.00 20.00
8 Battle Droid C .30 .75
9 Battle Droid C .30 .75
10 Boba Fett, Young Mercenary R 6.00 12.00
11 Bodyguard Droid U .75 1.50
12 Bodyguard Droid U .75 1.50
13 Captain Antilles R 6.00 12.00
14 Chagrian Mercenary Commander U .75 1.50
15 Chewbacca of Kashyyk VR 15.00 25.00
16 Clone Trooper C .30 .75
17 Clone Trooper C .30 .75
18 Clone Trooper Commander U .75 1.50
19 Clone Trooper Gunner C .30 .75
20 Dark Side Adept U .75 1.50
21 Darth Tyranus R 6.00 12.00
22 Darth Vader VR 18.00 30.00
23 Destroyer Droid R 6.00 12.00
24 Devaronian Soldier C .30 .75
25 Emperor Palpatine, Sith Lord VR 18.00 30.00
26 General Grievous, Jedi Hunter VR18.00 30.00
27 General Grievous, Supreme Commander R 6.00 12.00
28 Gotal Fringer U .75 1.50
29 Grievous Wheel Bike VR 15.00 25.00
30 Human Mercenary U .75 1.50
31 Iktotchi Tech Specialist U .75 1.50
32 Jedi Knight U .75 1.50
33 Mace Windu, Jedi Master VR 18.00 30.00
34 Medical Droid R 6.00 12.00
35 Mon Mothma VR 10.00 20.00
36 Muun Guard U .75 1.50
37 Neimoidian Soldier U .75 1.50
38 Neimoidian Soldier U .75 1.50
39 Obi-Wan Kenobi, Jedi Master R 6.00 12.00
40 Polis Massa Medic C .30 .75
41 R2-D2, Astromech Droid VR 15.00 25.00
42 Royal Guard U .75 1.50
43 San Hill R 6.00 12.00
44 Senate Guard U .75 1.50
45 Separatist Commando C .30 .75
46 Shaak Ti R 6.00 12.00
47 Sly Moore R 6.00 12.00
48 Stass Allie R 6.00 12.00
49 Super Battle Droid C .30 .75
50 Super Battle Droid C .30 .75
51 Tarfful R 6.00 12.00
52 Tion Medon R 6.00 12.00
53 Utapaun Soldier C .30 .75
54 Utapaun Soldier C .30 .75
55 Utapaun Soldier C .30 .75
56 Wat Tambor R 6.00 12.00
57 Wookiee Berserker C .30 .75
58 Wookiee Scout U .75 1.50
59 Yoda, Jedi Master R 7.50 15.00
60 Yuzzem C .30 .75
61 Zabrak Fringer C .30 .75

2005 Star Wars Universe Miniatures

COMPLETE SET (61)	150.00	300.00
RELEASED ON AUGUST 19, 2005		
1 Abyssin Black Sun Thug C	.30	.75
2 Acklay U	.75	1.50
3 Admiral Ackbar VR	10.00	20.00
4 ASP-7 U	.75	1.50
5 AT-ST R	7.50	15.00
6 B'omarr Monk R	7.50	15.00
7 Baron Fel VR	18.00	30.00
8 Battle Droid U	.75	1.50
9 Battle Droid U	.75	1.50
10 Bith Rebel C	.30	.75
11 Chewbacca, Rebel Hero R	7.50	15.00
12 Clone Trooper C	.30	.75
13 Clone Trooper on BARC Speeder R	10.00	20.00
14 Dark Side Marauder U	.75	1.50
15 Dark Trooper Phase III U	.75	1.50
16 Darth Maul on Speeder VR	12.50	25.00
17 Darth Vader, Jedi Hunter R	7.50	15.00
18 Dash Rendar R	7.50	15.00
19 Dr. Evazan VR	10.00	20.00
20 Dressellian Commando C	.30	.75
21 Elite Clone Trooper U	.75	1.50
22 Flash Speeder U	.75	1.50
23 Gonk Power Droid C	.30	.75
24 Grand Admiral Thrawn VR	18.00	30.00
25 Guri R	7.50	15.00
26 Hailfire Droid U	.75	1.50
27 Han Solo, Rebel Hero R	7.50	15.00
28 Kaminoan Ascetic C	.30	.75
29 Kyle Katarn VR	10.00	20.00
30 Lando Calrissian, Hero of Taanab R	7.50	15.00
31 Lobot R	6.00	12.00
32 Luke Skywalker on Tauntaun R	10.00	20.00
33 Luke Skywalker, Jedi Master VR	18.00	30.00
34 New Republic Commander U	.75	1.50
35 New Republic Trooper C	.30	.75
36 Nexu U	.75	1.50
37 Nien Nunb R	6.00	12.00
38 Nightsister Sith Witch U	.75	1.50
39 Noghri U	.75	1.50
40 Nom Anor R	7.50	15.00
41 Nute Gunray R	6.00	12.00
42 Obi-Wan on Boga VR	12.50	25.00
43 Ponda Baba R	6.00	12.00
44 Prince Xizor VR	10.00	20.00
45 Princess Leia, Rebel Hero VR	10.00	20.00
46 Rancor VR	20.00	35.00
47 Reek U	.75	1.50
48 Rodian Black Sun Vigo U	.75	1.50
49 Shistavanen Pilot U	.75	1.50
50 Stormtrooper C	.30	.75
51 Stormtrooper Commander U	.75	1.50
52 Super Battle Droid C	.30	.75
53 Super Battle Droid Commander U	.75	1.50
54 Tusken Raider on Bantha U	.75	1.50
55 Vornskr C	.30	.75
56 Warmaster Tsavong Lah VR	15.00	25.00
57 Wedge Antilles R	7.50	15.00
58 X-1 Viper Droid U	.75	1.50
59 Young Jedi Knight C	.30	.75
60 Yuuzhan Vong Subaltern U	.75	1.50
61 Yuuzhan Vong Warrior C	.30	.75

2006 Star Wars Champions of the Force Miniatures

COMPLETE SET (61)	120.00	250.00
RELEASED ON JUNE 6, 2006		
1 Arcona Smuggler C	.30	.75
2 Barriss Offee R	6.00	12.00
3 Bastila Shan VR	10.00	20.00
5 Clone Commander Bacara R	6.00	12.00
6 Clone Commander Cody R	7.50	15.00
7 Clone Commander Gree R	6.00	12.00
8 Corran Horn R	6.00	12.00
9 Coruscant Guard C	.30	.75
10 Crab Droid U	.60	1.50
11 Dark Jedi U	.60	1.50
12 Dark Jedi Master U	.60	1.50
13 Dark Side Enforcer U	.60	1.50
14 Dark Trooper Phase I C	.30	.75
15 Dark Trooper Phase II U	.60	1.50
16 Dark Trooper Phase II VR	10.00	20.00
17 Darth Bane VR	12.50	25.00
18 Darth Malak VR	12.50	25.00
19 Darth Maul, Champion of the Sith R	7.50	15.00
20 Darth Nihilus VR	10.00	20.00
21 Darth Sidious, Dark Lord of the Sith R	6.00	12.00
22 Depa Billaba R	6.00	12.00
23 Even Piell R	6.00	12.00
24 Exar Kun VR	12.50	25.00
25 General Windu R	6.00	12.00
26 Gundark Fringe U	.60	1.50
27 HK-47 VR	10.00	20.00
28 Hoth Trooper with Atgar Cannon R	6.00	12.00
29 Jacen Solo VR	10.00	20.00
30 Jaina Solo VR	10.00	20.00
31 Jedi Consular U	.60	1.50
32 Jedi Guardian U	.60	1.50
33 Jedi Padawan U	.60	1.50
34 Jedi Sentinel U	.60	1.50
35 Jedi Weapon Master C	.30	.75
36 Kashyyyk Trooper C	.30	.75
37 Luke Skywalker, Young Jedi VR	12.50	25.00
38 Mas Amedda R	7.50	15.00
39 Massassi Sith Mutant U	.60	1.50
41 Octuparra Droid R	6.00	12.00
42 Old Republic Commander U	.60	1.50
43 Old Republic Trooper U	.60	1.50
44 Old Republic Trooper C	.30	.75
45 Queen Amidala R	6.00	12.00
46 Qui-Gon Jinn, Jedi Master R	7.50	15.00
47 R5 Astromech Droid C	.30	.75
48 Republic Commando Boss U	.60	1.50
49 Republic Commando Fixer C	.30	.75
50 Republic Commando Scorch C	.30	.75
51 Republic Commando Sev C	.30	.75
52 Saleucami Trooper C	.30	.75
53 Sandtrooper C	.30	.75
54 Sith Assault Droid U	.60	1.50
55 Sith Trooper C	.30	.75
56 Sith Trooper C	.30	.75
57 Sith Trooper Commander U	.60	1.50
58 Snowtrooper with E-Web Blaster R	6.00	12.00
59 Ugnaught Demolitionist C	.30	.75
60 Ulic Qel-Droma VR	7.50	15.00
61 Utapau Trooper C	.30	.75
62 Varactyl Wrangler C	.30	.75
63 Yoda of Dagobah VR	12.50	25.00

2006 Star Wars Bounty Hunters Miniatures

COMPLETE SET (60)	150.00	300.00
RELEASED ON SEPTEMBER 23, 2006		
1 4-LOM, Bounty Hunter R	6.00	12.00
2 Aqualish Assassin C	.30	.75
3 Ayy Vida R	6.00	12.00
4 Basilisk War Droid U	.60	1.50
5 Bib Fortuna R	6.00	12.00
6 Bith Black Sun Vigo U	.60	1.50
7 Boba Fett, Bounty Hunter VR	15.00	40.00
8 BoShek R	6.00	12.00
9 Bossk, Bounty Hunter R	7.50	15.00
10 Boushh R	6.00	12.00
11 Calo Nord R	6.00	12.00
12 Chewbacca w/C-3PO VR	10.00	18.00
13 Commerce Guild Homing Spider Droid U	.60	1.50
14 Corellian Pirate U	.60	1.50
15 Corporate Alliance Tank Droid U	.60	1.50
16 Dannik Jerriko VR	7.50	15.00
17 Dark Hellion Marauder on Swoop Bike U	.60	1.50
18 Dark Hellion Swoop Gang Member C	.30	.75
19 Defel Spy C	.30	.75
20 Dengar, Bounty Hunter R	7.50	15.00
21 Djas Puhr R	6.00	12.00
22 Droid Starfighter in Walking Mode R	7.50	15.00
23 E522 Assassin Droid U	.60	1.50
24 Gamorrean Thug C	.30	.75
25 Garindan R	6.00	12.00
26 Han Solo, Scoundrel VR	7.50	15.00
27 Huge Crab Droid U	.60	1.50
28 Human Blaster-for-Hire C	.30	.75
29 IG-88, Bounty Hunter VR	15.00	25.00
30 ISP Speeder R	6.00	12.00
31 Jango Fett, Bounty Hunter VR	15.00	30.00
32 Klatooinian Hunter C	.30	.75
33 Komari Vosa R	7.50	15.00
34 Lord Vader VR	10.00	20.00
35 Luke Skywalker of Dagobah R	7.50	15.00
36 Mandalore the Indomitable VR	12.50	25.00
37 Mandalorian Blademaster U	.60	1.50
38 Mandalorian Commander U	.60	1.50
39 Mandalorian Soldier C	.30	.75
40 Mandalorian Supercommando C	.30	.75
41 Mandalorian Warrior C	.30	.75
42 Mistryl Shadow Guard U	.60	1.50
43 Mustafarian Flea Rider R	6.00	12.00
44 Mustafarian Soldier C	.30	.75
45 Nikto Gunner on Desert Skiff VR	10.00	20.00
46 Nym VR	7.50	15.00
47 Princess Leia, Hoth Commander R	7.50	15.00
48 Quarren Bounty Hunter C	.30	.75
49 Rebel Captain U	.60	1.50
50 Rebel Heavy Trooper U	.60	1.50
51 Rebel Snowspeeder U	.60	1.50
52 Rodian Hunt Master U	.60	1.50
53 Talon Karrde VR	7.50	15.00
54 Tamtel Skreej VR	7.50	15.00
55 Tusken Raider Sniper C	.30	.75
56 Utapaun on Dactillion VR	7.50	15.00
57 Weequay Leader U	.60	1.50
58 Weequay Thug C	.30	.75
59 Young Krayt Dragon VR	10.00	20.00
60 Zuckuss R	7.50	15.00

2007 Star Wars Alliance and Empire Miniatures

COMPLETE SET (60)	100.00	200.00
RELEASED IN MAY 2007		
1 Admiral Piett R	5.00	10.00
2 Advance Agent, Officer U	.60	1.50
3 Advance Scout C	.30	.75
4 Aurra Sing, Jedi Hunter VR	10.00	20.00
5 Biggs Darklighter VR	7.50	15.00
6 Boba Fett, Enforcer VR	12.50	25.00
7 C-3PO and R2-D2 R	5.00	10.00
8 Chadra-Fan Pickpocket U	.60	1.50
9 Chewbacca, Enraged Wookiee R	5.00	10.00
10 Darth Vader, Imperial Commander VR	12.50	25.00
11 Death Star Gunner U	.60	1.50
12 Death Star Trooper C	.30	.75
13 Duros Explorer C	.30	.75
14 Elite Hoth Trooper C	.30	.75
15 Ephant Mon VR	7.50	15.00
16 Ewok Hang Glider R	5.00	10.00
17 Ewok Warrior C	.30	.75
18 Gamorrean Guard C	.30	.75
19 Han Solo in Stormtrooper Armor R	5.00	10.00
20 Han Solo on Tauntaun VR	10.00	20.00
21 Han Solo Rogue R	5.00	10.00
22 Heavy Stormtrooper U	.60	1.50
23 Human Force Adept C	.30	.75
24 Imperial Governor Tarkin R	5.00	10.00
25 Imperial Officer U	.60	1.50
26 Ithorian Commander U	.60	1.50
27 Jabba, Crime Lord VR	7.50	15.00
28 Jawa on Ronto VR	7.50	15.00
29 Jawa Trader U	.60	1.50
30 Lando Calrissian, Dashing Scoundrel R	5.00	10.00
31 Luke Skywalker, Champion of the Force VR	12.50	25.00
32 Luke Skywalker, Hero of Yavin R	5.00	10.00
33 Luke's Landspeeder VR	7.50	15.00
34 Mara Jade, Jedi R	5.00	10.00
35 Mon Calamari Tech Specialist C	.30	.75
36 Nikto Soldier C	.30	.75
37 Obi-Wan Kenobi, Force Spirit VR	7.50	15.00
38 Princess Leia R	5.00	10.00
39 Quinlan Vos, Infiltrator VR	10.00	20.00
40 Rampaging Wampa VR	7.50	15.00
41 Rebel Commando C	.30	.75
42 Rebel Commando Strike Leader U	.60	1.50
43 Rebel Leader U	.60	1.50
44 Rebel Pilot C	.30	.75
45 Rebel Trooper U	.60	1.50
46 Rodian Scoundrel U	.60	1.50
47 Scout Trooper U	.60	1.50
48 Snivvian Fringer C	.30	.75
49 Snowtrooper C	.30	.75
50 Storm Commando R	5.00	10.00
51 Stormtrooper C	.30	.75
52 Stormtrooper Officer U	.60	1.50
53 Stormtrooper on Repulsor Sled VR	10.00	20.00
54 Talz Spy Fringe U	.60	1.50
55 Trandoshan Mercenary U	.60	1.50
56 Tusken Raider C	.30	.75
57 Twi'lek Rebel Agent U	.60	1.50
58 Wicket R	5.00	10.00
59 Wookiee Freedom Fighter C	.30	.75
60 Yomin Carr R	6.00	12.00

2007 Star Wars The Force Unleashed Miniatures

COMPLETE SET (60)	350.00	800.00
RELEASED IN 2007		
1 Darth Revan VR	50.00	80.00
2 Kazdan Paratus R	4.00	10.00
3 Shaak Ti, Jedi Master VR	8.00	20.00
4 Chewbacca of Hoth VR	4.00	10.00
5 Elite Hoth Trooper C	4.00	10.00
6 Golan Arms DF.9 Anti-Infantry Battery UC	4.00	10.00
7 Han Solo in Carbonite VR	4.00	10.00
8 Han Solo of Hoth VR	4.00	10.00
9 Hoth Trooper Officer UC	4.00	10.00
10 Hoth Trooper with Repeating Blaster Cannon UC	4.00	10.00
11 Juno Eclipse R	4.00	10.00
12 K-3PO R	4.00	10.00
13 Luke Skywalker, Hoth Pilot Unleashed R	4.00	10.00
14 Luke Skywalker and Yoda VR	6.00	15.00
15 Luke's Snowspeeder VR	6.00	15.00
16 Master Kota R	6.00	15.00
17 Mon Calamari Medic C	4.00	10.00
18 Obi-Wan Kenobi, Unleashed R	4.00	10.00
19 Princess Leia of Cloud City R	4.00	10.00
20 Rebel Marksman UC	4.00	10.00
21 Rebel Troop Cart UC	4.00	10.00
22 Rebel Trooper on Tauntaun R	4.00	10.00
23 Rebel Vanguard UC	4.00	10.00
24 2-1B R	4.00	10.00
25 Vader's Secret Apprentice, Redeemed R	8.00	20.00
26 Verpine Tech Rebel C	4.00	10.00
27 Wedge Antilles, Red Two Rebel R	4.00	10.00
28 Wookiee Warrior Rebel C	4.00	10.00
29 Admiral Ozzel R	4.00	10.00
30 AT-AT Driver UC	4.00	10.00
31 Dark trooper UC	4.00	10.00
32 Darth Vader, Unleashed VR	4.00	10.00
33 Emperor's Shadow Guard UC	4.00	10.00
34 Evo Trooper UC	4.00	10.00
35 Felucian Stormtrooper Officer UC	4.00	10.00
36 Gotal Imperial Assassin C	4.00	10.00
37 Imperial Navy trooper C	4.00	10.00
38 Raxus Prime Trooper C	4.00	10.00
39 Snowtrooper C	4.00	10.00
40 Star Destroyer Officer UC	4.00	10.00
41 Stormtrooper UC	4.00	10.00
42 TIE Crawler UC	4.00	10.00
43 Vader's Apprentice, Unleashed VR	4.00	10.00
44 Wookiee Hunter AT-ST R	6.00	15.00
45 Garm Bel Iblis R	4.00	10.00
46 Amanin Scout UC	4.00	10.00
47 Boba Fett, Mercenary VR	30.00	50.00
48 Caamasi Noble C	4.00	10.00
49 Cloud Car Pilot C	4.00	10.00
50 Felucian Warrior on Rancor VR	20.00	40.00
51 Junk golem UC	4.00	10.00
52 Knobby white spider UC	4.00	10.00
53 Maris Brood VR	6.00	15.00
54 Muun Tactics Broker C	4.00	10.00
55 Mynock UC	4.00	10.00
56 PROXY R	4.00	10.00
57 Telosian Tank Droid UC	4.00	10.00
58 Uggernaught R	4.00	10.00
59 Ugnaught Boss UC	4.00	10.00
60 Ugnaught Tech UC	4.00	10.00

2008 Star Wars Legacy of the Force Miniatures

COMPLETE SET (60)	300.00	700.00
RELEASED MARCH 28, 2008		
1 Nomi Sunrider VR	6.00	15.00
2 Old Republic Recruit C	4.00	10.00
3 Old Republic Scout C	4.00	10.00
4 Darth Caedus VR	15.00	30.00
5 Darth Krayt VR	15.00	30.00
6 Darth Nihl VR	4.00	10.00
7 Darth Talon VR	30.00	50.00
8 Lumiya, the Dark Lady R	4.00	10.00
9 Republic Commando Training Sergeant U	4.00	10.00
10 Darth Tyranus, Legacy of the dark side R	4.00	10.00
11 Bothan Noble U	4.00	10.00
12 Deena Shan R	4.00	10.00
13 Elite Rebel Commando U	4.00	10.00
14 General Dodonna R	4.00	10.00
15 Luke Skywalker, Legacy of the Light Side R	4.00	10.00
16 Rebel Honor Guard C	4.00	10.00
17 Twi'lek Scout C	4.00	10.00
18 Antares Draco R	5.00	12.00
19 Emperor Roan Fel VR	4.00	10.00
20 Imperial Knight U	4.00	10.00
21 Imperial Knight U	4.00	10.00
22 Imperial Pilot C	4.00	10.00
23 Imperial Security Officer U	4.00	10.00
24 Jagged Fel R	4.00	10.00
25 Marasiah Fel R	4.00	10.00
26 Moff Morlish Veed VR	4.00	10.00
27 Moff Nyna Calixte R	4.00	10.00
28 Noghri Commando U	4.00	10.00
29 Shadow Stormtrooper U	4.00	10.00
30 Corellian Security Officer U	4.00	10.00
31 Galactic Alliance Scout C	4.00	10.00
32 Galactic Alliance Trooper C	4.00	10.00
33 Han Solo, Galactic Hero R	4.00	10.00
34 Kyle Katarn, Jedi Battlemaster VR	4.00	10.00
35 Leia Organa Solo, Jedi Knight VR	4.00	10.00
36 Luke Skywalker, Force Spirit VR	4.00	10.00
37 Mara Jade Skywalker VR	6.00	15.00
38 Shado Vao R	4.00	10.00
39 Wolf Sazen VR	4.00	10.00
40 Cade Skywalker, Bounty Hunter VR	4.00	10.00
41 Deliah Blue R	4.00	10.00
42 Dug Fringer U	4.00	10.00
43 Duros Scoundrel C	4.00	10.00
44 Gotal Mercenary C	4.00	10.00
45 Guard Droid C	4.00	10.00
46 Human Bodyguard C	4.00	10.00
47 Human Scoundrel C	4.00	10.00
48 Human Scout C	4.00	10.00
49 Jariah Syn R	4.00	10.00
50 Kel Dor Bounty Hunter C	4.00	10.00
51 Rodian Blaster for Hire U	4.00	10.00
52 Trandoshan Mercenary C	4.00	10.00
53 Boba Fett, Mercenary Commander VR	4.00	10.00
54 Canderous Ordo R	4.00	10.00
55 Mandalorian Gunslinger U	4.00	10.00
56 Mandalorian Trooper U	4.00	10.00
57 Yuuzhan Vong Elite Warrior U	4.00	10.00
58 Yuuzhan Vong Jedi Hunter U	4.00	10.00
59 Yuuzhan Vong Shaper U	4.00	10.00
60 Yuuzhan Vong Warrior C	4.00	10.00

2008 Star Wars The Clone Wars Miniatures

COMPLETE SET (40)	200.00	400.00
RELEASED ON NOVEMBER 4, 2008		
1 Darth Sidious Hologram VR	4.00	10.00
2 Ahsoka Tano VR	10.00	25.00
3 Anakin Skywalker Champion of Nelvaan R	4.00	10.00
4 Anakin Skywalker on STAP VR	4.00	10.00
5 ARC Trooper Sniper U	4.00	10.00
6 Barriss Offee, Jedi Knight R	4.00	10.00
7 Captain Rex VR	4.00	10.00
8 Clone Trooper on Gelagrub R	4.00	10.00
9 Commander Gree R	4.00	10.00
10 Elite Clone Trooper Commander U	4.00	10.00
11 Elite Clone Trooper Grenadier C	4.00	10.00
12 Galactic Marine U	4.00	10.00
13 General Aayla Secura R	6.00	15.00
14 Heavy Clone Trooper C	4.00	10.00
15 Mon Calamari Knight U	4.00	10.00
16 Odd Ball R	4.00	10.00
17 PadmÉ Amidala Senator VR	5.00	12.00
18 Star Corps Trooper U	4.00	10.00
19 Wookiee Scoundrel C	4.00	10.00
20 Yoda on Kybuck VR	4.00	10.00
21 Battle Droid C	4.00	10.00
22 Battle Droid C	4.00	10.00
23 Battle Droid Sniper U	4.00	10.00
24 Chameleon Droid R	4.00	10.00
25 Durge, Jedi Hunter VR	10.00	25.00
26 General Grievous, Droid Army Commander VR	4.00	10.00
27 Heavy Super Battle Droid C	4.00	10.00
28 IG-100 MagnaGuard U	4.00	10.00
29 Neimoidian Warrior C	4.00	10.00
30 Quarren Isolationist U	4.00	10.00
31 Rocket Battle Droid U	4.00	10.00
32 Super Battle Droid C	4.00	10.00
33 Techno Union Warrior C	4.00	10.00
34 Aqualish Warrior C	4.00	10.00
35 Gha Nachkt R	4.00	10.00
36 Human Soldier of Fortune C	4.00	10.00
37 IG-86 Assassin Droid U	4.00	10.00
38 Nelvaanian Warrior U	4.00	10.00
39 Trandoshan Scavenger U	4.00	10.00
40 Utapaun Warrior C	4.00	10.00

2008 Star Wars The Clone Wars Miniatures Starter

COMPLETE SET (6)	20.00	50.00
RELEASED ON NOVEMBER 4, 2008		
1 General Obi-Wan Kenobi	3.00	8.00
2 Clone Trooper	3.00	8.00
3 Clone Trooper Commander	3.00	8.00
4 Count Dooku of Serenno	3.00	8.00
5 Security Battle Droid	3.00	8.00
6 Super Battle Droid Commander	3.00	8.00

2009 Star Wars Galaxy at War Miniatures

COMPLETE SET (40)	60.00	160.00
RELEASED ON OCTOBER 27, 2009		
1 501st Clone Trooper C	1.50	4.00
2 A4-Series Lab Droid U	1.50	4.00
3 Admiral Yularen VR	1.50	4.00
4 Aqualish Technician C	1.50	4.00
5 ARF Trooper C	1.50	4.00
6 Asajj Ventress, Strike Leader R	1.50	4.00
7 AT-TE Driver C	1.50	4.00
8 B3 Ultra Battle Droid U	1.50	4.00
9 Battle Droid C	1.50	4.00
10 Battle Droid Sergeant U	1.50	4.00
11 Cad Bane VR	1.50	4.00
12 Captain Argyus VR	1.50	4.00
13 Captain Mar Tuuk VR	1.50	4.00
14 Captain Rex, 501st Commander R	1.50	4.00
15 Clone Trooper Pilot C	1.50	4.00
16 Clone Trooper Sergeant U	1.50	4.00
17 Clone Trooper with Night Vision C	1.50	4.00
18 Clone Trooper with Repeating Blaster U	1.50	4.00
19 Commander Ahsoka R	1.50	4.00
20 Commander Cody R	1.50	4.00
21 Commando Droid C	1.50	4.00
22 Commando Droid C	1.50	4.00
23 Commando Droid Captain U	1.50	4.00
24 Elite Senate Guard U	1.50	4.00
25 General Grievous, Scourge of the Jedi R	1.50	4.00
26 General Skywalker R	1.50	4.00
27 General Whorm Loathsom VR	1.50	4.00
28 Hondo Ohnaka VR	1.50	4.00
29 IG-100 MagnaGuard Artillerist U	1.50	4.00
30 IG-100 MagnaGuard U	1.50	4.00
31 Jedi Master Kit Fisto R	1.50	4.00
32 LR-57 Combat Droid U	1.50	4.00
33 Nahdar Vebb VR	1.50	4.00
34 Obi-Wan Kenobi, Jedi General R	1.50	4.00
35 R7 Astromech Droid U	1.50	4.00
36 Rodian Trader C	1.50	4.00
37 Senate Commando C	1.50	4.00
38 Treadwell Droid U	1.50	4.00
39 Wat Tambor, Techno Union Foreman VR	1.50	4.00
40 Weequay Pirate C	1.50	4.00

2009 Star Wars Imperial Entanglements Miniatures

COMPLETE SET (40)	180.00	450.00
RELEASED ON MARCH 17, 2009		
1 Bothan Commando C	4.00	10.00
2 C-3PO, Ewok Deity VR	4.00	10.00
3 General Crix Madine R	4.00	10.00
4 General Rieekan VR	5.00	12.00
5 Leia, Bounty Hunter VR	4.00	10.00
6 Luke Skywalker, Rebel Commando VR	8.00	20.00
7 Rebel Commando Pathfinder U	4.00	10.00
8 Rebel Trooper C	4.00	10.00
9 R2-D2 with Extended Sensor R	4.00	10.00
10 Veteran Rebel Commando C	4.00	10.00
11 Arica R	4.00	10.00
12 Darth Vader, Legacy of the Force VR	8.00	20.00
13 Emperor Palpatine on Throne VR	10.00	25.00
14 Imperial Dignitary U	4.00	10.00
15 Moff Tiaan Jerjerrod R	4.00	10.00
16 181st Imperial Pilot U	4.00	10.00
17 Sandtrooper C	4.00	10.00
18 Sandtrooper Officer U	4.00	10.00
19 Scout Trooper C	4.00	10.00
20 Shock Trooper U	4.00	10.00
21 Snowtrooper C	4.00	10.00
22 Snowtrooper Commander U	4.00	10.00
23 Stormtrooper C	4.00	10.00
24 Thrawn Mitth'raw'nuruodo R	4.00	10.00
25 Kyp Durron R	4.00	10.00
26 Bacta Tank U	4.00	10.00
27 Bespin Guard C	4.00	10.00
28 Chiss Mercenary C	4.00	10.00
29 Dash Rendar, Renegade Smuggler VR	6.00	15.00
30 Duros Scout C	4.00	10.00
31 Ewok Scout C	4.00	10.00
32 Jawa Scavenger C	4.00	10.00
33 Lobot, Computer Liaison Officer R	4.00	10.00
34 Logray, Ewok Shaman R	4.00	10.00
35 Mercenary Commander U - resembling Airen Cracken	4.00	10.00
36 Mouse Droid U	4.00	10.00
37 Twi'lek Black Sun Vigo U	4.00	10.00
38 Ugnaught Droid Destroyer U	4.00	10.00
39 Whiphid Tracker U	4.00	10.00
40 Xizor VR	8.00	20.00

2009 Star Wars Jedi Academy Miniatures

COMPLETE SET (40)	200.00	450.00
RELEASED ON JUNE 30, 2009		
1 Anakin Solo R	4.00	10.00
2 Antarian Ranger C	4.00	10.00
3 Cade Skywalker, Padawan R	4.00	10.00
4 Crimson Nova Bounty Hunter UC	4.00	10.00
5 Darth Maul, Sith apprentice VR	10.00	25.00
6 Darth Plagueis VR	10.00	25.00
7 Darth Sidious, Sith Master R	4.00	10.00
8 Death Watch Raider C	4.00	10.00
9 Disciples of Ragnos C	4.00	10.00
10 Exceptional Jedi Apprentice UC	4.00	10.00
11 Felucian UC	4.00	10.00
12 Grand Master Luke Skywalker R	6.00	15.00
13 Grand Master Yoda R	5.00	12.00
14 Heavy Clone Trooper C	4.00	10.00
15 HK-50 Series Assassin Droid UC	4.00	10.00
16 Imperial Sentinel U	4.00	10.00
17 Jedi Battlemaster UC	4.00	10.00
18 Jedi Crusader UC	4.00	10.00
19 Jensaarai Defender UC	4.00	10.00
20 Kol Skywalker VR	4.00	10.00
21 Krath War Droid C	4.00	10.00
22 Kyle Katarn, Combat Instructor R	4.00	10.00
23 Leia Skywalker, Jedi KnightR	4.00	10.00
24 Master K'Kruhk VR	4.00	10.00
25 Naga Sadow VR	6.00	15.00
26 Peace Brigade Thug C	4.00	10.00
27 Praetorite Vong Priest UC	4.00	10.00
28 Praetorite Vong Warrior C	4.00	10.00
29 Qui-Gon Jinn, Jedi Trainer R	4.00	10.00
30 R4 Astromech Droid C	4.00	10.00
31 Reborn C	4.00	10.00
32 Rocket Battle Droid C	4.00	10.00
33 Sith apprentice UC - resembling Darth Bandon	4.00	10.00
34 Sith Lord U	4.00	10.00
35 Stormtrooper C	4.00	10.00
36 The Dark Woman VR	8.00	20.00
37 The Jedi ExileVR	10.00	25.00
38 Vodo-Siosk Baas VR	6.00	15.00
39 Youngling C	4.00	10.00
40 Yuuzhan Vong Ossus Guardian UC	4.00	10.00

2010 Star Wars Dark Times Miniatures

COMPLETE SET (40)	75.00	200.00
RELEASED ON JANUARY 26, 2010		
1 4-LOM, Droid Mercenary R	1.50	4.00
2 501st Legion Clone Commander UC	1.50	4.00
3 501st Legion Clone Trooper C	1.50	4.00
4 501st Legion Stormtrooper C	1.50	4.00
5 ARF Trooper UC	1.50	4.00
6 A'Sharad Hett VR	6.00	15.00
7 Bomo Greenbark VR	1.50	4.00
8 Bossk, Trandoshan Hunter R	1.50	4.00
9 Boushh, Ubese Hunter R	1.50	4.00
10 Chewbacca, Fearless Scout VR	1.50	4.00
11 Dass Jennir VR	4.00	10.00
12 Dengar, Hired Killer R	1.50	4.00
13 EG-5 Jedi Hunter Droid UC	3.00	8.00
14 Elite Sith Assassin UC	1.50	4.00
15 Emperor's Hand UC	1.50	4.00
16 Ferus Olin VR	1.50	4.00
17 Gungan Bounty Hunter C	1.50	4.00
18 Human Engineer C	1.50	4.00
19 IG-88, Assassin Droid	3.00	8.00
20 Imperial Engineer C	1.50	4.00
21 Imperial Inquisitor UC	1.50	4.00
22 Imperial Sovereign Protector UC	1.50	4.00
23 Jax Pavan VR	1.50	4.00
24 Jedi Watchman C	1.50	4.00
25 Kir Kanos VR	4.00	10.00
26 K'Kruhk VR	1.50	4.00
27 Kota's Elite Militia UC	1.50	4.00
28 Kota's Militia C	1.50	4.00
29 Major Maximilian Veers R	1.50	4.00
30 Mandalorian Jedi Hunter UC	1.50	4.00
31 Merumeru R	1.50	4.00
32 Rodian Brute C	1.50	4.00
33 Rodian Raider C	1.50	4.00
34 Talz Chieftain UC	1.50	4.00
35 Talz Warrior C	1.50	4.00
36 Togorian Soldier UC	1.50	4.00
37 Trandoshan Elite Mercenary UC	4.00	10.00
38 Trianii Scout UC	1.50	4.00
39 T'Surr C	1.50	4.00
40 Zuckuss, Bounty Hunter C	5.00	12.00

2010 Star Wars Masters of the Force Miniatures

COMPLETE SET (40)	115.00	280.00
RELEASED APRIL 6, 2010		
1 Cay Qel-Droma VR	6.00	15.00
2 Jedi Healer UC	2.50	6.00
3 Jedi Instructor - resembling Coleman Trebor UC	2.50	6.00
4 Jedi Sith Hunter UC	2.50	6.00
5 Lord Hoth VR	2.50	6.00
6 Freedon Nadd VR	2.50	6.00
7 Kit Fisto, Jedi Master R	2.50	6.00
8 Master Windu R	2.50	6.00
9 Plo Koon, Jedi Master R	4.00	10.00
10 Rodian Diplomat UC	2.50	6.00
11 Saesee Tiin, Jedi Master R	6.00	15.00
12 Voolvif Monn VR	10.00	25.00
13 Battle Droid Officer C	2.50	6.00
14 Anakin Skywalker, Force Spirit R	2.50	6.00
15 General Han Solo R	2.50	6.00
16 Lando Calrissian, Rebel Leader R	2.50	6.00
17 Rebel Soldier C	2.50	6.00
18 Red Hand Trooper UC	2.50	6.00
19 Yoda, Force Spirit VR	2.50	6.00
20 Arden Lyn VR	2.50	6.00
21 Darth Vader, Sith apprentice R	2.50	6.00
22 Ganner Rhysode VR	2.50	6.00
23 Blood Carver Assassin C	2.50	6.00
24 Chiss Trooper UC	2.50	6.00
25 Ewok Warrior C	2.50	6.00
26 Gamorrean Bodyguard C	2.50	6.00
27 Ghhhk UC	3.00	8.00
28 Grievous, Kaleesh Warlord VR	2.50	6.00
29 Houjix C	2.50	6.00
30 K'lor'slug UC	3.00	8.00
31 Kaminoan Medic UC	2.50	6.00
32 Kintan Strider C	2.50	6.00
33 Mantellian Savrip C	2.50	6.00
34 Molator UC	2.50	6.00
35 Monnok UC	2.50	6.00
36 Ng'ok UC	3.00	8.00
37 Sullustan Scout C	2.50	6.00
38 Toydarian Soldier C	2.50	6.00
39 Far-Outsider C	2.50	6.00
40 Taung Warrior C	2.50	6.00

Miscellaneous
PRICE GUIDE

HOT WHEELS

2014 Hot Wheels Star Wars Character Cars Black Cards 1:64

1	Darth Vader	10.00	20.00
2	R2-D2	5.00	10.00
3	Luke Skywalker	5.00	10.00
4	Chewbacca	4.00	8.00
5	Yoda	5.00	10.00
6	Tusken Raider	5.00	10.00
7	501st Clone Trooper	8.00	15.00
8	Stormtrooper	4.00	8.00
9	Darth Maul	4.00	8.00
10	Boba Fett	6.00	12.00
11	Chopper (Star Wars Rebels)	5.00	10.00
12	The Inquisitor (Star Wars Rebels)	4.00	8.00
13	C-3PO	8.00	15.00
14	Wicket the Ewok	5.00	10.00
15	Kanan Jarrus (Star Wars Rebels)	4.00	8.00
16	Zeb (Star Wars Rebels)	4.00	8.00
17	Kylo Ren	5.00	10.00
18	BB-8	8.00	15.00
19	General Grievous	6.00	12.00
20	Han Solo (The Force Awakens)	8.00	15.00
21	First Order Stormtrooper	6.00	12.00
22	Obi-Wan Kenobi	12.00	25.00
23	Rey	8.00	15.00
24	Jabba the Hutt	10.00	20.00
25	Admiral Ackbar	10.00	20.00
26	First Order Flametrooper	6.00	12.00
27	Battle Droid	6.00	12.00
28	Sabine Wren (Star Wars Rebels)	10.00	20.00
29	Clone Shock Trooper		
	(UER #27)		
30	C-3PO (The Force Awakens)	8.00	15.00
31	Sidon Ithano (The Force Awakens)	8.00	15.00
32	Jango Fett	6.00	12.00

2014 Hot Wheels Star Wars Character Cars Blue Cards 1:64

1	Darth Vader	4.00	8.00
2	R2-D2		
3	Luke Skywalker		
4	Chewbacca		
5	Yoda		
6	Tusken Raider	4.00	8.00
7	501st Clone Trooper	4.00	8.00
8	Stormtrooper	4.00	8.00
9	Darth Maul	5.00	10.00
10	Boba Fett	4.00	8.00
11	Chopper (Star Wars Rebels)		
12	The Inquisitor (Star Wars Rebels)	3.00	6.00
13	C-3PO	6.00	12.00
14	Wicket the Ewok	4.00	8.00
15	Kanan Jarrus (Star Wars Rebels)	5.00	10.00
16	Zeb (Star Wars Rebels)		
17	Kylo Ren		
18	BB-8		
19	General Grievous		
20	Han Solo (The Force Awakens)		
21	First Order Stormtrooper		
22	Obi-Wan Kenobi		
23	Rey		
24	Jabba the Hutt		
25	Admiral Ackbar		
26	First Order Flametrooper		
27	Battle Droid		
28	Sabine Wren (Star Wars Rebels)		
29	Clone Shock Trooper		
	(UER #27)		
30	C-3PO (The Force Awakens)		
31	Sidon Ithano (The Force Awakens)		
32	Jango Fett		

2014 Hot Wheels Star Wars Saga Walmart Exclusives 1:64

1	Gearonimo (The Phantom Menace)	5.00	10.00
2	Nitro Scorcher (Attack of the Clones)	6.00	12.00
3	Duel Fueler (Revenge of the Sith)	8.00	15.00
4	Motoblade (A New Hope)		
5	Spectyte (Empire Strikes Back)	10.00	20.00
6	Ballistik (Return of the Jedi)	4.00	8.00
7	Brutalistic (The Clone Wars)	4.00	8.00
8	Jet Threat 3.0 (Star Wars Rebels)	12.00	25.00

2014-16 Hot Wheels Star Wars Exclusives 1:64

1	Darth Vader (w/lightsaber box)		
	(2014 SDCC Exclusive)	80.00	150.00
2	R2-KT	40.00	80.00
	(2015 Star Wars Celebration Make-a-Wish Foundation Exclusive)		
3	First Order Stormtrooper		
	(2015 SDCC Exclusive)	25.00	50.00
4	Carships Trench Run Set		
	(2016 SDCC Exclusive)	50.00	100.00
5	Boba Fett Prototype Armor		
	(2016 Star Wars Celebration Exclusive)	25.00	50.00

2014-16 Hot Wheels Star Wars Target Exclusive 5-Packs 1:64

1	Character Cars (Battle-Damaged Stormtrooper	25.00	50.00
	Luke Skywalker/Darth Vader/Yoda/Chewbacca)		
2	Light Side vs. Dark Side (Luke Skywalker	15.00	30.00
	Obi-Wan Kenobi/Anakin Skywalker/Emperor Palpatine/Kylo Ren)		
3	Heroes of the Resistance (Chewbacca/Han Solo/Rey	20.00	40.00
	Poe Dameron/Maz Kanata)		

2015 Hot Wheels Star Wars Walmart Exclusives 1:64

1	Obi-Wan Kenobi		
	(Jedi Order Scorcher)	4.00	8.00
2	Darth Maul		
	(Sith Scoopa di Fuego)	5.00	10.00
3	Clone Trooper		
	(Galactic Republic Impavido 1)	4.00	8.00
4	General Grievous		
	(Separatists Sinistra)	4.00	8.00
5	Luke Skywalker		
	(Rebel Alliance Enforcer)	4.00	8.00
6	Darth Vader		
	(Galactic Empire Prototype H-24)	5.00	10.00
7	Poe Dameron		
	(Resistance Fast Felion)	4.00	8.00
8	Kylo Ren		
	(First Order Ettorium)	4.00	8.00

2015-16 Hot Wheels Star Wars Character Cars Black Carded 2-Packs 1:64

1	Chewbacca & Han Solo	5.00	10.00
2	R2-D2 & C-3PO (weathered)	4.00	8.00
3	Obi-Wan Kenobi & Darth Vader	20.00	40.00
4	501st Clone Trooper & Battle Droid	4.00	8.00
5	Emperor Palpatine vs. Yoda	8.00	15.00
6	Darth Vader & Princess Leia	10.00	20.00
7	Captain Phasma & First Order Stormtrooper	5.00	10.00
8	Rey vs. First Order Flametrooper	8.00	15.00
9	BB-8 & Poe Dameron	10.00	20.00
10	Han Solo vs. Greedo	12.00	25.00
11	Boba Fett & Bossk		
12	Luke Skywalker vs. Rancor		
13	Stormtrooper & Death Trooper (Rogue One)	8.00	15.00

2015-16 Hot Wheels Star Wars Character Cars Blue Carded 2-Packs 1:64

1	Chewbacca & Han Solo	6.00	12.00
2	R2-D2 & C-3PO (weathered)	6.00	12.00
3	Obi-Wan Kenobi & Darth Vader	6.00	12.00
4	501st Clone Trooper & Battle Droid	8.00	15.00
5	Emperor Palpatine vs. Yoda		
6	Darth Vader & Princess Leia	6.00	12.00
7	Captain Phasma & First Order Stormtrooper		
8	Rey vs. First Order Flametrooper		
9	BB-8 & Poe Dameron		
10	Han Solo vs. Greedo	8.00	15.00
11	Boba Fett & Bossk		
12	Luke Skywalker vs. Rancor		
13	Stormtrooper & Death Trooper (Rogue One)	10.00	20.00

2015-16 Hot Wheels Star Wars Tracksets 1:64

1	TIE Factory Takedown (w/Ezra Bridger car)	12.00	25.00
2	Throne Room Raceway (w/Luke Skywalker car)	12.00	25.00
3	Death Star Battle Blast (w/X-Wing inspired vehicle)	10.00	20.00
4	Blast & Battle Lightsaber Launcher (w/Darth Vader car)	8.00	15.00
5	Starkiller Base Battle (w/Finn car)		
6	Rancor Rumble set (w/Gamorrean Guard car)	15.00	30.00

2017 Hot Wheels Star Wars 40th Anniversary Carships 1:64

NNO Millennium Falcon	6.00	12.00
NNO TIE Advanced XI Prototype	6.00	12.00
NNO TIE Fighter	5.00	10.00
NNO X-Wing Fighter	5.00	10.00
NNO Y-Wing Fighter	8.00	15.00

2017 Hot Wheels Star Wars 40th Anniversary Character Cars 1:64

NNO Biggs Darklighter		
(Celebration Exclusive)	12.00	25.00
NNO Chewbacca	6.00	12.00
NNO Darth Vader	8.00	15.00
NNO Luke Skywalker		
NNO Princess Leia	6.00	12.00
NNO R2-D2	5.00	10.00
NNO Stormtrooper	6.00	12.00

2017 Hot Wheels Star Wars 40th Anniversary Starships 1:64

NNO Millennium Falcon	8.00	15.00
NNO Star Destroyer	10.00	20.00
NNO TIE Advanced X1 Prototype	6.00	12.00
NNO TIE Fighter	6.00	12.00
NNO X-Wing Fighter	6.00	12.00
NNO Y-Wing Fighter	8.00	15.00

2017 Hot Wheels Star Wars The Last Jedi 2-Packs 1:64

NNO BB-8 & Poe Dameron	8.00	15.00
NNO Boba Fett & Bossk	6.00	12.00
NNO Jabba the Hutt & Han Solo in Carbonite	12.00	25.00
NNO Kylo Ren & Snoke	15.00	30.00
NNO R2-D2 & C-3PO	8.00	15.00
NNO Rey (Jedi Training) & Luke Skywalker	15.00	30.00

2017 Hot Wheels Star Wars The Last Jedi Carships 1:64

NNO First Order TIE Fighter	6.00	12.00
NNO Kylo Ren's TIE Silencer		
NNO Millennium Falcon		
NNO Poe's X-Wing Fighter		
NNO Resistance Ski Speeder		
NNO Y-Wing Fighter		

2017 Hot Wheels Star Wars The Last Jedi Character Cars 1:64

2017 Hot Wheels Star Wars The Last Jedi Character Cars 1:64

NNO BB-8
NNO BB-9E
NNO C-3PO
NNO Captain Phasma
NNO Chewbacca
NNO Darth Vader
NNO Elite Praetorian Guard
NNO Finn
NNO First Order Executioner
NNO First Order Stormtrooper
NNO Kylo Ren
NNO Luke Skywalker
NNO R2-D2
NNO Rey (Jedi Training)

2017 Hot Wheels Star Wars The Last Jedi Character Cars All-Terrain 1:64

NNO BB-8
NNO Darth Vader
NNO Luke Skywalker
NNO Stormtrooper

2017 Hot Wheels Star Wars The Last Jedi Starships 1:64

NNO First Order Heavy Assault Walker
NNO First Order Special Forces TIE Fighter
NNO First Order Star Destroyer
NNO Kylo Ren's TIE Silencer
NNO Kylo Ren's TIE Silencer (boxed)
(SDCC Exclusive)
NNO Millennium Falcon
NNO Poe's Ski Speeder
NNO Resistance Bomber
NNO Resistance X-Wing Fighter

1999 LEGO Star Wars Episode I

7101 Lightsaber Duel	25.00	50.00
7111 Droid Fighter	15.00	30.00
7121 Naboo Swamp	20.00	40.00
7131 Anakin's Podracer	25.00	50.00
7141 Naboo Fighter	40.00	80.00
7151 Sith Infiltrator	30.00	60.00
7161 Gungan Sub	60.00	120.00
7171 Mos Espa Podrace	80.00	150.00

1999 LEGO Star Wars Episode IV

7110 Landspeeder	20.00	40.00
7140 X-wing Fighter	60.00	120.00
7150 TIE Fighter & Y-wing	80.00	150.00

1999 LEGO Star Wars Episode V

7130 Snowspeeder	40.00	80.00

1999 LEGO Star Wars Episode VI

7128 Speeder Bikes	25.00	50.00

2000 LEGO Star Wars Episode I

7115 Gungan Patrol	25.00	50.00
7124 Flash Speeder	15.00	30.00
7155 Trade Federation AAT	40.00	80.00
7159 Star Wars Bucket	30.00	75.00
7184 Trade Federation MTT	30.00	75.00

2000 LEGO Star Wars Episode IV

7190 Millennium Falcon	150.00	300.00

2000 LEGO Star Wars Episode V

7144 Slave I	50.00	100.00

2000 LEGO Star Wars Episode VI

7104 Desert Skiff	20.00	40.00
7134 A-wing Fighter	25.00	50.00
7180 B-wing at Rebel Control Center	30.00	60.00

2000 LEGO Star Wars Minifigure Pack

3340 Emperor Palpatine, Darth Maul and Darth Vader Minifig Pack - Star Wars #1	40.00	80.00
3341 Luke Skywalker, Han Solo and Boba Fett Minifig Pack - Star Wars #2	40.00	80.00
3342 Chewbacca and 2 Biker Scouts Minifig Pack - Star Wars #3	12.00	25.00
3343 2 Battle Droids and Command Officer Minifig Pack - Star Wars #4	12.00	25.00

2000 LEGO Star Wars Technic

8000 Pit Droid	20.00	40.00
8001 Battle Droid	25.00	50.00
8002 Destroyer Droid	120.00	200.00

2000 LEGO Star Wars Ultimate Collector Series

7181 TIE Interceptor	300.00	600.00
7191 X-wing Fighter	450.00	900.00

2001 LEGO Star Wars Episode I

7126	Battle Droid Carrier	20.00	40.00
7186	Watto's Junkyard	50.00	100.00

2001 LEGO Star Wars Episode IV

7106	Droid Escape	15.00	30.00
7146	TIE Fighter	60.00	120.00

2001 LEGO Star Wars Episode VI

7127	Imperial AT-ST	20.00	40.00
7166	Imperial Shuttle	40.00	80.00

2001 LEGO Star Wars Technic

8007	C-3PO	50.00	100.00
8008	Stormtrooper	20.00	50.00

2001 LEGO Star Wars Ultimate Collector Series

10018	Darth Maul	200.00	400.00
10019	Rebel Blockade Runner	700.00	1,400.00

2002 LEGO Star Wars Episode I

7203	Jedi Defense I	15.00	30.00
7204	Jedi Defense II	20.00	40.00

2002 LEGO Star Wars Episode II

7103	Jedi Duel	15.00	30.00
7113	Tusken Raider Encounter	20.00	40.00
7133	Bounty Hunter Pursuit	30.00	60.00
7143	Jedi Starfighter	30.00	60.00
7153	Jango Fett's Slave I	125.00	250.00
7163	Republic Gunship	125.00	250.00

2002 LEGO Star Wars Episode IV

7142	X-wing Fighter	100.00	200.00
7152	TIE Fighter & Y-wing		

2002 LEGO Star Wars Episode V

7119	Twin-Pod Cloud Car	25.00	50.00

2002 LEGO Star Wars Episode VI

7139	Ewok Attack	40.00	80.00
7200	Final Duel I	30.00	60.00
7201	Final Duel II	20.00	40.00

2002 LEGO Star Wars Miniature Building Set

3219	Mini TIE Fighter	15.00	30.00

2002 LEGO Star Wars Product Collection

65081	R2-D2 & C-3PO Droid Collectors Set	50.00	100.00
65145	X-wing Fighter TIE Fighter & Y-wing Fighter Collectors Set		
65153	Jango Fett's Slave I with Bonus Cargo Case		

2002 LEGO Star Wars Technic

8009 R2-D2	30.00	60.00
8010 Darth Vader	60.00	120.00
8011 Jango Fett	40.00	80.00
8012 Super Battle Droid	20.00	40.00

2002 LEGO Star Wars Ultimate Collector Series

7194 Yoda	300.00	600.00
10026 Naboo Starfighter Special Edition	300.00	600.00
10030 Imperial Star Destroyer	1,200.00	2,000.00

2003 LEGO Star Wars Episode II

4482 AT-TE	120.00	250.00
4478 Geonosian Fighter	90.00	150.00
4481 Hailfire Droid	60.00	120.00

2003 LEGO Star Wars Episode IV

4477 T-16 Skyhopper	20.00	40.00

2003 LEGO Star Wars Episode V

4483 AT-AT	250.00	500.00
4479 TIE Bomber	100.00	200.00
10123 Cloud City	600.00	1,000.00

2003 LEGO Star Wars Episode VI

4475 Jabba's Message	25.00	50.00
4476 Jabba's Prize	80.00	150.00
4480 Jabba's Palace	100.00	200.00

2003 LEGO Star Wars Miniature Building Set

4484 X-Wing Fighter & TIE Advanced	20.00	40.00
4485 Sebulba's Podracer & Anakin's Podracer	10.00	20.00
4486 AT-ST & Snowspeeder	20.00	40.00
4487 Jedi Starfighter & Slave I	12.00	25.00
4488 Millennium Falcon	25.00	50.00
4489 AT-AT	12.00	25.00
4490 Republic Gunship	8.00	15.00
4491 MTT	10.00	20.00

2003 LEGO Star Wars Product Collection

4207901 Star Wars MINI Bonus Pack		

2003 LEGO Star Wars Ultimate Collector Series

10129 Rebel Snowspeeder	600.00	1,200.00

2004 LEGO Star Wars Episode IV

4501 Mos Eisley Cantina	100.00	200.00
7262 TIE Fighter and Y-Wing	30.00	60.00

2004 LEGO Star Wars Episode V

4500 Rebel Snowspeeder	25.00	50.00
4502 X-wing Fighter	100.00	200.00
4504 Millennium Falcon	120.00	250.00

2004 LEGO Star Wars Legends

10131 TIE Fighter Collection	150.00	300.00

2004 LEGO Star Wars Miniature Building Set

4492 Star Destroyer	20.00	40.00
4493 Sith Infiltrator	8.00	15.00
4494 Imperial Shuttle	15.00	30.00
4495 AT-TE	12.00	25.00
6963 X-wing Fighter	15.00	30.00
6964 Boba Fett's Slave I	12.00	25.00
6965 TIE Interceptor	12.00	25.00

2004 LEGO Star Wars Product Collection

65707 Bonus/Value Pack

2004 LEGO Star Wars Ultimate Collector Series

10134 Y-wing Attack Starfighter	600.00	1,000.00

2005 LEGO Star Wars Episode III

6966 Jedi Starfighter	8.00	15.00
6967 ARC Fighter	8.00	15.00
6968 Wookiee Attack		
7250 Clone Scout Walker	30.00	60.00
7251 Darth Vader Transformation	50.00	100.00
7252 Droid Tri-Fighter	20.00	40.00
7255 General Grievous Chase	60.00	120.00
7256 Jedi Starfighter and Vulture Droid	40.00	80.00
7257 Ultimate Lightsaber Duel	100.00	200.00
7258 Wookiee Attack	60.00	120.00
7259 ARC-170 Fighter	60.00	120.00
7260 Wookiee Catamaran	50.00	100.00
7261 Clone Turbo Tank	120.00	250.00
7283 Ultimate Space Battle	150.00	300.00

2005 LEGO Star Wars Episode IV

7263 TIE Fighter	50.00	100.00
10144 Sandcrawler	200.00	400.00

2005 LEGO Star Wars Episode VI

7264 Imperial Inspection	100.00	200.00

2005 LEGO Star Wars Product Collection

65771 Episode III Collectors' Set	100.00	200.00
65828 Bonus/Value Pack		
65844 Bonus/Value Pack		
65845 Bonus/Value Pack		

2005 LEGO Star Wars Exclusives

PROMOSW002 Anakin Skywalker

  (2005 International Toy Fair Exclusive)

PROMOSW003 Luminara Unduli (2005 International Toy Fair Exclusive)

SW117PROMO Darth Vader (2005 Nurnberg Toy Fair Exclusive)

TF05 Star Wars V.I.P. Gala Set

  (2005 International Toy Fair Exclusive)

2005 LEGO Star Wars Ultimate Collector Series

10143 Death Star II	400.00	800.00

2006 LEGO Star Wars Episode III

6205 V-wing Fighter	25.00	50.00
72612 Clone Turbo Tank (non-light-up edition)	150.00	300.00

2006 LEGO Star Wars Episode IV

6211 Imperial Star Destroyer	150.00	300.00

2006 LEGO Star Wars Episode V

6209 Slave I	80.00	150.00
6212 X-wing Fighter	80.00	150.00

2006 LEGO Star Wars Episode VI

6206 TIE Interceptor	50.00	100.00
6207 A-wing Fighter	30.00	60.00
6208 B-wing Fighter	30.00	60.00
6210 Jabba's Sail Barge	200.00	350.00

2006 LEGO Star Wars Product Collection

66142 Bonus/Value Pack

66150 Bonus/Value Pack

66221 Bonus/Value Pack

2006 LEGO Star Wars Ultimate Collector Series

10174	Imperial AT-ST	275.00	550.00
10175	Vader's TIE Advanced	350.00	700.00

2007 LEGO Star Wars Episode I

7660	Naboo N-1 Starfighter with Vulture Droid	20.00	40.00
7662	Trade Federation MTT	150.00	300.00
7663	Sith Infiltrator	25.00	50.00
7665	Republic Cruiser	100.00	200.00

2007 LEGO Star Wars Episode III

7654	Droids Battle Pack	25.00	50.00
7655	Clone Troopers Battle Pack	25.00	50.00
7656	General Grievous Starfighter	40.00	80.00
7661	Jedi Starfighter with Hyperdrive Booster Ring	60.00	120.00

2007 LEGO Star Wars Episode IV

7658	Y-wing Fighter	50.00	100.00
7659	Imperial Landing Craft	50.00	100.00

2007 LEGO Star Wars Episode V

7666	Hoth Rebel Base	100.00	200.00
10178	Motorised Walking AT-AT	300.00	600.00

2007 LEGO Star Wars Episode VI

7657	AT-ST	80.00	150.00

2007 LEGO Star Wars Legends

7664	TIE Crawler	50.00	100.00

2007 LEGO Star Wars Minifigure Pack

4521221	Gold chrome plated C-3PO	250.00	500.00
PROMOSW004	Star Wars Celebration IV Exclusive/500*	600.00	1,000.00

2007 LEGO Star Wars Ultimate Collector Series

10179	Ultimate Collector's Millennium Falcon	3,000.00	5,000.00

2008 LEGO Star Wars The Clone Wars

7669	Anakin's Jedi Starfighter	40.00	80.00
7670	Hailfire Droid & Spider Droid	30.00	60.00
7673	MagnaGuard Starfighter	30.00	80.00
7674	V-19 Torrent	80.00	150.00
7675	AT-TE Walker	120.00	250.00
7676	Republic Attack Gunship	175.00	350.00
7678	Droid Gunship	30.00	60.00
7679	Republic Fighter Tank	80.00	150.00
7680	The Twilight	80.00	150.00
7681	Separatist Spider Droid	50.00	100.00
8031	V-19 Torrent	10.00	20.00
20006	Clone Turbo Tank	20.00	40.00

2008 LEGO Star Wars Episode III

7671	AT-AP Walker	40.00	80.00

2008 LEGO Star Wars Episode V

8029	Mini Snowspeeder	6.00	12.00

2008 LEGO Star Wars Legends

7667	Imperial Dropship	30.00	60.00
7668	Rebel Scout Speeder	25.00	50.00
7672	Rogue Shadow	120.00	250.00

2008 LEGO Star Wars Miniature Building Set

8028	TIE Fighter	6.00	15.00

2008 LEGO Star Wars Miscellaneous

COMCON001 Clone Wars

(2008 SDCC Exclusive)

2008 LEGO Star Wars Ultimate Collector Series

10186	General Grievous	120.00	200.00
10188	Death Star	225.00	450.00

2009 LEGO Star Wars The Clone Wars

7748	Corporate Alliance Tank Droid	25.00	50.00
7751	Ahsoka's Starfighter and Droids	80.00	150.00
7752	Count Dooku's Solar Sailer	40.00	80.00
7753	Pirate Tank	50.00	100.00
8014	Clone Walker Battle Pack	30.00	60.00
8015	Assassin Droids Battle Pack	12.00	25.00
8016	Hyena Droid Bomber	25.00	50.00
8018	Armored Assault Tank (AAT)	100.00	200.00
8019	Republic Attack Shuttle	60.00	120.00
8033	General Grievous' Starfighter	8.00	15.00
8036	Separatist Shuttle	30.00	60.00
8037	Anakin's Y-wing Starfighter	80.00	150.00
8039	Venator-Class Republic Attack Cruiser	175.00	350.00
10195	Republic Dropship with AT-OT Walker	300.00	600.00
20007	Republic Attack Cruiser	12.00	25.00
20009	AT-TE Walker	10.00	20.00
20010	Republic Gunship	15.00	30.00
30004	Battle Droid on STAP	10.00	20.00
30006	Clone Walker	10.00	20.00
COMCON010	Mini Republic Dropship Mini AT-TE Brickmaster Pack		

(SDCC 2009 Exclusive)

2009 LEGO Star Wars Episode IV

7778	Midi-scale Millennium Falcon	60.00	120.00
8017	Darth Vader's TIE Fighter	60.00	120.00
10198	Tantive IV	150.00	300.00

2009 LEGO Star Wars Episode V

7749	Echo Base	40.00	80.00

2009 LEGO Star Wars Episode VI

7754	Home One Mon Calamari Star Cruiser	100.00	200.00
8038	The Battle of Endor	100.00	200.00
30005	Imperial Speeder Bike	12.00	25.00

2009 LEGO Star Wars Minifigure Pack

4547551	Chrome Darth Vader	120.00	250.00

2009 LEGO Star Wars SDCC Exclusives

COMCON004	Collectible Display Set 1
COMCON005	Collectible Display Set 2
COMCON006	Collectible Display Set 4
COMCON007	Collectible Display Set 5
COMCON008	Collectible Display Set 3
COMCON009	Collectible Display Set 6
COMCON011	Holo-Brick Archives

2009 LEGO Star Wars Product Collection

66308	3 in 1 Superpack	

2010 LEGO Star Wars The Clone Wars

8085	Freeco Speeder	20.00	40.00
8086	Droid Tri-Fighter	25.00	50.00
8093	Plo Koon's Jedi Starfighter	25.00	50.00
8095	General Grievous' Starfighter	40.00	80.00
8098	Clone Turbo Tank	120.00	250.00
8128	Cad Bane's Speeder	25.00	50.00
30050	Republic Attack Shuttle	10.00	20.00

2010 LEGO Star Wars Episode III

8088	ARC-170 Starfighter	80.00	150.00
8091	Republic Swamp Speeder	30.00	60.00
8096	Emperor Palpatine's Shuttle	60.00	120.00

2010 LEGO Star Wars Episode IV

8092	Luke's Landspeeder	50.00	100.00
8099	Midi-Scale Imperial Star Destroyer	60.00	120.00

2010 LEGO Star Wars Episode V

8083	Rebel Trooper Battle Pack	12.00	25.00
8084	Snowtrooper Battle Pack	12.00	25.00
8089	Hoth Wampa Cave	50.00	100.00
8097	Slave I	100.00	200.00
8129	AT-AT Walker	150.00	300.00
20018	AT-AT Walker	12.00	25.00

2010 LEGO Star Wars Legends

8087	TIE Defender	80.00	150.00

2010 LEGO Star Wars Miniature Building Set

20016	Imperial Shuttle	10.00	20.00

2010 LEGO Star Wars Minifigure Pack

2853590	Chrome Stormtrooper	40.00	80.00
2853835	White Boba Fett Figure	60.00	120.00

2010 LEGO Star Wars Miscellaneous

BOBAFETT1 White Boba Fett minifig and Star Wars Book

2010 LEGO Star Wars Product Collection

66341	Star Wars Super Pack 3 in 1		
66364	Star Wars Super Pack 3 in 1		
66366	Star Wars Super Pack 3 in 1		
66368	Star Wars Super Pack 3 in 1		

2010 LEGO Star Wars Ultimate Collector Series

10212	Imperial Shuttle	350.00	700.00
10215	Obi-Wan's Jedi Starfighter	100.00	200.00

2011 LEGO Star Wars The Clone Wars

7868	Mace Windu's Jedi Starfighter	60.00	120.00
7869	Battle for Geonosis	40.00	80.00
7913	Clone Trooper Battle Pack	25.00	50.00
7914	Mandalorian Battle Pack	15.00	30.00
7930	Bounty Hunter Assault Gunship	50.00	100.00
7931	T-6 Jedi Shuttle	40.00	80.00
7957	Sith Nightspeeder	25.00	50.00
7959	Geonosian Starfighter	40.00	80.00
7964	Republic Frigate	120.00	250.00
20021	Bounty Hunter Assault Gunship	10.00	20.00
30053	Republic Attack Cruiser	8.00	15.00

2011 LEGO Star Wars Episode I

7877	Naboo Starfighter	25.00	50.00
7929	The Battle of Naboo	20.00	40.00
7961	Darth Maul's Sith Infiltrator	50.00	100.00
7962	Anakin Skywalker and Sebulba's Podracers	60.00	120.00
30052	AAT	8.00	15.00

2011 LEGO Star Wars Episode IV

7965	Millennium Falcon	200.00	400.00

2011 LEGO Star Wars Episode V

7879 Hoth Echo Base	150.00	300.00
20019 Slave I	15.00	30.00

2011 LEGO Star Wars Episode VI

7956 Ewok Attack	20.00	40.00
30054 AT-ST	10.00	20.00

2011 LEGO Star Wars Legends

7915 Imperial V-wing Starfighter	20.00	50.00

2011 LEGO Star Wars Miniature Building Set

30051 Mini X-wing	8.00	15.00
30055 Vulture Droid	8.00	15.00

2011 LEGO Star Wars Minifigure Pack

2856197 Shadow ARF Trooper	40.00	80.00

2011 LEGO Star Wars Exclusive

PROMOSW007 Star Wars Miniland Figures

(2011 Toy Fair Collector's Party Exclusive)

2011 LEGO Star Wars Product Collection

66377 Star Wars Super Pack 3 in 1	60.00	120.00
66378 Star Wars Super Pack 3 in 1		
66395 Star Wars Super Pack 3 in 1	60.00	120.00
66396 Star Wars Super Pack 3 in 1		

2011 LEGO Star Wars Seasonal Set

COMCON015 Advent calendar		
(2011 SDCC Exclusive)	60.00	120.00
7958 Star Wars Advent Calendar	30.00	60.00

2011 LEGO Star Wars Ultimate Collector Series

10221 Super Star Destroyer	600.00	1,100.00

2012 LEGO Star Wars The Clone Wars

9488 Elite Clone Trooper & Commando Droid Battle Pack	15.00	30.00

9491 Geonosian Cannon	25.00	50.00
9498 Saesee Tiin's Jedi Starfighter	30.00	60.00
9515 Malevolence	120.00	250.00
9525 Pre Vizsla's Mandalorian Fighter	60.00	120.00
30059 MTT	8.00	15.00

2012 LEGO Star Wars Episode I

9499 Gungan Sub	80.00	150.00
30057 Anakin's Pod Racer	6.00	12.00
30058 STAP	8.00	15.00
5000063 Chrome TC-14	25.00	50.00
COMCON019 Sith Infiltrator		
(2012 SDCC Exclusive)	80.00	150.00

2012 LEGO Star Wars Episode III

9494 Anakin's Jedi Interceptor	60.00	120.00
9526 Palpatine's Arrest	80.00	150.00

2012 LEGO Star Wars Episode IV

9490 Droid Escape	30.00	60.00
9492 TIE Fighter	100.00	200.00
9493 X-wing Starfighter	100.00	200.00
9495 Gold Leader's Y-wing Starfighter	80.00	150.00
COMCON024 Luke Skywalker's Landspeeder Mini	120.00	250.00
(2012 NYCC Exclusive)		

2012 LEGO Star Wars Episode V

CELEBVI Mini Slave I

(2012 Star Wars Celebration VI Exclusive)   100.00   200.00

2012 LEGO Star Wars Episode VI

9489	Endor Rebel Trooper & Imperial Trooper Battle Pack	25.00	50.00
9496	Desert Skiff	50.00	100.00
9516	Jabba's Palace	100.00	200.00

2012 LEGO Star Wars Miniature Building Set

30056	Star Destroyer	8.00	15.00

2012 LEGO Star Wars Minifigure Pack

5000062	Darth Maul	15.00	30.00

2012 LEGO Star Wars The Old Republic

9497	Republic Striker-class Starfighter	40.00	80.00
9500	Sith Fury-class Interceptor	100.00	200.00

2012 LEGO Star Wars Planet Set

9674	Naboo Starfighter & Naboo	10.00	20.00
9675	Sebulba's Podracer & Tatooine	8.00	15.00
9676	TIE Interceptor & Death Star	15.00	30.00
9677	X-wing Starfighter & Yavin 4	10.00	20.00
9678	Twin-Pod Cloud Car & Bespin	10.00	20.00
9679	AT-ST & Endor	8.00	15.00

2012 LEGO Star Wars Product Collection

66411	Super Pack 3-in-1		
66431	Super Pack 3-in-1		
66432	Super Pack 3-in-1		

2012 LEGO Star Wars Seasonal Set

9509	Star Wars Advent Calendar	30.00	60.00

2012 LEGO Star Wars Ultimate Collector Series

10225	R2-D2	200.00	400.00
10227	B-Wing Starfighter	175.00	350.00

2013 LEGO Star Wars The Clone Wars

11905	Brickmaster Star Wars: Battle for the Stolen Crystals parts		
30240	Z-95 Headhunter	8.00	15.00
30241	Mandalorian Fighter	8.00	15.00
30242	Republic Frigate	8.00	15.00
30243	Umbaran MHC	8.00	15.00
75002	AT-RT	25.00	50.00
75004	Z-95 Headhunter	40.00	80.00
75012	BARC Speeder with Sidecar	60.00	120.00
75013	Umbaran MHC (Mobile Heavy Cannon)	40.00	80.00
75022	Mandalorian Speeder	40.00	80.00
75024	HH-87 Starhopper	50.00	100.00

2013 LEGO Star Wars Episode II

75000	Clone Troopers vs. Droidekas	20.00	40.00
75015	Corporate Alliance Tank Droid	30.00	60.00
75016	Homing Spider Droid	25.00	50.00
75017	Duel on Geonosis	50.00	100.00
75019	AT-TE	100.00	200.00
75021	Republic Gunship	150.00	300.00
5001709	Clone Trooper Lieutenant	8.00	15.00

2013 LEGO Star Wars Episode V

75014	Battle of Hoth	80.00	150.00
5001621	Han Solo (Hoth)	8.00	15.00

2013 LEGO Star Wars Episode VI

75003	A-wing Starfighter	30.00	60.00
75005	Rancor Pit	100.00	200.00
75020	Jabba's Sail Barge	120.00	250.00

2013 LEGO Star Wars The Old Republic

75001	Republic Troopers vs. Sith Troopers	20.00	40.00
75025	Jedi Defender-class Cruiser	60.00	120.00

2013 LEGO Star Wars Originals

75018	JEK-14's Stealth Starfighter	80.00	150.00
COMCON032	Jek-14 Mini Stealth Starfighter		
	(2013 SDCC Exclusive)	120.00	250.00
MAY2013	Holocron Droid	12.00	25.00
TRU03	Mini Jek-14 Stealth Fighter		
	(2013 Toys R Us Exclusive)	12.00	25.00
YODACHRON	Yoda Chronicles Promotional Set		

2013 LEGO Star Wars Planet Set

75006	Jedi Starfighter & Planet Kamino	12.00	25.00
75007	Republic Assault Ship & Planet Coruscant	8.00	15.00
75008	TIE Bomber & Asteroid Field	12.00	25.00

75009	Snowspeeder & Hoth	25.00	50.00
75010	B-Wing Starfighter & Planet Endor	20.00	40.00
75011	Tantive IV & Planet Alderaan	25.00	50.00

2013 LEGO Star Wars Product Collection

66449	Super Pack 3-in-1	80.00	150.00
66456	Star Wars Value Pack	100.00	200.00
66473	LEGO Star Wars Super Pack	120.00	250.00

2013 LEGO Star Wars Promotional Set

NYCC2013	Yoda display box		
	(2013 NYCC Exclusive)		
YODA	Yoda minifig, NY I Heart Torso	120.00	250.00

2013 LEGO Star Wars Seasonal Set

75023	Star Wars Advent Calendar		

2013 LEGO Star Wars Ultimate Collector Series

10236	Ewok Village	175.00	350.00
10240	Red Five X-wing Starfighter	150.00	300.00

2014 LEGO Star Wars The Clone Wars

75045	Republic AV-7 Anti-Vehicle Cannon	50.00	100.00
75046	Coruscant Police Gunship	50.00	100.00

2014 LEGO Star Wars Episode I

75058	MTT	80.00	150.00

2014 LEGO Star Wars Episode III

30244	Anakin's Jedi Interceptor	8.00	15.00
30247	ARC-170 Starfighter	8.00	15.00
75035	Kashyyyk Troopers	20.00	40.00
75036	Utapau Troopers	20.00	40.00
75037	Battle on Saleucami	25.00	50.00
75038	Jedi Interceptor	50.00	100.00
75039	V-Wing Starfighter	30.00	60.00
75040	General Grievous' Wheel Bike	40.00	80.00
75041	Vulture Droid	40.00	80.00
75042	Droid Gunship	60.00	120.00
75043	AT-AP	100.00	200.00
75044	Droid Tri-Fighter	25.00	50.00

2014 LEGO Star Wars Episode IV

75034	Death Star Troopers	25.00	50.00
75052	Mos Eisley Cantina	60.00	120.00
75055	Imperial Star Destroyer	200.00	400.00

2014 LEGO Star Wars Episode V

75049 Snowspeeder	50.00	100.00
75054 AT-AT	150.00	300.00

2014 LEGO Star Wars Episode VI

30246 Imperial Shuttle	12.00	25.00
75050 B-Wing	40.00	80.00

2014 LEGO Star Wars MicroFighters

75029 AAT	15.00	30.00
75028 Clone Turbo Tank	20.00	40.00
75030 Millennium Falcon	25.00	50.00
75031 TIE Interceptor	15.00	30.00
75032 X-Wing Fighter	15.00	30.00
75033 Star Destroyer	12.00	25.00

2014 LEGO Star Wars Minifigure Pack

5002122 TC-4	15.00	30.00

2014 LEGO Star Wars The Old Republic

5002123 Darth Revan	25.00	50.00

2014 LEGO Star Wars Original Content

5051 Jedi Scout Fighter	60.00	120.00

2014 LEGO Star Wars Product Collection

66479 Value Pack		
66495 Star Wars Value Pack		
66512 Rebels Co-Pack		
66514 Microfighter Super Pack 3 in 1		
66515 Microfighter Super Pack 3 in 1		

2014 LEGO Star Wars Toys R Us Exclusives

TRUGHOST The Ghost micro-model	10.00	20.00
TRUTIE TIE Fighter		
TRUXWING X-wing		

2014 LEGO Star Wars Rebels

75048 The Phantom	80.00	150.00
75053 The Ghost	100.00	200.00
COMCON039 The Ghost Starship		
(2014 SDCC Exclusive)	80.00	150.00
FANEXPO001 The Ghost Starship		
(2014 Fan Expo Exclusive)	60.00	120.00

2014 LEGO Star Wars Seasonal Set

5056 Star Wars Advent Calendar		

2014 LEGO Star Wars Ultimate Collector Series

75059 Sandcrawler	175.00	350.00

2015 LEGO Star Wars Buildable Figures

75107 Jango Fett	20.00	40.00
75108 Clone Commander Cody	12.00	25.00
75109 Obi-Wan Kenobi	20.00	40.00
75110 Luke Skywalker	25.00	50.00
75111 Darth Vader	25.00	50.00
75112 General Grievous	40.00	80.00

2015 LEGO Star Wars The Clone Wars

75087 Anakin's Custom Jedi Starfighter	25.00	50.00

2015 LEGO Star Wars Episode I

75080 AAT	20.00	40.00
75086 Battle Droid Troop Carrier	30.00	60.00
75091 Flash Speeder	20.00	40.00
75092 Naboo Starfighter	30.00	60.00
75096 Sith Infiltrator	50.00	100.00

2015 LEGO Star Wars Episode II

75085 Hailfire Droid	25.00	50.00

2015 LEGO Star Wars Episode IV

75081 T-16 Skyhopper	25.00	50.00
5002947 Admiral Yularen	10.00	20.00

2015 LEGO Star Wars Episode VI

30272 A-Wing Starfighter	10.00	20.00
75093 Death Star Final Duel	50.00	100.00
75094 Imperial Shuttle Tydirium	60.00	120.00

2015 LEGO Star Wars The Force Awakens

30276 First Order Special Forces TIE Fighter	6.00	12.00
75099 Rey's Speeder	12.00	30.00
75100 First Order Snowspeeder	25.00	50.00
75101 First Order Special Forces TIE Fighter	40.00	80.00
75102 Poe's X-wing Fighter	50.00	100.00
75103 First Order Transporter	60.00	120.00
75104 Kylo Ren's Command Shuttle	60.00	120.00
75105 Millennium Falcon	100.00	200.00
5002948 C-3PO	10.00	20.00
30UNIQUE15 Force Friday Commemorative Brick		

2015 LEGO Star Wars Legends

75079 Shadow Troopers	15.00	30.00
75088 Senate Commando Troopers	10.00	20.00
75089 Geonosis Troopers	20.00	40.00

2015 LEGO Star Wars Magazine Gift

SW911506 Snowspeeder	8.00	15.00
SW911508 Mini Slave I		
SW911509 Imperial Shooter	8.00	15.00
SW911510 Micro Star Destroyer and TIE Fighter		
SW911511 Jedi Weapon Stand		
SWCOMIC1 Mini X-Wing Starfighter	15.00	30.00

2015 LEGO Star Wars MicroFighters

75072 ARC-170 Starfighter	15.00	30.00
75073 Vulture Droid	12.00	25.00
75074 Snowspeeder	12.00	25.00
75075 AT-AT	20.00	40.00
75076 Republic Gunship	12.00	25.00
75077 Homing Spider Droid	15.00	30.00

2015 LEGO Star Wars Product Collection

66533 Microfighter 3 in 1 Super Pack	25.00	50.00
66534 Microfighter 3 in 1 Super Pack	25.00	50.00
66535 Battle Pack 2 in 1	50.00	100.00
66536 Luke Skywalker and Darth Vader	50.00	100.00

2015 LEGO Star Wars Exclusives

CELEB2015 Tatooine Mini-build		
(2015 Star Wars Celebration Exclusive)	50.00	100.00
FANEXPO2015 Tatooine Mini Build		

(2015 Fan Expo Exclusive)	80.00	150.00
SDCC2015 Dagobah Mini Build		
(2015 SDCC Exclusive)	100.00	200.00
TRUWOOKIEE Wookiee Gunship		
(2015 Toys R Us Exclusive)	8.00	15.00
TRUXWING Poe's X-wing Fighter		
(2015 Toys R Us Exclusive)	10.00	20.00

2015 LEGO Star Wars Rebels

30274 AT-DP	8.00	15.00
30275 TIE Advanced Prototype	8.00	15.00
75078 Imperial Troop Transport	12.00	25.00
75082 TIE Advanced Prototype	20.00	40.00
75083 AT-DP	50.00	100.00
75084 Wookiee Gunship	50.00	100.00
75090 Ezra's Speeder Bike	15.00	30.00
75106 Imperial Assault Carrier	80.00	150.00
5002938 Stormtrooper Sergeant	8.00	15.00
5002939 The Phantom	8.00	15.00

2015 LEGO Star Wars Seasonal Set

75097 Star Wars Advent Calendar		

2015 LEGO Star Wars Ultimate Collector Series

75060 Slave I	120.00	250.00
75095 TIE Fighter	100.00	200.00

2016 LEGO Star Wars Battlefront

75133 Rebel Alliance Battle Pack	20.00	40.00
75134 Galactic Empire Battle Pack	15.00	30.00

2016 LEGO Star Wars Buildable Figures

75113	Rey	12.00	25.00
75114	First Order Stormtrooper	12.00	25.00
75115	Poe Dameron	12.00	25.00
75116	Finn	10.00	20.00
75117	Kylo Ren	12.00	25.00
75118	Captain Phasma	15.00	30.00
75119	Sergeant Jyn Erso	15.00	30.00
75120	K-2SO	15.00	30.00
75121	Imperial Death Trooper	12.00	25.00

2016 LEGO Star Wars Episode III

75135	Obi-Wan's Jedi Interceptor	30.00	75.00
75142	Homing Spider Droid	25.00	50.00
75151	Clone Turbo Tank	50.00	100.00

2016 LEGO Star Wars Episode IV

75136	Droid Escape Pod	20.00	40.00

2016 LEGO Star Wars Episode V

75137	Carbon-Freezing Chamber	20.00	40.00
75138	Hoth Attack	25.00	50.00

2016 LEGO Star Wars The Force Awakens

30277	First Order Star Destroyer	8.00	15.00
30278	Poe's X-wing Fighter	6.00	12.00
30279	Kylo Ren's Command Shuttle	6.00	12.00
30602	First Order Stormtrooper	10.00	20.00
30605	Finn (FN-2187)	6.00	12.00
75131	Resistance Trooper Battle Pack	10.00	20.00
75132	First Order Battle Pack	10.00	20.00
75139	Battle on Takodana	25.00	50.00
75140	Resistance Troop Transporter	30.00	75.00
75148	Encounter on Jakku	25.00	50.00
75149	Resistance X-wing Fighter	60.00	120.00
5004406	First Order General	8.00	15.00

2016 LEGO Star Wars Magazine Gift

SW911607	Millennium Falcon	6.00	12.00
SW911608	Landspeeder	6.00	12.00
SW911609	Naboo Starfighter	6.00	12.00
SW911610	Probe Droid	6.00	12.00
SW911611	AAT	6.00	12.00
SW911612	Acklay	6.00	12.00
SW911613	TIE Bomber	6.00	12.00

SW911614	Yoda's Hut	6.00	12.00
SW911615	AT-AT	6.00	12.00
SW911616	MTT	6.00	12.00
SW911617	Palpatine's Shuttle	6.00	12.00

2016 LEGO Star Wars MicroFighters

75125	Resistance X-wing Fighter	12.00	25.00
75126	First Order Snowspeeder	10.00	20.00
75127	The Ghost	12.00	25.00
75128	TIE Advanced Prototype	12.00	25.00
75129	Wookiee Gunship	8.00	15.00
75130	AT-DP	12.00	25.00

2016 LEGO Star Wars Miscellaneous

11912 Star Wars: Build Your Own Adventure parts

2016 LEGO Star Wars Originals

75145	Eclipse Fighter	20.00	40.00
75147	StarScavenger	20.00	40.00

2016 LEGO Star Wars Product Collection

66542	Microfighters Super Pack 3 in 1	12.00	25.00
66543	Microfighters Super Pack 3 in 1	15.00	30.00
5005217	Death Star Ultimate Kit		

2016 LEGO Star Wars Promotional Set

6176782	Escape the Space Slug	75.00	150.00
TRUFALCON	Millennium Falcon		
	(2016 Toys R Us Exclusive)		

2016 LEGO Star Wars Rebels

75141	Kanan's Speeder Bike	25.00	50.00
75150	Vader's TIE Advanced vs. A-wing Starfighter	50.00	100.00
75157	Captain Rex's AT-TE	50.00	100.00
75158	Rebel Combat Frigate	60.00	120.00
5004408	Rebel A-wing Pilot	6.00	12.00

2016 LEGO Star Wars Rogue One

75152	Imperial Assault Hovertank	25.00	50.00
75153	AT-ST Walker	30.00	60.00
75154	TIE Striker	25.00	50.00
75155	Rebel U-wing Fighter	30.00	75.00
75156	Krennic's Imperial Shuttle	60.00	120.00

2016 LEGO Star Wars Seasonal Set

75146	Star Wars Advent Calendar	30.00	75.00

2016 LEGO Star Wars Ultimate Collector Series

75098	Assault on Hoth	200.00	400.00
75159	Death Star	250.00	500.00

2017 LEGO Star Wars BrickHeadz

41498	Boba Fett & Han Solo in Carbonite	
	NYCC Exclusive	

2017 LEGO Star Wars Buildable Figures

75523	Scarif Stormtrooper	12.00	25.00
75524	Chirrut Imwe	15.00	30.00
75525	Baze Malbus	12.00	25.00
75526	Elite TIE Fighter Pilot	15.00	30.00
75528	Rey	15.00	30.00
75529	Elite Praetorian Guard	20.00	40.00
75530	Chewbacca	25.00	50.00
75531	Stormtrooper Commander	12.00	25.00
75532	Scout Trooper & Speeder Bike	20.00	40.00

2017 LEGO Star Wars The Clone Wars

75168	Yoda's Jedi Starfighter	20.00	40.00

2017 LEGO Star Wars Episode I

75169	Duel on Naboo	12.00	25.00

2017 LEGO Star Wars Episode II

75191	Jedi Starfighter (w/hyperdrive)	60.00	120.00

2017 LEGO Star Wars Episode III

75183	Darth Vader Transformation	20.00	40.00

2017 LEGO Star Wars Episode IV

75173	Luke's Landspeeder	25.00	50.00

2017 LEGO Star Wars Episode VI

75174	Desert Skiff Escape	20.00	40.00
75175	A-Wing Starfighter	30.00	60.00

2017 LEGO Star Wars The Force Awakens

75166	First Order Transport Speeder Battle Pack	15.00	30.00
75178	Jakku Quadjumper	25.00	50.00
75180	Rathtar Escape	50.00	100.00

2017 LEGO Star Wars The Last Jedi

30497	First Order Heavy Assault Walker	8.00	15.00
75176	Resistance Transport Pod	20.00	40.00
75177	First Order Heavy Scout Walker	30.00	75.00
75179	Kylo Ren's TIE Fighter	50.00	100.00
75187	BB-8	100.00	200.00
75188	Resistance Bomber	75.00	150.00
75189	First Order Heavy Assault Walker	150.00	300.00
75190	First Order Star Destroyer	150.00	300.00

2017 LEGO Star Wars Legends

75182	Republic Fighter Tank	15.00	30.00

2017 LEGO Star Wars Magazine Gift

- SW911618 Flash Speeder
- SW911719 Kanan Jarrus
- SW911720 The Ghost
- SW911721 Imperial Combat Driver
- SW911722 TIE Advanced
- SW911723 Vulture Droid
- SW911724 A-Wing
- SW911725 Sandcrawler
- SW911726 Imperial Snowtrooper
- SW911727 Rey's Speeder
- SW911728 First Order Snowspeeder

2017 LEGO Star Wars MicroFighters

75160	U-Wing	8.00	15.00
75161	TIE Striker	8.00	15.00
75162	Y-Wing	8.00	15.00
75163	Krennic's Imperial Shuttle	8.00	15.00

2017 LEGO Star Wars Originals

75167	Bounty Hunter Speeder Bike Battle Pack	12.00	25.00
75185	Tracker I	30.00	75.00
75186	The Arrowhead	60.00	120.00

2017 LEGO Star Wars Promotional

30611	R2-D2	12.00	25.00
CELEB2017	Detention Block Rescue	120.00	250.00
TRULEIA	Princess Leia		

2017 LEGO Star Wars Rebels

75170	The Phantom	20.00	40.00

2017 LEGO Star Wars Rogue One

30496	U-Wing Fighter	6.00	12.00
40176	Scarif Stormtrooper	12.00	25.00
40268	R3-M2	8.00	15.00
75164	Rebel Trooper Battle Pack	15.00	30.00
75165	Imperial Trooper Battle Pack	15.00	30.00
75171	Battle on Scarif	30.00	75.00
75172	Y-Wing Starfighter	30.00	75.00

2017 LEGO Star Wars Seasonal

75184	Star Wars Advent Calendar	30.00	60.00

2017 LEGO Star Wars Ultimate Collector Series

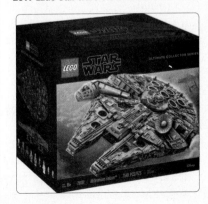

75144	Snowspeeder	120.00	250.00
75192	Millennium Falcon		

1993-97 Micro Machines Star Wars Planet Playsets

65872 Ice Planet Hoth	15.00	40.00
65995 Cloud City (w/Twin-Pod Cloud Car)	8.00	20.00
65858A Planet Tatooine (1994)	10.00	25.00
65858B Planet Tatooine (1996)	8.00	20.00
65859A Planet Dagobah (1994)	10.00	25.00
65859B Planet Dagobah (1996)		
65871A Death Star from A New Hope (1994)	10.00	25.00
65871B Death Star from A New Hope (1996)	5.00	12.00
65873A Planet Endor (w/Imperial AT-ST)(1993)	8.00	20.00
65873B Planet Endor (w/Imperial AT-ST)(1997)	6.00	15.00

1993-98 Micro Machines Star Wars Vehicle 3-Packs

65123 Imperial Landing Craft/Death Star/S-Swoop	8.00	20.00
65124 Outrider Tibanna/Gas Refinery/V-35 Landspeeder	6.00	15.00
65886 Star Wars A New Hope (silver)		
65886 Star Wars A New Hope #1	6.00	15.00
65887 Star Wars Empire Strikes Back #2		
65887 Star Wars Empire Strikes Back (silver)	5.00	12.00
65888 Star Wars Return of the Jedi (silver)		
65888 Star Wars Return of the Jedi #3		
65897 Star Wars A New Hope #4		
65898 Star Wars Empire Strikes Back #5	5.00	12.00
65899 Star Wars Return of the Jedi #6		
66111 TIE Interceptor/Imperial Star Destroyer/Rebel Blockade Runner	5.00	12.00
66112 Landspeeder/Millennium Falcon/Jawa Sandcrawler	8.00	20.00
66113 Darth Vader's TIE Fighter/Y-Wing Starfighter/X-Wing Starfighter	5.00	12.00
66114 Snowspeeder/Imperial AT-AT/Imperial Probot	15.00	40.00
66115 Rebel Transport/TIE Bomber/Imperial AT-ST	6.00	15.00
66116 Escort Frigate/Slave I/Twin-Pod Cloud Car	5.00	12.00
66117 Desert Sail Barge/Mon Calamari Star Cruiser/Speeder Bike and Rebel Pilot		

66118 Speeder Bike and Imperial Pilot/Imperial Shuttle Tydirium/TIE Starfighter		
66119 Super Star Destroyer Executor	10.00	25.00
A-Wing Starfighter/B-Wing Starfighter		
66137 Lars Family Landspeeder/Death Star II/T-16 Skyhopper	8.00	20.00
66138 Bespin Cloud City/Mon Calamari Rebel Cruiser/Escape Pod	6.00	15.00
66139 A-Wing Starfighter/Y-Wing Starfighter/TIE Starfighter	10.00	25.00
66155 2 Red Squad X-Wings/Green Squad X-Wing		

1994 Micro Machines Star Wars Fan Club Pieces

18279 Han Solo and the Millennium Falcon	6.00	15.00
28450 Darth Vader and Imperial Star Destroyer	6.00	15.00

1994-96 Micro Machines Star Wars Gift Sets

64624 Bronze Finish Collector's Gift Set	12.00	30.00
65836 Rebel Force Gift Set	6.00	15.00
65837 Imperial Force Gift Set	5.00	12.00
65847 11-Piece Collector's Gift Set	10.00	25.00
65851 A New Hope	5.00	12.00
65852 Empire Strikes Back		
65853 Return of the Jedi	8.00	20.00
65856 Rebel Force Gift Set 2nd Edition	6.00	15.00
65857 Imperial Force Gift Set 2nd Edition		
67079 Star Wars Trilogy Gift Set	15.00	40.00
68042 Rebel vs. Imperial Forces		

1994-97 Micro Machines Star Wars Collector's Sets

64598 Galaxy Battle Collector's Set 2nd Edition	8.00	20.00
64601 Master Collector's Edition (19 Items)	15.00	40.00
64602 Galaxy Battle Collector's Set	10.00	25.00
66090 Droids	10.00	25.00
68048 Master Collector's Edition (40 Items)	8.00	20.00

1994-99 Micro Machines Star Wars Transforming Action Sets

65694 TIE Fighter Pilot/Academy	10.00	25.00
65695 Royal Guard/Death Star II	15.00	40.00
65811 C-3PO/Cantina	10.00	25.00
65812 Darth Vader/Bespin	10.00	25.00
65813 R2-D2/Jabba's Palace	12.00	30.00
65814 Stormtrooper/Death Star	12.00	30.00
65815 Chewbacca/Endor	10.00	25.00
65816 Boba Fett/Cloud City	15.00	40.00
65817 Luke Skywalker/Hoth	10.00	25.00
66551 Jar Jar Binks/Naboo	6.00	15.00
66552 Battle Droid/Trade Federation Droid Control Ship		
66553 Darth Maul/Theed Generator	30.00	80.00
66554 Gungan Sub/Otoh Gunga		
67094 Star Destroyer/Space Fortress	15.00	40.00
67095 Slave I/Tatooine	10.00	25.00
68063 Yoda/Dagobah	12.00	30.00
68064 Jabba/Mos Eisley Spaceport	15.00	40.00

1995 Micro Machines Star Wars Action Fleet Playsets

67091 Ice Planet Hoth (w/Battle-Damaged Snow Speeder	10.00	25.00
Luke Skywalker on Tauntaun		
Wampa Ice Creature/Rebel Pilot/Princess Leia/2-1B Droid)		
67092 The Death Star (w/Darth Vader's Battle-Damaged TIE	10.00	25.00
Fighter/Imperial Pilot		
Imperial Gunner/Darth Vader/Stormtrooper/Imperial Royal Guard/Emperor Palpatine)		
67093 Yavin Rebel Base (w/Battle-Damaged	12.00	30.00
X-Wing/Wedge Antilles/R2 Unit		
Luke Skywalker/Han Solo/Princess Leia/Rebel Sentry)		
68177 Naboo Hangar Final Combat	20.00	50.00
(w/Obi-Wan Kenobi/Darth Maul/Qui-Gon Jinn)		

1995 Micro Machines Star Wars Gold Classic

67085 X-Wing Fighter and Slave I	12.00	30.00
67086 Imperial Shuttle		
67088 Millennium Falcon and TIE Fighter	30.00	80.00

1995-03 Micro Machines Star Wars Action Fleet Vehicles

46846 AT-TE		
46848 Solar Sailer		
46849 Millennium Falcon	12.00	30.00
46850 X-Wingfighter		
47045 Luke Skywalker's Snowspeeder		
47224 Imperial AT-AT	8.00	20.00
47287 Republic Gunship		
47305 Slave I	5.00	12.00
47356 TIE Advance X1		
47414 Naboo N-1 Starfighter		
47425 Republic Assault Ship	30.00	80.00
47766 Anakin's Speeder		
47767 Zam Wessel Speeder		
47768 Homing Spider Droid	4.00	10.00
47994 Jedi Starfighter	8.00	20.00
47995 Star Destroyer		
47997 Mon Calamari Cruiser	8.00	20.00
66989 Rancor (w/Gamorrean Guard and Luke Skywalker)	10.00	25.00
66990 Virago (w/Prince Xizor and Guri)	10.00	25.00
66991 X-Wing Starfighter (w/Wedge and R2 Unit)		
66992 Y-Wing Starfighter (red)(w/Gold Leader and R2 Unit)		
66993 A-Wing Starfighter (green)(w/Rebel pilot and Mon Mothma)	8.00	20.00
66994 B-Wing Starfighter (w/Rebel pilot and Admiral Ackbar)	10.00	25.00
66995 TIE Fighter (w/Imperial pilot and Grand Moff Tarkin)		
66996 Bespin Twin-Pod Cloud Car (w/Cloud Car pilot and Lobot)		
66997 Y-Wing Starfighter (blue)(w/Blue Leader and R2 Unit)	10.00	25.00
66998 X-Wing Starfighter (w/Jek Porkins and R2 Unit)		
67014 Jabba's Sail Barge (w/Jabba the Hutt/Saelt Marae and R2-D2	12.00	30.00
67031 Luke's X-Wing Starfighter (w/Luke and R2-D2)	15.00	40.00
67032 Darth Vader's TIE Fighter (w/Darth Vader and Imperial pilot)		
67033 Imperial AT-AT (w/Imperial drive and snowtrooper)	10.00	25.00
67034 A-Wing Starfighter (w/C-3PO and Rebel pilot)	6.00	15.00
67035 Imperial Shuttle Tydirium (w/Han Solo and Chewbacca)		
67036 Rebel Snowspeeder (w/Luke Skywalker and Rebel gunner)		
67039 Jawa Sandcrawler (w/Jawa and scavenger droid)	8.00	20.00
67040 Y-Wing Starfighter (w/Gold Leader and R2 Unit)	8.00	20.00
67041 Slave I (w/Boba Fett and Han Solo)	12.00	30.00
67058 TIE Interceptor (w/2 Imperial pilots)	8.00	20.00
67059 TIE Bomber (w/Imperial pilot and Imperial Naval pilot)	10.00	25.00
67077 Landspeeder and Imperial AT-ST 2-Pack	10.00	25.00
(w/Luke Skywalker/Obi-Wan Kenobi/Imperial Driver/Stormtrooper)		
67098 Luke's X-Wing from Dagobah (w/Luke Skywalker and R2-D2)	8.00	20.00
(1998 Toy Fair Magazine Exclusive)		
67100 Millennium Falcon (w/Han Solo and Chewbacca)		
67101 Rebel Blockade Runner (w/Princess Leia and Rebel trooper)	8.00	20.00
67102 Incom T-16 Skyhopper (w/Luke Skywalker and Biggs Darklighter)	6.00	15.00
67103 Imperial Landing Craft (w/Sandtrooper and Imperial Officer)	15.00	40.00
67105 TIE Defender (w/Imperial pilot and Moff Jerjerrod)	30.00	80.00
67106 E-Wing Starfighter (w/Rebel pilot and R7 Unit)		
68131 Naboo Starfighter (w/Anakin)		
68132 Trade Federation MTT (w/Battle Droid)	25.00	60.00
68133 Sebulba's Pod Racer (w/Sebulba)		
68134 Republic Cruiser (w/Qui-Gon Jinn)	12.00	30.00
68135 Droid Fighter (w/Daultry Dofine)		
68136 Gungan Sub (w/Qui-Gon Jinn)	4.00	10.00
68137 Flash Speeder (w/Naboo Royal Guard)		
68138 Trade Federation Landing Ship (w/Battle Droid)		
68140 Mars Guo's Pod Racer (w/Mars Guo)		
68180 Gian Speeder and Theed Palace (w/Captain Panaka/Naboo Foot Soldier/2 Battle Droids)		
79050 Anakin's Pod Racer (w/Anakin)		
79967 Royal Starship (w/Rick Olie)	25.00	60.00
79968 Droid Control Ship (w/Neimoidian Commander)		
79971 Trade Federation Tank (w/Battle Droid)	12.00	30.00
79972 Sith Infiltrator (w/Darth Maul)	30.00	80.00
1327CM6 Darth Vader's TIE Fighter (w/Darth Vader and Imperial pilot)		

1996 Micro Machines Star Wars Adventure Gear

68031 Vader's Lightsaber (w/Death Star Trench/X-Wing	8.00	20.00
Imperial Gunner/Grand Moff Tarkin/Darth Vader		
68032 Luke's Binoculars (w/Yavin Rebel Base/Y-Wing	8.00	20.00
Luke Skywalker/R5 Droid/Wedge Antilles		

1996 Micro Machines Star Wars Epic Collections

66281	Heir to the Empire	8.00	20.00
66282	Jedi Search	6.00	15.00
66283	The Truce at Bakura	8.00	20.00

1996 Micro Machines Star Wars Exclusives

66091	Balance of Power (Special Offer)		
68060	Star Wars Trilogy (Special Giveaway)	20.00	50.00

1996 Micro Machines Star Wars Shadows of the Empire

66194	Stinger/IG-2000/Guri/Darth Vader/Asp	5.00	12.00
66195	Virago/Swoop with Rider/Prince Xizor/Emperor Palpatine	6.00	15.00
66196	Outrider/Hound's Tooth/Dash Rendar/LE-B02D9	10.00	25.00

1996 Micro Machines Star Wars X-Ray Fleet

67071	Darth Vader's TIE Fighter/A-Wing Starfighter		
67072	X-Wing Starfighter/Imperial AT-AT		
67073	Millennium Falcon/Jawa Sandcrawler	6.00	15.00
67074	Boba Fett's Slave I/Y-Wing Starfighter		

1996-97 Micro Machines Star Wars Action Sets

65878	Millennium Falcon (w/Y-Wing/Mynock/Han Solo/Chewbacca	20.00	50.00
	Lando Calrissian/Nien Nunb/Leia		
65996	Rebel Transport (w/X-Wing/Rebel mechanic/General Rieekan/Major Derlin		

1996-98 Micro Machines Star Wars Character Sets

66081	Imperial Stormtroopers	10.00	25.00
66082	Ewoks	10.00	25.00
66083	Rebel Pilots	6.00	15.00
66084	Imperial Pilots	6.00	15.00
66096	Jawas	5.00	12.00
66097	Imperial Officers	6.00	15.00
66098	Echo Base Troops	5.00	12.00
66099	Imperial Naval Troops	8.00	20.00
66108	Rebel Fleet Troops	8.00	20.00
66109	Tusken Raiders	6.00	15.00
66158	Classic Characters	8.00	20.00
67112	Endor Rebel Strike Force	10.00	25.00
67113	Imperial Scout Troopers	5.00	12.00
67114	Bounty Hunters	10.00	25.00

1996-98 Micro Machines Star Wars Mini Heads

68021	Boba Fett/Admiral Ackbar/Gamorrean Guard	5.00	12.00
68022	Greedo/Nien Nunb/Tusken Raider	5.00	12.00
68023	Jawa/Yoda/Leia	5.00	12.00
68024	Bib Fortuna/Figrin D'an/Scout Trooper	4.00	10.00
68038	Darth Vader Set	5.00	10.00
68046	C-3PO Set		
NNO	Pizza Hut Set		

1996-99 Micro Machines Star Wars Battle Packs

68011	Rebel Alliance	6.00	15.00
68012	Galactic Empire	6.00	15.00
68013	Aliens and Creatures	6.00	15.00
68014	Galactic Hunters	6.00	15.00
68015	Shadow of the Empire	6.00	15.00
68016	Dune Sea	6.00	15.00
68017	Droid Escape	6.00	15.00
68018	Desert Palace	6.00	15.00
68035	Endor Adventure	8.00	20.00
68036	Mos Eisley Spaceport	12.00	30.00
68037	Cantina Encounter	6.00	15.00
68090	Cantina Smugglers and Spies	8.00	20.00
68091	Hoth Attack	10.00	25.00
68092	Death Star Escape	6.00	15.00
68093	Endor Victory	12.00	30.00
68094	Lars Family Homestead	8.00	20.00
68095	Imperial Troops	15.00	40.00
68096	Rebel Troops	10.00	25.00

1996-99 Micro Machines Star Wars Die-Cast Vehicles

66267 Death Star	10.00	25.00
66268 A-Wing Starfighter		
66269 Snowspeeder		
66270 TIE Bomber	8.00	20.00
66271 Landspeeder		
66272 Executor (w/Star Destroyer)	6.00	15.00
66273 Slave I		
66520 Royal Starship	5.00	12.00
66523 Gian Speeder		
66524 Trade Federation Battleship	6.00	15.00
66525 Sith Infiltrator	4.00	10.00
66526 Republic Cruiser		
66527 Trade Federation Tank	6.00	15.00
66528 Sebulba's Pod Racer		
79021 Trade Federation Droid Starfighter		
66261A X-Wing Starfighter (bubble)		
66261B X-Wing Starfighter (stripe)		
66262A Millennium Falcon (bubble)	5.00	12.00
66262B Millennium Falcon (stripe)	8.00	20.00
66263A Imperial Star Destroyer (bubble)	4.00	10.00
66263B Imperial Star Destroyer (stripe)	4.00	10.00
66264A TIE Fighter (bubble)		
66264B TIE Fighter (stripe)		
66265A Y-Wing Starfighter (bubble)		
66265B Y-Wing Starfighter (stripe)		
66266A Jawa Sandcrawler (bubble)	6.00	15.00
66266B Jawa Sandcrawler (stripe)	4.00	10.00

1996-99 Micro Machines Star Wars Electronic Action Fleet Vehicles

73419 AT-AT (w/Snowtrooper and Imperial Driver)	15.00	40.00
79072 FAMBAA		
79073 Trade Federation Tank		

1996-99 Micro Machines Star Wars Series Alpha

73421 X-Wing Starfighter	8.00	20.00
73422 Imperial Shuttle	10.00	25.00
73423 Rebel Snowspeeder	6.00	15.00
73424 Imperial AT-AT	8.00	20.00
73430 Twin-Pod Cloud Car		
73431 Y-Wing Starfighter		
73432 B-Wing Starfighter		
97033 Naboo Fighter		
97034 Droid Fighter		
97035 Sith Infiltrator	25.00	60.00
97036 Royal Starship		

1997 Micro Machines Star Wars Classic Duels

68301 TIE Fighter vs. X-Wing Starfighter	
68302 TIE Interceptor vs. Millennium Falcon	

1997 Micro Machines Star Wars Double Takes

75118 Death Star (w/Millennium Falcon/Obi-Wan Kenobi/Owen Lars	30.00	80.00
Ronto and Jawas/Beru Lars/2 Scurriers		

1997-98 Micro Machines Star Wars Flight Controllers

73417 Luke Skywalker's X-Wing Starfighter		
73418 Darth Vader's TIE Fighter	10.00	25.00
73440 Y-Wing Starfighter	8.00	20.00
73441 TIE Interceptor	8.00	20.00

1998-99 Micro Machines Star Wars Action Fleet Mini Scenes

68121 STAP Invasion (w/STAP/Jar Jar Binks/Battle Droid)	5.00	12.00
68122 Destroyer Droid Ambush (w/Destroyer Droid/Obi-Wan Kenobi/TC-14)	4.00	10.00
68123 Gungan Assault (w/Gungan/Kaadu/Battle Droid)	4.00	10.00
68124 Sith Pursuit (w/Sith speeder/Darth Maul/Qui-Gon Jinn)		
79025 Trade Federation Raid (w/Trade Federation MTT Ikopi/Jar Jar Binks/Qui-Gon Jinn)	5.00	12.00
79026 Throne Room Reception (w/Throne Room/Sio Bibble/Nute Gunray)	6.00	15.00
79027 Watto's Deal (w/Watto's Shop/Anakin/Pit droid)		
79028 Generator Core Duel (w/generator core Darth Maul/Obi-Wan Kenobi	8.00	20.00

1998-99 Micro Machines Star Wars Platform Action Sets

66541	Pod Race Arena	8.00	20.00
66542	Naboo Temple Ruins	6.00	15.00
66543	Galactic Senate	6.00	15.00
66544	Galactic Dogfight	10.00	25.00
66545	Theed Palace		
66546	Tatooine Desert		

1999 Micro Machines Star Wars Deluxe Platform Action Sets

66561	Royal Starship Repair	30.00	80.00
66562	Theed Palace Assault	100.00	200.00

1999 Micro Machines Star Wars Deluxe Action Sets

68156	Pod Racer Hangar Bay (w/pit droid and pit mechanic)		
68157	Mos Espa Market (w/Anakin Skywalker and C-3PO)	8.00	20.00
68158	Otoh Gunga (w/Obi-Wan Kenobi and Jar Jar Binks)		
68159	Theed Palace		

1999 Micro Machines Star Wars Mega Platform Set

66566	Trade Federation MTT/Naboo Battlefield	25.00	60.00

1999 Micro Machines Star Wars Pod Racer

66531	Pack 1 (w/Anakin and Ratts Tyrell)	5.00	12.00
66532	Pack 2 (w/Sebulba and Clegg Holdfast)	5.00	12.00
66533	Pack 3 (w/Dud Bolt and Mars Guo)	5.00	12.00
66534	Pack 4 (w/Boles Roor and Neva Kee)	5.00	12.00
66548A	Build Your Own Pod Racer Green (Galoob)	5.00	12.00
66548B	Build Your Own Pod Racer Yellow (Galoob)	5.00	12.00
97023A	Build Your Own Pod Racer Black (Hasbro)	5.00	12.00
97023B	Build Your Own Pod Racer Blue (Hasbro)	5.00	12.00

1999 Micro Machines Star Wars Pod Racing Gravity Track

66566	Beggar's Canyon Challenge		
66570	Boonta Eve Challenge	15.00	40.00
66577	Arch Canyon Adventure		

1999 Micro Machines Star Wars Turbo Pod Racers

68148	Gasgano	
68149	Ody Mandrell	

2002 Micro Machines Star Wars Action Fleet Movie Scenes

32549	Dune Sea Ambush (w/Tusken Raider/Bantha/Luke's Landspeeder)	5.00	12.00
32553	Tatooine Droid Hunter (w/Dewback/Sandtrooper/Escape Pod)	6.00	15.00
32554	Imperial Endor Pursuit (w/Luke Skywalker/Scout Trooper/2 speeder bikes/AT-ST) 6.00		15.00
32557	Mos Eisley Encounter (w/Ranto/Jawa/Black Landspeeder)	5.00	12.00

2015 Micro Machines Star Wars The Force Awakens Playsets

1	First Order Stormtrooper (w/Poe Dameron and transport)	6.00	15.00
2	Millennium Falcon (w/smaller Millennium Falcon and stormtrooper) 8.00		20.00
3	R2-D2 (w/Chewbacca/2 snowtroopers and transport)	5.00	12.00
4	Star Destroyer (w/Kylo Ren/Finn/X-Wing/TIE Fighter)	12.00	30.00

2015 Micro Machines Star Wars The Force Awakens Vehicles

1	Battle of Hoth (ESB)	5.00	12.00
2	Clone Army Raid (AOTC)	4.00	10.00
3	Desert Invasion	4.00	10.00
4	Droid Army (ROTS)	5.00	12.00
5	Endor Forest Battle (ROTJ)	6.00	15.00
6	First Order Attacks	4.00	10.00
7	First Order TIE Fighter Attack	4.00	10.00
8	Galactic Showdown	5.00	12.00
9	Imperial Pursuit (ANH)	4.00	10.00
10	Inquisitor's Hunt (Rebels)	4.00	10.00
11	Speeder Chase	5.00	12.00
12	Trench Run (ANH)	6.00	15.00

Marvel STAR WARS (1977-1986)

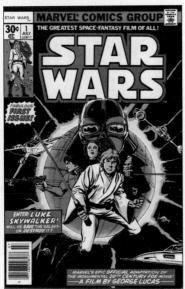

1	July 1977/"Star Wars: A New Hope" adaptation Part 1	75.00	200.00
1	July 1977/Star Wars 35-cent price variant	4,000.00	8,000.00
1	July 1977/Star Wars Newsstand reprint, 30-cent cover price, "reprint" on cover	15.00	40.00
1	July 1977/Star Wars Whitman reprint, diamond price type, no UPC, 35-cent cover price	15.00	40.00
1	July 1977/Star Wars Whitman reprint, diamond price type, no UPC, 35-cent cover price, "reprint" on cover	15.00	40.00
2	August 1977/"Star Wars: A New Hope" adaptation Part 2	20.00	50.00
2	August 1977/Star Wars Whitman variant, diamond price type, with UPC, 30-cent cover price	20.00	50.00
2	August 1977/Star Wars 35-cent price variant	1,000.00	3,000.00
2	August 1977/Star Wars Newsstand reprint, 30-cent cover price, "reprint" on cover	8.00	20.00
2	August 1977/Star Wars Whitman reprint, diamond price type, no UPC, 35-cent cover price	8.00	20.00
2	August 1977/Star Wars Whitman reprint, diamond price type, no UPC, 35-cent cover price, "reprint" on cover	8.00	20.00
3	September 1977/"Star Wars: A New Hope" adaptation Part 3	12.00	30.00
3	September 1977/Star Wars Whitman variant, diamond price type, with UPC, 30-cent cover price	12.00	30.00
3	September 1977/Star Wars 35-cent price variant	1,000.00	3,000.00
3	September 1977/Star Wars Newsstand reprint, 30-cent cover price, "reprint" on cover	6.00	15.00
3	September 1977/Star Wars Whitman reprint, diamond price type, no UPC, 35-cent cover price	6.00	15.00
3	September 1977/Star Wars Whitman reprint, diamond price type, no UPC, 35-cent cover price, "reprint" on cover	6.00	15.00
4	October 1977/"Star Wars: A New Hope" adaptation Part 4	12.00	30.00
4	October 1977/Star Wars Whitman variant, diamond price type, no UPC, 30-cent cover price	12.00	30.00
4	October 1977/Star Wars 35-cent price variant	1,000.00	3,000.00
4	October 1977/Star Wars Newsstand reprint, 30-cent cover price, "reprint" on cover	6.00	15.00
4	October 1977/Star Wars Whitman reprint, diamond price type, no UPC, 35-cent cover price	6.00	15.00
4	October 1977/Star Wars Whitman reprint, diamond price type, no UPC, 35-cent cover price, "reprint" on cover	6.00	15.00
5	November 1977/"Star Wars: A New Hope" adaptation Part 5	12.00	30.00
5	November 1977/Star Wars Whitman variant, diamond price type, no UPC	12.00	30.00
5	November 1977/Star Wars Newsstand reprint, "reprint" on cover	6.00	15.00
5	November 1977/Star Wars Whitman reprint, diamond price type, no UPC, "reprint" on cover	6.00	15.00
6	December 1977/"Star Wars: A New Hope" adaptation Part 6	12.00	30.00
6	December 1977/Star Wars Whitman variant, diamond price type, no UPC	12.00	30.00
6	December 1977/Star Wars Newsstand reprint, "reprint" on cover	6.00	15.00
6	December 1977/Star Wars Whitman reprint, diamond price type, no UPC, "reprint" on cover	6.00	15.00
7	January 1978	8.00	20.00
7	January 1978/Star Wars Whitman variant, diamond price type, no UPC	8.00	20.00
8	February 1978	8.00	20.00
8	February 1978/Star Wars Whitman variant, diamond price type, no UPC	8.00	20.00
9	March 1978	8.00	20.00
9	March 1978/Star Wars Whitman variant, diamond price type, no UPC	8.00	20.00
10	April 1978	8.00	20.00
10	April 1978/Star Wars Whitman variant, diamond price type, no UPC	8.00	20.00
11	May 1978	8.00	20.00
11	May 1978/Star Wars Whitman variant, diamond price type, with UPC	8.00	20.00
11	May 1978/Star Wars Whitman variant, diamond price type, no UPC	8.00	20.00
12	June 1978	8.00	20.00
12	June 1978/Star Wars Whitman variant, diamond price type, no UPC	8.00	20.00
13	July 1978	8.00	20.00
13	July 1978/Star Wars Whitman variant, diamond price type, no UPC	8.00	20.00
14	August 1978	8.00	20.00
14	August 1978/Star Wars Whitman variant, diamond price type, with UPC	8.00	20.00
15	September 1978	8.00	20.00
15	September 1978/Star Wars Whitman variant, diamond price type, no UPC	8.00	20.00
16	October 1978	8.00	20.00
16	October 1978/Star Wars Whitman variant, diamond price type, no UPC	8.00	20.00
17	November 1978	8.00	20.00
17	November 1978/Star Wars Whitman variant, diamond price type, no UPC	8.00	20.00
18	December 1978	8.00	20.00
18	December 1978/Star Wars Whitman variant, diamond price type, no UPC	8.00	20.00
19	January 1979	8.00	20.00
20	February 1979	8.00	20.00
21	March 1979	6.00	15.00
22	April 1979	6.00	15.00
23	May 1979	6.00	15.00
23	May 1979/Star Wars Whitman variant, diamond price type, no UPC	6.00	15.00
24	June 1979	6.00	15.00
25	July 1979	5.00	12.00
26	August 1979	5.00	12.00
27	September 1979	5.00	12.00
28	October 1979	5.00	12.00
29	November 1979	5.00	12.00
30	December 1979	5.00	12.00
31	January 1980	5.00	12.00
32	February 1980	5.00	12.00
33	March 1980	5.00	12.00
34	April 1980	5.00	12.00
35	May 1980	5.00	12.00
36	June 1980	5.00	12.00
37	July 1980	5.00	12.00
38	August 1980	5.00	12.00
39	September 1980/"The Empire Strikes Back" adaptation - Part 1	8.00	20.00
40	October 1980/"The Empire Strikes Back" adaptation - Part 2	8.00	20.00
41	November 1980/"The Empire Strikes Back" adaptation - Part 3	8.00	20.00
42	December 1980/"The Empire Strikes Back" adaptation - Part 4, "Bounty Hunters" cover w/Boba Fett	30.00	80.00
43	January 1981/"The Empire Strikes Back" adaptation - Part 5	8.00	20.00
44	February 1981/"The Empire Strikes Back" adaptation - Part 6	8.00	20.00
45	March 1981	5.00	12.00
46	April 1981	5.00	12.00
47	May 1981	5.00	12.00
48	June 1981	5.00	12.00
49	July 1981/"The Last Jedi" story title on cover	20.00	50.00
50	August 1981/Giant-Size issue	5.00	12.00
51	September 1981	5.00	12.00
52	October 1981	5.00	12.00
53	November 1981	5.00	12.00
54	December 1981	5.00	12.00
55	January 1982	5.00	12.00
56	February 1982	5.00	12.00
57	March 1982	5.00	12.00
58	April 1982	5.00	12.00
59	May 1982	5.00	12.00
60	June 1982	5.00	12.00
61	July 1982	5.00	12.00
62	August 1982	5.00	12.00
63	September 1982	5.00	12.00
64	October 1982	5.00	12.00
65	November 1982	5.00	12.00
66	December 1982	5.00	12.00

67	January 1983	5.00	12.00
68	February 1983/Boba Fett cover	30.00	80.00
69	March 1983	5.00	12.00
70	April 1983	5.00	12.00
71	May 1983	5.00	12.00
72	June 1983	5.00	12.00
73	July 1983	5.00	12.00
74	August 1983	5.00	12.00
75	September 1983	5.00	12.00
76	October 1983	5.00	12.00
77	November 1983	5.00	12.00
78	December 1983	5.00	12.00
79	January 1984	5.00	12.00
80	February 1984	5.00	12.00
81	March 1984/Boba Fett appearance	10.00	25.00
82	April 1984	5.00	12.00
83	May 1984	5.00	12.00
84	June 1984	5.00	12.00
85	July 1984	5.00	12.00
86	August 1984	5.00	12.00
87	September 1984	5.00	12.00
88	October 1984	5.00	12.00
89	November 1984	5.00	12.00
90	December 1984	5.00	12.00
91	January 1985	5.00	12.00
92	February 1985/Giant-Size issue	8.00	20.00
93	March 1985	6.00	15.00
94	April 1985	6.00	15.00
95	May 1985	6.00	15.00
96	June 1985	6.00	15.00
97	July 1985	6.00	15.00
98	August 1985	6.00	15.00
99	September 1985	6.00	15.00
100	October 1985/Giant-Size issue	10.00	25.00
101	November 1985	8.00	20.00
102	December 1985	8.00	20.00
103	January 1986	8.00	20.00
104	March 1986	8.00	20.00
105	May 1986	8.00	20.00
106	July 1986	10.00	25.00
107	September 1986/Final issue	30.00	80.00

Marvel STAR WARS Annual

1	Star Wars Annual 1979	6.00	15.00
2	Star Wars Annual 1982	6.00	15.00
3	Star Wars Annual 1983	6.00	15.00

STAR WARS: RETURN OF THE JEDI MINI-SERIES (1983-1984)

1	October 1983/"Return of the Jedi" adaptation Part 1	4.00	10.00
2	November 1983/"Return of the Jedi" adaptation Part 2	3.00	8.00
3	December 1983/"Return of the Jedi" adaptation Part 3	3.00	8.00
4	January 1984/"Return of the Jedi" adaptation Part 4	3.00	8.00

JOURNEY TO STAR WARS: THE FORCE AWAKENS - SHATTERED EMPIRE (2015)

1	November 2015	1.50	4.00
1	November 2015/Blank Cover Variant	3.00	8.00
1	November 2015/1:20 Hyperspace Variant	3.00	8.00
1	November 2015/1:25 Movie Photo Variant	3.00	8.00
1	November 2015/1:25 Marco Checchetto Variant	5.00	12.00
2	December 2015	1.50	4.00
2	December 2015/1:25 Movie Photo Variant	4.00	10.00

2	December 2015/1:25 Kris Anka Variant	4.00	10.00
3	December 2015	1.50	4.00
3	December 2015/1:25 Movie Photo Variant	4.00	10.00
3	December 2015/1:25 Mike Deodato Jr. Variant	4.00	10.00
4	December 2015	1.50	4.00
4	December 2015/1:25 Movie Photo Variant	4.00	10.00
4	December 2015/1:25 Sara Pichelli Variant	4.00	10.00

Marvel STAR WARS (2015-)

1	March 2015	3.00	8.00
1	March 2015/Blank Cover Variant	4.00	10.00
1	March 2015/Skottie Young "Baby" Variant	3.00	8.00
1	March 2015/Luke Skywalker Action Figure Variant	6.00	15.00
1	March 2015/1:15 Movie Photo Variant	4.00	10.00
1	March 2015/1:20 Sara Pichelli Variant	4.00	10.00
1	March 2015/1:25 "Two Suns" Variant	3.00	8.00
1	March 2015/1:25 Bob McLeod Variant	4.00	10.00
1	March 2015/1:50 Alex Ross Variant	20.00	50.00
1	March 2015/1:50 J. Scott Campbell Variant	15.00	40.00
1	March 2015/1:100 Joe Quesada Variant	15.00	40.00
1	March 2015/1:200 Alex Ross Sketch Variant	30.00	80.00
1	March 2015/1:500 Joe Quesada Sketch Variant	75.00	200.00
1	April 2015/2nd printing	4.00	10.00
1	April 2015/3rd printing	4.00	10.00
1	June 2015/4th printing	4.00	10.00
1	July 2015/5th printing	4.00	10.00
1	September 2015/6th printing (double cover)	6.00	15.00
1	7th printing	4.00	10.00
2	April 2015	4.00	10.00
2	April 2015/Han Solo Action Figure Variant	30.00	80.00
2	April 2015/Sergio Aragones Variant	3.00	8.00
2	April 2015/1:25 Leinil Francis Yu Variant	6.00	15.00
2	April 2015/1:25 Howard Chaykin Variant	6.00	15.00
2	April 2015/1:100 John Cassaday Sketch Variant	20.00	50.00
2	May 2015/2nd printing	4.00	10.00
2	June 2015/3rd printing	3.00	8.00
2	July 2015/4th printing	3.00	8.00
2	August 2015/5th printing	3.00	8.00

2	6th printing	3.00	8.00
3	May 2015	2.50	6.00
3	May 2015/Obi-Wan Kenobi Action Figure Variant	2.50	6.00
3	May 2015/1:25 Leinil Francis Yu Variant	6.00	15.00
3	May 2015/1:100 John Cassaday Sketch Variant	15.00	40.00
3	July 2015/2nd printing	2.00	5.00
3	July 2015/3rd printing	2.00	5.00
3	4th printing	2.00	5.00
4	June 2015	2.50	6.00
4	June 2015/Chewbacca Action Figure Variant	2.50	6.00
4	June 2015/1:25 Giuseppe Camuncoli Variant	5.00	12.00
4	June 2015/1:100 John Cassaday Sketch Variant	15.00	40.00
4	2nd printing	2.00	5.00
5	July 2015	2.00	5.00
5	July 2015/C-3PO Action Figure Variant	2.50	6.00
5	July 2015/1:100 John Cassaday Sketch Variant	15.00	40.00
5	2nd printing	2.00	5.00
6	August 2015	2.00	5.00
6	August 2015/R2-D2 Action Figure Variant	3.00	8.00
6	2nd printing	2.00	5.00
6	3rd printing	2.00	5.00
7	September 2015	2.00	5.00
7	September 2015/Stormtrooper Action Figure Variant	2.50	6.00
7	September 2015/1:25 Simone Bianchi Variant Cover	3.00	8.00
7	September 2015/1:25 Tony Moore Variant Cover	3.00	8.00
7	September 2015/1:100 John Cassaday Sketch Variant	15.00	40.00
8	October 2015	2.00	5.00
8	October 2015/Tusken Raider Action Figure Variant	2.50	6.00
8	October 2015/1:50 John Cassaday Variant	6.00	15.00
8	October 2015/1:100 Stuart Immonen Sketch Variant	15.00	40.00
9	November 2015	2.00	5.00
9	November 2015/Star Destroyer Commander Action Figure Variant	2.50	6.00
9	November 2015/1:100 Stuart Immonen Sketch Variant	15.00	40.00
10	December 2015	2.00	5.00
10	December 2015/Jawa Action Figure Variant	2.50	6.00
10	December 2015/1:100 Stuart Immonen Sketch Variant	15.00	40.00
11	January 2016	2.00	5.00
11	January 2016/Luke Skywalker: X-Wing Pilot Action Figure Variant	2.50	6.00
11	January 2016/1:100 Stuart Immonen Sketch Variant	15.00	40.00
12	January 2016	2.00	5.00
12	January 2016/Greedo Action Figure Variant	2.50	6.00
12	January 2016/1:100 Stuart Immonen Sketch Variant	15.00	40.00
13	February 2016	2.00	5.00
13	February 2016/R5-D4 Action Figure Variant	2.50	6.00
13	February 2016/Clay Mann Variant	2.50	6.00
13	March 2016/2nd printing	2.00	5.00
14	March 2016	2.00	5.00
14	March 2016/Hammerhead Action Figure Variant	2.50	6.00
14	March 2016/Clay Mann Variant	2.50	6.00
14	April 2016/2nd printing	2.00	5.00
15	March 2016	2.00	5.00
15	March 2016/Snaggletooth Action Figure Variant	2.50	6.00
15	March 2016/1:100 Mike Mayhew Sketch Variant	15.00	40.00
15	May 2016/2nd printing	2.00	5.00
16	April 2016	2.00	5.00
16	April 2016/Death Star Droid Action Figure Variant	2.50	6.00
16	April 2016/1:25 Stuart Immonen Variant	4.00	10.00
16	April 2016/1:25 Leinil Francis Yu Variant	4.00	10.00
16	April 2016/1:100 Terry Dodson Sketch Variant	15.00	40.00
17	May 2016	2.00	5.00
17	May 2016/Walrus Man Action Figure Variant	2.50	6.00
17	May 2016/1:25 Leinil Francis Yu Variant	4.00	10.00
17	May 2016/1:100 Terry Dodson Sketch Variant	15.00	40.00
18	June 2016	2.00	5.00
18	June 2016/Power Droid Action Figure Variant	2.50	6.00
18	June 2016/1:100 Leinil Francis Yu Sketch Variant	20.00	50.00
19	July 2016	2.00	5.00
19	July 2016/Leia Organa: Bespin Gown Action Figure Variant	3.00	8.00
19	July 2016/1:100 Leinil Francis Yu Sketch Variant	15.00	40.00
20	August 2016	2.00	5.00
20	August 2016/Yoda Action Figure Variant	4.00	10.00
20	August 2016/1:100 Mike Mayhew Sketch Variant	15.00	40.00
21	September 2016	2.00	5.00
21	September 2016/Stormtrooper: Hoth Battle Gear Action Figure Variant	3.00	8.00
21	September 2016/1:100 David Aja Sketch Variant	20.00	50.00
22	October 2016	2.00	5.00
22	October 2016/Dengar Action Figure Variant	2.50	6.00
22	October 2016/1:100 Mike Deodato Sketch Variant	20.00	50.00
23	November 2016	2.00	5.00
23	November 2016/Rebel Soldier: Hoth Battle Gear Action Figure Variant	2.50	6.00
23	November 2016/1:25 Jorge Molina Variant	5.00	12.00
23	November 2016/1:100 Mike Deodato Sketch Variant	20.00	50.00
24	December 2016'	2.00	5.00
24	December 2016/Lobot Action Figure Variant	2.50	6.00
24	December 2016/1:100 Mike Deodato Sketch Variant	20.00	50.00
25	January 2017	2.00	5.00
25	January 2017/IG-88 Action Figure Variant	2.50	6.00
25	January 2017/1:100 Mike Deodato Sketch Variant	20.00	50.00
26	February 2017'	2.00	5.00
26	February 2017/2-1B Action Figure Variant	2.50	6.00
26	February 2017/Qui-Gon Jinn Action Figure Variant	20.00	50.00
26	February 2017/1:100 Mike Deodato Sketch Variant	20.00	50.00
27	March 2017'	2.00	5.00
27	March 2017/R2-D2 with Sensorscope Action Figure Variant	2.50	6.00
27	March 2017/Star Wars 40th Anniversary Variant	4.00	10.00
28	April 2017'	2.00	5.00
28	April 2017/C-3PO Removable Limbs Action Figure Variant	2.50	6.00
28	April 2017/Star Wars 40th Anniversary Variant	4.00	10.00
29	May 2017'	2.00	5.00
29	May 2017/Luke Skywalker: Hoth Battle Gear Action Figure Variant	2.50	6.00
29	May 2017/Star Wars 40th Anniversary Variant	3.00	8.00
30	June 2017'	2.00	5.00
30	June 2017/AT-AT Commander Action Figure Variant	2.50	6.00
30	June 2017/Star Wars 40th Anniversary Variant	3.00	8.00
31	July 2017'	2.00	5.00
31	July 2017/Luke Skywalker: Bespin Fatigues Action Figure Variant	2.50	6.00
31	July 2017/Star Wars 40th Anniversary Variant	3.00	8.00
32	August 2017'	2.00	5.00
32	August 2017/FX-7 Medical Droid Action Figure Variant	2.50	6.00
32	August 2017/Star Wars 40th Anniversary Variant	3.00	8.00
33	September 2017'	2.00	5.00
33	September 2017/Bespin Security Guard Action Figure Variant	2.50	6.00
33	September 2017/Star Wars 40th Anniversary Variant	3.00	8.00
34	October 2017'	2.00	5.00
34	October 2017/Han Solo: Hoth Outfit Action Figure Variant	2.50	6.00
34	October 2017/Star Wars 40th Anniversary Variant	3.00	8.00
35	October 2017'	2.00	5.00
35	October 2017/Ugnaught Action Figure Variant	2.50	6.00
35	October 2017/Star Wars 40th Anniversary Variant	3.00	8.00
36	November 2017'	2.00	5.00
36	November 2017/Leia Organa: Hoth Outfit Action Figure Variant	3.00	8.00
36	November 2017/Star Wars 40th Anniversary Variant	3.00	8.00
37	December 2017'	2.00	5.00
37	December 2017/Rebel Commander Action Figure Variant	2.50	6.00
37	December 2017/Star Wars 40th Anniversary Variant	3.00	8.00

Marvel STAR WARS ANNUAL (2015-)

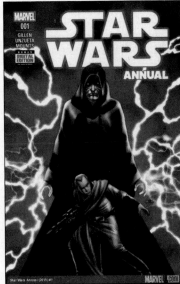

1	February 2016	2.00	5.00
1	February 2016/Blank Cover Variant	3.00	8.00
2	January 2017'	2.00	5.00
2	January 2017/Elsa Charretier Variant	2.00	5.00
3	November 2017'	2.00	5.00
3	November 2017/Rod Reis Variant	2.00	5.00

Marvel DARTH VADER (2015-2016)

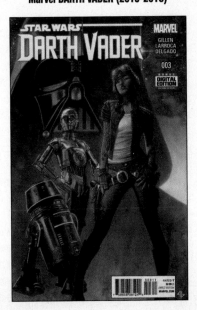

1	April 2015	4.00	10.00
1	April 2015/Blank Cover Variant	3.00	8.00
1	April 2015/Skottie Young "Baby" Variant	2.50	6.00
1	April 2015/Darth Vader Action Figure Variant	3.00	8.00
1	April 2015/1:15 Movie Photo Variant	4.00	10.00
1	April 2015/1:25 John Cassaday Variant	5.00	12.00
1	April 2015/1:25 Whilce Portacio Variant	6.00	15.00
1	April 2015/1:25 Mike Del Mundo Variant	8.00	20.00
1	April 2015/1:50 J. Scott Campbell Variant	15.00	40.00
1	April 2015/1:50 Alex Ross Variant	20.00	50.00
1	April 2015/1:200 Alex Ross Sketch Variant	80.00	150.00
1	2nd printing	2.00	5.00
1	3rd printing	2.00	5.00
1	4th printing	2.00	5.00
1	5th printing	2.00	5.00
2	April 2015	4.00	10.00
2	April 2015/1:25 Dave Dorman Variant	5.00	12.00
2	April 2015/1:25 Salvador Larroca Variant	5.00	12.00
2	2nd printing	4.00	10.00
2	3rd printing	4.00	10.00
2	4th printing	3.00	8.00
2	5th printing	3.00	8.00
3	May 2015/1st appearance of Dr. Aphra, 0-0-0 & BT-1	10.00	25.00
3	May 2015/1:25 Salvador Larroca Variant	40.00	100.00
3	2nd printing	4.00	10.00
3	3rd printing	4.00	10.00
3	4th printing	4.00	10.00
4	June 2015	2.50	6.00
4	June 2015/1:25 Salvador Larroca Variant	6.00	15.00
4	2nd printing	2.00	5.00
4	3rd printing	2.00	5.00
4	4th printing	2.00	5.00
5	July 2015	2.50	6.00
5	July 2015/1:25 Salvador Larroca Variant	4.00	10.00
5	2nd printing	2.00	5.00
6	August 2015	2.50	6.00
6	2nd printing	2.00	5.00
7	September 2015	2.50	6.00
8	October 2015	2.50	6.00
9	November 2015	2.50	6.00
9	November 2015/1:25 Adi Granov Variant	6.00	15.00
10	December 2015	2.50	6.00
11	December 2015	2.50	6.00
12	January 2016	2.50	6.00
13	January 2016	2.50	6.00
13	January 2016/Clay Mann Variant	2.50	6.00
13	2nd printing	2.50	6.00
14	February 2016	2.50	6.00
14	February 2016/Clay Mann Variant	2.50	6.00
14	2nd printing	2.50	6.00
15	March 2016	2.50	6.00
15	April 2016/Clay Mann Variant	2.50	6.00
15	May 2016/1:25 Francesco Francavilla Variant	6.00	15.00
15	June 2016/1:100 Mark Brooks Sketch Variant	20.00	50.00
15	2nd printing	2.50	6.00
16	April 2016	2.50	6.00
16	2nd printing	2.00	5.00
17	May 2016	2.50	6.00
18	May 2016	2.50	6.00
19	June 2016	2.50	6.00
20	July 2016	2.50	6.00
20	July 2016/Inspector Thanoth Action Figure Variant	2.50	6.00
20	July 2016/"The Story Thus Far" Reilly Brown Variant	2.50	6.00
20	2nd printing	2.00	5.00
21	August 2016	2.50	6.00
21	August 2016/Tulon Action Figure Variant	2.50	6.00
21	2nd printing	2.00	5.00
22	August 2016	2.50	6.00
22	August 2016/Cylo Action Figure Variant	2.50	6.00
22	2nd printing	2.00	5.00
23	September 2016	2.50	6.00
23	September 2016/BT-1 Action Figure Variant	2.50	6.00
23	2nd printing	2.00	5.00
24	October 2016	2.50	6.00
24	0-0-0 (Triple-Zero) Action Figure Variant	2.50	6.00
25	December 2016/final issue	2.50	6.00
25	December 2016/Doctor Aphra Action Figure Variant	4.00	10.00
25	December 2016/Adi Granov Variant	2.50	6.00
25	December 2016/Jamie McKelvie Variant	3.00	8.00
25	December 2016/Karmome Shirahama Variant	3.00	8.00
25	December 2016/Salvador Larroca Variant	2.50	6.00
25	December 2016/1:25 Chris Samnee Variant	6.00	15.00
25	December 2016/1:25 Sara Pichelli Variant	6.00	15.00
25	December 2016/1:25 Cliff Chiang Variant	7.00	18.00
25	December 2016/1:50 Michael Cho Variant	20.00	50.00
25	December 2016/1:100 Joe Quesada Variant	40.00	100.00
25	December 2016/1:200 Joe Quesada Sketch Variant	80.00	150.00

Marvel DARTH VADER ANNUAL (2015-2016)

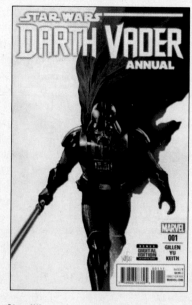

1	February 2015	3.00	8.00
1	February 2015/Blank Cover Variant	3.00	8.00

Marvel STAR WARS: THE FORCE AWAKENS (2016-)

1	August 2016/"Star Wars: The Force Awakens " adaptation Part 1	2.00	5.00
1	August 2016/Blank Cover Variant	4.00	10.00
1	August 2016/1:15 Movie Photo Variant	5.00	12.00
1	August 2016/1:25 Phil Noto Variant	10.00	25.00
1	August 2016/1:50 John Cassaday Variant	12.00	30.00
1	August 2016/1:75 Esad Ribic Sketch Variant	20.00	50.00
1	August 2016/1:100 Joe Quesada Variant	150.00	400.00
1	August 2016/1:200 John Cassaday Sketch Variant	20.00	50.00
1	August 2016/1:300 Joe Quesada Sketch Variant	400.00	800.00
2	September 2016/"Star Wars: The Force Awakens " adaptation Part 2	1.50	4.00
2	September 2016/1:15 Movie Photo Variant	4.00	10.00
2	September 2016/1:25 Chris Samnee Variant	6.00	15.00
2	September 2016/1:75 Mike Mayhew Sketch Variant	30.00	80.00
3	October 2016/"Star Wars: The Force Awakens" adaptation Part 3	1.50	4.00
3	October 2016/1:15 Movie Photo Variant	4.00	10.00
3	October 2016/1:75 Mike Deodato Jr. Sketch Variant	30.00	80.00
4	November 2016/"Star Wars: The Force Awakens" adaptation Part 4	1.50	4.00
4	November 2016/1:15 Movie Photo Variant	4.00	10.00
4	November 2016/1:75 Mike Del Mundo Sketch Variant	30.00	80.00
5	December 2016/"Star Wars: The Force Awakens" adaptation Part 5	1.50	4.00
5	December 2016/1:15 Movie Photo Variant	6.00	15.00
5	December 2016/1:75 Rafael Albuquerque Sketch Variant	50.00	120.00
6	January 2017/"Star Wars: The Force Awakens" adaptation Part 6	1.50	4.00
6	January 2017/1:15 Movie Photo Variant	6.00	15.00
6	January 2017/1:25 Esad Ribic Variant	10.00	25.00
6	January 2017/1:75 Paolo Rivera Variant	30.00	80.00